# VBScript Programmer's Reference, Second Edition

# VBScript Programmer's Reference, Second Edition

Adrian Kingsley-Hughes
Kathie Kingsley-Hughes
Daniel Read

**WILEY**

Wiley Publishing, Inc.

**VBScript Programmer's Reference, Second Edition**

Published by
Wiley Publishing, Inc.
10475 Crosspoint Boulevard
Indianapolis, IN 46256
www.wiley.com

For general information on our other products and services please contact our Customer Care Department within the United States at (800) 762-2974, outside the United States at (317) 572-3993 or fax (317) 572-4002.

*Wiley also publishes its books in a variety of electronic formats. Some content that appears in print may not be available in electronic books.*

Library of Congress Card Number:

ISBN: 0-7645-5993-1

Printed in the United States of America

10  9  8  7  6  5  4  3

*Library of Congress Cataloging-in-Publication Data*

Kingsley-Hughes, Adrian.
   VBScript programmer's reference / Adrian Kingsley-Hughes, Kathie
Kingsley-Hughes, Daniel Read.—2nd ed.
      p.   cm.
   Includes index.
   ISBN 0-7645-5993-1 (paper/website)
   1. VBScript (Computer program language).   2. HTML (Document markup language).
3. World Wide Web.   I. Kingsley-Hughes, Kathie.   II. Read, Daniel, 1969-   III. Title
   QA76.73.V27K56   2004
   005.2'762—dc22
                                                          2004007671

To my kids—you guys are great!
            —Adrian

To my parents, for their loving support and enduring patience. And to my kids, for being just so cool!
                                                            —Kathie

# About the Authors

## *Adrian Kingsley-Hughes*

Adrian Kingsley-Hughes has made his living as a technology writer for the last six years, with many books and articles to his name. He can also be found teaching classes on the Web, where he has successfully taught technology skills to thousands of learners, with his own special brand of knowledge, experience, wit, and poor spelling.

## *Kathie Kingsley-Hughes*

Kathie Kingsley-Hughes has worked in IT training for many years. In addition to writing, she now works as a courseware developer and e-trainer, specializing in Internet technologies. She also runs a Web development company in the United Kingdom.

## *Daniel Read*

Daniel Read is a software developer living and working in Atlanta, GA, USA. He currently works for Connecture Inc., an Atlanta-based software consulting firm specializing in the insurance industry. Daniel also publishes and writes essays for developer.*, a Web-based magazine for software professionals (`DeveloperDotStar.com`).

# Credits

**Vice President and Executive Group Publisher**
Richard Swadley

**Vice President and Executive Publisher**
Bob Ipsen

**Vice President and Publisher**
Joseph B. Wikert

**Executive Editorial Director**
Mary Bednarek

**Acquisitions Editor**
Katie Mohr

**Editorial Manager**
Kathryn A. Malm

**Senior Production Editor**
Fred Bernardi

**Development Editor**
Eileen Bien Calabro

**Production Editor**
Felicia Robinson

**Technical Reviewer**
Wiley-Dreamtech India Pvt Ltd

# Acknowledgments

A book is hard work, and a second edition even harder! The process involves a lot more people than just those listed on the cover. My sincerest thanks goes out to everyone who made this book possible, from the first idea of a second edition through to getting it onto the shelves.

—Adrian

Many thanks to family, friends, and colleagues, who have been very supportive during the writing of this book. A big thank you to all the editors, tech reviewers, and production staff who worked so hard on this edition.

—Kathie

I thank my fellow authors Adrian and Kathie and also the fine editorial staff at Wiley/WROX.

—Daniel

# Contents

# Contents

# Contents

# Contents

# Contents

# Contents

# Contents

# Introduction

Imagine having the ability to write code quickly and easily in a text editor without having to worry about complex development environments.

Imagine not having the hassles of compiling code or distributing complex set-up programs.

Imagine being able to deploy your code in a wide variety of ways.

Imagine learning one language that allows you to code for server-side Internet, client-side Internet, and desktop.

Stop imagining. VBScript gives you all this and much more.

VBScript is an absolutely superb language to be able to "speak" in. It's quick and easy to learn, powerful, flexible, and cheap. This makes it a winning language for both experienced programmers and those starting out in their programming careers. If you are an experienced programmer you can enjoy writing code free from complex development environments and the need for compiling. On the other hand, if you are a beginner you can get started programming, needing nothing more than a little knowledge and a text editor.

Knowledge and experience in VBScript can open many technology doors too. Having a good grounding in VBScript can lead you into areas such as Internet development, network administration, server-side coding, and even other programming languages (Visual Basic being the most popular route to take because the languages are so similar in syntax). With VBScript you can also create applications that look and feel like programs written using complex programming languages, such as C++. Also worth bearing in mind is that support for scripting is now embedded into every installation of the newer Windows operating systems—a dormant power that you can tap into with VBScript know-how. By writing some simple script in a text editor you can do a variety of tasks—such as copy and move files, create folders and files, modify the Windows registry, and lots more. One easy-to-use scripting language can do it all.

We believe that VBScript is a skill that many people will find both useful and rewarding, no matter whether they are involved in the IT industry, a SOHO PC user, a student, or simply a home user. Knowing and using VBScript can save you time and, more importantly, money.

## Who This Book Is For

This book is the one-stop book for anyone who is interested in learning VBScript. How you use it depends on your previous programming/scripting knowledge and experience:

- ❏ If you are a complete beginner who has heard about VBScript and have come this far, it's great. You've come to the best possible place. As a beginner you have a fascinating journey ahead of you. We suggest that you go through this book from cover to cover to get the best from it.

❑ If you already have IT and programming experience and want to learn VBScript (perhaps for Active Server Pages (ASP) or Windows Scripting Host (WSH)) then you too have come to the right place. Your background in programming will mean that you will already be familiar with most of the terms and techniques we will be covering here. For you, the task of learning another language is made simpler by this. If you know what you plan of using VBScript for (say ASP or WSH), then you can read with this in mind and skip certain chapters for speed.

❑ Network administrators are likely to find this book not only useful, but also an enormous timesaver because they can use VBScript to write powerful logon scripts or automate boring, repetitive, time-consuming, and error-prone tasks using WSH.

❑ You're already using VBScript and just want to fill some of the blanks or bought this new edition just to keep right up to date. You will no doubt find new information and you might want to read certain chapters more than others.

## What This Book Covers

As you'd expect, a book on VBScript covers VBScript. To be precise, this book covers VBScript right up to the latest version (version 5.6). However, VBScript is a tool that can be used in a variety of different ways and by a variety of different applications. Therefore, along with covering VBScript in detail, this book also covers technologies that are linked to and associated with VBScript. These include technologies such as server-side technologies like Active Server Pages (ASP), client-side Dynamic HTML (DHTML), and Windows Script Host (WSH). Likewise, if you come from a Visual Basic background then most of what we will cover in the first third of the book (variables, data types, procedures, flow control, and so on) will be familiar to you. We'll also show you how to get deep into the Windows operating system and make changes with just a few lines of code.

## How This Book Is Structured

Take a quick look at the table of contents of this edition and you will see that it is broken up into three broad sections:

❑ First, the book begins with chapters that are core VBScript—basically how VBScript works as a language.

❑ Second, the book looks at how to make use of VBScript within other technologies (such as WSH or ASP). These chapters look at more advanced examples of VBScript code in action.

❑ Finally, the book has a detailed and comprehensive reference section in the form of a series of appendices. This reference section can be used either as a standalone reference section or to give you greater insight into how the VBScript from earlier chapters works.

How you decide to progress through the book really depends on your current skill level with regards to VBScript or other programming languages and what you want to do. If you want to use VBScript client-side on the Web then you can; if you want, skip any or all chapters relating to server-side VBScript. On the other hand you might be a server-side developer and not be currently interested in client-side VBScript. Again, that's just fine. It's your book—use it the way that is best for you.

If you're not sure as to the best way to approach this book, we suggest that you read it from beginning to end, so that you benefit fully. Don't worry too much about actually remembering everything you read—that's not the point. The book is a reference, which means you can refer back to it again and again. Make notes in the book as you go along, as this will help you remember better and also help you to find key parts you've read before.

# What You Need to Use This Book

VBScript is possibly a low-cost solution to many of your scripting/programming needs. The good news is that if you (and your end users) use a Microsoft Windows operating system, you already have everything you need to be able to make full use of this book (or you can go online to download it).

All the code writing that you will be doing can be done using the Windows Notepad application that you already have installed. We will make a few suggestions as to other tools you can use that may make life easier for you, but a text editor is all you really need.

The Microsoft Scripting Web site contains documentation relating to VBScript that is available for download. You may like to download these too to augment your reading here.

If you are not using Windows XP you might want to download the latest VBScript engine—point your browser at `http://www.microsoft.com/scripting`.

# Conventions

To help you get the most from the text and keep track of what's happening, we've used a number of conventions throughout the book.

> **Boxes like this one hold important, not-to-be forgotten information that is directly relevant to the surrounding text.**

*Tips, hints, tricks, and asides to the current discussion are offset and placed in italics like this.*

As for styles in the text:

❑ We *highlight* important words when we introduce them

❑ We show keyboard strokes like this: Ctrl+A

❑ We show file names, URLs, and code within the text like so: `persistence.properties`

❑ We present code in two different ways:

```
In code examples we highlight new and important code with a gray background.
```

```
The gray highlighting is not used for code that's less important in the
present context, or has been shown before.
```

# Source Code

As you work through the examples in this book, you may choose either to type in all the code manually or to use the source code files that accompany the book. All of the source code used in this book is available for download at http://www.wrox.com. Once at the site, simply locate the book's title (either by using the Search box or by using one of the title lists) and click the Download Code link on the book's detail page to obtain all the source code for the book.

> *Because many books have similar titles, you may find it easiest to search by ISBN; for this book the ISBN is 0-764-55993-1.*

Once you have downloaded the code, just decompress it with your favorite compression tool. Alternately, you can go to the main Wrox code download page at http://www.wrox.com/dynamic/books/download.aspx to see the code available for this book and all other Wrox books.

# Errata

We make every effort to ensure that there are no errors in the text or in the code. However, no one is perfect, and mistakes do occur. If you find an error in one of our books, like a spelling mistake or faulty piece of code, we would be very grateful for your feedback. By sending in errata you may save another reader hours of frustration and at the same time you will be helping us provide even higher quality information.

To find the errata page for this book, go to http://www.wrox.com and locate the title using the Search box or one of the title lists. Then, on the book details page, click the Book Errata link. On this page you can view all errata that has been submitted for this book and posted by Wrox editors. A complete book list including links to each book's errata is also available at www.wrox.com/misc-pages/booklist.shtml.

If you don't spot "your" error on the Book Errata page, go to www.wrox.com/contact/techsupport.shtml and complete the form there to send us the error you have found. We'll check the information and, if appropriate, post a message to the book's errata page and fix the problem in subsequent editions of the book.

# p2p.wrox.com

For author and peer discussion, join the P2P forums at p2p.wrox.com. The forums are a Web-based system for you to post messages relating to Wrox books and related technologies and interact with other readers and technology users. The forums offer a subscription feature to e-mail you topics of interest of your choosing when new posts are made to the forums. Wrox authors, editors, other industry experts, and your fellow readers are present on these forums.

At http://p2p.wrox.com you will find a number of different forums that will help you not only as you read this book, but also as you develop your own applications. To join the forums, just follow these steps:

**1.** Go to p2p.wrox.com and click the Register link.

2. Read the terms of use and click `Agree`.

3. Complete the required information to join as well as any optional information you wish to provide and click `Submit`.

4. You will receive an e-mail with information describing how to verify your account and complete the joining process.

*You can read messages in the forums without joining P2P but in order to post your own messages, you must join.*

Once you join, you can post new messages and respond to messages other users post. You can read messages at any time on the Web. If you would like to have new messages from a particular forum e-mailed to you, click the `Subscribe to this Forum` icon by the forum name in the forum listing.

For more information about how to use the Wrox P2P, be sure to read the P2P FAQs for answers to questions about how the forum software works as well as many common questions specific to P2P and Wrox books. To read the FAQs, click the `FAQ` link on any P2P page.

# 1

# A Quick Introduction to Programming

## Overview

A chapter covering the basics of VBScript is the best place to begin this book. Well, this is because of the type of language VBScript is and the kind of people we see turning to it. In this chapter we are going to try and give you a crash course in programming basics. You might not need this chapter because you've come to VBScript with programming skills from another language (Visual Basic, C, C++, Delphi, C#) and are already both familiar with and comfortable using programming terminology. In that case, feel free to skip this chapter and move on to the next one. However, if you come from a nonprogramming background then this chapter will give you the firm foundation you need to begin using VBScript confidently.

If you're still reading, chances are you fall into one of three distinct categories:

❑   You're a Network/Systems administrator who probably wants to use VBScript and the Windows Script Host to write logon scripts and automate administration tasks.

❑   You might be a Web designer who feels the need to branch out and increase their skill set, perhaps in order to do some ASP work.

❑   You're interested in programming (possibly Visual Basic) and want to check out programming before getting too deeply involved.

Programming is a massive subject. Over the years countless volumes have been written about it, both in print and on the Internet. In this chapter, in a single paragraph, we might end up introducing several unfamiliar concepts. We'll be moving pretty fast, but if you read along carefully, trying out your hand at the examples along the way, you'll be just fine.

Also, please bear in mind that there's going to be a lot that we don't cover here, such as:

❑   Architecture

❑   System design

❑   Database design

❑    Documenting code

❑    Advanced testing and rollout

Think of this chapter as a brief introduction to the important building blocks of programming. It certainly won't make you an expert programmer overnight, but what it hopefully will give you is the know-how you'll need in order to get the most out of the rest of the book.

# Variables and Data Types

In this section, we're going to be moving quickly through some of the most basic concepts of programming. In particular:

❑    Variables

❑    Comments

❑    Using built-in VBScript functions

❑    Syntax issues

The first thing you need to know about is variables. Quite simply, a variable is a place in the computer memory where your script holds a piece (or pieces) of information. Since computers work with data, we'll be using that word instead of information but the concept is the same. The data stored in a variable can be pretty much anything. It may be something simple, like a small number, like 4. It can be more complex, like a floating-point number such as 2.3. Or it could be a much bigger number like 981.12932134. Or it might not be a number at all and could be a word or a combination of letters and numbers. In fact, a variable can store pretty much anything you want it to store.

Behind the scenes, the variable is a reserved section of the computer's memory, a temporary place to store data. Memory is temporary—things stored there are not stored permanently. For permanent storage you use the hard drive. Since memory is a temporary storage area, and since variables are stored in the computer's memory, they are therefore also temporary. Your script will use variables to store data temporarily that the script needs to keep track of for later use. If your script needs to store that data permanently, it would store it in a file or database on the computer's hard disk.

In order to make it easier for the computer to keep track of the millions of bits of data that are stored in memory at any given moment, the memory is broken up into chunks. Each of those chunks is exactly the same size, and is given a unique address. Don't worry about what the memory addresses are or how you use them because you won't need to know any of that to use VBScript, but it is useful to know that a variable is a reserved set of one or more chunks. Also, different types of variables take up different amounts of memory.

In your VBScript program, a variable usually begins its lifecycle by being declared (or dimensioned) before use.

*Note: It is not required that you have to declare all of the variables you use. VBScript by default allows you to use undeclared variables. However, we strongly recommend that you get into the good habit of declaring all of the variables you use in your scripts. Declaring variables before use makes code easier to read and to debug later.*

By declaring variables you also give them a name in the process. Here's an example of a variable declaration in VBScript.

```
Dim YourName
```

By doing this, what you in factdoing is giving the computer an instruction to reserve some memory space for you and give that chunk the name `YourName`. From now on, the computer (or, more accurately, the VBScript script engine) keeps track of that memory for you, and whenever you use the variable name `YourName`, it will know what you're talking about.

Variables are essential to programming. Without them you have no way to hold all the data that your script will be handling. Every input into the script, output from the script, and process within the script uses variables. They are the computer's equivalent of the sticky notes that we leave all over the place with little bits of information on them. All the notes are important (otherwise why write them?) but they are also temporary. Some might become permanent (so you take a phone number and write it down in your address book or PDA), while others are thrown away after use (say, after reminding you do something). This is how it works with variables too. Some hold data that you might later want to keep, while others are just used for general housekeeping and are disposed of as soon as they're used.

In VBScript, whenever you have a piece of information that you need to work with, you declare a variable using the exact same syntax that we showed you a moment ago. At some point in your script, you're going to need to do something with the memory space you've allocated yourself (otherwise, what would be the point of declaring it?) And what you do with a variable is place a value in it. This is called "initializing" the variable. Sometimes you initialize a variable with a default value. Other times, you might ask the user for some information, and initialize the variable with whatever the user enters. Alternatively, you might open a database and use a previously stored value to initialize the variable.

> Note: When we say "database"we don't necessarily mean an actual database but any store or data—it might be an Internet browser cookie or a text file that we get the data from.

Initializing the variable gives you a starting point. After it has been initialized, you can begin making use of the variable in your script.

Here's a very simple VBScript example.

```
Dim YourName
' Above we dimensioned the variable
YourName = InputBox("Hello! What is your name?")
' Above we ask for the user's name and initialize the variable
MsgBox "Hello " & YourName & "! Pleased to meet you."
' Above we display a greeting containing the user's name
```

Quite rightly, you're now probably wondering what all this code means. Last time we showed you one line and now it's grown to six.

> All of the examples in this chapter are designed so that you can run them using the Windows Script Host (WSH). The WSH is a scripting host that allows you to run VBScript programs within Windows. WSH will allow you to try out these example programs for yourself. You may already have WSH installed. To find out, type the above example script into a text editor, save the file as TEST.VBS (it must have the

*. VBS extension, and not a* `.TXT`*), and double-click the file in Windows Explorer. If the script runs, then you're all set. If Windows does not recognize the file, then you'll need to download and install WSH from* `http://msdn.microsoft.com/scripting`*.*

You already know what the first line of code does. It declares a variable for use called `YourName`.

The second line in our code is a comment. In VBScript, any text that is preceded by the single quote character ( ' ) is treated as a comment. What this means is that the VBScript script engine will completely ignore the text. So, if the VBScript engine just ignores any text typed after the single quote character, why bother typing it in at all? It doesn't contribute to the execution of the script, right? This is absolutely correct, but don't forget one of the most important principles of programming: It is not just computers that may have to read script. It is equally important to write a script with human readers in mind as it is to write with the computer in mind.

Of course, none of this means that we are for one moment forgetting that when we are writing our scripts, we must write them with the computer (or, more specifically, the script engine) in mind. If we don't type the code correctly (that is, if we don't use the proper syntax), the script engine won't be able to execute the script. However, humans are also involved in programming. Once you've written some useful scripts, you're probably going to have to go back to make some changes to a script you wrote six months or a year ago. If you didn't write that code with human readers in mind as well as a computer reader, it could be pretty difficult to figure out what you were thinking and how you decided to solve the problems at the time you wrote the script. Things can get worse. What happens when you or one of your coworkers has to make some changes to a script you wrote many months ago? If you did not write that script to be both readable and maintainable, others that useyour code will encounter difficulties deciphering thecode—no matter how well written the actual computer part of the code is.

Adding comments to your code is just one part of making sure code is clear and readable. There are many other things that you can do:

- ❑ Choosing clear, meaningful variable names
- ❑ Indenting code for clarity
- ❑ Making effective use of white space
- ❑ Organizing the code in a logical manner

All of these aid human-readability and we'll be covering all of these later, but clear, concise comments are by far the most important. However, too much of a good thing is never good and the same is true for comments. Overburdening code with comments doesn't help. Remember that if you are scripting for the Web that all the code, including the comments, are downloaded to the browser and so unnecessary comments may adversely affect download times.

We'll discuss some good commenting principles later in this chapter, but for now just be aware of the fact that the comment we have in line 2 of our script is not really a good comment for everyday use. This is because, to any semi-experienced programmer, it is all too obvious that what we are doing is declaring the `YourName` variable on the line above. However, throughout this book you will often see the code commented in a similar way. This is because the point of our code is to instruct the reader in how a particular aspect of VBScript programming works. The best way for us to do that is to add comments to the code directly. It removes ambiguity and keeps the code and comments together.

Also worth noting is that comments don't have to be on a separate line. Comments can also follow the code, like so :

```
Dim YourName ' initialize the variable
YourName = InputBox("Hello! What is your name?") ' ask for the user's name
MsgBox "Hello " & YourName & "! Pleased to meet you." ' display a greeting
```

This works in theory but it isn't as clear as keeping the comments on separate lines in the script.

OK, back to the script. Take a look at line 3.

```
YourName = InputBox("Hello! What is your name?")
```

Here we are doing two things at once. First, we're initializing the variable. We could do it directly, like this:

```
YourName = "Fred"
```

However, the drawback with this is that we are making the arbitrary decision that everyone is called Fred, which is ideal for some applications but not for others. If we wanted to assign a fixed value to a variable, such as a tax rate, this would be fine.

```
Dim TaxRate
TaxRate = 17.5
```

However, we want to do something that gives the user a choice, which is why we employ the use of a function, called InputBox. We'll be looking at this function and all the others in later chapters, but for now all you need to know is that InputBox is used to display a message in a dialog box, and it waits for the user to input text or click a button. The InputBox generated is displayed in Figure 1-1.

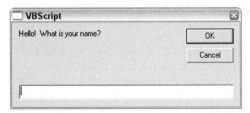

**Figure 1-1**

The clever bit is what happens to the text that the user types into the input box displayed—it is stored in the variable YourName.

Line is another comment. Line 5 is more code. Now that we've initialized this variable, we're going to do something useful with it. MsgBox is another built-in VBScript function that you will probably use quite a lot during the course of your VBScript programming. Using the MsgBox function is a good way to introduce the programming concept of passing function parameters, also known as *arguments*. Some functions don't require you to pass parameters to them while others do. This is because some functions (take the Date function as an example—this returns the current date based on the system time) do not need any additional information from you in order to do their job. The MsgBox function, on the other hand, displays a piece of information to the user in the form of a dialog box, like the one shown in Figure 1-2.

**Figure 1-2**

You have to pass `MsgBox` a parameter because on its own it doesn't have anything useful to display (in fact, it will just bring up a blank pop-up box). The `MsgBox` function actually has several parameters, but for now we're just going to look at one. All of the other parameters are optional parameters.

Take another look at line 5 and you'll probably notice the ampersand (`&`). The ampersand is a VBScript operator, and is used to concatenate (join) pieces of text together. To concatenate simply means to "string together." This text can take the form of either a literal or a variable. A literal is the opposite of a variable. A variable is so named because it is exactly that—a variable—and can change throughout the lifetime of the script (a script's lifetime is the time from when it starts executing, to the time it stops executing). Unlike a variable, a literal cannot change during the lifetime of the script. Here is line 5 of the script again.

```
MsgBox "Hello " & YourName & "! Pleased to meet you."
```

An operator is a symbol or a word that you use within your code that is usually used to change or test a value. Other operators include the standard mathematical operators (+, -, /, *), and the equals sign (=), which can actually be used in either a comparison or an assignment. So far, we have used the equals sign as an assignment operator. Later on you'll find out more about operators.

Let's now take a closer look at variables. Remember how we said that a variable is a piece of reserved memory? One question you might have is how does the computer know how large to make that piece of memory? Well, again, in VBScript this isn't something that you need to worry about and it is all handled automatically by the VBScript engine. You don't have to worry in advance about how big or small you need to make a variable. You can even change your mind and the VBScript engine will dynamically change and reallocate the actual memory addresses that are used up by a variable. For example, take a quick look at this VBScript program.

```
' First declare the variable
Dim SomeVariable

' Initialize it with a value
SomeVariable = "Hello, World!"
MsgBox SomeVariable

' Change the value of the variable to something larger
SomeVariable = "Let's take up more memory than the previous text"
MsgBox SomeVariable
```

```
' Change the value again
SomeVariable = "Bye!"
MsgBox SomeVariable
```

Each time the script engine comes across a variable, the engine assigns it the smallest chunk of memory it needs. Initially the variable contains nothing at all so needs little space but as we initialize it with the string "Hello, World!" the VBScript engine asks the computer for more memory to store the text. But again it asks for just what it needs and no more. (Memory is a precious thing and not to be wasted.) Next, when we assign more text to the same variable, the script engine must allocate even more memory, which it again does automatically. Finally, when we assign the shorter string of text, the script engine reduces the size of the variable in memory to conserve memory.

One final note about variables: Once you've assigned a value to a variable, you don't have to throw it away in order to assign something else to the variable as well. Take a look at this example.

```
Dim SomeVariable

SomeVariable = "Hello"
MsgBox SomeVariable

SomeVariable = SomeVariable & ", World!"
MsgBox SomeVariable

SomeVariable = SomeVariable & " Goodbye!"
MsgBox SomeVariable
```

Notice how in this script, we each time keep adding the original value of the variable and adding some additional text to it. We tell the script engine that this is what we wanted to do by also using the name of the SomeVariable variable on the right side of the equals sign, and then concatenating its existing value with an additional value using the ampersand (&) operator. Adding onto the original value works with numbers too (as opposed to numbers in strings) but you have to use the + operator instead of the & operator.

```
Dim SomeNumber

SomeNumber = 999
MsgBox SomeNumber

SomeNumber = SomeNumber + 2
MsgBox SomeNumber

SomeNumber = SomeNumber + 999
MsgBox SomeNumber
```

Here are the resulting message boxes generated by this code. The first is shown in Figure 1-3.

**Figure 1-3**

The second message box is shown in Figure 1-4.

**Figure 1-4**

Figure 1-5 shows the final message box.

**Figure 1-5**

There are several different types of data that you can store in variables. These are called data types and so far we've seen two:

❑ String

❑ Integer

*Note: We've also seen a single-precision floating-point number too in the tax rate example.*

We'll be covering all of them later on in the book. For now, just be aware that there are different data types and that they can be stored in variables.

# Flow Control

When you run a script that you have written, the code executes in a certain order. This order of execution is also known as *flow*. In simple scripts such as the ones we looked at so far, the statements simply execute from the top to down. The script engine starts with the first statement in the script, executes this, then moves on to the next one, then the next one, and so on until the script reaches the end. The execution occurs this way because the simple programs we've written so far do not contain any branching or looping code.

# Branching

Take a look at a script that we used earlier.

```
Dim YourName
'Above we initialized the variable
```

```
YourName = InputBox("Hello! What is your name?")
'Above we ask for the user's name and initialize the variable
MsgBox "Hello " & YourName & "! Pleased to meet you."
'Above we display a greeting containing the user's name
```

If you save this script in a file with a .vbs file and then execute it using the Windows Script Host, all of the statements will be executed in order from the first statement to the last.

Note that we say that all of the statements will be executed. However, this isn't what you always want. There are techniques that we can use to cause some statements to be executed, and some not, depending on certain conditions. This technique is called *branching*.

VBScript supports a few different branching constructs, and we will cover all of them in detail in a later chapter on flow control, but we're only going to cover the simplest and most common one here, which is the If...Else...End If construct.

Take a look at this modified code example.

```
Dim YourName
Dim Greeting

YourName = InputBox("Hello! What is your name?")

If YourName = "" Then
    Greeting = "OK. You don't want to tell me your name."
Else
    Greeting = "Hello, " & YourName & ", great to meet you."
End If

MsgBox Greeting
```

OK, let's take a trip through the code.

```
Dim YourName
Dim Greeting
```

Here we declare the two variables that we are going to be using.

```
YourName = InputBox("Hello! What is your name?")
```

Here we ask the user for some input, again using the InputBox function. This function expects one required parameter, the prompt text (the text that appears on the input box). It can also accept several optional parameters. Here we're only going to use the one required parameter.

Note that the parameter text that we passed "Hello! What is your name?" is displayed as a prompt for the dialog box. The InputBox function returns the value that the user types in, if any. If the user does not type anything in, or clicks the Cancel button (both do the same thing), then InputBox will return a zero-length string, which is a strange kind of programming concept that basically means that it returns text that doesn't actually contain any text. Our script stores the result of the InputBox function in the YourName variable.

Next we come to the actual loop we are going to use.

```
If YourName = "" Then
    Greeting = "OK. You don't want to tell me your name."
Else
    Greeting = "Hello, " & YourName & ", great to meet you."
End If
```

This code presents the VBScript engine with an option that is based on what the user typed (or didn't type) into the input box. The first line tests the input from the user. It tests to see if the input that is stored in the variable YourName is a zero-length string. If it is, the next line of code is run and the variable Greeting is assigned a string.

Figure 1-6 shows the message displayed if the user doesn't type his or her name into the InputBox.

Figure 1-6

What happens if the user does (as we expect) type something into the input box? Well, this is where the next line comes in.

```
Else
```

You can actually begin to read the code and in fact doing this helps it to make sense. What the whole loop actually means is that if the value of variable YourName is a zero-length string then assign the variable Greeting with one value; however, if it contains something else, do something else (assign Greeting a different value).

The final line of the code uses the MsgBox function to display the value of the variable Greeting.

Notice that both lines of code assign a value to the Greeting variable. However, only one of these lines will actually execute in any one running of the script. This is because our If...Else...End If block makes an either/or decision. Either a given condition is True, or it is False. There's no way it can be neither (not a string that contains text nor a zero-length string) or both (a zero-length string that contains text). If it is True, then the script engine will execute the code between the If and Else statements. If it is False, then it will execute the code between the Else and End If statements.

So, what the complete script does is test the input, and then executes different code, depending on the result of that test, and hence the term branching. Depending on the test of the input, the flow of execution is either going to go one way, or the other. Using this allows your script to adapt to the unpredictable nature of the input. Compare out intelligent script to this one, which by comparison looks pretty lame.

```
Dim YourName
Dim Greeting
```

```
YourName = InputBox("Hello! What is your name?")

Greeting = "Hello, " & YourName & ", great to meet you."

MsgBox Greeting
```

This script is just plain dumb because it does not contain any branching logic to test the input; so when the user does something unpredictable, like clicking the Cancel button, or not entering any name at all, the script does not have the ability to adapt. Compare this to our intelligent script, which is capable of adapting to the unpredictability of input by testing it with If...Else...End If branching.

Before we move on to looping, we should mention a few other things about If...Else...End If.

First, the block of code containing the If...Else...End If is known as a block of code. A block is a section of code that has a beginning and an end, and it usually contains keywords or statements at both the beginning and the end. In the case of If...Else...End If, the If statement marks the beginning of the block, while the End If marks the end of the block.

The script engine requires these beginning and ending statements, and if you omit them, the script engine won't understand your code and won't allow your script to execute. Over the course of this book you will encounter many different types of code blocks in VBScript.

> Note: Sometimes, just to confuse matters, the term "block of code" is often used informally to describe any group of lines of code.

Second, notice also that the lines of code that are inside the block itself are indented by 4spaces. This is an extremely important concept but not for the reason you might think. This indenting has nothing whatsoever to do with the script engine—it doesn't care whether you add 4spaces, 44spaces, or none at all. This indenting is for the benefit of any humans who might be reading your code. For example, the following script is completely legal and will execute just fine.

```
Dim YourName
        Dim Greeting

    YourName = InputBox("Hello! What is your name?")

If YourName = "" Then
        Greeting = "OK. You don't want to tell me your name."
  Else
Greeting = "Hello, " & YourName & ", great to meet you."
                                End If


            MsgBox Greeting
```

This code is, however, very difficult to read. As a general rule of thumb, you indent code by 4 spaces whenever a line or series of lines is subordinate to the lines above and below it. For example, the lines after the If clause and the Else clause belong inside the If...Else...End If block, so we indent them to visually suggest this.

Presentation, while having no bearing whatsoever on how the computer or script engine handles your code, is very important when it comes to how humans read it. The presentation of your code should visually suggest its logical structure. In other words, without even reading it, we can look at the code and get a sense for how it is organized and how it works. By seeing the indentations inside the If...Else...End If block, we cannot just read the code but "see" the branching logic at that point in the code. Indenting is only one element of programming style, but learning and following proper style and layout is essential for any programmer who wants to be taken seriously.

Third, the Else part of the block is optional. Sometimes you want to test for a certain condition, and if that condition is True, execute some code, but if it's False, there's no code to execute. For example, we could add another If...End If block to our script.

```
Dim YourName
Dim Greeting

YourName = InputBox("Hello! What is your name?")

If YourName = "" Then
    Greeting = "OK. You don't want to tell me your name."
Else
    Greeting = "Hello, " & YourName & ", great to meet you."
End If

If YourName = "Fred" Then
    Greeting = Greeting & " Nice to see you Fred."
End If

MsgBox Greeting
```

Fourth, If...Else...End If can be extended through the use of the ElseIf clause, and through nesting. *Nesting* is the technique of placing a block of code inside of another block of code of the same type.

The following variation on our script illustrates both concepts.

```
Dim YourName
Dim Greeting

YourName = InputBox("Hello! What is your name?")

If YourName = "" Then
    Greeting = "OK. You don't want to tell me your name."
ElseIf YourName = "abc" Then
    Greeting = "That's not a real name."
ElseIf YourName = "xxx" Then
    Greeting = "That's not a real name."
Else
    Greeting = "Hello, " & YourName & ", great to meet you."

    If YourName = "Fred" Then
        Greeting = Greeting & " Nice to see you Fred."
    End If

End If

MsgBox Greeting
```

Once again, see how the way that the code has been indented helps us to identify which lines of code are subordinate to the lines above them. As code gets more and more complex, proper indenting of the code becomes vital as it will become harder to follow.

Finally (and this may seem obvious by now), even though the branching logic you are adding to the code tells the script to execute certain lines of code while not executing others, all the code must still be interpreted by the script engine (including the code that's not executed). If any of the code that's not executed contains any syntax errors, the script engine will still produce an error message to let you know.

# Looping

Branching allows you to tell the script to execute some lines of code, but not others. Looping, on the other hand, allows you to tell the script to execute some lines of code over and over again. This is particularly useful in two situations:

❑    When you want to repeat a block of code until a condition is `True` or `False`

❑    When you want to repeat a block of code a finite number of times

There are many different looping constructs, but here we're going to focus on only two of them:

❑    The basic `Do...Loop While` loop

❑    The basic `For...Next` loop

We'll being by taking a look at the `Do...Loop While` construct and how it can be used to repeatedly execute a block of code until a certain condition is met. Take a look at this modification of our example script:

```
Dim Greeting
Dim YourName
Dim TryAgain

Do
    TryAgain = "No"

    YourName = InputBox("Please enter your name:")

    If YourName = "" Then
        MsgBox "You must enter your name to continue."
        TryAgain = "Yes"
    Else
        Greeting = "Hello, " & YourName & ", great to meet you."
    End If

Loop While TryAgain = "Yes"

MsgBox Greeting
```

Notice the block of code that starts with the word `Do` and ends with the line that starts with the word `Loop`. The indentation should make this code block easy to identify. This is the definition of our loop. The code inside the loop will keep being executed until at the end of the loop the `TryAgain` variable equals `"No"`.

We are using the `TryAgain` variable to control the loop. The loop starts at the word `Do`. At the end of the loop, if the `TryAgain` variable equals `"Yes"`, then all the code, starting at the word `Do`, will execute again.

Notice that at the top of the loop we initialize the `TryAgain` variable to `"No"`. It is absolutely essential that this initialization take place inside the loop (that is, between the `Do` and `Loop` statements). This way, the variable is reinitialized every time a loop occurs. If you didn't do this, you would end up with what's called an infinite loop. They are always bad. At best, the user is going to have to exit out of the program in an untimely (and inelegant) way because, as the name suggests, the loop is infinite. At worse, it can crash the system. You want neither and you want to try to avoid both in your code.

It's time to take a look at why the `TryAgain = "No"` line is essential to preventing an infinite loop. We'll go through the script line by line.

```
Do
```

This first line starts the loop. This tells the script engine that we are starting a block of code that will define a loop. The script engine will expect to find a Loop statement somewhere further down in the script. This is similar to the `If...End If` code block because the script engine expects the block to be defined with beginning and ending statements. The `Do` statement on a line all by itself means that the loop will execute at least once. Even if the `Loop While` statement at the end of the block does not result in a loop around back to the `Do` line, the code inside this block is going to be executed at least one time.

```
Do
     TryAgain = "No"
```

Let's move on to the second line of code. Here we are initializing our "control" variable. We call it the "control" variable because this variable will ultimately control whether or not the loop loops around again. We want to initialize this variable to `"No"` so that, by default, the loop will not loop around again. Only if a certain condition is met inside the loop will we set `TryAgain` to `"Yes"`. This is yet another strategy in our ever-vigilant desire to expect the unexpected.

```
Do
     TryAgain = "No"

     YourName = InputBox("Please enter your name:")
```

This line of code should look familiar. We are using the `InputBox` function to ask the user to enter a name. We store the return value from the function in the `YourName` variable. Whatever the user types in, unless they type nothing, will be stored in this variable. Put another way, our script is receiving some external input—and remember that we said input is always unpredictable.

```
Do
     TryAgain = "No"

     YourName = InputBox("Please enter your name:")

     If YourName = "" Then
          MsgBox "You must enter your name to continue."
```

```
        TryAgain = "Yes"
    Else
        Greeting = "Hello, " & YourName & ", great to meet you."
    End If
```

Now we are testing our input. The line If YourName = "" Then tests to see if the user typed in their name (or at least some text). If they typed something in, the code immediately after the Else line will execute. If they didn't type in anything (or if they clicked the Cancel button), then the YourName variable will be empty, and the code after the If line will execute instead.

If the user didn't type anything into the input box, we will display a message informing them that they have done something we didn't want them to. We then set the TryAgain variable (our control variable) to "Yes" and send them around the loop once more and ask the users for their name again (wherein this time they will hopefully type something into the input box).

If the user did type in their name, then we initialize our familiar Greeting variable. Note that in this case, we do not change the value of the TryAgain variable. This is because there is no need to loop around again because the user has entered a name. The value of TryAgain is already equal to "No", so there's no need to change it.

```
Do

    TryAgain = "No"

    YourName = InputBox("Please enter your name:")

    If YourName = "" Then
        MsgBox "You must enter your name to continue."
        TryAgain = "Yes"
    Else
        Greeting = "Hello, " & YourName & ", great to meet you."
    End If

Loop While TryAgain = "Yes"

MsgBox Greeting
```

Now we encounter the end of our loop block. What this Loop line is essentially telling the script engine is "If the TryAgain variable equals "Yes" at this point, then go back up to the Do line and execute all that code over again." If the user entered his or her name, then the TryAgain variable will be equal to "No". Therefore, the code will not loop again, and will continue onto the last line.

```
    MsgBox Greeting
```

If the user did not enter his or her name, then TryAgain would be equal to "Yes", which would mean that the code would again jump back to the Do line. This is where the reinitialization of the TryAgain variable to "No" is essential because if it wasn't done then there's no way for TryAgain to ever equal anything but "Yes". And if TryAgain always equals "Yes", then the loop will keep going around and around forever. This results in total disaster for your script, and for the user.

Next we'll take a quick look at the `For...Next` loop. In this kind of loop, we don't need to worry about infinite loops because the loop is predefined to execute only a certain number of times.

Here's a simple (if not very useful) example.

```
Dim Counter

MsgBox "Let's count to ten. Ready?"

For Counter = 1 to 10
    MsgBox Counter
Next

MsgBox "Wasn't that fun?"
```

This loop is similar to the previous loop. The beginning loop block is defined by the `For` statement, and the end is defined by the `Next` statement. This loop is different because you can predetermine how many times it will run; in this case, it will go around exactly ten times. The line `For Counter = 1 to 10` essentially tells the script engine, "Execute this block of code as many times as it takes to count from 1 to 10, and use the `Counter` variable to keep track of your counting. When we've gone through this loop ten times, stop looping and move on."

Notice that every time the loop goes around (including the first time through), the `Counter` variable holds the value of the current count. The first time through, `Counter` equals 1, the second time through it equals 2, and so on up to 10. It's important to note that after the loop is finished, the value of the `Counter` variable will be 11, one number higher than the highest value in our `For` statement. The reason for this is that the `Counter` variable is incremented at the end of the loop, after which the `For` statement tests the value of index to see if it is necessary to loop again.

Giving you a meaningful example of how to make use of the `For...Next` loop isn't easy because you haven't been exposed to much VBScript just yet, but here's an example that shows you don't need to know how many times the loop needs to run before you run it.

```
Dim Counter
Dim WordLength
Dim WordBuilder

WordLength = Len("VBScript is great!")

For Counter = 1 to WordLength
    MsgBox Mid("VBScript is great!", Counter, 1)
    WordBuilder = WordBuilder & Mid("VBScript is great!", Counter, 1)
Next

MsgBox WordBuilder
```

For example, the phrase `"VBScript is great!"` has exactly 18 letters. If you first calculated the number of letters in the phrase, you could use that number to drive a `For...Next` loop. However, this code uses the VBScript `Len()` function to calculate the length of the phrase used. Inside the loop, it uses the `Mid()` function to pull one letter out of the phrase one at a time and display them separately. The position of that letter is controlled by the counter variable, while the number of letters extracted is defined by the `length` argument at the end. It also populates the `WordBuilder` variable with each loop, adding each new letter to the previous letter or letters, rebuilding the phrase.

Here's a variation of the last example: here giving the user the opportunity to type in a word or phrase to use, proving that there's nothing up our sleeve when it comes to knowing how many times to loop the code.

```
Dim Counter
Dim WordLength
Dim InputWord
Dim WordBuilder

InputWord = InputBox ("Type in a word of phrase to use")

WordLength = Len(InputWord)

For Counter = 1 to WordLength
    MsgBox Mid(InputWord, Counter, 1)
    WordBuilder = WordBuilder & Mid(InputWord, Counter, 1)
Next

MsgBox WordBuilder & " contains " & WordLength & " characters."
```

Figure 1-7 shows the final summary message generated by the code. Notice how well the information is integrated.

**Figure 1-7**

# Operators

An operator acts on one or more operands when comparing, assigning, concatenating, calculating, and performing logical operations.

Say you want to calculate the difference between two variables X and Y and save the result in variable Z. These variables are the operands and to find the difference you use the subtraction operator like this:

```
Z = X - Y
```

Here we used the assignment operator (=) to assign the difference between X and Y, which was found by using the subtraction operator (-).

Operators are one of the single-most important parts of any programming language. Without them, you would not be able to assign values to variables or perform calculations or comparisons. In fact, you wouldn't be able to do much at all.

There are different types of operators and they each serve a specific purpose:

❑ The assignment (=) operator is the most obvious and is simply used for assigning a value to a variable or property.

❑ The arithmetic operators are all used to calculate a numeric value, and are normally used in conjunction with the assignment operator and/or one of the comparison operators.

❑ The concatenation operators are used to concatenate ("join together") expressions.

❑ The comparison operators are used for comparing variables and expressions against other variables, constants, or expressions.

❑ The logical operators are used for performing logical operations on expressions; all logical operators can also be used as bitwise operators.

❑ The bitwise operators are used for comparing binary values bit –by bit; all bitwise operators can also be used as logical operators.

## Operator Precedence

When you have a situation where more than one operation occurs in an expression, the operations are normally performed from left to right. However, there are several rules.

Operators from the arithmetic group are evaluated first, then concatenation, comparison, and finally logical operators. This is the set order in which operations occur (operators in brackets have the same precedence):

❑ ∩,−, (*, /), \, Mod, (+, −)

❑ &

❑ =, <>, <, >, <=, >=, Is

❑ Not, And, Or, Xor, Eqv, Imp

This order can be overridden by using parentheses. Operations in parentheses are evaluated before operations outside the parentheses, but inside the parentheses, the normal precedence rules still apply.

Take a look at the following two statements.

```
A = 5 + 6 * 7 + 8
A = (5 + 6) * (7 + 8)
```

They look the same but they're not. According to operator precedence, multiplication is performed before addition, so the top line gives A the value 55 (6 * 7 = 42 + 5 + 8 = 55). By adding parentheses, we force the additions to be evaluated first and A becomes equal to 165.

# Organizing and Reusing Code

So far, the scripts we've worked with have been fairly simple in structure. The code has been all together in one unit. We haven't been doing anything all that complicated, so it has been easy to see all the code right there in front of us, in just a few lines. The execution of the code is easy to follow because it starts at the top of the file, with the first line, and then continues downward until it reaches the last line. Sometimes, at certain points, choices made will have redirected the code using branching, or sections of code will have been repeated using loops.

However, when you come to writing a script that will actually do something useful, it is likely your code is going to get quite a bit more complex. As you add more and more code to the script, it will become harder and harder to read it all in one chunk. If printed on paper, your scripts would probably stretch across multiple pages. As the code gets more and more complex, it becomes easier for bugs and errors to creep-in, and the poor layout of the code will make these harder to find and fix. The most common technique programmers use to manage complexity is called *modularization*. This is a big, fancy word, but the concept behind it is really quite simple.

Modularization is the process of organizing your code into modules, which we can also think of as building blocks. You can apply the principles of modularity to create your own personal set of programming building blocks, which you can then use to build programs that are more powerful, more reliable, easier to debug, and easier for you and your fellow programmers to maintain and reuse. When you take your code and divide it up into modules, your ultimate goal is to create what are known as black boxes. A *black box* is any kind of device that has a simple, well-defined interface and that performs some discrete, well-defined function. A black box is so called because you don't need to see what's going on inside it. All you need to know is what it does, what its inputs are, and (sometimes) what its outputs are.

A wristwatch is a good example of a black box. It has inputs (buttons) and outputs (time) and does a simple function well while at the same time you don't need to worry about how the innards of the watch work in order to be able to tell the time.

The most basic kind of black box programmers use to achieve modularity is the procedure. A *procedure* is a set of code that (ideally) performs a single function. Good examples of procedures are:

- ❏   Code that adds two numbers together
- ❏   Code that processes a string input
- ❏   Code that handles saving to a file

Bad examples include:

- ❏   Code that takes an input, processes it, and also handles saving to a file
- ❏   Code that handles file access and database access

We have been using procedures throughout this chapter, but they have been procedures that VBScript provides for us. Some of these procedures require input, some don't. Some of these procedures return a value, some don't. But all of the procedures we have used so far (`MsgBox()`, `InputBox()`, and so on) are black boxes. They perform one single well-defined function, and they perform it without you having to worry about how they perform their respective functions. In just a moment, we're going to see how to extend the VBScript language by writing our own procedures.

Before we begin though, it's time to get some of the terminology cleared up. *Procedure* is a generic term that can be used to describe either a function or a subprocedure. We touched on some of this confusing terminology earlier, but a *function* is simply a procedure that returns a value. Len() is a function. You pass it some text, and it returns the number of characters in the string (or the number of bytes required to store a variable) back to you. Functions do not always require input, but they often do.

A *subprocedure* is a procedure that does not return a value. We have been using MsgBox() as a subprocedure. We pass it some text, and it displays a message on the screen comprising of that text. It does not return any kind of value to our code. All we need to know is that it did what we asked it to do. Just like functions, procedure may or may not require input.

Some of the code that follows will look familiar to you—that's because we've already shown it to you earlier. Here's how to turn code into a function.

```
Function PromptUserName

    ' This Function prompts the user for their name.
    ' If the user enters nothing it returns a zero-length string.
    ' It incorporates various greetings depending on input by the user.
    Dim YourName
    Dim Greeting

    YourName = InputBox("Hello! What is your name?")

    If YourName = "" Then
        Greeting = "OK. You don't want to tell me your name."
    ElseIf YourName = "abc" Then
        Greeting = "That's not a real name."
    ElseIf YourName = "xxx" Then
        Greeting = "That's not a real name."
    Else
        Greeting = "Hello, " & YourName & ", great to meet you."

        If YourName = "Fred" Then
            Greeting = Greeting & " Nice to see you Fred."
        End If

    End If

    MsgBox Greeting

    PromptUserName = YourName

End Function
```

The first thing to take note of in the code is the first and last lines. While not groundbreaking, the first and last lines are what defines a function. The first line defines the beginning of the function and gives it a name while the last line defines the end of the function. Based on our earlier discussion of code blocks, this should be a familiar convention by now. Looking at this now you should begin to realize that a procedure is nothing but a special kind of code block. The code has to tell the script engine where it begins, and where it ends. Notice also that we have given the function a clear, useful name that precisely describes what this function does. Giving your procedures good names is one of the keys to writing programs that are easy to read and maintain.

Notice also how we added a comment to the beginning of the procedure to describe what it does. Notice that the comment does not describe how the function does what it does, only what it does. The code that uses this function does not care how the function accomplishes its task; it only cares about inputs, outputs, and predictability. It is vitally important that you add clear, informative comments such as this to the beginning of your procedures, since they make it easy to determine what the function does. The comment also performs one other valuable service to you and any other developer who wants to call this function—it says that the function may return a zero-length string if the user does not enter his name.

Finally, notice how, in the second to last line, we treat the function name `PromptUserName` as if it were a variable. When using functions (as opposed to subprocedures, which do not return a value), this is how you give the function its return value. In a sense, what happens is that the function name itself is a variable within the procedure.

Here is some code that uses the `PromptUserName` function.

```
Dim Greeting
Dim VisitorName

VisitorName = PromptUserName

If VisitorName <> "" Then
    Greeting = "Goodbye, " & VisitorName & ". Nice to have met you."

Else
    Greeting = "I'm glad to have met you, but I wish I knew your name."
End If

MsgBox Greeting
```

If you are using Windows Script Host as the host for this code, bear in mind that this code and the `PromptUserName` function itself must be in the same `.vbs` script file.

```
Dim PartingGreeting
Dim VisitorName

VisitorName = PromptUserName

If VisitorName <> "" Then
    PartingGreeting = "Goodbye, " & VisitorName & ". Nice to have met you."

Else
    PartingGreeting = "I'm glad to have met you, but I wish I knew your name."
End If

MsgBox PartingGreeting

Function PromptUserName

    ' This Function prompts the user for their name.
```

```
    ' It incorporates various greetings depending on input by the user.
    Dim YourName
    Dim Greeting

    YourName = InputBox("Hello! What is your name?")

    If YourName = "" Then
        Greeting = "OK. You don't want to tell me your name."
    ElseIf YourName = "abc" Then
        Greeting = "That's not a real name."
    ElseIf YourName = "xxx" Then
        Greeting = "That's not a real name."
    Else
        Greeting = "Hello, " & YourName & ", great to meet you."

        If YourName = "Fred" Then
            Greeting = Greeting & " Nice to see you Fred."
        End If

    End If

    MsgBox Greeting

    PromptUserName = YourName

End Function
```

As you can see, calling the `PromptUserName` function is pretty straightforward. Once you have written a procedure, calling it is no different than calling a built-in VBScript procedure.

Procedures afford several key advantages that are beyond the scope of this discussion. However, here are a few of the most important ones:

❑ Code such as the code we put in the `PromptUserName` function can be thought of as "generic," meaning that it can be applied to a variety of uses. Once you have created a discreet, well-defined, generic function such as `PromptUserName`, you are free to reuse it any time you wish to prompt the user for their name. Once you've written a well-tested procedure, you never have to write that code again. Any time you need it, you just call the procedure. This is known as code reuse.

❑ When you call a procedure to perform a task rather than writing the code "in-line," it makes that code much easier to read and maintain. Increasing the readability, and therefore the manageability and maintainability, of your code is a good enough reason by itself to break a block of code out into its own procedure.

❑ When code is isolated into its own procedure, it greatly reduces the effects of changes to that code. This goes back to the idea of the black box. As long as the procedure itself maintains its predictable inputs and outputs, changes to the code inside of a procedure are insulated from harming the code that calls the procedure. You can make significant changes to the procedure, but as long as the inputs and outputs are predictable and remain unchanged, the code will work just fine.

# Top-Down versus Event-Driven

Before we leave this introduction to programming, it will be helpful to you if we shed light on the fact that you will encounter two different *models* of programming in this book:

❑   Top-down programs

❑   Event-driven programs

The differences between top-down and event-driven have to do with both the way you organize your code and how and when that code gets executed at runtime. As you get deeper into programming in general, and VBScript in particular, this will become clearer, so don't be alarmed if it seems a little vague and doesn't completely sink-in right now.

What we have been doing so far in this chapter is writing very simple top-down style programs. The process is simple to follow:

❑   We write some code.

❑   The code is saved it in a script file.

❑   Windows Script Host is used to execute the script.

❑   The Script Host starts executing at the first line and continues to the last line.

❑   If a script file contains some procedure definitions (such as our `PromptUserName` function), then the Script Host will only execute those procedures if some other code calls them.

❑   Once the Script Host reaches the last line of code, the lifetime of the script ends.

Top-down programs are very useful for task-oriented scripts. For example, you might write a script to search your hard drive for all the files with the extension `.HTM` and copy all the names and file locations to a file, formatted in HTML to act as a sitemap. Or you might write a script that gets executed every time Windows starts and which randomly chooses a different desktop wallpaper bitmap file for that session of Windows. Top-down programming is perfect for these kinds of scripts.

Event-driven code is different, and is useful in different contexts. As the name implies, event-driven code only gets executed when a certain "event" occurs. Until the event occurs, the code won't get executed. If a given event does not occur during the lifetime of the script, the code associated with that event won't be executed at all. If an event occurs, and there's no code associated with that event, then the event is essentially ignored.

Event-driven programming is the predominant paradigm in Windows programming. Most of the Windows programs you use every day were written in the event-driven model. This is because of the graphical nature of Windows programs. In a graphical user interface (GUI), you have all sorts of buttons, drop-down lists, fields in which to type text, and so on. For example, the word processor program Microsoft Word is totally jam-packed with these. Every time a user clicks a button, chooses an item in a list, or types some text into a field, an event is "raised" within the code. The person who wrote the program may or may not have decided to write code in response to that event. However, if the program is well written, an item such as a button for saving a file, which the user expects to have code behind it, will indeed have code behind it (for example, code to save the file).

When a GUI-based program starts, there is almost always some top-down style code that executes first. This code might be used to read a setting stored in the registry, prompt the user for a name and password, load a particular file at startup or prompt to take the user through the setting up stages if this is the first time the application has been run, and so on. Then a "form" typically comes up. The form contains all the menus, buttons, lists, and fields that make up the user interface of the program. At that point, the top-down style coding is done, and the program enters what is known as a wait state. No code is executing at this point and the program just waits for the user to do something. From here on , it's pretty much all about events.

When the user begins to do something, the program comes to life again. Say the user clicks on a button. The program raises the Click event for the button that the user clicked. The code attached to that event starts to execute, performs some operations, and when it's finished, the program returns to its wait state. In-between event occurrences, the program just sits there, doing nothing.

As far as VBScript is concerned, the event-driven model is used heavily in scripting for the Web. Scripts that run inside of HTML Web pages are all based on events. One script may execute when the page is loaded, while another script might execute when the user clicks on a link or graphic. These "mini scripts" are embedded in the HTML file, and are blocked-out in a syntax very similar to the one we used to define the PromptUserName function in the previous section.

As you progress through the second half of this book, the finer points of event-driven programming will become much clearer to you. However, just so you can see an example at this point, type the code below into your text editor, save the file with a .HTM extension, and then select Open from the File menu in Internet Explorer 5.0 or higher to open the file.

```
<html>
<head>
<title>Simple VBScript Example</title>
<script language="vbscript">
    Sub ButtonClicked
        window.alert("You clicked on the button!")
    End Sub
</script>
</head>
<body>
  <button name="Button1" type=BUTTON onclick="ButtonClicked">
  Click Me If You Can!!!
  </button>
</body>
</html>
```

Figure 1-8 shows the result of clicking on the button on the page. In this case it's only a message box but it could be much more.

# Coding Guidelines

It's a really good idea to get into healthy programming habits right from the beginning. As you continue to hone your programming skills and possibly learn multiple languages, these habits will serve you well. Your programs will be easier for you and your fellow developers to read, understand, and modify, and they will also contain fewer bugs.

**Figure 1-8**

When you first get started writing code, you have to concentrate so hard on just getting the syntax correct for the computer that it will be easy for you to forget about all the things you need to do in order to make sure your code is human friendly as well. However, attentiveness early on will pay huge dividends in the long run.

## Expect the Unexpected

Always remember that anything that can happen probably will happen. The idea here is to code defensively—preparing for the unexpected. You don't need to become totally fixated on preparing for all contingencies and remote possibilities, but you can't ignore them either. You especially have to worry about the unexpected when receiving input from the user, from a database, or from a file. Whenever you're about to perform an action on something, ask yourself questions: What could go wrong here? What happens if the file is flagged Read Only? What happens if the file isn't there? What happens if the user doesn't run the program from the right folder? What happens if the database table doesn't have any records? What happens if the registry keys I was expecting aren't there? What happens if the user doesn't have the proper permission to carry out the operation? If you don't know what might go wrong with a given operation, find out through research or trial and error. Get others to try out your code and get their feedback on how it worked for them, on their system configuration, and operating system. Don't leave it up to your users to discover how well (or not) your script reacts to something unexpected. A huge part of properly preparing for the unexpected is the implementation of proper error handling, which we discuss in detail later.

## Always Favor the Explicit over the Implicit

When you are writing code, constantly ask yourself Is my intent clear to someone reading this code? Does the code speak for itself? Is there anything mysterious here? Are there any hidden meanings? Are the variable names too similar to be confusing? Even though something is obvious in your mind at the moment you are typing in the code, it doesn't mean it will be obvious to you six months or a year from now—or to someone else tomorrow. Always endeavor to make your code as self-documenting as possible, and where you fall short of that goal (which even the best programmers do—self-documenting code can be an elusive goal), use good comments to make things more clear. Be wary of using too many generics in code, such as x, y, and z as variable names and Function1, Function2, and Function3 as function names. Instead, make them explicit. Use variable names such as UserName and TaxRate. When naming a variable, use a name that will make it clear what that variable is used for. Be careful using abbreviations. Don't make variable names too short, but don't make them too long either (10–16 characters is a good length, but ideal length is largely a matter of preference). Even though VBScript is not case-sensitive, use mixed case to make it easier to distinguish multiple words within the variable name (for example, UserName is easier to read than username).

When naming procedures, try to choose a name that describes exactly what the procedure does. If the procedure is a function that returns a value, indicate what the return value is in the function name (for example, PromptUserName). Try to use good verb–noun combinations to describe first, what action the procedure performs, and second, what the action is performed on (for example, SearchFolders, MakeUniqueRegistryKey, or LoadSettings). Good procedure names tend to be longer than good variable names. Don't go out of your way to make them longer, but don't be afraid to either. Fifteen to thirty characters for a procedure name are perfectly acceptable (they can be a bit longer since you generally don't type them nearly as much). If you are having trouble giving your procedure a good name, that might be an indication that the procedure is not narrow enough—a good procedure does one thing, and does it well.

That said, if you are writing scripts for Web pages that will be downloaded to a user's browser, it is sometimes necessary to use shorter variable and procedure names. Longer names mean larger files to download. Even if you sacrifice some readability in order to make the file smaller, you can still make an effort to make the names as descriptive as possible. There may, however, be times with Web scripts where you might not want the code to be clear and easy to understand (at least for others). We'll look at techniques that you can employ to make scripts harder to follow for "script snoopers" while still allowing you to work with them and modify them later.

# Modularize Your Code into Procedures, Modules, Classes, and Components

When you are writing code, you should constantly evaluate whether any given block of code might be better if you moved it to its own function or subprocedure. Is the code you're working on rather complex? If so, break it into procedures. Are you using lots of And's and Or's in an If...End If statement? Consider moving the evaluation to its own procedure. Are you writing a block of code that you think you might need again in some other part of the script, or in another script? Move it to its own procedure. Are you writing some code that you think someone else might find useful? Move it. This isn't a science and there are no hard and fast rules for code—after all, only you know what you want it to do. Only you know if parts are going to be reused later. Only you know how complex something will turn out. However, always keep an eye out for possible modularization.

# Use the "Hungarian" Variable Naming Convention

You might hear programmers (especially C++ programmers) mention this quite a bit. While this is a bit out of scope of this introductory discussion, it is still worth mentioning nonetheless. The Hungarian naming convention involves giving variable names a prefix that indicates what the scope and data type of the variable are intended to be. So as not to confuse matters, we have not been using the Hungarian convention in this chapter, but you will find that most programmers prefer this convention. Properly used, it makes your programs much clearer and easier to write and read. We will list the standard prefixes for scope and data type in Appendix B.

## Don't Use One Variable for More Than One Job

This is a big no-no and a common mistake of both beginner and experienced programmers alike (but the fact that experienced programmers might have a bad habit does not make it any less bad). Each variable in your script should have just one purpose. It might be very tempting to just declare a bunch of generic variables with fuzzy names at the beginning of your script and then use them for multiple purposes throughout your script—but don't do it. This is one of the best ways to introduce very strange, hard to track down bugs into your scripts. Giving a variable a good name that clearly defines its purpose will help prevent you from using it for multiple purposes. The moral here is that while reusing variables might seem like a total timesaver, it isn't and can lead to hours of frustration and wasted time looking for the problem.

## Always Lay Out Your Code Properly

Always remember that good code layout adds greatly to readability later. Don't be tempted to save time early on by writing messy, hard to follow code because as sure as day turns to night, you will suffer if you do.

Without reading a single word, you should be able to look at the indentations of the lines to see which ones are subordinate to others. Keep related code together by keeping them on consecutive lines. Also, don't be frightened of white space in your code. Separate blocks of unrelated code by putting a blank line between them. Even though the script engine will let you, avoid putting multiple statements on the same line.

Also, remember to use the line continuation character (_) to break long lines into multiple shorter lines.

The importance of a clean layout that visually suggests the logic of the underlying code cannot be overemphasized.

## Use Comments To Make Your Code More Clear and Readable, but Don't Overuse Them

When writing code, strive to make it as self-documenting as possible. You can do this by following the guidelines set out earlier. However, self-documenting code is hard to achieve and no one is capable of 100% self-documenting code. Everyone writes code that can benefit from a few little scribbles to serve as reminders in the margins. The coding equivalents of these scribbles are comments. But how can you tell a good comment from a bad comment?

Generally speaking, a good comment operates at the level of intent. A good comment answers the questions What was the programmer trying to achieve with the code? Where does this code block fit in with the overall script? Why did the programmer write this code? The answers to these questions fill in the blanks that can never be filled by even the best, most pedantic self-documenting code. Good comments are also generally "paragraph-level" comments. Your code should be clear enough that you do not need a comment for each and every line of code it contains, but a comment that quickly and clearly describes the purpose for a block of code allows a reader to scan through the comments rather than reading every line of code. The idea is to keep the person who might be reading your code from having to pore over every line to try and figure out why the code exists. Commenting every line (as you probably noticed with the earlier examples) makes the code hard to follow and breaks up the flow too much.

Bad comments are generally redundant comments, meaning they repeat what the code itself already tells you. Try to make your code as clear as possible so that you don't need to repeat yourself with comments. Redundant comments tend to add clutter and do more harm than good. Reading the code tells you the how; reading the comments should tell you the why.

Finally, it's a good idea to get into the habit of adding "tombstone" or "flower box" comments at the top of each script file, module, class, and procedure. These comments typically describe the purpose of the code, the date it was written, the original author, and a log of modifications.

```
' Adrian Kingsley-Hughes
' 27 Oct 2003
' This script prompts the user for their name.
' It incorporates various greetings depending on input by the user.
'
' Added alternative greeting
' Changed variable names to make them more readable
```

# Summary

In this chapter we've taken a really fast-paced journey through the basics of programming. We've tried to distill a whole subject (at least a book) into one chapter. We've covered an awful lot of ground but we've also skimmed over or totally passed by a lot of stuff too. However, the information in this chapter will have given you the basics you need to get started programming with VBScript and the knowledge and confidence you need to be able to talk about programming with other programmers in a language they understand.

# What VBScript Is—and Isn't!

## Overview

VBScript–(or Microsoft's Visual Basic Scripting Edition) is a powerful interpreted scripting language that brings active scripting to a variety of environments, both client and server side. But VBScript is part of a bigger programming world—the world of Visual Basic.

What we are going to do in this chapter is to give you a peek into this bigger programming world and show you how VBScript fits in with the bigger picture. As the chapter name suggests, we'll be looking at what VBScript is and also what it isn't (this, hopefully, will dispel any myths that you might have read about VBScript).

Before we go any further, we should spend a little time clearing up a few points and getting the terminology, not just the terminology of VBScript but also that of related terminology, clear.

## Windows Script

Windows Script is the technology that provides the backbone for scripting on the Windows platform. Windows Script itself provides two separate script engines for use within the Windows operating system:

❑ Visual Basic Scripting Edition

❑ Microsoft JScript

Both of these scripting languages can be embedded and used together side by side if you want—there is no restriction on using only one language within your project, although this does make for more complex code and we don't recommend that you do this.

Windows Script also provides an array of supporting technologies that make it easier for user of Windows Script to do so. These include tools such as debuggers and script encoders.

# Version Information

The latest version of Windows Script is version 5.6. This is the version that we will be using throughout the book, as it is the latest, most fully featured, and contains all the latest security patches. Code written for Windows Script Engine 5.6 might work for earlier versions but cannot be guaranteed.

Version 5.6 introduced integration with Windows XP, tighter security controls, and a new object model. Windows Script has gone through many versions, each with a different host application behind it.

| Version | Host Application |
| --- | --- |
| 1.0 | Microsoft Internet Explorer 3.0 |
| 2.0 | Microsoft Internet Information Server 3.0 |
| 3.0 | Microsoft Internet Explorer 4.0<br>Microsoft Internet Information Server 4.0<br>Microsoft Windows Scripting Host 1.0<br>Microsoft Outlook 98 |
| 4.0 | Microsoft Visual Studio 6.0 |
| 5.0 | Microsoft Internet Explorer 5.0<br>Microsoft Internet Information Server 5.0 |
| 5.5 | Microsoft Internet Explorer 5.5 |
| 5.6 | Microsoft Visual Studio .NET |

# VBScript Is a Subset of VB

VBScript is a subset of Microsoft's Visual Basic. What this means is that if you are already using Visual Basic and come to VBScript you will find similarities in the syntax. The same is true if you make the leap from VBScript to Visual Basic (although you will have to learn how to use the development environment in Visual Basic). Likewise, if you come to VBScript from VB, don't expect it to look or feel too much like it. Certainly don't expect a VB-like integrated development environment (IDE) to work with. Also, don't expect to be able to do everything that you can in VB with VBScript.

However, the fact that VBScript is a subset of Visual Basic certainly makes it a compelling language to learn both as a stand-alone tool to use in day-to-day problem solving and as a language to learn that is both simple to pick up and has all the advantages of Visual Basic without the hassle of an IDE and the cost of purchasing the software.

Reinforcing their commitment to VBScript, Microsoft has released a script editor with their Microsoft Office 2003 suite.

# VBScript Is a Scripting Language

VBScript is a scripting language, as opposed to a programming language. The difference can be vague but the key test is what happens to the source code before it becomes the end product—for example, what is actually "run" and thought of as the program or application. The end product for a programming language is usually a compiled binary executable program, while for a scripting language the end product is still the source code. What this means is that VBScript source code and the VBScript end product are basically the same thing—a plain-text file readable and editable using any text editor (such as the trustworthy old Windows Notepad application included with all Windows versions). No special development environment is needed and the script in the file is not protected in any way.

# VBScript Is Interpreted at Runtime

Interpreted is another fuzzy term. It is vague because any language you care to think about can be either compiled or interpreted. This is because for any computer language you could write both a compiler and an interpreter. As long as the language itself is properly formed, all the compiler/interpreter does is make it machine-readable.

Now you might be beginning to see why VBScript is interpreted—because it isn't compiled!

> Note: Compiled means recoded into an executable format that have the .exe file extension. Programs written in languages such as C++ need to be compiled into an executable before distributed to the user.

Instead of building a compiler, an interpreter was written that takes the high-level VBScript "source code" and interprets it as the source code is processed. The interpreter in this case is the VBScript scripting engine, which is both very versatile and easily accessible for a variety of applications.

This doesn't mean that VBScript is never compiled. All computer languages are compiled at some point, otherwise the computer wouldn't know what to do with it and how to respond to it. The language the computer uses is the lowest level possible - the 1's and 0's language of machine language or binary language. Different sequences of 1's and 0's mean different things. One binary sequence may tell the computer to add two numbers together while another sequence tells it to store a value in a particular memory address. It's pretty hard to imagine it, but everything you ask a computer to do is ultimately digested into 1's and 0's.

A long time ago, if you wanted to write a program the only option available to you was to write it in binary language. As you can imagine, this wasn't easy or convenient. Over time, more advanced programming languages were invented. With each language, more and more higher levels of abstraction were added, which meant that programmers could use syntax that was closer to that of the English language. However, while programming languages have become cleverer, computers still continue to use machine language.

Plain text is easily readable by a human (although they might not understand what it means).

```
Dim Counter
Dim WordLength
Dim InputWord
Dim WordBuilder

InputWord = InputBox ("Type in a word or phrase to use")

WordLength = Len(InputWord)
```

```
For Counter = 1 to WordLength
    MsgBox Mid(InputWord, Counter, 1)
    WordBuilder = WordBuilder & Mid(InputWord, Counter, 1)
Next

MsgBox WordBuilder & " contains " & WordLength & " characters."
```

When code is compiled, what happens is that the higher level language that the programmer understands and writes is turned into the binary language that the computer understands. The main difference between "normal" programming languages and interpreted scripting languages is not whether the source code is compiled, but when compilation takes place. Take languages such as C and C++ that are commonly known as compiled languages, not because this distinguishes them from noncompiled languages but because they are compiled to machine code at design time (at the time the program was written).

This is where scripting languages differ. They are compiled (or, more accurately, interpreted) when they are executed, and hence runtime. This means that right up until runtime the script remains as plain text. Even during runtime, the actual file isn't altered; all the work in interpreting it is done in memory and has no effect whatsoever on the actual source file.

Compare this to a C++ program which if you were to look at the compiled code it would make no sense at all because it as already been processed into machine language. This means that the edit–debugging cycle for scripting languages is usually shorter than that of compiled code, because you do not have to go through the separate step of compiling the code at design time. Compiled code looks nothing like plain-text script.

Here is just part of a simple piece of C++ code that does the classic "Hello, World!".

```
MZP □    □ □ ÿÿ   ,         @ →                ⌐ °┼´  Í!¸⌐Lí!□□ This program must be run under Win32
$7
PE  L□□  ‾£<        à  ˪
⌐| □⌐ p  ┼ ┼ ⌐ @ ┼ ┐ ˩  ˩   €⌐ –  ˪ ┼  ┼┼  ┼ @⌐1 0⌐Ö| P⌐ ⌐           ⌐ h‼
⌐ ↑                      .text □□ □   Š⌐ –      ‵.data  p  ⌐ d □⌐     @ À.tls  ┼ ┼⌐ ⌐ ô⌐
@ À.rdata ┼ ⌐ ⌐ ö⌐    @ P.idata ┼ 0⌐ – ø⌐    @ @.edata ┼ @⌐ ⌐ þ⌐    @ @.rsrc ┼ P⌐ ⌐ ⌐
@ @.reloc        ‵□
□    □□           @  P
```

Not exactly bedtime reading, is it?

All the runtime interpretation of script is carried out by a scripting engine. The scripting engine is a special program that understands how to interpret the text in the script and turn that into machine-understandable commands. In this respect it is similar to any other design-time compiler, with the single exception that users never get to see runtime compilation errors of C++ executable programs, but if you make a mistake in script and don't test it, they will.

## Runtime Compilation—Disadvantages

Compiling a program at runtime does bring with it a few disadvantages that are worth bringing out into the open at the beginning.

First of all, it's going to be slower. This has to be said early and there's no disputing it. This is simply because the system has to do more at runtime—it has to interpret the code. And remember that it has to do this each and every time the code is run. However, because you are not normally dealing with programs that span many thousands of lines of code, this step, albeit adding to the load, is normally quite fast.

> Note: Don't try asking which is faster—VBScript or JScript/JavaScript; you'll never get a straight answer because it's so subjective. For all intents and purposes you can say that VBScript and JScript are, speed wise, identical. It prevents a lot of arguments.

Second, a compiled program, once compiled into binary language, is afforded protection from snooping and change. This protects both the application and the developer or company that owns the code. Curious users or malicious hackers cannot read the code to find out how things work, make changes, or "borrow" code for their own applications. Because a script is plain text, it isn't afforded such protection and anyone who can gain access to the file can read it and make changes.

Some will argue that this transparency of code is what has made script so popular (in the same way the ease in reading and making alterations to Web pages made HTML a huge success). Transparent code makes it easier for others to find it, read it, copy it, and ultimately learn from it.

> Note: Later on in the book we'll be examining ways that you can protect your intellectual property from unwanted snooping using a variety of techniques.

Finally, when you compile code at design time you can catch and debug any syntax errors you come across, whereas syntax errors in script aren't caught until runtime. Remember that even expert programmers make syntax errors occasionally when they write code. It's human nature. The design-time compiler or runtime script engine expects you to write code that follows stringent rules of syntax. You must do things right. You can't misspell variable names or have ambiguity over parameters passed. Everything has to be right. And even if you are an expert, simple typos can creep in and wreak havoc. The more complicated the code, the more likely it becomes it will contain a mistake—accept this and plan accordingly. What that ultimately boils down to is one word—testing. Test all code and never rely on thinking that it looks OK or the fact that it worked last time. Script errors when seen by the end user reflect badly on the programmer.

# Runtime Compilation—Advantages

With the downsides come the upsides. Here are the advantages of using script over compiled languages.

One of the main advantages of script code being plain text is that it can be embedded with other types of code, for example:

- ❑ HTML
- ❑ XHTML
- ❑ XML
- ❑ Other script languages

As you've probably guessed, the classic example of this is Web scripting where you are free to mix scripts based on different languages (VBScript and JavaScript for example) with HTML (a markup language that handles the content), and CSS (a style-sheet language handling formatting all in one file).

Here is a simple example of VBScript code incorporated into a simple HTML Web page.

```
<html>
<head>
<script language="vbscript">
    Sub ButtonClicked
        window.alert("You clicked on the button!")
    End Sub
</script>
</head>
<body>
  <button name="Button1" type=BUTTON onclick="ButtonClicked">
  Click Me If You Can!!!
  </button>
</body>
</html>
```

Even if you don't know much about VBScript just yet, you can probably understand what this code does (easiest way for you to figure it out is type the code out into Windows Notepad, save it with a .HTM file extension and run it in Internet Explorer).

In the same way you can mix script, HTML and XML (a markup language that handles data structure) in another file. These files can then be downloaded over the Internet in a Web browser where it is executed. If you want the same level of flexibility in a compiled language, it would be very hard (or at least expensive) to achieve.

Scripting is ideally suited for quick, ad hoc solutions. For example, say you wanted to write a small application to back up certain files stored on a hard drive. This is an ideal job for script. Of course, you could do the same job by hand but if the task was one that was going to be repeated on a regular basis, then an automatic solution would be faster and more accurate. Creating a simple script to solve such problems can be much faster and easier than doing the same thing in a compiled language. Also, compiled solutions would take up greater disk space and would not be platform-independent.

Finally, because scripting does not require a complicated IDE, such as those required to program with Visual Basic and Visual C++, scripting languages are easier to learn.

Scripting can be an excellent gateway into the vast, exciting, and lucrative world of programming. Scripting languages are much easier to learn and far more forgiving to mistakes than do compiled languages, and they are great for solving simple tasks. Also, because VBScript has its roots firmly in the BASIC programming language, it is especially quick and easy for the nonprogrammer to pick up and begin using.

# Advantages of Using VBScript

There are other advantages to using VBScript as a programming language:

❑ Good platform coverage. A powerful aspect to VBScript is that it can be run in many environments. Currently there are VBScript script engines for the 32-bit Windows API, 16-bit Windows API, and the Macintosh. VBScript is also integrated into Microsoft Internet Explorer and the latest Windows operating systems. Over the Internet, VBScript can be run both on the client side (through the browser, for example) or server side (using Microsoft's Internet Information Service).

❑    The ability to implement VBScript in your own applications. Add to all that the fact that VBScript is appearing in a variety of other tools and applications thanks to the fact you can license the VBScript source implementation from Microsoft, completely free of charge, for use in your products and applications. We'll look at what this means in greater detail later in this chapter.

## Is VBScript Right for You?

How do you know if VBScript is right for you? In fact, it's just answering a few simple questions should help you come to the right decision.

❑    Are you new to programming? If yes, VBScript is a good entry choice. It's powerful and has a lot of features for you to use (because it is based on a fully fledged programming language—Visual Basic) while still remaining low cost and easy to learn.

❑    Do you want to learn ASP (Active Server Pages)? If the answer is yes, then VBScript is pretty much a must. While you don't have to use VBScript for ASP, you'll find the learning curve steeper because so much ASP-related material uses VBScript as the language of choice.

❑    Do you want to leverage your existing VB skills? If the answer is yes, diversifying into VBScript can open up new avenues to you, such as server-side ASP and client-side Web development. VBScript can also be used to automate tasks and carry out administrative functions on desktops using Windows Script. In this case VBScript can be superior to VB because you can quickly write and debug small files and deploy them over a network to carry out such tasks.

But how do you know if VBScript is the right tool for you to be using? Faced with many different programming languages to choose from, it can be hard to come to the right decision, especially if you don't understand the capabilities of each language.

Fortunately, it's easy to find out if VBScript is the right choice for the project you have in mind. For example, VBScript isn't for you if you want to end up with a compiled executable program, if you want to make extensive use of file I/O, or if speed or graphical manipulation is important to you.

This isn't an exhaustive list by far, but it does cover the areas of programming best left to another language. However, this isn't to say that VBScript can't handle graphical manipulation or file I/O—it can do both—it's just that it's not ideally suited to those applications and other languages exist that can do the job much better. This doesn't reflect badly on VBScript in any way, it's just a case of using the right tools for the right job.

For example, VBScript is for you if you want to quickly prototype code, you write code to carry out repetitive processes (such as backup or deleting files) or administrative functions (such as registry tweaks), you want to use ASP, you are a Web developer who builds Web pages aimed at Internet Explorer users either on the Internet or Intranet, or you are developing an application and want to include scripting support for it.

## How VBScript Fits In with the Visual Basic Family

VBScript (sometimes referred to as VBS), Visual Basic for Applications, Visual Basic (VBA), Visual Basic—what's the difference between them all?

# Visual Basic

Let's begin by taking a look at Visual Basic. VBScript and VBA are both subsets of Visual Basic itself, which is a stand-alone, hybrid language (that is hybrid between compiled and interpreted.), complete with its own IDE. This IDE includes all the things you'd expect of an IDE—language editor, form designer, debugging tools, code project managers, controls to integrate into applications, wizards, and so on, to aid the developer. Visual Basic provides a full set of language features and includes the ability to access the Windows API, allowing VB applications to access key functions of the Windows operating system.

> *Note: Is it a hybrid language? It's not accurate to call VB a compiled language. It is more of a hybrid between a compiled language and an interpreted language. Applications written in VB are indeed compiled, but they rely on a very large "runtime library" to work. This runtime library consists of a set of DLL files (`Asycfilt.dll`, `Comcat.dll`, `Msvbvm60.dll`, `Oleaut32.dll`, `Olepro32.dll`, and `Stdole2.tlb`) that have to be installed on the system that wants to run the VB application. This isn't a big problem because the program that builds the installer includes these files; the problem is just that even the smallest VB application distribution becomes bigger than 1MB when these files are included. This situation is changed in Visual Basic .NET (VB.NET) with the introduction of the Common Language Runtime Framework.*

Let's add another bit of confusion. Although VBA is considered a subset to VB based on the functionality that it offers, VB actually uses VBA at its core because the VBA library defines both the VB language itself and allows other applications (such as Microsoft Word) to host Visual Basic capabilities. So you could look at the Visual Basic IDE as just another host.

# Visual Basic for Applications

Visual Basic for Applications is an "embedded" version of Visual Basic. VBA allows developers with an existing application to provide a powerful tool to enable customization and extension of the application. The biggest and best example of this is the Microsoft Office suite of applications, Microsoft Word, Microsoft Excel, Microsoft Outlook, and Microsoft Access. These applications all support VBA and come fully equipped with a VBA IDE similar to that provided by VB Using the VBA IDE you can write code that goes well beyond the basic features offered by these applications and design custom tools to handle pretty much any job you want carry out.

VBA is quite fast, but not as fast as Visual Basic. VBA code is compiled by the host application into interpreted P-code in a similar way that VB version 4.0 and earlier was capable of.

The main thing to remember here though is that VBA can only live and work within the host applications. You can't write a small application in VBA, distribute it, and expect it to work stand-alone. Neither can you distribute a whole Microsoft application with it! VBA is irrevocably bound to the host application. You can, however, distribute VBA to others who have the host application, but you must bear in mind that the hosts must be the same to ensure all functionality is present. There would be no point, for example, distributing VBA code that worked on a spreadsheet and expect it to work in a word processor.

# VBScript

Syntactically, VBScript is similar to both VB and VBA. If you've used either before, the syntax that we use in VBScript code should be pleasantly familiar to you. However, it is quite different in other important respects.

VBScript, like VBA, needs a hosting application. However, VBScript depends on a scripting host that can interpret, compile and execute plain-text VBScript code at runtime. VBScript began life as a browser scripting language but nowadays it isn't just a Microsoft alternative to Netscape's JavaScript (called LiveScript in the early days), where Microsoft wanted VB developers to be able to embed code into plain-text HTML pages and have it run at runtime. Nowadays the support for VBScript goes way beyond scripting for the Internet Explorer browser and has found many new hosts—including the Windows operating system itself. However, it is important to remember that VBScript, like VBA, needs a host. We'll be learning a lot more about these hosts later on in the book.

## Is VBScript a "Real" Programming Language?

Many people worry about this needlessly. They have heard or read that serious C++ or VB developers don't think that VBScript, or any scripting language, is "real" programming, and as such isn't worth learning. This is absolutely wrong. It's just a matter of picking the right tool for the job. If you were going to develop a new word processor, Web browser or accounting system, choosing VBScript as the main tool would be unwise for a variety of reasons. However, including VBScript support in that application, so that the end user might automate repetitive tasks would be a major bonus. Also, let's face it, it's not every day that you want to write something major. Sometimes programming skills come into play to solve much smaller problems, which is where VBScript can come in useful. Also, try embedding C++ code into an HTML or ASP page—that's not going to work, no matter how "real" you think it is.

The basic fact of the matter is that Microsoft didn't come up with VBScript as a replacement for all other development tools—although a free tool that did that would be cool. VBScript is designed to supplement and augment other languages and to provide a low-impact, easy solution to some tasks while leaving the big stuff to the more powerful languages.

Think of VBScript as an important tool in today's programmer toolkit and you won't go far wrong.

## What Can You Do with VBScript?

VBScript is a powerful language, but on its own it can't do anything. In order to make it do something you need a host because the code itself isn't compiled. As we've already mentioned, a host is an application that can interpret, compile, and execute plain-text VBScript code.

## Windows Script Host

The Windows Script Host (WSH—previously called the Windows Scripting Host) is just one host that allows you to run VBScript. This host allows you to run VBScript directly from within the Windows operating system. The concept of WSH is similar to that of the DOS batch file or Unix Shell scripting. You can also choose how these scripts are run:

- ❑ From the command line (or a DOS command window)
- ❑ Within Windows (for example, by double-clicking on the script file)

WSH is perfect for a variety of common network and administrative tasks, such as making registry changes and creating network logon scripts.

The great thing about WSH is that you can run script just as simply as you run any other program installed on the system. It looks just like any other compiled application to the user, but under the hood it is powered by script.

WSH also comes complete with a set of objects that allow the programmer access to the Windows file system and environment.

> Note: WSH scripts don't have to be written in VBScript. In fact, any language that conforms to the ActiveX scripting specification can be used. This includes, Perl, Jscript, and Python.

WSH is the perfect way to try out many of the code examples that appear in this book. Remember though that some scripts will depend on certain hosts. For example, client-side Web scripts will require Microsoft Internet Explorer browser while Active Server Pages (ASP) script will need Microsoft's Internet Information Server (IIS) or Personal Web Server (PWS) or equivalent to run. WSH is supported on all Windows operating systems from Windows 98 to Windows XP.

# Windows Script Components

A Windows Script Component (WSC) is a COM component that combines XML with script code. These are run server side and can perform a variety of tasks, such as performing middle-tier business logic, accessing and manipulating databases, adding transaction processing to applications (in conjunction with Microsoft Transaction Server), and used to add interactive effects to a Web page in conjunction with DHTML Behaviors.

Previously, this level of control and application was only available to C++, Visual Basic, and Delphi developers.

# Client-Side Web Scripting

Client-side Web scripting is probably the VBScript host that offers you, as the developer, the greatest reach in terms of potential users. Web use is on the increase daily and now even the simplest HTML page often contains script code. The script code in HTML pages is downloaded into the browser with the corresponding HTML code that defines the structure of the page (and any CSS that might be used for formatting). This code is then interpreted by the visitor's browser.

Script can not only be used to make Web pages look compelling to the visitor to the site but can also be used to add functional features to a page, help to reduce server load and page load times, and maximize on bandwidth.

# Server-Side Web Scripting

Server-side Web scripting is done using ASP pages. These pages are HTML pages that contain specially formatted script code.

This, unlike client-side script, is then processed at the server when a request is made for the page and the output is sent to the browser that made the request. Pages created with ASP can, just like ordinary HTML pages, contain script that is processed client side by the browser.

The host for ASP is installed on the server. In order to take advantage of ASP on the Internet you will need access to a server running an appropriate host, such as IIS.

Here is a simple ASP example (don't worry about what it means just yet. In fact it is a simple ASP-based counter for a Web page).

```
<%
Set FS=Server.CreateObject("Scripting.FileSystemObject")
Set RS=FS.OpenTextFile(Server.MapPath("counter.txt"), 1, False)
fcount=RS.ReadLine()
RS.Close

fcount=fcount+1

Set RS=FS.OpenTextFile(Server.MapPath("counter.txt"), 2, False)
RS.Write fcount
RS.Close

Set RS=Nothing
Set FS=Nothing

%>
<html>
<body>
<p>
This page has been visited <%=fcount%> times.
</p>
</body>
</html>
```

However, if you don't have access to an ASP capable server, you can always download PWS for Windows 95, Windows 98, and Windows Me or Install IIS on Windows NT, Windows 2000, and Windows XP Professional. Using this you can develop your own ASP and view them in any Web browser you have installed on your system.

# Remote Scripting

Remote scripting is a technology that allows you to treat all ASP pages as if they were COM objects. This allows the client to "call" scripts that are embedded in ASP pages on the server. This means you can allow scripts to be run server side as if they were client side. The advantage of this is that large, complicated code doesn't have to be downloaded to the user's browser, speeding up the process as well as protecting any proprietary code from prying eyes and alteration.

# HTML Applications

An HTML Application (HTA) is a Web page that runs in its own window outside of the browser window. This offers many advantages over running a script from within the browser itself:

HTAs run outside the browser and as such are considered "trusted" and are subject to different security constraints.

HTAs can be used to build stand-alone graphical applications that may be run without the need for a Web server, network, or Internet connection to work.

HTAs are likely to be of great interest to WSH programmers who were previously limited to using pop-up dialog boxes to communicate with the user, instead enabling them to create an effective interface using HTML.

## Add VBScript to Your Applications

Imagine wanting to give users of your application the power to automate general functions within that application using a simple-to-learn scripting language. Would that be something you'd be interested in? How much would that be worth to you? Read on if you are interested.

Adding the ability for the user to be able to control and customize an application using script is a compelling one. Adding a solution that has been designed in-house is one possibility, but that is likely to be difficult and probably second rate. Now, Visual Basic, C++, Delphi, and other developers can add VBScript support directly to their applications using the free Microsoft Script Control (MSC). Adding the MSC adds support not only for VBScript but also for JScript, Perl, and other ActiveX-enabled scripting languages—all by adding a few extra lines of code to the application. The ActiveX control you need (the Microsoft Windows Script Control) is freely available for download from the Microsoft site at `http://www.microsoft.com/scripting`. And don't think you have to download a massive component—the current file size is just 205kB. It is supported in Windows 98, Windows Me, Windows 2000, and Windows XP.

*Note: The Windows Script Control is currently available only in the English and German languages.*

# Tool of the Trade—Tools for VBScript

We've already said that VBScript has no development environment; so, what tools should you use for VBScript?

Well, if you don't want to spend money on an editor, just use plain old Windows Notepad that comes with every install of Windows. It's fast, easy-to-use, and reliable and does the job just fine. However, it's primitive and not customized for any specific coding or scripting application.

So, if you want more, you might have to spend a little cash (depending on what you choose). There are literally hundreds of text editors on the market that allow you to edit text and a lot more. Some come with advanced clipboard control, auto-indenting, color-coded syntax, auto-backup, and many more functions.

## Text Editor Listing

Here are a selection of editors—some free, some shareware, some commercial—that exist. Any would be ideal for VBScript writing and the final choice you make will be based on personal preference.

UltraEdit-32
Shareware
IDM Computer Solutions, Inc
`http://www.ultraedit.com/`

Programmer's File Editor
Freeware
Alan Phillips
http://www.lancs.ac.uk/people/cpaap/pfe/

TextPad
Shareware
Helios Software Solutions
http://www.textpad.com/

EditPlus Text Editor
Shareware
ES-Computing
http://www.editplus.com/

Jedit
Freeware
Slava Pestov
http://www.jedit.org

Edit Pad
Shareware
Jan Goyvaerts
http://www.just-great-software.com/

Vim
Charityware
http://www.vim.org/

FrontPage
Commercial
Microsoft
http://www.microsoft.com

HomeSite
Commercial
Macromedia
http://www.macromedia.com/software/homesite/

If you don't like any of these, then fire-up your browser, log on to your favorite search engine or shareware site, and start looking! There are literally hundreds out there, so take your pick!

# Summary

Now that you've read this chapter you should have a pretty good idea of what VBScript is, what it isn't, and how VBScript fits in with the Visual Basic family of languages. We've also introduced the VBScript hosts that you can use and touched upon the fact that if you develop applications in another language you can add VBScript support to them for free.

Well, now you've had a brief introduction to programming and taken a tour of VBScript, it's time to take a look at the detailed nitty-gritty of the language, beginning with variables and data types.

# Data Types

## Overview

This chapter will introduce VBScript data types, which is closely linked to the subject of Chapter 4, "Variables and Procedures." A *variable* is a name given to a location in memory where some data used by a program is stored. For example, a variable with the name `Color` might store the value `"Blue"`. The variable called `Color` is pointer to a location in the computer's memory where the value `"Blue"` is stored.

Variables can hold a wide range of data: numbers, dates, text, and other more specialized categories. The different "categories" into which values can be divided—numbers, dates, text, and so on—are called *data types*.

Data types help a programming language compiler generate the proper machine instructions from the code that a programmer types in. Even if you did not know a lot about how compilers work, you could imagine that the instructions given to your computer for adding two numbers together are different from the instructions for displaying character text on the screen.

While your success as a VBScript programmer does not depend on your understanding of low-level details such as compilers and machine instructions, it is critical to understand how VBScript handles data types and variables, including the particulars of VBScript's "universal" data type, the `Variant`. VBScript has some features and behaviors that are unique and, on the surface, confusing. That is why, even if you are familiar with other programming languages, it is important to read and absorb this chapter.

## Scripting Languages as Loosely Typed

Programming languages come in two flavors when it comes to how data types are handled.

A *strongly typed* language forces the programmer to declare, in advance, the data type of every variable so that the compiler will know exactly what kind of value to expect in that variable. If the programmer declares a variable with a numeric data type, the compiler expects that variable to hold a number, and produces an error if the programmer violates that assumption by trying to, for instance, store a date in that variable.

In a *loosely typed* language, the programmer does not have to declare in advance the data type of a variable. Usually, in fact, a loosely typed language does not even provide a way to declare the data type. Scripting languages like VBScript are very often loosely typed. They use a generic, "universal" super data type that can hold any type of data.

The opposite of a scripting language is a *compiled language*. Code written in a compiled language is processed in advance by a compiler, which produces an optimized binary executable file—like the .EXE files you are no doubt accustomed to seeing on your computer. A scripting language is not compiled in advance, but rather "on the fly." The process for a compiled language is:

1. Write the code in plain text
2. Compile the code to produce an executable file
3. Run the compiled executable file
4. The program runs

Instead of a compiler, most scripting languages, including VBScript, have the concept of a *runtime engine*, which "interprets" the code "at runtime" instead of compiling it in advance. The process for a scripting language goes a bit differently:

1. Write the code in plain text
2. Execute the script file
3. The scripting runtime engine compiles the code "on the fly"
4. The program runs

The delayed compilation that comes with a scripting language goes hand-in-hand with the loose typing of the language. This is an oversimplification, but since code is compiled on the fly, the compiler can examine the data being placed into a variable and what kinds of operations are being performed on the variable to arrive at an educated guess for what the data type of that variable should be.

The concepts of loose typing, a universal data type, and educated guessing about data types at runtime lead to some interesting scenarios and behaviors when you execute the VBScript code you have written. Throughout this chapter, we will closely examine these details to ensure that you will not fall into any programming traps related to VBScript's unique way of working with variables and data types.

# Why Data Types Are Important

Let's consider for a moment the Visual Basic programmer's perspective on data types. It may seem odd to suddenly change the subject to a different programming language, but VBScript and Visual Basic are actually very closely related and often used together. You can think of Visual Basic as the parent of VBScript. VBScript syntax is derived directly from Visual Basic, and in many cases Visual Basic and VBScript syntax are identical.

However, the reason for bringing up Visual Basic is that, in a discussion of data types, the concepts are simpler to explain and easier to grasp when presented in the context of Visual Basic. What's more, these concepts translate directly when we return in the next section to the discussion of VBScript's `Variant` data type and its peculiarities.

You will remember from the previous section that Visual Basic is a strongly typed language, which means that a Visual Basic programmer must declare a specific data type for each variable used in his or her program. For example, here is a variable declaration in Visual Basic. What this line of code means is that the programmer is telling the computer to reserve space in memory for a variable called `OrderTotal` and that the data type that will be stored in that variable is the `Currency` data type. (The `Currency` type is used to store numeric values that represent an amount of money.)

```
Dim OrderTotal As Currency
```

By declaring the `OrderTotal` variable with the `Currency` data type, the programmer is signaling his or her intention to store *only* numeric amounts of money in this variable. He does not plan to try to store a date or a customer's name in the `OrderTotal` variable. And if he did, the Visual Basic compiler would produce an error. Take a look at the next two lines of code, which assign two different values to the `OrderTotal` variable.

```
OrderTotal = 695.95
OrderTotal = "Bill's Hardware Store"
```

The first line of code works fine, because a numeric value is being stored in the variable. However, the second line of code will produce an error because the type of data going into the variable does not match the declared data type. A strongly typed language also makes a line of code like the following produce an error.

```
OrderTotal = 695.95 + "Bill's Hardware Store"
```

This strongly typed syntax produces several technical benefits in the compilation and performance of a Visual Basic application. However, since this book is about VBScript, we're not going to get into that. What we do want to talk about though are benefits that translate directly to VBScript—namely, the predictability and clarity that strong typing brings to programming.

A programmer always wants to accomplish at least two things: fulfilling the requirements for the program (in other words, building a program that will do what it is supposed to do) and producing a program that is free of bugs and mistakes. Code that is clear, readable, understandable, and predictable will always be easier for human beings to read, understand, and change. Code that is easy to read, understand, and change is always more likely to fulfill the requirements and more likely to be free of bugs than code that is not.

A Visual Basic programmer must declare a variable for a specific purpose, give the variable a specific name, and declare the intention to store only a specific type of data in that variable. If all of the elements of a program are this neatly segmented, given good specific names like `OrderTotal`, and used in a very consistent manner, the program is likely to do what it's supposed to do without a lot of bugs.

Things are a little different, though, for the VBScript programmer. VBScript does not have any syntax for declaring a variable with the `Currency` data type, or any other specific data type. All VBScript variables have the same data type, `Variant`. The following line of code shows what the same variable declaration would look like in VBScript.

```
Dim OrderTotal
```

The syntax is almost the same, but VBScript does not support the `As` keyword for declaring a data type. This means that the VBScript programmer is free to put any kind of data in this variable he or she wants. The following two lines of VBScript code are both equally valid in VBScript. Unlike in Visual Basic, the second line of code will not produce an error.

```
OrderTotal = 695.95
OrderTotal = "Bill's Hardware Store"
```

Believe it or not, the second line of code that seems so ridiculous does not produce an error in VBScript. As mentioned a moment ago, in Visual Basic this line definitely produces an error when `OrderTotal` is declared with the `Currency` data type. However, in VBScript this line of code results in the value `"695.95Bill's Hardware Store"` stored in the `OrderTotal` variable.

```
OrderTotal = 695.95 + "Bill's Hardware Store"
```

The reason for these seemingly strange VBScript behaviors will become clear as we dig deeper into the `Variant` data type and its subtypes. Before we get there, however, there is a lesson to take away from this comparison of Visual Basic and VBScript variables and data types: even though VBScript does not inherently offer the benefits that come with the rigidity of Visual Basic's strong typing and declared data types, VBScript programmers can still realize these benefits. Realizing the benefits takes two things.

First, we must understand how the `Variant` data type works—in particular, how the `Variant` subtypes correspond almost exactly to the Visual Basic data types. There are specific ways to control the subtype of a `Variant` variable so that your programming techniques won't be that much different than if you were programming in Visual Basic. We'll learn these techniques in this chapter.

Second, when we program in VBScript, we must *pretend* we are programming in Visual Basic. We must pretend that each variable we declare has been declared with a specific data type. Just because the VBScript runtime engine does not care if we store the value `"Bob's Hardware Store"` in the `OrderTotal` variable does not mean that we can't be careful to ensure that our code never does that. In fact, when we introduce the "Hungarian naming convention" later in this chapter you'll see a way that you can declare your intention for each variable to hold a specific data type even though VBScript will not enforce that intention in the way that Visual Basic would.

# The Variant: VBScript's Only Data Type

As mentioned in the previous sections, the `Variant` is the only data type supported in VBScript. Programmers in other nonscripting languages who are accustomed to a wide range of data types that are enforced by a compiler might find this disconcerting. However, the good news is that the `Variant` is also very flexible. Because the `Variant` subtype feature allows you to store many different data types and still keep track of what the data type should be, your scripts can handle just about any kind of data you need: numbers, strings (text), and dates, plus other more complex data types such as objects and arrays.

At this point, please flip back to the end of the book and check out Appendix K, "The Variant Subtypes." This appendix contains two tables that can be of great use to you as you read along with this chapter and as you write VBScript code on your own.

The first table contains a list of all of the possible subtypes of the `Variant` data type. For each subtype, you can see the equivalent Visual Basic data type, followed by some information about some special functions that you can use to test for and control what the subtype is in each of your `Variant` variables. For now, don't worry too much about these function-related columns (we'll get to these very soon). Just take a look at the list of subtypes and how they line up with the Visual Basic data types.

The second table is a list of all of the native Visual Basic data types. As you saw in the first table, all of these data types have an equivalent `Variant` subtype (that is, except for the `Variant` data type itself, which is pretty much the same in Visual Basic as it is in VBScript). Take a few moments and look through this second table. Notice what kinds of values can be stored in each of the data types. The properties of each Visual Basic data type are exactly the same as the equivalent `Variant` subtype.

Keep a bookmark in Appendix K, as you'll want to refer to it as you progress through this chapter.

Returning now to this chapter, let's discuss in more detail the concept of a subtype. A *subtype*, as the name suggests, is a type within a type. You can think of the `Variant` itself as the parent data type and the subtype as the child. The parent data type is always `Variant`, but the child subtype can be one of the many types listed in the aforementioned table in Appendix K. A `Variant` variable has exactly one subtype; in other words, the `Variant`'s subtype can only be one type at time. For example, the subtype cannot be both a `String` and a `Long` at the same time.

The subtype changes depending on what kind of data your code puts into the variable. As a rule, the subtype and the type of data will always be compatible. For example, it is impossible to have a subtype of `Long` with the value `"Hello"` stored in it. If the value of `"Hello"` was placed into the variable, then the subtype will automatically be `String`. The `Variant` will, like a chameleon, automatically change its subtype based on the type of data placed into it. This subtype change process has a fancy name: *type coercion*.

Even with the fancy name, this subtype concept may seem fairly straightforward. However, there are some real pitfalls waiting for you. And we haven't even brought up implicit versus explicit type coercion. Starting in the next section, we will dig deep into subtypes and type coercion. The investment in reading time (and perhaps trying out the examples) will be well worth it.

# Testing For and Coercing Subtypes

There are two built-in VBScript functions that allow you to check what the subtype is for any `Variant` variable. These functions are `VarType()` and `TypeName()`. These two functions do pretty much the same thing, but `VarType()` returns a numeric representation of the subtype, and `TypeName()` returns a text representation. Take a look at the last two columns of the subtypes table in Appendix K, and you'll see the different values that `VarType()` and `TypeName()` will return for each of the subtypes. Notice also that there are *named constant* equivalents for each of the values that `VarType()` returns.

> A named constant is similar to a variable, in that it represents a certain value, but constants cannot be changed at runtime like variables can. You can use a named constant in place of an actual value, which improves the understandability of your code. For example, it's much clearer to write
>
> If `VarType(MyVariable)` = `vbString` Then
>
> rather than
>
> If `VarType(MyVariable)` = 8 Then
>
> VBScript comes with some built-in named constants, and you can also declare your own. We cover constants later in this chapter.

As you can see in the third column of the subtypes table, VBScript also provides some functions that you can use to force (or coerce) the `Variant` to have a specific subtype, assuming that the value stored in the variable is legal for that subtype. These conversion functions are especially useful when you need to pass data of a certain data type to a VB/COM object that expects data of a specific data type. This is also useful when you want to ensure that the value stored in a `Variant` variable is treated in a certain way.

For example, the value 12 can be stored in a `Variant` variable with either a `String` subtype or one of the numeric subtypes, such as `Long`. If you want to make sure that the number 12 is treated as a number, and not text, you can use the `CLng()` conversion function to force the subtype to be `Long` and not `String`.

A `Variant` variable automatically chooses its subtype whenever you place a new value into it. It does this by examining the value placed into it and making its best guess as to what the appropriate subtype is. Sometimes, though, the `Variant`'s best guess is not quite what you expect. You can control this apparent lack of predictability by being careful and explicit in your code.

## Automatic Assignment of String Subtype

Let's look at some code examples that will demonstrate the principles that we have been talking about here.

> All of the examples in this chapter are tailored so that they can be run by the Windows Script Host (WSH). The WSH is a scripting host that allows you to run VBScript programs within Windows. WSH will allow you to try out these example programs for yourself. If you are running a newer version of Windows such as Windows 2000 or Windows XP, you should already have the WSH installed. If you are running an older version of Windows, you may or may not have the WSH installed.
>
> To find out, follow the example below by attempting to run the script. To run the script, simply double-click the `.VBS` file in Windows Explorer. If the script runs, then

> you're all set. If Windows does not recognize the file, then you'll need to download
> and install WSH from:
>
> `http://msdn.microsoft.com/scripting`
>
> For more information on the Windows Script Host, you can skip ahead to Chapter 12.

Run the script below using the WSH. You can type it in yourself, but it's much easier to download the code for this book from the Wrox Web site. All of the scripts in this chapter are available as individual `.VBS` files. Throughout the book, before each code example, we will identify the filename in which the script is contained. This script can be found in `SUBTYPE_STRING.VBS`.

```
Dim varTest
varTest = "Hello There"
MsgBox TypeName(varTest)
```

Running this code results in the dialog box shown in Figure 3-1.

Figure 3-1

This makes sense. We placed a text (also known as `"String"`) value into the variable `varTest`, and VBScript automatically decided that the variable should have the `String` subtype. VBScript `Variant` variables are smart this way. VBScript takes an educated guess about what the appropriate subtype should be and sets it accordingly. However, the intelligence built into the `Variant` can also be dangerous, which we'll see as we continue to examine the subtleties of subtypes and type coercion.

Dealing with string values such as `"Hello There"` is generally straightforward—unless your string value looks like a number, as in the following examples. The script file for the first example is `SUBTYPE_STRING2.VBS`.

```
Dim varTest
varTest = "12"
MsgBox TypeName(varTest)
```

Running this code results in the exact same dialog box (Figure 3-2) as in the previous example where we used the string `"Hello There"`.

Figure 3-2

49

## Coercing String to Long

At first glance, it may seem like VBScript's `Variant` is not that smart after all. Why does the `TypeName()` function return `"String"` when we clearly passed it a numeric value of 12? This is because we placed the value 12 in quotes. VBScript is doing only what we told it to do. By placing the number in quotes, we are telling VBScript to treat the value as a string, not a number. Here are three variations that will tell VBScript that we mean for the value to be treated as a number: SUBTYPE_NUMBER.VBS, SUBTYPE_NUMBER2.VBS, and SUBTYPE_NUMBER3.VBS, respectively.

```
Dim varTest
varTest = 12
MsgBox TypeName(varTest)
```

```
Dim varTest
varTest = CInt("12")
MsgBox TypeName(varTest)
```

```
Dim varTest
varTest = "12"
varTest = CInt(varTest)
MsgBox TypeName(varTest)
```

All three scripts result in the dialog box shown in Figure 3-3.

**Figure 3-3**

All these three examples achieve the same thing: coercing the `varTest` variable to have the `Integer` subtype. The first example results in the `Integer` subtype because we did not enclose the value 12 in quotes, as we did previously. Omitting the quotes tells VBScript that we want the number to be treated as a number, not as text.

The second example uses the `CInt()` conversion function to transform the string value `"12"` into an integer value *before* placing it in the variable. This tells the VBScript that we want the subtype to be `Integer` right from the start.

The third example does basically the same thing as the second but uses two lines of code instead of one. All three examples represent valid ways to make sure that the value we are placing in the variable is treated as a numeric `Integer` value and not text. However, the first example is better for two reasons: one, because it is more straightforward and succinct; and two, because it is theoretically faster as we're not making the extra call to the `CInt()` function.

Note that this code would be redundant.

```
Dim varTest
varTest = CInt(12)
```

Because we do not have quotes around the 12, the subtype will automatically be Integer, and so the CInt() call is unnecessary. However, this code has a different effect.

```
Dim varTest
varTest = CLng(12)
```

This tells VBScript to make sure that the subtype of the variable is Long. The same numeric value of 12 is stored in the variable, but instead of being classified as an Integer, it is classified as a Long. Generally speaking, in a VBScript program this distinction between Integer and Long is not so important, but the distinction *would* be significant if you were passing the value to a VB/COM function that required a Long. When passing variables between VBScript and VB/COM, it is more important to be particular about data types. (If you remember from the lists of data types earlier in this chapter, Integer and Long are distinguished by the fact that the Long type can hold larger values.)

By default, the Variant subtype will be Integer when a whole number within the Integer range is placed in the variable. However, if you place a whole number outside of this range into the variable, it will choose the Long subtype, which has a much larger range (−2,147,483,648 to 2,147,483,647). You will find that the Long data type is used far more often than the Integer in VB/COM components and ActiveX controls, so you may need to use the CLng() function often to coerce your Variant subtypes to match, although this is not always necessary—when you are passing Variant variables to a COM/VB function, VBScript often takes care of the type coercion for you implicitly (more on this later in the chapter).

Given that VBScript chooses the Integer subtype by default instead of the Long, you would also expect it to choose the Single by default instead of the Double when placing floating-point numbers into a Variant variable, since the Single takes up less resources than the Double. However, this is not the case. When floating-point numbers (that is, numbers with decimal places) are assigned to a Variant variable, the default subtype is Double.

Also, as we'll see later, in the section called *Implicit Type Coercion*, when you are placing the result of a mathematical expression into an uninitialized Variant variable, VBScript will choose the Double subtype.

## Hungarian Notation Variable Prefixes

You may have noticed that we named the variable in the last code examples using the var prefix. This might look strange if you have not seen *Hungarian notation* before. Hungarian notation is a naming convention for variables that involves the use of prefixes in front of variable names in order to convey the data type of the variable, as well as its "scope." (We will discuss scope in the next chapter.)

A data type prefix can tell you the programmer (and other programmers who are reading or modifying your code) what type of data you *intend* for a variable to hold. In other words, Variant variables *can* hold any kind of data, but in practice, any given variable *should* generally hold only one kind of data.

In Visual Basic, since it is a strongly typed language, each variable can hold the type of data only for which it is declared. For example, a Visual Basic variable declared with the Long data type can hold *only* whole numbers within the lower and upper ranges of the Long data type. In VBScript, however, where every variable is a Variant, any given variable can hold any kind of data.

Remember earlier we said that when we code in VBScript, we want to pretend we are programming in Visual Basic? This is one example of this pretending technique. If we use Hungarian prefixes to signal what kind of data we intend for a variable to hold, it makes it a lot easier to avoid accidentally placing the value "Bill's Hardware Store" in the OrderTotal variable.

Here is a short list of data type prefixes that are commonly used (see Appendix B):

- var—Variant
- str—String
- int—Integer
- lng—Long
- byt—Byte
- sng—Single
- dbl—Double
- cur—Currency
- obj—Object
- bool—Boolean

The var prefix is best used when you don't know exactly what type of data might end up in the variable, or when you intend for that variable to hold different kinds of data at different times. This is why we're using the var prefix often in this chapter where we're doing all sorts of playing around with data types. In normal practice, however, you will want your variables to have one of the other more specific prefixes listed above or in Appendix B.

## Automatic Assignment of the Date Subtype

Let's look at a similar example, this time using date/time values (SUBTYPE_DATE.VBS).

```
Dim varTest
varTest = "5/16/99 12:30 PM"
MsgBox TypeName(varTest)
```

Running this code results in the dialog box shown in Figure 3-4.

Figure 3-4

The variable assignment results in a subtype of String, although you might expect it to be Date. We get the String subtype because we put the date/time value in quotes. We saw this principle in action in the previous set of examples when we put the number 12 in quotes in the variable assignment. Once again, there are different ways that we can force the subtype to be Date instead of String (SUBTYPE_DATE2.VBS).

```
Dim varTest
varTest = #5/16/99 12:30 PM#
MsgBox TypeName(varTest)
```

Or (SUBTYPE_DATE3.VBS).

```
Dim varTest
varTest = CDate("5/16/99 12:30 PM")
MsgBox TypeName(varTest)
```

Running either of these examples produces the dialog box shown in Figure 3-5.

**Figure 3-5**

The first example surrounds the date/time value in # signs instead of quotes. This is the VBScript way of identifying a date *literal*. A literal is any value that's expressed directly in your code, as opposed to being expressed via a variable or named constant. The number 12 and the string "Hello There" that we used in previous examples are also literals. By enclosing the date/time in # signs rather than quotes, we are telling VBScript to treat the value as a Date, not as a String. As a result, when the Date literal gets stored in the Variant variable, the subtype comes out as Date. The second example uses the CDate() conversion function to achieve the same thing. Once again, the first version is theoretically faster since it does not require an extra function call.

## The "Is" Functions

Often you are not exactly sure what type of data a variable might hold initially, and you need to be sure of what type of data it is before you try to use a conversion function on it. This is important because using a conversion function on the wrong type of data can cause a runtime error. For example, try this code (SUBTYPE_DATE4_ERROR.VBS).

```
Dim varTest
varTest = "Hello"
varTest = CLng(varTest)
```

This code will cause a runtime error on line 3: "Type Mismatch". Not a nice thing to happen when your code is trying to accomplish something. Obviously, this little code sample is pretty silly, because we knew that the variable contained a String when we tried to convert it to a Long. However, you often do not have control over what value ends up in a variable. This is especially true when you are:

❑   accepting input from the user

❑   reading data from a database

❑   reading data from a file

You can often get around these "Type Mismatch" errors by using one of the "Is" functions that are listed in the fourth column of the Variant subtypes table in Appendix K. For example, here is some code that asks the user his or her age. Since we don't have any control over what the user types in, we need to verify that he or she actually typed in a number (GET_TEST_AGE.VBS).

```
Dim lngAge

lngAge = InputBox("Please enter your age in years.")

If IsNumeric(lngAge) Then
    lngAge = CLng(lngAge)
    lngAge = lngAge + 50
    MsgBox "In 50 years, you will be " & CStr(lngAge) & _
        " years old."
Else
    MsgBox "Sorry, but you did not enter a valid number."
End If
```

Notice how we use the IsNumeric() function to test whether or not the user actually entered a valid number. Since we're planning to use the CLng() function to coerce the subtype, we want to avoid a "Type Mismatch" error. What we have not stated explicitly is that the subtype of the variable does not have to be numeric in order for IsNumeric() to return True. IsNumeric() examines the actual value of the variable, rather than its subtype. The subtype of the variable and the value of the variable are two different things.

This behavior is actually what allows us to use IsNumeric() to avoid a "Type Mismatch" error. If IsNumeric() examined the subtype, it would not be quite so useful. In line 3 of the previous example, the subtype of the lngAge variable is String, yet IsNumeric() returns True if the variable has a number in it. That's because IsNumeric() is considering the *value* of lngAge, not the subtype. We can test the value before trying to convert the variable's subtype to a different subtype to make sure we don't get that "Type Mismatch" error. This points to a general principle: never trust or make assumptions about data that comes from an external source, in particular from user entry.

The function IsDate() works in exactly the same way as IsNumeric() (GET_TEST_BIRTH.VBS).

```
Dim datBirth

datBirth = InputBox("Please enter the date on which " & _
    " you were born.")

If IsDate(datBirth) Then
    datBirth = CDate(datBirth)
    MsgBox "You were born on day " & Day(datBirth) & _
        " of month " & Month(datBirth) & " in the year " & _
        Year(datBirth) & "."
Else
    MsgBox "Sorry, but you did not enter a valid date."
End If
```

> Note: **Day()**, **Month()**, and **Year()** are built-in VBScript functions that you can use to return the different parts of a date. These functions are covered in detail in Appendix A.

An exception to the previous statement about the "Is" functions: not all of the "Is" functions work strictly on the value, as IsNumeric() and IsDate() do. The functions IsEmpty(), IsNull(), and IsObject() examine the subtype of the variable, not the value. We will cover these three functions later in the chapter.

Before we move on, a brief jump-ahead regarding the use of the If statement in the last code example.

This line of code

```
If IsNumeric(lngAge) Then
```

is functionally equivalent to this line

```
If IsNumeric(lngAge) = True Then
```

And likewise, this line

```
If Not IsNumeric(lngAge) Then
```

is functionally equivalent to this line

```
If IsNumeric(lngAge) = False Then
```

However, when using the Not operator, you want to be sure you are using it only in combination with expressions that return the Boolean values True and False (such as the IsNumeric() function). This is because the Not operator can also be used as a "bitwise" operator (see Appendix A) when used with numeric (non-Boolean) values.

# Implicit Type Coercion

So far, we have been discussing *explicit* type coercion using conversion functions. We have not yet discussed a phenomenon called *implicit* type coercion. Explicit type coercion refers to when you the programmer are deliberately changing subtypes using the conversion functions and variable assignment techniques described earlier.

Implicit type coercion is when a Variant variable changes its subtype automatically. Sometimes, implicit type coercion can work in your favor, and sometimes it can present a problem. While this material about type coercion may seem like something you can skip, it is vitally important to understand how this works so that you can avoid hard-to-find bugs in your VBScript programs.

## Implicit Type Coercion in Action

Remember the example code that asks the user for his or her age that we used in the previous section? Here it is again (GET_TEST_AGE.VBS).

```
Dim lngAge

lngAge = InputBox("Please enter your age in years.")

If IsNumeric(lngAge) Then
    lngAge = CLng(lngAge)
    lngAge = lngAge + 50
    MsgBox "In 50 years, you will be " & CStr(lngAge) & _
        " years old."
Else
    MsgBox "Sorry, but you did not enter a valid number."
End If
```

Notice how we use the CLng() and CStr() functions to explicitly coerce the subtypes. Well, in the case of this particular code, these functions are not strictly necessary. The reason is that VBScript's implicit type coercion would have done approximately the same thing for us. Here's the code again, without the conversion functions (GET_TEST_AGE_IMPLICIT.VBS).

```
Dim lngAge

lngAge = InputBox("Please enter your age in years.")

If IsNumeric(lngAge) Then
    lngAge = lngAge + 50
    MsgBox "In 50 years, you will be " & lngAge & _
        " years old."
Else
    MsgBox "Sorry, but you did not enter a valid number."
End If
```

Because of implicit type coercion, this code works exactly the same way as the original code. Take a look at this line (the fourth line in the above script).

```
lngAge = lngAge + 50
```

We did not explicitly coerce the subtype to Long, but the math still works as you'd expect. Let's run this same code, but with some TypeName() functions thrown in so that we can watch the subtypes change (GET_TEST_AGE_TYPENAME.VBS).

```
Dim lngAge

lngAge = InputBox("Please enter your age in years.")

MsgBox "TypeName After InputBox: " & TypeName(lngAge)

If IsNumeric(lngAge) Then
    lngAge = lngAge + 50
```

```
        MsgBox "TypeName After Adding 50: " & TypeName(lngAge)
        MsgBox "In 50 years, you will be " & lngAge & _
            " years old."
    Else
        MsgBox "Sorry, but you did not enter a valid number."
    End If
```

If the user enters, for example, the number 30, this code will result in the dialog boxes, in order, shown in Figures 3-6 to 3-8.

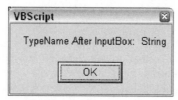

**Figure 3-6**

**Figure 3-7**

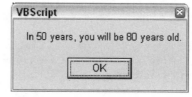

**Figure 3-8**

The first call to the TypeName() function shows that the subtype is String. That's because data coming back from the InputBox() function is always treated as String data, even when the user types in a number. Remember that the String subtype can hold just about any kind of data. However, when numbers and dates (and Boolean True/False values) are stored in a variable with the String subtype, they are not treated as numbers or dates (or as Boolean values)—they are treated simply as strings of text with no special meaning. This is why when our code tries to do math on the String value, VBScript must first coerce the subtype to a numeric one.

It's as if the VBScript compiler behind the scenes is following logic such as this:

1.  The variable holds a string value.

2.  The code is trying to perform math with the variable.

3. Math requires numeric values. Does the variable hold a numeric value?

4. It does, so do implicit type coercion to change the variable to a numeric subtype.

5. Now that we are sure we are working with a numeric value, do the math the code is asking for.

The second call to the TypeName() function comes *after* we add 50 to it, and shows that the subtype is Double. Wait a minute—Double? Why Double? Why not one of the whole number subtypes, such as Integer or Long? We didn't introduce any decimal places in this math. Why would VBScript implicitly coerce the subtype into Double? The answer is because VBScript determined that this was the best thing to do, and since we're trusting VBScript to do the type coercion for us implicitly, we have to accept its sometimes mysterious ways.

Since we did not use a conversion function to explicitly tell VBScript to change the variable to one subtype or another, it evaluated the situation and chose the subtype that it thought was best. VBScript automatically knew that we wanted the value in the variable to be a number. It knew this because our code added 50 to the variable. VBScript says, "Oh, we're doing some math. I better change the subtype to a numeric one before I do the math, because I can't do math on strings."

This is pretty straightforward. What isn't so straightforward is that it chose the Double subtype instead of Long or Integer or Byte. This gets to exactly why we're getting into the discussion about implicit type coercion: you have to be careful, because it can be tricky to predict exactly which subtype VBScript will choose.

> Before we move one, let's note that there is one other instance of implicit type coercion in our current example. The coercion is incidental, but useful to be aware of. It occurs on this line:
>
> ```
> MsgBox "In 50 years, you will be " & lngAge & " years old."
> ```
>
> At the time this line executes, we have just finished adding the number 50 to our variable, and the subtype is numeric. When we use the concatenation operator (&) to insert the value of the variable into the sentence, VBScript implicitly changes the subtype to **String**. This is similar to the way in which the subtype is changed from **String** to **Double** when we performed a mathematical operation on it. However, this coercion is not permanent. Since we did not assign a new value to the variable, the subtype does not change.

## Avoiding Trouble with Implicit Type Coercion

While you have to be aware of implicit type coercion, there is no reason to fear it. VBScript is not going to arbitrarily go around changing subtypes on its own. There is a logic to what VBScript does. Implicit type coercion only happens when you assign a new value to a variable that does not fit the current subtype. Generally, once a Variant variable has a subtype (based on the value first placed within it, or based on a subtype that your code explicitly coerced), it will keep that subtype as you place new values in the variable.

One way to be sure that implicit type coercion won't cause you any problems is to be careful about using each variable you declare for exactly one purpose. Don't declare generic, multipurpose variables that you use for different reasons throughout your script. If you are going to ask the user for his or her age and then later ask the user for the birth date, don't declare a single generic variable called varInput. Instead, declare *two* variables, one called lngAge and another called datBirthDate. This makes your code more clear and understandable and helps make sure you don't get in trouble with implicit type coercion.

Where you do need to watch out for implicit type coercion is when you're dealing with a mixture of data types. We saw this in our example: when the data came back from the InputBox() function, it was a string. Then we did some math on it, which turned it into a number. Give this code a try (IMPLICIT_COERCION.VBS).

```
Dim lngTest

lngTest = CLng(100)
MsgBox "TypeName after initialization: " & TypeName(lngTest)

lngTest = lngTest + 1000
MsgBox "TypeName after adding 1000: " & TypeName(lngTest)

lngTest = lngTest * 50
MsgBox "TypeName after multiplying by 50: " & _
    TypeName(lngTest)

lngTest = "Hello"
MsgBox "TypeName after assigning value of 'Hello': " & _

    TypeName(lngTest)
```

If you run this code, you'll see that the first three calls to the TypeName() function reveal that the subtype is Long. Then, after we change the value of the variable to "Hello", the subtype is automatically coerced into String. What this code illustrates is that once the subtype is established as Long, it stays Long as long as we keep changing the value to other numbers. VBScript has no reason to change it, because the values we put in it remain in the range of the Long subtype. However, when we place text in the variable, VBScript sees that the new value is not appropriate for the Long subtype, and so it changes it to String.

That said, these kinds of mixed-type situations should be rare, and you should try to avoid them. The best way to avoid them is to declare specific variables for specific purposes. Don't mix things up with a single, multipurpose variable like the last code does.

This example reinforces the reason that we use the Hungarian subtype prefix in the variable name. By placing that lng prefix on the variable name, we indicate that we intend for this variable to hold Long numeric values only. The code at the end of our example violates this by changing the value to something nonnumeric. VBScript allows this, because it can't read your mind, but that's not the point.

On the contrary, the fact that the VBScript allows us to store any type of data we please in any variable increases the need for subtype prefixes. The point is to protect our code from strange errors creeping in. Six months from now, if we or someone else were modifying this code, the lng prefix would make it clear that the original intent was for the variable to hold Long numeric values.

In the next example, we will look at how implicit type coercion can happen with numeric variables as the size of the number increases. Give this code a try (IMPLICIT_COERCION_NUMBER.VBS).

```
Dim intTest

intTest = CInt(100)
MsgBox "TypeName after initialization to 100: " & _
    TypeName(intTest)

intTest = intTest + 1000000
MsgBox "TypeName after adding 1,000,000: " & _
    TypeName(intTest)

intTest = intTest + 10000000000
MsgBox "TypeName after adding another 10,000,000,000: " & _
    TypeName(intTest)
```

Running this code results in the three dialog boxes shown in Figures 3-9 to 3-11.

**Figure 3-9**

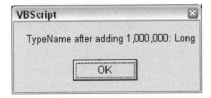

**Figure 3-10**

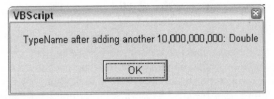

**Figure 3-11**

Notice that we initialize the variable with a value of 100, and use the CInt() function to coerce the subtype into Integer. The first call to the TypeName() function reflects this. Then we add 1,000,000 to the variable. The next call to the TypeName() function reveals that VBScript coerced the subtype to Long. Why did it do this? Because we exceeded the upper limit of the Integer subtype, which is 32,767.

VBScript will promote numeric subtypes when the value exceeds the upper or lower limits of the current numeric subtype. Finally, we add another 10 billion to the variable. This exceeds the upper limit of the `Long` subtype, so VBScript upgrades the subtype to `Double`.

## Avoiding Trouble with the "&" and "+" Operators

Throughout this chapter you have seen example code that uses the & operator to *concatenate* strings together. This is a very common operation in VBScript code. VBScript also allows you to use the + operator to concatenate strings. However, this usage of the + operator should be avoided. This is because the + operator, when used to concatenate strings, can cause unwanted implicit type coercion. Try this code (PLUS_WITH_STRING.VBS).

```
Dim strFirst
Dim lngSecond

strFirst = CStr(50)
lngSecond = CLng(100)
MsgBox strFirst + lngSecond
```

The resulting dialog box will display the number 150, which means that it added the two numbers mathematically rather than concatenating them. Now, this is admittedly a very silly example, but it illustrates that the + operator has different effects when you are not using it in a strictly mathematical context. The + operator uses the following rules when deciding what to do:

❑ If both variables have the `String` subtype, then VBScript will concatenate them.

❑ If both variables have any of the numeric subtypes, then VBScript will add them.

❑ If one of the variables has a numeric subtype, and the other has the `String` subtype, then VBScript will attempt to add them. If the variable with the `String` subtype does not contain a number, then a `"Type Mismatch"` error will occur.

Your best bet is to not worry about these rules and remember only these:

❑ Use the + operator *only* when you explicitly want to perform math on numeric values.

❑ *Always* use the & operator to concatenate strings.

❑ Never use the + operator to concatenate strings.

# Empty and Null

You may have noticed that we have not mentioned the first two subtypes in our table of subtypes: `Empty` and `Null`. These two subtypes are special in that they do not have a corresponding specific Visual Basic data type. In fact, it's a bit of a misnomer to call these subtypes, because they are actually special values that a `Variant` variable can hold. When the subtype of a variable is `Empty` or `Null`, its value is also either `Empty` or `Null`.

This is different from the other subtypes, which describe only the type of value that the variable holds, not the value itself. For example, when the subtype of a variable is `Long`, the value of the variable can be 0, or 15, or 2,876,456, or one of about 4.3 billion other numbers (−2,147,483,648 to 2,147,483,647). However, when the subtype of a variable is `Empty`, its value is also always a special value called `Empty`. In the same fashion, when the subtype of a variable is `Null`, the value is always a special value called `Null`.

`Empty` is a special value that can only be held in a `Variant` variable. In Visual Basic, variables declared as any of the specific data types cannot hold the value of `Empty`—only variables declared as `Variant` can hold the value. In VBScript of course, all variables are `Variant` variables. A `Variant` variable is "empty," and has the `Empty` subtype, after it has been declared, but before any value has been placed within it. In other words, `Empty` is the equivalent of "not initialized." Once any type of value has been placed into the variable, it will take on one of the other subtypes, depending on what the value is.

Let's take a look at some examples. First, SUBTYPE_EMPTY.VBS.

```
Dim varTest
MsgBox TypeName(varTest)
```

This simple example results in the dialog box shown in Figure 3-12.

Figure 3-12

The subtype is `Empty` because we have not yet placed any value in it. `Empty` is both the initial subtype and the initial value of the variable. However, `Empty` is not a value that you can really do anything with. You can't display it on the screen or print it on paper. It only exists to represent the condition of the variable not having had any value placed in it. Try this code (SUBTYPE_EMPTY_CONVERT.VBS).

```
Dim varTest
MsgBox CLng(varTest)
MsgBox CStr(varTest)
```

The code will produce, in succession, the two dialog boxes shown in Figures 3-13 and 3-14.

Figure 3-13

Figure 3-14

The first box displays a 0 because `Empty` is 0 when represented as a number. The second box displays nothing because `Empty` is an "empty" or "zero length" string when represented as a `String`.

Once you place a value in a `Variant` variable, it is no longer empty. It will take on another subtype, depending on what type of value you place in it. This is also true when you use a conversion function to coerce the subtype. However, if you need to, you can force the variable to become empty again by using the `Empty` keyword directly.

```
varTest = Empty
```

You can also test for whether a variable is empty in either of two ways.

```
If varTest = Empty Then
    MsgBox "The variable is empty."
End If
```

Or

```
If IsEmpty(varTest) Then
    MsgBox "The variable is empty."
End If
```

The `IsEmpty()` function returns a `Variant` value of the `Boolean` subtype with the value of `True` if the variable is empty, and `False` if not.

The value/subtype of `Null`, in a confusing way, is similar to the value/subtype of `Empty`. The distinction may seem esoteric, but `Empty` indicates that a variable is uninitialized, whereas `Null` indicates the absence of valid data. `Empty` means that no value has been placed into a variable, whereas a `Variant` variable can only have the value/subtype of `Null` after the value of `Null` has been placed into it.

In other words, a variable can only be `Null` if the `Null` value has explicitly been placed into it. `Null` is a special value that is most often encountered in database tables. A column in a database is `Null` when there is no data in it, and if your code is going to read data from a database, you have to be ready for `Null` values. Certain functions might also return a `Null` value.

Another way to think about it is that `Empty` generally happens by default—it is implicit, because a variable is empty until you place something in it. `Null`, on the other hand, is explicit—a variable can only be `Null` if some code made it that way.

The syntax for assigning and testing for `Null` values is similar to the way the `Empty` value/subtype works. Here is some code that assigns a `Null` value to a variable.

```
varTest = Null
```

However, you cannot directly test for the value of `Null` using the equals (=) operator in the same way that you can with `Empty`—you can use only the `IsNull()` function to test for a `Null` value. This is because `Null` represents invalid data, and when you try to make a direct comparison using invalid data, the result is always invalid data. Try running this code (NULL_BOOLEAN.VBS).

```
'This code does not work like you might expect
Dim varTest

varTest = Null
If varTest = Null Then
    MsgBox "The variable has a Null value."
End If
```

You did not see any pop-up dialog box here. That's because the expression If varTest = Null always returns False. If you want to know if a variable contains a Null value, you must use the IsNull() function (NULL_BOOLEAN_ISNULL.VBS).

```
Dim varTest

varTest = Null
If IsNull(varTest) = True Then
    MsgBox "The variable has a Null value."
End If
```

As mentioned, often your code has to be concerned with receiving Null values from a database or a function. The reason we say that you need to be concerned is that, since Null is an indicator of invalid data, Null can cause troubles for you if you pass it to certain functions or try and use it to perform mathematical operations. We saw this just a moment ago when we tried to use the expression If varTest = Null. This unpleasantness occurs in many contexts where you try to mix in Null with valid data. For example, try this code (NULL_INVALID_ERROR.VBS).

```
Dim varTest
varTest = Null
varTest = CLng(varTest)
```

Running this code produces an error on line 3: "Invalid Use of Null". This is a common error with many VBScript functions that don't like Null values to be passed into them. Sometimes, though, you can experience unwanted behavior without an error message to tell you that you did something wrong. Take a look at the odd behavior that results from this code (NULL_IMPLICIT.VBS).

```
Dim varTest
Dim lngTest
varTest = Null
lngTest = 2 + varTest
MsgBox TypeName(lngTest)
```

Running this code results in the dialog box shown in Figure 3-15.

**Figure 3-15**

Did you see what happened here? When we added the number 2 to the value Null, the result was Null. Once again when you mix invalid data (Null) with valid data (the number 2, in this case), you always end up with invalid data.

The following code uses some ADO (ActiveX Data Objects) syntax that you might not be familiar with (see Chapter 18), but here's an example of the type of thing you want to do when you're concerned that a database column might return a Null value.

```
strCustomerName = rsCustomers.Fields("Name").Value
If IsNull(strCustomerName) Then
    strCustomerName = ""
End If
```

Here we are assigning the value of the "Name" column in a database table to the variable strCustomerName. If the Name column in the database allows Null values, then we need to be concerned that we might end up with a Null value in our variable. So we use IsNull() to test the value. If IsNull() returns True, then we assign an empty string to the variable instead. Empty strings are much more friendly than Null. This kind of defensive programming is an important technique. Here's a handy shortcut that achieves the same exact thing as the above code.

```
strCustomerName = "" & rsCustomers.Fields("Name").Value
```

Here we are appending an empty string to the value coming from the database. This takes advantage of VBScript's implicit type coercion behavior. Concatenating an empty string with a Null value transforms that value into an empty string, and concatenating an empty string to a valid string has no effect at all, so it's a win-win situation: if the value is Null, it gets fixed, and if it's not Null, it's left alone.

A caution for Visual Basic programmers: you may be accustomed to being able to use the Trim$() function to transform Null database values into empty strings. VBScript does not support the "$" versions of functions such as Trim(), UCase(), and Left(). As you may know, when you don't use the "$" versions of these functions in Visual Basic, they return a Variant value. This behavior is the same in VBScript, since all functions return Variant values. Therefore, Trim(Null) always returns Null. If you still want to be able to trim database values as you read them in, you need to both append an empty string and use Trim(), like so:

```
strName = Trim("" & rsCustomers.Field("Name").Value)
```

# The Object Subtype

So far, we have not discussed the Object subtype. As the name suggests, a variable will have the Object subtype when it contains a reference to an object. An *object* is a special construct that contains *properties* and *methods*. A property is analogous to a variable, and a method is analogous to a function or procedure. An object is essentially a convenient way of encompassing both data (in the form of properties) and functionality (in the form of methods). Objects are always created at runtime from a *class*, which is a template from which objects are created (or *instantiated*).

For example, you could create a class called Dog. This Dog class could have properties called Color, Breed, and Name, and it could have methods called Bark and Sit. The class definition would have code to implement these properties and methods. Objects created at runtime from the Dog class would be able to set and read the properties and call the methods. A class typically exists as part of a component. For example, you might have a component called Animals that contains a bunch of different classes like Dog, Elephant, and Rhino. The code to create and use a Dog object would look something like this:

```
Dim objMyDog

Set objMyDog = WScript.CreateObject("Animals.Dog")

objDog.Name = "Buddy"
objDog.Breed = "Poodle"
objDog.Color = "Brown"
objDog.Bark
objDog.Sit
```

Don't worry if this is going over your head at this point. We discuss objects and classes in much greater detail throughout the book, starting in Chapter 8. Our point in this section is simply to illustrate how variables with the object subtype behave. Let's look at some code that actually uses a real object: in this case the FileSystemObject, which is part of a collection of objects that allow your VBScript code to interact with the Windows file system. (We discuss FileSystemObject and its cousins in detail in Chapter 7.) The script file for this code is OBJECT_SIMPLE.VBS.

```
Dim objFSO
Dim boolExists

Set objFSO = _
    WScript.CreateObject("Scripting.FileSystemObject")

boolExists = objFSO.FileExists("C:\autoexec.bat")
MsgBox boolExists
```

In this code, we create a FileSystemObject object and store it in the variable called objFSO. We then use the FileExists function of the object to test for the existence of the autoexec.bat file. Then we display the result of this test in a dialog box. (Note the use of the Set keyword. When changing the value of an object variable, you must use Set.)

Now that you've seen an object in action, let's take a look at two concepts that are germane to this chapter: the IsObject() function, and the special value of Nothing. The script file for this code is OBJECT_ISOBJECT.VBS.

```
Dim objFSO
Dim boolExists

Set objFSO = _
    WScript.CreateObject("Scripting.FileSystemObject")

If IsObject(objFSO) Then
    boolExists = objFSO.FileExists("C:\autoexec.bat")
    MsgBox boolExists
End If
```

This illustrates the use of the `IsObject()` function, which is similar to the other "Is" functions that we studied earlier in the chapter. If the variable holds a reference to an object (in other words, if the subtype is `Object`), then the function will return `True`. Otherwise, it will return `False`.

Nothing is a special value that applies only to variables with the `Object` subtype. An object variable is equal to the value `Nothing` when the subtype is `Object`, but the object in the variable either has been destroyed or has not yet been instantiated. The `Nothing` value is similar to the `Null` value. When testing for whether an object variable is equal to the value `Nothing`, you do not use the = operator, as you normally would to test for a specific value. Instead, you have to use the special operator `Is`. However, when you want to destroy an object, you have to use the `Set` keyword in combination with the = operator.

If that sounds confusing, don't worry, because it is confusing. Let's look at an example (OBJECT_SET_NOTHING.VBS).

```
Dim objFSO
Dim boolExists

Set objFSO = _
    WScript.CreateObject("Scripting.FileSystemObject")

If IsObject(objFSO) Then
    boolExists = objFSO.FileExists("C:\autoexec.bat")
    MsgBox boolExists
    Set objFSO = Nothing
    If objFSO Is Nothing Then
        MsgBox "The object has been destroyed, which " & _
            "frees up the resources it was using."
    End If
End If
```

Why would you want to destroy an object using the `Set <variable> = Nothing` syntax? It's a good idea to do this when you are done with using an object, because destroying the object frees up the memory it was taking up. Objects take up a great deal more memory than do normal variables. Also, for reasons too complex to go into here, keeping object variables around longer than necessary can cause fatal memory errors. It's a good idea to develop a habit of setting all object variables equal to `Nothing` immediately after you are done with them.

# The Error Subtype

We left the `Error` subtype for last because it is seldom used. However, there's a remote chance that you might end up coming across a component or function that uses the `Error` subtype to indicate that an error occurred in the function. We are not necessarily endorsing this methodology, but what you might encounter is a function that returns a `Variant` value that will contain either the result of the function or an error number.

Imagine a function called `GetAge()` that returns a person's age in years. This function would take a date as a parameter, and return to you the person's age, based on the computer's current system date. If an error occurred in the function, then the return value would instead contain an error number indicating what went wrong. For example:

```
Dim datBirth
Dim lngAge

datBirth = _
    InputBox("Please enter the date on which you were born.")

If IsDate(datBirth) Then
    lngAge = GetAge(datBirth)
    If Not IsError(lngAge) Then
        MsgBox "You are " & lngAge & " years old."
    Else
        If lngAge = 1000 Then
            'This error means that the date was greater
            'than the current system date.
            MsgBox "That date was greater than the " & _
                "current system date."
        Else
            'An unknown error occurred.
            MsgBox "The error " & lngAge & _
                " occurred in the GetAge() function"
        End If
    End If
Else
    MsgBox "You did not enter a valid date."
End If
```

Keep in mind that GetAge() is a totally fictional function, and you cannot actually run this code (unless you wanted to write a GetAge() function yourself using Visual Basic). The point here is only to illustrate how someone might use the Error subtype, and how your code might have to respond to it. We say *might* since the Error subtype and the error-returning technique illustrated above is unorthodox and seldom used.

You could not easily implement the use of the Error subtype yourself in VBScript because the VBScript does not support the CVErr() conversion function, as Visual Basic does. (The CVErr() function coerces the subtype of a Variant variable to Error.) Therefore, without the aid of Visual Basic, you could never coerce the subtype of a variable to be Error. In other words, VBScript code cannot create a variable with the subtype of Error.

There is a 99% probability that as a VBScript programmer you will never have to worry about the Error subtype.

# Arrays as Complex Data Types

Our discussion so far has focused on variables that hold a single value. However, VBScript can work with two other types of data that are more complex than anything we've looked at so far: objects and arrays. We are not going to discuss objects in this chapter, since they are covered throughout the book, beginning in Chapter 7. However, we are going to take a detailed look at arrays.

# What Is an Array?

An *array*, as the name suggests, is a matrix of data. While a normal variable has one "compartment" in which to store one piece of information, an array has multiple compartments in which to store multiple pieces of information. As you can imagine, this comes in very handy. Even though you might not know it, you are probably already very familiar, outside the context of VBScript, with all sorts of matrices. A spreadsheet is a matrix. It has rows and columns, and you can identify a single "cell" in the spreadsheet by referring to the row number and column letter where that cell resides. A Bingo game card is also a matrix. It has rows of numbers that span five columns, which are headed by the letters B-I-N-G-O. A database table is a matrix–once again, rows and columns.

An array can be a very simple matrix, with a single column (an array column is called a *dimension*), or it can be much more complex, with up to 60 dimensions. Arrays are typically used to store repeating instances of the same type of information. For example, suppose your script needs to work with a list of names and phone numbers. An array is perfect for this. Rather than trying to declare separate variables for each of the names and phone numbers in your list (which would be especially challenging if you did not know in advance how many names were going to be in the list), you can store the entire list in one variable.

# Arrays Have Dimensions

A VBScript array can have up to 60 *dimensions*. Most arrays have either one or two dimensions. A one-dimensional array is best thought of as a list of rows with only one column. A two-dimensional array is a list of values with multiple columns (the first dimension) and rows (the second dimension). Beyond two dimensions, however, the matrix-based rows/columns analogy starts to break down, and the array turns into something much more complex. We're not going to discuss multidimensional arrays much here. Luckily, for the needs of your average script, a two-dimensional array is absolutely sufficient.

Note that a two-dimensional array does not mean that you are limited to two columns. It only means that the array is limited to an $x$ and a $y$ axis. A one-dimensional array really does have two dimensions, but it is limited to a single column. A two-dimensional array can have as many columns and rows as the memory of your computer will allow. For example, here is graphical representation of a one-dimensional array, in the form of a list of colors.

```
Red
Green
Blue
Yellow
Orange
Black
```

And here is a two-dimensional array, in the form of a list of names and phone numbers.

```
Williams    Tony      404-555-6328
Carter      Ron       305-555-2514
Davis       Miles     212-555-5314
Hancock     Herbie    616-555-6943
Shorter     Wayne     853-555-0060
```

An array with three dimensions is more difficult to represent graphically. Picture a three-dimensional cube, divided up into slices. After three dimensions, it becomes even more difficult to hold a picture of the array's structure in your mind.

# Array Bounds and Declaring Arrays

It's important to make a distinction between the number of dimensions that an array has, and the *bounds* that an array has. The phone list array above has two dimensions, but it has different upper and lower bounds for each dimension. The upper bound of an array determines how many "compartments" that dimension can hold. Each of the compartments in an array is called an *element*. An element can hold exactly one value, but an array can have as many elements as your computer's memory will allow. Here is the phone list array again, but with each of the elements numbered.

```
          0            1          2
   0   Williams     Tony      404-555-6328
   1   Carter       Ron       305-555-2514
   2   Davis        Miles     212-555-5314
   3   Hancock      Herbie    616-555-6943
   4   Shorter      Wayne     853-555-0060
```

The lower bound of the first dimension (the columns) is 0, and the upper bound is 2. The lower bound of the second dimension (the rows) is once again 0, and the upper bound is 4. The lower bound of an array in VBScript is *always* 0 (unlike Visual Basic arrays, which can have any lower bound that you wish to declare). Arrays with a lower bound of 0 are said to be zero based. This can become a bit confusing, because when you are accessing elements in the array, you have to always remember to start counting at 0, which is not always natural for people. So even though there are three columns in the first dimension, the upper bound is expressed as 2—because we started numbering them at 0. Likewise, even though there are five rows in the second dimension, the upper bound is expressed as 4.

When you declare an array, you can tell VBScript how many dimensions you want, and what the upper bound of each dimension is. There is no need to tell VBScript what you want the lower bound to be because the lower bound is always 0. For example, here is a declaration for an array variable for the list of colors from the previous section.

```
Dim astrColors(5)
```

The list of colors is one dimensional (that is, it has only one column) and it has six elements. So the upper bound of the array is 5—remember that we start counting at 0. Notice the Hungarian prefix (see Appendix B) that we used for our variable name: astr. For a normal string variable name, we would just use the str prefix. We add an extra "a" in order to convey that this variable is an array. It is very useful for someone reading your code to know that a variable you are using is an array. An additional example: an array of Long numbers would have this prefix—alng. For more information on subtypes and arrays, see the last section of this chapter.

Moving on to the declaration of variables with more than one dimension, here is a declaration for an array variable for our two-dimensional phone list.

```
Dim astrPhoneList(2,4)
```

When we add another dimension, we add a comma and another upper bound definition to the declaration. Since our phone list has three columns, the upper bound of the first dimension is 2. And since it has five rows, the upper bound of the second dimension is 4.

Starting in the next section, we're going to cumulatively build a script that will illustrate three things about arrays: how to declare and populate an array; how to add dimensions and elements to an array dynamically; and how to loop through an array and access all of its contents. The variable declaration for astrPhoneList is our first building block. Before we start adding more building blocks, we need to discuss array subscripts.

## Accessing Arrays with Subscripts

In order to read from or write to an array element, you have to use a *subscript*. A subscript is similar to the column letter and row number syntax that you use in a spreadsheet program. It's also much like the $x, y$ coordinates you learned about in geometry class. Here's our phone list array again, with the elements numbered for convenience.

|   | 0 | 1 | 2 |
|---|---|---|---|
| 0 | Williams | Tony | 404-555-6328 |
| 1 | Carter | Ron | 305-555-2514 |
| 2 | Davis | Miles | 212-555-5314 |
| 3 | Hancock | Herbie | 616-555-6943 |
| 4 | Shorter | Wayne | 853-555-0060 |

The last name "Williams" is stored in subscript 0, 0. The first name "Miles" is stored in subscript 1, 2. The phone number "305-555-2514" is stored in subscript 2, 1. You get the idea.

So now we can add some code that will populate the astrPhoneList array variable with the data for our phone list (ARRAY_LIST_STATIC.VBS).

```
Dim astrPhoneList(2,4)

'Add the first row
astrPhoneList(0,0) = "Williams"
astrPhoneList(1,0) = "Tony"
astrPhoneList(2,0) = "404-555-6328"

'Add the second row
astrPhoneList(0,1) = "Carter"
astrPhoneList(1,1) = "Ron"
astrPhoneList(2,1) = "305-555-2514"

'Add the third row
astrPhoneList(0,2) = "Davis"
astrPhoneList(1,2) = "Miles"
astrPhoneList(2,2) = "212-555-5314"
```

```
'Add the fourth row
astrPhoneList(0,3) = "Hancock"
astrPhoneList(1,3) = "Herbie"
astrPhoneList(2,3) = "616-555-6943"

'Add the fifth row
astrPhoneList(0,4) = "Shorter"
astrPhoneList(1,4) = "Wayne"
astrPhoneList(2,4) = "853-555-0060"
```

First, this code declares the array variable `astrPhoneList`. Since we know in advance that we want this array to have three columns (one each for last name, first name, and phone number), and five rows (one for each of the names in our list), we declare the array with the dimensions we want: (2,4). Then, we add the data to the array, one element/subscript at a time.

When we declared the array variable with the upper bounds (2,4), VBScript made space in memory for all of the compartments, and the rest of the code puts data into the empty compartments. We use subscripts to identify the compartment we want for each piece of data. We're careful to be consistent by making sure that last names, first names, and phone numbers each go into the same column across all five rows.

But what happens when we don't know in advance how many elements we're going to need in our array? This is where the *dynamic array* comes in. A dynamic array is one that is not preconstrained to have certain upper bounds, or even a certain number of dimensions. You can declare the array variable once at design time, then change the number of dimensions and the upper bound of those dimensions dynamically at runtime. In order to declare a variable as a dynamic array, you just use the parentheses without putting any dimensions in them.

```
Dim astrPhoneList()
```

The parentheses after the variable name tells VBScript that we want this variable to be an array, but the omission of the upper bounds signals that we don't know at design time how many elements we're going to need to store in it. This is a very common occurrence—perhaps more common than knowing in advance how many elements you're going to need.

If you're going to open a file or database table and feed the contents into an array, you might not know at design time how many items will be in the file or database table. Since the number of columns in a database table is relatively fixed, you can safely hard-code an assumption about the number of columns. However, you would not want to assume how many rows are in the table. The number of rows in a database table can potentially change frequently. Even if you know how many rows there are right at this moment, you would not want to hard-code that assumption. So the dynamic array solves that dilemma by allowing us to resize the array at runtime.

In order to change the number of dimensions in a dynamic array you have to use the `ReDim` statement. You can use the `ReDim` statement anywhere in any code that is in the same scope as the dynamic array variable (for more about "scope," see Chapter 4).

However, there is one caveat to keep in mind with `ReDim`: using `ReDim` all by itself clears out the array at the same time that it resizes it. If you stored some data in the array, and then used `ReDim` to resize it, all the data you previously stored in the array would be lost. Sometimes that's a good thing, sometimes it's not—it depends on the program you're writing. In those cases where you don't want to lose the data in the array as you resize it you want to use the Preserve keyword. Using the Preserve keyword ensures that the data you've already stored in the array stays there when you resize it. (However, if you make the array *smaller* than it already was, you will of course lose the data that was in the elements you chopped off, even if you use the Preserve keyword.)

Below is our phone list code, this time with two changes. First, we've changed the declaration of the array variable so that it is a dynamic array. Second, we've changed the code that populates the array so that it uses the ReDim statement with the Preserve keyword to add rows to the array as we go (ARRAY_LIST_DYNAMIC.VBS).

```
Dim astrPhoneList()

'Add the first row
ReDim Preserve astrPhoneList(2,0)
astrPhoneList(0, 0) = "Williams"
astrPhoneList(1, 0) = "Tony"
astrPhoneList(2, 0) = "404-555-6328"

'Add the second row
ReDim Preserve astrPhoneList(2,1)
astrPhoneList(0, 1) = "Carter"
astrPhoneList(1, 1) = "Ron"
astrPhoneList(2, 1) = "305-555-2514"

'Add the third row
ReDim Preserve astrPhoneList(2,2)
astrPhoneList(0, 2) = "Davis"
astrPhoneList(1, 2) = "Miles"
astrPhoneList(2, 2) = "212-555-5314"

'Add the fourth row
ReDim Preserve astrPhoneList(2,3)
astrPhoneList(0, 3) = "Hancock"
astrPhoneList(1, 3) = "Herbie"
astrPhoneList(2, 3) = "616-555-6943"

'Add the fifth row
ReDim Preserve astrPhoneList(2,4)
astrPhoneList(0, 4) = "Shorter"
astrPhoneList(1, 4) = "Wayne"
astrPhoneList(2, 4) = "853-555-0060"
```

There is one caveat when using the Preserve keyword: you can only resize the last dimension in the array. If you attempt to resize any dimension other than the last dimension, VBScript will generate a runtime error. That's why, when working with two-dimensional arrays, it's best to think of the first dimension as the columns, and the second dimension as the rows. You will generally know how many columns you need in an array at design time, so you won't have to resize the columns dimension.

It's the number of rows that you generally won't be sure about. For example, in our phone list array, we know that we need three columns: one for the last name, one for the first name, and one for the phone number. So we can hard code these at design time and dynamically resize the rows dimension at runtime.

Regardless, make sure that the dimension you want to resize with `ReDim Preserve` is the *last* dimension in your array.

Note that when you declare a variable with the parentheses at the end of the variable name—for example, `varTest()`—that variable can *only* be used as an array. However, you can declare a variable *without* the parentheses at the end, and still use the `ReDim` statement later to turn it into a dynamic array. Then you can assign a normal number to the variable again to stop it from being an array. However, using a variable for multiple purposes in this manner can be confusing and might allow bugs to creep into your code. If you need a variable to be both an array and not an array, you might consider declaring two separate variables instead of using one variable for two purposes.

## Looping through Arrays

Now that we've declared an array, sized it appropriately, and filled it up with data, let's do something useful with it. Below is our code, this time with some new additions. We've added a few more variables, and we've added a block of code at the end that loops through the array and displays the contents of the phone list (`ARRAY_LIST_DISPLAY.VBS`).

```
Dim astrPhoneList()
Dim strMsg
Dim lngIndex
Dim lngUBound

'Add the first row
ReDim Preserve astrPhoneList(2,0)
astrPhoneList(0, 0) = "Williams"
astrPhoneList(1, 0) = "Tony"
astrPhoneList(2, 0) = "404-555-6328"

'Add the second row
ReDim Preserve astrPhoneList(2,1)
astrPhoneList(0, 1) = "Carter"
astrPhoneList(1, 1) = "Ron"
astrPhoneList(2, 1) = "305-555-2514"
'Add the third row
ReDim Preserve astrPhoneList(2,2)
astrPhoneList(0, 2) = "Davis"
astrPhoneList(1, 2) = "Miles"
astrPhoneList(2, 2) = "212-555-5314"

'Add the fourth row
ReDim Preserve astrPhoneList(2,3)
astrPhoneList(0, 3) = "Hancock"
astrPhoneList(1, 3) = "Herbie"
astrPhoneList(2, 3) = "616-555-6943"

'Add the fifth row
ReDim Preserve astrPhoneList(2,4)
astrPhoneList(0, 4) = "Shorter"
astrPhoneList(1, 4) = "Wayne"
astrPhoneList(2, 4) = "853-555-0060"
```

```
'Loop through the array and display its contents
lngUBound = UBound(astrPhoneList, 2)

strMsg = "The phone list is:" & vbNewLine & vbNewLine

For lngIndex = 0 to lngUBound
   strMsg = strMsg & astrPhoneList(0, lngIndex) & ", "
   strMsg = strMsg & astrPhoneList(1, lngIndex) & " - "
   strMsg = strMsg & astrPhoneList(2, lngIndex) & vbNewLine
Next

MsgBox strMsg
```

Running this script results in the dialog box shown in Figure 3-16.

**Figure 3-16**

Let's examine the additions to our code. First, we've added three new variables.

```
Dim strMsg
Dim lngIndex
Dim lngUBound
```

These are used in the new block of code at the end of the script. The strMsg variable stores the text version of the phone list that we build dynamically as we loop through the array. The lngIndex variable is used to keep track of which row we are on inside the loop. Finally, lngUBound is used to store the count of rows in the array.

Turning our attention to the new block of code, first we use the UBound() function to read how many rows are in our array.

```
lngUBound = UBound(astrPhoneList, 2)
```

The UBound() function is very useful in this type of situation because it keeps us from having to hard-code in our loop an assumption about how many rows the array has. For example, if we added a sixth row to the array, the loop-and-display code would not need to change at all because we used the UBound() function to keep from assuming the number of rows.

The UBound() function takes two arguments. The first argument is the array variable that you wish the function to measure. The second argument is the number for the dimension you wish to have a count on. In our code, we passed in the number 2, indicating the second dimension—that is, the rows in the phone list array. If we had wanted to count the number of columns, we would have passed the number 1. Notice that this argument is 1 based, not 0 based. This is a little confusing, but that's the way it is.

Next we initialize the strMsg variable.

```
strMsg = "The phone list is:" & vbNewLine & vbNewLine
```

As we go through the loop, we continually append to the end of this variable, until we have a string of text that we can feed to the MsgBox() function. We initialize it before we start the loop. vbNewLine is a special named constant that is built into VBScript that you can use whenever you want to add a line break to a string of text. (You can learn more about named constants and why they're so important in Chapter 4.)

Next we have our loop.

```
For lngIndex = 0 to lngUBound
    strMsg = strMsg & astrPhoneList(0, lngIndex) & ", "
    strMsg = strMsg & astrPhoneList(1, lngIndex) & " - "
    strMsg = strMsg & astrPhoneList(2, lngIndex) & vbNewLine
Next
```

We're going to ignore for now the exact syntax of the loop, since loop structure and syntax is covered in detail in Chapter 5. If the syntax is unfamiliar to you, don't worry about that for now. Let's point out a few things, though. First, notice that we are using the lngUBound variable to control how many times we go through our loop.

Second, notice that the lngIndex variable automatically increases by 1 each time we go through the loop. It starts out at 0, and then for each row in the array, it increases by 1. This allows us to use lngIndex for the row subscript when we read from each element of the array. This illustrates another good thing to know about array subscripts: you don't have to use literal numbers as we had been in all of our previous examples; you can use variables as well.

Finally, when the loop is done, we display the phone list in the dialog box shown in Figure 3-16.

```
MsgBox strMsg
```

# Erasing Arrays

You can totally empty out an array using the Erase statement. The Erase statement has slightly different effects with fixed size and dynamic arrays. With a fixed size array, the data in the array elements is deleted, but the elements themselves stay there—they're just empty. With a dynamic array, the Erase statement completely releases the memory the array was taking up. The data in the array is deleted, and the elements themselves are destroyed. To get them back, you would have to use the ReDim statement on the array variable again. Here's an example.

```
Erase astrPhoneList
```

## Using VarType() with Arrays

The Microsoft VBScript documentation has an error in its description of the VarType() function in regards to arrays. It states that when you use the VarType() function to determine the subtype of an array variable, the number returned will be a combination of the number 8192 and the normal VarType() return value for the subtype (see the table in Appendix K for a list of all the subtype return values and their named constant equivalents). The named constant equivalent for 8192 is vbArray.

According to the documentation, you can subtract 8192 from the VarType() return value to determine that actual subtype. This is only partially correct. The VarType() function does indeed return 8192 (vbArray) plus another subtype number—but that other subtype number will always be 12 (vbVariant). The subtype of a VBScript array can *never be anything but* Variant.

Give this code a try and you'll see that no matter what types of values you try to place in the array (String, Date, Long, Integer, Boolean, and so on), you'll never get the message box in the Else clause to display (ARRAY_VARTYPE_NOMSG.VBS).

```
Dim strTest(1)
Dim lngSubType

strTest(0) = CLng(12)
strTest(1) = "Hello"

lngSubType = VarType(strTest) - vbArray

If lngSubType = vbVariant Then
   MsgBox "The Subtype is Variant."
Else
   MsgBox "The subtype is: " & lngSubType
End If
```

A final note for Visual Basic developers: since we are discussing complex data types, keep in mind that User Defined Types (UDTs) are not supported in VBScript. You cannot define UDTs with the Type statement, nor can you work with UDT variables exposed by VB components.

# Summary

In this chapter we covered the ins and outs of VBScript data types, including one of the "complex" data types, arrays. VBScript supports only one data type, the Variant, but the Variant data type supports many "subtypes."

A Variant variable always has exactly one subtype. Subtypes are determined either implicitly or explicitly. Implicit setting of the subtype occurs when you assign a value to a variable. Sometimes VBScript will change the subtype of a variable "behind your back" without your realizing it. It is important to understand when and why VBScript implicitly coerces subtypes. Sometimes you can use implicit type coercion to your advantage. In addition, as a VBScript programmer you can explicitly set the subtype of a variable using conversion functions such as CLng().

You can test for the subtype of a Variant variable using functions such as IsNumeric() and IsNull(). In addition, you can obtain the name of a variable's subtype using the VarType() function.

Often it is important to test the subtype rather than making assumptions about it. Errors and unwanted behavior can result in certain circumstances if you are not careful with the subtype of your variables.

VBScript also has some "special" subtypes such as Empty, Null, and Object, and it is important for a VBScript programmer to understand these subtypes.

In this chapter we also covered arrays, which, along with objects, are a form of complex data type. An array is considered "complex" because it can hold many values at the same time. Arrays hold multiple values in a "dimensional" structure. Most commonly, arrays are two dimensional, much like a grid or database table. However, arrays can also have more than two dimensions. Data can be placed into and read from arrays using "subscripts," which is a convention for referring to a particular location within the dimensional array structure.

# Variables and Procedures

## Overview

In the preceding chapters, you've seen a lot of variables in the sample code, and you should understand the basic concept of a variable by now, but there are some topics that we have not explicitly discussed. These topics include rules for naming and declaring variables, as well as variable scope and lifetime, which we will cover here. If you are already an experienced programmer in another language, you can skim over much of this material, but there is some information that is particular to VBScript that you would do well to take in.

## Option Explicit

You might not be able to guess it based on the code examples we've presented so far, but declaring variables in VBScript is optional. That's right, you can just start using a new variable anywhere in your code without having declared it first. There is no absolute requirement that says that you must declare the variable first. As soon as VBScript encounters a new nondeclared variable in your code, it just allocates memory for it and keeps going. Here's an example (The script file for this code is OPTION_EXPL_NO_DECLARE.VBS; all code examples for this book are downloadable from the wrox.com Web site.).

```
lngFirst = 1
lngSecond = 2
lngThird = lngFirst + lngSecond
MsgBox lngThird
```

Even though we did not explicitly declare any of the three variables, VBScript does not care. The code runs as you'd expect, and a dialog box comes up at the end displaying the number 3. This sounds pretty convenient. This convenience comes at a very high price. Take a look at this code (OPTION_EXPL_MISSPELLING.VBS).

```
lngFirst = 1
lngSecond = 2
lngThird = lngFirst + lgnSecond
MsgBox lngThird
```

Isn't this the same code as the previous example? Look again. Do you notice the misspelling in the third line? This is an easy mistake to make while you're typing in line after line of script code. The trouble is that this misspelling does not cause VBScript any trouble at all. It just thinks the misspelling is yet another new variable, so it allocates memory for it and gives it the initial subtype of `Empty`. When you ask VBScript to do math on an empty variable, it just treats the variable as a zero. So when this code runs, the dialog box displays the number 1, rather than the number 3 we were expecting.

Easy enough to find the error and fix it in this simple do-nothing script, but what if this script contained dozens, or even hundreds, of lines of code? What if instead of adding 1 to 2 to get 3, we were adding 78523.6778262 to 2349.25385 and then dividing the result by 4.97432? Would you be able to notice a math error by looking at the result? If you were storing these numbers in variables, and you accidentally misspelled one of the variables in your code, you could end up with a math error that you might not notice for weeks—or worse yet, your boss or customer might find the error for you.

So what can we do to prevent this? The answer is a statement called `Option Explicit`. What you do is place the statement `Option Explicit` at the top of your script file, before any other statements appear. This tells VBScript that our code requires that all variables be explicitly declared before they can be used. Now VBScript will no longer let you introduce a new variable right in the middle of your code without declaring it first. Here's an example (`OPTION_EXPL_ERROR.VBS`).

```
Option Explicit

Dim lngFirst
Dim lngSecond
Dim lngThird

lngFirst = 1
lngSecond = 2
lngThird = lngFirst + lgnSecond
MsgBox lngThird
```

Notice that we have added the `Option Explicit` statement to the top of our code. Since we have added `Option Explicit`, we must now declare all of our variables before we use them, which is what you see on the three lines following `Option Explicit`. Finally, notice that we have left our misspelling on the second-to-last line. We did this in order to illustrate what happens when you try to use an undeclared variable. If you try and run this code, VBScript will halt the execution with the following error: `Variable is undefined: 'lgnSecond'`. This is a good thing.

As long as we use `Option Explicit`, VBScript will catch our variable-related typing errors.

One thing that's very nice about `Option Explicit` is that it applies to the entire script file in which it resides. We have not discussed this too much so far in this book, but a single script file can contain multiple procedures, functions, and class definitions, and each class definition can itself contain multiple procedures and functions (we cover VBScript classes in Chapter 8). As long as you place `Option Explicit` at the top of the script file, all of the code within the file is covered.

Start a good habit today: every single time you start a new script file, before you do anything else, type the words `Option Explicit` at the top of the file. This will prevent silly typing errors from seriously messing up your code, and your fellow script developers (and customers) will appreciate it.

# Naming Variables

VBScript has a few rules for what names you can give to a variable. The rules are pretty simple, and leave you plenty of room to come up with clear, useful, understandable variable names.

> **Rule Number 1: VBScript variable names must begin with an alpha character.**

An *alpha character* is any character between "a" and "z" (capital or lowercase). Non-alpha characters are pretty much everything else: numbers, punctuation marks, mathematical operators, and other special characters. For example, these are legal variable names:

- ❏ `strName`
- ❏ `Some_Thing`
- ❏ `Fruit`

And these are illegal variable names:

- ❏ `+strName`
- ❏ `99RedBalloons`
- ❏ `@Test`

> **Rule Number 2: Numbers and the underscore (_) character can be used within the variable name, but all other non-alphanumeric characters are illegal.**

VBScript does not like variable names that contain characters that are anything but numbers and letters. The lone exception to this is the underscore (_) character. (Some programmers find the underscore character to be useful for separating distinct words within a variable name (for example, `customer_name`), while other programmers prefer to accomplish this by letting the mixed upper and lower case letters accomplish the same thing (for example, `CustomerName`). For example, these are legal variable names:

- ❏ `lngPosition99`
- ❏ `Word1_Word2_`
- ❏ `bool2ndTime`

And these are illegal variable names:

- ❏ `str&Name`
- ❏ `SomeThing@`
- ❏ `First*Name`

> **Rule Number 3: VBScript variable names cannot exceed 255 characters.**

Hopefully, your variable names will not exceed 20 characters or so, but VBScript allows them to be as long as 255 characters.

These rules for variable naming should be pretty easy to follow, but it is important to make a distinction between coming up with variable names that are legal, and coming up with variable names that are clear, useful, and understandable. The fact that VBScript will *allow* you to use a variable name such as `X99B2F012345` does not necessarily mean that it's a good idea to do so.

A variable name should make the purpose of the variable clear. If you're going to store the user's name in a variable, a name like `strUserName` is a good one because it removes any doubt as to what the programmer intended the variable to be used for. Good variable names not only decrease the chances of errors creeping into your code, but also make the code itself easier for humans to read and understand.

Another principle that a large percentage of programmers have found useful is the "Hungarian naming convention," which we have mentioned a couple times before, and which we have been using throughout this and the preceding chapters. This convention simply involves using a prefix on the variable name to indicate what type of data the programmer intends for that variable to store.

For example, the variable name `strUserName` indicates not only that the variable should hold the user's name, but also that the subtype of the variable should be `String`. Similarly, the variable name `lngFileCount` indicates not only that the variable should hold a count of the number of files, but also that the subtype of the variable should be `Long`.

Appendix B of this book contains additional guidelines for naming variables, including a list of suggested data type prefixes.

# Procedures and Functions

At this point we will introduce the concept of procedures and functions, which are essential building blocks for more complex scripts. Procedures and functions allow you to *modularize* the code in your script into named blocks of code that perform specific functions. Modularization allows you to think about a more complex problem in a structured way, increases the readability and understandability of your code, and creates opportunities to reuse the same code multiple times within the same script.

Sometimes the word *procedure* is used in the generic sense to refer to either a procedure or a function, but we will do our best in this chapter to use the term procedure in the specific sense. A function is a named block of code that returns a value to the calling code, while a procedure is a named block of code that does *not* return a value to the calling code. Let's break down some of the new concepts in that last sentence.

❑ *A named block of code*: When we use the term block of code, we are referring to a grouping of lines of code that are related in some logical way, that work together to perform a certain programming task. We call procedures and functions "named" blocks of code because we put an explicit boundary around the code and give it a name. For example, we might separate a block of code that processes a customer's order into a procedure with the name `ProcessCustomerOrder()`.

❑ *Calling code*: When we say "the calling code" we mean the code that *calls* a procedure or function. One of the primary purposes of naming a block of code is that other code can invoke that block of a code using the name. Throughout the preceding chapters, we have been looking at code that uses the MsgBox() procedure to display a value in a dialog box. The script code that invokes the MsgBox() procedure is referred to as the *calling code*, and MsgBox() is the procedure being *called*.

❑ *Returning a value*: Some named blocks of code can return a value to the calling code. A procedure does not return a value, whereas a function does. Sometimes you need a value to be returned by a block of code, and sometimes you do not. As we have been using it, the MsgBox() procedure does not return a value (though it can if you ask it to—MsgBox() is interesting as it can be used as either a procedure or a function). We just pass MsgBox() a value to display, it displays the value to the user, and when the user clicks the OK button, the subsequent code continues executing. On the other hand, the CLng() function returns a value to the calling code. For example, in the code below we would say that the CLng() function is returning a value of 12 with the Long subtype and that returned value is stored in the lngCount variable.

```
lngCount = CLng("12")
```

## Procedure Syntax

A procedure is declared with the following syntax.

```
[Public|Private] Sub  Name ([Argument1],[ArgumentN])

    [code inside the procedure]

End Sub
```

A named block of code that is a procedure is identified with Sub keyword. ("Sub" is short for "subprocedure," which is another way of saying "procedure.") You can optionally precede the Sub keyword with the keywords of Public or Private, but these keywords are really relevant only within a class where you want some procedures to be visible outside the class and other procedures to be not visible (see Chapter 8).

In a normal script file (that is, one that is not a class or a Windows Script Component), the keywords Public and Private do not really do anything for you since no procedures, functions, or variables can be visible to any other scripts in other files. If you do not specify one or the other, Public is the default.

The ending boundary of the procedure must be defined with the keywords End Sub. Between the Sub and End Sub boundaries, normal VBScript syntax rules apply.

The rules for naming a procedure are the same as those for naming variables (see earlier). It is a good idea, however, to use clear, purposeful names that make it obvious what the purpose of the procedure is and what the code inside of it does. A good technique is to use verb–noun combinations such as ProcessOrder or GetName.

*Arguments* (also known as *parameters*) are optional for a procedure, and you can use as many arguments as you would practically need (though a procedure with too many arguments is a sure sign of a poorly designed procedure that is doing too much; see under section *Design Strategies for Procedures and Functions*). An argument is a value that you wish to "pass into" the procedure so that the code inside the procedure will have access to it. The argument list must be surrounded by parentheses, and arguments should be separated by commas if a procedure has more than one argument. If a procedure does not have any arguments, the parentheses after the procedure name should be omitted.

Here is a bare-bones procedure that does not use any arguments (PROCEDURE_SIMPLE.VBS).

```
Option Explicit

SayHelloToBill

Sub SayHelloToBill
    MsgBox "Hello, Bill. Welcome to our script."
End Sub
```

The first line in this example is not part of the procedure definition, but rather is the calling code that invokes the procedure. A procedure just sits there doing nothing unless there is some other code to call it.

Notice that we have omitted the Public/Private keywords and that there are no parentheses after the procedure name since it does not take any arguments. Also notice that the code inside of the procedure is indented; this is not required, but is a common convention since it makes the code easier to read. The indentation suggests the hierarchical relationship between the procedure and the code within it.

Here is a similar procedure that takes one argument (PROCEDURE_ARGUMENT.VBS).

```
Option Explicit

GreetUser "Bill"

Sub GreetUser(strUserName)
    MsgBox "Hello, " & strUserName & _
        ". Welcome to our script."
End Sub
```

Notice how the addition of the strUserName argument, along with an adjustment to the procedure name, allows us to make the procedure more generic, which in turn makes it more reusable.

# Function Syntax

The syntax for a function is identical to that of a procedure, except that you change the keyword Sub to the keyword Function.

```
[Public|Private] Function  Name([Argument1],[ArgumentN])

    [code inside the function]

End Function
```

The rules for naming, Public/Private, and the declaration of arguments are the same as for procedures. As we've said, the distinction between a function and a procedure is that a function returns a value. Here is an example that illustrates the syntax for a function and how the code within a function sets the return value for the function (FUNCTION_SIMPLE.VBS).

```
Option Explicit

Dim lngFirst
Dim lngSecond

lngFirst = 10
lngSecond = 20

MsgBox "The sum is: " & AddNumbers(lngFirst, lngSecond)

Function AddNumbers(lngFirstNumber, lngSecondNumber)

    AddNumbers = lngFirstNumber + lngSecondNumber

End Function
```

AddNumbers may not be the most useful function in the world, but it serves well to illustrate a few things. First, notice that this function has two arguments, lngFirstNumber and lngSecondNumber. The arguments are used inside of the function. Second, notice that the way the return value is specified is by referring to the name of the function within the code of the function. That's what is going on in this line.

```
AddNumbers = lngFirstNumber + lngSecondNumber
```

It's as if there is a nondeclared variable inside of the function that has the same exact name as the function itself. To set the return value of the function, you set the value of this invisible variable. You can do this from anywhere inside the function, and you can change the return value of the function repeatedly just as you can with a normal variable. If you set the return value more than once inside the function, the last such line of code to execute before exiting from the function is the one that sets the value.

Let's join together a procedure and a function in order to demonstrate how functions and procedures can be used together in a nested fashion (PROCEDURE_FUNCTION_NESTED.VBS).

```
Option Explicit

GreetUser

Sub GreetUser
    MsgBox "Hello, " & GetUserName & _
        ". Welcome to our script."
End Sub
Function GetUserName
    GetUserName = InputBox("Please enter your name.")
End Function
```

Notice how the GreetUser procedure calls the GetUserName function. Functions and procedures can work together in this way, which is how programs are built. Break your code up into specific modular building blocks of procedures and functions that do very specific things and then string the building blocks together in a logical manner.

This example brings up a good opportunity to introduce an important principle that we will discuss in more detail in the "Design Strategies for Procedures and Functions" section of this chapter. There is a flaw in our nested procedure–function design. The `GreetUser` procedure has an unnecessary *coupling* to the `GetUserName` function. What this means is that `GreetUser` "knows about" and depends on the `GetUserName` function. It depends on it because it makes a call to it; `GreetUser` won't know whom to greet if it does not ask `GetUserName` for a name.

Some amount of "coupling" amongst code modules is necessary and good, but coupling is also something that you want to avoid if you don't need it. The more couplings in your program, the more complex it is. Some complexity is inevitable, but you want to reduce complexity as much as possible. When functions and procedures are coupled together in a haphazard manner, you get what is famously known as "spaghetti code"—that is, code in which it is impossible to trace the logic because the logic twists and turns in a seemingly random pattern.

Here's a different version of the same script that eliminates the unnecessary coupling.

```
Option Explicit

GreetUser GetUserName

Sub GreetUser(strUserName)
    MsgBox "Hello, " & strUserName & _
        ". Welcome to our script."
End Sub

Function GetUserName
    GetUserName = InputBox("Please enter your name.")
End Function
```

The logic of the program is the same, but now we have *decoupled* `GreetUser` and `GetUserName`. We did this by restoring the `strUserName` argument to `GreetUser` and instead using the code at the top of the script to put the two functions together without either function "knowing about" the other. Here is the interesting line of code in this script.

```
GreetUser GetUserName
```

The return value from the `GetUserName` function is fed as the `strUserName` argument of the `GreetUser` function.

One final note about function syntax: programmers familiar with other languages may have noticed that there is no way to declare the data type of a function's return value. This makes sense if you remember that VBScript supports only one data type—the `Variant`. Since all variables are `Variant`s, there is no need for syntax that specifies the data type of a function.

One way that many VBScript programmers choose to help with code clarity in this regard is to use the same Hungarian type prefixes in front of their function names as they do for their variable names. For example, `GetUserName` could be renamed `strGetUserName`. However, if you choose to follow this convention, it is extra important to name your variables and functions so that they are easy to tell apart. Using the verb–noun convention for function names helps, such that it becomes obvious that `strUserName` is a variable and `strGetUserName` is a function.

# Calling Procedures and Functions

In the preceding examples of procedures and functions, you may have noticed some differences in the syntax for calling a procedure as opposed to a function. There are indeed differences, and the VBScript compiler is very particular about them.

Here is one way to call a procedure.

```
GreetUser "Bill"
```

Here is another.

```
Call GreetUser("Bill")
```

These two conventions are functionally equivalent, and whichever you choose is largely a matter of taste. Some would argue that the second convention (using the Call keyword) is more clear, but both conventions are equally common and Visual Basic and VBScript programmers over time become very accustomed to one or the other.

The next example, however, is not legal for calling a procedure and will produce a compilation error.

```
GreetUser("Bill")
```

Likewise, this example is also illegal for calling a procedure.

```
Call GreetUser "Bill"
```

When calling a procedure (as opposed to a function), if you choose not to use the Call keyword, then you cannot use parentheses around the argument value you are passing to the procedure. Conversely, if you do wish to use the Call keyword, then the parentheses are required.

The rules for calling functions are a bit different. If you want to receive the return value from a function, then you must *not* use the Call keyword and you must use parentheses around the argument list, like so:

```
lngSum = AddNumbers(10,20)
```

This syntax is illegal because it omits the parentheses.

```
lngSum = AddNumbers 10,20
```

And this is illegal as well because you cannot use the Call keyword when receiving the return value.

```
lngSum = Call AddNumbers(10,20)
```

You can, however, use the Call keyword if you do not wish to receive the return value of the function, but you have to use the parentheses.

```
Call AddNumbers(10,20)
```

You could also omit the Call keyword and still ignore the return value, but you must omit the parentheses in that case.

```
AddNumbers 10,20
```

This begs the question: why would you ever want to call a function if you did not want the return value? The code in the preceding two examples might compile, but it looks awfully silly. Generally speaking, functions are functions because they return values and we call functions because we want the values they return.

However, there are cases where it makes sense to ignore the return value and call a function as if it were a procedure. The way we have been using MsgBox is a good example of this. MsgBox can be used as either a procedure or a function, depending on why you need it. MsgBox has dual purpose. It can just display a message for you, which is how we've been using it, or you can use it as a function to find out which button a user clicked on the dialog box. Here is a script that illustrates the two ways of using MsgBox (MSGBOX_DUAL.VBS).

```
Option Explicit

Dim lngResponse
Dim strUserName

lngResponse = MsgBox("Would you like a greeting?", vbYesNo)

If lngResponse = vbYes Then
    strUserName = GetUserName
    GreetUser strUserName
End If

Sub GreetUser(strUserName)
    MsgBox "Hello, " & strUserName & _
        ". Welcome to our script."
End Sub

Function GetUserName
    GetUserName = InputBox("Please enter your name.")
End Function
```

In this line of code we are using MsgBox as a function.

```
lngResponse = MsgBox("Would you like a greeting?", vbYesNo)
```

MsgBox has some optional arguments, one of which is the second argument that allows you to specify if you want the dialog box to offer more buttons than just the OK button. This use of the MsgBox function produces the dialog box shown in Figure 4-1.

If the user clicks the Yes button, the MsgBox function will return a certain value (defined as vbYes in this example). If the user clicked Yes, then the familiar GreetUser procedure will eventually be called, in which you can see how we can call MsgBox as a procedure instead of as a function.

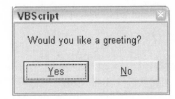

**Figure 4-1**

*Note: vbYesNo and vbYes from the example are built-in VBScript "named constants," which are like variables with fixed, unchangeable values. (We will cover named constants later in this chapter.)*

## Optional Arguments

As we just saw with the `MsgBox` function in the previous section, procedures and functions can have optional arguments. If an argument is optional, then you don't have to pass anything to it. Generally, an optional argument will have a default value if you don't pass anything. Optional arguments will always appear at the end of the argument list; mandatory arguments must come first, followed by any optional arguments.

However, the procedures and functions you write yourself using VBScript cannot have optional arguments. The built-in VBScript procedures you call (such as `MsgBox`) can have optional arguments, but your own VBScript procedures cannot. If you need to, you can get around this by defining mandatory arguments and interpreting a certain value (such as Null) to indicate that the caller wants that argument to be ignored. This kind of "fake" optional argument can help you sometimes in a bind, but this technique is generally discouraged.

## Exiting a Procedure or Function

A procedure or function will exit naturally when the last line of code inside of it is done executing. However, sometimes you want to terminate a procedure sooner than that. In this case, you can use either of the statements `Exit Sub` (for procedures) or `Exit Function` (for functions). The code will stop executing wherever the `Exit` statement appears and the flow of the code will return to the caller.

With the simple functions we have been using as examples, there has not been an obvious place where you would want to use `Exit Sub` or `Exit Function`. Usually these statements are used inside of more complex code in situations where you have reached a logical stopping point or dead end in the logic. That said, many programmers discourage the use of these statements in favor of using a code structure that does not require them. Take this code, for example (`EXIT_SUB.VBS`).

```
Option Explicit

GreetUser InputBox("Please enter your name.")
Sub GreetUser(strUserName)
    If IsNumeric(strUserName) or IsDate(strUserName) Then
        MsgBox "That is not a legal name."
        Exit Sub
    End If
```

```
    MsgBox "Hello, " & strUserName & _
        ". Welcome to our script."
End Sub
```

Notice the `Exit Sub` in the `GreetUser` procedure. We have added some logic that tests to make sure the name is not a number or date, and if it is, we inform the user and use `Exit Sub` to terminate the procedure. However, many programmers would argue that there is a better way to do this that does not require the use of `Exit Sub`, as in this example (`EXIT_SUB_NOT_NEEDED.VBS`).

```
Option Explicit

GreetUser InputBox("Please enter your name.")

Sub GreetUser(strUserName)
    If IsNumeric(strUserName) or IsDate(strUserName) Then
        MsgBox "That is not a legal name."
    Else
        MsgBox "Hello, " & strUserName & _
            ". Welcome to our script."
    End If
End Sub
```

Notice that instead of using `Exit Sub` we have used an `Else` clause. The principle at work here is to design the procedure to have only one exit point, that being the implicit exit point at the end of the procedure. By definition, procedure or function with an `Exit` statement has more than one exit point, which some programmers would argue is poor design. The logic behind this principle is that procedures with multiple exit points are more prone to bugs and harder to understand.

# Variable Declaration and Scope

The issue of variable *scope* and *lifetime* is closely tied concepts. A variable's scope is a boundary within which a variable is valid and accessible. The boundary within which a variable is declared is directly related to the lifetime of that variable. Script code that is executing outside of a variable's scope cannot access that variable. There are three types of scope that a VBScript variable can have:

❑ *Script-level scope*: Script-level scope means that the variable is available to all of the scripts within a script file. Variables that are declared outside of the boundaries of a VBScript procedure, function, or class automatically have script-level scope.

❑ *Procedure-level scope*: Procedure-level scope (also known as "local" scope) means that the variable is available only within the procedure or function in which it is declared. Other code outside of the procedure, even if that code resides within the same script file, cannot access a procedure-level variable.

❑ *Class-level scope*: A class is a special construct that contains a logic grouping of properties and methods. In VBScript, classes are defined within a script using the `Class...End Class` block definition statements. A variable that is declared using the `Private` statement within the class definition, but outside of any of the procedures or functions within the class, has class-level scope. This means that other code within the class can access the variable, but code outside of the class definition, even if that code resides in the same script file, cannot access the variable. Class-level scope will be covered in Chapter 8.

There are three statements that you can use to declare variables: `Dim`, `Private`, and `Public`. (The `ReDim` statement that we introduced in the previous chapter also falls into this category of statements, but it is specifically used for the "redimensioning" of already declared array variables.) These declaration statements are used in different situations, depending on the scope of the variable being declared:

❑ `Dim`: This statement is generally used to declare variables at either the script level or the procedure level. Any variable declared at the script level is automatically available to the entire script file, regardless of whether `Dim`, `Private`, or `Public` was used to declare it. In order to declare a variable inside of a procedure (also known as a *local variable*), you must use `Dim`. Using `Public` and `Private` is not allowed inside of a procedure. If used at the class level, then `Dim` has the exact same effect as `Public`.

❑ `Private`: The `Private` statement can be used at either the script level or the class level, but not inside of procedures or functions. If used at the script level, it has the exact same effect as using `Dim` or `Public`. Any variable declared at the script level is automatically available to the entire script file, regardless of whether `Dim`, `Private`, or `Public` was used to declare it. Although VBScript does not require it, many programmers prefer to use the `Private` statement to declare variables at the script level, and to reserve `Dim` for local variables within procedures and functions. In order to declare a private class-level variable, you must use `Private`. Any variable declared at the class level with either `Dim` or `Public` is automatically available as a public property of the class.

❑ `Public`: The `Public` statement can be used to declare variables with script-level scope, but it has the exact same effect as either `Dim` or `Private`. The only place that `Public` is really meaningful is at the class level. A variable declared at the class level with `Public` is made available as a public property of the class. The reason that `Public` is not meaningful at the script level is that, with the exception of "script components" (see Chapter 13), variables within a script are not available outside the script file in which they reside. Therefore, the only place it really makes sense to use `Public` is for creating public properties for a class. However, note that many VBScript programmers discourage the use of `Public` variables in a class and prefer instead to use a combination of a `Private` class-level variable and `Property Let`, `Set`, and `Get` procedures (see Chapter 8).

We packed a lot of rules into these three points (and again, the examples we'll be getting to soon will make the rules clearer), so the following guidelines might make it easier to keep track of when to use `Dim`, `Private`, and `Public`.

Use `Dim` either at the procedure level to declare variables that are local to that procedure or at the script level. `Dim` is sort of the all-purpose keyword for declaring variables. Within non-class-based scripts and within scripts that will not be used as Windows Script Components, `Private` and `Public` don't have any effect different than that of `Dim`.

If you wish, you can use `Private` at the script level (instead of `Dim`) to declare variables that will be available to the whole script. Use of `Private` becomes more important at the class level to declare variables that are available only within a class.

Use `Public` only to declare public properties for a class, but consider also the option of using a `Private` variable in combination with `Property Let/Set` and `Get` procedures. Even though `Dim` has the same effect as `Public` at the class level, it is more explicit, and therefore preferable, to not use `Dim` at the class level.

VBScript allows you to put more than one variable declaration on the same line. From a style standpoint, it is generally preferable to limit variable declarations to one per line, as our example scripts have, but this is not an absolute rule. For example, script programmers who are writing scripts that will be downloaded over the Web as part of an HTML file often prefer to put multiple declarations on a single line since it makes the file a little smaller. Sometimes, though, a programmer simply prefers to have more than one variable within a single declaration. This is one of those stylistic things on which programmers simply differ. It's nothing to get worked up about.

Here is an example of a valid multi-variable declaration.

```
Dim strUserName, strPassword, lngAge
```

And here is one using `Private` instead of `Dim`. The rules are the same whether you are using `Dim`, `Private`, or `Public`.

```
Private strUserName, strPassword, lngAge
```

Note, however, that you cannot mix declarations of differing scope on the same line. If you wanted to declare some `Private` and `Public` variables within a class, for instance, you would have to have two separate lines.

```
Private strUserName, strPassword
Public lngAge, datBirthday, boolLikesPresents
```

Finally, VBScript does have limitations on the number of variables you can have within a script or procedure. You cannot have more than 127 procedure-level variables in any given procedure, and you cannot have any more than 127 script-level variables in any given script file. This should not cause you any trouble, however. If you are using this many variables within a script or procedure, you might want to rethink your design and break that giant procedure up into multiple procedures.

# Variable Lifetime

A variable's lifetime is closely tied to its scope. Lifetime, as the term suggests, refers to the time that a variable is in memory and available for use. A variable with procedure-level scope is only alive as long as that procedure is executing. A variable with script-level scope is alive as long as the script is running. A variable with class-level scope is alive only while some other code is using an object based on that class.

By limiting a variable's scope, you also limit its lifetime. Here is an important principle to keep in mind: you should limit a variable's lifetime, and therefore its scope, as much as you can. Since a variable takes up memory, and therefore operating system and script engine resources, you should keep it alive only as long as you need it.

By declaring a variable within the procedure in which it will be used, you keep the variable from taking up resources when the procedure in which it resides is not being executed. If you had a script file that contained ten procedures and functions, and you declared all of your variables at the script level, you would not only create some pretty confusing code, but also cause your script to take up more resources than necessary.

Really, though, resource consumption is not the most important reason for limiting variable scope. The most important reason is that limiting scope decreases the chance for programming errors and makes code more understandable and maintainable. If you have a script with several procedures and functions, and all of your variables are declared at the script level so that any of those procedures and functions can change the variables, then you've created a situation in which any code can be changing any variable at any time, and this can become very difficult for a programmer to keep up with.

It is best to design your scripts and classes so that you have the fewest possible number of variables that are available to all of the procedures and functions in your script or class. Instead, make use of local variables and procedure parameters as much as possible so that each procedure only has visibility to the data that it absolutely needs.

Let's look at an example that illustrates variable scope and lifetime in a non-class-based script (SCOPE.VBS).

```
Option Explicit

Private datToday

datToday = Date
MsgBox "Tommorrow's date will be " & AddOneDay(datToday) & "."

Function AddOneDay(datAny)

    Dim datResult

    datResult = DateAdd("d", 1, datAny)
    AddOneDay = datResult

End Function
```

This script contains a function called AddOneDay(). The variable datResult is declared with Dim inside the function and has procedure-level scope, which means that it is not available to any of the code outside of the function. The variable datToday is declared with Private and has script-level scope. The variable datResult will be active only while the AddOneDay() function is executing, whereas the datToday variable will be active for the entire lifetime of the script.

# Design Strategies for Scripts and Procedures

Take another look at our last example (SCOPE.VBS). Note that we could have instead designed this script this way (SCOPE_BAD_DESIGN.VBS).

```
Option Explicit

Private datToday

datToday = Date
AddOneDay
MsgBox "Tommorrow's date will be " & datToday & "."
Sub AddOneDay()
    datToday = DateAdd("d", 1, datToday)
End Sub
```

This code is 100% legal and valid, and the ultimate result is the same as the original. Since datToday has script-level scope, it is available to the code inside of AddOneDay (which we've now changed from a function to a procedure), we simply designed AddOneDay to change datToday directly. It does work, but this kind of technique creates some problems.

First, we have lost the reusability of the AddOneDay function. Now AddOneDay is "tightly coupled" to the script-level variable datToday. If we want to copy AddOneDay and paste it into another script so we can reuse it, we've made our job a whole lot more difficult. When it was a stand-alone function with no knowledge of any data or code outside of itself, it was totally portable, generic, and reusable.

Second, while this simple situation in this simple script might seem innocent enough, try to imagine a more complex script with a couple dozen script-level variables. Imagine also a couple dozen procedures (no functions), and all of the procedures make changes to the script-level variables. Imagine these procedures calling each other and all of the script-level variables changing values rapidly. In imagining this script, hopefully you can also imagine that the logic of this script would be very chaotic and difficult to keep track of. There would be a lot of strange, hard to find bugs. Fixing one bug could easily create three others.

Keep in mind that we are not suggesting that you not use script-level variables or that you never change their values. It's all in *how* you go about doing it. The strategy you want to employ is to *limit* the number of places in your script that directly read and change script-level variables.

A great way to accomplish this is to think of the code at the top of your script file as the "main" code, the code that controls the overall logic of the script. Lets call this code the puppet master. Then think of the procedures, functions, and classes inside of your script as puppets that have very specific jobs to do, but only do them when asked to by the puppet master code. Furthermore, the puppets are also kind of dumb. They don't know the big picture. The puppet master code keeps them in the dark by only giving them the information (by way of their arguments) they absolutely need in order to do their respective jobs. The puppet master forbids each puppet from changing any data outside of its very specific scope.

Some puppets are smarter than others, and the smarter puppets can enlist the help of the other puppets when necessary. In other words, sometimes one of the puppets might have a job that's somewhat complex, and it needs to call on one or more other puppets. At the lowest level you have very dumb puppets that do one very specific thing and don't get help from any other puppets.

Let's bring this back down to earth with an example, followed by some general principles. First, take a look at this script (SENTENCE_NO_PROCS.VBS).

```
Option Explicit

Dim strSentence
Dim strVerb
Dim strNoun
'Start the sentence
strSentence = "The "

'Get a noun from the user
strNoun = InputBox("Please enter a noun (person, " & _
    "place, or thing).")
```

```
'Add the noun to the sentence
strSentence = strSentence & Trim(strNoun) & " "

'Get a verb from the user
strVerb = InputBox("Please enter a past tense verb.")

'Add the verb to the sentence
strSentence = strSentence & Trim(strVerb)

'Finish the sentence
strSentence = strSentence & "."

'Display the sentence
MsgBox strSentence
```

This essentially useless script goes through a series of steps to build a simple sentence based on input from the user. All of the code is in a single block with no procedures or functions, and the code shares access to script-level variables. Here is the same procedure broken into procedures and functions along the lines of our puppet master and puppets metaphor (SENTENCE_WITH_PROCS.VBS).

```
Option Explicit

Dim strSentence

strSentence = GetThe
strSentence = strSentence & GetNoun & " "
strSentence = strSentence & GetVerb
strSentence = strSentence & GetPeriod
DisplayMessage strSentence

Function GetThe
    GetThe = "The "
End Function

Function GetNoun
    GetNoun = Trim(InputBox("Please enter a noun (person, place, or
thing)."))
End Function

Function GetVerb
    GetVerb = Trim(InputBox("Please enter a past tense verb."))
End Function

Function GetPeriod
    GetPeriod = "."
End Function
Sub DisplayMessage(strAny)
    MsgBox strAny
End Sub
```

In this version we have a single script-level variable with a block of code at the top that coordinates the logic leading to the goal of the script: to build a sentence and display it to the user. The code at the top of the script uses a series of functions and one procedure to do the real work. Each function and procedure has a very specific job and makes no use of any script-level data. All of the functions and procedures are "dumb" in that they do not have any "knowledge" of the big picture. This makes them less error prone, easier to understand, and more reusable.

Another benefit is that you do not have to read the whole script in order to understand what's going on in this script. All you have to do is read these five lines and you have the entire big picture.

```
strSentence = GetThe
strSentence = strSentence & GetNoun & " "
strSentence = strSentence & GetVerb
strSentence = strSentence & GetPeriod
DisplayMessage strSentence
```

If, after getting the big picture, you want to dive into the specific details of how a particular step is accomplished, you know exactly where in the script to look. Even though this is a silly example not rooted in the real world, hopefully it illustrates the technique of strategically modularizing your scripts.

Here are some general principles to aid you in your script designs:

❑ Simple script files that perform one specific job with a limited amount of code can be written as a single block of code without any procedures or functions.

❑ As script files become more complex, look for ways to break the logic down into subparts using procedures, functions, and/or classes.

❑ As you break the logic into subparts, keep the coordinating code at the top of the script file.

❑ Design each procedure and function so that it has a very specific job and so that it does only that job. Give the procedure a good descriptive name that indicates what job it does.

❑ Design each procedure and function so that it does not need to have any "knowledge" of the script file's "big picture." In other words, individual procedures and functions should be "dumb," only knowing how to do their specific job.

❑ As much as possible, keep the procedures and functions from reading from or writing to script-level variables. When procedures and functions need access to some data that is stored in a script-level variable, include it as an argument rather than accessing the script-level variable directly.

❑ If the value of a script-level variable needs to be changed, use the coordinating code at the top of the script file to make the change.

# ByRef and ByVal

There is one concept we skipped while introducing arguments for procedures and functions: passing arguments *by reference* versus passing arguments *by value*. An argument is defined either by reference or by value depending on how it is declared in the procedure or function definition. A by reference argument is indicated with the ByRef keyword, whereas a by value argument can either be indicated with the ByVal keyword or by not specifying either ByRef or ByVal—that is, if you do not specify one or the other explicitly, ByVal is the default.

So what does all this mean exactly? You have probably noticed that when a variable is passed to a procedure or function as an argument that the code within the procedure can refer to that argument by name like any other variable. Specifying that an argument is by value means that the code within the procedure cannot make any permanent changes to the value of the variable. With by value, the code in the procedure can change the variable, but as soon as the procedure terminates, the changes to that variable/argument are discarded. On the other hand, with by reference, the changes are permanent and reflected in the calling code's copy of that variable.

Let's look at some examples. Here is a procedure with two arguments, one `ByVal` and one `ByRef` (BYREF_BYVAL.VBS).

```
Option Explicit

Dim lngA
Dim lngB

lngA = 1
lngB = 1

ByRefByValExample lngA, lngB

MsgBox "lngA = " & lngA & vbNewLine & _
    "lngB = " & lngB

Sub ByRefByValExample(ByRef lngFirst, ByVal lngSecond)
    lngFirst = lngFirst + 1
    lngSecond = lngSecond + 1
End Sub
```

Running this code produces the dialog box shown in Figure 4-2.

**Figure 4-2**

First, notice that the `lngA` and `lngB` variables are declared at the script level, outside of the `ByRefByValExample` procedure and that both are initialized to a value of 1. Second, notice that the `lngFirst` argument is declared as `ByRef`, and `lngSecond` as `ByVal`. Third, notice that both arguments are incremented by 1 inside of the procedure. Fourth, notice that in the dialog box only `lngA` (which was passed by reference) has a value of 2 after the procedure terminates.

Only `lngA` was changed because only `lngA` was passed by reference. Since `lngB` was passed by value, and changes made to it inside of the `ByRefByValExample` procedure are not reflected in the variable outside of the procedure.

Most of the time (we could even say almost all of the time), you will want to use `ByVal` for your procedure and function arguments. For many of the same reasons discussed in the previous sections about variable scope and lifetime, it is just plain safer and straightforward to use ByVal. There is nothing inherently wrong with ByRef, and there are sometimes good reasons to use it that are too involved to get into, but stick with ByVal until you run into a situation where you feel you need ByRef.

For example, here is a script that is using ByRef even though it does not have to (BYREF.VBS).

```
Option Explicit

Dim strWord

strWord = "aligator"
AppendSuffix strWord
MsgBox strWord

Sub AppendSuffix(ByRef strAny)
    strAny = strAny & "XXX"
End Sub
```

Here is a better example that eliminates the need for ByRef (BYVAL.VBS).

```
Option Explicit

Dim strWord

strWord = "aligator"
strWord = AppendSuffix(strWord)
MsgBox strWord

Function AppendSuffix(ByVal strAny)
    AppendSuffix = strAny & "XXX"
End Function
```

This example changes the procedure to a function such that the ByRef keyword is no longer needed. Note also that the ByVal keyword in this example is optional; leaving it out has the same effect since ByVal is the default.

# Literals and Named Constants

In this section we will introduce a concept that has some controversy amongst programmers. When is it okay to use literals in your code, and when is it better to use a named constant instead? On one extreme, you have programmers who never use named constants in place of literals. On the other extreme, you have programmers who never use literals anywhere. In the middle, there is a balance that allows for some use of literals, but leans toward the use of named constants when doing so would increase clarity and reduce the likelihood of typing mistakes.

After reading the discussion given in the next section, you should have a good feel for where you stand on the literals and named constants controversy.

# What is a Literal?

A *literal* is any piece of static data that appears in your code that is not stored in a variable or named constant. Literals can be strings of text, numbers, dates, or Boolean values. For example, the word `"Hello"` in the following code is a literal.

```
Dim strMessage

strMessage = "Hello"
MsgBox strMessage
```

The date `08/31/69` in the following code is also a literal.

```
Dim datBirthday

datBirthday = #08/31/69#
MsgBox "My birthday is " & datBirthday & "."
```

The string `"My birthday is"` is also a literal. Literals do not need to be stored in a variable to be considered a literal. And for one more example, the value `True` in the following code is also a literal.

```
Dim boolCanShowMsg

boolCanShowMsg = True
If boolCanShowMsg Then
    MsgBox "Hello there."
End If
```

Many times, literals are just fine in your code, especially for simple scripts without a lot of code or complexity. Programmers use literals all the time. They are not inherently bad. However, there are many instances when the use of a named constant is preferable to using a literal.

# What is a Named Constant?

A *named constant* is similar to a variable, except that its value cannot be changed at runtime. A variable is dynamic. While the code is running, any code within a variable's scope can change the value of it to something else. A named constant, on the other hand, is static. Once defined, it cannot be changed by any code during runtime—hence the name "constant."

You define a constant in your code using the `Const` statement. Here's an example (NAMED_CONSTANT .VBS).

```
Option Explicit

Const GREETING = "Hello there, "

Dim strUserName
strUserName = InputBox("Please enter your name.")
If Trim(strUserName) <> "" Then
  MsgBox GREETING & strUserName & "."
End If
```

If the user types in the name "William", then this code results in the dialog box shown in Figure 4-3.

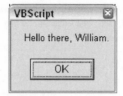

**Figure 4-3**

The Const statement defines the named constant called GREETING. The name of the constant is in all capital letters because this is the generally accepted convention for named constants. Defining constant names in all capital letters makes them easy to differentiate from variables, which are generally typed in either all lower case or mixed case. (Note, however, that VBScript is *not* case-sensitive. There is nothing in VBScript that enforces any capitalization standard. These are stylistic conventions only, adopted to make the code easier to read, understand, and maintain.) Additionally, since constants are usually written in all capital letters, distinct words within the constant's name are usually separated by the underscore (_) character, as in this example (NAMED_CONSTANT2.VBS).

```
Option Explicit

Const RESPONSE_YES = "YES"
Const RESPONSE_NO = "NO"

Dim strResponse

strResponse = InputBox("Is today a Tuesday? Please answer Yes or No.")
strResponse = UCase(strResponse)
If strResponse = RESPONSE_YES Then
   MsgBox "I love Tuesdays."
ElseIf strResponse = RESPONSE_NO Then
   MsgBox "I will gladly pay you Tuesday for a hamburger today."
Else
   MsgBox "Invalid response."
End If
```

Constants also have scope, just like variables. While you cannot use the Dim statement to declare a constant, you can use Private and Public in front of the Const statement. However, these scope qualifications are optional. A constant declared at the script level automatically has script-level scope (meaning it is available to all procedures, functions, and classes within the script file.) A constant declared inside of procedure or function automatically has procedure-level scope (meaning that other code outside of the procedure cannot use the constant).

You can also declare multiple constants on one line, like so:

```
Const RESPONSE_YES = "YES", RESPONSE_NO = "No"
```

Finally, you cannot use variables or functions to set the value of a constant, because that would require the value to be set at runtime. The value of a constant must be defined at design time with a literal value, as in the aforementioned examples.

# Using Named Constants in Place of Literals?

Some programmers will answer this question with "always." There is a school of thought that says that your code should never contain any literals. Other programmers never use named constants, either out of a lack of knowledge of their benefits, or out of just plain laziness. However, there is a reasonable middle ground. In a moment, we will look at some guidelines that might help us find this middle ground. However, first, let's examine some of the benefits that named constants can afford your code.

❑ Named constants can decrease bugs. If you are repeating the same literal value many times throughout your code, the probability of misspelling that literal goes up every time you type it. If you type the constant's name in place of the literal throughout your code, you could just as easily misspell that, but the script engine would catch this error at runtime (as long as you are using `Option Explicit`), whereas a misspelling of the literal itself might go unnoticed for quite some time.

❑ Named constants can increase clarity. Some of the literals we used in our previous examples were mostly clear all by themselves, and adding a constant did not really make their meaning more clear. However, using a literal in your code can often hide meaning when the purpose of the literal is not immediately apparent from reading the code. This is especially true with literals that are numbers. A number by itself does not suggest its purpose for being in the code, and using a constant in its place can make that meaning clear.

❑ If the literal being replaced by the constant is especially long, or otherwise cumbersome to type, then using the constant makes it a lot easier to type your code. For example, if you needed to insert a large multi-paragraph legal disclaimer at various points in your scripts, it would be a good idea to replace that large block of text with a short named constant that's much easier to type.

> **Named Constant Rule #1: If you are using a literal only once, it's probably okay to use it instead of creating a named constant.**

Named Constant Rule #1 is especially true when you consider constants used in HTML-embedded script code, which must be downloaded over the Web. If you always used named constants in place of literals in client-side Web scripting, you could easily increase the size of the file that the user has to download to a point that is noticeable. And even in a server-side Web scripting scenario (where the script code is not downloaded to the user's browser), using constants everywhere can slow down the script execution. This is because the script engine has to process all the constants before it can execute the code that uses them.

However, if you are using the same literal over and over throughout the script, then replacing it with a named constant can really increase the readability of the code, and reduce mistakes from misspellings of the literal. A great technique in server-side Web ASP (Active Server Pages) scripting (see Chapter 14) is to put named constants in an "include" file that can be reused in multiple scripts. Named constants are important, but sometimes you have to weigh the tradeoff.

> **Named Constant Rule #2: If using the constant in place of a literal makes the meaning of the code more clear, use the constant.**

As we mentioned, Named Constant Rule #2 is especially true for literals that are numbers. If you are working with arrays with multiple dimensions, then using named constants in place of the array subscripts is a really good idea (see the next section of this chapter). If you are checking numeric codes that have different meanings based on the number, it's a great idea to use constants in place of the numbers, because the meaning of the numbers by themselves will probably not be clear. The same principle holds true of dates with a special meaning, or odd strings of characters whose meaning is not clear just from looking at them.

# Built-In VBScript Constants

Many VBScript hosts, such as the Windows Script Host and Active Server Pages, support the use of constants that are built into VBScript. These are especially helpful for two reasons: first, it can be hard to remember a lot of the seemingly arbitrary numbers the many of the VBScript functions and procedures use as parameters and return values; and second, using these named constants makes your code a lot easier to read. We saw some examples of built-in named constants related to the VarType() and MsgBox() functions.

Appendix D of this book contains a list of many of the named constants that VBScript provides for you for free. You'll notice that many of these constants are easy to identify by the prefix vb. Also, you'll notice that these constants are usually written in mixed case, rather than all upper case. By way of example, lets take a look at some constants you can use in an optional parameter of the MsgBox() function (see Appendix A for details on the MsgBox() function).

Thus far, we have used the first parameter of MsgBox() multiple times throughout the book. This first parameter is the message that we want displayed in the dialog box. The MsgBox() function also takes several optional parameters, the second of which is the "buttons" parameter, which lets you define different buttons and icons to appear on the dialog box. Here's an example.

```
MsgBox "The sky is falling!", 48
```

This code produces the dialog box shown in Figure 4-4.

**Figure 4-4**

By passing the number 48 as the second parameter of MsgBox(), we told it that we wanted the exclamation point icon to appear on the dialog box. Instead of using the not-so-clear number 48, we could have used the vbExclamation named constant instead.

```
MsgBox "The sky is falling!", vbExclamation
```

This code results in the exact same dialog box, but it's much more clear from reading the code what we're trying to do.

# Summary

In this chapter we dove deeper into some of the details of VBScript variables. VBScript does not force you to declare variables before using them, but it is highly recommended that you include the `Option Explicit` statement at the top of all of your scripts so that VBScript will force variable declaration. Whether using `Option Explicit` or not, VBScript has some rules for how you can name variables, including that variable names must start with a letter and cannot include most special characters.

In this chapter we also formally introduced procedures and functions, including the syntax for defining them and design principles on how to best make use of them. Once we introduced the concept of using procedures and functions to put boundaries around certain blocks of code, we explained how those boundaries define variable scope and lifetime.

We discussed the `ByRef` and `ByVal` keywords that can be used when declaring arguments for a procedure or function. We closed out the chapter by introducing named constants, which can, and often should, be used in your code in place of literal values.

# 5

# Control of Flow

VBScript code executes in a top-down manner. The runtime engine starts at the top of a script and processes one line at time until it reaches the end of the script. However, this does not mean that every single line of code in that script will execute, and furthermore, some lines of code will execute more than once—thousands of times even. Some lines are skipped because of *branching logic* that tells the runtime engine to skip a certain block of code. Other lines are executed multiple times because of *looping logic* that repeats the same block of code over and over.

Branching logic is implemented in VBScript with statements such as `If`, `Else`, and `Select Case`. Loops are defined with the `For`, `Do`, and `While` statements. The sections in this chapter will prepare you with all of the information you need on branching and looping, which are as essential to programming as variables. If you are relatively new to programming, this will be an important chapter. Like all of the chapters up to this point, this chapter explains essential programming fundamentals while also teaching you the VBScript-specific techniques and syntax.

If you are an experienced programmer in another language, you might only skim this chapter for some of the VBScript particulars. VBScript's branching and looping capabilities are basically the same as any mature procedural language. If you are looking only for syntax details, the language reference in Appendix A might be your best source of information.

## Branching Constructs

*Branching* is the process of making a decision in your code and then, based on that decision, executing one block of code, but not others. If you have been reading along since the beginning of the book, you have seen the most common branching construct, `If...End If`, many times already. In this chapter, we will cover in detail `If...End If` along with another branching construct, `Select...End Select`.

`If...End If` and `Select...End Select` are both used to define a *code block*, which is a section of code that is bounded by beginning and ending statements. In the case of an `If` block, the beginning of it is defined by an `If` statement, and the end is defined by an `End If` statement. `Select...End Select` follows the same pattern. VBScript requires that both the beginning and the ending statements be there. If you forget to include the ending statement, VBScript will produce a syntax error at runtime.

It's a good idea to get in the habit of typing both the beginning and ending statements first, before you type the code that goes between them. This ensures that you will not forget to type the ending statement, especially if the code that goes between the statements is rather involved. This is also especially helpful if you're going to be nesting multiple code blocks within each other.

# The "If" Branch

The `If...End If` construct can be very simple, or it can become fairly complicated. In its simplest form, it requires this syntax.

```
If <expression> Then
    <other code goes here>
End If
```

In place of `<expression>` you can use anything that results in a `True` or `False` answer (also known as a Boolean expression). This can be a mathematical equation.

```
If 2 + 2 = 4 Then
    <other code goes here>
End If
```

Or it can be a function that returns `True` or `False`.

```
If IsNumeric(varAny) Then
    <other code goes here>
End If
```

Or it can use more complicated Boolean logic.

```
If strMagicWord = "Please" And _
    (strName = "Hank" Or strName = "Bill") Then

    <other code goes here>
End If
```

You can also use the `Not` statement to reverse the `True` or `False` result of the expression.

```
If Not IsNumeric(varAny) Then
    <other code goes here>
End If
```

We can add another dimension to the `If` construct by adding an `Else` block. The `Else` block will be executed if the result of the `If` expression is `False`.

```
If IsNumeric(varAny) Then
    <other code goes here>
Else
    <some other code goes here>
End If
```

Many times, however, the decision you are trying to make does not involve a simple either/or evaluation. In that case, you can add as many ElseIf blocks as you like.

```
If IsNumeric(varAny) Then
    <other code goes here>
ElseIf IsDate(varAny) Then
    <some other code goes here>
ElseIf IsEmpty(varAny) Then
    <some other code goes here>
Else
    <some other code goes here>
End If
```

If the first expression returns False, then the execution moves to the first ElseIf evaluation. If that returns False, then the execution moves on to the second ElseIf evaluation. If that returns False, then the execution falls into the code in the Else block. The ElseIf line must end with the word Then, just as the initial If line must. The Else block is always optional and must come last.

```
If IsNumeric(varAny) Then
    <other code goes here>
ElseIf IsDate(varAny) Then
    <some other code goes here>
ElseIf IsEmpty(varAny) Then
    <some other code goes here>
End If
```

You can also nest If...End If blocks within each other.

```
If IsNumeric(varAny) Then
    If varAny > 0 Then
        <code goes here>
    ElseIf varAny < 0 Then
        <code goes here>
    Else
        <code goes here>
    End If
Else
    <some other code goes here>
End If
```

You can nest as deeply as you like, but beware of nesting too deeply, because the logic of the code can become unmanageable and hard to follow.

Keep in mind that a Select...End Select block (which we will introduce in the next section) is often an alternative to an If...End If block with a lot of ElseIf clauses in the middle. However, the ElseIf construct is more flexible, because each different ElseIf line can evaluate something totally different, whereas a Select...End Select block must consider different possible results to the *same* expression. Because the If...ElseIf...End If is more flexible, you can always use it in place of Select...End Select. However, the reverse is not true. Select...End Select can *only* be used to evaluate different variations of the *same* expression.

Here is a sequence of `ElseIf` blocks that evaluate totally different expressions.

```
If boolFirst Then
    <other code goes here>
ElseIf boolSecond Then
    <some other code goes here>
ElseIf boolThird Then
    <some other code goes here>
ElseIf lngTest = 1 Then
    <some other code goes here>
ElseIf strName = "Bill" Then
    <some other code goes here>
End If
```

# The "Select Case" Branch

As we mentioned in the previous section, the `Select...End Select` construct is useful when you are evaluating different possible results to the same expression. `Select...End Select` has the following syntax.

```
Select Case <expression>
    Case <possibility 1>
        <code goes here>
    Case <possibility 2>
        <other code goes here>
    Case <possibility 3>
        <other code goes here>
    Case <possibility  n>
        <other code goes here>
    Case Else
        <other code goes here>
End Select
```

Notice that we are evaluating the same expression multiple times, whereas the `If...ElseIf...End If` block allows you to evaluate different expressions. Notice also that after all of the tests are made, we can include an optional `Case Else` block that will be executed if none of the other possibilities return `True`. Let's look at a more concrete example.

```
Select Case VarType(varAny)
    Case vbString
        <code goes here>
    Case vbLong
        <code goes here>
    Case vbBoolean
        <code goes here>
    Case Else
        <code goes here>
End Select
```

The first line evaluates the expression `VarType(varAny)`; then each subsequent `Case` statement checks for each of many possible results. Finally, if none of the `Case` statements evaluates to `True`, then the

`Case Else` block will be executed. Note that we could accomplish this same thing with an `If...ElseIf...End If` block.

```
If VarType(varAny) = vbString Then
    <code goes here>
ElseIf VarType(varAny) = vbLong Then
    <code goes here>
ElseIf VarType(varAny) = vbBoolean Then
    <code goes here>
Else
    <code goes here>
End If
```

However, this has the disadvantage that the expression `VarType(varAny)` will be executed for *every* `ElseIf` block, whereas with the `Select...End Select`, it is evaluated only once, which is more efficient. Some programmers would also argue that the `Select Case` block is more elegant and readable than a series of `ElseIf` statements.

It is a good idea to always consider including a `Case Else` block in your `Select Case` blocks—even if you cannot conceive of a situation where the `Case Else` would be executed. This is a good idea for two reasons.

First, if the input data or code for your script changes unexpectedly, and the `Case Else` block does suddenly start executing, your code will catch it—whereas without the `Case Else` block you might never catch it. This is useful when you are expecting a limited set of input values that you are checking for, with the `Case Else` block catching any other input data that does not match the expected set of values.

Second, including a `Case Else` block can add documentation to the code as to why the `Case Else` block is never intended to be executed. It's a common convention to include a `Case Else` block that contains nothing other than a comment stipulating why the programmer expects the `Else` condition to never exist. Here's an example that uses both a comment and an error message.

```
Select Case lngColor
    Case vbRed
        <code goes here>
    Case vbGreen
        <code goes here>
    Case vbBlue
        <code goes here>
    Case Else
        'We never use anything but Red, Green, and Blue
        MsgBox "Illegal color encountered: " & lngColor, _
                vbExclamation
End Select
```

You can also nest `Select...End Select` blocks within one another, and you can nest `If...End If` blocks (or any other kind of code) inside the `Select...End Select` as well.

```
Select Case VarType(varAny)
    Case vbString
        Select Case varAny
```

```
            Case "Test1"
                If Trim(strUserName) = "" Then
                    <code goes here>
                Else
                    <code goes here>
                End If
            Case "Test2"
                <code goes here>
            Case "Test3"
                <code goes here>
        End Select
    Case vbLong
        <code goes here>
    Case vbBoolean
        <code goes here>
    Case Else
        <code goes here>
End Select
```

# Loop Constructs

Branching is the process of making a decision on whether to execute one block of code or another. Looping is the process of repeating the same block of code over and over.

VBScript provides four looping constructs that you can use in different situations. In the view of most Visual Basic and VBScript programmers, however, one of these loop constructs, the `While...Wend` loop, has been supplanted by the more intuitive, powerful, and flexible `Do...Loop` loop. For this reason, in this chapter we will emphasize the remaining three loops. However, in the interest of completeness, we will cover the syntax for the `While...Wend` loop at the end of the chapter.

Once you remove `While...Wend` from consideration, each of the remaining three loop constructs is ideal for a different type of loop. Each of the following sections will explain the syntax for these loops, as well as when you would use one loop or another.

## For...Next

The `For...Next` loop is ideal for two situations: first, when you want to execute a block of code repeatedly a known, finite number of times; and second, when you want to execute a block of code once for each element in a complex data structure such as an array, file, or database table. (However, the `For Each...Next` loop is specifically designed for another kind of complex data structure, the *collection*.)

Let's first look at how to use the `For...Next` loop to execute a block of code a known number of times (FOR_LOOP_SIMPLE.VBS).

```
Option Explicit

Dim lngIndex

For lngIndex = 1 To 5
    MsgBox "Loop Index: " & lngIndex
Next
```

Running this code produces, in succession, the five dialog boxes shown in Figure 5-1 through 5-5.

**Figure 5-1**

**Figure 5-2**

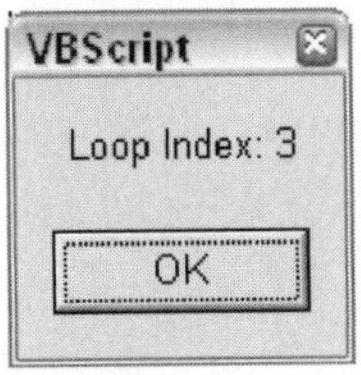

**Figure 5-3**

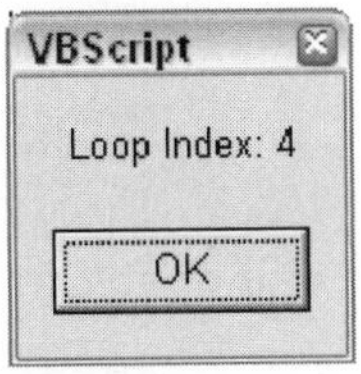

**Figure 5-4**

**Figure 5-5**

This is pretty straightforward. The first thing you'll notice is that in order to use the For...Next loop, you need a loop variable—also known as a loop index. The variable lngIndex serves this purpose. The statement For lngIndex = 1 To 5 means that this loop will execute five times. As you can see from the dialog boxes that appear, the value of lngIndex matches each step in the traversal from the number 1 to the number 5. After looping for the fifth time, the loop stops and the code moves on. Note that you don't need to start at 1 in order to loop five times (FOR_LOOP_NOT_ONE.VBS).

```
Option Explicit

Dim lngIndex

For lngIndex = 10 To 14
    MsgBox "Loop Index: " & lngIndex
Next
```

This will still loop five times, but instead of starting at 1, it will start at 10. As the loop iterates, lngIndex will have a value of 10, then 11, then 12, and so on to 14.

You can also use the Step keyword to skip numbers (FOR_LOOP_STEP.VBS).

```
Option Explicit

Dim lngIndex

For lngIndex = 10 To 18 Step 2
    MsgBox "Loop Index: " & lngIndex
Next
```

Once again, this will still loop five times, but, because we specified Step 2, it will skip every other number. On the first loop, lngIndex will have a value of 10, then 12, then 14, and so on to 18. You can use any increment you like with the Step keyword (FOR_LOOP_STEP_100.VBS).

```
Option Explicit

Dim lngIndex

For lngIndex = 100 To 500 Step 100
    MsgBox "Loop Index: " & lngIndex
Next
```

You can also use the Step keyword to cause the loop to go backwards (FOR_LOOP_BACKWARDS .VBS).

```
Option Explicit

Dim lngIndex

For lngIndex = 5 To 1 Step -1
    MsgBox "Loop Index: " & lngIndex
Next
```

Because we used a negative number with the Step keyword, the loop goes downward through the numbers. Notice that in order for this to work, the increment range must specify the larger number first.

You are not limited to using negative numbers with the Step keyword. The loop itself can loop through negative numbers, like this (FOR_LOOP_NEGATIVE.VBS):

```
Option Explicit

Dim lngIndex
For lngIndex = -10 To -1
    MsgBox "Loop Index: " & lngIndex
Next
```

Or like this (FOR_LOOP_NEGATIVE2.VBS):

```
Option Explicit

Dim lngIndex

For lngIndex = -10 To -20 Step -2
    MsgBox "Loop Index: " & lngIndex
Next
```

You can also nest loops inside one another (FOR_LOOP_NESTED.VBS).

```
Option Explicit

Dim lngOuter
Dim lngInner

For lngOuter = 1 to 5
    MsgBox "Outer loop index: " & lngOuter

    For lngInner = 10 to 18 Step 2
        MsgBox "Inner loop index: " & lngInner
    Next
Next
```

So what do you do when you *don't* know exactly how many times you want to loop? This is a common situation. It often comes up when you need to traverse an array (see Chapter 3), a string, or any other kind of structure. Let's look at an example (EXTRACT_FILE_NAME.VBS).

```
Option Explicit

Dim lngIndex
Dim lngStrLen
Dim strFullPath
Dim strFileName

'This code will extract the filename from a path

strFullPath = "C:\Windows\Temp\Test\myfile.txt"
lngStrLen = Len(strFullPath)

For lngIndex = lngStrLen To 1 Step -1
    If Mid(strFullPath, lngIndex, 1) = "\" Then
```

```
        strFileName = Right(strFullPath, _
            lngStrLen - lngIndex)
        Exit For
    End If
Next

MsgBox "The filename is: " & strFileName
```

Running this code produces the dialog box shown in Figure 5-6.

**Figure 5-6**

We've added some new elements in this example. The Len() function is a built-in VBScript function that returns the number of characters in a string. The Mid() function extracts one or more bytes from the middle of a string. The first parameter is the string to extract from; the second parameter is the character at which to start the extraction; the third parameter is how many characters to extract. The Right() function is similar to Mid(), except that it extracts a certain number of the rightmost characters in a string. Finally, the Exit For statement breaks you out of a loop. This is very handy when you know that you don't need to loop anymore.

Notice how we use the length of the strFullPath variable to drive how many times we need to loop. When we started, we did not know how many times we needed to loop, so we used the length of the structure we needed to traverse (in the case, a string) to tell us how many times to loop. Notice also how we loop backwards so that we can search for the last backslash character ("\") in the strFullPath variable. Once we've found the backslash, we know where the filename begins. Once we've used the Right() function to extract the filename into the strFileName variable, we don't need the loop anymore (we've accomplished our goal), so we use Exit For to break out of the loop. Exit For jumps the execution of the code to the very next line after the Next statement.

> Note: The above example was provided for the purpose of demonstrating how to use a For...Next loop to move through a data structure of a size that is unknown at design time. This is not necessarily the best way to extract a filename from a full pathname. This, for example, would be much faster (EXTRACT_FILE_NAME_NO_LOOP.VBS).

```
Option Explicit

Dim strFileName
Dim strFullPath

strFullPath = "C:\MyStuff\Documents\Personal\resume.doc"
strFileName = Right(strFullPath, _
    Len(strFullPath) - InStrRev(strFullPath,"\"))

MsgBox "The filename is: " & strFileName
```

There is almost always more than one way to solve the same problem. Loops are very handy and an integral part of programming, but they are also expensive from a performance standpoint. The second example is better for two reasons: one, there are less lines of code; and two, since it does not use a loop to repeat the same lines of code over and over, it find the answer much faster.

# For Each. . . Next

The `For Each...Next` loop is a special kind of loop that is specifically used for traversing collections. A "collection," as the name suggests, is a collection of data, almost like an array. A "collection" is most often a collection of objects of the same type (even though "collections" can be collections of virtually any kind of data).

For example, built into the VBScript "runtime objects" `FileSystemObject` (see Chapter 7) is the `Folder` object, which represents a directory in a file system. The `Folder` object has a `Files` collection, which is exposed as a property on the `Folder` object. Inside the `Folder.Files` collection are zero or more `File` objects. You can use a `For Each...Next` loop to move through each of the `File` objects in the `Folder.Files` collection.

With the `For Each...Next` loop, you cannot directly control how many times the loop will go around. This is dependent upon how many objects are in the collection you are traversing. However, you can still use the `Exit For` statement to break out of the loop at any time. You can figure out when to use `Exit For` by testing for some condition, or using an extra counter variable to count how many times you've gone through the loop.

Let's look at an example that uses the `FileSystemObject` and related objects, which we introduce formally in Chapter 7. In this example (`FSO_FIND_FILE.VBS`), we will attempt to locate the `AUTOEXEC.BAT` file on our system. (Don't worry—it's safe to try out this code—there is no danger of harming your `AUTOEXEC.BAT` file.)

```
Option Explicit

Dim objFSO
Dim objRootFolder
Dim objFileLoop
Dim boolFoundIt

Set objFSO = _
    WScript.CreateObject("Scripting.FileSystemObject")
Set objRootFolder = objFSO.GetFolder("C:\")
Set objFSO = Nothing

boolFoundIt = False
For Each objFileLoop In objRootFolder.Files

    If UCase(objFileLoop.Name) = "AUTOEXEC.BAT" Then
        boolFoundIt = True
        Exit For
    End If

Next
```

```
Set objFileLoop = Nothing
Set objRootFolder = Nothing

If boolFoundIt Then
    MsgBox "We found your AUTOEXEC.BAT file in " & _
        "the C:\ directory."
Else
    MsgBox "We could not find AUTOEXEC.BAT in " & _
        "the C:\ directory."
End If
```

Don't worry about any syntax that may be unfamiliar to you. Concentrate instead on the syntax of the `For Each...Next` loop block. The `objRootFolder` variable holds a reference to a `Folder` object. A `Folder` object has a `Files` collection. The `Files` collection is a collection of `File` objects. So what VBScript is telling us to do is "take a look at each `File` object in the `Files` collection." Each time the loop goes around, the loop variable, `objFileLoop`, will hold a reference to a different `File` object in the `Files` collection. If the `Files` collection is empty, then the loop will not go around at all. Notice how we use the `Exit For` statement to break out of the loop once we've found the file we're looking for.

The last script example is intended to demonstrate the use of the `For Each...Next` loop to traverse a collection of objects. Just as in the previous section, using a loop in this way is not necessarily the best way to see if a file exists. For example, this is much faster and more compact (`FSO_FIND_FILE_NO_LOOP.VBS`).

```
Option Explicit

Dim objFSO

Set objFSO = _
    WScript.CreateObject("Scripting.FileSystemObject")

If objFSO.FileExists("C:\AUTOEXEC.BAT") Then
    MsgBox "We found your AUTOEXEC.BAT file in the " & _
        "C:\ directory."
Else
    MsgBox "We could not find AUTOEXEC.BAT in " & _
        "the C:\ directory."
End If

Set objFSO = Nothing
```

You might be getting the idea that we're trying to send the message that you should not use loops, that there is always a better way. This is not the case. Loops are extremely useful and many well-written scripts will use them often. Programming is most often about using some kind of data, and often meaningful data is stored in complex structures like arrays and collections. If you need to root around inside that data to do what you need to do, the loop is your friend. However, as we mentioned, many times a loop seems like the obvious solution, but there may be a more elegant, less expensive alternate solution.

Before we move on to the `Do` loop, please note that even though the `For Each...Next` loop is most often used to loop through collections, it can also be used to loop through all of the elements of an array. No matter how many elements or dimensions the array has, the `For Each...Next` loop will touch each and every one of them. Here is an example of using the `For Each...Next` loop to traverse a single dimension array (`FOR_EACH_ARRAY.VBS`).

```
Option Explicit

Dim astrColors(3)
Dim strElement

astrColors(0) = "Red"
astrColors(1) = "Green"
astrColors(2) = "Blue"
astrColors(3) = "Yellow"

For Each strElement In astrColors
    MsgBox strElement
Next
```

# Do Loop

Do loop is the most versatile of all of the loop constructs. This is because you can easily make it loop as many times as you like based on any criteria you like. (However, you'd have to go through some trouble to use it to traverse a collection—For Each...Next is much better for that.) The power of the Do loop is in the use of the While and Until keywords. You can use While or Until at either the beginning of the loop or the end of the loop to control whether the loop will go around again. Let's look at a simple script that uses a Do loop (DO_WHILE.VBS).

```
Option Explicit

Dim boolLoopAgain
Dim lngLoopCount
Dim strResponse

boolLoopAgain = False
lngLoopCount = 0
Do
    boolLoopAgain = False
    lngLoopCount = lngLoopCount + 1

    strResponse = InputBox("What is the magic word?")
    If UCase(Trim(strResponse)) = "PLEASE" Then
        MsgBox "Correct! Congratulations!"
    Else
        If lngLoopCount < 5 Then
            MsgBox "Sorry, try again."
            boolLoopAgain = True
        Else
            MsgBox "Okay, the word we wanted was 'Please'."
        End If
    End If

Loop While boolLoopAgain
```

Using a Do loop in this way to process user input is a common technique. You need to ask the user something, but he or she might enter illegal data. You need a way to check the input and, if necessary, loop back and ask the user to enter it again.

**117**

Notice how the Do statement marks the beginning of the loop block, and how the Loop statement defines the end of the block. The While statement, however, places a condition on the Loop statement. The loop will only go around again if the expression following the While statement is True. In this case, our expression is a variable called boolLoopAgain, which has the Boolean subtype, but it could be any expression that evaluates to or returns a True or False response.

Notice also how we initialize the boolLoopAgain variable to False before the loop starts. This accomplishes two things: it establishes the subtype of the variable as Boolean, and it guarantees that the loop will only go around again if some piece of code inside the loop explicitly sets the variable to True. If the user guesses wrong, then we set boolLoopAgain to True, guaranteeing that the loop will go around at least one more time and so we can ask the user to guess again.

Finally, notice how we use a loop counter variable, lngLoopCount, to make sure that the loop does not go around forever and drive the user crazy if he or she can't guess the magic word. Using a loop counter variable is optional, and not part of the Do . . . Loop syntax, but it's a good idea if there's a chance that the loop might go around indefinitely.

Using this particular loop structure—with the Do statement by itself at the beginning, and the While condition attached to the Loop statement at the end—has an important implication: because we did not place a condition on the Do statement, the code inside the loop is guaranteed to execute *at least once*. This is what we want in this case, because if we did not execute the code at least one time, the user would never get asked the question "What is the magic word?"

Sometimes, though, you only want the code inside the loop to execute if some precondition is True; if that precondition is False, then you don't want the loop to execute at all. In that case, we can place the While statement at the beginning of the loop. If the Do While condition is False, then the loop will not go around even once.

In the following example, we are going to use the FileSystemObject to open a text file. We will access the text file using a TextStream object. When you open a file in the form of a TextStream object, the TextStream object uses a "pointer" to keep track of it's place in the file as you move through it. When you first open the file, the pointer is at the beginning of the file. (The pointer is not physically placed in the file—it exists only in memory in the TextStream object.) You can move through the file line by line using the TextStream.ReadLine method.

Each time you call ReadLine, the pointer moves one line down in the file. When the pointer moves past the last line in the file, the TextStream.AtEndOfStream property will have a value of True. That's when we know we are done reading the file. There is a possible problem, though: when we open a text file, we're not sure if it actually contains any data. It might be empty. If it is, then we don't want to call ReadLine, because this will cause an error. However, we'll know that the file is empty if the AtEndOfStream property is True right after opening the file. We can handle this nicely by placing the calls to ReadLine inside of a Do loop.

If you want to try out this code yourself, just create a text file and put the following lines in it (the downloadable code contains a file called TESTFILE.TXT).

```
Line 1
Line 2
Line 3
Line 4
Line 5
```

Save the file to your hard drive in the same location as the script below (DO_WHILE_READ_FILE.VBS). The script assumes that TESTFILE.TXT is in the same directory as the script file. While you're reading this code, don't worry if you're not familiar with the particulars of the FileSystemObject and TextStream objects, which are covered in detail in Chapter 7. Just pay attention to the way we use the While condition in conjunction with the Do statement.

```
Option Explicit

Dim objFSO
Dim objStream
Dim strText

Set objFSO = _
    WScript.CreateObject("Scripting.FileSystemObject")
Set objStream = objFSO.OpenTextFile("testfile.txt")
Set objFSO = Nothing

strText = ""
Do While Not objStream.AtEndOfStream
    strText = strText & objStream.ReadLine & vbNewLine
Loop
Set objStream = Nothing

If strText <> "" Then
    MsgBox strText
Else
    MsgBox "The file is empty."
End If
```

Running this code results in the dialog box shown in Figure 5-7.

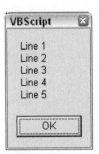

**Figure 5-7**

You can see that by placing the While condition at the *beginning* of our loop, we can decide whether or not we want the loop to go around even once. If the file is empty, then we don't want to try reading any lines. Since there is no condition on the Loop statement, though, when the loop reaches the end, the code will jump back up to the Do line. However, if the Do While expression returns False, the loop will not execute again, and the code will jump back down to the line immediately following the Loop line.

The objStream.AtEndOfStream property will be True only when the end of the file is reached. As long as we have not reached the end of the file, we want to keep looping. If we start out at the end of the file because the file is empty, we don't want to loop at all.

Going back to our first Do loop example, for the record, note that we *could* have put the While statement with the Do in our first example and accomplished the same thing (DO_WHILE2.VBS).

```
Option Explicit

Dim boolLoopAgain
Dim lngLoopCount
Dim strResponse

boolLoopAgain = True
lngLoopCount = 0
Do While boolLoopAgain
    boolLoopAgain = False
    lngLoopCount = lngLoopCount + 1

    strResponse = InputBox("What is the magic word?")
    If UCase(Trim(strResponse)) = "PLEASE" Then
        MsgBox "Correct! Congratulations!"
    Else
        If lngLoopCount < 5 Then
            MsgBox "Sorry, try again."
            boolLoopAgain = True
        Else
            MsgBox "Okay, the word we wanted was 'Please'."
        End If
    End If
Loop
```

Compare our first Do loop example with this one. Both examples accomplish exactly the same thing: the loop executes at least once, and it will only loop again if the code inside the loop says that we should. The difference with this second technique is that we started off by initializing boolLoopAgain to True, which guarantees that the loop will execute at least once.

As you can see, the Do loop is quite versatile, and how you accomplish one thing or another is largely a matter of preference. That said, one could make a pretty good argument that the first version of this code is preferable because the Do statement all by itself makes it obvious that the loop is going to execute at least once, whereas this second example is a little bit tricky.

> **All else being equal, if there are two ways of coding something, the more explicit method is almost always preferable.**

So the first question you need to answer when considering the use of the Do loop is, do I want the code to execute at least once, no matter what? If the answer to this question is yes, then it's best to place your condition at the end of the loop. Otherwise, put the condition at the beginning of the loop.

However, there is a second question: should you use the While statement for the condition, or its cousin, the Until statement? The answer to this second question is also largely a matter of preference. Although the While and Until statements are slightly different, they pretty much do the same thing. The main difference is one of semantics, and people generally fall into the habit of using one or the other, based on which syntax makes the most intuitive sense to them. However, one will usually tend to be more clear than another in a given situation.

Here's how Microsoft's VBScript documentation describes the Do loop (we added the **bold** emphasis).

*Repeats a block of statements **while** a condition is True or **until** a condition becomes True.*

As you can see, the distinction between While and Until is rather fuzzy. The easiest way to explain the difference is to modify our previous two examples replacing While with Until. You'll see that the consideration of whether to execute the loop *at least once* remains the same. However, the implementation is slightly different. Here's our first example, modified to use Until instead of While (DO_UNTIL.VBS).

```
Option Explicit

Dim boolLoopAgain
Dim lngLoopCount
Dim strResponse

boolLoopAgain = False
lngLoopCount = 0
Do
    boolLoopAgain = False
    lngLoopCount = lngLoopCount + 1

    strResponse = InputBox("What is the magic word?")
    If UCase(Trim(strResponse)) = "PLEASE" Then
        MsgBox "Correct! Congratulations!"
    Else
        If lngLoopCount < 5 Then
            MsgBox "Sorry, try again."
            boolLoopAgain = True
        Else
            MsgBox "Okay, the word we wanted was 'Please'."
        End If
    End If

Loop Until boolLoopAgain = False
```

It may look like the same code, but the difference is that we must test for a False value in our Until clause, whereas we tested for a True value in our While clause. When you read the line Loop While boolLoopAgain, does it make more sense than Loop Until boolLoopAgain = False? If the While syntax makes more sense to you, maybe we can fix that by changing the name of our variable (DO_UNTIL_BETTER_NAME.VBS).

```
Option Explicit

Dim boolStopLooping
Dim lngLoopCount
Dim strResponse

boolStopLooping = True
```

```
lngLoopCount = 0
Do
    boolStopLooping = True
    lngLoopCount = lngLoopCount + 1

    strResponse = InputBox("What is the magic word?")
    If UCase(Trim(strResponse)) = "PLEASE" Then
        MsgBox "Correct! Congratulations!"
    Else
        If lngLoopCount < 5 Then
            MsgBox "Sorry, try again."
            boolStopLooping = False
        Else
            MsgBox "Okay, the word we wanted was 'Please'."
        End If
    End If

Loop Until boolStopLooping = True
```

Does the Until syntax make a little more sense now? The point is you can use either While or Until to accomplish what you need to—it's just a matter of what makes more sense in a given situation. Let's look at our file reading example again, this time using Until instead of While (DO_UNTIL_READ_FILE.VBS).

```
Option Explicit

Dim objFSO
Dim objStream
Dim strText

Set objFSO = _
    WScript.CreateObject("Scripting.FileSystemObject")
Set objStream = objFSO.OpenTextFile("testfile.txt")
Set objFSO = Nothing

strText = ""
Do Until objStream.AtEndOfStream
    strText = strText & objStream.ReadLine & vbNewLine
Loop
Set objStream = Nothing

If strText <> "" Then
    MsgBox strText
Else
    MsgBox "The file is empty."
End If
```

The Until syntax might make this more clear. People sometimes have an easier time thinking in terms of positives, and the syntax Do While Not objStream.AtEndOfStream may be more or less clear to you than Do Until objStream.AtEndOfStream. It's up to you, though. VBScript doesn't care. And if you use good variable names, stick to straightforward logic, and make good use of indenting and white space, your fellow programmers most likely won't care either.

Before we move on to `While...Wend`, we need to mention the `Exit Do` statement. Like `Exit For`, you can use `Exit Do` to break out of a `Do` loop at any point. You can have as many `Exit Do` statements inside your loop as you like. Here's an example, yet another variation on our "magic word" example (`DO_WHILE3.VBS`).

```
Option Explicit

Dim boolLoopAgain
Dim lngLoopCount
Dim strResponse

boolLoopAgain = False
lngLoopCount = 0
Do
    boolLoopAgain = False
    lngLoopCount = lngLoopCount + 1

    strResponse = InputBox("What is the magic word?")
    If UCase(Trim(strResponse)) = "PLEASE" Then
        MsgBox "Correct! Congratulations!"
        Exit Do
    Else
        If lngLoopCount < 5 Then
            MsgBox "Sorry, try again."
            boolLoopAgain = True
        Else
            MsgBox "Okay, the word we wanted was 'Please'."
            Exit Do
        End If
    End If

Loop While boolLoopAgain
```

Instead of setting `boolLoopAgain` to `False`, we just execute an `Exit Do`, which has the same effect in that we won't go around the loop again. When the `Exit Do` statement executes, the code jumps out of the loop, to the line of code immediately following the last line of the loop block (in our example, there is not any code after our loop, so the script ends). However, while this example illustrates the proper syntax for `Exit Do`, we have not necessarily made our magic word code any better by using it.

Remember the procedures and functions discussion in Chapter 4? When discussing the `Exit Sub` and `Exit Function` statements, we said that you should use them carefully and that there is usually a way to organize your code so that you do not have to use them. The potential problem with using `Exit Sub` and `Exit Function` is that the logic can become hard to follow because of the jumping out of the flow. The same principle applies to `Exit Do`.

If you compare the original magic word code to this new version, in the original we used the `boolLoopAgain` statement in conjunction with `If` conditions to control the loop. The logic flows from top to bottom in a linear fashion. Our new code with the `Exit Do` statements has lost that elegance and clarity.

A final note about `Exit Do` (and the other loop `Exit` statements as well): if you are working with nested loops, an `Exit Do` executed in the *inner* loop *does not* break out of the *outer* loop as well—only from the loop in which the `Exit Do` was executed.

# While. . . Wend

As we mentioned at the beginning of the chapter, the `While...Wend` loop is an older loop syntax from early versions of BASIC and Visual Basic. The `Do` loop (see previous section) is often preferred by programmers over the `While...Wend` loop, which is not nearly as versatile. This is not to say that it is not perfectly valid to use it, and many programmers use it often. It works fine, it's simple, and Microsoft certainly has not given any indication that they plan to remove support for it. It has simply fallen out of vogue. In the interest of completeness, here's an example of the `While...Wend` syntax (`WHILE_WEND.VBS`).

```
Option Explicit

Dim lngCounter

lngCounter = 0
While lngCounter <= 20
    lngCounter = lngCounter + 1
    '<other code goes here>
Wend
```

Unlike the `Do` loop, you do not have the option of using either `While` or `Until`, nor can you place the condition at the end of the loop. The condition for whether to loop again can only be placed at the beginning of the loop, as you see here. Finally, a significant limitation of the `While...Wend` loop is that there is no equivalent to `Exit For` or `Exit Do`, meaning you cannot forcibly break out of the loop.

# Summary

In this chapter we covered the topic of "control of flow," which involves branching and looping. Branching is the technique of checking conditions, making a decision, and executing (or not executing) a block of code based on that decision. Following are the branching constructs in VBScript.

```
If ... ElseIf ... Else ... End If

Select Case ... End Select
```

Looping is the technique of repeating the same block of code over again. The looping constructs in VBScript are as follows.

```
For ... Next
For Each ... Next
Do ... Loop While
Do While ... Loop
Do ... Loop Until
Do Until ... Loop
While ... Wend
```

# 6

# Error Handling and Debugging

## Overview

No explanation or tutorial of a programming language is complete without a thorough coverage of *error handling*. It is of course important to learn the syntax of a language and to use correct logic in your programs. What truly gives a program or script professional polish—what separates throwaway from production quality—is error handling.

Writing a computer program, even a simple one, is a delicate matter. You have to get the syntax exactly write. You have to place the quote marks and the parentheses just so. You have to name the files in a particular way. You have to follow a certain kind of logic. What's more, your program does not exist in a vacuum. A VBScript program can interact directly or indirectly with the scripting host, the operating system, the user, the network, and the Internet. A script is beset by the possibility of full disks, invalid user entry, scrambled file formats, and the electricity suddenly dropping out.

Things can, and will, go wrong.

Error handling is the programmer's line of defense against this inherent unpredictability. The term error handling refers not only to how a program responds when an error occurs, but also to how it prevents errors from happening in the first place.

The subject of debugging goes hand-in-hand with that of error handling. *Debugging*, as the name suggests, is the process of detecting, locating, and removing bugs from a program. The removing part of that process is most often the easiest part. The real art of debugging is in the use of tools and techniques for the detecting and locating processes. Basic proficiency with debugging brings with it a reduction in frustration and an increase in productivity.

This chapter will dive deep into the closely related subjects of error handling and debugging. If you are a new programmer, this chapter explains not only the VBScript mechanics of error handling and debugging, but also the universal principles and techniques at work. If you are an experienced programmer in other programming languages, this chapter is still worth your while; error handling and debugging in VBScript are quite unique and likely different from your experience with other languages.

Note that error handling associated with the Script Control (Chapter 18) is slightly different than with other hosts. Although error handling within the Script Control works similarly to other scripting hosts, there is also the possibility of handling errors via the host (for example the VB application itself), with a distinction between compilation and runtime errors. For more specific information, consult Chapter 18 on Script Control.

# Types of Errors

There are three types of errors that can burrow their way into your lovingly crafted VBScript code. *Syntax errors* will halt the execution of the script. *Runtime errors* will invoke an error handler, giving you the opportunity to do something about the error—or at least display it attractively. Finally, *logical errors* will most commonly contaminate data in your application, cause strange behavior for users and administrators, and often cause other errors to occur.

# Syntax Errors

VBScript, like all other programming or scripting languages, follows set rules for construction of statements. Before the script is run, the scripting engine parses all of the code, converting it into tokens. When an unrecognizable structure or an expression is encountered (for example, if you mistype a keyword or forget to close a loop), a syntax error is generated. Luckily, syntax errors can usually be caught during development phase, with minimal testing of the code.

Here is an example script that, when run under the Windows Script Host, produces the syntax error displayed in Figure 6-1.

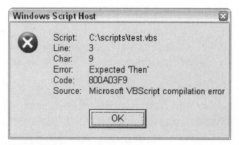

**Figure 6-1**

```
Option Explicit

Dim x
If x > 0
    MsgBox "That number is high enough."
End If
```

Most of the time, the information in the error display will make it obvious where the problem is—in this case, a missing Then keyword on line 4. How the syntax error is displayed depends on which host the script is run under. For example, a syntax error for an ASP (Active Server Page) script run under Internet Information Services (IIS) would be displayed on an error page in the browser.

Syntax errors (and runtime errors) are easier to spot than logic errors (which we will look at shortly) because they always result in an error message being generated. Needless to say, with proper understanding of VBScript, syntax errors are not a major concern. Syntax errors tend to pop-up in several circumstances:

- ❑ When something is missing from the code—parentheses, keywords (especially in blocks), statement elements, or when the keywords are simply out of place

- ❑ When a keyword is misspelled or used incorrectly

- ❑ When you try to use a Visual Basic or VBA keyword or function that is not implemented by VBScript

- ❑ When you use keywords that are not supported by a particular version of the scripting engine (certain keywords may be phased out, and others added)

As you may expect, dynamic code executed using the Eval, Execute, and ExecuteGlobal functions is not parsed at the same time as normal script code. Dynamic code is not parsed until the call to one of these functions, and so syntax errors in dynamic code are not reported until that time. Special attention has to be paid when generating dynamic code. Ideally, you would be able to test all of your dynamically generated code before releasing to users, but since dynamic code often includes input from outside sources, it is not always possible to anticipate syntax errors.

Appendix E shows all 53 of VBScript's syntax errors and their codes. All of these errors, with an exception of the first two—Out of Memory and Syntax Error—are relatively easy to diagnose and correct, though sometimes diagnosis can be tricky when you have a lot of nested parentheses or quote marks.

# Runtime Errors

The second, and most common type of error is the runtime error. A runtime error occurs when a command attempts to perform an action that is invalid. A runtime error is different from a syntax error in that the offending code looks syntactically fine to the script engine, but has some kind of problem when it is executed. That is, the error does not necessarily appear while you are programming, but rather when you or one of your users is running the script.

Runtime errors can be divided into three categories: native VBScript runtime errors, non-VBScript runtime errors, and variable declaration runtime errors related to the Option Explicit directive. In all three cases, the result is the same: an error occurs while the script is running. What differentiates the three types is what causes an error—and how an error could be prevented.

## Native VBScript Runtime Errors

For example, a runtime error occurs if you try to divide by zero (ERR_DIVIDE_BY_ZERO.VBS).

```
Option Explicit

Dim x
x = 200/0
MsgBox "The answer is: " & x
```

This code, run under the Windows Script Host, produces the error displayed in Figure 6-2.

Windows Script Host
Script: C:\scripts\test.vbs
Line: 3
Char: 1
Error: Division by zero
Code: 800A000B
Source: Microsoft VBScript runtime error
OK

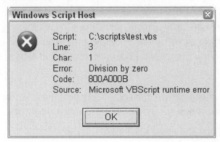

**Figure 6-2**

Figure 6-3 shows the same error from the same script, but this time the script was launched from the command line (see Chapter 12).

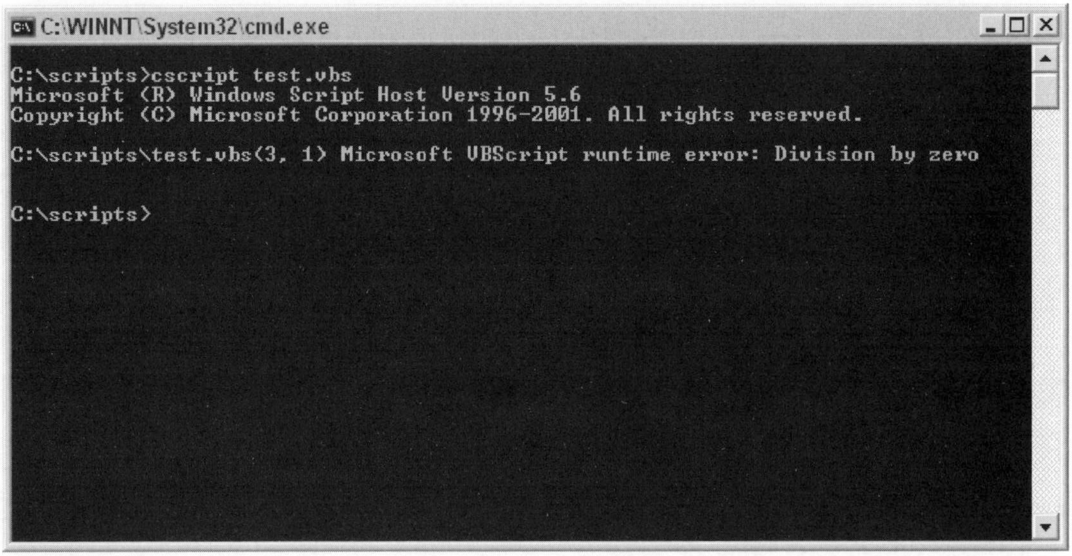

C:\WINNT\System32\cmd.exe
C:\scripts>cscript test.vbs
Microsoft (R) Windows Script Host Version 5.6
Copyright (C) Microsoft Corporation 1996-2001. All rights reserved.
C:\scripts\test.vbs(3, 1) Microsoft VBScript runtime error: Division by zero
C:\scripts>

**Figure 6-3**

As you can see, as with the syntax error, the default error display gives fairly specific information about what went wrong. What distinguishes this example from a syntax error is that there is nothing wrong with the syntax of this code. Instead, the code is trying to do something that computers don't like: dividing by zero.

Another common example of a runtime error is passing the `Null` value to a function that does not like nulls, as in this example.

```
Option Explicit

Dim x
x = Null
MsgBox x
```

This code will produce an `Invalid use of Null` runtime error on line 4. The `MsgBox` function does not accept `Null` as a valid input value. `Null` values often cause problems when passed to built-in VBScript functions; so when your script takes in data from user input, a file, or a database, it is important to make sure that you test for `Null` values. One common technique is to take advantage of VBScript's implicit type coercion (see Chapter 3) to get rid of the `Null`.

```
Option Explicit

Dim x
x = GetValueFromDatabase()
MsgBox "" & x
```

`GetValueFromDatabase` is a fictional function that might return a `Null`. This code accounts for this fact by appending an empty string to the value of `x`. When VBScript executes this code, the concatenation of the empty string causes the `Null` subtype of `x` to be converted to the `String` subtype. A little defensive programming can prevent many runtime errors from ever occurring.

The tricky thing with runtime errors such as these is that it takes some time for a programmer in any language or platform to learn the particular things that can cause runtime errors. Unfortunately, it would take an entire book, at least the size of this, one to cover all of the possible scenarios for runtime errors, especially when you consider all of the hosts under which VBScript can be run and all of the commercial and custom components that VBScript can use.

Here are two tips to help you with runtime errors: one, the first time you use a function, read the documentation for that function to look for possible traps that could lead to runtime errors, and then code defensively to prevent those errors. And two, if you are plagued by a runtime error you don't have an explanation for, search online knowledge bases and discussion forums; chances are someone has already encountered that error and can tell you what's causing it.

## Non-VBScript Runtime Errors

The two examples of runtime errors we have looked at so far—a divide by zero error and a `Null` value passed to the `MsgBox` function—are produced by the VBScript runtime engine (which you can tell by the `Source` value of `Microsoft VBScript runtime error` in Figure 6-2). However, not all runtime errors will come from VBScript itself. In fact, depending on the complexity of the project, it is safe to say that most errors you encounter as a VBScript programmer will not be produced by the VBScript engine.

Instead, runtime errors will often come from other sources—namely, scripting hosts such as IIS and external components such as Microsoft's ActiveX Data Objects (ADO) component. Runtime errors can even be raised by other VBScript scripts since any script can use the `Err.Raise` method to generate runtime errors. (`Err.Raise` is covered later in this chapter.)

The method of dealing with non-VBScript runtime errors is the same as for native VBScript runtime errors. Ideally, the error message itself will give you enough information to make the cause of the error obvious. For example, Microsoft's ADO database access component (see Appendix L) has a runtime error with the description `The specified table does not exist`. The cause of this error is pretty clear from the description; evidently, the offending code referred to a database table that does not exist, perhaps the result of a misspelling in the code.

However, ADO also has several other runtime errors with descriptions such as `Unspecified error`, `Operation aborted`, and even `Errors occurred`. What are you supposed to do when faced with such ambiguous information? Unfortunately, the only way to work past these errors is through a combination of detective work and trial-and-error. When a runtime error does not offer useful hints as to what's going on, your best bet is to turn to online knowledge bases such as the one at microsoft.com and online discussion forums such as those offered at p2p.wrox.com.

Start by searching these resources for information about the error. If you can't find instances of people having encountered and fixed the error before, then post a description of your problem so that other developers can offer help. When you post, be sure to include code samples and as much information as possible about the context of what you are trying to do. The annoyance of runtime errors is an unfortunate downside of being a programmer, but not an insurmountable one, especially with the help of your fellow developers around the world.

## Errors Related to Option Explicit

As discussed in Chapter 4, the use of the Option Explicit statement is critical to your success as a VBScript programmer. It is your best defense against strange, difficult to detect errors that can result from misspellings of variable names and mistakes related to a variable's scope. When using Option Explicit, if your code refers to a variable that has not be declared (or that has not been declared with the correct scope) then VBScript will produce an error, thereby allowing you the opportunity to fix a problem that otherwise may not have been detected at all.

However, the error you receive in these situations will be a runtime error—not a syntax error as you might expect. VBScript will report only the Variable is undefined runtime error when the offending code is executed—*not* when the code is compiled by the script engine. What this means is that it is important to test your code fully before releasing it into a production environment. Let's quickly look at an example.

The following Windows Script Host script (OPT_EXPL_ERROR.VBS), which uses the Option Explicit statement, has a missing variable declaration for the lngDay variable in the SpecialNovemberProcessing procedure.

```
Option Explicit

Dim datToday
Dim lngMonth

datToday = Date()
lngMonth = DatePart("m", datToday)
If lngMonth = 11 Then
    SpecialNovemberProcessing(datToday)
End If

Private Sub SpecialNovemberProcessing(datAny)
    lngDay = DatePart("d", datAny)
    MsgBox "Today is day " & lngDay & " of November."
End Sub
```

As you can see from the code, the SpecialNovemberProcessing procedure will only be called when the month of the current system date is November. If you run this code when your system date is anything other than November, then VBScript will not detect the variable declaration problem with lngDay in SpecialNovemberProcessing. If you wrote this code and tested it with a non-November month, then SpecialNovemberProcessing would never be called. However, after you have released the code to production and November finally rolls around, this code will produce a `Variable is undefined` runtime error, and you will have an embarrassing production error on your hands. If you are reading these words in a month that is not November, and you would like to see this behavior in action, first run this script and you will see that no error is produced. Then, change the `11` in this line to match whatever month your system clock says it is.

```
If lngMonth = 11 Then
```

Run the script after making the change, and you'll see that VBScript generates a `Variable is undefined` runtime error.

The way to prevent this from happening is to fully test your code to make sure that all paths of execution are exercised. Check your code for procedures and functions that are called only under certain conditions, and then force those conditions to exist so that you can make sure all of your code executes properly.

# Logic Errors

You can think of logic errors as hidden errors. Logic errors, in general, will not produce any kind of error message. Instead, a logic error will produce what programmers usually call "undesirable results." For example, if you write a sales tax calculation script for processing orders on your ASP-based Web site, and that script incorrectly calculates the tax amount, that's a logic error—otherwise known as a *bug*. No error message is produced, but the program is wrong all the same. One could definitely make an argument that logic errors are the worst kind of error since they can go undetected for a long time, and, as in the example of miscalculated sales tax, can even cause serious legal and financial problems.

The computer generally cannot detect a logic error for you. Only careful examination, testing, and validation of program code can detect logic errors. The best way to deal with logic errors is to avoid them in the first place. The oldest and most common method for logic error prevention is requirements and design specifications, which are detailed descriptions (in the form of words and/or diagrams) of how a program needs to work. A requirements specification stays as close to normal human vocabulary as possible, without describing actual technical details, so that nontechnical subject matter experts can verify the requirements. A design specification is generally produced after the requirements specification and describes the details of the technical implementation that will "solve" the requirements.

By producing specifications, you can theoretically avoid logic errors by ensuring that you fully understand the problem and the proposed solution *before* you start writing code. However, even with perfect specifications, logic errors can still creep into code. The programmer might accidentally use a "plus" operator instead of "minus," or a "greater than" operator instead of "less than." The programmer might forget to implement the special sales tax processing rules for a particular locale, even if those rules are clearly spelled out in the specifications. Logic errors can also result from improper use of the programming language. For example, a VBScript programmer who does not understand the subtleties of the `Variant` subtypes and implicit type coercion described in Chapter 3 could introduce logic errors into a script.

Because some amount of logic errors is inevitable in all but the most trivial programs, thorough testing of program code is essential. The programmer himself or herself has the first responsibility to perform some basic testing of his or her code, and ideally the programmer will have professional testers who can follow up with more methodical and thorough testing. Ideally, such testing is based on the requirements and design specifications on which the code is based.

In addition to upfront specifications and after-the-fact testing, another preventative measure against logic errors is what is known as defensive programming. Defensive programming is about checking assumptions about the expected program flow and either (a) generating runtime errors when those checks fail, or (b) including extra code that fixes the problem. For example, if you are writing a function that takes a numeric argument, and your logic requires that the argument must be greater than zero, include a double-check at the top of the function that ensures that the argument is greater than zero. If the check fails, you can choose to generate a custom runtime error or, depending on the situation, do something to fix the offending numeric argument. (We discuss custom runtime errors later in this chapter.)

Finally, the greater the complexity, the more likely that logic errors will be introduced. If you are working on a particularly complex problem, break the problem down into manageable chunks, in the form of procedures, functions, classes, and so on, as discussed in Chapter 4. When the solution to a problem is decomposed into smaller modules, it becomes easier to hold in your head all at once while simultaneously allowing you to focus your attention on one small aspect of the problem at a time.

# Error Visibility and Context

A key aspect of understanding and managing runtime errors is knowledge of where your code is running and what happens when an error occurs. In the following sections we will briefly describe some of the more typical situations. Later in the chapter we will introduce "error handling" techniques, which can be used to catch errors when they occur and control what happens after that point.

## Windows Script Host Errors

Throughout the book so far, the example scripts we've been using are intended to be run under the Windows Script Host (WSH), which is a scripting host built into Windows. As we have seen in Figures 6-1, 6-2, and 6-3, WSH has an automatic error display mechanism. For "interactive" scripts where the person running the script is sitting in front of the computer launching the script, this default error display may be sufficient. If an error occurs, WSH displays it in a dialog box (or as plain text on the command line, depending on how the script was launched), and the human operator can decide what to do at that point.

However, often a WSH script runs automatically, perhaps on a schedule, with no human operator sitting in front of the computer. In this case, you can control to some degree what happens when an error occurs instead of using WSH's default error display mechanism. The section *Handling Errors* later in this chapter discusses various techniques.

## Server-Side ASP Errors

A server-side ASP error can occur when IIS is processing ASP code. Even though ASP code is used for producing Web sites, the code actually runs on the server to produce Web pages and other Web-friendly files that are pushed out to the browser. It is important to distinguish this from client-side VBScript that actually runs inside of the Internet Explorer browser (see next section).

However, even though the code is executed on the server, paradoxically the default mechanism of displaying an error is inside the Web browser. If you think about it, this makes sense. Without the browser, IIS is basically invisible. Its whole purpose is to push content to the browser. There is no terminal in which to display an error on the server, and even if there was, most of the time no one is sitting there watching the server.

However, IIS does not leave you powerless when it comes to error display. The section later in this chapter called *Presenting and Logging Errors* describes a technique you can use to display how and whether detailed error information is displayed in the browser when a server-side error occurs.

# Client-Side VBScript Errors in Internet Explorer

Since client-side VBScript code runs inside of the Internet Explorer browser, naturally you would expect errors to be displayed within the browser. That is the case, but your users very likely will have their browsers set up so that they never see a client-side VBScript (or JavaScript or JScript for that matter) error when it occurs. Figure 6-4 shows the Advanced tab on the Internet Options dialog box for Internet Explorer, with the "Display a notification about every script error" option highlighted.

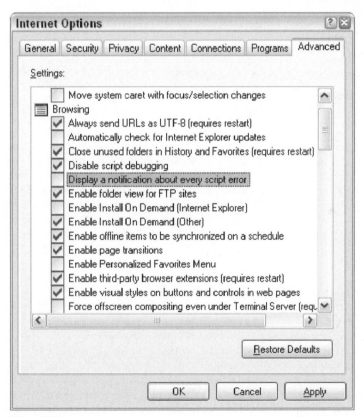

**Figure 6-4**

As you can see, users may or may not have error display turned on in the browser. It's safe to assume that your users do not have this option turned on because having it turned on becomes annoying after awhile. If an error message popped up in your browser every time you browsed to a Web page with a client-side script error, you would be driven crazy clicking the OK button all the time. When error display is turned off, a small yellow triangle with an exclamation point (!) will appear in the status bar at the bottom of the browser window.

This will be the user's only indication that an error has occurred, and the actual error message will only come up if the user happens to notice the yellow icon and clicks on it. However, it is important to consider the likely possibility that users of your Web page will not care what the error is. There is nothing that they can do about it anyway. All they know is that the page is not working. This situation underlines the importance of thoroughly testing all of your browser-based VBScript code.

# Handling Errors

What exactly does "error handling" mean? In the purest definition, error handling means take an active, rather than passive, approach to responding to errors. This means having extra code built into your script to deal with errors in case they occur. This can take the form of a "global" error handling scheme that does something such as:

- ❑ displaying the error to a user
- ❑ logging the error to a file, database, or the Windows Event Log
- ❑ e-mailing the error to a system administrator
- ❑ paging the system administrator
- ❑ some combination of all of the these

In addition to a general error handling scheme, you can trap for specific errors at specific points. For example, trying to connect to a database is a common point where errors occur. The password entered by the user might be wrong, or the database might have reached the maximum allowable connections. Knowing that connecting to a database is error prone, the experienced VBScript programmer will put a specific error trap in his or her code in the place where the code attempts a database connection.

The remainder of this section will introduce the elements necessary for handling errors in your VBScript programs.

## The Err Object

The Err object is what is described in the Microsoft VBScript documentation as an "intrinsic object with global scope," which means that it is always available to any VBScript code. There is no need to declare a variable to hold an Err object and no need to instantiate it using CreateObject or New. There is exactly one Err object in memory at all times while a VBScript program is running.

The Err object contains information about the last error that occurred. If no error has occurred, the Err object will still be available, but it will not contain any error information. Error information is stored in the properties of the Err object; some of which are given in the table.

The properties and methods of the Err object are described in more detail in Appendix E.

The Err object also has two methods. The first is the Clear method, which erases all of the properties of the Err object so that the information about the last error is thrown away. The second is the Raise

| | |
|---|---|
| Description | Holds a textual description of the last error that occurred |
| Number | Holds the number of the last error that occurred |
| Source | Holds a textual description of the source of the last error that occurred; usually this is the name of the component from where the error originated |
| HelpFile | If the source of the error has an associated Windows help file, holds the pathname of the help file |
| HelpContext | If the source of the error has an associated Windows help file, holds a unique identifier |

method, which you can use in your VBScript code to generate custom runtime errors. The next section about the On Error statements goes into more detail on how you can use the Err object and its properties and methods to handle errors in your VBScript programs. In addition, the section later in this chapter called *Generating Custom Errors* explains the use of the Err.Raise method.

## Using the On Error Statements

Unfortunately, VBScript does not have the robust, structured error handling mechanism offered by other programming languages such as Visual Basic, C++, Java, and the .NET languages. This is one of VBScript's most glaring shortcomings. It is not a stretch to characterize VBScript's error handling mechanism as awkward and limiting. In fact, if you don't understand how it works and use it properly, it can cause you to not even be aware that dozens of errors might be occurring in your code.

By default, a VBScript program does not have any error handling at all. All of the example scripts we have had in the book so far are in this default state. As described at the beginning of this chapter, if an error occurs, whatever error display mechanism the script host uses takes over and, in most cases, simply displays the error information to the user.

The most useful way to think about VBScript error control is that there is a switch that controls the error control setting for the entire script. The default position of the switch is On. When the switch is On, any error that occurs will immediately be reported. When the switch is Off, any error that occurs will essentially be ignored (that is, unless you specifically check to see if an error occurred). This WSH script (ERR_DIVIDE_BY_ZERO.VBS) from the beginning of the chapter that causes a divide by zero error is using the default On position.

```
Option Explicit

Dim x
x = 200/0
MsgBox "The answer is: " & x
```

When the script engine tries to execute line 4, it hits the divide by zero error and immediately displays the error, as shown in Figures 6-2 and 6-3.

If you want to flip the error control switch to the Off position, you can add the On Error Resume Next statement to the top of the script, like so (ERR_DBZ_RESUME_NEXT.VBS):

```
Option Explicit
On Error Resume Next

Dim x
x = 200/0
MsgBox "The answer is: " & x
```

If you run this code, instead of displaying the divide by zero error, VBScript ignores that error and continues executing the next line. The message box pops up, but since the value of x was never initialized, the value shown after "The answer is: " is blank. The divide by zero error still occurred, but with the switch in the Off position, VBScript won't tell us about it.

You can see now how flipping the global error control switch to the Off position with On Error Resume Next could get you into trouble. What if the x = 200/0 line was part of a much larger algorithm calculating the price of an expensive product sold by your company? If you had used On Error Resume Next in this manner to suppress error, then you might never find the error and the price of the product could be way off.

So we are not trying to say that On Error Resume Next is inherently bad. What we are trying to say is that because On Error Resume Next globally suppresses errors for your entire script—including all procedures, functions, classes, and (with ASP) include files—it is very dangerous and must be used carefully. We can propose with confidence the following two rules.

> Unless you have a very good reason, never suppress all errors by simply placing the **On Error Resume Next** statement at the top of your script.

And

> If, in the body of your script, you use the **On Error Resume Next** statement to temporarily disable error reporting, make sure you use a corresponding **On Error GoTo 0** statement to enable it again.

What is On Error GoTo 0? Just as On Error Resume Next flips the error reporting to the switch to the Off position, On Error GoTo 0 turns it back on. Our second rule states explicitly what is implicit in the first rule: in general, don't use On Error Resume Next by itself, without a subsequent On Error GoTo 0 statement to flip the switch back to On.

Used together with the Err object (introduced in the previous section), the two On Error statements can be used to add specific error traps to your code. The following script (ERR_TRAP.VBS) demonstrates an error trap using `On Error Resume Next` and `On Error GoTo 0` together. The example also demonstrates the `Err.Raise` method, but we'll be saving detailed discussion of `Err.Raise` until the *Generating Custom Errors* section later in this chapter. The script also contains an incomplete procedure called `DisplayError()`, which we will populate with real code in the next section.

```
Option Explicit
Dim x

On Error Resume Next
x = GetValueFromDatabase()
If Err.Number = 0 Then
    MsgBox "The value of x is: " & x
Else
    DisplayError
End If
On Error GoTo 0

Private Function GetValueFromDatabase()

    'Deliberately create an error for
    'demonstration purposes.
    Err.Raise vbObjectError + 1000, _
        "GetValueFromDatabase()", _
        "A database error occurred."

End Function

Private Sub DisplayError()
    'Stub procedure. We will fill this in
    'with a proper error display.
    MsgBox "An error occurred."
End Sub
```

The part of this code that we want to focus on is the block that begins with the `On Error Resume Next` statement and ends with the `On Error GoTo 0` statement. By surrounding this block of code with these two statements, the programmer who wrote this code is saying "There is a good chance an error might occur right here, so I'm going to set a trap for it." The line of code that the programmer is worried about is this one.

```
x = GetValueFromDatabase()
```

We created this fake `GetValueFromDatabase()` function to illustrate the point that database-related calls are often prone to errors. When databases are involved, there are just a lot of things that could go wrong—more so than in most other situations. The same could be said of interactions with the Windows file system, the Internet, e-mail, networks, or external components with which you are not familiar. Over time, programmers develop a sixth sense about hot spots for errors.

In this case, the programmer was correct: our fake `GetValueFromDatabase()` function does raise an error (the details of the `Err.Raise` method call will be covered in the *Generating Custom Errors* section later in this chapter). Whenever an error occurs, the `Err` object's properties are populated with information about the error. Generally, you can count on the fact that if an error occurs, the `Err.Number` property will be some number greater than or less than zero. So the line immediately after the call to `GetValueFromDatabase()` checks the `Err.Number` property.

If the error number is zero, then the code assumes that no error occurred and proceeds with its normal path of execution—in this case, displaying the value of the variable x. If an error does occur, the script attempts to gracefully display the error before continuing. (We'll put some meaningful code in this `DisplayError` procedure in the next section, *Presenting and Logging Errors*.)

What your script does after an error occurs really depends on the situation. You might want to log the error to a file. You may want to hide the error from the user. You may want to retry the operation a few times before giving up. You may want to send an e-mail to the system administrator. You may want to continue execution of the script after the error or stop the script. The choice is up to the programmer.

The key point here is this: if the programmer had not set this trap for this error and taken the action he or she chose (in this case, displaying the error), he or she would not have had any control over the situation. The VBScript host would have followed its default error handling path, as illustrated with the script errors at the beginning of this chapter. In summary, here are the steps for setting an error trap.

1.  Use the `On Error Resume Next` statement on the line immediately before the line you suspect might raise an error. This assumes that you have been careful not to use `On Error Resume Next` to turn off error handling for the whole script.

2.  On the line immediately after the suspect line, check the value of `Err.Number`. If it is zero, you can safely assume that no error has occurred and proceed as normal. If it is anything other than zero, an error has occurred and you have to "handle" the error somehow. There are many choices for what to do, including displaying the error information to the user, logging it, e-mailing it, using a `Do` loop with a retry counter variable to try again a few times, or hide the error completely by ignoring it.

3.  After you have handled the error, it is very important to use the `On Error GoTo 0` statement to put VBScript back into its default mode of handling errors for you. If you do not follow the `On Error Resume Next` statement with a corresponding `On Error GoTo 0` statement, then you will, without realizing it, suppress errors later in your script.

It is unfortunate that VBScript's error handling is designed such that the programmer is forced to watch out for error "hot spots" and set traps to catch the errors so that they can be "handled" elegantly—rather than having VBScript or its host take over and stop your script dead in its tracks. The more robust error handling schemes of other programming languages have ways of setting "generic traps" for errors so that you are always in control. VBScript does not have such a facility.

You may have already seen the big problem here: if VBScript does not give us a way of generically trapping errors, are we supposed to put specific error traps after every single line of code we write? Obviously, doing this for *every* line of code is not practical, but unfortunately you *do* have to use these error traps in places where errors are likely. You just have to trust, given proper use of VBScript, that your calls to generic functions like `MsgBox()` and `InStr()` are not going to raise errors, but when dealing with those "hot spots" mentioned earlier, error traps are a good idea for production code.

It's not quite as bad as it sounds. Within any given script, you will have some hot spots, but hopefully not so many that you go crazy writing traps. In closing, here is an illustration of a section of script code with several possible hot spots in a row.

```
On Error Resume Next

DoTheFirstThing()
If Err.Number <> 0 Then
    HandleError()
    Exit Sub
End If

DoTheSecondThing()
If Err.Number <> 0 Then
    HandleError()
    Exit Sub
End If

DoTheThirdThing()
If Err.Number <> 0 Then
    HandleError()
    Exit Sub
End If

On Error GoTo 0
```

What we have done here is created a larger section of code with multiple traps, but we've used only one pair of On Error Resume Next and On Error GoTo 0 statements to block out the whole thing. As you can see, the If block that checks Err.Number is the same each time, so while we have more code than we'd like, Copy and Paste makes adding the extra code relatively painless.

## Presenting and Logging Errors

As discussed in the previous section, when you have "trapped" an error, you have to do something with it. This "doing something" is usually referred to as "handling" the error, which means you are going to respond to the error in some specific way other than letting the VBScript host handle the error on your behalf.

The most common error handling technique is to display the error to your users. As demonstrated at the beginning of this chapter, if you do not use the On Error Resume Next statement, VBScript's default error handling, depending on the host, is generally to display the error to the user somehow. So if VBScript will display the error for you, why add your own error handling and display code? There are two good reasons: control and cosmetics.

If you do not use the error trapping technique described in the previous section, then you are giving all error handling control to the VBScript host. Yes, the host will display the error for you, but it will also stop your script at the exact point the error occurred. If you had a file open, you won't get a chance to close it. If you were in the middle of a database update, your connection to the database, and your data, will be thrown away. If you were in the middle of collecting a large amount of information from the user, all of that work on the user's part will be lost. Allowing the VBScript host to handle all errors for you is often not the best technique.

The second reason mentioned, cosmetics, has to do with how the error is displayed. The error display in, for instance, the WSH, is not the most friendly in the world. Your users might miss the important information buried in the daunting error display dialog box. By writing your own procedure to display errors in your WSH scripts, you can present a more professional face to your users. Let's add some code to the DisplayError procedure we saw in one of the example scripts (ERR_TRAP.VBS) from the previous section.

```
Private Sub DisplayError(lngNumber, strSource, strDescription)
    MsgBox "An error occurred. Please write down " & _
        "the error information displayed below " & _
        "and contact your system administrator:" & _
        vbNewLine & vbNewLine & _
        "Error Description: " & strDescription & vbNewLine & _
        "Error Number: " & lngNumber & vbNewLine & _
        "Error Source: " & strSource, _
        vbExclamation
End Sub
```

This looks like a lot of code, but really we're just stringing together a nice, friendly message with line breaks and white space, as shown in Figure 6-5. Other than the improved appearance, we're basically displaying the same information that VBScript would have by default.

**Figure 6-5**

Beyond displaying the error, you have other options as well. In fact, if your script runs unattended, you might not want to display the error at all since there is no one sitting there to click the OK button. One of the most popular techniques is to log the error to a file, a database, or the Windows Event Log. You can also e-mail the error to a system administrator, or even page the system administrator on his or her beeper. You could get really fancy and send a message to a Web site that reboots the server in your back office. How elaborate you get, and what ways you choose to respond, is really dependent upon the situation—in particular, how important the script is and what bad things might happen if an error occurs without anyone noticing.

There is unfortunately not enough space in this chapter to demonstrate all of the possible techniques for logging, e-mailing, and so on, but none of these ideas is beyond the capabilities of VBScript and the companion components described in this book and elsewhere. You can use the `FileSystemObject` library (see Chapter 7) to open an error log file and append to the end of it. You can use Microsoft Outlook and Exchange to send an e-mail or beeper message. You can use IIS to redirect to another Web page.

The key thing to keep in mind is to retain control of your application, its behavior, and its appearance by taking a proactive stance about what you want to do when errors occur.

## Server-Side ASP Errors

One common VBScript-related error handling situation bears special mention: the display of server-side ASP errors using IIS. As described earlier in this chapter, by default, IIS will by default push ASP syntax and runtime errors out to the browser. IIS uses a built-in template HTML page for displaying a server-side error in the browser. Figure 6-6 shows a divide by zero runtime error for an ASP page.

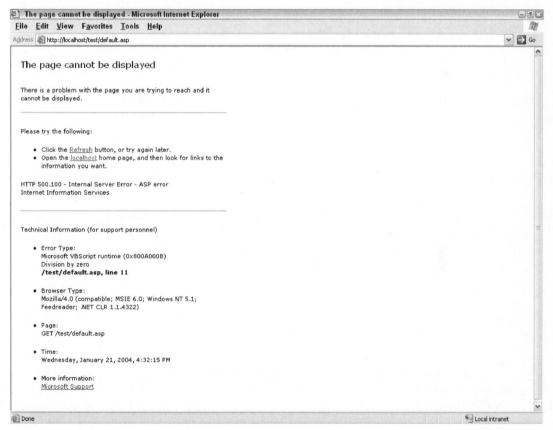

**Figure 6-6**

As you can see, the normal error information is displayed as you would expect (although it's kind of buried in the fine print of the page): the error number, description, source, and so on. In addition, the display includes information about the page that caused the error and about the requesting browser. It's nice that IIS has this built-in error display feature, but this default page is not the most attractive in the world, and almost certainly does not fit in with the look and feel of the rest of your Web site.

You do not, however, have to keep this default error display page. For each Web site hosted by your IIS server, you can set up custom error handler pages for each type of error that can occur. As you can see in Figure 6-6, the error type for a server-side ASP code error is `HTTP 500.100 - Internal Server Error - ASP error`. This page is used to display ASP and VBScript runtime errors, as well as errors raised by other code called by your ASP code. If you want to provide an error display page of your own, you can replace the default error page in IIS for 500.100 ASP errors (and many other kinds of errors as well, though errors other than 500.100 are not in the scope of this discussion).

Figure 6-7 shows the Web site properties screen for the IIS default Web site. Each Web site configured in IIS has its own unique properties, so you can set up different custom error display pages for each of your Web sites. For the Web site properties in Figure 6-7, the default 500.100 error page is configured. By clicking on the `Edit Properties` button, you can point to a different error display file. (See Chapter 17 or the IIS documentation for more information about configuring your Web site.)

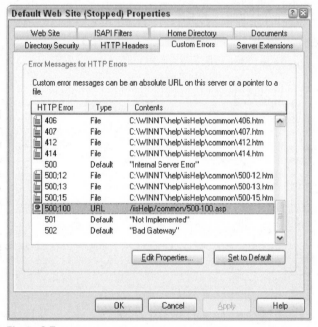

**Figure 6-7**

Before you can replace the default page, however, you must create a custom error display page. The best way to go about this is to make sure you understand the basics of ASP. If you do not, Chapter 17 in this book can get you started. If you have at least a basic grasp of basic ASP concepts, then the best thing to do is to use the default `500-100.asp` Web page, the location of which is highlighted in Figure 6-7, as a guide.

The key is to use the `Server.GetLastError` method to get a reference to an `ASPError` object, which is very similar to the native VBScript `Err` object. The `ASPError` object has properties like `Number`, `Description`, and `Source`, just like the `Err` object. In addition, the `ASPError` object it has properties called `ASPCode` and `ASPDescription` that return more detailed information if the error was an ASP-specific error raised by IIS. There are even `File`, `Line`, and `Column` properties to provide information on exactly where the error occurred. The following code snippet illustrates how to get a reference to an `ASPError` object.

```
<%
Option Explicit

Dim objASPError

Set objASPError = Server.GetLastError
%>
```

It's a safe assumption (though not a guarantee) that `Server.GetLastError` will return a fully populated `ASPError` object—otherwise this ASP page would not have been called. Now that you have a reference to an `ASPError` object, you can embed code like the following within the HTML of your new custom error page to display the various properties of the `ASPError` object.

```
Response.Write "Number: " & _
     Server.HTMLEncode(objASPError.Number) & "<br>"
Response.Write "Description: " & _
     Server.HTMLEncode(objASPError.Description) & "<br>"
Response.Write "Source: " & _
     Server.HTMLEncode(objASPError.Source) & "<br>"
```

This is a very simple example, and, as you will see if you read the default `500-100.asp` file, you can get quite elaborate. A custom error page is a great way to centralize your error handling code. Keep in mind that since this is *your* ASP error display page on *your* Web site, you can use the error information in the `ASPError` object any way you like. You could provide an input field and a button to allow the user to type in comments and e-mail them and the error information to you. You might even decide to hide the ugly details of the error from your users, replacing it with a simple `Sorry, the Web site had a problem` message, and logging the error in the background. You can also include code for handling specific errors, taking different actions depending on the error number. As in any error handling situation, it's all up to you.

If your Web site already has an established look and feel, it's a good idea to design your error page to match the rest of your Web site. This will reduce the surprise of your users if ASP errors do occur on your Web site since the error display won't make them feel like they've been suddenly kicked out of your Web site.

# Generating Custom Errors

So far in this chapter we have been discussing how, when, and why to react to errors coming out of other people's code. However, VBScript also provides the ability to "raise" errors yourself. Any VBScript code you write can at any time stop execution and generate an error. The key to this ability is the `Raise` method of the `Err` object we introduced earlier in this chapter.

# Using Err.Raise

You might remember that the `Err` object is always available and is of global scope. That means you can refer to it any time you want without having to declare a variable for it. The following code demonstrates a call to `Err.Raise`.

```
Err.Raise vbObjectError + 10000, _
    "MyScript.MyFunction", _
    "The Age argument of MyFunction may not be greater than 150."
```

In this code example we are using the first three arguments of the `Err.Raise` method.

The first argument is the error number. You are free to any error number between 0 and 65535, but using zero is not recommended since, as we illustrated earlier in this chapter, many programmers will consider 0 as the absence of an error. In addition, Microsoft strongly recommends that you add the value of the `vbObjectError` constant to your error number. The detailed explanation of why this is necessary is out of the scope of this book, but to summarize, adding `vbObjectError` to your error number makes sure your error number will not clash with "official" Microsoft error numbers.

The second argument is the error source. This is an optional parameter that many people omit or leave blank, but if you are raising an error from a specific script, page, and/or function, including some kind of description of where the error originated, is a good idea. A programmer who receives your error (maybe even yourself) will thank you someday for filling in the `Source` argument.

The third argument is the error description. It's a good idea to be as specific as possible in your description. Include any additional information you can think of that would be helpful to someone trying to diagnose and eradicate the cause of your error. Remember those useless ADO error descriptions we mentioned earlier in the chapter? Don't stick yourself or your fellow programmers with useless messages like `Errors occurred` or `Undefined error`.

The `Err.Raise` method accepts two additional arguments that are seldom used in a VBScript context: `helpfile` and `helpcontext`. If your VBScript project does have a companion Windows help file, by all means include the path to it in the `helpfile` argument. And if your help file has a specific section that explains the cause and solution for your custom error, then providing the "context id" for that section is a great idea too.

## When Not to Use Err.Raise

Now that you know *how* to generate a custom error, the obvious follow-up questions are *why* and *when* to raise a custom error. First, though, let's talk about when it's *not* a good idea to raise custom errors. Errors are generally created for the benefit of other programmers. When something goes wrong (like a lost database connection), or when a programmer tries to do something illegal (like dividing by zero), an error is the most common way to inform a program or programmer of that fact.

However, your users generally do not appreciate errors. Ideally, the only time a user should see an error is when something unexpected occurred either in your script or in a script or component being used by your script. Furthermore, you want errors to make it only as far as the user's eyes when you did not have a specific way of dealing with the error. (For example, if your script received an error indicating a lost database connection, you could try to reconnect to the database rather than stopping your script and displaying the error to the user.)

It is useful to distinguish between an error and a "problem message." Certainly, there are times that you must communicate bad news to your user, or ask your user to fix some problem. You see this all the time on Web pages with forms. If you forget to fill in a certain field, the Web page will tell you about it so that you can fix the problem. This kind of "problem message" is different from an error.

Remember the script at the beginning of this chapter that caused a divide by zero error? What if you had a script asking the user to enter a number which your script will divide into 100, like so:

```
Option Explicit

Dim x, y

x = InputBox("Please enter a number to divide into 100.")
y = 100 / x
MsgBox "100 divided by " & x & " is " & y & "."
```

What if the user enters 0? With this code as-is, run under the WSH, the user will see an unfriendly divide by zero error, as seen in Figure 6-2.

What if, instead, you tested the value that the user typed in before attempting the division, as in this script (PROBLEM_MESSAGE.VBS)?

```
Option Explicit

Dim x, y

x = InputBox("Please enter a number to divide into 100.")
If x <> 0 Then
    y = 100 / x
    MsgBox "100 divided by " & x & " is " & y & "."
Else
    MsgBox "Please enter a number other than zero."
End If
```

This time, the user sees a nice, friendly "problem message" instead of an ugly, scary error. Users would always prefer to see a cordial message that informs them of what they can do to fix a problem rather than an error that leaves them feeling stupid and helpless.

The point of all this is to say that it is not a good idea to abuse Err.Raise by using it to inform your users of when they have done something wrong. Instead, as described in the next section, use Err.Raise to catch programming problems or to report problems in the environment. The following script (ERR_MSG_UGLY.VBS) illustrates how not to use Err.Raise. The error description is sarcastic, but it reflects how your users will feel if you use Err.Raise in this way.

```
Option Explicit

Dim x, y

x = InputBox("Please enter a number to divide into 100.")
If x <> 0 Then
    y = 100 / x
    MsgBox "100 divided by " & x & " is " & y & "."
Else
    Err.Raise vbObjectError + 15000, _
        "ERR_MSG_UGLY.VBS", _
```

```
                "Hey, stupid, you can't enter a zero! It will " & _
                "cause a divide by zero error!"
    End If
```

# When to Generate Custom Errors

Now that we've discussed *how* to generate custom errors—and when *not* to—the question that is left is when *should* you generate a custom error? The answer has to do with assumptions. Whenever we write computer programs, we are forced to operate on a set of assumptions. Different types of programs running in different type of environments have different sets of assumptions, but assumptions are always there.

Certain assumptions are foundational: you assume a certain operating system and computer configuration; you assume the ability to open files for reading and writing; you assume a certain database configuration; you assume that the Customer table is structured in a certain way; you assume that the Web server works in a certain way. Other assumptions are more specific, and often take the form of rules; for example, you assume that the CustomerID argument passed into your LoadCustomer function is never less than or equal to zero and that the number will match an actual record in the Customer table.

The concept rules is closely related to the concept of assumptions. For example, there is a rule that you cannot divide by zero. If you try to use VBScript (or just about any other programming language) to divide by zero, VBScript is going to generate an error. To put it another way, VBScript "assumes" that you are not going to try to divide by zero, and if you do, VBScript is going to generate an error.

And therein lies the key point when it comes to assumptions, rules, and errors: rather than simply trusting that all VBScript programmers will *never* attempt to divide by zero (which would no doubt cause troubles at the operating system and even CPU levels), the VBScript compiler/runtime engine double checks any division operation to make sure that the code is not attempting to divide by zero. If the code is attempting it, VBScript generates an error: dividing by zero is not allowed.

A rule was broken; an assumption failed. Generate an error. That is the most basic answer to the questions of *when* and *why* to generate custom errors.

Before we look at a specific example, let's reconsider the previous section, which explained that it is *not* a good idea to use custom errors as a way to tell your users about things they have done wrong. Instead, we suggested using more friendly and helpful "problem messages," which are not the same as "errors" per se. The distinction between this advice from the previous section about when *not* to use errors to report a problem and the advice in this section about when you *do* want to use errors to report a problem is one of "audience."

Take another look at this ERR_MSG_UGLY.VBS script.

```
Option Explicit

Dim x, y

x = InputBox("Please enter a number to divide into 100.")
If x <> 0 Then
    y = 100 / x
```

```
        MsgBox "100 divided by " & x & " is " & y & "."
    Else
        Err.Raise vbObjectError + 15000, _
            "ERR_MSG_UGLY.VBS", _
            "Hey, stupid, you can't enter a zero! It will " & _
            "cause a divide by zero error!"
    End If
```

Besides the obviously rude wording of the error message, the reason this technique is undesirable is that the "audience" of the error in this script is the user. Ideally, we don't want to use errors to communicate with our users. If we must report bad news to the user or tell him or her that he or she did something against the assumptions/rules of our script, we want to do this in a more friendly and helpful manner. The reason we say that the "audience" of this script is the user is that the Err.Raise method is being used in code that is directly interacting with a user—as opposed to lower level code, in a subprocedure or class method.

However, when the "audience" of a block of code is other code (or to put it another way, the programmer himself or herself), then an error is appropriate—because we can assume that the programmer is equipped to do something about an error. Take a look at this reworking of the script (ERR_MSG_NICE.VBS).

```
Option Explicit

Dim x, y

x = InputBox("Please enter a number to divide into 100.")

On Error Resume Next
y = DivideNumbers(100, x)
If Err.Number = (vbObjectError + 15000) Then
    On Error GoTo 0
    MsgBox "Please enter a number other than zero."
Else
    On Error GoTo 0
    MsgBox "100 divided by " & x & " is " & y & "."
End If

Private Function DivideNumbers(dblNumber, dblDivideBy)

    If dblDivideBy = 0 Then
        Err.Raise vbObjectError + 15000, _
            "ERR_MSG_NICE.DivideNumbers()", _
            "Division by zero not allowed."
    Else
        DivideNumbers = dblNumber / dblDivideBy
    End If

End Function
```

Notice that we have moved our division code into a function called DivideNumbers. Our script has two logical sections now. In terms of "audience," the top part of the script is at the "outer edge" of the script, directly interacting with the user. The DivideNumbers function, on the other hand, is lower down in the script, interacting only with other code. Since the "audience" of the lower level `DivideNumbers` function is other code, if something goes wrong, the best way for `DivideNumbers` to tell the other code about it is with a runtime error.

However, the "outer edge" code that is interacting with the user anticipates that this error could come back from the `DivideNumbers` function and has a trap to catch it if it does. The whole purpose of the error trap is to turn the unfriendly runtime error into a friendly "problem message" for the user. The "outer edge" code and the lower level code are communicating the same problem in two different ways based on the "audience."

The other thing to take notice of with the `DivideNumbers` function is that it is *proactively* verifying assumptions. This is what programmers call *defensive programming*, which involves anticipating problems and failed assumptions as early as possible. It is as if the programmer of `DivideNumbers` said to himself or herself, "The primary purpose of this function is to divide two numbers. The division operation has an assumption/rule that division by zero is not allowed. Therefore, I am going to test this assumption, and if the test fails, I will raise an error." This is one of the primary situations in which it is good to generate custom errors from your code.

Before moving on, let's consider another situation in which generating a runtime error would be appropriate. In the example above, the `DivideNumbers` function is doing a before-the-fact verification of an assumption. In other situations you must instead report failed assumptions after the fact.

Consider a function called `GetCustomerName`, which takes a `CustomerID` argument and returns a customer name as a string. The function uses the `CustomerID` value to query the `Customer` table in a database. If the customer record is found based on the `CustomerID` argument, the function returns the customer's name from the database record. What if, however, no `Customer` record was found with that `CustomerID`?

One way to handle this is for `GetCustomerName` to use `Err.Raise` to generate a custom `No Customer record with specified CustomerID` runtime error. Then the code that called `GetCustomerName` can respond to this error in whatever way is appropriate given the situation. There are other examples you can think of along these lines. If a procedure called `OpenFile` can't find the specified file, it might generate a `File Not Found` error. If a procedure called `WriteFile` is denied access to the specified file based on security settings in the file system, it might generate a `Permission denied` error.

At this point, we have discussed *how* to generate custom errors using `Err.Raise`, *when* and *why* to generate them, and when *not* to. Other than the syntax rules for the `Err.Raise` method, none of the restrictions or suggestions we have offered are built into VBScript itself. Instead, we have primarily laid out philosophical principles and techniques followed by programmers in many different languages. Learning and understanding these principles and techniques is an essential part of writing programs with a professional polish.

# Debugging

The term *debugging* refers to the activity of a programmer trying to figure out the cause of a problem (or "bug") in his or her program, and then taking steps to eliminate the problem. There are two steps to this process: first, identifying the problem; and second, fixing the problem. Even though in the formal sense the term debugging refers to both steps (*finding* followed by *fixing*), our discussion in this section will focus on the first step, which involves a certain amount of detective work and puzzle solving.

# What is a Debugger?

A *debugger* is a tool to help programmers follow the logic of their code as it runs. This can aid not only in finding bugs, but also in simply understanding a program. If you can follow along with the code as it runs, you can more easily see how it works—especially if the program's logic twists and turns in ways that are difficult to comprehend by simply reading the code.

A debugger sits in between the compiler and/or runtime engine and the actual running program. Without a debugger, you write the code, compile it, and then run the resulting binary program. (In the case of VBScript, the compiling step is invisible; the scripting engine compiles the code for you when you run it.) When running the program, you can't tell exactly what's going on in the background—the program just runs according to the logic laid out in the code. A debugger, however, gives you a window into what's actually going on in the background as the code is run line by line.

A typical debugger gives you various tools to help in watching and interacting with your code as it executes:

❑ *A way to specify a certain line of code on which to pause program execution.* The line of code you specify is called a *breakpoint*. For example, if the problem you are having is deep down in the code in your `CalculatePrice` function, you would mark a certain line in the `CalculatePrice` function as a breakpoint. The program would run up until the breakpoint is reached, at which point the program pauses execution, showing you the breakpoint line.

❑ *A way to step through your code one line at a time.* Once the debugger has paused the program at a certain line because of a watch or breakpoint, the debugger allows you to slowly and deliberately execute the code one line at a time. This allows you to follow along with the logic of the program as it executes. Debuggers usually have three "step" options: *Step Into*, *Step Over*, and *Step Out*. Which one you use depends on what you want to do—or more specifically, exactly which code you want to see. *Step Into* will bring the debugger into a procedure or function, if one is being called and if the code for it is in the scope of the debugger (in other words, you can't Step Into the VBScript `MsgBox` function, since that code is not available). This is useful when you suspect the procedure being called might have a problem. *Step Over* will do the opposite: if the line you are on calls a procedure or function, the debugger will execute it without stepping into it. This is useful when you are confident that the procedure being called is not part of the problem you're debugging. Finally, *Step Out* will finish the execution of a lower level procedure or function and then pause again at the next line of code after the call to that procedure or function. This is useful if you've stepped into a procedure and then decided that you don't need to step through the rest of it.

❑ *A way to view the value of all of the variables active at any given point in the code.* While code execution is paused, mostly any debugger will have some way to view all of the variables active at that point in the code and what their values are. A good debugger will even allow you to change the value of a variable so that you can experiment and observe the effects as you step through the code.

❑ *A way to view the "call stack."* The call stack is the nested sequence of function and procedure calls that have led to a certain point in the code. For example, if the debugger has paused because of a breakpoint or watch in the low-level `CalculatePrice` function, the debugger's call stack window would show you that the `Main` procedure called the `LoadOrder` procedure, which called the `CalculateOrder` procedure, which called the `CalculateLineItem` procedure, which called the `CalculatePrice` function in which the debugger is paused. This tells you how you got to where you are.

Please note that the Microsoft Script Debugger discussed below does not have two options that developers may be accustomed to having in a debugger. First, the Script Debugger does not have a "Locals Window," which is a graphical display of all of the variables active at a breakpoint. (You can, however, use the Command Window in the Script Debugger to view the value of any in-scope variables.) Second, the Script Debugger does not have "Watch" functionality, which is a way to set up a dynamic breakpoint whenever a certain variable changes value in a certain way.

## Options for Debugging VBScript Code

The following forthcoming sections explore the details of debugging your VBScript code under the following scenarios:

❑   Scripts hosted by the Windows Script Host (WSH)

❑   Client-side Web scripts running in Internet Explorer (IE)

❑   Server-side Active Server Pages (ASP) Web scripts running under Internet Information Services (IIS)

❑   When a debugger is not available or convenient

Microsoft offers a freely downloadable product called the Microsoft Script Debugger, which offers all of the standard debugging features described in the previous section. This debugger is integrated with the three major VBScript hosts covered in this book: Windows Script Host, Internet Explorer, and Internet Information Services/ASP.

Before we get into the details of the Microsoft Script Debugger, the next section, *Debugging Without a Debugger*, describes concepts and techniques you can use when you do not have a debugger available. Sometimes you may find yourself in a situation where the use of a debugger is not practical or possible. This situation is common with scripts that somehow run across a network. For example, you may need to debug an ASP page hosted on another server to which you do not have access.

However, even if you are planning to use the Microsoft Script Debugger under WSH, IE, or IIS, you will most likely find the *Debugging Without a Debugger* section worthwhile since it contains techniques that are quite useful even when you are using a debugger.

## Debugging without a Debugger

Often times the VBScript programmer is without the benefits of a debugger. In these times, there are some basic techniques that can assist with debugging, whether the goal is finding a problem or just understanding how a program works. Not all techniques, however, are available or useful in all hosts. As we discuss the techniques, we will identify which techniques are available in the three most common VBScript hosts: WSH, IIS with ASP, and IE.

Some of these techniques are useful when a debugger *is* available. In addition, you do not necessarily need to wait to implement these techniques until you have a problem that needs debugging. Once you have determined which of these techniques can be useful to you, build them into your application from the beginning.

## Using a Global Debug Flag

This is a technique available in any host, though the implementation will be different depending on the host. The purpose of a global debug flag is to allow you to run your script in two different "modes": debug mode and production mode. In debug mode, the script may, for instance, output various messages about what is going on in the program (see later), whereas in production mode, those messages would be suppressed. Debug mode is for the benefit of only the programmer or tester, not for end users.

A global debug flag is simply a Boolean variable that has global scope in your script. For example, you might call this variable gblnDebug. Many people prefer to implement a debug flag as a named constant, in which case you might instead call it DEBUG_MODE. (As we discuss debug flags, we'll use the named constant convention since a named constant is more reliable in that its value cannot be changed while the script is running.) In some hosts, such as IIS with ASP, you don't use a variable at all, but rather a custom property of the Application object (see later).

Once you have defined a global debug flag, anywhere in your script you can insert code that executes only when the flag is equal to True. It's important to have only one place in your script that sets the value of the flag so that it is consistently either On or Off throughout the script. The code to implement the other techniques discussed later, such as outputting debug messages, would go inside of an If...End If block that checks the value of the debug flag.

Here is a simple example of a debug flag implemented in a WSH script (WSH_NODEBUG_FLAG.VBS).

```
Option Explicit

Private Const DEBUG_MODE = True

If DEBUG_MODE Then
    MsgBox "Script starting."
End If

MsgBox "Non-debug script code executing here."

If DEBUG_MODE Then
    MsgBox "Script ending."
End If
```

Here we have a named constant called DEBUG_MODE that, since it is declared at the top of the script, has global scope. Then, we have two debug messages at the beginning of the script and the end of the script. (See the next section for more information about debug messages.) These messages will only be displayed when DEBUG_MODE is True. The programmer can then change the value of the DEBUG_MODE constant to True or False, depending on whether he or she wants to see the debug messages or not. Of course, you have to be careful to make sure you set the flag to False before releasing a script to production.

Implementing a debug flag in with ASP or IE is a little trickier. With ASP, the most common technique is to use the Application_OnStart procedure in the global.asa file to add a custom property to the Application object's Contents collection. (See Chapter 17 for more information on these ASP concepts.) Then, anywhere in your ASP application, you can check the value of the debug flag on the Application object. Here is an example of what the code would look like in global.asa to create and set the debug flag.

```
Sub Application_OnStart
    Application("DEBUG_MODE") = True
End Sub
```

Since the `Contents` collection is the default property of the `Application` object, it is conventional to not refer to it directly. Instead, as you see here, just follow the `Application` with parentheses. The `Contents` collection will automatically add a property called `DEBUG_MODE` with the specified value (in this case `True`). Again, just as with the WSH example, the programmer changes the value of the flag to switch back and forth between debug mode and production mode. Finally, since the `Application_OnStart` procedure executes only when the Web site is stopped and restarted, many programmers will also create a special-purpose ASP page to change the value of the flag while the application is running.

Using a debug flag in IE is tricky because your scripts are running in the browser on a client machine. How you implement a debug flag for visibility within IE depends on how you are producing your Web pages. If your pages are static or generated by some kind of publishing tool, you will need to declare a variable in each page or template, and then change the value through `Search` and `Replace`, or whatever makes sense given your toolset.

If your pages are dynamically generated through ASP, then it's a little easier. Make sure that each HTML page you produce includes a declaration for the debug flag variable with page-level scope, which will ensure that all of the scripts on your page can read the variable to, for instance, include debug messages in the page output. One way to accomplish this is to put the variable declaration and value setting in an *include file* that is used by all of your ASP pages. To make maintenance of the flag as easy as possible, tie the setting of its value to a `"DEBUG_MODE"` flag on the `Application` object, as described earlier.

## Outputting Debug Messages

What a debugging tool offers is visibility into the information inside of a program, such as variable values and when they change and the path(s) of execution through the code. You do not have that visibility when a debugger is not available to you. So what you need is a way to gain some visibility. The best way to do this is with debug messages.

Debug messages can be used for any number of purposes, depending on what information you need. For example, you can output debug messages in the form of log entries, which together provide a view into the sequence of events in your script. A log entry type debug message might report significant program events such as the beginning and ending of a script, an entry into a certain function, a connection to a database, the opening of a file, or the changing of certain variables.

Another use of debug messages is to track the changing of important variables. If you suspect that a certain variable is, because of a logic error in your code, changing to the wrong value at the wrong time, you can output a message each time the value is changed. This can substitute for the "watch" feature of a real debugger.

Finally, debug messages are useful for displaying the total *state* of your program. For example, in an ASP program you could output all of the values stored on the `Request`, `Response`, `Session`, and/or `Application` objects at the bottom of each page (see later). Or, if you are using an array or `Dictionary` to store a series of values, you could output all of the values in a debug message.

Debug messages can take different forms. Like debug flags, the implementation depends on the host. The simplest way to output a debug message is with the `MsgBox` function, which displays a dialog box and pauses the execution of the code until the OK button is clicked. However, the MsgBox function is really useful only for scripts running in WSH or IE.

For WSH scripts, it's actually preferable to use the Echo method of the Wscript object (see Chapter 12 for detailed information on the intrinsic WSH objects) instead of MsgBox. The advantage of this is that you can choose to run the script either with wscript.exe, in which case the Echo method will display the message with a dialog box, or with cscript.exe, in which case the message will be output to the console window (see Chapter 12). If you use Echo a lot in your script, running it under cscript keeps you from having to click the OK button over and over.

This code fragment shows a debug message implemented with the Echo method.

```
If DEBUG_MODE Then
    WScript.Echo "Current order status: " & gstrOrderStatus
End If
```

Yet another way to output debug messages in WSH is to use the StdOut property of the WScript object, which is implemented as a TextStream object (see Chapter 7). However, you can use only StdOut with WSH scripts that are exclusively run in the console window with cscript.exe. Using StdOut under wscript.exe will cause an error. Here is a code fragment that uses StdOut for debug messages.

```
Dim objStdOut

If DEBUG_MODE Then
    objStdOut = WScript.StdOut
End If

...

If DEBUG_MODE Then
    objStdOut.WriteLine "Current order status: " & _
        gstrOrderStatus
End If
```

Finally, in WSH scripts you can also use the LogEvent method of the WshShell object to add events to the Windows Event Log. LogEvent can be used under wscript.exe or cscript.exe. Chapter 17 describes the LogEvent method in detail.

Since ASP scripts run on the server, MsgBox is not a good way to implement debug messages when IIS is the host. In addition, the WSH WScript and WshShell objects are not available in ASP. Instead, with ASP the best thing to do is either to include debug messages in the body of the HTML page or to log them to a file, database, or the Windows Event Log.

One powerful technique is to create an include file for use in all of your ASP pages that will include a standard section of debug info at the bottom of every generated HTML page. When the Web site is running in debug mode, the HTML will include the debug section. When in production mode, the debug section is omitted so that your users never see it.

This debug info section could be as simple or as fancy as you require. Most commonly, programmers will at least include information such as the names and values of all of the properties in the Contents collections of the Session and Application objects and the values stored in the Form, Cookies,

`QueryString`, and `ServerVariables` properties of the `Request` object (see Chapter 17). If you have any other variables that store particularly important information, then you can include the values of these variables as well.

## Homemade Assertions

VBScript unfortunately does not support a feature called *assertions*, which is included in many other languages, including Visual Basic. An assertion is a test of an assumption in the form of a `True/False` expression. For example, if in a complex algorithm you wanted to make sure that a certain variable is equal to a certain value at a certain point, in order to verify that the algorithm is working properly, you could add an assertion that tests the value of the variable. The assertion expression is evaluated only when the program is running in debug mode. In a language with a debugger and full support for assertions, the failure of the assertion would trigger a breakpoint pause in the debugger.

Even though VBScript does not natively support assertions, you can still "roll your own." The following code fragment illustrates an assertion in a WSH script.

```
If DEBUG_MODE Then
    If gstrOrderStatus <> "PENDING" Then
        WScript.Echo "***INVALID ORDER STATUS***"
    End If
End If
```

## Inserting Temporary Test Code

Finally, you can also include test code that you want to execute only while in debug mode. This is especially useful when you are trying to track down a stubborn logic bug in your code. A good debugger would allow you to pause the code at a certain point and execute test code that is not normally part of the program. Once again, if you do not have a debugger, you can use a debug flag to execute only test code while running in debug mode.

```
If DEBUG_MODE Then
    'Test code to illegally change order status
    'to verify status tracking logic.
    'A status of NEW would not normally be allowed
    'at this point.
    gstrOrderStatus = "NEW"
End If
```

You might also want to mark these blocks of test code with a unique value in a comment so that you can use your editor's `Search` function to find and eliminate them later.

# Debugging WSH Scripts with the Microsoft Script Debugger

In this section we will introduce the basics of activating the Microsoft Script Debugger for scripts running under the WSH. We will only explain how to *activate* the debugger when running a WSH script. Since the usage of the Script Debugger, once activated, is basically the same no matter which host you're running under, usage details are covered separately in a later section called *Using the Microsoft Script Debugger*. This section also assumes that you have read the earlier section called *What Is a Debugger?* which explains the basic terms and concepts of a debugging tool.

If you have not done so yet, you can download the Script Debugger for free from `msdn.microsoft.com/scripting` (be sure to get the version that matches your version of Windows). Even though the installation program does not require it, it's a good idea to reboot your machine after installing the Script Debugger.

Unlike IE and ASP/IIS scripts (see next two sections), enabling the debugger is not a configuration option. The WSH is automatically aware of the debugger. However, the WSH `wscript.exe` and `cscript.exe` programs require special command line switches in order to enable the debugger when running a script. (See Chapter 12 for more details on `wscript.exe` and `cscript.exe`.)

Normally, for non-command-line scripts if you want to run a WSH script, you would probably just double-click the `.VBS` file in Windows Explorer. However, if you want to debug a non-command-line WSH script, you have to launch the script using `wscript.exe` directly. The most straightforward way to do this is with the `Run` option on the Windows `Start` menu. If you work with command line scripts, you are already accustomed to launching your scripts with `cscript.exe`. In that case, all that's required to enable the debugger is to add an additional switch to your normal `cscript.exe` command lines.

Both `wscript.exe` and `cscript.exe` accept two debugging related switches. The behavior is the same for both `wscript.exe` and `cscript.exe`. The `//x` switch will launch the script in the debugger, making an automatic breakpoint on the first line of the script. The `//d` switch will launch the script as normal, but in a "debug aware" mode, meaning that the debugger will only be activated if one of two things happens: if an unhandled error occurs or if the `Stop` statement is encountered.

Let's look at a few examples. We're going to use `wscript.exe` for these examples, but everything said applies equally to `cscript.exe`.

Before we get into the examples, however, we have to mention one quirk with the WSH and the Script Debugger: in order for debugging to work, the Script Debugger must already be running when you launch the script. You will have to start the Script Debugger manually before you launch your script for debugging. The executable file for the latest version of the Script Debugger that runs under Windows 2000 and Windows XP is `msscrdbg.exe`. The default installation location is `C:\Program Files\Microsoft Script Debugger`, but may be installed in a different folder on your computer.

Once you've located `msscrdbg.exe`, double-click it to launch the debugger. You may wish to create a shortcut for it to make it easier to launch in the future. The examples in this section assume that you already have the debugger running.

Our first example will illustrate how to launch a script in the debugger with a script that does not have any preset breakpoints or runtime errors. The downloadable code for this chapter includes a script called `WSH_DEBUG_X.VBS`. Place this file in a folder on your hard drive and use the `Start ⇨ Run` menu option with this command.

```
wscript //x c:\scripts\WSH_DEBUG_X.VBS
```

You will of course have to change the path for the script to match where you've placed it on your hard drive. When you run this command, you should see a window like the one shown in Figure 6-8.

This is the Script Debugger in an active debugging session. The `//x` command line switch tells WSH to run the script in the debugger with a breakpoint on the very first line. When you use the `//x` switch, you

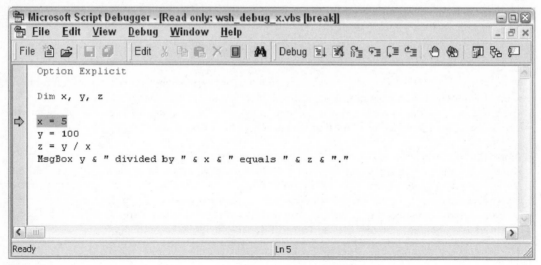

**Figure 6-8**

are in essence saying that you wish to debug your whole script from the very beginning. With //x, it is not necessary to manually specify any breakpoints.

The section called *Using the Microsoft Script Debugger* will describe all of the debugging options you have at this point, so feel free to skip ahead to that section or just play around with some of the options on the Debug menu or toolbar. When you are done, you can click the Run or Stop Debugging menu or toolbar option before moving on to the next example.

If you imagine that this script was much larger, you could also imagine that you might not want to use the //x switch to debug the script starting right at the top. Instead, you might only want the debugger to come up if (a) an error occurs, or (b) WSH reaches a manual breakpoint that you have inserted into the code. The //d switch is intended for these two situations.

Let's look at situation (a) first. The script WSH_DEBUG_ERR.VBS contains a divide by zero error. Run this command from the Start ⇨ Run menu (notice that we're using the //d switch now instead of the //x switch).

```
wscript //d c:\scripts\WSH_DEBUG_ERR.VBS
```

As you can see in Figure 6-9, this time the debugger stops on the line with the divide by zero error. This gives you the programmer the opportunity to use the debugger to observe what happened to cause the error and experiment with ways to fix it. Since we used the //d switch, if this script had not contained any errors, we would have never seen the debugger at all. The //d switch says to WSH "Only bring up the debugger if I need it," whereas the //x switch says "Bring up the debugger no matter what, and break on the first line."

Finally, we can also use the //d switch when we want the debugger to come up on a preset breakpoint. For this purpose, VBScript offers the Stop statement, which is a command to tell the host to activate the

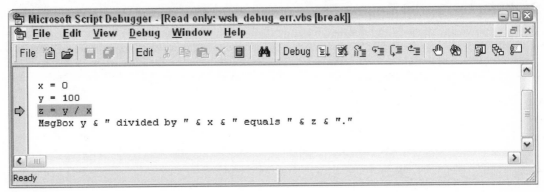

**Figure 6-9**

debugger, pausing execution on the line with the `Stop` statement. If no debugger is available, the `Stop` statement is ignored. For example, if you run a WSH script that contains a `Stop` statement without using the `//d` switch, WSH will ignore the `Stop` statement and will not bring up the debugger.

Setting a manual breakpoint with the `Stop` statement is useful when you want a script to run up to a certain point where you want to pause execution. If you are debugging a fairly large script, this ability is a huge timesaver, especially if the point from which you want to debug is deep down in the script. The file `WSH_DEBUG_STOP.VBS` contains a `Stop` statement. If you run it with this command line, you will see that the debugger will come up with a breakpoint on exactly the line with the `Stop` statement.

```
wscript //d c:\scripts\WSH_DEBUG_STOP.VBS
```

You've now seen how you can control the activation of a debugging session for WSH scripts in the Script Debugger. The following two sections will explain the same concepts for IE Web page scripts and ASP pages. If you wish to get into the details of how the Script Debugger works once you have started a debugging session, you may wish to skip ahead to the section called *Using the Microsoft Script Debugger*.

## Debugging Client-Side Web Scripts with the Microsoft Script Debugger

In this section we will introduce the basics of activating the Microsoft Script Debugger for client-side Web scripts running in IE. We will only explain how to *activate* the debugger for a script embedded in a Web page opened in IE. Since the usage of the Script Debugger, once activated, is basically the same no matter which host you're running under, usage details are covered separately in a later section called *Using the Microsoft Script Debugger*. This section also assumes that you have read the previous section called *What Is a Debugger?* which explains the basic terms and concepts of a debugging tool.

If you have not done so yet, you can download the Script Debugger for free from `msdn.microsoft .com/scripting` (be sure to get the version that matches your version of Windows). Even though the installation program does not require it, it's a good idea to reboot your machine after installing the Script Debugger.

## Enabling the Script Debugger

Once you've downloaded and installed the Script Debugger, the first thing you have to do if you want to debug VBScript in a client-side Web page is to enable the debugging option in IE. Figure 6-10 shows the `Advanced` tab of the `Internet Options` dialog box for IE 6. Notice that the option `Disable script debugging` has been unchecked. This enables the debugger. The next question is how to get it to come up so that you can do some debugging.

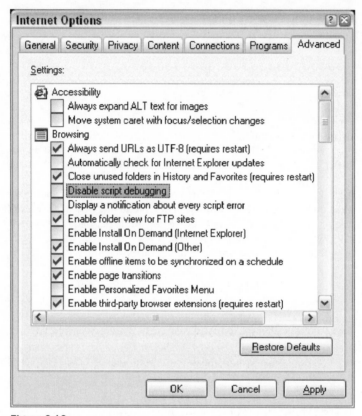

Figure 6-10

## Activating the Debugger with an Error

Once the Script Debugger is installed and enabled, any time an error occurs in any of the VBScript code embedded in a page, you will have an opportunity to activate the debugger. Take a look at this HTML page, which contains a script with a divide by zero error (`IE_DEBUG_ERR.HTML`).

```
<!DOCTYPE HTML PUBLIC "-//W3C//DTD HTML 4.0 Transitional//EN">
<html>
    <head>
        <meta http-equiv="Content-Type" content="text/html;
        charset=UTF-8" />
        <title>VBScript Programmer's Reference - IE Debugger
```

```
              Example</title>
          <script type="text/vbscript" language="VBScript">
            Sub cmdTest_OnClick
                Dim x, y, z
                x = 0
                y = 100
                z = y / x
                txtResult.Value = z
            End Sub
          </script>
      <head>
      <body>
      <h2>IE Script Debugger Example: Activate Debugger with
          Error<br></h2>
      This button will call a script that contains a coding error.<br>
      If the IE "Disable script debugging" option is turned off, the
      debugger will active on the line of code with the error.
      </h2>
      <input type="button" name="cmdTest" value="Run Test"><br><br>
      <b>Test Result:</b> <input type="text" name="txtResult"
          id="txtResult">
      </body>
  </html>
```

Notice that we have a button called cmdTest that activates the script called cmdTest_OnClick. cmdTest_OnClick contains a divide by zero error. (If you are not familiar with the basics of embedding VBScript in an HTML page, please consult Chapter 10.) This code will produce the Web page shown in Figure 6-11.

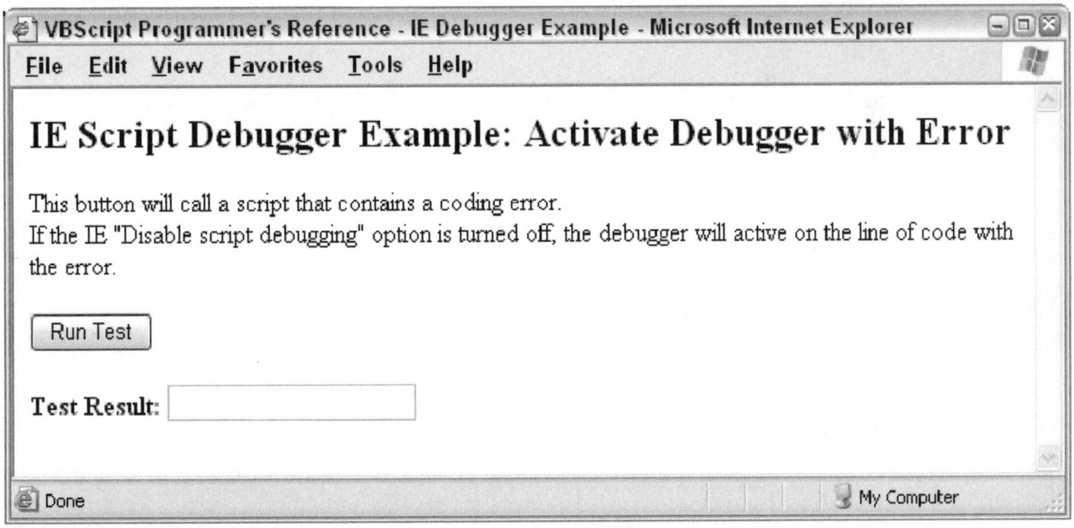

Figure 6-11

If you click the Run Test button, you should see a dialog box like the one shown in Figure 6-12.

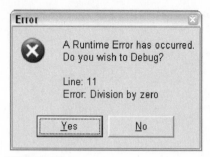

**Figure 6-12**

If you click the Yes button, you should see a window like the one shown in Figure 6-13.

```
Microsoft Script Debugger - [Read only: file://C:\scripts\IE_DEBUG_ERR.HTML [break]]
 File   Edit   View   Debug   Window   Help

File  📄 📂 🔲 🔄   Edit  ✂ 📋 📋 ✕ 🔲  🔍   Debug 📊 📊 📊 📊 📊 📊  ✋ 👋  📋 📋 📋

   <!DOCTYPE HTML PUBLIC "-//W3C//DTD HTML 4.0 Transitional//EN">
   <html>
       <head>
           <meta http-equiv="Content-Type" content="text/html; charset=UTF-8" />
           <title>VBScript Programmer's Reference - IE Debugger Example</title>
           <script type="text/vbscript" language="VBScript">
               Sub cmdTest_OnClick
                   Dim x, y, z
                   x = 0
                   y = 100
⇨                  z = y / x
                   MsgBox z
               End Sub
           </script>
       <head>
       <body>
       <h2>IE Script Debugger Example: Activate Debugger with Error<br></h2>
       This button will call a script that contains a coding error.<br>
       If the IE "Disable script debugging" option is turned off, the
       debugger will active on the line of code with the error.
       </h2>
       <input type="button" name="cmdTest" value="Run Test">

Ready                                    Ln 11
```

**Figure 6-13**

As you can see in Figure 6-13, the line with the error is highlighted, with an arrow off to the left pointing to the same line. These indicators mean that the code has paused execution at this point. We now have an active debugging session for this Web page. The section called *Using the Microsoft Script Debugger* will describe all of the debugging options you have at this point, so feel free to skip ahead to that section or just play around with some of the options on the Debug menu or toolbar. When you are done, you can click the Run or Stop Debugging menu or toolbar option before moving on to the next example.

## Activating the Debugger with the Stop Statement

You can also force the activation of the Script Debugger using the Stop statement. Stop is a special VBScript keyword that applies only when script debugging is enabled in the current host (in this case, IE). If no debugger is active, the VBScript runtime engine ignores the Stop statement. (However, particularly for client-side scripts, you don't want to leave any stray Stop statements in your code because your end users might end up looking at a debugger and wondering what the heck is going on.)

Following is a code snippet from another version of the same page from the previous section, this time with the divide by zero error removed and the Stop statement inserted into the code (IE_DEBUG_STOP .HTML).

```
<script type="text/vbscript" language="VBScript">
    Sub cmdTest_OnClick
        Dim x, y, z
        Stop
        x = 5
        y = 100
        z = y / x
        txtResult.Value = z
    End Sub
</script>
```

If you click the Run Test button on this page, the Script Debugger will come up automatically, with execution paused on the line with the Stop statement. The Stop statement is one of two ways to set a *breakpoint* in your code. The Stop statement is useful when you're editing your script and know in advance that you want to set a breakpoint at a certain point in the script. The next section explains how to set a breakpoint once the page is already open in IE.

## Activating the Debugger with a Manual Breakpoint

If you already have a Web page with a script open in IE, you can use the View ⇨ Script Debugger ⇨ Open menu in IE to open the debugger before the script starts executing. However, this technique works only if you are debugging a script that is executed "on demand"—for instance, with the click of a button on the page. If the script is one that runs automatically when the page is loaded, you'll have to use the Stop statement to set a breakpoint.

The page IE_DEBUG_MANUAL.HTML (which, like all examples in this book, is downloadable from wrox.com) is just like the page examples used in the previous example, except that it does not contain a Stop statement or divide by zero error. If you open this page in IE, you can use the View ⇨ Script Debugger ⇨ Open menu to open the debugger. The debugger window will open, displaying the page with our cmdTest_OnClick procedure.

At this point, you can use the Toggle Breakpoint menu option or toolbar button to set a breakpoint on any line in the script you wish. Then return to the browser and click the Run Test button. The Script Debugger window will come back and paused on the line where you set your breakpoint.

# Debugging ASP with the Microsoft Script Debugger

In this section we will introduce the basics of activating the Microsoft Script Debugger for server-side ASP pages running in IIS. We will only explain how to *activate* the debugger for ASP pages. Since the usage of the Script Debugger, once activated, is basically the same no matter which host you're running under, usage details are covered separately in a later section called *Using the Microsoft Script Debugger*.

This section also assumes that you have read the earlier section called *What Is a Debugger?* which explains the basic terms and concepts of a debugging tool. This section also assumes that you are familiar with the basics of administering IIS.

If you have not done so yet, you can download the Script Debugger for free from `msdn.microsoft` `.com/scripting` (be sure to get the version that matches your version of Windows). Even though the installation program does not require it, it's a good idea to reboot your machine after installing the Script Debugger.

What about the Visual Interdev debugger? Visual Interdev, an ASP development tool that ships with Microsoft Visual Studio, also includes a debugger that ASP programmers can use to debug ASP Web sites. Programmers who have Visual Interdev available may choose to use that debugger instead of the free Script Debugger. The Visual Interdev debugger does offer some functionality not offered by the Script Debugger, namely the Locals window, watches, and "Advanced Breakpoints." Launching the debugger in Interdev is a little different than as described in this section (please consult the Visual Interdev documentation), but once the debugger is activated, the general capabilities and techniques described in this section and the *Using the Microsoft Script Debugger* section (given later) apply equally well to Visual Interdev and the Script Debugger.

## Enabling ASP Debugging

In order for your IIS-hosted Web site to allow debugging of ASP pages, you must explicitly enable this capability. This can be accomplished using the IIS administration tool, which on the latest versions of Windows is available through the "Administrative Tools" Control Panel applet.

❏ Right-click on the Web site you wish to debug and choose the `Properties` menu option.

❏ Go to the `Home Directory` tab.

❏ Click the `Configuration` button in the lower right corner of the `Home Directory` tab. This will bring up the `Application Configuration` dialog box.

❏ On the `Application Configuration` dialog box, click the `Debugging` tab.

❏ On the `Debugging` tab, make sure the `Enable ASP server-side script debugging` option is selected. (You can ignore the `Enable ASP client-side script debugging` option; it does nothing.)

After enabling this option (if it was not already enabled), it's a good idea to reboot your machine before trying to use the Script Debugger with ASP. Under ideal circumstances, these steps described are all that is required to enable ASP debugging. It is possible, however, that you will have some trouble getting the Script Debugger to work with ASP. Many developers have posted messages in Internet discussion groups attesting to their troubles getting it to work.

If you are having trouble, the Microsoft "Knowledge Base" (`support.microsoft.com`) does have some articles that may help you. Using the Knowledge Base Search function, search for article IDs 252895, 192011, 244272, 284973, and 312880. If you are still experiencing trouble, try the discussion groups at `p2p.wrox.com` or `communities.microsoft.com`.

Finally, be sure to turn off the `Enable ASP server-side script debugging` option for your Web site before you release the Web site to users. You do not want the debugger to launch when actual users are browsing your Web site. In fact, it's a good idea to perform ASP debugging only on your development machine and never on the actual server hosting your production Web site.

## Activating the Debugger

Just as with WSH and IE script debugging, the Script Debugger with ASP pages is activated under two circumstances: when an unhandled runtime error occurs and when IIS encounters a `Stop` statement in a page's VBScript code.

The previous two sections of this chapter on WSH and IE debugging demonstrate how the debugger activates upon encountering a runtime error, such as a divide by zero error. This works exactly the same with ASP debugging. If ASP debugging is enabled for your site's ASP code and IIS encounters a line of code that causes an unhandled runtime error, then the debugger will come up with a breakpoint on that line. If you want to see this work, modify the `asp_debug_stop.asp` page (described later) by commenting out the `Stop` statement and changing the value of x to 0, which will trigger a divide by zero error.

The downloadable code for this chapter includes a file called `asp_debug_stop.asp` that is intended to demonstrate how to activate the Script Debugger with ASP using the `Stop` statement. To try out this example you will need to install the `asp_debug_stop.asp` file in IIS. Make sure that you install it on a machine that, as described in the previous section, (a) has IIS installed, (b) has the Script Debugger installed, and (c) has at least one running Web site (the "Default Web Site" will do) with server-side ASP debugging enabled.

This is what the top of `asp_debug_stop.asp` looks like, before the `<HTML>` tag.

```
<%@ Language=VBScript %>
<% Option Explicit %>
<%
Dim strResult

Call Main()

Sub Main
    Dim x, y, z

    Stop
    x = 5
    y = 100
    z = y / x
    strResult = z
End Sub
%>
```

Notice the `Stop` statement inside the `Main` procedure. As with any other script, this will cause the debugger to pause at this point in the code.

Once you have `asp_debug_stop.asp` installed under a running Web site on your machine, use IE to browse to that page using `http://localhost/` as the beginning of the URL. As soon as you do, the Script Debugger should come up, paused with a breakpoint on the line with the `Stop` statement. This means that you are now in an active debugging section, with the functionality described in the next section, *Using the Microsoft Script Debugger*, available to you.

If for some reason the debugger does not come up, but the page *does* successfully come up in the browser, please consult the previous section, *Enabling ASP Debugging*, for configuration and troubleshooting tips.

# Using the Microsoft Script Debugger

The three previous sections describe how to activate the Script Debugger into a debugging session under the WSH, IE, and IIS. Once you have activated the debugger, the activities you can perform are pretty much the same regardless of which of these hosts you are running under. The following sections will describe the basics of the Script Debugger functionality, including why and when a particular function is useful. This should not be considered comprehensive documentation of the Script Debugger.

The examples in the following sections are based on a WSH script debugging session with the file WSH_DEBUG_EXAMPLE.VBS, which is part of the downloadable code for this chapter. Where necessary, we will point out relevant differences in debugging activities under IE and/or IIS.

If you wish to follow along with the examples, start a debugging session with using the //x command line switch with wscript.exe, as described above in the section called *Debugging WSH Scripts with the Microsoft Script Debugger*. (If you wish, you could also run it under cscript.exe.) Running the script with the //x switch will activate the debugger, paused at the very first line of code, as shown in Figure 6-14. Remember that, as mentioned before, when debugging a WSH script, the Script Debugger must already be running when you launch the script.

Also, for your reference, here is the code for WSH_DEBUG_EXAMPLE.VBS.

```
Option Explicit

Const FILE_NAME = "WSH_DEBUG_TEST_FILE.TXT"
Const COPY_SUFFIX = "_COPY"
Const OVERWRITE_FILE = True

'***** Main Code

Dim objFSO
Dim strExtension
Dim blnFileExists
Dim strNewFileName
Dim strScriptPath

Set objFSO = CreateObject("Scripting.FileSystemObject")
strScriptPath = GetScriptPath()
blnFileExists = VerifyFile(strScriptPath, FILE_NAME)

If blnFileExists Then
    strExtension = GetExtension(FILE_NAME)
    strNewFileName = MakeNewFileName(FILE_NAME, _
        strExtension, COPY_SUFFIX)
    CopyFile strScriptPath & FILE_NAME, _
```

Figure 6-14

```
            strScriptPath & strNewFileName, _
            OVERWRITE_FILE
    Else
        On Error GoTo 0
        Err.Raise vbObjectError + 10000, _
            "WSH_DEBUG_EXAMPLE.VBS", _
            "Expected file " & FILE_NAME & " not found."
    End If

    '***** Supporting procedures and functions

    Private Sub CopyFile(strFileName, strNewFileName, blnOverwrite)
```

```
        objFSO.CopyFile strFileName, strNewFileName, blnOverwrite
End Sub

Private Function GetExtension(strFileName)
    GetExtension = objFSO.GetExtensionName(strFileName)
End Function

Private Function GetScriptPath
    Dim strPath

    strPath = objFSO.GetAbsolutePathName(WScript.ScriptFullName)
    strPath = Left(strPath, _
        Len(strPath) - Len(objFSO.GetFileName(strPath)))
    GetScriptPath = strPath
End Function

Private Function VerifyFile(strPath, strFileName)
    VerifyFile = objFSO.FileExists(strPath & strFileName)
End Function

Private Function MakeNewFileName(strFileName, strExtension, strSuffix)
    MakeNewFileName = Left(strFileName, Len(strFileName) _
        - (1 + Len(strExtension))) & strSuffix & _
        "." & strExtension
End Function
```

The code is a bit more complex than it needs to be, but that is deliberate in order to create interesting debugging opportunities for the examples given later.

## Setting Breakpoints

WSH_DEBUG_EXAMPLE.VBS does not contain any manual breakpoints using the Stop statement. However, since we launched the script using the //x switch, the debugger has set an automatic breakpoint on the first line of the script. You can easily identify the breakpoint since it is highlighted in yellow and has a yellow arrow next to it in the left column of the debugger window.

Now that we are in a debugging session, we can set more breakpoints in the script for this session. To set a breakpoint, use your mouse or your keyboard arrow keys to put the cursor on some other line below the current line. For example, put it on this line.

```
If blnFileExists Then
```

Once the cursor is on the line of your choosing, click the *Toggle Breakpoint* option on the *Debug* menu or toolbar. Your line should now be highlighted in red with a red circle in the column to the left. The purpose of a breakpoint is to tell the debugger to pause execution on the specified line. This implies that the debugger is running through the code, which is different than your stepping through the code one line at a time (see next section). If you are stepping through the code, breakpoints don't really do anything for you since you are by definition stopping on each line of code.

Therefore, to see your new breakpoint in action, click the *Run* option on the *Debug* menu or toolbar. Clicking the *Run* option is, in effect, telling the debugger to run through the code, only stopping if the debugger encounters one of three things: it reaches a breakpoint like the one we just defined, it reaches an unhanded error, or it reaches the end of the script (in which case the debugging session ends). After you click the *Run* option, code execution should pause on the breakpoint you defined. The only reason the breakpoint would not work is if you chose a line that is inside of a conditional If...Then or Select Case block that does not get executed.

Breakpoints are useful when you want to skip down to examine a deeper part of the script. You could just step down to the line you want to examine, but that could become very tedious in any script that is more than a few lines. A breakpoint, in combination with the *Run* option, is a quick way to jump down to a particular section of the script.

## Stepping through Code

It is important to understand that the yellow-highlighted line of code with the yellow arrow (see Figure 6-14) *has not been executed yet*. The debugger pauses on a line of code *before* executing it. Once the debugger is paused on a certain line of code, you have the ability to "step through" the code. "Stepping" means executing each line of code one at a time. If you click one of the debugger's "step" options, the highlighted line of code will be executed and the highlight will move down to the next line.

The Script Debugger provides three different kinds of stepping.

*Step Into* means that you wish to execute the currently highlighted line of code. The "into" part of Step Into means that if that line of code calls a procedure or function within the scope of the debugger, the debugger will "step into" that function, pausing on the first line of code in that procedure or function. (This is in contrast to "Step Over," which is described below.) Notice that we did not say that the debugger will step into *every* procedure or function—only those that are "in the scope of the debugger," which means that the code for the function must be available to the debugger. In general (setting aside the availability of "symbolic debug info" for external components, which is outside the scope of this book), this means that the procedure or function must be within the same script you are debugging.

Let's look at a Step Into example. To try out the example, start a debug session with the WSH_DEBUG_EXAMPLE.VBS script and use the //x option. When the script comes up in the debugger, set a breakpoint on this line of code and click the Run option.

```
blnFileExists = VerifyFile(FILE_NAME)
```

The debugger will pause on this line since you set a breakpoint on it. If you now click the Step Into option on the Debug menu or toolbar, the debugger will pause execution on the first line within the VerifyFile function.

*Step Over* means that you wish to execute the currently highlighted line of code *without* stepping into any procedures or functions called by that line. For example, if the highlighted line calls a function that you are already familiar and comfortable with, then stepping into that function would be a waste of your time. In this situation, you want to use the Step Over option instead of Step Into.

Going back to the previous example, if you had clicked Step Over instead of Step Into, the debugger would go to the next line after the highlighted line without pausing on any of the lines in the VerifyFile function. Keep in mind that the VerifyFile function is still executed; the difference is that the debugger does not bring you into VerifyFile.

*Step Out* means that you want the debugger to execute the rest of the current procedure or function without going through it line by line. The debugger will then pause on the next line after the line that called the procedure or function you are stepping out of. In the previous example, if you used `Step Into` to go into the `VerifyFile` function, you could use `Step Out` to complete the execution of the `VerifyFile` function and then pause again at the line after the `VerifyFile` call, which is this line.

```
If blnFileExists Then
```

The `Step Out` option is particularly useful when you accidentally click `Step Into` instead of `Step Over`. A quick click of `Step Out` will get you back to where you were as if you had used `Step Over` instead of `Step Into`.

Keep in mind that even when using `Step Over`, if the procedure or function you are stepping over has an unhandled error inside of it, the debugger will pause on the line of code that is about to cause the error. The debugger will always stop for unhandled errors.

## Using the Command Window

The `Command Window` is one of the most powerful features of the Script Debugger. While the debugger is paused on a line of code, you can use the `Command Window` to view the value of in-scope variables, change the value of those variables, and execute actual VBScript code while the main script is paused. To enable the `Command Window`, choose the `Command Window` option on the `View` menu. Let's look at some examples.

*If you followed along with the previous example and wish to follow along with the next example, restart WSH_DEBUG_EXAMPLE.VBS with a fresh debugging session using the //x option.*

Set a breakpoint on this line in the script and click the `Run` option.

```
If blnFileExists Then
```

This line of code, where we have paused execution with our breakpoint, comes after this line.

```
blnFileExists = VerifyFile(strScriptPath, FILE_NAME)
```

This means that at the point we have paused, the value of `blnFileExists` has already been set by the `VerifyFile` function. Presuming that everything is set up correctly and WSH_DEBUG_TEST_FILE.TXT is in the same directory as our script, `blnFileExists` should have a value of `True`. While the debugger is paused, we can prove this using the `Command Window`. The `Command Window` supports a special function using the question mark character (?) that will display the value of any in-scope variable. If you type `? blnFileExists` into the `Command Window` and press the Enter key, the `Command Window` will display the value of `True`, as shown in Figure 6-15.

Using the `?` operator is one of the most typical things you will do in the `Command Window`. Together with breakpoints, this is a powerful capability that allows you to see the overall state of your entire script at any point you wish. But viewing the value of a variable is not the only thing you can do in the `Command Window`.

Suppose we want to test to make sure that the `Err.Raise` call in the `Else` block is working as we expect. Making sure that you exercise all of the logic pathways through your code is an important part of

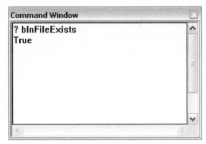

Figure 6-15

testing your scripts before releasing them. Under normal circumstances, the `Else` block would not be tested unless we renamed or removed the `WSH_DEBUG_TEST_FILE.TXT` file. However, using the `Command Window`, we can change the value of `blnFileExists` to `False` just to make sure the `Else` block will be executed at least once. To do this, type `blnFileExists = False` into the `Command Window`, just as if you were typing a normal line of VBScript code, and press the Enter key. This operation is shown in Figure 6-16.

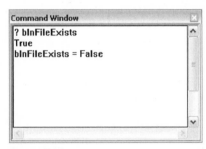

Figure 6-16

Now we have changed the value of `blnFileExists` right in the middle of our debugging session. If you click the `Run` option, the debugger will break on the `Err.Raise` call (since this amounts to an unhandled runtime error). At this point you can use the `Command Window` to examine the value of the `Err` object to see what error is occurring, as shown in Figure 6-17.

This should give you an idea of the power of the `Command Window`. In addition to doing simple things like changing the value of variables, you can call methods on in-scope objects in your script, and call other procedures and functions within the script. You can even write and execute a mini-script right in the `Command Window`, as shown in Figure 6-18.

Keep in mind that you can also use the `Command Window` to access the "intrinsic objects" available in the VBScript host. The `Err` object is an example of an intrinsic object that is available in all hosts, but each host has a unique set of intrinsic objects that are available only in that host. For example, WSH has the `WScript` object. ASP/IIS has the `Request` and `Response` objects. These objects, like any other object in scope while the debugger is paused, can be accessed through the `Command Window`.

## Viewing the Call Stack

A *call stack* is a hierarchical list of the chain of execution within a program. As one function calls another function that calls another function, VBScript is keeping track of this calling order so that as each function

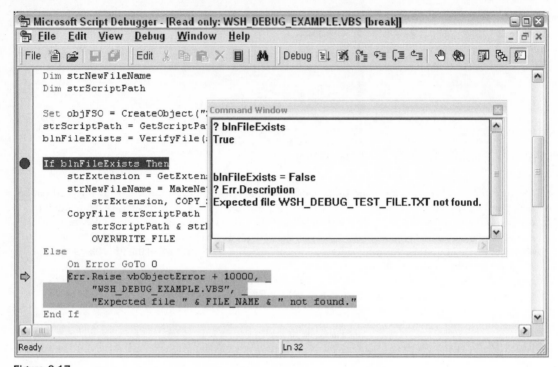

Figure 6-17

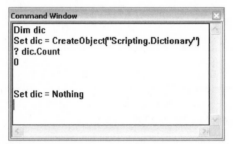

Figure 6-18

completes, VBScript can go backwards "up the stack." Sometimes when you are paused inside of a procedure or function you might not be exactly sure how the path of execution got to that point. This is where the Call Stack window in the Script Debugger can help. Let's look at an example.

*If you followed along with the previous example and wish to follow along with the next example, restart WSH_DEBUG_EXAMPLE.VBS with a fresh debugging session using the //x option.*

Set a breakpoint on this line of code inside of the GetScriptPath function.

```
strPath = objFSO.GetAbsolutePathName(WScript.ScriptFullName)
```

Click the Run option, and the debugger will pause on this line of code. Now click the Call Stack option on the View menu. The Call Stack window will come up and should look something like Figure 6-19.

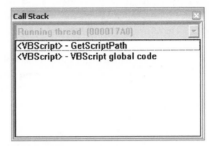

**Figure 6-19**

The call stack reads from the bottom up (That's why they call it a stack, like a stack of plates or books—first thing in goes on the bottom, last thing in goes on top.). In Figure 6-19, "VBScript global code" means that the path of execution started in the "root" of the script, outside of any named procedure or function. Above that, the line with "GetScriptPath" tells us that right now we are in the GetScriptPath function. This simple example does not look like much, but when you have a complex script with many levels of procedures and functions calling each other, the Call Stack window is very helpful for getting your bearings.

# Summary

In this chapter, we covered quite a lot of ground. First, we discussed why it is important to care about errors, error handling, and debugging. Second, we covered the different types of errors a script can encounter: syntax errors, runtime errors, and logic errors. Third, we looked at the three primary VBScript hosts (WSH, IE, and IIS) and how errors and error handling are different between them.

Fourth, we introduced the concept of "error handling," which means taking a proactive stance as a programmer to ensure that you are testing risky assumptions and that your script will at least fail gracefully if things go horribly wrong. The key points included the use of the Err object, the two On Error statements, which toggle VBScript's default error handling mode, and techniques for logging and displaying errors. For logging and displaying errors, we presented general techniques as well as some that are specific to an ASP application.

Fifth, we discussed the concept of generating custom errors. In addition to explaining how the Err.Raise method can be used to generate your own runtime errors, we went into when it is better to *not* use Err.Raise and to use a "problem message" instead. We also introduced strategies for when and how to use Err.Raise.

The second half of the chapter moved away from errors and error handling into debugging. Debugging is the activity of trying to figure out the cause of a problem or error in a script and then taking steps to fix it. One of the most important tools in debugging is called a *debugger*. A debugger is a tool that allows you to interactively execute a program line by line, including the ability to see the values of variables and even change them. We introduced general debugging terms such as breakpoints, stepping through code, and call stacks.

After this general debugging overview, we explained various debugging techniques that do not involve a debugging tool. Some of these techniques, such as using MsgBox to display the value of a variable at a certain point, are fairly simple. Others are more comprehensive and are ideally built into the infrastructure of your script-based program from the beginning. Even though this section was called *Debugging Without a Debugger*, many of the techniques are equally useful even if you do have a debugger at your disposal.

To close out the chapter, we covered the freely downloadable Microsoft Script Debugger in great detail. To start with, we explained how the debugger can be used with the three major VBScript hosts (WSH, IE, and IIS). Each host interacts with the debugger differently. In particular, the techniques for enabling the debugger are different from host to host.

After discussing the host-specific Script Debugger details, we concluded with an introduction to the features offered by the Script Debugger that can help you find problems in a script or just understand the code better. These features are the same no matter which host you are using.

Bugs, errors, exceptions, and failed assumptions are inevitable. If you want your programs to have a professional polish, and if you want to make the process of finding and eliminating the inevitable problems to be as short and painless as possible, this is an important chapter to read. A thorough understanding of errors, error handling, and debugging is the mark of a professional programmer.

# The Scripting Runtime Objects

## Overview

This chapter will introduce some powerful objects that are available for use in your VBScript code. You can think of these as utility objects, as they are designed to be reusable in a variety of situations. We will introduce in this chapter the `Dictionary` object, which is a useful and more versatile replacement for arrays, as well as the family of objects in the `FileSystemObject` hierarchy. The objects in the `FileSystemObject` object collection offer pretty much everything you need for interacting with the Windows file system.

This chapter will start off with a brief overview of the basic syntax, rules, and recommendations for using objects in VBScript. For those who have been working through the previous chapters on VBScript fundamentals, the first sections of this chapter will continue along that course. The rest of the chapter will introduce some powerful objects you will find useful in many of your scripts. If you are already familiar with the basics of using objects in VBScript, and if you are looking primarily for how-to information on the runtime objects, you may wish to skip ahead to those sections of the chapter.

## What Are Runtime Objects?

Why do we refer to these as "runtime objects?" These objects are labeled *runtime* because they exist in a separate component, apart from the core VBScript interpreter. They are not an official part of the VBScript language. In fact, since they are in a separate component (commonly referred to as the "scripting runtime"), they can also be invoked from Visual Basic or any other COM-enabled language.

That said, these runtime objects are going to be automatically available to you pretty much anywhere you would use VBScript, be it within Office, Active Server Pages, or the Windows Script Host. So while it's interesting to know that these runtime objects are not officially part of VBScript, it is not essential knowledge. However, the distinction is helpful given that the official Microsoft scripting documentation has the runtime objects information in a separate section labeled "Script Runtime".

# The Built-In Objects: Debug, Err, and RegExp

Going back to that "runtime objects" distinction, there are two other similar objects that we won't be considering in this chapter. We refer to these objects as "built-in object" because, unlike the runtime objects, these *are* an inherent part of VBScript. None of the built-in objects will be covered in this chapter. For information on the Debug and Err objects, please refer to the error handling chapter, Chapter 6. For information on the RegExp object and its cousin the Match object, please refer to Chapter 9, which covers regular expressions in detail.

# Creating Objects

Throughout the example scripts in this chapter, we will be using the scripting runtime objects to accomplish various tasks. In this section we will quickly go over the syntax for creating (also known as *instantiating*) objects. Objects are a bit different than other data types because objects must be created explicitly. With a normal numeric variable, for instance, you just use the equals ( = ) operator to put a number into it. With objects, however, you must first use a separate command to create the object, after which you can use the object in your code.

When an object is instantiated, a copy of that type of object is created in memory, with a pointer (also known as a *reference*) to the object stored in the variable you have declared for it. This copy of the object is dedicated to the code that created it. To create an object, you must declare a variable for it, and then use the Set command in conjunction with the CreateObject function. Here is an example (CREATE_OBJECT.VBS).

```
Option Explicit

Dim objDict

Set objDict = CreateObject("Scripting.Dictionary")

MsgBox "The Dictionary object holds this many items: " & _
    objDict.Count
```

This code declares a variable to hold the object (objDict), and then uses the Set command and the CreateObject function to instantiate the object. The MsgBox line then displays the value of the object's Count property. The Set command must be used whenever initializing the value of an object variable. This is the only use for the Set command.

The CreateObject command actually does the real work of creating the object. Whenever you use CreateObject, you must pass into it the name of the object you wish to instantiate, in this case Scripting.Dictionary. Scripting is the name of the library in which the object's class lives (in this case the scripting runtime library), and Dictionary is the class name of the object. Whenever you wish to instantiate an object of a particular type, you just have to know the library and class name of the object so that you can pass it to CreateObject. The documentation for any object you wish to use should tell you this information.

Not all objects can be instantiated directly in this way. Many libraries, including the scripting runtime, have certain objects that can only be created directly by another object in the library. With these types of objects, you cannot use the CreateObject function to instantiate them. Instead, one of the other objects in the library must create them for you. We'll be getting to the details of the FileSystemObject later in this chapter, but we'll jump ahead just briefly to give an example of an object type that cannot be directly instantiated.

The Folder object in the `FileSystemObject` is not directly creatable. Only the `CreateFolder` or `GetFolder` methods can give you a `Folder` object. The following code illustrates how this works using the `GetFolder` method (NOT_DIRECTLY_CREATABLE.VBS).

```
Option Explicit

Dim objFSO
Dim objFolder

Set objFSO = CreateObject("Scripting.FileSystemObject")
Set objFolder = objFSO.GetFolder("C:\")

If objFolder.IsRootFolder Then
    MsgBox "We have opened the root folder."
End If
```

# Properties and Methods

Objects have two different elements that you can access with your code: *properties* and *methods*. A property is, like a variable, a placeholder for a value associated with that object. A property may hold any type of data, from strings to numbers to dates. A property may also hold a reference to another object. Some properties are read-only, while others can be set with your code. To find out which ones are read-only and which ones can be changed, you need to familiarize yourself with the object through its documentation.

We saw two examples of properties in the previous section: the `Dictionary` object's `Count` property and the `Folder` object's `IsRootFolder` property. We'll see more later in this chapter.

A method is simply a procedure or function that is attached to an object. You can call methods just as you would any other procedure or function (see Chapter 4). We saw one example of a method in the last code example from the previous section: the `FileSystemObject`'s `GetFolder` method, which is a function that returns a `Folder` object.

Just as in the previous examples, when calling a property or method of an object you must use the name of the variable that holds the object, followed by a period, and then by the name of the property or method.

# The "With" Keyword

The `With` keyword is a handy shortcut that can save you some typing. When you are referring to the same object more than once in a block of code, you can surround the block of code with the `With...End With` construct. Here is an example (WITH_BLOCK.VBS).

```
Option Explicit

Dim objFSO
Dim objFolder
```

```
Set objFSO = CreateObject("Scripting.FileSystemObject")
Set objFolder = objFSO.GetFolder("C:\Program Files")

With objFolder
    MsgBox "Here are some properties from the " & _
        "Folder object:" & _
        vbNewLine & vbNewLine & _
        "Path: " & .Path & vbNewLine & _
        "DateCreated: " & .DateCreated & vbNewLine & _
        "DateLastAccessed: " & .DateLastAccessed & _
        vbNewLine & _
        "DateLastModified: " & .DateLastModified
End With
```

Notice how we surround the last block of code with `With` and `End With`. In the `With` statement, we refer to the `objFolder` object variable, which allows us within that block of code to refer to the `Path`, `DateCreated`, `DateLastAccessed`, and `DateLastModified` properties without having to refer to the `objFolder` variable by name each time. The `With` statement is a convenience that can save you some typing and make your code look a bit cleaner.

# Objects Can Have Multiple References

Behind the scenes, an object variable does not really contain the copy of the object. The object itself is held elsewhere in the computer's memory, and the variable only holds a *reference* to the object. The reason this technical distinction is important is that you need to be aware of when you are dealing with two different objects versus when you are dealing with two references to the same object. Take a look at this example (REF_TWO_OBJECTS.VBS).

```
Option Explicit

Dim objDict1
Dim objDict2

Set objDict1 = CreateObject("Scripting.Dictionary")
Set objDict2 = CreateObject("Scripting.Dictionary")

objDict1.Add "Hello", "Hello"

MsgBox "The first Dictionary object holds this many " & _
    "items: " & objDict1.Count & vbNewLine & _
    "The second Dictionary object holds this many " & _
    "items: " & objDict2.Count
```

This code produces the dialog box shown in Figure 7-1.

We have two variables, `objDict1` and `objDict2`, and we have used `Set` and `CreateObject` to instantiate two separate `Dictionary` objects. Then we used the `Dictionary` object's `Add` method to add a string to `objDict1` (we'll be getting to the details of the `Dictionary` object later in this chapter). Notice, however, that we did not add any items to `objDict2`. This is reflected in the dialog box, where

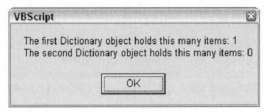

**Figure 7-1**

we see that objDict1 has a Count of 1 whereas objDict2 has a Count of 0, since we did not add anything to objDict2. Now, however, take a look at this code (REF_ONE_OBJECT.VBS).

```
Option Explicit

Dim objDict1
Dim objDict2

Set objDict1 = CreateObject("Scripting.Dictionary")
Set objDict2 = objDict1
objDict1.Add "Hello", "Hello"

MsgBox "The first Dictionary object holds this many " & _
    "items: " & objDict1.Count & vbNewLine & _
    "The second Dictionary object holds this many " & _
    "items: " & objDict2.Count
```

This code produces the dialog box shown in Figure 7-2.

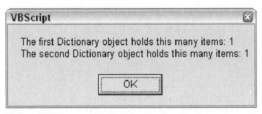

**Figure 7-2**

Notice that we only used CreateObject one time, with objDict1. The next line is the key line of code in this example.

```
Set objDict2 = objDict1
```

This line sets objDict2 equal to objDict1, which means that two variables are holding references to *the same object*. That is why the Count properties of both objDict1 and objDict2 have a value of 1, even though we only called the Add method on objDict1. Since both variables hold references to the same object, it does not matter which variable you use to make a change to that object—both variables will reflect the change.

# Object Lifetime and Destroying Objects

When it comes to the issue of variable lifetime (see Chapter 4), object variables are a little different than other kinds of variables. The key to understanding this difference lies in the two facts we introduced in the previous section of this chapter: first, an object variable only holds a reference to the object, not the object itself; and second, multiple variables can each hold a reference to the same object.

An object will stay active in memory as long as one or more variables are holding a reference to it. As soon as the *reference count* goes down to zero, the object will destroy itself automatically. An object can lose its reference to an object in one of two ways: first, if a variable goes out of scope (see Chapter 4), and second, if a line of code explicitly empties out the object by setting it to the special value of Nothing. Let's look at an example (REF_NOTHING.VBS).

```
Option Explicit

Dim objDict1
Dim objDict2

Set objDict1 = CreateObject("Scripting.Dictionary")
'The object now exists and has a reference count of 1
Set objDict2 = objDict1
'The object now has a reference count of 2

objDict1.Add "Hello", "Hello"

MsgBox "The first Dictionary object holds this many " & _
    " items: " & objDict1.Count & vbNewLine & _
    "The second Dictionary object holds this many " & _
    "items: " & objDict2.Count

Set objDict1 = Nothing
'The object still exists because objDict2 still
'holds a reference
Set objDict2 = Nothing
'The object's reference count has now gone down to 0,
'so it has been destroyed.
```

As you read this code, follow along with the comments to see the reference count and lifetime of the object. Notice how we use this syntax to eliminate a variable's reference to the object.

```
Set objDict1 = Nothing
```

Nothing is a special value, which can only be used with object variables. By setting an object variable to Nothing, you are basically saying "I don't need this object reference anymore." It is important to note that the two line of code we added to this script setting the two variables to Nothing are, in this specific example, unnecessary. They are unnecessary because, as we said, an object will be destroyed automatically when the reference variables naturally go out of scope. objDict1 and objDict2 go out of scope when the script ends, so in this short script the Nothing lines are not necessary.

However, it is important to use Nothing in longer scripts. This principle to keep in mind is that you do not want to have objects in memory any longer than you need them. Objects take up a relatively large amount of resources, so you want to instantiate them right before you need them and destroy them as soon as you don't need them anymore. This example script from Chapter 4 illustrates this principle (FSO_FIND_FILE.VBS from Chapter 4).

```
Option Explicit

Dim objFSO
Dim objRootFolder
Dim objFileLoop
Dim boolFoundIt

Set objFSO = _
    WScript.CreateObject("Scripting.FileSystemObject")
Set objRootFolder = objFSO.GetFolder("C:\")
Set objFSO = Nothing

boolFoundIt = False
For Each objFileLoop In objRootFolder.Files
    If UCase(objFileLoop.Name) = "AUTOEXEC.BAT" Then
        boolFoundIt = True
        Exit For
    End If
Next
Set objFileLoop = Nothing
Set objRootFolder = Nothing

If boolFoundIt Then
    MsgBox "We found your AUTOEXEC.BAT file in " & _
        "the C:\ directory."
Else
    MsgBox "We could not find AUTOEXEC.BAT in " & _
        "the C:\ directory."

End If
```

Take a look at this line in relation to the rest of the script.

```
Set objFSO = Nothing
```

The reason for this line is that at that point we don't need objFSO anymore. The only reason we needed it was to call the GetFolder method to get a Folder object. Once we have the Folder object, objFSO is of no more use to us in this script, so we follow the principle of limiting object lifetime as much as possible to objFSO to Nothing.

*For more information on the Nothing keyword, the Is Nothing statement, and the IsObject function, please see Chapter 3.*

# The Dictionary Object

In Chapter 3, we introduced the array, which is a unique data type that allows you to store multiple separate values in a single variable. The Dictionary object offers similar functionality, but in a different way. You may remember the phone list example from Chapter 3. The phone list was a simple two-dimensional array of names and phone numbers, as shown in the table below. The left column and top row show the subscripts of the array.

| | 0 | 1 | 2 |
|---|---|---|---|
| 0 | Williams | Tony | 404-555-6328 |
| 1 | Carter | Ron | 305-555-2514 |
| 2 | Davis | Miles | 212-555-5314 |
| 3 | Hancock | Herbie | 616-555-6943 |
| 4 | Shorter | Wayne | 853-555-0060 |

One problem with this data structure is that there is not an easy way to search the array—for example, a search for a certain name by phone number or a certain phone number by name. One way would be to loop through the whole array and check the appropriate "columns" to see if we have found the "row" we want. There are also other, more advanced ways to search this array, but they have to be programmed manually.

The Dictionary object solves this problem by providing an *associative array*, which means that each item (or "row," if it helps you to think about it that way) in the array has a unique *key* associated with it. So instead of having to search for an item in the dictionary, we can simply ask for it using the key. A Dictionary object can hold any type of data, from simple data type such as strings and dates to complex data types such as arrays and objects.

In this chapter, we will cover the basics of the Dictionary object, including an overview and examples. For a complete reference of the Dictionary object's properties and methods, please consult Appendix F.

## Overview

Let's use our phone list example to show how things can be done differently using a Dictionary object instead of an array. In this example, we are going to get a little fancy and store arrays of phone list entries in a dictionary, and for each entry, we will use the phone number as the key. This will allow us to keep the list information structured (separated into last name, first name, and phone number) while also giving us the ability to find a row quickly using the phone number as the key.

Later, in Chapter 8, when we discuss the creation of your own VBScript classes, we'll extend our phone list yet again by using a custom PhoneEntry class for each entry instead of the array.

This code will populate the dictionary with our phone list (DICT_FILL_LIST.VBS).

```
Option Explicit

Const LAST = 0
Const FIRST = 1
Const PHONE = 2

Dim dicPhoneList

Set dicPhoneList = CreateObject("Scripting.Dictionary")
FillPhoneList
```

```
Sub FillPhoneList

    Dim strItemAdd(2,0)
    Dim strKey

    'Populate the list, using phone number as the key.
    'Add values to temp array, then add temp
    'array to dictionary.
    strItemAdd(LAST, 0) = "Williams"
    strItemAdd(FIRST, 0) = "Tony"
    strItemAdd(PHONE, 0) = "404-555-6328"
    strKey = strItemAdd(PHONE, 0)
    dicPhoneList.Add strKey, strItemAdd

    strItemAdd(LAST, 0) = "Carter"
    strItemAdd(FIRST, 0) = "Ron"
    strItemAdd(PHONE, 0) = "305-555-2514"
    strKey = strItemAdd(PHONE, 0)
    dicPhoneList.Add strKey, strItemAdd

    strItemAdd(LAST, 0) = "Davis"
    strItemAdd(FIRST, 0) = "Miles"
    strItemAdd(PHONE, 0) = "212-555-5314"
    strKey = strItemAdd(PHONE, 0)
    dicPhoneList.Add strKey, strItemAdd

    strItemAdd(LAST, 0) = "Hancock"
    strItemAdd(FIRST, 0) = "Herbie"
    strItemAdd(PHONE, 0) = "616-555-6943"
    strKey = strItemAdd(PHONE, 0)
    dicPhoneList.Add strKey, strItemAdd

    strItemAdd(LAST, 0) = "Shorter"
    strItemAdd(FIRST, 0) = "Wayne"
    strItemAdd(PHONE, 0) = "853-555-0060"
    strKey = strItemAdd(PHONE, 0)
    dicPhoneList.Add strKey, strItemAdd

End Sub
```

First, we declare some named constants to make our array subscripts more clear. Then we declare a script-level variable called dicPhoneList for our Dictionary, which we instantiate using the CreateObject function. Then we call the FillPhoneList procedure, which populates the script-level Dictionary. For each list entry, FillPhoneList builds a simple array, which we declared as a local variable, sets the key using the phone number, and stores the entry in the dictionary.

Notice that the Add method takes two arguments. The first is the key for the item you wish to add and the second is the item value itself, in this case an array that holds one phone list entry, including last name, first name, and phone number.

Now let's extend this script to do something useful with our Dictionary object (DICT_RETRIEVE_LIST.VBS).

```
Option Explicit

Const LAST = 0
Const FIRST = 1
Const PHONE = 2

Dim dicPhoneList

Set dicPhoneList = CreateObject("Scripting.Dictionary")
FillPhoneList
SearchPhoneList

Sub FillPhoneList

    Dim strItemAdd(2,0)
    Dim strKey

    'Populate the list, using phone number as the key.
    'Add values to temp array, then add temp
    'array to dictionary.

    strItemAdd(LAST, 0) = "Williams"
    strItemAdd(FIRST, 0) = "Tony"
    strItemAdd(PHONE, 0) = "404-985-6328"
    strKey = strItemAdd(PHONE, 0)
    dicPhoneList.Add strKey, strItemAdd

    strItemAdd(LAST, 0) = "Carter"
    strItemAdd(FIRST, 0) = "Ron"
    strItemAdd(PHONE, 0) = "305-781-2514"
    strKey = strItemAdd(PHONE, 0)
    dicPhoneList.Add strKey, strItemAdd

    strItemAdd(LAST, 0) = "Davis"
    strItemAdd(FIRST, 0) = "Miles"
    strItemAdd(PHONE, 0) = "212-555-5314"
    strKey = strItemAdd(PHONE, 0)
    dicPhoneList.Add strKey, strItemAdd

    strItemAdd(LAST, 0) = "Hancock"
    strItemAdd(FIRST, 0) = "Herbie"
    strItemAdd(PHONE, 0) = "616-555-6943"
    strKey = strItemAdd(PHONE, 0)
    dicPhoneList.Add strKey, strItemAdd

    strItemAdd(LAST, 0) = "Shorter"
    strItemAdd(FIRST, 0) = "Wayne"
    strItemAdd(PHONE, 0) = "853-555-0060"
    strKey = strItemAdd(PHONE, 0)
    dicPhoneList.Add strKey, strItemAdd

End Sub

Sub SearchPhoneList
```

```
      Dim strPhone
      Dim strItemRead

      strPhone = InputBox("Please enter a phone number " & _
          "(XXX-XXX-XXXX) with which to search the list.")

      If dicPhoneList.Exists(strPhone) Then
          strItemRead = dicPhoneList.Item(strPhone)
          MsgBox "We found that entry:" & vbNewLine & _
              vbNewLine & _
              "Last: " & strItemRead(LAST,0) & vbNewLine & _
              "First: " & strItemRead(FIRST,0) & vbNewLine & _
              "Phone: " & strItemRead(PHONE,0)
      Else
          MsgBox "That number was not found in the " & _
              "phone list."
      End If

End Sub
```

We have added a new procedure called `SearchPhoneList`. This procedure asks the user for a phone number in the proper format, and checks the dictionary to see if there is an entry for that number. If there is, the code displays the entry in a dialog box. We use the `Exists` method to check to see if the number was used as a key value in the dictionary. `Exists` will return `True` if the key has a match in the dictionary, `False` if not. If `Exists` returns `True`, then the code can use the `Item` property with confidence to retrieve the phone list entry.

Notice that when we retrieve the array from the dictionary we put it into a variable (`strItemRead`) *before* we start using the array subscripts to get the values from inside the array. This is an optional technique, but one that makes your code a little easier to read. It's optional because VBScript can figure out for us that there is an array stored in the dictionary item without our having to feed the array into the `strItemRead` "holding variable" first. The following alternative syntax achieves the exact same result without the extra variable.

```
  If dicPhoneList.Exists(strPhone) Then
      With dicPhoneList
          MsgBox "We found that entry:" & vbNewLine & _
              vbNewLine & _
              "Last: " & .Item(strPhone)(LAST,0) & _
              vbNewLine & _
              "First: " & .Item(strPhone)(FIRST,0) & _
              vbNewLine & _
              "Phone: " & .Item(strPhone)(PHONE,0)

      End With
  Else
      MsgBox "That number was not found in the " & _
          "phone list."
  End If
```

This is the key syntax in this example (Notice that the code at this point is inside of a `With` block.).

```
.Item(strPhone)(LAST,0)
```

Since we know in advance that there is an array stored in the dictionary, we can just follow the call to the Item property with the array subscripts we want. VBScript does the work behind the scenes. The "holding variable" is optional. Different programmers will prefer one convention over the other, and you can choose which ever you prefer.

## Three Different Ways to Add

Let's look at some additional syntactic variations that are possible with the Dictionary object. All of the following are valid ways to add a new item to a dictionary.

```
dicAnimals.Add "12345", "Cat"

dicAnimals.Item("45678") = "Dog"

dicAnimals("98765") = "Goldfish"
```

The first line is the syntax we've demonstrated already, using the Add method. This is the most explicit syntax, but somehow not as much fun as the methods used in the second or third lines. The second and third lines both take advantage of two particular behaviors of the Dictionary object: one, since Item is a property (as opposed to a method), you can bypass the Add method and just set the Item property directly using the equals operator ( = ); and the other, if you pass a key value to the Item property that is *not* found in the dictionary, the dictionary object will add that key to the dictionary behind the scenes.

Behavior number two makes possible the syntax in those second and third lines. However, this trick is a double-edged sword. This same behavior also holds true when you are simply *reading* from the Item property. If you use a line like the following to retrieve a value from a dictionary, and the key you pass in does not exist in the dictionary already, then you just added an empty item to the dictionary even though you probably did not intend to.

```
strAnimalName = dicAnimals.Item("72645")
```

That is why it is important to use the Exists method first to ensure that the key you are about to use is really in the dictionary.

```
If dicAnimals.Exists("72645") Then
    strAnimalName = dicAnimals.Item("72645")
End If
```

Finally, going back to that third syntax of adding to a dictionary:

```
dicAnimals("98765") = "Goldfish"
```

What this syntax is taking advantage of is the fact that the Item property is the *default property* of the Dictionary object. When a property is an object's default property, referring to it by name is optional. The second syntax refers to it by name, the third takes the shortcut. All three of these syntactical conventions are valid and acceptable.

# The CompareMode Property

The `CompareMode` property controls which "mode" the dictionary's `Item` property will use when comparing key values for equality. The options are "Text" (1; `vbTextCompare`; the default), "Binary" (0; `vbBinaryCompare`), and "Database" (2; `vbDatabaseCompare`).

The main thing you have to think about when it comes to the `CompareMode` property is whether or not you want your key comparisons in the `Item` method to be case sensitive. If case *insensitive* is fine, then you can accept default value of `vbTextCompare` (1). If, on the other hand, you want comparisons to be case sensitive, change this property to `vbBinaryCompare` (0). Take a look at the following code.

```
dicAnimals.Add "abc", "Cat"
dicAnimals.Add "def", "Dog"
dicAnimals.Add "ABC", "Goldfish"
```

If you use `vbTextCompare`, then the third line of this code will produce an error that you are trying to add a duplicate key to the dictionary. This will occur because with `vbTextCompare` `"abc"` and `"ABC"` are seen as equivalent. If, however, you use `vbBinaryCompare`, then the third line will *not* produce an error because `"abc"` and `"ABC"` are seen as distinct values.

# The Item Property

We have seen the `Item` property in action in several of the earlier examples. `Item` is the gateway to the data storage inside the `Dictionary` object. To read from the `Item` property, you can access it directly with a particular key, or you can *enumerate* the `Items` collection with a `For Each` loop to access each dictionary item in order. `Item` can be used in three ways:

❑ To add a new item to the dictionary; if key value is not already in the dictionary, it will be added automatically

❑ To update the value of an item already in the dictionary

❑ To read or retrieve the value of an item already in the dictionary

Whenever accessing the `Item` property directly (as opposed to indirectly with a `For Each` loop), you must pass the `Key` argument, which can be any unique string or integer. The key value determines which item in the dictionary will be written to or read from.

Following is an example syntax for the `Item` property.

```
'Add an item to the dictionary
dicAnimals.Item("1234") = "Cat"

'Update an item already in the dictionary
dicAnimals.Item("1234") = "Feline"

'Read an item from the dictionary
strAnimalName = dicAnimals.Item("1234")
```

`Item` is the default property, which means that referring to it by name is optional.

# The Exists Method

You can use the `Exists` method to check if a key is already in the dictionary. If you are not positive that the key is in the dictionary, it is important to use the `Exists` method before reading from the `Item` property. This is because the `Item` property will add the key if there is not a match. It is also wise to check the `Exists` method before calling the `Remove` method, since `Remove` will raise an error if the key does not exist in the dictionary.

In this example given previously in this chapter, we check `Exists` before accessing `Item`.

```
If dicAnimals.Exists("72645") Then
    strAnimalName = dicAnimals.Item("72645")
End If
```

# The FileSystemObject Library

The remainder of this chapter is dedicated to the `FileSystemObject` (FSO) library. This chapter does not contain a complete and detailed reference for all of the FSO objects, properties, and methods. Appendix F does, however, contain a complete reference. If you need quick lookup for a particular property or method, Appendix F is the place. As for *this* chapter, in the following sections we will start with an overview of the FSO library, after which we will demonstrate, including example code, some common tasks such as opening and reading a text file; writing to a text file; and creating and copying files and folders.

## Why FileSystemObject?

Quite often scripts need the ability to create a file, read a file, find a file or folder, check for the existence of a certain drive, etc. For security reasons, none of this functionality is built into the core VBScript language. However, all of this functionality and more is available from the scripting runtime's `FileSystemObject` library. The `FileSystemObject` is a kind of "master object" that serves as the access point for a family of objects. All of the objects in the `FileSystemObject` hierarchy work together to provide functionality for accessing and manipulating the Windows file system.

The `FileSystemObject` (FSO) objects are intended for use with the Windows Script Host, Active Server Pages, and other "safe" hosts. By default, access to the `FileSystemObject` is blocked from scripts running inside of the Internet Explorer browser. These security settings can be changed to allow browser scripts to use the `FileSystemObject`, but it is not recommended that you do so. It is also not recommended that you ask your users to do so.

The FSO object model consists of the following objects and collections.

## Using Collections

The `FileSystemObject` hierarchy contains a few `Collection` type objects—a subject we have not yet discussed. What is a `Collection`? A `Collection` is a special type of object much like the `Dictionary` object, in that it stores a key-indexed group of data. VBScript does not natively support generic `Collection` objects, but many COM-based libraries, such as the scripting runtime we've been discussing in this chapter, will use `Collection` objects.

| Object or Collection | Description |
| --- | --- |
| FileSystemObject | This is the main, or "root," object. To use any of the FSO objects, you must first create a FileSystemObject, at which point you can use its properties and methods to perform various functions and access the other objects. Example properties and methods: CopyFile, CreateFolder, FileExists, Drives |
| Drive | A Drive object represents a logical or physical drive mapped on the host computer. The drive can be a hard disk, CD-ROM drive, or even a RAM drive. Example properties and methods: DriveLetter, AvailableSpace, RootFolder |
| Drives | A Drives Collection is a child of FileSystemObject and holds zero or more Drive objects. The only way to obtain a reference to a valid Drives object is through the FileSystemObject.Drives property. All drives are included, regardless of type. Removable-media drives do not need to have media inserted to appear. Drives has two properties: Count and Item |
| File | A File object represents a file that exists in a folder on a drive. There are two ways to obtain a File object: one is from the FileSystemObject.GetFile method and the other is from the Folder.Files collection. The File object is easily confused with the TextStream object, which represents a "stream" of text going into or coming out of a file, but not the file itself. Example properties and methods: DateCreated, ParentFolder, Copy, Delete |
| Files | The Files collection is a child of the Folder object. The only way to obtain a valid Files object is through the Folder.Files property. Only has two properties: Count and Item |
| Folder | A Folder represents a folder on a drive. You can obtain a reference to a Folder object through the Drive.RootFolder and the CreateFolder, GetFolder, and GetSpecialFolder methods of FileSystemObject. Example properties and methods: IsRootFolder, ParentFolder, Drive, Files, SubFolders |
| Folders | The Folders collection stores a list of Folder objects. You can obtain a Folders object only through the Folder.SubFolders property. Only has two properties and one method: Count, Item, and Add. The Add method allows you to add a new subfolder (as a Folder object) to the collection |

*continues*

| Object or Collection | Description |
|---|---|
| TextStream | A TextStream object represents a series of text, either being read from a file, written to a file, or going to or coming from the Windows "standard i/o." You can obtain a TextStream object via the File.OpenAsTextStream, Folder.CreateTextFile methods, as well as the CreateTextFile, OpenTextFile, and GetStandardStream methods of FileSystemObject. Internally, a TextStream object has a line pointer and a character pointer. When reading or writing a file as a TextStream, you move through the file from top to bottom *only once*, character-by-character and/or line-by-line. Example properties and methods: Read, Write, ReadLine, WriteLine, AtEndOfLine |

There is no real mystery to a Collection if you understand the Dictionary. Like Dictionary, Collection has Count and Item properties, and you can iterate the Item property using a For Each loop. However, Collection does not have some of the niceties of the Dictionary such as the Exists and RemoveAll methods. You'll see examples of the syntax throughout the remainder of this chapter as we discuss FSO collections such as Drives, Folders, and Files.

# Understanding FileSystemObject

The FSO objects are a little strange to some programmers at first because the root object, FileSystemObject, is the access point for everything else. Before you can do anything with drives or folders or files, you must first create a FileSystemObject. Either directly or indirectly, everything you want, you have to start by going through FileSystemObject. Take a look at the properties, and especially, methods of FileSystemObject and you will see all of the tasks it can perform and data it can provide.

The most important thing to keep in mind is that if you want access to any object other than FileSystemObject itself, then you have to get that object directly or indirectly through one or more of the properties and methods of FileSystemObject. Sometimes you have to "drill down" through the levels of objects to get what you want, and at other times, FileSystemObject will have a method that does exactly what you need.

Let's look at two examples that accomplish the same task. Our goal is to locate the AUTOEXEC.BAT file and display the date and time it was last changed. This first example uses an indirect, drill-down methodology (GET_AUTOEXEC_1.VBS).

```
Option Explicit

Dim objFSO
Dim objCDrive
Dim objRootFolder
Dim objFileLoop
Dim objAutoExecFile
```

```
Set objFSO = CreateObject("Scripting.FileSystemObject")
Set objCDrive = objFSO.GetDrive("C")
Set objRootFolder = objCDrive.RootFolder

For Each objFileLoop in objRootFolder.Files
    If UCase(objFileLoop.Name) = "AUTOEXEC.BAT" Then
        Set objAutoExecFile = objFileLoop
        Exit For
    End If
Next

If IsObject(objAutoExecFile) Then
    MsgBox "The autoexec.bat was last changed on: " & _
        objAutoExecFile.DateLastModified
Else
    MsgBox "Could not find autoexec.bat."
End If
```

This code starts at the top of the hierarchy, drills into the drive level, then the folder level, then the file level—a lot of trouble to find one file, especially when we know right where the file should be. But there is a much simpler way to solve the same problem, one which takes advantage of the direct method provided by FileSystemObject (GET_AUTOEXEC_2.VBS).

```
Option Explicit

Dim objFSO
Dim objAutoExecFile

Set objFSO = CreateObject("Scripting.FileSystemObject")
Set objAutoExecFile = objFSO.GetFile("C:\autoexec.bat")

MsgBox "The autoexec.bat was last changed on: " & _
    objAutoExecFile.DateLastModified
```

If you find yourself going to a lot of trouble to accomplish a task, take a step back, look through the various FSO objects, properties, and methods, and you might find a more direct way.

## Creating a Folder

There are two different ways to create a folder. Which one you choose depends on what you are doing otherwise in your script. If you are already working with a Folder object that represents the folder in which you want to create the new folder, you can use the Folder.SubFolders.Add method, like so (FSO_CREATE_FOLDER.VBS):

```
Option Explicit

Dim FSO
Dim objFolder

Set FSO = CreateObject("Scripting.FileSystemObject")
Set objFolder = FSO.GetFolder("C:\")
```

```
If Not FSO.FolderExists("C:\TestVBScriptFolder") Then
    objFolder.SubFolders.Add "TestVBScriptFolder"
    MsgBox "The C:\TestVBScriptFolder folder was " & _
        "created successfully."

End If
```

*Note: if you run this script on your computer, you can run the FSO_CLEANUP.VBS script to remove the folder that was created.*

The above example, as mentioned, is the most practical if you already have a `Folder` object that you are working with. However, there is a quicker way to create a new folder if you don't otherwise have any need for a `Folder` object. The following code simply uses the `FileSystemObject.CreateFolder` method (FSO_CREATE_FOLDER_QUICK.VBS).

```
Option Explicit

Dim FSO

Set FSO = CreateObject("Scripting.FileSystemObject")

FSO.CreateFolder("C:\TestVBScriptFolder")

MsgBox "The C:\TestVBScriptFolder folder was " & _
    "created successfully."
```

*Note: if you run this script on your computer, you can run the FSO_CLEANUP.VBS script to remove the folder that was created.*

This script accomplishes the same thing, but without using the `Folder` object. As mentioned previously, with FSO you can often perform the same task using one of `FileSystemObject`'s methods or one of the other FSO objects.

## Copying a File

Copying a file is pretty simple. The `FileSystemObject` object has a method called `CopyFile` exactly for this purpose. The following script copies a file that is assumed to exist in the same directory as the script file (FSO_COPY_FILE.VBS). If you downloaded all of the code for this chapter in the same directory, the file we are copying should be there.

```
Option Explicit

Dim FSO

Set FSO = CreateObject("Scripting.FileSystemObject")

If FSO.FileExists("TEST_INPUT_FILE.TXT") Then
    FSO.CopyFile "TEST_INPUT_FILE.TXT", _
        "TEST_INPUT_FILE_COPY.TXT", True
End If
```

*Note: if you run this script on your computer, you can run the FSO_CLEANUP.VBS script to remove the file that was created.*

Notice that we check `FileExists` first because if the file we are copying does not exist then `CopyFile` will raise an error. Also notice that we have passed `True` for the `overwrite` argument, which means that we want to overwrite the file if it already exists. If you did not want to overwrite it, you would want to use `FileExists` to check first.

The previous example assumes that the source and destination are both in the same directory as our script. You can also use full pathnames for both the file being copied and the target file.

```
FSO.CopyFile "\\ A_Network_Folder\Customers.xls", _
    "C:\MyFolder\Spreadsheets\Customers.xls", True
```

You can also omit the filename from the target path if you want to use the same filename. In fact, omitting the filename is a requirement if you use wildcard characters in the source path:

```
FSO.CopyFile "\\A_Network_Folder\*.xls", _
    "C:\MyFolder\Spreadsheets\", True
```

Notice the trailing backslash ("\") that we have on the target path. This is critical because it signals the `CopyFile` method that `Spreadsheets` is a folder. Without the trailing backslash, `CopyFile` will assume that `Spreadsheets` is a file we want it to create. Note also that wildcard characters are not allowed for the target path.

After you have copied a file, you can access it using either the `FileSystemObject.GetFile` method (which returns a `File` object) or find the file in the `Folder.Files` collection. Or, if the file you've copied is a text file and you need to read from or write to the file, you can open it as a `TextStream` (see the "Reading a Text File" and "Writing to a Text File" sections below).

## Copying a Folder

Copying a folder is much like copying a file, but it's a bit more complex because a folder can contain multiple items, including subfolders and files. Also, you might want to copy more than one folder, in which case you may be able to use wildcard characters to identify the folders you want to copy. Here is a simple example:

```
Option Explicit

Dim FSO

Set FSO = CreateObject("Scripting.FileSystemObject")

If FSO.FolderExists("C:\TestVBScriptFolder") Then
    FSO.CopyFolder "C:\TestVBScriptFolder", _
        "C:\Program Files\", True
End If
```

*Note: if you run this script on your computer, you can run the FSO_CLEANUP.VBS script to remove the folder that was created.*

Since we did not include any wildcard characters in the source path, the CopyFolder method assumes that TestVBScriptFolder is the one we want to copy, and it will look for a folder with exactly that name. If, however, we had wanted to copy any folders in the C:\ folder that start with the string TestVBScript, we could use wildcard characters.

```
FSO.CopyFolder "C:TestVBScript*", _
    "C:Program Files\", True
```

However, it is important to understand that the wildcard characters used with the CopyFolder method are *only* used to match folders—not files. If you want to copy some files and not others, then you must use the CopyFile method (see previous section).

You also have to be careful when copying folders with multiple files and subfolders into an existing hierarchy of identical folders and files. If any of those folders and files have the read-only attribute turned on, then the CopyFolder method will raise an error, even if you pass True for the overwrite argument. If you suspect that some target folders or files might have the read-only attribute turned on, you can use the Folder.Attributes and/or File.Attributes property to check first (see Appendix F).

# Reading a Text File

It is often necessary to open a text file and either retrieve a specific piece of data from it, or simply feed the entire file contents into another data structure. We'll look at examples for both of these situations. Both of the scripts in this section assume that a file called TEST_INPUT_FILE.TXT exists in the same directory as the scripts. If you downloaded all of the code for this chapter, you should have everything you need.

You can see the contents of TEST_INPUT_FILE.TXT as follows. Each field is separated by a Tab character. Each line ends with a standard Windows end-of-line character-pair.

```
OrderID=456    CustID=123    ItemID=765
OrderID=345    CustID=987    ItemID=149
OrderID=207    CustID=923    ItemID=592
```

First, let's look at an example script that opens this file and looks for a specific piece of data (FSO_READ_FILE_SEEK.VBS). There is a lot of code here that has to do with parsing the data in the file, so if you want to focus on how we actually open and read the file, follow the objStream variable, which holds a TextStream object. The interesting part of this code is in the GetCustIDForOrder function, which opens a text file, searches for some particular data, and returns it.

```
Option Explicit

Const ORDER_ID_TO_FIND = "345"
Dim strCustID

strCustID = ""
strCustID = GetCustIDForOrder(ORDER_ID_TO_FIND)
```

```
If strCustID <> "" Then
    MsgBox "The CustomerID for Order " & _
        ORDER_ID_TO_FIND & " is: " & strCustID
Else
    MsgBox "We could not find OrderID " & _
        ORDER_ID_TO_FIND & "."
End If

Function GetCustIDForOrder(strOrderIDSeek)

    Const TristateFalse = 0
    Const ForReading = 1
    Const ORDER_FIELD = "OrderID="
    Const CUST_FIELD = "CustID="
    Const FILE_NAME = "TEST_INPUT_FILE.TXT"

    Dim FSO
    Dim objStream
    Dim strLine
    Dim lngFirstTab
    Dim lngSecondTab
    Dim strOrderID
    Dim strCustID

    strCustID = ""

    Set FSO = CreateObject("Scripting.FileSystemObject")

    If FSO.FileExists(FILE_NAME) Then
        Set objStream = FSO.OpenTextFile(FILE_NAME, _
            ForReading, False, TristateFalse)
    Else
        MsgBox "Could not find " & FILE_NAME & "."
        GetCustIDForOrder = ""
        Exit Function
    End If

    Do While Not objStream.AtEndOfStream
        strLine = objStream.ReadLine
        lngFirstTab = InStr(Len(ORDER_FIELD), strLine, _
            vbTab, vbBinaryCompare)
        strOrderID = Mid(strLine, Len(ORDER_FIELD) + 1, _
            lngFirstTab - Len(ORDER_FIELD) - 1)
        If strOrderID = strOrderIDSeek Then
            lngSecondTab = InStr(lngFirstTab + 1, strLine, _
                vbTab, vbBinaryCompare)
            strCustID = Mid(strLine, lngFirstTab + _
                Len(CUST_FIELD) + 1, _
                lngSecondTab - (lngFirstTab + _
                Len(CUST_FIELD)))
            Exit Do
        End If
    Loop
```

```
      objStream.Close
      GetCustIDForOrder = strCustID

End Function
```

After using `FileExists` to ensure that our input file is where we expect it to be, we use this line to open the file as a `TextStream` object:

```
Set objStream = FSO.OpenTextFile("TEST_INPUT_FILE.TXT", _
    ForReading, False, TristateFalse)
```

We tell the `OpenTextFile` method which file we want to open, that we want to open it for reading (as opposed to writing), that we don't want to create it if it does not exist, and that we want to open it in ASCII mode. (Please see Appendix F for a detailed explanation of these arguments.) After this point, we have an open `TextStream` object in our `objStream` variable. The line pointer and the character position pointer are both at the beginning of the file. When processing a file, you have three options:

❑   Use the `ReadAll` method to feed the entire file into a string variable, after which you can parse the variable using a variety of methods

❑   Use a loop and the `Read` method to move through the file, one character at a time

❑   Use a loop and the `ReadLine` method to move through the file one line at a time, parsing each line as necessary

Which method you choose depends on what is in the file, how it is structured (if it is structured), and what you need to do with the data. Our example file is structured as a series of fields that repeat on a line-by-line basis. So we opted to use the `ReadLine` method:

```
Do While Not objStream.AtEndOfStream
    strLine = objStream.ReadLine
    ...<<code ommitted>>...
Loop
objStream.Close
```

By setting up our `Do` loop this way, we ensure two things: one, that we only start the loop if the file we opened is not totally empty; and the other, that we will stop looping once we have read the last line of the file. The other thing that makes this work is that when we call the `ReadLine` method, the line pointer in `objStream` automatically moves ahead by one. A `TextStream` object always moves the pointers ahead automatically as you read the file. Finally, notice that we call the `Close` method on the `TextStream` object as soon as we are done with it; it's a good idea to call the `Close` method for any file you open.

We'll only comment briefly on these lines, which we omitted from the previous code snippet of the `ReadLine` loop.

```
lngFirstTab = InStr(Len(ORDER_FIELD), strLine, _
    vbTab, vbBinaryCompare)
strOrderID = Mid(strLine, Len(ORDER_FIELD) + 1, _
    lngFirstTab - Len(ORDER_FIELD) - 1)
If strOrderID = strOrderIDSeek Then
    lngSecondTab = InStr(lngFirstTab + 1, strLine, _
        vbTab, vbBinaryCompare)
```

```
        strCustID = Mid(strLine, lngFirstTab + _
            Len(CUST_FIELD) + 1, _
            lngSecondTab - (lngFirstTab + _
            Len(CUST_FIELD)))
    Exit Do
End If
```

What we're doing here is using the InStr, Mid, and Len functions to parse the contents of each line, looking for specific known field markers. Other similar functions such as Left and Right are useful also, depending on the situation. You can learn about the details of how these functions work in Appendix A.

The particular techniques employed in this code depend on the fact that we know how the file should be structured. We know the field names and the fact that the field delimiter is the Tab character. For a production-quality script, we would also want to include some defensive code to ensure graceful handling of files that are not formatted as expected.

## Writing to a Text File

Creating a new text file is about as straightforward as reading from one. The steps are simple: open a new text file in a specified location, write data to it, and close the file. All of this is done through the TextStream object. This simply demonstrates the three steps (FSO_CREATE_FILE.VBS):

```
Option Explicit

Dim FSO
Dim objStream

Const TristateFalse = 0
Const FILE_NAME = "CREATE_FILE_TEST.TXT"

Set FSO = CreateObject("Scripting.FileSystemObject")

Set objStream = FSO.CreateTextFile(FILE_NAME, _
    True, TristateFalse)

With objStream
    .WriteLine "Test Line 1"
    .WriteLine "Test Line 2"
    .WriteLine "Test Line 3"
    .Close
End With

MsgBox "Successfully created " & FILE_NAME & "."
```

*Note: if you run this script on your computer, you can run the FSO_CLEANUP.VBS script to remove the file that was created.*

Because in this case we are creating a new, blank text file, we use the FileSystemObject.CreateTextFile method. We pass True for the overwrite argument so that if a file of the same name is already there it will be replaced by our new file. Then we use the TextStream.WriteLine method to add one line at a time to the file. We could have also used the Write method to add the data all at one or a little bit at a time (adding multiple lines at once if we liked). The `WriteBlankLines` method is also available. Finally, we use the `Close` method to close the file.

Sometimes you need to write to a file that already exists rather than create a new one. Unfortunately, the `TextStream` object, as is, only supports two ways to write to an existing file: one, appending data to the end of an existing text file, and the other, starting at the beginning of an existing file, which throws out all existing data in the file. The following example demonstrates how to append to an existing file. As for the ability to start writing at the beginning (which unfortunately means you also have to throw out all existing data in the file), this is of course not that useful; you might as well just use `CreateTextFile` to open a new blank file.

So let's take a look at an example of appending to an existing file (`FSO_APPEND_FILE.VBS`). This script assumes that you have run `FSO_CREATE_FILE.VBS` first.

```
Option Explicit

Dim FSO
Dim objStream

Const ForAppending = 8
Const TristateFalse = 0
Const FILE_NAME = "CREATE_FILE_TEST.TXT"

Set FSO = CreateObject("Scripting.FileSystemObject")

If Not FSO.FileExists(FILE_NAME) Then
    MsgBox "Could not find " & FILE_NAME & ". " & _
        "Please run FSO_CREATE_FILE.VBS first."
Else
    Set objStream = FSO.OpenTextFile(FILE_NAME, _
        ForAppending, False, TristateFalse)

    With objStream
        .WriteLine "Appended Line 1"
        .WriteLine "Appended Line 2"
        .WriteLine "Appended Line 3"
        .Close
    End With

    MsgBox "Successfully appended to " & FILE_NAME & "."
End If
```

This code is very similar to the code for creating a new text file. Instead of using `CreateTextFile`, we use `OpenTextFile`, passing it the `ForAppending` value for the `iomode` argument (see Appendix F). Then we use the `WriteLine` and `Close` methods just as before. Adding new data to the file is basically the same as for creating a new file, except that you are instead adding to the end of an existing file. In some cases, you might prefer to get all of the new data into a single string variable and passing to the `Write` method.

There are two common writing-related tasks that the `TextStream` object *does not* support: first, inserting data at the beginning of an existing file, and second, adding data somewhere in the middle of an existing file. To accomplish these, you have to write some code of your own to open the file for reading, get the contents into one or more variables, close the file, add or remove whatever data you need, and then write it all back as a new file.

# Summary

We started this chapter with an overview of the basic syntax and techniques for using objects in VBScript. This overview included an explanation of the `CreateObject` function, object lifetime reference counts, and object destruction.

We also introduced in this chapter the "scripting runtime objects," which is a set of objects that exist in a separate library apart from core VBScript, but which are nonetheless available almost anywhere VBScript can be hosted. The scripting runtime is divided into the `Dictionary` object and the `FileSystemObject`, which acts as the gateway to family of related objects. The focus in this chapter is to explain why these objects are useful, how they are designed, and how to perform common tasks. For a complete reference of the scripting runtime objects, please consult Appendix F.

The `Dictionary` object provides an associated array, allowing you to store a series of data of any type: strings, numbers, arrays, objects, etc. Each item added to a `Dictionary` object must be given a key value, which must be unique within the dictionary. The key can then be used to retrieve the item from the dictionary later.

The `FileSystemObject` library offers a variety of objects that allow you to interact with the Windows file system. Features include: creating and editing text files; creating folders; copying, moving, and deleting files and folders; "drilling down" into the hierarchy of drives, folders, subfolders, and files; reading file attributes; and more.

# 8

# Classes in VBScript (Writing Your Own COM Objects)

## Overview

One of the most exciting features added to VBScript version 5 is the ability to write classes, bringing VBScript one step closer to the object-oriented paradigm, and giving VBScript programmers a powerful programming tool. Granted, classes defined in VBScript do not have the more properly object-oriented capability of Java, C++, or even Visual Basic classes, but they do let the VBScript programmer take advantage of a few of the benefits available when programming in these other languages.

The ability to create objects from classes defined in VBScript gives programmers increased power and flexibility for creating complex scripts, more reusable code, and even Script-based components. This chapter will explain in detail how to unlock these capabilities.

If you've skipped previous chapters and are not familiar with how to use COM objects from VBScript, then you might benefit from reading the first sections of Chapter 7 before tackling this chapter. This chapter will assume that you are familiar with the basics of instantiating objects and calling their properties and methods.

## Objects, Classes, and Components

Before we get too far into how to write your own classes in VBScript, and where you can make use of them, we'll start by covering some terminology. Few technical terms in recent years have been misused, obscured, morphed, and confused more than *class*, *object*, and *component*. Often the terms are used interchangeably, even though they do have distinct meaning. This lack of clarity drives object-oriented purists crazy, but it also makes these waters difficult for beginners to navigate. Let's clear the fog a little bit.

In the strict sense, an *object* is an in-memory representation of a complex data and programming structure that can exist only while a program is running. A good analogy is an array, which is also a complex data structure that exists only at runtime. When in a programming context we refer to an array, it is clear to most people that we mean the in-memory data structure. Unfortunately, when someone uses the word object, it is not always clear that they are using the strict definition of the term, referring to a construct in memory at runtime.

An object is different from an array in several ways, but most importantly, an object not only stores data (in the form of *properties*), but also has "behavior"—that is, "things it knows how do when asked"—which are exposed as *methods*. Properties can store any kind of data, and methods can be either procedures or functions. The idea of bringing the data and the behavior together in an object is that you can design your program such that the data that needs to be manipulated and the code that manipulates it can be close to each other.

A *class* is a template for an object. While an object exists only in memory at runtime, a class is a block of code that you work with at design time. A class is the code, and an object is the use of that code while a program is running. If you want to be able to use an object at runtime, you have to first define a class at design time. Objects are created at runtime based on templates provided by classes. For example, you could write a class called Customer. Once the class definition is saved, you could then use other code to create a thousand Customer objects in memory. This concept is illustrated in Figure 8-1.

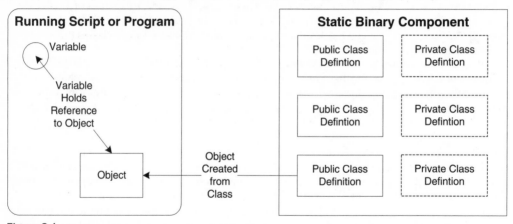

Figure 8-1

Many people, however, use the terms class and object interchangeably, like so: "I coded the Customer object, then I created a thousand Customer objects and sorted them by total sales." As we mentioned, this can create some confusion for beginners, but over time you can learn to use the context to figure out what is meant.

A *component* is nothing more than a packaging mechanism, a way of compiling one or more related classes into a binary file that can be distributed to one or more computers. You can see that the class used to create the object in Figure 8-1 is stored inside of a component. In the Windows operating system, a component usually takes the form of a .DLL or .OCX file. The scripting runtime library that we introduced in Chapter 7 is a perfect example of a component.

When a programmer writes some classes that are related to each other in some way, and he or she wants people to be able to use those classes to create objects at runtime, she would probably package and distribute the classes as a component. A single program or script might make use of dozens of different classes from different components.

Components are not the only way to make use of classes, however. Figure 8-1 shows only one possible scenario (albeit a very common one). In a Visual Basic application, for example, you can write classes that are compiled within the application itself, and are never exposed to the outside world. The classes exist only inside that application, and the sole purpose is to serve the needs of that application. In that case, we would not consider those classes to be part of a component.

However, people are finding that it is often much more productive and forward thinking to package their classes into a component that can exist outside of the application. The thinking is that you might find a use for one or more of those classes later, and having them in a more portable component makes them much easier to reuse. In VBScript, you can use both techniques: you can create classes within a script that can only be used by that script (which we will cover in this chapter), or you can package your classes as a Windows Script Component (see Chapter 13).

# The Class Statement

The key to creating VBScript classes is the `Class` statement. Similar to the way the `Function...End Function` or `Sub...End Sub` statement pairs are used to block off the boundaries of a procedure, the `Class` and `End Class` statements are used to block off the boundaries of a class. You can use multiple blocks of `Class...End Class` blocks in a single script file to define multiple classes (however, classes cannot be nested).

If you are coming to VBScript from another language, such as Visual Basic, you are probably accustomed to classes being stored in their own separate files. However, this is not the case with VBScript classes. In general, a VBScript class must be defined in the same script file as the script code that creates an instance of it.

This may seem like a pretty big limitation—since part of the purpose of creating a class is easy code portability and centralized reuse—but there are two other options. First, you can package one or more VBScript classes in a Windows Script Component, which we discuss in detail in Chapter 13. Second, you can use the Active Server Pages (ASP) #INCLUDE directive to include VBScript classes in your ASP scripts, which we discuss in Chapter 14. In this chapter, however, we are going to limit ourselves to the discussion of classes that are defined within the same script file as the code that makes use of the class.

Other than this same-script-file difference, Visual Basic programmers will not have any trouble adjusting to VBScript classes. Except for the differences between the Visual Basic and VBScript languages, the structure and techniques for VBScript classes are pretty much the same as for Visual Basic. Here is the fundamental syntax for the `Class` statement.

```
Class MyClass

    <rest of the class code will go here>

End Class
```

You would, of course, replace `MyClass` with the name of the class you are defining. This class name must be unique within the script file, as well as within any classes that are brought into the same scope through "include directives." The class name must also not be the same as any of the VBScript reserved words (such as `Function` or `While`).

# Defining Properties

When a script creates an object based on a class, properties are the mechanisms through which data is stored and accessed. Through properties, data can be either stored in the object or retrieved from the object.

## Private Property Variables

The best way to store the value of a property is in a private property variable. This is a variable that is defined at the class level (at the beginning of the class). This variable is private (that is, it is not directly accessible to code outside of the class) and holds the actual value of the property. Code that is using a class will use `Property Let`, `Set`, and `Get` procedures to interact with the property, but these procedures are merely gatekeepers for the private property variable.

You define a private property variable like so:

```
Class Customer

    Private mstrName

    <rest of the class code will go here>

End Class
```

In order for the variable to have private, class-level scope, it must be declared with the `Private` statement. The "m" prefix is the "Hungarian" notation to indicate that the scope of the variable is "*m*odule level," which is another way of saying "class level." Some texts will advocate the use of the "c" prefix (as in `cstrName`) to indicate *c*lass-level scope. However, we do not recommend this approach as it is easily confused with the prefix that Visual Basic programmers often use for the `Currency` data type.

## Property Let

A `Property Let` procedure is a special kind of procedure that allows code outside of a class to place a value in a private property variable. A `Property Let` procedure is similar to a VBScript `Sub` procedure in that it does not return a value. Here is the syntax.

```
Class Customer

    Private mstrName

    Public Property Let CustomerName(strName)
        mstrName = strName
    End Property

End Class
```

Notice that instead of using the `Sub` or `Function` statements to define the procedure, `Property Let` is used. A `Property Let` procedure must accept at least one argument. Omitting this argument would defeat the whole purpose of the `Property Let` procedure, which is to allow outside code to store a value in the private property variable. Notice how the code inside the property procedure saves that strName value passed into the procedure in the private property variable mstrName. You are not required to have any code at all inside the procedure, but not storing the value passed into the procedure in some sort of class-level variable or object would tend to, once again, defeat the whole purpose of the Property Let procedure.

Conversely, you can have as much additional code in the procedure as you like. In some cases, you might wish to do some sort of validation before actually assigning the passed-in value in the private property variable. For example, if the length of the customer name value was not allowed to exceed 50 characters, you could verify that the strName argument value does not exceed 50 characters, and, if it did, use the Err.Raise method (see Chapter 6) to inform the calling code of this violation.

Finally, a property procedure must end with the End Property statement (just as a Function procedure ends with End Function, and a Sub procedure ends with End Sub). If you wished to break out of a property procedure, you would use the Exit Property statement (just as you would use Exit Function to break out of a Function, and Exit Sub to break out of a Sub).

## Property Get

A Property Get procedure is the inverse of a Property Let procedure. While a Property Let procedure allows code outside of your class to write a value to a private property variable, a Property Get procedure allows code outside of your class to read the value of a private property variable. A Property Get procedure is similar to a VBScript Function procedure in that it returns a value. Here is the syntax.

```
Class Customer

    Private mstrName

    Public Property Let CustomerName(strName)
        mstrName = strName
    End Property

    Public Property Get CustomerName()
        CustomerName = mstrName
    End Property

End Class
```

Like a VBScript Function procedure, a Property Get procedure returns a value to the calling code. This value will typically be the value of a private property variable. Notice how the name of the Property Get procedure is the same as the corresponding Property Let procedure. The Property Let procedure stores a value in the private property variable, and the Property Get procedure reads it back out.

The Property Get procedure does not accept any arguments. VBScript will allow you to add an argument, but if you are tempted to do this, then you will also have to add an additional argument to the property's corresponding Property Let or Property Set procedure (if there is one). This is because a Property Let/Set procedure must always have *exactly one more* argument than its corresponding Property Get procedure.

Adding an extra argument to a Property Let/Set procedure is extremely awkward, and asking the code that uses your class to accommodate more than one argument in a Property Let procedure is very bad form. If you feel you have a need for a `Property Get` procedure to accept an argument, you are much better off adding an extra property to fulfill whatever need the `Property Get` argument would have fulfilled.

If your `Property Get` procedure returns a reference to an object variable, then you may wish to use the `Set` statement to return the value. For example:

```
Class FileHelper

    'Private FileSystemObject object
    Private mobjFSO

    Public Property Get FSO()
        Set FSO = mobjFSO
    End Property

End Class
```

However, since all VBScript variables are `Variant` variables, the `Set` syntax is not strictly required. This syntax would work just as well.

```
Class FileHelper

    'Private FileSystemObject object
    Private mobjFSO

    Public Property Get FSO()
        FSO = mobjFSO
    End Property

End Class
```

It's a good idea to use the `Set` syntax, though, since it makes it clearer that the corresponding `Property Get` procedure is returning a reference to an object variable.

# Property Set

A `Property Set` procedure is very similar to a `Property Let` procedure, but the `Property Set` procedure is used exclusively for object-based properties. When the property needs to store an object (as opposed to a variable with a numeric, `Date`, `Boolean`, or `String` subtype), you can provide a `Property Set` procedure instead of a `Property Let` procedure. Here is the syntax for a `Property Set` procedure.

```
Class FileHelper

    'Private FileSystemObject object
    Private mobjFSO

    Public Property Set FSO(objFSO)
        Set mobjFSO = objFSO
    End Property

End Class
```

Functionally, `Property Let` and `Property Set` procedures do the same thing. However, the `Property Set` procedure has two differences:

- ❑ It makes it clearer that the property is an object-based property (any technique that makes the intent of the code more explicit is preferable over any other equally correct technique).

- ❑ Code outside of your class must use the `Set Object.Property = Object` syntax in order to write to the property (also a good thing, since this is the typical way of doing things).

For example, here is what code that is using an object based on the above class might look like.

```
Dim objFileHelper
Dim objFSO

Set objFSO = _
    WScript.CreateObject("Scripting.FileSystemObject")
Set objFileHelper = New FileHelper
Set objFileHelper.FSO = objFSO
```

Notice that when the last line writes to the `FSO` property, it uses the `Set` statement. This is required because the `FileHelper` class used a `Property Set` procedure for the `FSO` property. Without the `Set` statement at the beginning of the last line, VBScript would produce an error. When a property on a class is object based, it is typical to use a `Property Set` procedure. Most programmers using your class will expect this.

That said, since all VBScript variables are Variant variables, it is perfectly legal to use a `Property Let` procedure instead. However, if you provide a `Property Let` procedure *instead* of a `Property Set` procedure, code that is using your class *will not* be able to use the `Set` statement to write to the property (VBScript will produce an error if they do), and this will be a trip-up for programmers who are accustomed to using the `Set` syntax. If you want to be very thorough, and cover both bases, you can provide both a `Property Let` and a `Property Set` for the same property, like so:

```
Class FileHelper

    'Private FileSystemObject object
    Private mobjFSO

    Public Property Set FSO(objFSO)
        Set mobjFSO = objFSO
    End Property

    Public Property Let FSO(objFSO)
        Set mobjFSO = objFSO
    End Property

End Class
```

The `Set` syntax inside of the `Property Set` and `Let` is optional. Since you are writing directly to the Variant private property variable, you can use either. This example is the functional equivalent of the previous example.

```
Class FileHelper

    'Private FileSystemObject object
    Private mobjFSO

    Public Property Set FSO(objFSO)
        mobjFSO = objFSO
    End Property

    Public Property Let FSO(objFSO)
        mobjFSO = objFSO
    End Property

End Class
```

# Making a Property Read-Only

You can make a property on a class read-only in one of two ways:

❑ By providing only a `Property Get` procedure for the property

❑ By declaring the `Property Get` procedure as `Public` and the `Property Let` procedure as `Private`

Here is the first method.

```
Class Customer

    Private mstrName

    Public Property Get CustomerName()
        CustomerName = mstrName
    End Property

End Class
```

Notice the absence of a `Property Let` procedure. Since we have not provided a `Property Let` procedure, code outside of the class cannot write to the `CustomerName` property.

Here is the second method.

```
Class Customer

    Private mstrName

    Private Property Let CustomerName(strName)
        mstrName = strName
    End Property

    Public Property Get CustomerName()
        CustomerName = mstrName
    End Property

End Class
```

The `Property Get` procedure is declared with the `Public` statement, and the `Property Let` procedure is declared with the `Private` statement. By declaring the `Property Let` as `Private`, we have effectively hidden it from code outside of the class. Code inside of the class can still write to the property through the `Property Let` procedure, but in our simple example, this is of limited usefulness. This is because code inside of the class can write directly to the private property variable, so there is little need for the private `Property Let` procedure.

The exception to this would be when there is code inside of the `Property Let` procedure that is performing validations and/or transformations on the value being placed in the property. If this were the case, then there might be a benefit in code inside the class using the private `Property Let` procedure rather than writing directly to the private property variable.

The first method (providing only a `Property Get`) is the more typical method of creating a read-only property.

## Making a Property Write-Only

The two techniques for making a property write-only are the exact reverse of the two techniques for making a property read-only (see previous section):

❑ You can omit the `Property Get` procedure and provide only a `Property Let` procedure.

❑ You can declare the `Property Let` procedure with the `Public` statement, and declare the `Property Get` with the `Private` statement.

## Public Properties without Property Procedures

You can provide properties for your class without using `Property Let`, `Set`, and `Get` procedures at all. This is accomplished through the use of public class-level variables. For example, this code.

```
Class Customer

    Private mstrName

    Public Property Let CustomerName(strName)
        mstrName = strName
    End Property

    Public Property Get CustomerName()
        CustomerName = mstrName
    End Property

End Class
```

is the functional equivalent of this:

```
Class Customer

    Public Name

End Class
```

The second option looks a lot more attractive. It has a lot less code. From a functionality and syntax standpoint, the second option is perfectly legal. However, many VBScript programmers strongly prefer using private property variables in combination with `Property Let`, `Set`, and `Get` procedures, as we have discussed in the previous sections.

Other programmers prefer to use public class-level variables instead of `Property Let`, `Set`, and `Get` procedures. The main advantage of using public class-level variables to create class properties is that this method takes a lot less code. However, not using `Property Let`, `Set`, and `Get` procedures also has some serious disadvantages that you should consider.

Unless you want the code that uses your class to use awkward syntax like `objCustomer.mstrName = "ACME Inc."`, you cannot use Hungarian scope or subtype prefixes on your class-level variables. If you agree with the theory that Hungarian prefixes add value to your code, this tends to make the code less readable and understandable.

- ❑ You cannot use the techniques described in previous sections of this chapter for making properties read-only or write-only.

- ❑ Code outside of your class can write to any property at any time. If there are certain circumstances where it is valid to write to a certain property, and other circumstances where it is invalid to write to a certain property, the only way you can enforce this is through `Property Let` procedures that have code in them to check for these valid and invalid circumstances. You never know when code outside the class might be changing the values of properties.

- ❑ Without `Property Let` procedures, you cannot write code to validate or transform the value being written to a property.

- ❑ Without `Property Get` procedures, you cannot write code to validate or transform the value being read from a property.

That said, if you can live with these disadvantages, you certainly can declare your properties as public class-level variables and change them to use `Property Let`, `Set`, and `Get` procedures later if the need arises. However, one could make an argument that it's better to do it the "right" way from the start. This is one of those issues where good programmers will simply have a difference of opinion, but we think you'll find more programmers who prefer `Property Let`, `Set`, and `Get` procedures over public class-level variables.

Often, however, you are creating a simple class for use within a single script. In such situations, it may be more acceptable to take some shortcuts so that the code is simpler and easier to write. In these cases, you may decide to forgo `Property Let`, `Set`, and `Get` procedures and just use public variables.

# Defining Methods

A *method* is a different name for functions and procedures, which we have been discussing throughout this book. When a function or procedure is part of a class, we call it a method instead. If you know how to write `Function` and `Sub` procedures (see Chapter 4), then you know how to write methods for a class. There is no special syntax for methods, as there is for properties. Your primary consideration is whether to declare a `Function` or `Sub` in a class as `Public` or `Private`.

Simply put, a class method that is declared with the `Public` statement will be available to code outside or inside the class, and a method that is declared with the `Private` statement will be available only to code inside the class.

The example script `SHOW_GREETING.VBS` contains a class called `Greeting`, which can be used to greet the user with different types of messages. The class uses both public and private methods. As you can see in the code for the `Greeting` class, methods defined in a class use the same syntax as any other VBScript procedure or function. The only new consideration with class methods is whether to make them public or private—that is, visible to outside code, or not visible to outside code.

```
Class Greeting

    Private mstrName

    Public Property Let Name(strName)
        mstrName = strName
    End Property

    Public Sub ShowGreeting(strType)
        MsgBox MakeGreeting(strType) & mstrName & "."
    End Sub

    Private Function MakeGreeting(strType)
        Select Case strType
            Case "Formal"
                MakeGreeting = "Greetings, "
            Case "Informal"
                MakeGreeting = "Hello there, "
            Case "Casual"
                MakeGreeting = "Hey, "
        End Select
    End Function

End Class
```

Code that is outside of this class can call the `ShowGreeting` method, which is public, but cannot call the `MakeGreeting` method, which is private and for internal use only. The code at the top of the `SHOW_GREETING.VBS` example script makes use of the class.

```
Dim objGreet
Set objGreet = New Greeting

With objGreet
    .Name = "Dan"
    .ShowGreeting "Informal"
    .ShowGreeting "Formal"
    .ShowGreeting "Casual"
End With
Set objGreet = Nothing
```

Running this script results in the dialog boxes shown in Figures 8-2 through 8-4.

Figure 8-2

Figure 8-3

Figure 8-4

*Note to Visual Basic programmers: VBScript does not support the* `Friend` *keyword for defining properties and methods.*

# Class Events

An *event* is a special kind of method that is called automatically. In any given context, the objects you are working with may support one or more events. When an event is supported in a given context, you can choose to write an *event handler*, which is a special kind of method that will be called whenever the event "fires."

Any VBScript class that you write automatically supports two events: `Class_Initialize` and `Class_Terminate`. As with most events, providing event handler methods in your class is optional. If you include event handler methods in your class, then they will be called automatically; if you don't, then nothing will happen when these events fire—which is not a problem at all if you had no good reason to provide handler methods.

## The Class_Initialize Event

The `Class_Initialize` event "fires" in your class when some code instantiates an object that is based on your class. It will always fire when an object based on your class is instantiated, but whether your class contains any code to respond to it is up to you. If you do not wish to respond to this event, then you can simply choose to omit the event handler method for the event. An event handler is a subprocedure that is called automatically whenever the event that it is tied to fires. Here is an example class that contains a `Class_Initialize` event handler.

```
Class FileHelper

    'Private FileSystemObject object
    Private mobjFSO

    Private Sub Class_Initialize
        Set mobjFSO = _
            WScript.CreateObject( _
            "Scripting.FileSystemObject")
    End Sub

    '<<rest of the class goes here>>

End Class
```

As in this example, initializing class-level variables is a fairly typical use for a `Class_Initialize` event handler. If you have a variable that you want to make sure has a certain value when your class first starts, you can initialize it in the `Class_Initialize` event handler. You might also use the `Class_Initialize` event to do other preliminary things such as opening a database connection, or opening a file.

The syntax for blocking off the beginning and ending of the `Class_Initialize` event handler must be exactly as you see it in this example. Your code can do just about whatever you please inside the event handler, but you do not have the flexibility of giving the procedure a different name. The first line of the handler must be `Private Sub Class_Initialize`, and the last line must be `End Sub`. Really, the event handler is a normal VBScript subprocedure, but with a special name.

> *Technically, the event handler could also be declared with the* `Public` *statement (as opposed to* `Private`*, but event handlers are generally private. If you were to make it public, then code outside of the class could call it like any other method any time it liked, which would not generally be desirable.*

There can only be exactly one `Class_Initialize` event handler in a given class. You can omit it if you don't need it, but you can't have more than one.

## The Class_Terminate Event

The `Class_Terminate` event is the inverse of the `Class_Initialize` event (see previous section). Whereas the `Class_Initialize` event fires whenever an object based on your class is instantiated, the `Class_Terminate` event fires whenever an object based on your class is destroyed. An object can be destroyed in either of two ways:

❑   When some code explicitly assigns to the special value `Nothing` to the last object variable with a reference to the object

❑   When the last object variable with a reference to the object goes out of scope

When either of these things occurs, the `Class_Terminate` event will fire immediately before the object is actually destroyed. (For more information about object lifetime and references, please see Chapter 7.)

Here is the example `FileHelper` class that we saw in the previous section, this time with a `Class_Terminate` event handler added.

```
Class FileHelper

    'Private FileSystemObject object
    Private mobjFSO

    Private Sub Class_Initialize
        Set mobjFSO = _
        WScript.CreateObject("Scripting.FileSystemObject")
    End Sub

    Private Sub Class_Terminate
        Set mobjFSO = Nothing
    End Sub

    '<rest of the class goes here>

End Class
```

In this example, we are using the `Class_Terminate` event handler to destroy the object that we instantiated in the `Class_Initialize` event. This is not strictly necessary, since when the `FileHelper` object is destroyed, the private `mobjFSO` variable will go out of scope and the script engine will destroy it for us. However, some programmers prefer to explicitly destroy all objects that they instantiate.

You might also use the `Class_Terminate` event to close a database connection, close a file, or save some information in the class to a database or file. The same syntactical restrictions that apply to `Class_Initialize` event handlers apply to `Class_Terminate` event handlers.

# Class-Level Constants

For reasons that are unclear, VBScript does not support named constants declared at the class level. That is, you cannot use the `Const` statement within a class such that the constant variable would be available throughout the class, or from outside the class. For example, this code will produce a compile error.

```
Option Explicit

Dim objTest

Set objTest = new ConstTest
objTest.SayHello
Set objTest = Nothing

Class ConstTest

    Private Const TEST_CONST = "Hello there."

    Public Sub SayHello
        MsgBox TEST_CONST
    End Sub

End Class
```

The compile error will occur on this line.

```
Private Const TEST_CONST = "Hello there."
```

The reason is that this statement is scoped at the class-level, which means that it is declared within the class, but not within any of the properties or methods of the class. (The Const statement is legal within a property or method, but it will of course have only local scope within that property or method.) There is a workaround, however, as shown in this example.

```
Option Explicit

Dim objTest

set objTest = new ConstTest
objTest.SayHello

Class ConstTest

    Private TEST_CONST

    Private Sub Class_Initialize
        TEST_CONST = "Hello there."
    End Sub

    Public Sub SayHello
        MsgBox TEST_CONST
    End Sub

End Class
```

This workaround creates a pseudo-constant. Instead of declaring TEST_CONST with the Const statement, we declare it as a normal, private class-level variable (we could have made it public as well). Then in the Class_Initialize event handler, we give the TEST_CONST variable the "constant" value that we want. There is a danger in this, however, because code inside your class can still change the value of the TEST_CONST variable. However, using the all-caps naming convention might help prevent this from happening (most programmers are accustomed to equating all-caps with a named constant). You'll just have to make sure the code inside the class behaves itself.

Please note that in earlier versions of VBScript, class-level constants were also not supported. However, strangely, they would not cause a compile error; their values would simply be ignored. If you are using a version of VBScript that does not produce the compile error, you essentially still have the same problem, and the same workaround will do the trick.

# Class-Level Arrays

A previous version of VBScript had a bug with class-level arrays; you could declare a class-level array, but it would be ignored by the VBScript engine *as an array*. The array variable itself was not ignored, but the fact that you had declared it as an array *was* ignored. This occurred with variables declared as fixed or dynamic arrays. This bug appears to have been fixed with the latest versions of VBScript, so you only need to concern yourself with this if for some reason you are not able to upgrade your scripting engine to the latest version. If you are on a pre-XP version of Windows and want to ensure that you have the latest scripting version, you can download the newest version from `http://www.microsoft.com/scripting`.

If you are for some reason stuck with an older version that has this bug, then there is a workaround: declare the class-level variable as a normal variable (not as an array), and then use the `ReDim` statement in the `Class_Initialize` event handler to transform it into an array of the desired type and size. Then you can use the variable throughout the rest of your class as if it had been declared as an array all along.

Note that local constants and arrays (that is, those declared inside of class methods or property procedures) work fine. It's only class-level arrays and constants that will cause these problems for you.

# Building and Using a Sample VBScript Class

In Chapter 3, we showed how an array could be used to store a list of names and phone numbers. Later, in Chapter 7 we showed how we could store a phone list in a series of one-element arrays in the scripting runtime's `Dictionary` object. Now, for the remainder of this chapter, we will further adapt the phone list example to use VBScript classes. In much the same way as the example code from Chapter 7, the code we will develop now will accomplish the following:

❑   Provide a data structure to store a phone list entry

❑   Provide a data structure to store a list of phone list entries

❑   Provide a way to locate and display a phone list entry

The example script we will develop will have the following elements:

❑   A `ListEntry` class to store a single phone list entry. This class will also know how to display its own data.

❑   A `PhoneList` class that uses an internal `Dictionary` object to store a series of `ListEntry` objects. This class, which uses the phone number value as the key for the dictionary, will also support the retrieval and display of an individual entry.

❑   Supporting non-class-based code that will use the two aforementioned classes to populate a phone list and ask the user for a phone number to locate and display.

You might remember from the Chapter 7 example that all of this same functionality was provided, but it was all done without classes. With that in mind, the purpose of this chapter's evolution of the Chapter 7 code is to illustrate how classes can be used to create more generic and reusable code that is more tolerant to future changes. You can read, execute, and experiment with this script in the file PHONE_LIST_CLASS .VBS, which, along with all of the rest of the code for this book, can be downloaded from the `wrox.com` Web site.

First, let's take a look at the `ListEntry` class.

```
Class ListEntry

    Private mstrLast
    Private mstrFirst
    Private mstrPhone
```

```vbscript
        Public Property Let LastName(strLastName)
            If IsNumeric(strLastName) or _
                IsDate(strLastName) Then
                Err.Raise 32003, "ListEntry", _
                    "The LastName property may not " & _
                    "be a number or date."
            End If

            mstrLast = strLastName
        End Property
        Public Property Get LastName
            LastName = mstrLast
        End Property

        Public Property Let FirstName(strFirstName)
            If IsNumeric(strFirstName) or _
                IsDate(strFirstName) Then
                Err.Raise 32004, "ListEntry", _
                    "The FirstName property may not " & _
                    "be a number or date."
            End If

            mstrFirst = strFirstName
        End Property
        Public Property Get FirstName
            FirstName = mstrFirst
        End Property

        Public Property Let PhoneNumber(strPhoneNumber)
            mstrPhone = strPhoneNumber
        End Property
        Public Property Get PhoneNumber
            PhoneNumber = mstrPhone
        End Property

        Public Sub DisplayEntry
            MsgBox "Phone list entry:" & vbNewLine & _
                vbNewLine & _
                "Last: " & mstrLast & vbNewLine & _
                "First: " & mstrFirst & vbNewLine & _
                "Phone: " & mstrPhone
        End Sub

    End Class
```

This class has three properties: LastName, FirstName, and PhoneNumber. Each property is implemented using a private property variable, along with Property Let and Get procedures. Since we have provided both Let and Get procedures for each property, they can both read from and written to. Notice also that in the Property Let procedures for LastName and FirstName, we are checking to make sure that outside code does not store any numeric or date values in the properties. If an illegal value is passed in, the code raises an error (see Chapter 6).

Checking for numbers and dates is a somewhat arbitrary choice of something to validate; the primary purpose in this example is to illustrate how important it is to use your Property Let procedures to ensure that programmers do not store any data in a property that does not belong. This technique is especially important given VBScript's lack of data type enforcement; since all variables have the `Variant` data type, any variable can hold any value.

Please note that we could have chosen many other types of validation. We could have checked for data length (minimum or maximum), special characters that might be illegal, proper formatting, and so on. For example, we could have also added a check to the `PhoneNumber` `Property Let` that verifies the format XXX-XXX-XXXX. Or we could have added a "transformation" that coverts the phone number into that format if it already wasn't. What kinds of validations and transformations you choose depends on the situation. The point is to test the assumptions inherent in the rest of your code so as to avoid bugs and errors.

The `ListEntry` class has one method: `DisplayEntry`, which uses the `MsgBox` function to display the properties of a list entry. We chose to put this code in the `ListEntry` class because of the general principle that a class should provide functionality that it is "natural" for that class to know how to do. The `ListEntry` class "knows" the last name, first name, and phone number. Therefore, in order to keep the code that manipulates data as close as possible to where the data is stored, we put the `DisplayEntry` method on the `ListEntry` class.

In object-oriented parlance, this is called *separation of concerns* or *responsibility-based design*. Each class has a set of "things" it needs to "know" and to "know how to do." We want to design our classes so that the separations between them are logical. The less one class "knows" about other classes, the better.

However, sometimes there is functionality that we expressly *do not* want a class to know how to do. The idea is to keep our classes as generic as possible, so that they can be used in multiple ways in multiple contexts. We'll see examples of this as we continue to build our code.

Moving on, this is our second class, `PhoneList`.

```
Class PhoneList

    Private objDict

    Private Sub Class_Initialize
        Set objDict = CreateObject("Scripting.Dictionary")
    End Sub
    Private Sub Class_Terminate
        Set objDict = Nothing
    End Sub

    Public Property Get ListCount
        ListCount = objDict.Count
    End Property

    Public Function EntryExists(strPhoneNumber)
        EntryExists = _
            objDict.Exists(strPhoneNumber)
    End Function

    Public Sub AddEntry(objListEntry)
        If TypeName(objListEntry) <> "ListEntry" Then
```

```
            Err.Raise 32000, "PhoneList", _
                "Only ListEntry objects can be stored " & _
                "in a PhoneList class."
        End If
        'We use the PhoneNumber property as the key.
        If Trim("" & objListEntry.PhoneNumber) = "" Then
            Err.Raise 32001, "PhoneList", _
                "A ListEntry object must have a " & _
                "phone number to be added to the " & _
                "phone list."
        End If

        objDict.Add objListEntry.PhoneNumber, objListEntry
    End Sub

    Public Sub DisplayEntry(strPhoneNumber)
        Dim objEntry

        If objDict.Exists(strPhoneNumber) Then
            Set objEntry = objDict(strPhoneNumber)
            objEntry.DisplayEntry
        Else
            Err.Raise 32002, "PhoneList", _
                "The phone number '" & strPhoneNumber & _
                    "' is not in the list."
        End If
    End Sub

End Class
```

The first thing to notice about this class is that internally it is using a private `Dictionary` object to store the phone list. This is a powerful technique for two reasons: first, it illustrates how your classes can "borrow" the functionality of other classes; and second, the fact that we don't expose the internal `Dictionary` object to any code outside of the `PhoneList` class means that scripts that use the `PhoneList` class do not need to have any knowledge of how the `PhoneList` class stores the data. If we want to change the `Dictionary` to some other data storage method (such as an array, hash table, text file, and so on), we could do so without breaking any other code that uses the `PhoneList` class.

Next, as illustrated earlier in this chapter, notice we are using the `Class_Initialize` and `Class_Terminate` events to control the lifetime of the internal `Dictionary` object (`objDict`). This allows the rest of the class to be able to assume that there is always a `Dictionary` object to use.

Next, we have a `Property Get` procedure called `ListCount` and a method called `EntryExists`. The `ListCount` property is a "wrapper" for the `objDict.Count` property, and likewise `ExtryExists` is a wrapper for the `objDict.Exists` method. We could have chosen to expose other `Dictionary` properties and methods as well. However, we want to be careful about this because we don't want to lose our future flexibility to change out the `Dictionary` object with another data storage structure.

For example, we could make things really easy and just expose `objDict` as a property and let outside code use it directly as a dictionary. However, if we did that, outside code would become too "tightly coupled" to the internals of our class—meaning that outside code would have too much "knowledge" about how our class works internally. As much as possible, we want our `PhoneList` class to be a "black box"; you can use the functionality of a black box, you can know what goes in and what comes out, but you can see what's inside the box that makes it all work.

Next we have the AddEntry method. This method really does only one thing: it calls the dictionary's Add method, using the phone number of the list entry as the key for the dictionary.

```
objDict.Add objListEntry.PhoneNumber, objListEntry
```

Notice that we are storing the ListEntry object itself in the dictionary, just as in Chapter 7 we stored a phone list entry array in the dictionary.

However, this is the last line of the method. All of the code that comes before it is validation code. The idea here is that we want to test and document the assumptions made by this method. This method has two important implicit assumptions:

❑ That only ListEntry objects are stored in the PhoneList class

❑ That the PhoneNumber property will be used as the key

To test these assumptions, first we use the TypeName function check to make sure that the outside code is passing us a ListEntry object, and not some other kind of data. This is necessary because, given VBScript's lack of data type enforcement, we need to do our own validation. Second, we check to make sure that the ListEntry object has a non-blank value in the PhoneNumber property. This way we can make sure that we have something that can be used as a key.

There are other assumptions that we could have tested as well, but these are the two that would be most likely to produce strange bugs or error messages that would make it difficult for programmers using our classes to figure out what they are doing wrong. These clear error messages document for all concerned what the important assumptions are.

Finally, PhoneList has a method called DisplayEntry. Now wait a minute—didn't we also have a DisplayEntry method on the ListEntry class? Why two methods that apparently do the same thing? It all comes down to design options. There is not necessarily a "correct" way to design these classes. The DisplayEntry method of the PhoneList class "delegates" the responsibility of displaying of an entry to the ListEntry.DisplayEntry method, as you can see in these lines.

```
If objDict.Exists(strPhoneNumber) Then
    Set objEntry = objDict(strPhoneNumber)
    objEntry.DisplayEntry
```

So even though we have two methods, there is not really any duplication because the code that does the actual displaying only exists in the ListEntry class. The implicit design decision we made was to specialize the PhoneList class with methods (such as DisplayEntry) that allow programmers to do specific things with phone list entries (such as displaying them), as opposed to going with a more generic approach that just exposes the list of entries, allowing the outside code to do the work embodied in the three lines of code above—that is, finding the correct entry and telling it to display itself. Both designs are valid, and nothing in our chosen design would prevent us from extending these classes in any number of ways in the future.

Now that we have our two classes, lets look at some code that makes use of these classes (again, all of this code can be found in PHONE_LIST_CLASS.VBS).

```
Option Explicit

Dim objList

FillPhoneList
On Error Resume Next
objList.DisplayEntry(GetNumberFromUser)

If Err.Number <> 0 Then
    If Err.Number = vbObjectError + 32002 Then
        MsgBox "That phone number is not in the list.", _
            vbInformation
    Else
        DisplayError Err.Number, Err.Source, _
            Err.Description
    End If
End If

Public Sub FillPhoneList
    Dim objNewEntry

    Set objList = New PhoneList

    Set objNewEntry = New ListEntry
    With objNewEntry
        .LastName = "Williams"
        .FirstName = "Tony"
        .PhoneNumber = "404-555-6328"
    End With
    objList.AddEntry objNewEntry
    Set objNewEntry = Nothing

    Set objNewEntry = New ListEntry
    With objNewEntry
        .LastName = "Carter"
        .FirstName = "Ron"
        .PhoneNumber = "305-555-2514"
    End With
    objList.AddEntry objNewEntry
    Set objNewEntry = Nothing

    Set objNewEntry = New ListEntry
    With objNewEntry
        .LastName = "Davis"
        .FirstName = "Miles"
        .PhoneNumber = "212-555-5314"
    End With
    objList.AddEntry objNewEntry
    Set objNewEntry = Nothing
```

```
        Set objNewEntry = New ListEntry
        With objNewEntry
            .LastName = "Hancock"
            .FirstName = "Herbie"
            .PhoneNumber = "616-555-6943"
        End With
        objList.AddEntry objNewEntry
        Set objNewEntry = Nothing

        Set objNewEntry = New ListEntry
        With objNewEntry
            .LastName = "Shorter"
            .FirstName = "Wayne"
            .PhoneNumber = "853-555-0060"
        End With
        objList.AddEntry objNewEntry
        Set objNewEntry = Nothing

    End Sub

    Public Function GetNumberFromUser
        GetNumberFromUser = InputBox("Please enter " & _
            "a phone number (XXX-XXX-XXXX) with " & _
            "which to search the list.")
    End Function
```

Running this code and entering the phone number 404-555-6328 results in the dialog box shown in Figure 8-5.

**Figure 8-5**

Running the code again and entering an invalid phone number results in the dialog box shown in Figure 8-6.

**Figure 8-6**

220

The most important point to take away from this elaborate example can be found in these two simple lines of code (without the error handling related code).

```
FillPhoneList
objList.DisplayEntry(GetNumberFromUser)
```

These two lines represent the total logic of our script: create a phone list, fill it up, ask the user for a phone number to search for, and display the entry. This is the beauty of breaking our code up into separate classes and procedures. If we make our classes and procedures as generic as possible, then the code that actually strings them together to do something useful can be relatively simple and easy to understand and change—not to mention easy to reuse in any number of ways.

The `FillPhoneList` procedure creates a `PhoneList` object (`objList`) and fills it up with entries. If you use your imagination, you could picture the phone list entries coming from a database table, a file, or from user entry. `FillPhoneList` uses a "temporary object variable" called `objNewEntry`. For each entry in the list, it instantiates `objNewEntry`, fills it with data, then passes it to the `objList.AddEntry` method.

Notice that we use the `New` keyword in `FillPhoneList` to instantiate objects from our custom VBScript classes.

```
Set objList = New PhoneList
```

and

```
Set objNewEntry = New ListEntry
```

What happened to the `CreateObject` function? `CreateObject` is only for use in instantiating nonnative VBScript objects (such as `Dictionary` and `FileSystemObject`), whereas we must use `New` to instantiate a custom VBScript class that exists in the same script file. The reasons behind this are complex, so keep this simple rule in mind: if you are instantiating an object based on a custom VBScript class, use `New`; otherwise, use `CreateObject`.

The `GetNumberFromUser` function is very simple. It uses the `InputBox` function to prompt the user for a phone number and returns whatever the user entered. The code at the top of the script then passes this value to `objDict.DisplayEntry`. If the entry exists, the `ListEntry` object will display itself. If not, `objDict.DisplayEntry` will return an error.

What is important is *not* to dwell on the way in which we have used the `PhoneList` and `ListEntry` classes. Rather, what is important is to realize that our `PhoneList` and `ListEntry` classes can be used in any number of ways for any number of purposes. As new needs arise, the classes can be extended without breaking any code that is already using them. Any future programmers who come to our script will have a very easy time understanding what our script is doing. After all, it's all in these two lines of code.

```
FillPhoneList
objList.DisplayEntry(GetNumberFromUser)
```

If a programmer wants to further understand the low-level details of how the script works, he or she can choose to read the rest of the code, digging into the procedures and the classes. But in many cases, that would be unnecessary, unless the programmer needed to fix a bug or add some functionality. If all a programmer wants to know is *What does this script do?*, the answer is right there in those two simple lines.

# Summary

In this chapter we explained how to develop classes in native VBScript. This is a powerful ability that allows you to create scripts that are object oriented in nature, which, when properly designed, can give you greater understandability, maintainability, flexibility, and reuse. A VBScript class is defined using the `Class...End Class` block construct. In general, classes must be defined within the same script file as the code that will make use of them. (For an alternative technique, please see Chapter 13 for information on Windows Script Components.)

Classes can have properties and methods. Properties are defined using either public variables or special procedure constructs called `Property Let`, `Get`, and `Set` procedures. Using private property variables and different combinations of `Let`, `Get`, and `Set` procedures, you can control whether properties are read-only, write-only, or both. Methods are defined like normal procedures and functions, and can be either public or private.

The final section of this chapter gives a detailed class-based example, including explanations of the design and programming techniques. The example is an extension of the phone list examples used in Chapters 3 and 7.

# Regular Expressions

## Overview

Version 5 and above of VBScript fully support regular expressions in VBScript. Before that this was one feature that was sorely lacking within VBScript, and one that made it inferior to other scripting languages, including JavaScript.

## Introduction to Regular Expressions

Regular expressions provide powerful facilities for character pattern-matching and replacing. Before the addition of regular expressions to the VBScript engine, performing a search-and-replace task throughout a string required a fair amount of code, comprising mainly of loops, InStr, and Mid functions. Now it is possible to do all this with one line of code using a regular expression.

If you've programmed in the past using another language (C++, Perl, awk, or JavaScript—even Microsoft's own JScript had support for regular expression before VBScript did), regular expressions won't be new to you. However, one thing that experienced programmers need to know in order to leverage regular expressions in VBScript is that VBScript does not provide support for regular expression constants (like /a pattern/). Instead, VBScript uses text strings assigned to the Pattern property of a RegExp object. In many ways this is superior to the traditional method because there is no new syntax to learn. But if you are used to regular expressions from other languages, especially client-side JavaScript, this might be something that you may not expect.

> *Note: There are now many Windows based text editors that have followed in the footsteps of the Unix text editor vi and now support regular expression searches. These include UltraEdit-32 (www.ultraedit.com) and SlickEdit (www.slickedit.com).*

## Regular Expressions in Action

The quickest and easiest way to become familiar with regular expressions is to look at a few examples. Here is probably one of the simplest examples of regular expression in action—a simple find-and-replace example.

```
Dim re, s
Set re = New RegExp
re.Pattern = "France"
s = "The rain in France falls mainly on the plains."
MsgBox re.Replace(s, "Spain")
```

Nothing spectacular—it's just a simple find and replace, but it is a powerful foundation to build up from. Here's how the code works. First, we create a new regular expression object.

```
Set re = New RegExp
```

Then we set the key property on that object. This is the pattern that we want to match.

```
re.Pattern = "France"
```

And the following line is the string we will be searching.

```
s = "The rain in France falls mainly on the plains."
```

The last line is the powerhouse of the script and is the line that does the real work. It asks our regular expression object to find the first occurrence of `"France"` (the pattern) within the string held in variable s and to replace it with `"Spain"`. Once we've done that, we use a message box to show off our great find-and-replace skills.

```
MsgBox re.Replace(s, "Spain")
```

When the script is run, the final output should be as shown in Figure 9-1.

**Figure 9-1**

Now, it's all well and good hard-coding the string and search criteria straight from the start, but you can make it a lot more flexible by making the script accept the string and the find-and-replace criteria from an input.

```
Dim re, s, sc
Set re = New RegExp
s = InputBox("Type a string for the code to search")
re.Pattern = InputBox("Type in a pattern to find")
sc = InputBox("Type in a string to replace the pattern")
MsgBox re.Replace(s, sc)
```

This is pretty much the exact same code as we had before, but with three key differences. Instead of having everything hard-coded into the script, we introduce flexibility by using three input boxes in the code.

```
s = InputBox("Type a string for the code to search")
re.Pattern = InputBox("Type in a pattern to find")
sc = InputBox("Type in a string to replace the pattern")
```

The final change to the code is in the final line enabling the `Replace` method to make use of the `sc` variable.

```
MsgBox re.Replace(s, sc)
```

This lets you manually enter the string you want to be searched, as shown in Figure 9-2.

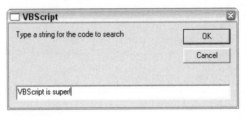

**Figure 9-2**

Then you can enter the pattern you want to find (see Figure 9-3).

**Figure 9-3**

Finally, enter a string to replace the pattern (see Figure 9-4).

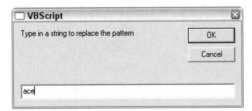

**Figure 9-4**

This let's you try out something that you might already be thinking. That is, what happens if you try to find and replace a pattern that doesn't exist in the string. In fact, nothing happens, as shown here. Type in the string as shown in Figure 9-5.

Next you enter a search for a pattern that doesn't exist (something that doesn't appear in the string). In Figure 9-6 we use the string "JScript".

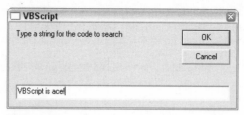

**Figure 9-5**

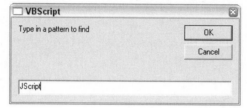

**Figure 9-6**

In the next prompt, enter a string to replace the nonexistent pattern. As no replacement will be carried out it can be anything. In Figure 9-7 we use the string "JavaScript."

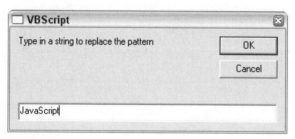

**Figure 9-7**

Notice what happens. Nothing. As you can see in Figure 9-8, the initial string is unchanged.

**Figure 9-8**

# Building on Simplicity

Obviously the examples that you've seen so far are quite simple ones, and to be honest, we could probably do everything we've done here just as easily using VBScript's string manipulation functions.

But what if we wanted to replace all occurrences of string? Or what if we wanted to replace all occurrences of string but only when they appear at the end of a word?

We need to make some tweaks to the code. Take a look at the following code.

```
Dim re, s
Set re = New RegExp
re.Pattern = "\bin"
re.Global = True
s = "The rain in Spain falls mainly on the plains."
MsgBox re.Replace(s, "in the country of")
```

This version has two key differences. First, it uses a special sequence (\b) to match a word boundary (we'll explore all the special sequences available in the *Regular Expression Characters* section ). This is demonstrated in Figure 9-9.

**Figure 9-9**

What if we left the \b out, like this?

```
Dim re, s
Set re = New RegExp
re.Pattern = "in"
re.Global = True
s = "The rain in Spain falls mainly on the plains."
MsgBox re.Replace(s, "in the country of")
```

Without this, the "in" part of the words "rain", "Spain", "mainly" and "plains" would be changed to "in the country of" also. This would give, as you can see in Figure 9-10, some very funny, but undesirable, results.

**Figure 9-10**

Second, by setting the Global property we ensure that we match all the occurrences of "in" that we want.

```
Dim re, s
Set re = New RegExp
re.Pattern = "in"
```

```
re.Global = True
s = "The rain in Spain falls mainly on the plains."
MsgBox re.Replace(s, "in the country of")
```

Regular expressions provide a very powerful language for expressing complicated patterns like these, so let's get on with learning about the objects that allow us to use them within VBScript.

# The RegExp Object

The RegExp object is the object that provides simple regular expression support in VBScript. All the properties and methods relating to regular expressions in VBScript are related to this object.

```
Dim re
Set re = New RegExp
```

This object has three properties and three methods. The three properties are:

❑   Global property

❑   IgnoreCase property

❑   Pattern property

The three methods are:

❑   Execute method

❑   Replace method

❑   Test method

# RegExp Properties

As mentioned before, the RegExp object has three properties that you can use. Let's take a look at the three properties associated with the RegExp object.Global property.

The Global property is responsible for setting or returning a Boolean value that indicates whether or not a pattern is to match all occurrences in an entire search string or just the first occurrence.

```
object.Global [= value ]
```

| | |
|---|---|
| **object** | Always a **RegExp** object |
| **value** | There are two possible values: **True** and **False** |
| | If the value of the **Global** property is **True** then the search applies to the entire string; if it is **False** then it does not. Default is **False**—not **True** as documented in some Microsoft sources |

The following example uses the Global property to ensure all occurrences of "in" were changed.

```
Dim re, s
Set re = New RegExp
re.Pattern = "\bin"
re.Global = True
s = "The rain in Spain falls mainly on the plains."
MsgBox re.Replace(s, "in the country of")
```

## IgnoreCase Property

The IgnoreCase property sets or returns a Boolean value that indicates whether or not the pattern search is case-sensitive.

```
object.IgnoreCase [= value ]
```

> **object**      Always a **RegExp** object
> **value**       There are two possible values: **True** and **False**
>                 If the value of the **IgnoreCase** property is **False** then the search is
> case sensitive; if it is **True** then it is not. Default is **False**—not **True** as documented
> in some Microsoft sources

Continuing with the example we looked at for the Global property earlier, if the string we want to match has "In" capitalized, we need to tell VBScript to ignore the case when it does the matching.

```
Dim re, s
Set re = New RegExp
re.Pattern = "\bin"
re.Global = True
re.IgnoreCase = True
s = "The rain In Spain falls mainly on the plains."
MsgBox re.Replace(s, "in the country of")
```

## Pattern Property

The Pattern property sets or returns the regular expression pattern being searched.

```
object.Pattern [= "searchstring"]
```

> **object**           Always a **RegExp** object
> **searchstring**     Regular string expression being searched for. May include any
> of the regular expression characters—optional

All the preceding examples used Pattern.

```
Dim re, s
Set re = New RegExp
```

```
re.Pattern = "\bin"
re.Global = True
s = "The rain in Spain falls mainly on the plains."
MsgBox re.Replace(s, "in the country of")
```

# Regular Expression Characters

The real power of regular expressions comes not from using strings as patterns, but from using special characters in the pattern. What follows is a table that shows the characters that can be used along with a description of what each of the characters does in code.

*Capitalized special characters do the opposite of their lower case counterparts.*

| Character | Description |
| --- | --- |
| \ | Marks the next character as either a special character or a literal |
| ^ | Matches the beginning of input |
| $ | Matches the end of input |
| * | Matches the preceding character zero or more times |
| + | Matches the preceding character one or more times |
| ? | Matches the preceding character zero or one time |
| . | Matches any single character except a newline character |
| (pattern) | Matches *pattern* and remembers the match. The matched substring can be retrieved from the resulting Matches collection, using Item [0]...[n]. To match the parentheses characters themselves, precede with slash—use "\(" or "\)" |
| (?:pattern) | Matches *pattern* but does not capture the match, that is, it is a noncapturing match that is not stored for possible later use. This is useful for combining parts of a pattern with the "or" character (\|). For example, "anomol(?:y\|ies)" is a more economical expression than "anomoly\|anomolies" |
| (?=pattern) | Positive lookahead matches the search string at any point where a string matching *pattern* begins. This is a noncapturing match, that is, the match is not captured for possible later use. For example, "Windows (?=95\|98\|NT\|2000\|XP)" matches "Windows" in "Windows XP" but not "Windows" in "Windows 3.1" |
| (?!pattern) | Negative lookahead matches the search string at any point where a string not matching *pattern* begins. This is a noncapturing match, that is, the match is not captured for possible later use. For example, "Windows (?!95\|98\|NT\|2000\|XP)" matches "Windows" in "Windows 3.1" but does not match "Windows" in "Windows XP" |
| x\|y | Matches either x or y |
| {n} | Matches exactly n times (n must always be a nonnegative integer) |

| Character | Description |
|---|---|
| {n,} | Matches at least n times (n must always be a nonnegative integer—note the terminating comma) |
| {n,m} | Matches at least n and at most m times (m and n must always be nonnegative integers) |
| [xyz] | Matches any one of the enclosed characters (xyz represents a character set) |
| [^xyz] | Matches any character not enclosed (^xyz represents a negative character set) |
| [a-z] | Matches any character in the specified range (a-z represents a range of characters) |
| [^m-z] | Matches any character not in the specified range (^m-z represents a negative range of characters) |
| \b | Matches a word boundary, that is, the position between a word and a space |
| \B | Matches a nonword boundary |
| \d | Matches a digit character. Equivalent to [0-9] |
| \D | Matches a nondigit character. Equivalent to [^0-9] |
| \f | Matches a form-feed character |
| \n | Matches a newline character |
| \r | Matches a carriage return character |
| \s | Matches any white space including space, tab, form-feed, and so on. Equivalent to "[\f\n\r\t\v]" |
| \S | Matches any nonwhite space character. Equivalent to "[^\f\n\r\t\v]" |
| \t | Matches a tab character |
| \v | Matches a vertical tab character |
| \w | Matches any word character including underscore. Equivalent to "[A-Za-z0-9_]" |
| \W | Matches any nonword character. Equivalent to "[^A-Za-z0-9_]" |
| \. | Matches . |
| \| | Matches \| |
| \{ | Matches { |
| \} | Matches } |
| \\ | Matches \ |
| \[ | Matches [ |
| \] | Matches ] |
| \( | Matches ( |

*Continues*

| Character | Description |
|---|---|
| \) | Matches ) |
| $num | Matches num, where num is a positive integer. A reference back to remembered matches (note the $ symbol—differs from some Microsoft documentation) |
| \n | Matches n, where n is an octal escape value. Octal escape values must be 1, 2, or 3 digits long |
| \uxxxx | Matches the ASCII character expressed by the UNICODE xxxx |
| \xn | Matches n, where n is a hexadecimal escape value. Hexadecimal escape values must be exactly two digits long |

Many of these codes are self-explanatory, but some examples would probably help with others. We've already seen a simple pattern:

```
re.Pattern = "in"
```

Often it's useful to match any one of a whole class of characters. We do this by enclosing the characters that we want to match in square brackets. For example, the following example will replace any single digit with a more generic term.

```
Dim re, s
Set re = New RegExp
re.Pattern = "[23456789]"
s = "Spain received 3 millimeters of rain last week."
MsgBox re.Replace(s, "many")
```

Figure 9-11 shows the output from this code.

**Figure 9-11**

In this case, the number "3" is replaced with the text "many". As you might expect, we can shorten this class by using a range. This pattern does the same as the preceding one but saves some typing.

```
Dim re, s
Set re = New RegExp
re.Pattern = "[2-9]"
s = "Spain received 3 millimeters of rain last week."
MsgBox re.Replace(s, "many")
```

Replacing digits is a common task. In fact, the pattern [0-9] (covering all the digits) is used so often that there is a shortcut for it: \d is equivalent to [0-9].

```
Dim re, s
Set re = New RegExp
re.Pattern = "\d"
s = "a b c d e f 1 g 2 h ... 10 z"
MsgBox re.Replace(s, "a number")
```

The string with the replaced characters is shown in Figure 9-12

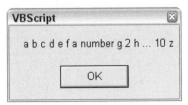

**Figure 9-12**

But what if you wanted to match everything except a digit? Then we can use negation, which is indicated by a circumflex (^) used within the class square brackets.

*Note: Using ^ outside the square brackets has a totally different meaning and is discussed after the next example.*

Thus, to match any character other than a digit we can use any of the following patterns.

```
re.Pattern = "[^0-9]" 'the hard way
re.Pattern = "[^\d]" 'a little shorter
re.Pattern = "[\D]" 'another of those special characters
```

The last option here uses another of the dozen or so special characters. In most cases these characters just save you some extra typing (or act as a good memory shorthand) but a few, like matching tabs and other nonprintable characters, can be very useful.

There are three special characters that anchor a pattern. They don't match any characters themselves but force another pattern to appear at the beginning of the input (^ used outside of [ ]), the end of the input ($), or at a word boundary (we've already seen \b).

Another way by which we can shorten our patterns is using repeat counts. The basic idea is to place the repeat after the character or class. For example, the following pattern, as shown in Figure 9-13, matches both digits and replaces them.

```
Dim re, s
Set re = New RegExp
re.Pattern = "\d{3}"
s = "Spain received 100 millimeters of rain in the last 2 weeks."
MsgBox re.Replace(s, "a whopping number of")
```

**Figure 9-13**

Without the use of the repeat count Figure 9-14 shows that the code would leave the "00" in the final string.

**Figure 9-14**

```
Dim re, s
Set re = New RegExp
re.Pattern = "\d"
s = "Spain received 100 millimeters of rain in the last 2 weeks."
MsgBox re.Replace(s, "a whopping number of")
```

Note also that we can't just set re.Global = True because we'd end up with four instances of the phrase "a whopping number of" in the result. The result is shown in Figure 9-15.

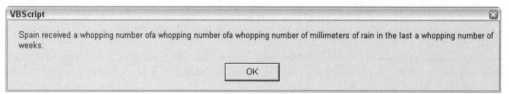

**Figure 9-15**

```
Dim re, s
Set re = New RegExp
re.Global = True
re.Pattern = "\d"
s = "Spain received 100 millimeters of rain in the last 2 weeks."
MsgBox re.Replace(s, "a whopping number of")
```

As the previous table shows, we can also specify a minimum number of matches {min,} or a range {min, max}. Again there are a few repeat patterns that are used so often that they have special short cuts.

```
re.Pattern = "\d+"        'one or more digits, \d{1, }
re.Pattern = "\d*"        'zero or more digits, \d{0, }
```

```
re.Pattern = "\d?"        'optional: zero or one, \d{0,1}

Dim re, s
Set re = New RegExp
re.Global = True
re.Pattern = "\d+"
s = "Spain received 100 millimeters of rain in the last 2 weeks."
MsgBox re.Replace(s, "a number")
```

The output of the last code is shown in Figure 9-16.

**Figure 9-16**

```
Dim re, s
Set re = New RegExp
re.Global = True
re.Pattern = "\d*"
s = "Spain received 100 millimeters of rain in the last 2 weeks."
MsgBox re.Replace(s, "a number")
```

The output of the preceding code is shown in Figure 9-17.

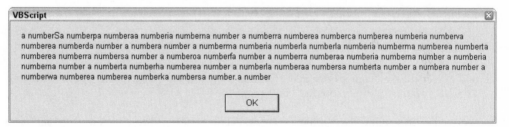

**Figure 9-17**

```
Dim re, s
Set re = New RegExp
re.Global = True
re.Pattern = "\d?"
s = "Spain received 100 millimeters of rain in the last 2 weeks."
MsgBox re.Replace(s, "a number")
```

The output of the preceding code is shown in Figure 9-18.

The last special characters we should discuss are remembered matches. These are useful when we want to use some or all of the text that matched our pattern as part of the replacement text—see the Replace method for an example of using remembered matches.

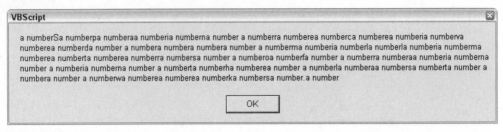

**Figure 9-18**

To illustrate this, and bring all this discussion of special characters together, let's do something more useful. We want to search an arbitrary text string and locate any URLs within it. To keep this example simple and reasonable in size, we will only be searching for the "http:" protocols, but we will be handling some of the vulgarities of DNS names, including an unlimited number of domain layers. Don't worry if you "don't speak DNS, " what you know from typing URLs into your browser will suffice.

Our code uses yet another of the `RegExp` object's methods that we'll meet in more detail in the next section. For now, we need only know that `Execute` simply performs the pattern match and returns each match via a collection. Here's the code.

```
Dim re, s
Set re = New RegExp
re.Global = True
re.Pattern = "http://(\w+[\w-]*\w+\.)*\w+"
s = "http://www.kingsley-hughes.com is a valid web address. And so is "
s = s & vbCrLf & "http://www.wrox.com. And "
s = s & vbCrLf & "http://www.pc.ibm.com - even with 4 levels."
Set colMatches = re.Execute(s)
For Each match In colMatches
    MsgBox "Found valid URL: " & match.Value
Next
```

As we'd expect, the real work is done in the line that sets the actual pattern. It looks a bit daunting at first, but it's actually quite easy to follow. Let's break it down.

Our pattern begins with the fixed string `http://`. We then use parentheses to group the real workhorse of this pattern. The following highlighted pattern will match one level of a DNS name, including a trailing dot.

```
re.Pattern = "http://(\w[\w-]*\w\.)*\w+"
```

This pattern begins with one of the special characters we looked at earlier, \w, which is used to match [a-zA-Z0-9], or in English, all the alphanumeric characters. Next we use the class brackets to match either an alphanumeric character or a dash. This is because DNS names can include dashes. Why didn't we use the same pattern before? Simple—because valid DNS names cannot begin or end with a dash. We allow zero or more characters from this expanded class by using the * repeat count.

```
re.Pattern = "http://(\w [\w-]*\w\.)*\w+"
```

After that, we again strictly want an alphanumeric character so our domain name doesn't end in a dash. The last pattern in the parentheses matches the dots (.) used to separate DNS levels.

*Note: we can't use the dot alone because that is a special character that normally matches any single character except a newline. Thus, we "escape" this character, by preceding it with a slash (\\).*

After wrapping all that in parentheses, just to keep our grouping straight, we again use the * repeat count. So the following highlighted pattern will match any valid domain name followed by a dot. To put it another way, it will match one level of a fully qualified DNS name.

```
re.Pattern = "http:// (\w[\w-]*\w\.)*\w+"
```

We end the pattern by requiring one or more alphanumeric characters for the top-level domain name (for example, the com, org, edu, and so on.).

```
re.Pattern = "http://(\w[\w-]*\w\.)*\w+"
```

# RegExp Methods

We've covered the properties of the RegExp object, so it's time to take a look at the methods. There are three methods associated with the RegExp object that we can look at.

## Execute Method

This method is used to execute a regular expression search against a specified string and returns a Matches collection. This is the trigger in the code to run the pattern matching on the string.

```
object.Execute(string)
```

| | |
|---|---|
| **object** | Always a **RegExp** object |
| **string** | The text string which is searched for—required |

The actual pattern for the regular expression search is set using the Pattern property of the RegExp object.

```
Dim re, s
Set re = New RegExp
re.Global = True
re.Pattern = "http://(\w+[\w-]*\w+\.)*\w+"
s = "http://www.kingsley-hughes.com is a valid web address. And so is "
s = s & vbCrLf & "http://www.wrox.com. And "
s = s & vbCrLf & "http://www.pc.ibm.com - even with 4 levels."
Set colMatches = re.Execute(s)
For Each match In colMatches
    MsgBox "Found valid URL: " & match.Value
Next
```

Note the difference with other languages that support regular expressions that treat the results of `Execute` as a Boolean to determine whether or not the pattern was found. As a result of this difference, you'll quite often see examples that have been converted from another language that simply don't work in VBScript!

*Note: Some of Microsoft's own documentation has been known to contain such errors, most of which though have hopefully been corrected by now.*

Remember the result of `Execute` is always a collection, possibly even an empty collection. You can use a test like `if re.Execute(s).count = 0`, or better yet use the `Test` method, which is designed for this purpose.

## Replace Method

This method is used to replace text found in a regular expression search.

```
object.Replace(string1, string2)
```

| | |
|---|---|
| **object** | Always a **RegExp** object. |
| **string1** | This is the text string in which the text replacement is to occur—required. |
| **string2** | This is the replacement text string—required. |

The `Replace` method returns a copy of `string1` with the text of `RegExp.Pattern` replaced with `string2`. If no match is found in the string, a copy of `string1` is returned unchanged.

```
Dim re, s
Set re = New RegExp
re.Pattern = "http://(\w+[\w-]*\w+\.)*\w+"
s = "http://www.kingsley-hughes.com is a valid web address. And so is "
s = s & vbCrLf & "http://www.wrox.com. And "
s = s & vbCrLf & "http://www.pc.ibm.com - even with 4 levels."
MsgBox re.Replace(s, "** TOP SECRET! **")
```

The output of the last code is shown in Figure 9-19.

**Figure 9-19**

The `Replace` method can also replace subexpressions in the pattern. In order to accomplish this we use the special characters $1, $2, and so on. in the replace text. These "parameters" refer to remembered matches.

### *Backreferencing*

A remembered match is simply part of a pattern. This is known as backreferencing. We designate which parts we want to be stored into a temporary buffer by enclosing them in parentheses. Each captured submatch is stored in the order in which it is encountered (from left to right in a regular expressions pattern). The buffer numbers where the submatches are stored begins at 1 and continues up to a maximum of 99 subexpressions. They are then referred to sequentially as $1, $2, and so on.

You can override the saving of that part of the regular expression using the noncapturing metacharacters "?:", "?=", or "?!".

In the following example we remember the first five words (consisting of one or more nonwhite space character) and then we display only four of them in the replacement text.

```
Dim re, s
Set re = New RegExp
re.Pattern = "(\S+)\s+(\S+)\s+(\S+)\s+(\S+)\s+(\S+)"
s = "VBScript is not very cool."
MsgBox re.Replace(s, "$1 $2 $4 $5")
```

The output of the preceding code is shown in Figure 9-20.

**Figure 9-20**

Notice how in the last code we have added a (\S+)\s+ pair for each word in the string. This is to give the code greater control over how the string is handled. With this we prevent the tail of the string being added to the end of the string displayed. Take great care when using backreferencing to make sure that the outputs you get are what you expect them to be to!

## Test Method

The Test method executes a regular expression search against a specified string and returns a Boolean value that indicates whether or not a pattern match was found.

```
object.Test(string)
```

| | |
|---|---|
| **object** | Always a **RegExp** object |
| **string** | The text string upon which the regular expression is executed—required |

The `Test` method returns `True` if a pattern match is found and `False` if no match is found. This is the preferred way to determine if a string contains a pattern. Note we often must make patterns case insensitive, as in the following example.

```
Dim re, s
Set re = New RegExp
re.IgnoreCase = True
re.Pattern = "http://(\w+[\w-]*\w+\.)*\w+"
s = "Some long string with http://www.wrox.com buried in it."
If re.Test(s) Then
    MsgBox "Found a URL."
Else
    MsgBox "No URL found."
End If
```

The output of the preceding code is shown in Figure 9-21.

**Figure 9-21**

# The Matches Collection

The Matches collection is a collection of regular expression `Match` objects.

A `Matches` collection contains individual `Match` objects. The only way to create this collection is using the `Execute` method of the `RegExp` object. It is important to remember that the `Matches` collection property is read-only, as are the individual `Match` objects.

When a regular expression is executed, zero or more `Match` objects result. Each `Match` object provides access to three things:

❑ The string found by the regular expression

❑ The length of the string

❑ An index to where the match was found

Remember to set the `Global` property to `True` or your `Matches` collection can never contain more than one member. This is an easy way to create a very simple but hard to trace bug!

```
Dim re, objMatch, colMatches, sMsg
Set re = New RegExp
re.Global = True
re.Pattern = "http://(\w+[\w-]*\w+\.)*\w+"
s = "http://www.kingsley-hughes.com is a valid web address. And so is "
s = s & vbCrLf & "http://www.wrox.com. As is "
s = s & vbCrLf & "http://www.wiley.com."
```

```
Set colMatches = re.Execute(s)
sMsg = ""
For Each objMatch in colMatches
    sMsg = sMsg & "Match of " & objMatch.Value
    sMsg = sMsg & ", found at position " & objMatch.FirstIndex & " of
the string."
    sMsg = sMsg & "The length matched is "
    sMsg = sMsg & objMatch.Length & "." & vbCrLf
Next
MsgBox sMsg
```

## Matches Properties

Matches is a simple collection and supports just two properties:

```
Count
Item
```

Count returns the number of items in the collection.

```
Dim re, objMatch, colMatches, sMsg
Set re = New RegExp
re.Global = True
re.Pattern = "http://(\w+[\w-]*\w+\.)*\w+"
s = "http://www.kingsley-hughes.com is a valid web address. And so is "
s = s & vbCrLf & "http://www.wrox.com. As is "
s = s & vbCrLf & "http://www.wiley.com."
Set colMatches = re.Execute(s)
MsgBox colMatches.count
```

The output of the preceding code is shown in Figure 9-22.

Figure 9-22

Item returns an item based on the specified key.

```
Dim re, objMatch, colMatches, sMsg
Set re = New RegExp
re.Global = True
re.Pattern = "http://(\w+[\w-]*\w+\.)*\w+"
s = "http://www.kingsley-hughes.com is a valid web address. And so is "
s = s & vbCrLf & "http://www.wrox.com. As is "
s = s & vbCrLf & "http://www.wiley.com."
Set colMatches = re.Execute(s)
MsgBox colMatches.item(0)
MsgBox colMatches.item(1)
MsgBox colMatches.item(2)
```

# The Match Object

Match objects are the members in a Matches collection. The only way to create a Match object is by using the Execute method of the RegExp object. When a regular expression is executed, zero or more Match objects can result.

Each Match object provides the following:

❑  Access to the string found by the regular expression

❑  The length of the string found

❑  An index to where in the string the match was found

## Match Properties

The Match object has three properties. All three properties are read-only:

❑  FirstIndex

❑  Length

❑  Value

### FirstIndex Property

The FirstIndex property returns the position in a search string where a match occurs.

```
object.FirstIndex
```

| | |
|---|---|
| **object** | **Always a Match object** |

The FirstIndex property uses a zero-based offset from the beginning of the search string. To put in plain English, the first character in the string is identified as character zero (0).

```
Dim re, objMatch, colMatches, sMsg
Set re = New RegExp
re.Global = True
re.Pattern = "http://(\w+[\w-]*\w+\.)*\w+"
s = "http://www.kingsley-hughes.com is a valid web address. And so is "
s = s & vbCrLf & "http://www.wrox.com. As is "
s = s & vbCrLf & "http://www.wiley.com."
Set colMatches = re.Execute(s)
sMsg = ""
For Each objMatch in colMatches
    sMsg = sMsg & "Match of " & objMatch.Value
    sMsg = sMsg & ", found at position " & objMatch.FirstIndex & " of the
string. "
    sMsg = sMsg & "The length matched is "
    sMsg = sMsg & objMatch.Length & "." & vbCrLf
Next
MsgBox sMsg
```

## Length Property

The Length property returns the length of a match found in a search string.

```
object.Length
```

| object | Always a **Match** object |
|---|---|

```
Dim re, objMatch, colMatches, sMsg
Set re = New RegExp
re.Global = True
re.Pattern = "http://(\w+[\w-]*\w+\.)*\w+"
s = "http://www.kingsley-hughes.com is a valid web address. And so is "
s = s & vbCrLf & "http://www.wrox.com. As is "
s = s & vbCrLf & "http://www.wiley.com."
Set colMatches = re.Execute(s)
sMsg = ""
For Each objMatch in colMatches
    sMsg = sMsg & "Match of " & objMatch.Value
    sMsg = sMsg & ", found at position " & objMatch.FirstIndex & "
of the string. "
    sMsg = sMsg & "The length matched is "
    sMsg = sMsg & objMatch.Length & "." & vbCrLf
Next
MsgBox sMsg
```

## Value Property

The Value property returns the value or text of a match found in a search string.

```
object.Value
```

| object | Always a **Match** object. |
|---|---|

```
Dim re, objMatch, colMatches, sMsg
Set re = New RegExp
re.Global = True
re.Pattern = "http://(\w+[\w-]*\w+\.)*\w+"
s = "http://www.kingsley-hughes.com is a valid web address. And so is "
s = s & vbCrLf & "http://www.wrox.com. As is "
s = s & vbCrLf & "http://www.wiley.com."
Set colMatches = re.Execute(s)
sMsg = ""
For Each objMatch in colMatches
    sMsg = sMsg & "Match of " & objMatch.Value
    sMsg = sMsg & ", found at position " & objMatch.FirstIndex & "
of the string. "
    sMsg = sMsg & "The length matched is "
    sMsg = sMsg & objMatch.Length & "." & vbCrLf
Next
MsgBox sMsg
```

# A Few Examples

We've covered a lot of theory in the past few pages. Theory is great but you might like to see regular expressions in action. Let's complete this chapter with a few examples of how you can make use of regular expressions to solve real life problems.

## Validating Phone Number Input

Validating inputs prevents bogus or dubious information being entered by a user. One piece of information that many developers need to make sure is a telephone number entered correctly. While we cannot write a script to actually check if a number is a valid phone number, we can use script and regular expressions to enforce a format on the input, which helps to eliminate false entry.

Here is a simple code sample for validating that a standard US phone number entered conforms to the format (XXX)XXX-XXXX.

```
Dim re, s, objMatch, colMatches
Set re = New RegExp
re.Pattern = "\([0-9]{3}\)[0-9]{3}-[0-9]{4}"
re.Global = True
re.IgnoreCase = True
s = InputBox("Enter your phone number in the following Format (XXX)XXX-XXXX:")
If re.Test(s) Then
    MsgBox "Thank you!"
Else
    MsgBox "Sorry but that number is not in a valid format."
End If
```

The code is simple, but again it is the pattern that does all the hard work. Depending on the input, you can get one of two possible output messages, shown in Figures 9-23 and 9-24.

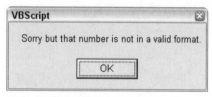

**Figure 9-23**

**Figure 9-24**

If you want to make this script applicable in countries with other formats you will have to do a little work on it, but customizing it wouldn't be difficult.

# Breaking Down URIs

Here is an example that can be used to break down a Universal Resource Indicator (URI) into its component parts. Take the following URI:

```
www.wrox.com:80/misc-pages/support.shtml
```

We can write a script that will break it down into the protocol (ftp, http, and so on), the domain address, and the page/path. To do this we can use the following pattern.

```
"(\w+):\/\/([^ /:]+)(:\d*)?([^# ]*)"
```

The following code will carry out the task.

```
Dim re, s
Set re = New RegExp
re.Pattern = "(\w+):\/\/([^ /:]+)(:\d*)?([^# ]*)"
re.Global = True
re.IgnoreCase = True
s = "http://www.wrox.com:80/misc-pages/support.shtml"
MsgBox re.Replace(s, "$1")
MsgBox re.Replace(s, "$2")
MsgBox re.Replace(s, "$3")
MsgBox re.Replace(s, "$4")
```

# Testing for HTML Elements

Testing for HTML elements is easy; all you need is the right pattern. Here is one that works for elements with both an opening and closing tag.

```
"<(.*)>.*<\/\1>"
```

How you script this depends on what you want to do. Here is a simple script just for demonstration purpose.

```
Dim re, s
Set re = New RegExp
re.IgnoreCase = True
re.Pattern = "<(.*)>.*<\/\1>"
s = "<p>This is a paragraph</p>"
If re.Test(s) Then
    MsgBox "HTML element found."
Else
    MsgBox "No HTML element found."
End If
```

# Matching White Space

Sometimes it can be really handy to be able to match white space, that is, lines that are either completely empty, or that only contain white space (spaces and tab characters). Here is the pattern you would need for that.

```
"^[ \t]*$"
```

That breaks down to the following:

^—Matches the start of the line.

[\t]*—Match zero or more space or tab (\t) characters.

$—Match the end of the line.

```
Dim re, s, colMatches, objMatch, sMsg
Set re = New RegExp
re.Global = True
re.Pattern = "^[ \t]*$"
s = " "
Set colMatches = re.Execute(s)
sMsg = ""
For Each objMatch in colMatches
    sMsg = sMsg & "Blank line found at position " & objMatch.FirstIndex
& " of the string."
Next
MsgBox sMsg
```

# Matching HTML Comment Tags

When you come to the section on Windows Script Host we'll show you how you can use VBScript and Widows Script Host to work with the file system. Once you can do this, reading and modifying files becomes within your reach. One good application of regular expressions might be to look for comment tags within an HTML file. You could then choose to remove these before making the files available on the Web.

Here is a script that can detect HTML comment tags.

```
Dim re, s
Set re = New RegExp
re.Global = True
re.Pattern = "^.*<!--.*-->.*$"
s = " <title>A Title</title> <!-- a title tag -->"
If re.Test(s) Then
    MsgBox "HTML comment tags found."
Else
    MsgBox "No HTML comment tags found."
End If
```

With a simple modification to the pattern and the use of `Replace` method, we can get the script to remove the comment tag altogether.

```
Dim re, s
Set re = New RegExp
re.Global = True
re.Pattern = "(^.*)(<!--.*-->)(.*$)"
s = " <title>A Title</title> <!-- a title tag -->"
If re.Test(s) Then
    MsgBox "HTML comment tags found."
Else
    MsgBox "No HTML comment tags found."
End If
MsgBox re.Replace(s, "$1" & "$3")
```

# Summary

In this chapter we've covered, in depth, regular expressions and how they fit into the world of VBScript. You've seen how regular expressions can be used to carry out effective, flexible pattern matching within text strings. You've also seen examples of what can be done by effectively integrating regular expressions with script together with examples of customizable find and replace within text strings as well as input validations.

Learning to use regular expressions can seem a bit daunting and even those comfortable with programming sometimes find regular expressions forbidding and choose instead less flexible solutions. However, the power and flexibility that regular expressions give to the programmer is immense and your efforts will be quickly rewarded!

# 10

# Client-Side Web Scripting

## Overview

In this chapter we are going to take VBScript straight to your Web site visitor's browser. We'll take a look at how VBScript and Internet Explorer can be combined on the client-side to create interesting and exciting HTML pages for your visitors.

Going straight for the client-side is the easiest, now-tech, no-special-server needed way to get VBScript enabled pages to the visitor. You can do it using any server, with no Active Server Pages (ASP) needed.

In this chapter you'll learn what you need to be able to deliver VBScript-enabled content straight to the browser, as well as find out how it works and what you can do with it. Let's start by exploring the tools you'll need to write client-side VBScript.

## Tools Of The Trade

Creating HTML Web pages requires nothing more than a text editor to type in your HTML code and a Web browser to view it. To check that visitors to your Web site see things the way you intend, you'll need to use the same browser or browsers as they will be using. This is easy when you are dealing with Netscape Navigator or Opera because you can have many different versions installed on the one system. Internet Explorer (IE) is a different case. Because it couples so tightly with the operating system, you can only have one version of Internet Explorer per machine.

*IE5 did have a compatibility mode that allowed you to launch IE5 acting as IE4. To use IE5's IE4 compatibility mode you did need to have IE4 installed on the machine prior to installing IE5, and choose the IE4 compatibility mode option during the IE5 setup. For more details, see Microsoft Knowledge Base article 197311. Note that IE6 has no such feature.*

To thoroughly test your Web pages you need to test using the same operating systems as your users. The same version of a browser may support different features or behave differently depending on the operating system. For example, IE4 on the Mac does not support ActiveX. Never assume that because something works on one browser or platform then it will work on them all.

It is quite possible to create all your pages using Windows Notepad. Many do and this has the advantage of being simple to use and also it's free with Windows. However, creating a whole Web site (especially if it is a large one) using just Notepad is needlessly complicated, when there are plenty of tools available specifically for Web page creation.

Most seasoned Web designers have some kind of HTML editor that they use and probably swear by. If you're planning on doing a lot of VBScripting and haven't decided on a tool to use, there are a few features that you might like to look out for. Features such as:

❑ Syntax highlighting

❑ Automatic code completion

❑ Inbuilt support for event scripting

Syntax highlighting makes the VBScript code much easier to read by color-coding-specific language keywords. Automatic code completion gives a list of available properties and methods associated with a HTML tag or an ActiveX control. Event scripting lists the events available for a particular tag or ActiveX control and will even write the code framework to handle the event.

Be careful of **WYSIWYG** HTML editors. Many WYSIWYG Web page design applications also have a tendency to rearrange your carefully crafted HTML tags and code. Because of this, many developers start off by building the skeleton of the Web site using a WYSIWYG page design tool and then switch back to Notepad or another simpler text-based editor to hand-code the scripts.

# How Browser Scripting Works

Client-side scripting gives the Web developer two separate abilities:

❑ The ability to manipulate elements within an HTML page

❑ The ability to interact with the user

It also provides the "glue" with which to bind and work with ActiveX components embedded in the page.

Client-side scripting, in the form of *JavaScript* 1.0, first emerged with the release of Netscape Navigator 2. Although very primitive and restrictive in comparison to the scripting capabilities of a modern Internet browser, it did mean that an HTML page was no longer just a static page consisting of information designed to be passively viewed by the end user, but that they were now active and able to act more like a conventional application.

Prior to Dynamic HTML (DHTML), the most important use of scripting was for the purposes of form validation. Forms have been supported since the very first browsers, back in the days when just being able to combine text and images on the same Web page was considered the pinnacle of excitement.

However, forms have always presented problems. The problem that most Web developers wish they could do something about was that there was no way to check whether the information the user had entered into a form field was actually valid—until after they had submitted it to the server. On receiving the submit form, the developer could easily check the validity of the data with a server-side component (usually a CGI program). However, it was always thought that it would be much more user-friendly and efficient to catch as many form errors as possible before getting to this stage. It would be much better if the user could be notified of any mistakes before the information was submitted to the server. Client-side scripting gives us the power to do precisely that.

Scripting in the earlier browsers also enabled a few simple special effects. The most popular amongst these were scrolling text in the status bar and image rollovers. However, once a page was loaded it was still essentially static. Some primitive responses to user interaction of the page were indeed possible, but nothing that could genuinely be called "dynamic" was possible. Any elements that were on the page were there to stay and could not be changed. Adding new elements to an existing page was also impossible.

As you will see in the next chapter, all this changed with DHTML, particularly that supported by Microsoft's Internet Explorer 4, 5, and 6.

Including script into your page simply involves using the <script> tag. In theory there is no restriction as to where you can place a script in an HTML page but normally you will place most of your scripts inside the <head> tag of an HTML page.

As a very simple example, the following script shows a message box when the page is loaded.

```
<html>
<head>
<title>A sample page</title>
<script language="VBScript">
    MsgBox "Hello World"
</script>

</head>

<body>
<h1>A page containing VBScript</h1>
</body>

</html>
```

Note that we use the language attribute to tell the browser to interpret the script as VBScript. JavaScript is the default language of Internet Explorer.

Notice something important about this script—The script is not connected to any event in the browser and as such fires as soon as the browser reaches it when parsing the page.

# Different Scripting Languages

The browser wars between Netscape and Microsoft have left us with a (sometimes confusing) array of scripting languages and standards.

The following table details which browser supports which languages.

| Browser Version | Microsoft | Netscape |
| --- | --- | --- |
| 2 | None | JavaScript 1.0 |
| 3 | JScript 1, VBScript 1 | JavaScript 1.1 |
| 4 | JScript 3, VBScript 3 | JavaScript 1.2/1.3/1.4 |
| 5 | JScript 5, VBScript 5 | None—no browser of this version |
| 6 | JScript 5, VBScript 5 | JavaScript 1.5 |
| 7 | | JavaScript 1.5 |

*This table relates to Windows Platforms only. Internet Explorer for the Macintosh does not support VBScript.*

Your choice of scripting language is ultimately limited by which browsers your pages must be compatible with. Although it is possible to include different client-side scripting languages in a page, it can quickly become confusing.

## Browser Wars—How Things Have Changed!

Things are a lot better nowadays than they were five years ago, with Internet Explorer currently commanding an enormous lead over the other browsers in terms of browser numbers in use. However, even with one browser having massive dominance over the others, it's still hard for developers to shed their browser burdens and develop for one browser alone. However, greater problems loom on the horizon for Web developers as a greater number of browsers (such as Opera and Mozilla) enter the market along with more diverse platforms (especially Linux-based platforms).

There is one group of developers that have it easier than others when it comes to deciding what standards to support—the Intranet developer. The Intranet developer is in the enviable position of being able to know pretty well what browser and scripting language others are using and can develop pages and scripts that are perfectly suited to the target browser that is used. This makes the Intranet developer's job a lot easier than that of an Internet developer.

## JavaScript, Jscript, and ECMAScript

JavaScript was first developed by Netscape and was first introduced to the development community in Netscape Navigator 2. Although named JavaScript, it in fact has no connection with the development of the Java language, although its syntax can resemble that of Java. The original name for JavaScript was *LiveScript* but this was quickly changed in order to make it sound cooler and because they wanted to reinforce the link that JavaScript could be used to control Java applets in a Web page. This did nothing to discourage the link between Java and JavaScript and it persists to this day.

Because Netscape owned the name JavaScript, when Microsoft released its version of JavaScript with IE3 it had to be called something else. Microsoft chose JScript. JScript 1 had a remarkably similar set of features to that of Netscape's JavaScript 1.0. With their next release, Microsoft jumped a version to JScript 3, which again is very similar to (although not totally compatible with) JavaScript 1.2. In keeping with the skipping of version numbers, IE5 saw the release of JScript 5, which incorporates some of the features of JavaScript 1.3. Netscape released JavaScript 1.3 and 1.4 with Netscape Communicator 4 and then skipped a browser version altogether and went straight to Netscape 6 and JavaScript 1.5.

All the subtle (and sometimes not so subtle) differences between Netscape's and Microsoft's versions of JavaScript produced no end of headaches for developers who weren't really interested in marketing hype and one-upmanship. They just wanted to get the job done and utilize the power the languages offered, while remaining as browser neutral as they were able. There's nothing more frustrating than spending time developing and designing an all-singing, all-dancing Web page, only to find that it needs to be significantly tweaked and rewritten to run on browser X, version Y, and platform Z.

To aid the developer, steps have been made toward compatibility between the various dialects of JavaScript, in the form of ECMAScript. The European Computer Manufacturers Association (ECMA) in December of 1999 released a standard for JavaScript ECMA-262, and hence ECMAScript. Microsoft's JScript 5 and Netscape's JavaScript 1.5 (along with the script engine supplied with the Opera browser) is fully compatible with ECMA-262. The Opera script engine goes further and even adds support for a number of nonstandardized JavaScript/JScript objects).

The future goes on to promise an updated and revamped ECMAScript (likely to be similar to JavaScript 1.3).

# VBScript

Given that we already have a fully featured scripting language in the form of JavaScript (in all of its forms and incarnations), why use VBScript?

Well, firstly, if you're a Visual Basic or VBA (Visual Basic for Applications, the version of Visual Basic supported with many Microsoft products, such as Microsoft Office) developer then you'll feel right at home with VBScript, which is a subset of VBA. With such similarity (and this book!), you'll quickly be ready to start creating sophisticated Web applications. JavaScript's syntax is arguably less intuitive and more obtuse than that of VBScript, and tends to be less forgiving of simple "mistakes" such as case sensitivity.

In terms of what VBScript and JavaScript can actually do, there is little to choose between the two. Almost everything that can be achieved in one language can be achieved in the other; however, sometimes clever and intuitive workarounds are necessary. Although not compliant with the ECMA standard at all (because it's a different language), Microsoft have made clear their intention that VBScript will continue to match JavaScript in terms of functionality.

There are important differences between VBScript and VBA. VBScript is an untyped language, which means that all variables are variants and don't have an explicit type (such as integer or string).

> *In fact, they do have subtypes that you can (and often need to) use. Conversion functions such as CLng, CStr, and CInt make explicit the subtype you're dealing with.*

If you are used to using VBA, one difference that you will certainly find when moving to VBScript is that error handling is a lot less powerful.

# Responding to Browser Events

Most of the client-side scripting you do will involve handling events raised by objects in the page. It could be the onLoad event of the page itself, onSubmit event of a form, the onClick event of an image, or an event raised by an ActiveX control that you have embedded in your page. The reference section of the book includes a listing of objects and the events they support.

## Adding an Event Handler

The easiest way to add an event handler in Internet Explorer is to define a Sub or Function to handle it inside a <script> block. The name for the Sub or Function must be of the form elementName_eventname. Also note in the following example the use of the VBScript Me object, which references the object (for example, an HTML tag or ActiveX control) that caused the event to fire.

```
<html>
<head>
<title>A sample page</title>
<script language="VBScript">
    Sub cmdFireEvent_onclick
        MsgBox Me.Name & " made me pop this message up!"
    End Sub
</script>

</head>

<body>
<input type="button" name="cmdFireEvent" value="Trigger">
</body>

</html>
```

Clicking on the button generates the message box displayed in Figure 10-1.

An alternative way of doing the same thing is to use the for and event properties of the <script> tag. All the code inside the <script> tags will execute when the event fires.

```
<html>
<head>
<title>A sample page</title>
<script for="cmdFireEvent" event="onclick"
language="VBScript">
    MsgBox Me.Name & " made me pop this message up!"
</script>

</head>

<body>
<input type="button" name="cmdFireEvent" value="Trigger">
</body>

</html>
```

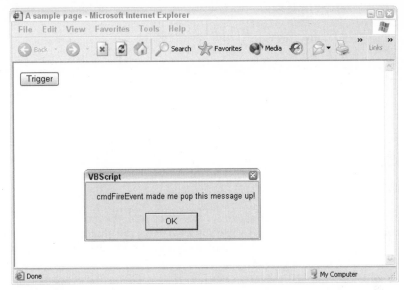

Figure 10-1

Different code, but as Figure 10-2 shows, the result is the same.

Figure 10-2

## Adding an Event Handler That Passes Parameters

If you want to pass parameters to your event handling subroutine, then you must define a `Sub` or `Function` and call that in your element's `onEvent` embedded inside the tag. You must not name your subroutine `elementName_EventName` or the browser will get confused with the first way we saw above of defining the event.

Because we are calling a separate subroutine (and not directly defining an event handler), the `Me` object if used inside our subroutine won't point to the element that caused the event to fire. It will, however, behave "correctly" in the procedure that calls the function; so from here we can pass `Me` to our `Sub` as one of its parameters.

*Take note that in IE3 there is no other way to discover which element was used to fire a particular subroutine within the script.*

```
<html>
<head>
<title>A sample page</title>
```

```
<script language="VBScript">
Sub DoSomething(theElement,theNumber)
    MsgBox theElement.Name & " made me fire"
    MsgBox "Today's number is the number " & theNumber
End Sub
</script>

</head>

<body>
<input type="button" name="cmdFireEvent" Value="Trigger" onClick="DoSomething
Me,99">
</body>

</html>
```

Here, our subroutine is called DoSomething, and it's called from the onclick event of our input
button with our two parameters. Me works fine in the event handler, but note however that if we were to
try to refer directly to Me in the DoSomething procedure, it would have no meaning since the
DoSomething procedure is a standalone Sub.

Figures 10-3 and 10-4 show the message boxes generated by this code.

**Figure 10-3**

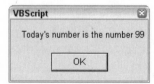

**Figure 10-4**

# Cancelling Events

Some events, such as those associated with link tags and forms, can be cancelled. If, for example, the user has entered an invalid value in a form, then we don't want the form to submit because we know that it will fail to process at the server-side if it contains bogus information. Instead, we want to stop the event in its tracks and notify the user.

To do this we normally need to return a value of `False` to cancel the action. As only functions (not subroutines) can have return values, we need to define our event handler code as a function.

```
<html>
<head>
<title>A sample page containing a form</title>
<script language="VBScript">
Function form1_onsubmit()
   ' Has the user entered something?
    If form1.txtNumber.value = "" Then
        MsgBox "You must enter a value!"
        form1_onsubmit = false
   ' Is it a valid number?
    ElseIf Not IsNumeric(form1.txtNumber.value) Then
        MsgBox "You must enter a number!"
        form1_onsubmit = false
   ' Is the value in the correct range?
    ElseIf form1.txtNumber.value > 10 Or _
        form1.txtNumber.value < 1 Then
        MsgBox "Invalid number!"
        form1_onsubmit = false
    Else
    'Form submit can continue
        MsgBox "Valid Number. Thank you!"
    End If
End Function
</script>

</head>

<body>
    <form action="" method="POST" id="form1" name="form1">
    Enter a number from 1 to 10
        <input type="text" id="txtNumber" name="txtNumber">
    <br>
        <input type="submit" value="Submit" id="submit1" name="submit1">
    </form>
</body>

</html>
```

Depending on the input, the script generates the appropriate message. The user can enter nothing, a number outside of the appropriate range or a number in the right range and the appropriate message is displayed accordingly. These are shown in Figures 10-5, 10-6, and 10-7 respectively.

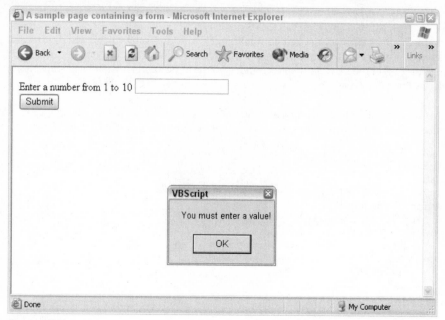

Figure 10-5

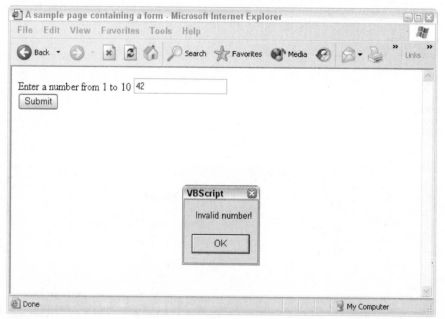

Figure 10-6

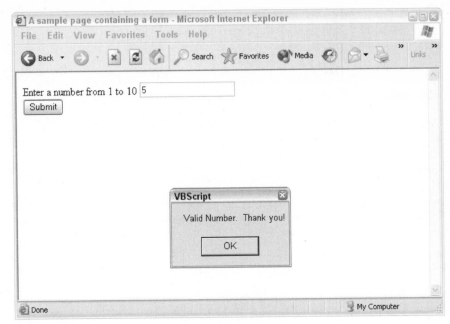

Figure 10-7

## The Order of Things

With most events in a script it's quite obvious when they will fire. You click a button, and the `onclick` event fires. However, there are some events that don't fire as a direct response to user interaction. The `window_onload` event is a good example of this. Any script in your page outside of a subprocedure or function will fire as the page is parsed by the browser. But which comes first, the `window_onload` or the parsed code? Also if you have a frameset and frames, what will be the order the `window_onloads` fire?

Let's take a look at a simple example. You'll need to create three HTML pages: a page containing the frameset tags and a page for each of the frames.

First we have the frameset page, which we'll call `EventOrder.htm`.

```
<html>
<head>
<title>A sample page containing script</title>
<script language="VBScript">
Dim sEventTracker
Dim iEventOrder
iEventOrder = 0

window.Parent.iEventOrder = window.Parent.iEventOrder + 1
window.Parent.sEventTracker = window.Parent.sEventTracker _
  & window.Parent.iEventOrder _
  & " Frameset - First code in Page" & Chr(13) & Chr(10)
Sub window_onload
```

```
    iEventOrder = iEventOrder + 1
    sEventTracker = sEventTracker & iEventOrder _
       & " Frameset window_onload" & Chr(13) & Chr(10)
End Sub
</script>

</head>

<frameset rows="50%,*">
    <frame src="top.htm" id="fraTop" name="fraTop">
    <frame src="bottom.htm" id="fraBottom" name="fraBottom">
        <noframes>
            <body>
            <p>This page uses frames, but your browser doesn't
               support them.</p>
            </body>
        </noframes>
</frameset>

</html>
```

Next we create the top frame page. Save this page as `top.htm`.

```
<html>
<head>
<title>A sample page containing script</title>
<script language="VBScript">
window.Parent.iEventOrder = window.Parent.iEventOrder + 1
window.Parent.sEventTracker = window.Parent.sEventTracker _
  & window.Parent.iEventOrder _
  & " Top frame - First code in Page" & Chr(13) & Chr(10)

Sub cmdCheckForm_onclick
    window.Parent.iEventOrder = window.Parent.iEventOrder + 1
    window.Parent.sEventTracker = window.Parent.sEventTracker _
    & window.Parent.iEventOrder _
    & " Top frame - cmdCheckForm_onclick" & Chr(13) & Chr(10)
    form1.txtEvents.Value = window.Parent.sEventTracker
End Sub

Sub window_onload
    window.Parent.iEventOrder = window.Parent.iEventOrder + 1
    window.Parent.sEventTracker = window.Parent.sEventTracker _
    & window.Parent.iEventOrder _
    & " Top frame - window_onload" & Chr(13) & Chr(10)
End Sub
</script>

</head>

<body>
<form action="some_form_handler.asp" method="post" id="form1" name="form1">
<textarea cols="60" name="txtEvents" rows="10"></textarea>
```

```
<input type="button" value="List Events" name="cmdCheckForm">
</form>

<script language="VBScript">
window.Parent.iEventOrder = window.Parent.iEventOrder + 1
window.Parent.sEventTracker = window.Parent.sEventTracker _
  & window.Parent.iEventOrder _
  & " Top frame - Second code in Page" & Chr(13) & Chr(10)
</script>
</body>

<html>
```

Finally, create the page for the bottom frame. Save this as `bottom.htm`.

```
<html>
<head>
<title>A sample page containg script</title>
<script language="VBScript">
window.Parent.iEventOrder = window.Parent.iEventOrder + 1
window.Parent.sEventTracker = window.Parent.sEventTracker _
  & window.Parent.iEventOrder _
  & " bottom frame - First code in Page" & Chr(13) & Chr(10)

Sub window_onload
   window.Parent.iEventOrder = window.Parent.iEventOrder + 1
   window.parent.sEventTracker = window.Parent.sEventTracker _
     & window.Parent.iEventOrder _
     & " bottom frame - window_onload" & Chr(13) & Chr(10)
End Sub
</script>

</head>

<body>
</body>
</html>
```

If you load the page containing the frameset, then click the list events button, the text area will be filled with details of the `window_onload` events and embedded scripts, listed in the order they fired. This is shown in Figure 10-8.

It's perhaps worth noting that the differences between browsers include not just the events each HTML tag has but the order they fire in. For example, if you run this code in IE3 you'll find the order in which events fire is different from that of IE5 and IE6. Although the events we've used in our examples are the same for IE4, IE5, and IE6, you will find other differences between them.

# Form Validation

The most common way on the Web to obtain information from the user is to use an HTML form populated with a variety of form elements (in case you're wondering, e-mail is another option). Using script, the HTML form can be manipulated and examined using its form object. An HTML page

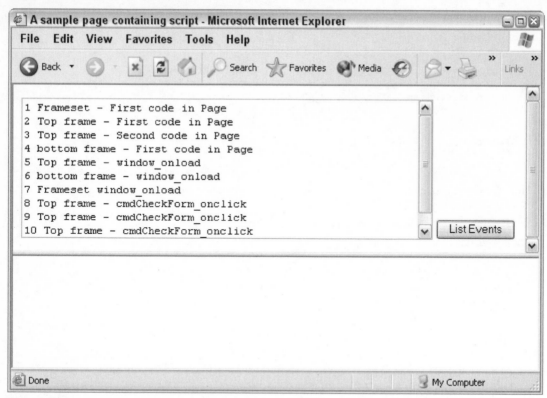

**Figure 10-8**

can have one or more forms that we can reference either by name or using the document object's forms array. In most cases it's easier just to refer to a form by name.

> *To insert an HTML form into a page the `<form>` tag is used along with the corresponding `</form>` close tag.*

The most important properties of the `<form>` tag are `Action` and `Method`. The `Action` property is the URL where the form will post to, for example an ASP page or a CGI script.

The `Method` property can be either `post` or `get`, and determines how the form's data is transmitted to the server when the form is submitted. If the `Method` property is set to `get`, then the data in the form's elements will be appended to the URL that was specified in the `Action` property. A form `Method` of `post` sends the form's data as a data stream to the server along with the `http` header.

Normally it is the form `post` method that is used most often. HTML 4.0 standard even deprecated the `get` method, although this doesn't stop it being used. The reason for this is because `get` places a character limit on how much data can be sent and is actually visible in the URL for your users to see, something which you may not want.

Having defined our form tags, we can then populate the form with the HTML controls (commonly referred to as *elements*) available. The most common controls are:

❑   Input boxes
❑   Radio buttons
❑   Select controls

The next thing we need to worry about is how we make sure what the user submits is valid data.

# Validating Numerical Input Box Values

The most common criteria for validation of an input box that's being used for the entry of numerical data are:

❑   That the field has been completed
❑   That it contains a numeric value
❑   That the numeric value is within an acceptable range
❑   That it is an integer

We saw a simple example of this earlier on when we looked at cancelling events. The following example describes another approach. If the value entered by the user into form1's element text1 is an integer between 1 and 10, then a message box tells us that it's valid. At this point (in real life at least, but not as far as the example is concerned) you would actually submit the form rather than inform the user using a message box the way we do here. The line "form1.submit" (which is currently commented out) in the following code will do this, although to use the code as supplied here you'll need to create the page some_form_handler.asp for yourself or provide an alternative way to process the form.

If the user has entered invalid data then the ValidInteger function returns a message describing the problem.

```
<html>
<head>
<title>A sample page containg script</title>
<script language="VBScript">
Function ValidInteger(sNumber, iMin, iMax)
    Dim iNumber
    ' Is it a number?
    If IsNumeric(sNumber) Then

        ' Is it an integer?
        If InStr(sNumber,".") = 0 Then

            ' Is it in the correct range?
            If CLng(sNumber) >= iMin And CLng(sNumber) <= iMax Then
            ValidInteger = ""
            Else
            ValidInteger = "You must enter an integer between " _
            & iMin & " and " & iMax
```

```
            End If
        Else
            ValidInteger = "You must enter a whole number"
        End If

        Else
            ValidInteger = "You must enter a number"
        End If
End Function


Sub cmdCheckForm_onclick
    Dim sValidity
    sValidity = ValidInteger(form1.text1.value,1,10)
    If sValidity = "" Then
        MsgBox "Valid"
        'form1.submit
    Else
        MsgBox sValidity
    End If

End Sub
</script>

</head>

<body>
<form action="some_form_handler.asp" method="post" id="form1" name="form1">
    <input id="text1" name="text1">
    <input type="button" value="Button" id="cmdCheckForm" name="cmdCheckForm">
</form>
</body>

</html>
```

The outputs generated by the script contained in this form are again reliant upon the input that the user gives it via the input box. Again, this example isn't very sophisticated but does serve as a starting point for more complex and relevant form validation scripts.

## Validating Radio Buttons

The only check for validity you can make with a radio button group is that one element has been selected by the user. You can define one of the elements to be checked by default, simply by putting checked inside one of the radio buttons' tags.

*In case you are not familiar with HTML, to define a group of radio buttons we simply create a number of radio buttons and give them the same name.*

Some things are too important to be left to defaults, though. Take the example of a radio group for selecting a credit card type. By not using a default, you know that the user has made a positive choice in setting their credit card type. Otherwise there is a danger that they could have missed the question, and we would end up with invalid information.

```
<html>
<head>
<title>A sample page containg script</title>
<script language="VBScript">
Function RadioGroupValid(radGroup)
    Dim iElement
    RadioGroupValid = False
    ' Loop through the radio buttons in the group
    For iElement = 0 To radGroup.Length - 1
        ' If one is checked then we have validity
        If radGroup(iElement).Checked = True _
            Then RadioGroupValid = True
    Next
End Function

Sub cmdCheckForm_onclick
    Dim sValidity
    If RadioGroupValid(form1.radCreditCard) Then
        MsgBox "You made a selection. Thank you!"
        'form1.submit
    Else
        MsgBox "You forgot to make a selection. Try again."
    End If
End Sub
</script>

</head>

<body>
<form action="some_form_handler.asp" method="post" id="form1" name="form1">
  Visa
  <input type="radio" id="radCreditCard" name="radCreditCard" value="Visa">
  <br>
  Master Card
  <input type="radio" id="radCreditCard" name="radCreditCard"
value="MasterCard">
  <br>
  American Express
  <input type="radio" id="radCreditCard" name="radCreditCard"
value="AmericanExpress">
  <br>
  Other
  <input type="radio" id="radCreditCard" name="radCreditCard" value="Other">
  <br>
  <input type="button" value="Test" id="cmdCheckForm" name="cmdCheckForm">
</form>
</body>

</html>
```

The code in the page loops through each of the radio buttons in the group and checks to see if one is selected. We could also find out how many elements there are in a group using the length property.

When the form is actually posted, the value sent will only be the value of the selected radio button. So if radio button 3 is selected then `radio1=AmericanExpress` will be submitted to the server and nothing else.

## Validating Select Controls and Dates

An HTML `select` element can be used in the same way as a Visual Basic combo box or a list box, depending on its `size` property. If the `size` property is set to 1 then it acts just like a drop-down combo box, but if its size is set to more than 1 then it becomes a list box.

One common use of the `select` element is to allow the user to enter a date. It has enormous advantages over using a text box for dates, the main one being its clarity and ease of use for the user. Take the difference between American and British date formatting. Each country has a different format and this has enormous scope for causing problems (in Britain 11/07/2003 is interpreted as the 11th day of July 2003; in America this is November 7th of 2003). Using `select` controls you can unambiguously pass the date that you mean without trusting the user to get it the right way around.

In the following example we validate the date defined by the user selecting from select boxes. We need to ensure that they don't select an invalid date, such as the 31st April or the 29th of February in a nonleap year.

```
<html>
<head>
<title>A sample page containing script</title>
<script language="VBScript">
Function CheckDate(sDay, sMonth, sYear)
    On Error Resume Next
    Dim Date1
    ' If invalid date an error will be raised
    Date1 = CDate(sDay & "/" & sMonth & "/" & sYear)
    ' If error number not 0 then invalid date
    If Err.number <> 0 Then
        Err.Clear
        ' Calc days in month by going to next month then
        ' subtract 1 day
        Date1 = DateAdd("m",1,sMonth & "/" & sYear)
        Date1 = DateAdd("d",-1,Date1)
        CheckDate = "There are only " & Day(Date1) _
        & " days in " & sMonth
    Else
        CheckDate = ""
    End If
End Function

Sub cmdCheckForm_onclick
    sDateValidityMessage = CheckDate(form1.cboDay.Value, _
        form1.cboMonth.Value, form1.cboYear.Value)
    If sDateValidityMessage <> "" Then
        MsgBox sDateValidityMessage
    Else
```

```
            MsgBox "That date is valid"
            'form1.submit
        End If
End Sub
</script>

</head>

<body>
<form action="some_form_handler.asp" method="post" id="form1" name="form1">
<select id="cboDay" name="cboDay" size="1">
<option value="1">1
<option value="2">2
<option value="3">3
<option value="4">4
<option value="5">5
<option value="6">6
<option value="7">7
<option value="8">8
<option value="9">9
<option value="10">10
<option value="11">11
<option value="12">12
<option value="13">13
<option value="14">14
<option value="15">15
<option value="16">16
<option value="17">17
<option value="18">18
<option value="19">29
<option value="20">20
<option value="21">21
<option value="22">22
<option value="23">23
<option value="24">24
<option value="25">25
<option value="26">26
<option value="27">27
<option value="28">28
<option value="29">29
<option value="30">30
<option value="31">31
</select>

<select id="cboMonth" name="cboMonth" size=1>
<option value="Jan">Jan
<option value="Feb">Feb
<option value="Mar">Mar
<option value="Apr">Apr
<option value="May">May
<option value="Jun">Jun
<option value="Jul">Jul
<option value="Aug">Aug
```

```
<option value="Sep">Sep
<option value="Oct">Oct
<option value="Nov">Nov
<option value="Dec">Dec
</select>

<select id="cboYear" name="cboYear" size=1>
<option value="2003">2003
<option value="2004">2004
<option value="2005">2005
<option value="2006">2006
<option value="2007">2007
<option value="2008">2008
</select>

<br>


<input type="button" value="Test" id="cmdCheckForm" name="cmdCheckForm">
</form>
</body>

</html>
```

Figure 10-9 shows the result on choosing a valid date, while Figure 10-10 shows the response to selecting an invalid date.

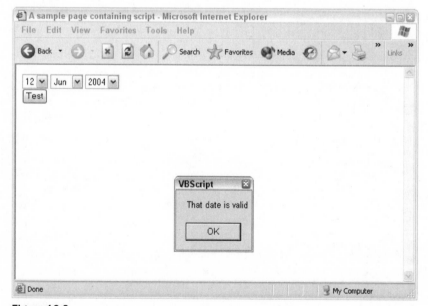

**Figure 10-9**

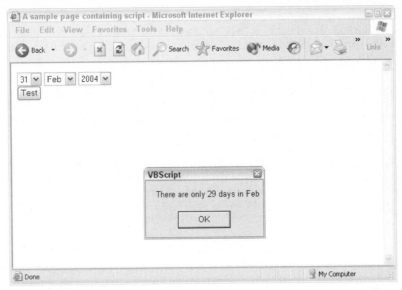

Figure 10-10

# The Document Object Model

VBScript cannot exist within a vacuum. It is a tool with which to leverage and manipulate the environment of its current context or host, whether that be Windows Script Host and the Windows system, Active Server Pages and Internet Information Server, or a Web page and the browser. But what are we actually manipulating? The answer is that we are manipulating the Document Object Model.

The *Document Object Model (DOM)* is an all-encompassing term for the programmatic interface to the hierarchy of objects available within a browser and the Web page it displays. It maps out each object's associated properties, methods, and events. Objects include the browser itself, a frame's window, the document or Web page within that frame, and the HTML, XHTML, and XML tags within the page, as well as any plug-ins or embedded ActiveX controls. The DOM also includes a number of collections of objects, such as the forms collection we have already seen in use.

Every browser version has its own DOM, and they vary considerably between Microsoft's Internet Explorer and Netscape's Navigator. There is also considerable variation between different versions of the same browser.

In an effort to bring about a common standard for the DOM, the *W3C* (the body that deals with Web standards) has released a number of standards for defining the DOM. The W3C's DOM (Level 0) approximated to the level supported by version 3 browsers.

Level 1 DOM specifications, released in October 1998, struck a balance between IE4's DOM and that of Netscape 4's, though IE4's was much closer to the specification. The changes from the Level 0 DOM to Level 1, particularly those supported by IE4, were quite dramatic. The Level 1 specification makes every element within a page a programmable object and exposes its attributes as properties. Microsoft's DOM in IE4 went even further, allowing pages to be updated even after they have been loaded. This puts the "Dynamic" in Dynamic HTML. Prior to this (with the exception of images), once the page was loaded into a browser no further changes were possible.

Level 2 was completed in November 2000. It extended on Level 1 with support for XML 1.0 with namespaces, adding support for Cascading Style Sheets (CSS), events such as user-interface events and tree manipulation events, and enhancing tree manipulation methods (tree ranges and traversal mechanisms). The DOM Level 2 HTML became a W3C Recommendation in January 2003.

The new DOM supported by IE5 and IE6 is a significantly evolutionary move on from that supported by IE4. Under IE4 almost all tags were programmable while under IE5 and IE6 all of the tags are individually programmable. Also, new methods introduced in IE5's DOM make dynamically manipulating the page easier in later versions of Internet Explorer than it was under IE4.

DOM Level 3 is currently under development. Level 3 will extend Level 2 by finishing support for XML 1.0 with namespaces, aligning the DOM Core with the XML Infoset, adding support for XML Base, and extending the user-interface events (keyboard). The Level 3 will also add support for validation, the ability to load, and save a document, will explore further mixed markup vocabularies and their implications on the DOM API ("Embedded DOM"), and will support XPath.

You can find the latest information on DOM specification developments on the W3C's Web site at `http://www.w3.org/DOM/`.

# The DOM in Action

DOM specifications are all well and good, but as programmers it's the practical implementation we're interested in. Before leaving this chapter it's worth taking a look at the DOM as implemented by IE6.

## The Window Object

Right at the top of the HTML, DOM hierarchy is the window object. If your page has no frames then there is just one window object. If the page contains frames then each frame has its own window object.

Each window object within a frameset has a parent window object, which is the window object of the page defining the frames. You can access any of the other window objects from script inside a page by using the window object's parent property. After you have a reference to the parent window object you can use that to access not only the window object's properties and methods, but also those of any HTML tags inside that window. You can also use it to access any global VBScript variables or functions.

Let's take a look at a simple frameset example. We will create three pages:

❑    The first defines a frameset

❑    The second is the left window's page

❑    The third is the right window's page

The first page we will call `TopFrame.htm`.

```
<html>
<head>
<title>A sample page containg script</title>
<script language="VBScript">
Dim sName
sName = "Top Frame"

Sub SayWhoIsThis()
    MsgBox "This is the top frame's subprocedure " _
    & "window.SayWhoIsThis"
End Sub
</script>

</head>

<frameset cols="50%,*">
  <frame src="LFrame.htm" name="LFrame">
  <frame src="RFrame.htm" name="RFrame">
</frameset>

</html>
```

The second page we will call Lframe.htm.

```
<html>
<head>
<script language="VBSCRIPT">
Dim sName
sName = "Left Frame"

Sub SayWhoIsThis()
    MsgBox "This is LFrame's subroutine window.SayWhoIsThis"
End Sub
</script>
<title>Left Frame</title>
</head>
  <body>
<H1>Left Frame</H1>
</body>
</html>
```

The third page we will call Rframe.htm.

```
<html>
<head>
<script language="VBSCRIPT">
Dim sName
sName = "Right Frame"

Sub SayWhoIsThis()
    MsgBox "This is RFrame's subroutine window.SayWhoIsThis"
End Sub
```

```
Sub button1_onclick
    MsgBox "window.sName = " & window.sName
    window.SayWhoIsThis
End Sub

Sub button2_onclick
    MsgBox "window.Parent.sName = " & window.parent.sName
    window.Parent.SayWhoIsThis
End Sub

Sub button3_onclick
    MsgBox "window.parent.LFrame.sName = " & window.Parent.LFrame.sName
    window.Parent.LFrame.SayWhoIsThis
End Sub

Sub button4_onclick
    MsgBox "window.Parent.LFrame.sName = " & window.Parent.frames(0).sName
   window.Parent.frames(0).SayWhoIsThis
End Sub
</script>
<title>Right Frame</title>
</head>

<body>
<h1>Right Frame</h1>
<input type="button" value="window" name="button1">
<input type="button" value="window.Parent" name="button2">
<input type="button" value="window.Parent.LFrame" name="button3">
<input type="button" value="window.Parent.frames(0)" name="button4">
</body>
</html>
```

If you load Topframe.htm into your browser you can try out the buttons in the right frame. These demonstrate accessing script in the window object of the right frame, its parent's window, and the left frame.

In the first button's onclick we are accessing the window of the current frame, so we normally don't need to explicitly say it is the window object we are referring to as this is implied. In other words, sName is the same as window.sName. Bear in mind that there are some contexts you will need to explicitly state if it's the window object you are referring to.

When the second button is clicked, the top frame page (that is, the right window's parent object), is referenced. This is very handy for defining global variables and functions when you have a multiframe page.

For the third button we access the sName and SayWhoIsThis function contained in the left frame. When the button is clicked we do this by referencing the frame called Lframe contained by the right window's parent window object. As you can see, navigating the DOM can get a little complex at times and vigilance and care is needed to prevent mistakes.

The fourth button does exactly the same as the third but in a different way to demonstrate another of the DOM's important features: collections.

## Collections

The `window` object has not only properties, methods, and events, but like many other objects in the DOM it also has collections. We know from the earlier example that a `window` object can have many child `window` objects, but where are these contained? The answer is in the frames collection. The frames collection is a zero-based array containing references to the frames defined by that window. So in `button4`'s code, you see that the left frame is `window.parent.frames(0)`, which is exactly the same as `window.parent.Lframe`.

Progressing along the DOM down the hierarchy, we come to the `document` object. Each `window` object will contain a `document` object. This can be referenced using the `window` object's `document` property. The `document` object acts as a container for all the `document` objects, such as HTML tags and ActiveX controls, inside your page. Just like the window object, the `document` object has a large number of collections associated with it.

Time to look at an example.

Here we create a simple page consisting of a paragraph and a table. Using script, we access collections and properties in the DOM by using the `document.all` collection to set references to various document objects in the page. An alternative would be to give all the tags names instead, but you'll find this isn't always possible. There will be times when you are unable know the name of a tag and need to access it using collections such as the `all` collection.

```
<html>
<head>
<title>A sample page containg script</title>
<script language="VBScript">
Sub button1_onclick
  Dim theWindow
  Dim theDocument
  Dim thePara
  Dim theTable
  Dim theRow
  Dim theCell

  Set theWindow = window

  Set theDocument = theWindow.document
  MsgBox theDocument.title

  Set thePara = theDocument.all(5)
  MsgBox thepara.innerText


  Set theTable = theDocument.all(6)
  MsgBox theTable.tagName

  Set theRow = theTable.rows(1)
  MsgBox theRow.name

  Set theCell = theRow.all(1)
  MsgBox theCell.innertext
```

```
      End Sub
      </script>

      </head>

      <body>
        <p>A boring paragraph</p>
        <table border="1" "name"="table1">
          <tr>
            <td>Cell 1</td>
            <td>Cell 2</td>
          </tr>
          <tr name="second_row_in_table1">
            <td>Cell 3</td>
            <td>Cell 4</td>
          </tr>
        </table>
      <input type="button" value="document.all" name="button1">
      </body>

      </html>
```

First, we dimension some variables, which we will set to reference document objects. You're probably thinking that we could reference the objects directly, but creating variables instead will make your code easier to read if you are accessing the property numerous times. Creating the reference to the window and document object is unnecessary for this example, but we've done it to emphasize what it is we are referencing in the DOM.

We set the variable theWindow to reference the window object for our page. Then we use object's document property to set a reference to the document for that page and to display the page's title.

We set the variable thePara to reference our paragraph contained in the document object. Why document.all(5) and not document.all(0)? Well, the all collection of an object references all objects contained by that object. The document includes the html tag, head tags, the script tags, the body tags, and so on. The collection starts at zero and as our paragraph is the sixth tag in the page it is document.all(5).

We then use the message box to show the innerText property of the paragraph object.

Next, we set theTable to reference the table in the page. It's the next tag after the paragraph, so it corresponds to document.all(6). We show a message box with the table's tagName property. The tagName is simply the tag definition, so for <table> it's TABLE, for a <p> it's P, and so on. See Figure 10-11 to see an example of the output.

Next we set theRow to reference the second row in the table. We do this using the rows collection of the table object.

Finally we obtain a reference to the second cell in the row by using the all collection of the row object. We might have used the cells collection, but this example demonstrates that it's not just documents that have the all collection. In fact, all objects have it if they contain other objects.

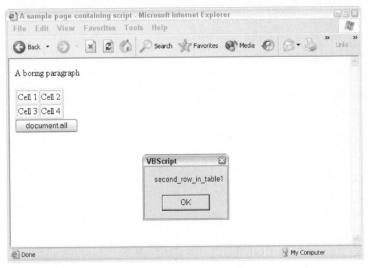

**Figure 10-11**

Hopefully, the examples in this section have demonstrated how to access objects in the DOM, and also shown that the DOM is a hierarchical collection of objects, with each object in the hierarchy being both an object inside another object and also a container for other objects.

# Summary

In this chapter we have taken a brief look at what client-side scripting can be put to work on. We have seen how to connect events raised by HTML objects to VBScript code. We've also noted relationship between VBScript and JavaScript. In reality neither language is better than the other; it's really determined by what browsers your pages must support and what your previous programming background consists of. VBScript makes an excellent choice for Visual Basic and Microsoft Office VBA programmers who are writing for Internet Explorer.

Validating forms client-side using VBScript was also demonstrated with a variety of common controls and types of data. Finally, we took a tour of the Document Object Model and the various standards associated with it, including those laid out by the W3C and implemented by Microsoft and Netscape.

In the next chapter you'll be shown lots of exciting techniques using the latest technologies available with IE5 and IE6.

# Super-Charged Client-Side Scripting

## Overview

In this chapter, we'll continue looking at client-side scripting, but we'll be looking at more advanced technologies that give much needed functionality and extensibility to client-side pages. This includes:

❑   Scriptlets

❑   Behaviors

❑   HTML components

Each of these are subjects broad and deep enough to be books of their own, so what we are going to be doing here is focusing on small, well-tested examples that cover the major techniques required for you to be able to begin making use of these technologies. In reality, to achieve maximum gain from these technologies you'd have to read masses of documentation—a lot of which is very poorly written. We'll show you here what is possible and how to go about doing it. We'll have achieved what we set out to do if, by the time you have finished this chapter, you are able to make any sense of the official documentation!

Microsoft's documentation is available as a free download at www.microsoft.com/scripting.

## Requirements

Even though these are advanced applications and tools, the main thing you still need is a good text editor to manage these technologies. The following table lists the applications you need to make use of the technologies.

| Technology | Requirements |
|---|---|
| Scriptlets | Internet Explorer 4 or later |
| Behaviors | Internet Explorer 5 or later |
| HTML Components | Internet Explorer 5 or later |

# Browser Security

The Internet Explorer browser is a security-*aware application*. Every component contained within the browser (flaws and bugs aside) is subject to the security settings defined for it. For detailed information about the security settings of your browser, refer to the documentation and help files.

Typically, the *zone* containing the components-server should be `Medium` (`Medium-Low` in IE5 and IE6) or `Low`. If the security level is more restrictive the components will not download on the client computer.

It is especially important to verify security settings when distributing an application that uses components. This is why these technologies are better suited for distribution in a corporate network setting than over the Internet to everyone. Asking a visitor to your site to change security settings in order to utilize something is, in today's security climate, absurd. For one thing, the security settings will be global. Secondly, how can they trust you?

# Scriptlets—Ancestors of Behaviors

Introduced in IE4, the scriptlet mechanism was the first browser technology to permit the design of components using DHTML. While developing a Web or an intranet project, you usually produce a lot of HTML and scripting functionalities. Without a technology to implement components, you're limited to reusing your code by cutting it from a source file and pasting it into another file (or you can include external scripting files using the `src` attribute of the `<script>` tag: a useful facility, not a component-based technology). Also, cutting and pasting code usually requires lot of adaptations to make the code work in the new context and there is enormous scope for things to go wrong and for errors to be introduced. On the other hand the usage of a component is straightforward. You include it in your context using its public interface made of properties, methods, and events—the usual stuff expected by an object-oriented programmer.

# What is a Scriptlet?

A *scriptlet* is a component developed using DHTML. What this actually means is that a scriptlet is an HTML file with a few extensions to allow the definition of properties, methods and events that permit its use as a component.

## The Hello World Scriptlet

To quickly show what a scriptlet is, we'll introduce the classic application "Hello, World!". The application's task is just to output the "Hello, World!" message using the technology under examination. To implement "Hello, World!" two files are required:

❑ The component file: `HELLOW.HTM`

❑ The client file: `CLIENT_HELLOW.HTM`

The following code shows the content of the CLIENT_HELLOW.HTM file.

```
<html>
<head>
<script language="VBScript">

Sub Hello()
    Document.All.myScriptlet.Hello
End Sub

</script>
</head>

<body onload="Hello()">

<OBJECT ID="myScriptlet"
    TYPE="text/x-scriptlet"
    DATA="hellow.htm"
    HEIGHT="0" WIDTH="0">
</OBJECT>

</body>
</html>
```

The scriptlet is identified by the name myScriptlet. This name has been used as the ID of an <OBJECT> tag included in the HTML file. The details of this tag are as follows:

```
<OBJECT ID="myScriptlet"
    TYPE="text/x-scriptlet"
    DATA="hellow.htm"
    HEIGHT="0" WIDTH="0">
</OBJECT>
```

*Note the HEIGHT and WIDTH parameters of the <OBJECT> tag have been set to zero. This is done so as to make the object invisible. There are cases where it might make sense to the object visible (say if the scriptlet contains visible objects as well) but that is not the case here.*

The following line calls the scriptlet code.

```
Document.All.myScriptlet.Hello
```

This line will require a scriptlet that exposes a Hello method. This very simple scriptlet is stored in the HELLOW.HTM file.

```
<script language="VBScript">

Sub public_Hello()
    MsgBox "Hello World!"
End Sub

</script>
```

So, what does our scriptlet comprise? It is an HTML file encapsulating the scripting code inside a `<script>` tag, which, in our case, contains just one VBScript function defined as `public_Hello`.

There are several points for you to take note of from this example:

❑ The `<OBJECT>` tag lets us insert a scriptlet into an HTML document using a special object type defined as `"text/x-scriptlet"`.

❑ The scriptlet code itself is contained in a separate HTML file specified in the `DATA` attribute of the `<OBJECT>` tag.

❑ The scriptlet is accessed for scripting through the `ID` specified for the `<OBJECT>` tag.

To run the scriptlet we simply run the client file (the file that contains the `<OBJECT>` tag. Figure 11-1 shows the scriptlet in action!

**Figure 11-1**

# The Prefix "public_" Exposes Scriptlet Members

VBScript offers a very simple way to define which code is exposed by the scriptlet to the container: a simple to follow naming convention.

❑ The procedures and functions become public methods of the scriptlet if their names are prefixed with `public_`.

❑ The global variables in the code become properties of the scriptlet if their names are prefixed with `public_` as well.

*It is important for you to note (especially if you have used JScript) that JScript offers a further mechanism called "Public Description Object" to define the public interface of a scriptlet. JScript is outside the scope of this book and, anyway, we don't need it to implement scriptlets.*

Further naming conventions:

| Prefix | Used to Expose |
|---|---|
| `public_` | Variables as read/write properties and procedures or functions as methods |
| `public_get_` | Functions as readable properties |
| `public_put_` | Functions as writable properties |

When a scriptlet member is exposed, its name in the host application does not have the prefix. Remember that the `Hello` function in the `HELLOW.HTM` scriptlet was defined as `public_Hello`.

```
Sub public_Hello()
```

While the `public_` prefix has been removed in the method call made by the host file `CLIENT_HELLOW.HTM`:

```
Document.All.myScriptlet.Hello ' and not
                             ' Document.All.myScriptlet.public_Hello
```

Scriptlets use prefixes to expose their public interface, but the host applications don't use the prefixes to access that interface. This is using quite an ambiguous syntax to simply declare a public interface.

# Packaging Code in a Scriptlet for Reuse

Scriptlets are a good mechanism to package reusable code into one module. The next example shows you the beginnings of a more complex example that exposes a few methods and a property.

## The Cookies Manager

The `Cookies Manager` is a scriptlet that exposes the following interface.

| Member Type | Name | Description |
| --- | --- | --- |
| Method | SetCookieKey (Key, Value) | Stores a value in a cookie and associates it with a specific key |
| Method | GetCookieKey (Key) | Returns the value of a specific key in a cookie |
| Method | RemoveCookieKey (Key) | Removes a specific key from a cookie |
| Property | KeyExists | True if the cookie key exists. |
| | | Usually checked after calling GetCookieKey or RemoveCookieKey |

Using this interface, the client can store, read, or remove a specific key stored in a cookie.

*An HTTP cookie is a small file stored on a client machine. By using cookies you can implement persistency among different sessions (so a user returning to the page will still find the values previously stored in the cookie). However, you cannot fully rely on this as many people do delete their cookies now on a regular basis.*

Here is the code of `COOKIESMANAGER.HTM` scriptlet.

```
<script language="VBScript">
<!--

Dim public_KeyExists
```

```
Sub public_SetCookieKey(sKey, sValue)
    Dim ck
    ck = sKey & "=" & sValue
    ck = ck & ";Expires=Thu 31-Dec-2020 12:00:00 GMT"
    Document.Cookie = ck
End Sub

Function public_GetCookieKey(sKey)

    public_KeyExists = True

    Dim iLoc
    iLoc = Instr(Document.Cookie, sKey)

    If iLoc = 0 Then
        public_GetCookieKey = ""
        public_KeyExists = False
    Else
        Dim sTemp
        sTemp = Right(Document.Cookie, Len(Document.Cookie) - iLoc + 1)

        Dim iKeyLen
        iKeyLen = Len(sKey)

        If Mid(sTemp, iKeyLen + 1, 1) <> "=" Then
            public_GetCookieKey = ""
            public_KeyExists = False
        Else
        Dim iNextSep
        iNextSep = Instr(sTemp, ";")

        If iNextSep = 0 Then iNextSep = Len(sTemp) + 1
        If iNextSep = (iKeyLen + 2) Then
            public_GetCookieKey = ""
        Else
            Dim iValLen
            iValLen = iNextSep - iKeyLen - 2
            public_GetCookieKey = Mid(sTemp, iKeyLen + 2, iValLen)
        End If
        End If
    End if

End Function

Sub public_RemoveCookieKey(sKey)
    Document.Cookie = sKey & "=NULL;Expires=Fri 31-Dec-1980 12:00:00 GMT"
End Sub

-->
</script>
```

We also need a new host application to display an example of using the Cookies Manager scriptlet. This is the code contained in the CLIENT_COOKIE.HTM.

```
<html>
<head>
<script language="VBScript">
<!--

  Sub btnGetName_onClick
    Dim sValue
    sValue = InputBox("Enter your name:")
    Document.All.myScriptlet.SetCookieKey "Name", sValue
    Document.All.Message.InnerHTML = "Please reload the page to see
the scriptlet in action ..."
  End Sub

-->
</script>

<script language="VBScript" for="window" event="onload">
<!--
  Dim sValue
  sValue = Document.All.myScriptlet.GetCookieKey("Name")

  If Document.All.myScriptlet.KeyExists Then
    Document.All.Main.InnerHTML = "Hello there " & sValue & "! Welcome back!"
  End If
-->
</script>

</head>
<body>

<OBJECT ID="myScriptlet"
    TYPE="text/x-scriptlet"
    DATA="cookiesManager.htm"
    HEIGHT="0" WIDTH="0">
</OBJECT>

<div id="Main">
<input TYPE="BUTTON" NAME="btnGetName" VALUE="Enter your name">
</div>

<br>

<div id="Message">
</div>

</body>
</html>
```

Let's take a quick run-through of what this application does.

❑   The first time you load the CLIENT_COOKIE.HTM file in the browser, you will just see a button, as shown in Figure 11-2.

❑   Clicking on the button results in a dialog box asking for your name, as shown in Figure 11-3.

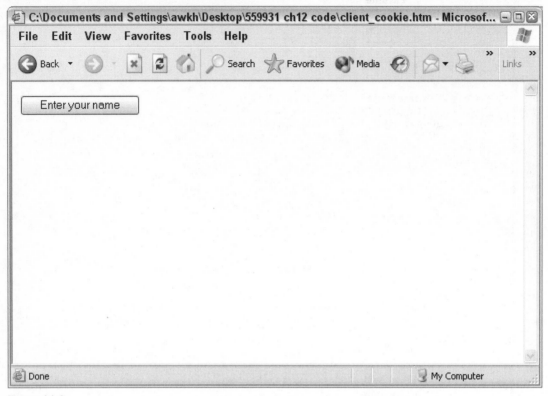

Figure 11-2

Figure 11-3

❑   After entering your name (or at least a text string) into the dialog box, the text in the document window will be updated and ask you to reload the page, as shown in Figure 11-4.

❑   After reloading the page the text displayed demonstrates that you have added persistence to the page using the Cookies Manager by displaying the text you entered into the dialog box in the browser (see Figure 11-5).

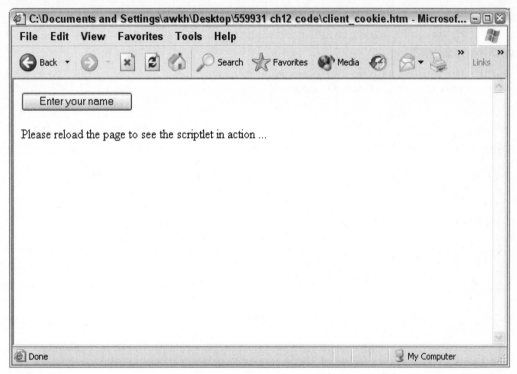

Figure 11-4

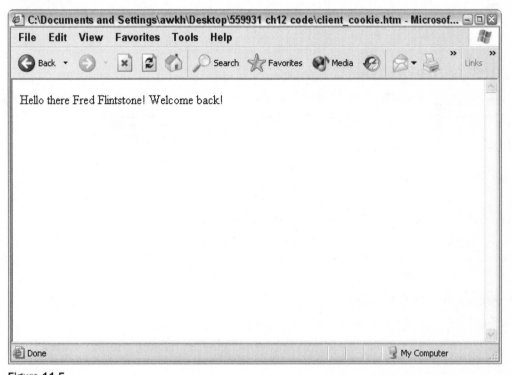

Figure 11-5

### How Does It Work?

The first time you load the page the cookie storing your name doesn't exist. In this case, the following <div> tag will be used to display a button.

```
<div id="Main">
<input TYPE="BUTTON" NAME="btnGetName" VALUE="Enter your name">
</div>
```

Once you've completed the process by entering a text string and then reloading the page, the same <div> will be dynamically filled with a new content by the VBScript code.

```
sValue = Document.All.myScriptlet.GetCookieKey("Name")

If Document.All.myScriptlet.KeyExists Then
    Document.All.Main.InnerHTML = "Hello there" & sValue & _
    "! Welcome back!"
End If
```

Using the Cookies Manager, your name has been stored in a cookie (very originally called "Name").

The Cookies Manager script extends the "Hello, World!" example by showing the following:

❑ How to implement properties (KeyExists)

❑ How to pass variables to methods (SetCookieKey, GetCookieKey, RemoveCookieKey)

❑ How to retrieve values from methods (GetCookieKey)

# Event Management

When the scriptlet is used in a host document, it is only logical that the host document can be notified about events raised from the scriptlet. A scriptlet can raise two types of events:

❑ Standard DHTML events

❑ Custom or nonstandard, events (that is, events defined by the scriptlet)

# Relationship to the Event Handler

Handlers have a one-to-one relationship with each other. This means that when one event handler is in the scriptlet and raises the event, another event handler is in the host document to capture the event raised by the scriptlet.

## Standard DHTML Events

The standard DHTML events exposed by the scriptlet are:

❑ onclick

❑ ondblclick

- ❏ onkeydown
- ❏ onkeypress
- ❏ onkeyup
- ❏ onmousedown
- ❏ onmousemove
- ❏ onmouseup

The following example shows an HTML file that contains a simple implementation of an event handler in the scriptlet for the onclick event that is triggered when the user clicks on the image that will be displayed on the page.

```
<html>

<head>
<title>Example</title>
</head>

<body>
<img src="myimage.gif" onclick="BubbleOnClick()">

<script language="VBScript">

Function BubbleOnClick()
    ' here you do something before raising event in the container object
    ' usually, what you do is check the frozen property to be sure that
    ' the container object is ready to handle events
    Window.External.BubbleEvent
    ' do something after raising the event, if required
End Function

</script>
</body>

</html>
```

The previous sample shows how to do the following:

- ❏ How to access the object container through the External property of the Window object
- ❏ How to raise the event in the object container using the BubbleEvent method

What happens if the scriptlet does not implement an event handler for a standard event using the BubbleEvent method? In this case the event will not be passed to the host application and will not be acted upon.

> *In a COM development environment the scriptlet container object will expose all standard events at design time, even if the scriptlet does not handle all of them.*

**287**

In the preceding context the scriptlet container object is the HTML document. The Event object is accessed via the Window.Event property. The Event object properties will give additional information on the specific event.

Here is an example (for clarity and brevity we've omitted the HTML skeleton that surrounds this code) that shows how to access the event additional information using the Window.Event property.

```
<script language="VBScript" for="document" event="onkeydown">
    Window.Status = "Key code = " & Window.Event.KeyCode
    Window.Status = Window.Status & "Shift status = " & _
    Window.Event.ShiftKey
</script>
```

## Custom Events

Custom events are used to:

❑   Expose more information about a standard DHTML event

❑   Notify the host document about DHTML events that are not among the events handled by the BubbleEvent method

❑   Notify the host document about changes in the internal state of the scriptlet

The following sample (again, free from HTML) shows how to notify a change in the internal state of the scriptlet.

```
<script language="VBScript">

Function public_put_Title(sNewTitle)
    public_Title = sNewTitle
    Window.External.RaiseEvent ("event_ontitlechange", Window.Document)
End Function

</script>
```

This simple example demonstrates the following:

❑   How to raise an event from the scriptlet the RaiseEvent method is required

❑   That there is a naming convention; the exposed event name is prefixed with event_

❑   That the object involved is passed as an argument to the RaiseEvent method

A special event is captured in the host document to run the host event handler: onscriptletevent. The following example shows this technique in action.

```
<script language="VBScript" for="myScriptlet"
    event=onscriptletevent(EventName, EventData)>
    MsgBox "This scriptlet has just raised the following event: " & EventName
</script>
```

All the custom events are subsequently handled by the onscriptletevent. As a result, a Select Case structure is normally used in the onscriptletevent handler to customize the actions taken based on different events.

## How Do You Know When a Scriptlet Is Ready?

In order to make sure everything works fine, the container object implements the property ReadyState and the event onreadystatechange that are used to ensure that specific code will be executed only when the scriptlet has been completely loaded into the container object.

The onreadystatechange event is fired multiple times while the scriptlet is loading. The final time it is fired indicates the point at which the scriptlet file has been fully loaded and its scripts can be called. The ReadyState property is used to test the current state. This property is read-only and it is available only at runtime. The ReadyState property returns an integer value indicating the loading state of the scriptlet.

| Value | Description |
| --- | --- |
| 1,2 | Scriptlet is still loading |
| 3 | Scriptlet has been loaded, but the page might not yet be fully functional |
| 4 | Scriptlet is completely loaded and functional |

# Scriptlet Model Extensions

Specific extensions have been introduced into the Dynamic HTML Object Model to help programmers design and implement scriptlets. All these extensions are available in the DHTML Window.External object.

| Properties | Methods |
| --- | --- |
| Frozen | BubbleEvent |
| SelectableContent | RasieEvent |
| Version | SetContextMenu |

Let's take a closer look at the properties and methods listed in the last table.

## Frozen Property

| | |
| --- | --- |
| Description | This property indicates whether the scriptlet container is ready to handle events |
| Syntax | aVariable = Window.External.Frozen |
| Remarks | While this property is True, events will not be received by the scriptlet container. When the container is ready to receive events the variable is set to False. This property is read-only |

## SelectableContent Property

| | |
|---|---|
| Description | This property specifies whether the user can select the contents of the scriptlet |
| Syntax | `Window.External.SelectableContent = boolean` |
| Remarks | By default, the value of this property is set to `False`, and the user cannot select objects in the scriptlet. If it is set to `True` then the user can select text or other objects contained in the scriptlet |

## Version Property

| | |
|---|---|
| Description | Returns the version and platform of the scriptlet container object. For example "`5.0 Win32`" is the value returned by the `Version` property when the scriptlet is hosted by IE6 for Windows 98/NT/2000/XP |
| Syntax | `ver = Window.External.Version` |
| Remarks | `Version` is returned in the following format `N.nnnn platform` |
| | Where |
| | `N` is an integer representing the major version number |
| | `nnnn` is any number of characters (except a space) representing the minor version number |
| | `platform` is the platform (`win32`, `mac`, `alpha`, and so on) |
| | The version property can be used to determine whether the page is being used as a scriptlet or as a standalone Web page. The following code: |
| | `Mode = (TypeName(Window.External.Version)`<br>`= "String")` |
| | If the value of `Mode` is `True`, the page is being used as a scriptlet, otherwise the page is being used as a standalone page |

## BubbleEvent Method

| | |
|---|---|
| Description | This method sends event notification for a standard event to the host document |
| Syntax | `Window.External.BubbleEvent` |
| Remarks | This method is used to pass a standard DHTML event from the scriptlet to the host document |

## RaiseEvent Method

| | |
|---|---|
| Description | This method is used to pass a custom event notification from the scriptlet to the host document |
| Syntax | `Window.External.RaiseEvent EventName, EventObject` |
| Parameters | `EventName`—a string identifying the event that is being passed. |
| | `EventObject`—a variant type that typically includes a reference to the object on the scriptlet that triggered the event |
| Remarks | This method is used to notify the host document about a nonstandard event. The `onscriptletevents` event is strictly related to this method |

## SetContextMenu Method

| | |
|---|---|
| Description | This method creates a context menu that is displayed when a user right-clicks a scriptlet in the scriptlet container object |
| Syntax | `Window.External.SetContextMenu MenuDefinition` |
| Parameters | `MenuDefinition` defines the command text and commands contained in the context menu |
| | A one-dimensional array in which the menu items are defined using sequences of two elements, n and n + 1 |
| | Element n is the command text. Shortcut keys are defined by preceding a letter with "&" |
| | Element n + 1 is the method to be called when the command is chosen |
| | You cannot pass parameters to the method |
| | Example—the following script defines a context menu with two commands: |

```
<script language="VBScript" for="Menu"
event="onClick">

Dim MenuItems(4)

MenuItems(0) = "&Cut text"

MenuItems(1) = "CutText"

MenuItems(2) = "Co&py text"

MenuItems(3) = "CopyText"

Window.External.SetContextMenu MenuItems

</script>
```

# Scriptlets Are Deprecated in IE5

This chapter shows examples of scriptlets that contain only code (no visible HTML tags). Originally scriptlets were introduced to contain HTML visible tags as well. You can actually use it by adopting the same techniques we've been looking at so far. The only thing to remember is not to set the WIDTH and HEIGHT parameters of the <OBJECT> tag to zero. If the scriptlet has visible parts then it will occupy a visible place in the layout of the HTML page that contains the component. The examples display thinking in "behaviors terms".

At the end of 1998, Microsoft deprecated the scriptlets technology. You can still use this technology but Microsoft suggests replacing it in your applications with HTC components (known as behaviors). As we will see later in this chapter, behaviors have a strong influence during the design of an application, suggesting the separation of the code that defines the behavior of an HTML tag from the tag itself (that's the reason why they're called behaviors!). We have chosen to present scriptlets as the original approach as it was these that evolved into behaviors (known as HTML components) and are still a widely used technology.

*Behaviors are not supported in IE4.*

## Behaviors

Introduced with the advent of Internet Explorer 5.0, behaviors are a fascinating mechanism that have the potential to bring a new programming paradigm in the DHTML world.

The behaviors technology is based on a concept: the behavior. The previous sentence could appear to be a truism, but it introduces a major point. As we will see, Microsoft overused the term behavior in different contexts (to indicate a concept, a technology label, and a keyword). We are now focusing on the first and most important occurrence: the behavior concept.

Unlike scriptlets that were created to group HTML elements and scripts together in an external HTML file, the behavior concept emphasizes the separation of script from HTML elements.

The behavior concept is implemented as an encapsulated component that is associated to an HTML element or, more frequently, to a (CSS) class of HTML elements.

## Which Technologies Implement Behaviors?

Currently two technologies allow us to implement behaviors:

❑   HTCs—HTML Components

❑   Binary behaviors

HTML components are simply text files with an HTC extension containing code scripts (VBScript or JScript) while binary behaviors are built using compiled languages such as C++ or Visual Basic.

*Binary behaviors do not fall within the scope of this book; they have been introduced to further clarify the relationship between the behavior concept and an HTML component.*

When the encapsulated component implementing a behavior is applied to an HTML element, that component then extends the behavior of the HTML element (that's where the term behavior comes from).

# Applying a Behavior to an HTML Element

There are two approaches you can follow to apply a behavior to an HTML element: Statically by using a CSS class, and Dynamically by using scripting.

## Applying a Behavior Statically

In IE5 and IE6 you can define a CSS class using a new property, `behavior`.

*The property is currently a Microsoft proposal to W3C.*

The following code defines a simple CSS class that will be used to apply a behavior to HTML elements.

```
<style>
.myClass {
    behavior: url(abehavior.htc);
}
</style>
```

After the declaration of such a CSS class, your HTML file could contain several different tags, for example:

```
<ul class="myClass">
    <li> an item </li>
    <li> an item </li>
</ul>

<div class="myClass">This is a div</div>
```

In the last example, a behavior has been applied to two different HTML elements.

❑    `<ul>`

❑    `<div>`

The behavior of both HTML elements will be extended by the code (either VBScript or JScript code) that is contained in the `somebehavior.htc` file.

The CSS property named behavior can be defined inline using the `<style>` attribute. In this case the programmer doesn't even need to declare a CSS class to apply the behavior. Also, if you wanted, a single specific element can be addressed. The following example demonstrates this technique:

```
<div style="behavior: url(somebehavior.htc)"> another div</div>
```

## Applying a Behavior Dynamically

A behavior can be applied through scripting in one of two ways: using the `AddBehavior` method or modifying the `Behavior` property of the `Style` object. The following code shows both ways in action.

```
<script language="VBScript">
    Sub ApplyOption1()
        Document.All.MyDiv.AddBehavior("somebehavior.htc");
    End Sub
```

```
     Sub ApplyOption2()
          Document.All.MyDiv.Style.Behavior = "url(somebehavior.htc)";
     End Sub
</script>

...

<div id="MyDiv">another div</div>
```

*Note that the* Behavior *property still expects the syntax* "url (somebehavior.htc)" *while the* AddBehavior *method doesn't require this syntax.*

## Remove a Behavior Attached Dynamically

Let's think about the lifecycle of the relationship between an attached behavior and the HTML elements. Behaviors attached employing CSS classes are automatically detached from the elements as soon as the element or elements are removed from the document tree. This is not the case when using any other method. Under these circumstances you will be required to use the RemoveBehavior method.

In all these cases it is not enough to just remove the elements themselves from the document tree. They will still maintain all the style sheet rules defined programmatically or by inline definitions (including the behavior rule itself).

So far, we have looked at what a behavior is as a concept and the ways that it can be used to augment and extend on HTML elements. As yet, we haven't examined any behavior implementation. We have already seen that behaviors could be implemented using VBScript through HTML components. It is time we looked at HTML components.

# HTML Components (HTCs)

An HTML component is an encapsulated component, which implements a behavior. An actual HTC is simply a file with an HTC extension. An HTC file contains VBScript code that is wrapped by HTML tags that define the public interface of the component.

# Extending HTML Elements Behavior

It is not too difficult to confuse HTML components with scriptlets. Microsoft has recommended that programmers replace scriptlets with HTML components because they are the newer and as such better evolution of this technology. HTML components are evolving into something that is very different and far removed from scriptlets themselves. The behavior concept (discussed earlier) is what makes the difference—and an enormous difference.

The main purpose of both scriptlets and HTML components is to make it easier for the programmer to reuse code. However, this produces the misconception that HTML components should replace scriptlets. Each of them in fact captures different code aspects and both of them should be used together in large projects that are component-based.

In contrast to scriptlets, the goal of HTML components is to extend HTML elements' behavior. Let's look at a few techniques that are used to extend HTML elements using HTML components:

❑    Adding properties

- ❑ Adding methods
- ❑ Exposing component events
- ❑ Handling HTML element events

Let's begin this journey by taking a look at a basic "Hello, World!" HTML component to get a feeling for how this technology actually works. The HTML component is stored in the HELLOW.HTC file.

```
<attach event="ondocumentready" ONEVENT="Hello()" />

<script language="VBScript">

Function Hello()
     MsgBox "Hello, World!"
End Function

</script>
```

The component has one line of code more than the analogue scriptlet sample. One thing that's important to note is that the prefix "public_" is not required (the prefix naming conventions are only required for scriptlets and are not required for HTML components).

In the case of this minimal sample, you will certainly find it more interesting to have a look at the HTML file that uses the component CLIENT_HTC_HELLOW.HTM.

```
<html>
<head>

<style>

.myClass  {
     behavior: url(hellow.htc);
}

</style>

</head>

<body class="myClass">

</body>
</html>
```

As you can see there is a total separation between scripting code (contained in one file) and HTML and CSS (contained in another).

If you think that we are exaggerating the minimalist nature of the actual HTML file, take a look at the following alternative for the client file (CLIENT_HTC_HELLOW2.HTM).

```
<html>
<body style="behavior: url(hellow.htc)">
</body>
</html>
```

This is an extremely minimalist file in terms of it being a complete HTML file. However, it can afford to be only four lines because the powerhouse is contained in the `.htc` file.

## Enhancement 1—Adding Properties

An HTML component can expose properties to the containing document by using the `<property>` element.

Here we have an example that implements an HTML component, which has a public interface made of only one property called `CryptedKey`. The example captures the essentials of the technique to exposes properties. The HTML component is contained in a file named CRYPTED.HTC.

```
<property name="CryptedKey" put="PutCK" get="GetCK" />

<script language="VBScript">

Dim cKey

Function PutCK(ByVal newValue)
    cKey = newValue Xor 43960
End Function

Function GetCK()
    GetCK = cKey Xor 43960
End Function

</script>
```

This sample shows you how to do the following:

- ❑ Declare the name of the property through the NAME attribute of the `<property>` tag
- ❑ Declare a function to make the property writable using the PUT attribute
- ❑ Declare a function to make the property readable using the GET attribute

The example uses the `Xor` function to crypt/decrypt the value of the property. Applying this crypt/decrypt transformation the example shows how it is possible to use read/write property functions that actually do something more than simply give access to an internal variable.

A client sample that uses the HTML component is shown next (`CLIENT_CRYPT.HTM`).

```
<html>
<head>

<style>

.myClass    {
    background: red;
    behavior: url(crypted.htc);
}

</style>

<script language="VBScript">
```

```
Sub WriteProp()
    Dim iKey
    iKey = CInt(InputBox("Enter the a number:"))
    Document.All.myDIV.CryptedKey = iKey
End Sub

Sub ReadProp()
    MsgBox Document.All.myDiv.CryptedKey
End Sub

</script>

</head>
<body>

<div class="myClass" ID="myDIV">This div has been enhanced with the CryptEd
property</div>

<input type="Button" onclick="VBScript:WriteProp" value="Change
Property"></input>
<input type="Button" onclick="VBScript:ReadProp" value="Read
Property"></input>

</body>
</html>
```

The example applies the behavior to a `<div>` element, identified by the "myDIV" ID. This is done using the following line of code.

```
MsgBox Document.All.myDiv.CryptedKey
```

The HTML component has actually enhanced the `<div>` adding to it the CryptedKey property that behaves as implemented. To check this you could generate an error by choice, changing a letter in the same line, as in:

```
MsgBox Document.All.myDiv.CryptKey
```

If you now click on the button labeled Read Property you will see the error message shown in Figure 11-6.

What the error message is telling you is that the CryptKey property it is not supported by the object. This is further evidence that you can actually extend HTML elements using behaviors.

## Overriding Standard Properties

It is possible to override the element's default behavior by specifying a name for the property that is the same as that of a property already defined for the element.

## Notify the HTML Element that the Property Value has Changed

When the value of the property has changed, the HTML element can be notified by firing the onpropertychange event calling the FireChange method.

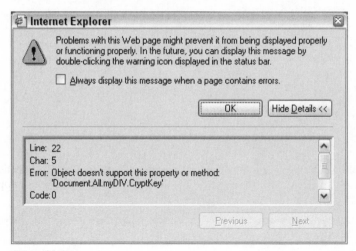

**Figure 11-6**

```
Function PutCK(ByVal newValue)
    cKey = newValue Xor 43960
    oCryptedKey.FireChange
End Function
```

The `oCryptedKey` identifier indicates the id of the `<property>` element that has been specified.

```
<property name="CryptedKey" put="PutCK" get="GetCK" id="oCryptedKey" />
```

To verify that the event has fired effectively, modify the `<div>` definition in the client.

```
<div class="myClass" id="myDIV" onpropertychange="MsgBox('!')">
This div has been enhanced with a Crypted property
</div>
```

## Enhancement 2—Adding Methods

To add new methods to an HTML element using an HTML component is easier than to adding properties.

As an example let's modify the `CRYPTED.HTC` component to expose a method named `DisplayCryptedValue`, which displays the internal value of the `CryptedKey` property in a dialog. A further element named `method` is available to expose methods. The resulting `CRYPTED.HTC` code looks as follows.

```
<property name="CryptedKey" put="PutCK" get="GetCK" id="oCryptedKey" />
<method name="DisplayCryptedValue" />

<script language="VBScript">

Dim cKey

Function PutCK(ByVal newValue)
    cKey = newValue Xor 43960
    oCryptedKey.FireChange
```

```
End Function

Function GetCK()
    GetCK = cKey Xor 43960
End Function

Sub DisplayCryptedValue()
    MsgBox cKey
End Sub

</script>
```

For this new, modified code to work the host application will require some modification to use the DisplayCryptedValue method. The following is the code for the modified host application (CLIENT_CRYPT2.HTM).

```
<html>
<head>

<style>

.myClass  {
    background: red;
    behavior: url(crypted.htc);
}

</style>

<script language="VBScript">

Sub WriteProp()
    Dim iKey
    iKey = CInt(InputBox("Enter a number:"))
    Document.All.myDIV.CryptedKey = iKey
End Sub

Sub ReadProp()
    MsgBox Document.All.myDiv.CryptedKey
End Sub

Sub DisplayCV()
    Document.All.myDIV.DisplayCryptedValue
End Sub

</script>

</head>
<body>

<div class="myClass" id="myDIV">This div has been enhanced with a Crypted
property</div>

<input type="Button" onclick="VBScript:WriteProp" value="Change
Property"></input>
<input type="Button" onclick="VBScript:ReadProp" value="Read
Property"></input>
```

```
<input type="Button" onclick="VBScript:DisplayCV" value="Display Crypted
Value"></input>

</body>
</html>
```

## Enhancement 3—Exposing Component Events

An HTML component is capable of defining its own events and then exposing them through the <event> element. This method of exposing custom events is clearly more powerful than the one offered by scriptlets (described earlier in this chapter). Actually, scriptlets are only capable of exposing one event—onscriptletevent. With HTML components you can expose any kind of event you want to the containing document. As an example we are going to enhance our CRYPTED.HTC code with an OnReadWarning event, which informs the container that somebody has accessed the CryptedKey property.

```
<property name="CryptedKey" put="PutCK" get="GetCK" id="oCryptedKey" />
<method name="DisplayCryptedValue" />
<event name="OnReadWarning" id="orw" />

<script language="VBScript">

Dim cKey

Function PutCK(ByVal newValue)
    cKey = newValue Xor 43960
    oCryptedKey.FireChange
End Function

Function GetCK()
    Dim oEvent
    Set oEvent = CreateEventObject()
    orw.Fire(oEvent)
    GetCK = cKey Xor 43960
End Function

Sub DisplayCryptedValue()
    MsgBox cKey
End Sub

</script>
```

This code shows the technique to fire a component event in.

```
Dim oEvent
Set oEvent = CreateEventObject()
orw.Fire(oEvent)
```

The CreateEventObject function is required to create an event object and the event object becomes the parameter of the Fire method of the <event> element. The <event> element is identified by its id attribute (orw). The <event> element also defines the name of the exposed event as well.

```
<event name="OnReadWarning" id="orw" />
```

It is again necessary to modify the client, but this time only one line of code needs to be changed.

```
<div class="myClass" id="myDIV" onreadwarning="MsgBox('Someone is reading
the property')">This div has been enhanced with a Crypted property</div>
```

To generate the event we launch the client application, assign a value to the property, and then read that value. The `onreadwarning` event will be raised and the application will inform you with the message shown in Figure 11-7.

Figure 11-7

## Enhancement 4—Handling HTML Element Events

HTML components offer a further mechanism to enhance HTML elements. They can attach handlers for the HTML element's events using the `<attach>` element. We will modify the `CRYPTED.HTC` example to handle the `onclick` event of the HTML elements to which the behavior is attached.

```
<property name="CryptedKey" put="PutCK" get="GetCK" id="oCryptedKey" />
<method name="DisplayCryptedValue" />
<event name="OnReadWarning" id="orw" />
<attach event="onclick" onevent="ClickHandler()" />

<script language="VBScript">

Dim cKey

Function PutCK(ByVal newValue)
    cKey = newValue Xor 43960
    oCryptedKey.FireChange
End Function

Function GetCK()
    Dim oEvent
    Set oEvent = CreateEventObject()
    orw.Fire(oEvent)
    GetCK = cKey Xor 43960
End Function

Sub DisplayCryptedValue()
    MsgBox cKey
End Sub

Function ClickHandler()
    MsgBox "You clicked on an element enhanced by the CRYPTED behavior"
End Function

</script>
```

The handler for the `onclick` event is declared in the following line.

```
<attach event="onclick" onevent="ClickHandler()" />
```

This time, no modifications are required in the code for the host application.

You can easily test the handler. Click on the `<div>` element to run the handler. This will produce a dialog box shown in Figure 11-8.

**Figure 11-8**

*When the specified event fires on an element to which the behavior is attached, the behavior's handler is called after the element's event handler (if any).*

## Attach Event Handlers through Scripting

Timing becomes a very critical issue when dealing with event handlers. Sometimes you need to attach an event handler that responds to specific events. It is possible to attach handlers through scripting using the `AttachEvent` method instead of the `<attach>` element.

The general technique to deal with dynamically attached event handlers is shown in the following lines of code.

```
<attach event="ondetach" onevent="DetachEvents()" />

<script language="VBScript">

Function DetachEvents()
    DetachEvent('onevent1', EvH1)
    DetachEvent('onevent2', EvH2)
End Function

Function EvH1()
    ' do something here
End Function

Function EvH2()
    ' do something here also
End Function

Function SomeTimeInTheBehavior()
    AttachEvent('onevent1', EvH1)
    AttachEvent('onevent2', EvH2)
    ' do something too
End Function

</script>
```

A `DetachEvent` method and an `ondetach` event have both been introduced in the example above. Event handlers that are attached using the `AttachEvent` method have to call the `DetachEvent` method to stop them from receiving any sent notifications. The HTML component will be notified with the `ondetach` event from the page to actually detach all the handlers attached through scripting.

## Multiple Behaviors

It is possible to apply multiple behaviors to an element either by using the `AddBehavior` method multiple times or using the syntax shown in the following example.

```
<style>

.myClass {
    behavior: url(b-one.htc), url(b-two.htc), url(b-three.htc);
}

</style>
```

But what about conflicts? Conflicts can happen when more than one behavior is applied to one element. For any conflicts resulting from applying multiple behaviors to an element, the following resolution rule is defined.

*Each subsequent behavior takes precedence over the previous behavior in the order in which the behavior is applied to the element.*

### Name Clashing Resolution and the COMPONENT Element

A further element can actually be helpful in cases where there are multiple behaviors. This is the `<component>` element. The `<component>` element allows us to give a name to the HTML component that can be used to access properties and methods through scripting (solving name clashing issues whenever multiple behaviors are applied to the same element).

```
<component name="Crypted">

<property name="CryptedKey" put="PutCK" get="GetCK" id="oCryptedKey" />
<method name="DisplayCryptedValue" />
<event name="OnReadWarning" id="orw" />
<attach event="onclick" onevent="ClickHandler()" />

<script language="VBScript">

Dim cKey

Function PutCK(ByVal newValue)
    cKey = newValue Xor 43960
    oCryptedKey.FireChange
End Function

Function GetCK()
    Dim oEvent
    Set oEvent = CreateEventObject()
    orw.Fire(oEvent)
    GetCK = cKey Xor 43960
End Function
```

```
Sub DisplayCryptedValue()
    MsgBox cKey
End Sub

Function ClickHandler()
    MsgBox "You clicked on an element enhanced by the CRYPTED behavior"
End Function

</script>

</component>
```

After using the <component> element it is possible to access the component properties and methods using the component name.

```
Sub ReadProp()
    MsgBox Document.All.myDiv.Crypted.CryptedKey
End Sub
```

This definitively solves the name clashing issue. Suppose we want to apply two behaviors (named, for example, bhone and bhtwo) both of which define a Description property to the same element (myDiv), it is possible to access both properties.

```
MsgBox Document.All.myDiv.bhone.Title & Document.All.myDiv.bhtwo.Title
```

The goal of this section was to introduce all the fundamental techniques to start you on your way using behaviors and HTML components. Experimenting with the preceding code and concepts can only help to further your understanding of these topics.

# Summary

The goal of this chapter is to give you an understanding of how much farther than a simple static Web page VBScript can take you. We've looked at sufficient code samples for you to be able to make use of many and reuse or adapt them to suit your own needs. We looked at the evolution of scriptlets into behaviors and their use through HTML components. With regard to scriptlets you saw how to:

❑   Implement properties

❑   Pass variables to methods

❑   Retrieve values from methods

❑   Manage events statically

❑   Manage events dynamically

❑   Use custom events

We then moved on to look at behaviors and saw how to:

❑   Apply a behavior statically

❑   Apply a behavior dynamically

❑   Remove attached behaviors

This then led us to learn that the goal of HTML components is to extend HTML elements' behavior. And, with regard to HTML components, we also covered:

❑   Adding properties

❑   Adding methods

❑   Exposing events

❑   Handling html element's events

❑   Enhancement techniques

Do remember that we've covered some enormous topics here. Whole volumes can (and have!) been devoted to the topics we have covered in this chapter and, so, if you want to go deeper and do more, refer to more specialized sources to further your learning. However, what we've provided here will give you a good foundation on which to build!

# 12

# Windows Script Host

## Overview

Ask programmers if they use VBScript and most will answer "Yes, for ASP" or "Yes, for client-side scripting on an intranet." But you need to remember that these are nothing more than contexts where VBScript can be used to solve problems that are in need of scripting solutions. Because VBScript is designed as an ActiveX Scripting engine, it can be used to provide scripting capability for any ActiveX Scripting host environment.

Two of the most common hosts are Active Server Pages (ASP) and Internet Explorer. Both of these hosts provide the programmer with a lot of power but both also come with certain limitations. An example is that Internet Explorer does not provide a capability for script to interact with the local computer (such as file system access, registry access, and so on) unless the user explicitly sets permissions for this (and doing this can cause enormous security risks. For this reason, this is usually done only for trusted sites and intranets). So what's the point of having extended power within the VBScript language when you can't do anything with it? Well, this is where Windows Script Host (WSH) comes in. WSH is a totally scripting language–neutral host interface that will work with any ActiveX Scripting engine. This means that programmers that want to use WSH can use VBScript, JScript, PerlScript, or any other scripting language that exposes the ActiveX Scripting interfaces. The WSH host interface thus provides Windows platforms with a powerful, yet easy-to-use scripting platform that can be accessed from both the Windows GUI and the command prompt.

In this chapter, you will be examining the following aspects of WSH:

- ❏ The tools required for WSH development
- ❏ What WSH can be used for
- ❏ The two methods of execution for WSH scripts
- ❏ The use of .WSH files to customize script behavior
- ❏ The WSH object model
- ❏ The .WSF file format, used for creating more advanced scripts
- ❏ Using WSH for disk and network administration

# Tools of the Trade

In order to begin making use of WSH you will need the following:

❑ The WSH engine.

❑ A text editor, such as Notepad (although you are free to make use of one that is designed with programming in mind—there are plenty of alternatives).

❑ If you wish to use a scripting language other than VBScript or JScript, you will also need to download and install the proper ActiveX Scripting engine (such as ActivePerl from ActiveState, http://www.activestate.com).

If your operating system is Windows 98, Windows Me, Windows NT 4.0 with Option Pack 4 installed, Windows 2000, or Windows XP, then you probably already have Windows Script Host (WSH 1.0 is provided as an optional component for Win98 and WinNT). However, you may want to ensure that you have the latest version in order to run the scripts included in this chapter. You can download it from the Microsoft Scripting Technologies Web site at http://msdn.microsoft.com/scripting/windowshost/. We suggest that you upgrade to the latest version, WSH 5.6 and Windows Script engine 5.6 for JScript and VBScript.

In addition, you may wish to install the WSH references locally. The complete WSH reference is also available for download from http://msdn.microsoft.com/scripting/windowshost/ as a single HTML Help file.

# What Is WSH?

Windows Script Host (WSH) is a Windows administration tool. WSH creates an environment for hosting scripts so that when a script arrives at a computer, WSH plays the part of the host. WSH makes objects and services available for the script and provides a set of guidelines within which the script is executed. Among other things, WSH manages security and invokes the appropriate script engine.

Since WSH is script language independent, WSH also provides the facility to write scripts in JScript, Perl, Python, REXX, or any other ActiveX Scripting Language (only the VBScript and JScript languages are available from Microsoft—other ActiveX Scripting engines are available from third parties).

WSH provides network administrators with a handy toolkit to use for access to machines scattered across a network of computers running various flavors of the Windows operating system family. Much of this access comes through the use of Active Directory Service Interfaces (ADSI) and Windows Management Instrumentation (WMI). ADSI provides a single set of COM interfaces that can be used with multiple directory services, such as the Lightweight Directory Access Protocol (LDAP), the Windows NT directory service, and Novell's Netware and NDS services. WMI is Microsoft's implementation of Web-Based Enterprise Management (WBEM), a standard method of providing access to management information such as applications installed on a given client, system memory, and other client information.

By developing WSH scripts that take advantage of ADSI and WMI, administrators can develop scripts that make it very easy to perform the following tasks and much more:

❑ Access and manipulate servers

❑ Add and remove users and change password

❑ Add network file shares

As the table shown previously shows,[Q1] the current version of WSH is version 5.6. This version was released with the release of Windows XP and brings with it significant changes over the previous version (version 2.0). The current release of WSH now includes a whole host of features that programmers will find appealing:

❑   Support for file inclusion

❑   Ability to use multiple languages within the same script

❑   Support for drag-and-drop functionality

❑   Argument handling

❑   Ability to run scripts remotely

❑   Enhanced access to external objects and type libraries

❑   Stronger debugging capability

❑   A mechanism for pausing script execution (useful for sinking events raised by controlled objects)

❑   Standard input/output and standard error support (only available via console-mode execution with cscript.exe)

❑   New processes can be treated as objects

❑   Access to the current working directory

❑   New, improved security model

WSH 1.0 operated by simply associating the file extensions for VBScript (.vbs) and JScript (.js) files with the actual script host. This meant that if you double-clicked on a script file, it would automatically execute. However, this had one major limitation—the association model did not allow for the use of code modules or for the integrating of multiple script languages in a single WSH script project. To appease programmers everywhere, Microsoft introduced a new type of script file (.wsf) in WSH 2.0, which utilized an XML syntax that provides much of the new functionality listed earlier.

This schema includes the tags <script>, <object>, and <job> among others. You'll be seeing how this all works later on in this chapter.

> *The file extension .wsf is only available with final release of WSH 2.0 and later. Developers working with the beta releases of WSH 2.0 will have to use the .ws file extension. We suggest that you upgrade to the version 5.6 script engines and WSH.*

# Types of Script Files

Stand-alone script files come in a few different formats, each having its own extension. The following table is a list of some common types.

The script type that you choose will ultimately depends on your needs. Most small projects only require the use of one file type while certain scenarios will mean that you could divide your overall problem into several smaller parts, writing a separate script for each part, with each script written in the most suitable scripting language.

| Extension | Script Type | Description |
|---|---|---|
| .bat | MS-DOS batch file | MS-DOS operating system batch file |
| .asp | ASP page | Active Server Page file |
| .htm | HTML file | Web page |
| .html | HTML file | Web page |
| .js | JScript file | Windows script |
| .vbs | VBScript file | Windows script |
| .wsf | Windows Script Host file | Container or project file for a Windows script. This is supported by WSH 2.0 and later |
| .wsh | Windows Script Host file | Property file for a script file; supported by WSH 1.0 and later |

This is where Windows Script Host files (WSF files) are useful. WSF files may include other script files as part of the script. This means that multiple WSF files can reference libraries of useful functions, which may be created and stored in a single place.

# Running Scripts with the Windows Script Host

WSH provides two interfaces that allow us to execute scripts on the command line or from within the Windows environment. These two interfaces each use different host programs for the VBScript engine:

❑   cscript.exe—Command line
❑   wscript.exe—Windows environment

The reason there are two host programs is that cscript.exe is designed for use from a console window (basically, an MS-DOS box within Windows) while wscript.exe is intended to interface directly with the Windows GUI itself. There is very little difference between them in terms of functionality.

## Command-Line Execution

The console interface for executing script files, cscript.exe, is called as follows:

Open the Run dialog (Start | Run) or a command window (in Windows 9x, this is done via Start | Programs | DOS Prompt; in Windows NT via Start | Programs | Command Prompt; and in XP via Start | All Programs | Accessories | Command Prompt).

Execute your script as follows.

```
cscript c:\folderName\YourScriptName.vbs
```

If you run `cscript.exe` with no arguments directly from an MS-DOS window, you will simply get the usage notes, as shown in Figure 12-1.

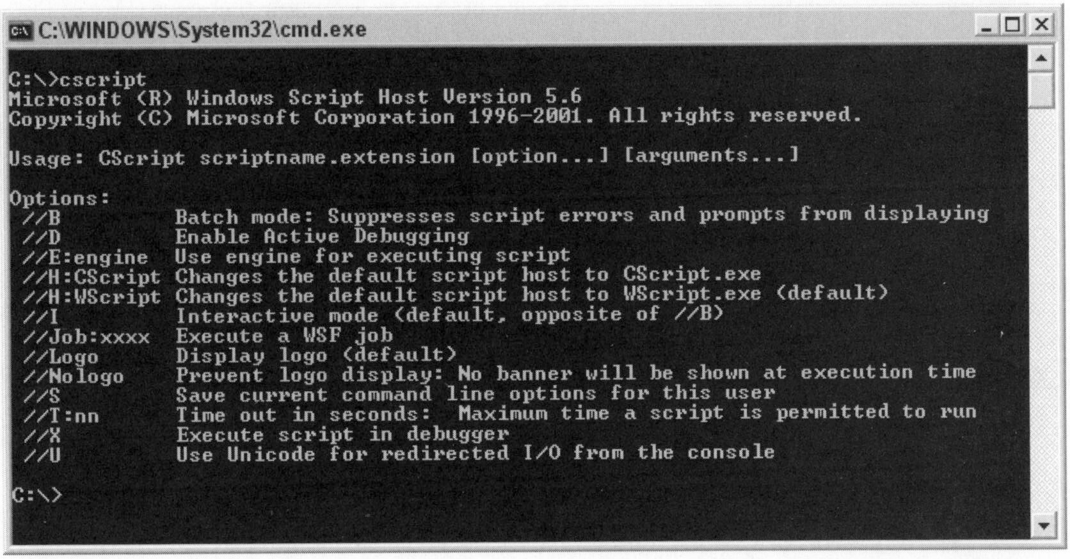

**Figure 12-1**

The usage syntax is as follows.

```
cscript scriptname.extension [option...] [arguments...]
```

The following command-line options are provided by `cscript.exe` to allow you to control various settings for the WSH environment.

| | |
|---|---|
| `//B` | Batch mode. This suppresses script errors and prompts from being displayed |
| `//D` | Enable active debugging |
| `//E:engine` | Use engine for executing script |
| `//H:Cscript` | Changes the default script host to `cscript.exe` |
| `//H:Wscript` | Changes the default script host to `wscript.exe` (default) |
| `//I` | Interactive mode (default, opposite of `//B`) |
| `//Job:xxxx` | Execute a WSF job |
| `//Logo` | Display logo (default) |
| `//Nologo` | Prevent logo from displaying. No banner will be shown at execution time |

*Continues*

| //S | Save current command line options for this user |
| --- | --- |
| //T:nn | Time out in seconds. Maximum time a script is permitted to run |
| //X | Execute script in debugger |
| //U | Use Unicode for redirected I/O from the console |

To use these, add them as switches at the command line. The following example executes the script in the debugger.

```
cscript MyScript.vbs //X
```

## Execution of WSH within the Windows Environment

The Windows GUI interface for script file execution, `wscript.exe`, allows us to execute files in several ways:

- ❑ If the file type is registered to execute within WSH, the script can be run by simply double-clicking on its icon in any folder-view window or on the desktop.
- ❑ Using the Run command dialog, simply type in the full path and name of the script.

From the Run dialog, you can invoke `wscript.exe`.

```
wscript c:\folderName\YourScriptName.vbs
```

If you run `wscript.exe` from an MS-DOS window, you'll get no output in the MS-DOS window. Instead you'll see the dialog box shown in Figure 12-2, which provides minimal customization options. This is the same dialog box displayed if `wscript.exe` is run from the Run command dialog.

When you click OK, nothing happens. The only way to customize script behavior on a system level is through the `cscript` options detailed earlier. This dialog is used for individual script customization through .wsh files, which we'll cover next.

The major difference between `cscript` and `wscript` really becomes apparent only when debugging a faulty script. This is because sending error messages to a console window is much quicker and easier to handle than perhaps endless error pop-ups produced by `wscript`. We'd recommend `cscript` for use when debugging scripts, and it is best to use the Echo method of the WScript object when printing debug output, as this can result in too many error messages being generated. In fact, it is possible that you get into loops where you can't exit from the error messages.

## Using .WSH Files to Launch Scripts

Maybe you don't need or want to modify the settings for every script you execute, but you do need to be able to control individual files. This is made possible by creating control files, which have the extension .wsh, that allow us to control settings for individual scripts. A .wsh file is a small configuration file roughly following the .ini file format of past Windows versions. These files are good for customizing the way a script is started up—you can have several different .wsh files for the one script.

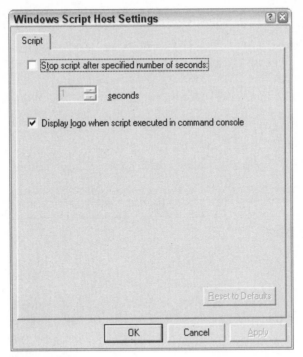

**Figure 12-2**

To create a `.wsh` file, right-click on a file associated with WSH (a file with a `.js`, `.vbs`, or `.wsf` extension), select `Properties`, and then the `Script` tab from the dialog box as shown in Figure 12-3.

This dialog box allows you to change the time-out default setting, and whether or not logo information should be displayed when the script is executed on the command line. When you apply or accept any changes you have made, a new file will be created, with the same name as the script in question, but containing the extension `.wsh`. This new file will record these custom settings in a format which the host engines use to set runtime options. Here is a `.wsh` file created from a script named `test.vbs`.

```
[ScriptFile]
Path=C:\test.vbs

[Options]
Timeout=25
DisplayLogo=0
```

In order to execute the script with these options, you would run the `test.wsh` file.

# Windows Script Host Intrinsic Objects

Every programming environment provides its own object model that developers can use to implement solutions, and WSH is no different. WSH contains a core set of objects, that in turn contains properties and methods, which can be used to access other computers on a network, import external scriptable objects for use within an application, or connect with Windows or the Windows shell.

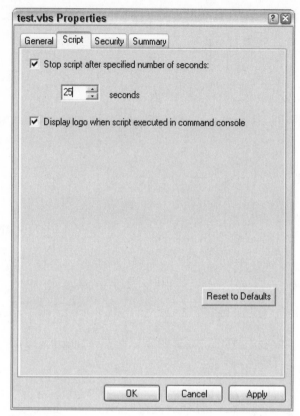

**Figure 12-3**

# The WScript Object

The root of the WSH object model is the WScript object. This object provides properties and methods that give the developer access to a variety of information, such as:

❑ Name and path information for the script file being executed

❑ Version of the Microsoft Scripting engines

❑ Links to external objects

❑ User interaction

❑ Ability to delay or terminate script execution

## WScript Properties

What follows are the properties for the WScript object. The WScript object has 11 properties:

❑ Arguments property

❑ FullName property

- ❑ `Interactive` property
- ❑ `Name` property
- ❑ `Path` property
- ❑ `ScriptFullName` property
- ❑ `ScriptName` property
- ❑ `StdErr` property
- ❑ `StdIn` property
- ❑ `StdOut` property
- ❑ `Version` property

### Arguments

The `Arguments` property contains the `WshArguments` object (a collection of arguments). Use a zero-based index to retrieve individual arguments from this collection.

```
Set objArgs = WScript.Arguments
For x = 0 to objArgs.Count - 1
    WScript.Echo objArgs(x)
Next
```

### FullName

The `FullName` property is a read-only string representing the fully qualified path of the host executable file (`cscript.exe` or `wscript.exe`). The following code uses the `FullName` property.

```
WScript.Echo WScript.FullName
```

This produces the output shown in Figure 12-4.

**Figure 12-4**

### Interactive

The `Interactive` property sets the script mode, or identifies the script mode. When used, this property returns a Boolean value. There are two possible modes available for use. These are batch and interactive.

In interactive mode (the default), the script provides user interaction. Input to and output from the WSH is enabled and the script can echo information to dialog boxes and can wait for the user to provide feedback. In batch mode, this type of user interaction is not supported and all input and output to WSH is disabled.

Script mode can be set using the WSH command-line switches `//I` (for interactive) and `//B` (for batch).

## Name

The `Name` property returns the name of the `WScript` object (the host executable file). This is a read-only string. The following code uses the `Name` property.

```
WScript.Echo WScript.Name
```

This produces the output shown in Figure 12-5.

**Figure 12-5**

## Path

The `Path` property returns the name of the directory containing the host executable file (`cscript.exe` or `wscript.exe`). This returns a read-only string.

The following VBScript code echoes the directory where the executable file resides.

```
WScript.Echo WScript.Path
```

## ScriptFullName

The `ScriptFullName` property returns the full path of the currently running script. This property returns a read-only string.

## ScriptName

The `ScriptName` property returns the file name of the currently running script. This property returns a read-only string. The following code echoes the name of the script being run, as shown in Figure 12-6.

```
WScript.Echo WScript.ScriptName
```

**Figure 12-6**

## StdErr

The `StdErr` property exposes the write-only error output stream for the current script. It returns an object representing the standard error stream. The `StdIn`, `StdOut`, and `StdErr`, streams can be accessed while using `cscript.exe` only. Note that attempting to access these streams while using `wscript.exe` produces an error.

## StdIn

The `StdIn` property exposes the read-only input stream for the current script. It returns an object representing the standard error stream. The `StdIn`, `StdOut`, and `StdErr` streams can be accessed while using `cscript.exe` only. Note that attempting to access these streams while using `wscript.exe` produces an error.

## StdOut

The `StdOut` property exposes the write-only error output stream for the current script. It returns an object representing the standard error stream. The `StdIn`, `StdOut`, and `StdErr` streams can be accessed while using `cscript.exe` only. Note that attempting to access these streams while using `wscript.exe` produces an error.

The following example makes use of all three of the built-in stream types to print a list of all files matching a particular extension. This is implemented by piping the output from the DOS `dir` command into the filter script, with an extension string passed as an argument.

```
' Usage: dir | cscript filter.vbs ext
'        ext: file extension to match
'
Dim streamOut, streamIn, streamErr
Set streamOut = WScript.StdOut
Set streamIn = WScript.StdIn
Set streamErr = WScript.StdErr

Dim strExt, strLineIn
Dim intMatch
strExt = WScript.Arguments(0)
intMatch = 0

Do While Not streamIn.AtEndOfStream
  strLineIn = streamIn.ReadLine
  If 0 = StrComp(strExt, Right(strLineIn, Len(strExt)), _
                 vbTextCompare) Then
    streamOut.WriteLine strLineIn
    intMatch = intMatch + 1
  End If
Loop

If 0 = intMatch Then
  streamErr.WriteLine "No files of type '" & strExt & "' found"
End If
```

Since this example uses `StdIn`, `StdOut`, and `StdErr` for all messaging, you could use it not only to print out matching files to the screen, but also to send output to a text file or another application with redirection or additional piping. For example, you could create a file containing all `.vbs` files in an entire directory tree, including all subdirectories, with the following command.

```
C:\wsh>dir /s | cscript filter.vbs vbs >> vbsfiles.txt
```

## Version

This property returns the version of WSH. The following code echoes the current version of WSH, as shown in Figure 12-7.

```
WScript.Echo WScript.Version
```

Figure 12-7

## WScript Methods

What follows is a listing of the `WScript` methods. The `WScript` object has seven methods:

- ❑ `CreateObject` method
- ❑ `ConnectObject` method
- ❑ `DisconnectObject` method
- ❑ `Echo` method
- ❑ `GetObject` method
- ❑ `Quit` method
- ❑ `Sleep` method

### CreateObject

This method of the `WScript` object is used to create a COM object.

```
object.CreateObject(strProgID[,strPrefix])
```

- ❑ `object`—`WScript` object.
- ❑ `strProgID`—String value indicating the programmatic identifier (`ProgID`) of the object you want to create.
- ❑ `strPrefix`—Optional. String value indicating the function prefix.

Objects created with the `CreateObject` method using the `strPrefix` argument are connected objects. The object's outgoing interface is connected to the script file after the object is created. Event functions are a combination of this prefix and the event name.

If you create an object and do not provide the `strPrefix` argument, you can still synchronize events on the object by using the `ConnectObject` method. When the object fires an event, WSH calls a subroutine with `strPrefix` attached to the beginning of the event name.

The following code uses the `CreateObject` method to create a `WshNetwork` object.

```
Set WshNetwork = WScript.CreateObject("WScript.Network")
```

### ConnectObject

This method connects the object's event sources to functions with a given prefix.

```
object.ConnectObject(strObject, strPrefix)
```

- ❏  `object`—WScript object.
- ❏  `strObject`—Required. String value indicating the name of the object you want to connect.
- ❏  `strPrefix`—Required. String value indicating the function prefix.

Connected objects are useful when you want to synchronize an object's events. The `ConnectObject` method connects the object's outgoing interface to the script file after creating the object. Event functions are a combination of this prefix and the event name.

```
WScript.ConnectObject RemoteScript, "remote_"
```

### DisconnectObject

This is used to disconnect a connected object's event sources.

```
object.DisconnectObject(obj)
```

- ❏  `object`—WScript object.
- ❏  `obj`—String value that indicate the name of the object to disconnect.

Disconnecting an object means that WSH will no longer respond to its events. It is important to note though that the object is still capable of firing events. Note also that the `DisconnectObject` method does nothing if the specified object is not already connected.

```
WScript.DisconnectObject RemoteScript
```

### Echo

This outputs text to either a message box or the command console window.

```
object.Echo [Arg1] [,Arg2] [,Arg3] ...
```

- ❏  `object`—WScript object.
- ❏  `Arg1`, `Arg2`, `Arg3`, ...—Optional. String value indicating the list of items to be displayed.

The `Echo` method gives a different type of output depending on which WSH engine you are using.

| WSH Engine | Text Output |
| --- | --- |
| `wscript.exe` | Graphical message box |
| `cscript.exe` | Command console window |

Figures 12-8 and 12-9 show an example of each output.

### GetObject

The `GetObject` method retrieves an existing object with the specified `ProgID`, or creates a new one from a file.

```
object.GetObject(strPathname [,strProgID], [strPrefix])
```

**Figure 12-8**

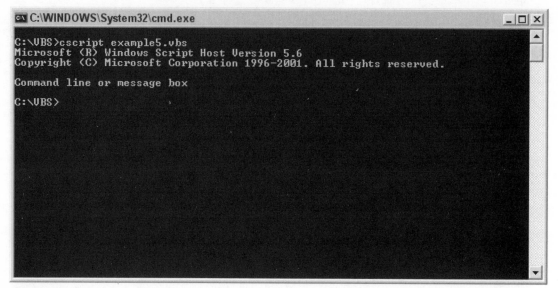

**Figure 12-9**

- ❑  object—WScript object.
- ❑  strPathname—A fully qualified path name of the file that contains the object persisted to disk.
- ❑  strProgID—Optional. The object's program identifier (ProgID).
- ❑  strPrefix—Optional. This is used when you want to synchronize the object's events. If you supply the strPrefix argument, WSH connects the object's outgoing interface to the script file after creating the object.

You use the GetObject method when an instance of the object exists in memory or when you want to create the object from a file. The GetObject method can be used with all COM classes, independent of the scripting language used to create the object.

If no current instance exists and you do not want the object created from a file, use the CreateObject method.

```
Dim MyObject As Object
Set MyObject = GetObject("C:\DRAWINGS\SCHEMA.DRW")
MyApp = MyObject.Application
```

## Quit

This method forces the script execution to immediately stop at any time.

```
object.Quit([intErrorCode])
```

❑   object—WScript object.

❑   intErrorCode—Optional. An integer value is returned as the process's exit code. If you omit the intErrorCode parameter, no value will be returned.

The Quit method can be used to return an optional error code. If the Quit method is the final instruction in your script (and you have no need to return a nonzero value), you can leave it out, and your script will terminate normally.

```
WScript.Quit 1

' This line of code is not executed.
MsgBox "This message will never be shown!"
```

Here is another example of the Quit method in action.

```
If Err.Number <> 0 Then
    WScript.Quit 1 ' some failure indicator
Else
    WScript.Quit 0 ' success
End If
WScript.Quit 1
```

## Sleep

This method suspends script execution for a specified length of time, and then continues execution.

```
object.Sleep(intTime)
```

❑   object—WScript object.

❑   intTime—This is an integer value indicating the interval (in milliseconds) that you want the script process to remain inactive for.

When using this method the thread running the script is suspended and CPU utilization is released. Execution resumes when the interval expires. To be triggered by an event, a script must be continually active because a script that has finished executing will certainly not detect an event. Events handled by the script will still be executed during a sleep.

Passing the Sleep method a 0 or −1 will not cause a script to be suspended indefinitely.

```
<package>
    <job id="vbs">
        <script language="VBScript">
        set WshShell = WScript.CreateObject("WScript.Shell")
        WshShell.Run "calc"
        WScript.Sleep 100
        WshShell.AppActivate "Calculator"
        WScript.Sleep 100
```

```
        WshShell.SendKeys "1{+}"
        WScript.Sleep 500
        WshShell.SendKeys "2"
        WScript.Sleep 500
        WshShell.SendKeys "~"
        WScript.Sleep 500
        WshShell.SendKeys "*9"
        WScript.Sleep 500
        WshShell.SendKeys "~"
        WScript.Sleep 2500
      </script>
    </job>
</package>
```

# The WshArguments Object

The use of arguments in programming tasks is a very useful mechanism for providing your script with input on which it can act. Think about working at a DOS prompt. Most command-line executable files use arguments in order to determine the right thing to do. For example, navigating within a directory structure.

```
c:\>cd wsh
```

In this instance, cd is the name of a DOS command (for change directory), while wsh is the name of the directory activated—it is an argument passed to cd.

Creating scripts that work with arguments is a good step toward writing reusable code. Developers creating scripts designed to execute on the command line may immediately see the benefits of working with the Arguments property. However, within WSH, there is another good reason to use this object, as this is how drag-and-drop functionality is implemented.

A final justification for the use of this object is that it allows developers to reuse script code within other scripts, by running the script in question as if it were executing on the command line, passing whatever arguments may be necessary at runtime.

## Accessing the WshArguments Object

This is accessed by using WScript.Arguments property.

```
Set objArgs = WScript.Arguments
```

## WshArguments Properties

The WshArguments object is a collection returned by the WScript object's Arguments property (WScript.Arguments).

There are three ways to access sets of command-line arguments:

❑   Access the entire set of arguments with the WshArguments object.

❑   Access the arguments that have names with the WshNamed object.

❑   Access the arguments that have no names with the WshUnnamed object.

The following example simply loops through the WshArguments collection, displaying each in turn.

```
Set objArgs = WScript. Arguments
For x = 0 to objArgs.Count - 1
    WScript.Echo objArgs(x)
Next
```

The interesting thing here is that this works in both `cscript` and `wscript`. You can try this out for yourself using the `echoargs.vbs` example. Execute on the command line, passing a few arguments:

```
c:\vbs\echoargs hello there
```

Figure 12-10 shows the output from the command line.

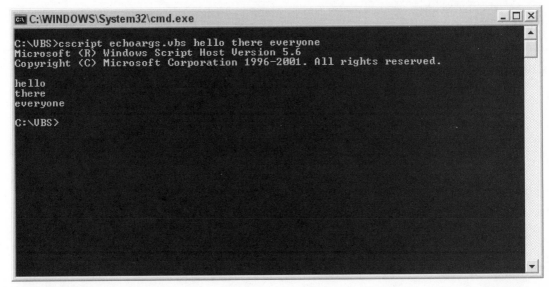

**Figure 12-10**

Now try dragging a file or two, then dropping them on `echoargs.vbs`. Figure 12-11 shows the output resulting from this.

**Figure 12-11**

## The WshShell Object

Windows Script Host provides a convenient way to gain access to system environment variables, create shortcuts, access Windows special folders such as the Windows Desktop, and add or remove entries from the registry. It is also possible to create more customized dialog boxes for user interaction by using features of the `Shell` object.

## Accessing the WshShell Object

Programmers should create an instance of the object WScript.Shell in order to be able to work with the properties listed in the next section. Further references to the WshShell object will refer to this created instance.

```
Set WshShell= WScript.CreateObject( "WScript.Shell" )
```

## WshShell Properties

The WshShell object has three properties:

- ❑  CurrentDirectory property
- ❑  Environment property
- ❑  SpecialFolders property

### CurrentDirectory

This property retrieves or changes the current active directory.

```
object.CurrentDirectory
```

- ❑  object—WshShell object.

The CurrentDirectory property returns a string that contains the fully qualified path of the current working directory of the active process.

```
Dim WshShell
Set WshShell = WScript.CreateObject("WScript.Shell")
WScript.Echo WshShell.CurrentDirectory
```

### Environment

This property returns the WshEnvironment object (a collection of environment variables).

```
object.Environment ([strType])
```

- ❑  object—WshShell object.
- ❑  strType—Optional. This specifies the location of the environment variable.

The Environment property contains the WshEnvironment object (a collection of environment variables). If strType is supplied, it specifies where the environment variable resides with possible values of:

- ❑  System
- ❑  User
- ❑  Volatile
- ❑  Process

If strType is not supplied, the Environment property returns different environment variable types depending on the operating system.

| Type of Environment Variable | Operating System |
| --- | --- |
| System | Microsoft Windows NT/2000/XP |
| Process | Windows 95/98/Me |

For Windows 95/98/Me, only one strType is permitted, Process. None of the others can be used in scripts.

The following table lists some of the variables that are provided with the Windows operating system.

| Name | Description | System | User | Process (NT/2000/XP) | Process (95/98/Me) |
| --- | --- | --- | --- | --- | --- |
| NUMBER_OF_PROCESSORS | Number of processors running on the machine. | x | — | X | — |
| PROCESSOR_ARCHITECTURE | Processor type of the user's workstation. | x | — | X | — |
| PROCESSOR_IDENTIFIER | Processor ID of the user's workstation. | x | — | X | — |
| PROCESSOR_LEVEL | Processor level of the user's workstation. | x | — | X | — |
| PROCESSOR_REVISION | Processor version of the user's workstation. | x | — | X | — |
| OS | Operating system on the user's workstation. | x | — | X | — |
| COMSPEC | Operating system on the user's workstation. | — | — | X | x |
| HOMEDRIVE | Primary local drive (usually this is C drive). | — | — | X | — |
| HOMEPATH | Default directory for users. | — | — | X | — |

*Continues*

| Name | Description | System | User | Process (NT/2000/XP) | Process (95/98/Me) |
|------|-------------|--------|------|----------------------|---------------------|
| PATH | PATH environment variable. | x | x | X | x |
| PATHEXT | Extensions for executable files (typically .com, .exe, .bat, or .cmd). | x | — | X | — |
| PROMPT | Command prompt (typically $P$G). | — | — | X | x |
| SYSTEMDRIVE | Local drive on which the system directory resides (typically c:\). | — | — | X | — |
| SYSTEMROOT | System directory (for example, c:\winnt). This is the same as WINDIR. | — | — | X | — |
| WINDIR | System directory (for example, c:\winnt). This is the same as SYSTEMROOT. | x | — | X | x |
| TEMP | Directory for storing temporary files (for example, c:\temp). | — | x | X | x |
| TMP | Directory for storing temporary files (for example, c:\temp). | — | x | X | x |

Note that scripts can access environment variables that have been set by other applications and that none of the variables listed above are available from the Volatile type.

Here is an example of how to use the variables listed in the table in your code. This returns the number of processors present on the system.

```
Set WshShell = WScript.CreateObject("WScript.Shell")
Set WshSysEnv = WshShell.Environment("SYSTEM")
WScript.Echo WshSysEnv("NUMBER_OF_PROCESSORS")
```

### SpecialFolders

This property returns a `SpecialFolders` object (a collection of special folders).

```
object.SpecialFolders(objWshSpecialFolders)
```

❑   object—WshShell object.

❑   objWshSpecialFolders—The name of the special folder.

The `WshSpecialFolders` object is a collection. This contains the entire set of Windows special folders, which include the Desktop folder, the Start Menu folder, and the My Documents folder.

The special folder name is used to index into the collection to retrieve the special folder you want. The `SpecialFolders` property returns an empty string if the requested folder (`strFolderName`) is not available. For example, Windows 95 does not have an `AllUsersDesktop` folder and returns an empty string if `strFolderName` is `AllUsersDesktop`.

The following special folders are available:

❑   AllUsersDesktop

❑   AllUsersStartMenu

❑   AllUsersPrograms

❑   AllUsersStartup

❑   Desktop

❑   Favorites

❑   Fonts

❑   MyDocuments

❑   NetHood

❑   PrintHood

❑   Programs

❑   Recent

❑   SendTo

❑   StartMenu

❑   Startup

❑   Templates

```
strDesktop = WshShell.SpecialFolders("StartMenu")
```

## WshShell Methods

The `WshShell` object has 11 methods. All these methods relate to the operating system shell and allow you control over the Windows registry, as well as being able to create pop-ups and shortcuts and activate and control running applications:

- ❑ AppActivate method
- ❑ CreateShortcut method
- ❑ ExpandEnvironmentStrings method
- ❑ LogEvent method
- ❑ Popup method
- ❑ RegDelete method
- ❑ RegRead method
- ❑ RegWrite method
- ❑ Run method
- ❑ SendKeys method
- ❑ Exec method

## *AppActivate*

Here you have a method that allows you to activate a specific application window already open.

```
object.AppActivate title
```

- ❑ object—WshShell object.
- ❑ title—Specifies which application to activate. This can be a string that contains the title of the application (as it appears in the title bar) or the application's Process ID.

The AppActivate method returns a Boolean value that identifies whether the procedure call is successful. This method is used to change the focus to the named application or window. It does not affect whether it is maximized or minimized. Focus moves away from the activated application window when the user takes action to change the focus (or closes the window).

To determine which application to activate, the specified title is compared to the title string of each running application. If no exact match exists, any application whose title string begins with title is activated. If an application still cannot be found, any application whose title string ends with title is activated. If more than one instance of the application named by title exists, one instance is arbitrarily activated. You do not have control over which one is chosen.

```
<package>
    <job id="vbs">
        <script language="VBScript">
        set WshShell = WScript.CreateObject("WScript.Shell")
        WshShell.Run "calc"
        WScript.Sleep 100
        WshShell.AppActivate "Calculator"
        WScript.Sleep 100
        WshShell.SendKeys "1{+}"
        WScript.Sleep 500
        WshShell.SendKeys "2"
        WScript.Sleep 500
```

```
        WshShell.SendKeys "~"
        WScript.Sleep 500
        WshShell.SendKeys "*3"
        WScript.Sleep 500
        WshShell.SendKeys "~"
        WScript.Sleep 2500
        </script>
    </job>
</package>
```

### CreateShortcut

This method can be used to either create a new shortcut or open an existing shortcut.

```
object.CreateShortcut(strPathname)
```

❑    object—WshShell object.

❑    strPathname—A string value indicating the pathname of the shortcut to create.

The CreateShortcut method returns either a WshShortcut object or a WshURLShortcut object. Calling the CreateShortcut method does not result in the creation of a shortcut. Instead, the shortcut object and changes you may have made to it are stored in memory until you save it to disk using the Save method. To create a shortcut, you must follow these steps:

❑    Create an instance of a WshShortcut object.

❑    Initialize its properties.

❑    Save it to disk with the Save method.

A common cause of problems is putting arguments in the TargetPath property of the shortcut object. This will not work. All arguments to the shortcut must be put in the Arguments property.

```
<package>
    <job id="vbs">
        <script language="VBScript">
        set WshShell = WScript.CreateObject("WScript.Shell")
        strDesktop = WshShell.SpecialFolders("Desktop")
        set oShellLink = WshShell.CreateShortcut(strDesktop & _
"\Shortcut Script.lnk")
        oShellLink.TargetPath = WScript.ScriptFullName
        oShellLink.WindowStyle = 1
        oShellLink.Hotkey = "CTRL+SHIFT+N"
        oShellLink.IconLocation = "notepad.exe, 0"
        oShellLink.Description = "Shortcut to Notepad"
        oShellLink.WorkingDirectory = strDesktop
        oShellLink.Save
        </script>
    </job>
</package>
```

### ExpandEnvironmentStrings

This method returns an environment variable's expanded value.

```
object.ExpandEnvironmentStrings(strString)
```

❑   object—WshShell object.

❑   strString—A string value indicating the name of the environment variable you want to expand.

This method expands environment variables defined in the PROCESS environment space only. Environment variable names must be enclosed between "%" characters and are not case-sensitive.

```
set WshShell = WScript.CreateObject("WScript.Shell")
WScript.Echo "The path to WinDir is " _
& WshShell.ExpandEnvironmentStrings("%WinDir%")
```

### LogEvent

The LogEvent method adds an event entry to a log file.

```
object.LogEvent(intType, strMessage [,strTarget])
```

❑   object—WshShell object.

❑   intType—Integer value representing the event type.

❑   strMessage—A string value that contains the log entry text.

❑   strTarget—Optional. A string value that indicates the name of the computer system where the event log is stored (the default is the local computer system). Applies to Windows NT/2000/XP only.

This method is used to return a Boolean value (True if an event is successfully logged, otherwise False). In Windows NT/2000/XP, events are logged in the Windows NT Event Log. In Windows 9x/Me, events are logged in WSH.log (which is located in the Windows directory).

There are six event types.

| Type | Value |
| --- | --- |
| 0 | SUCCESS |
| 1 | ERROR |
| 2 | WARNING |
| 4 | INFORMATION |
| 8 | AUDIT_SUCCESS |
| 16 | AUDIT_FAILURE |

```
Set WshShell = WScript.CreateObject("WScript.Shell")

'assume that rS contains a return code
'from another part of the code

if rS then
    WshShell.LogEvent 0, "Script Completed Successfully"
```

```
    else
        WshShell.LogEvent 1, "Script failed"
    end if
```

### Popup

This method is used to display text in a pop-up message box.

```
    intButton = object.Popup(strText,[nSecondsToWait],[strTitle],[nType])
```

- ❏ object—WshShell object.
- ❏ strText—A string value that contains the text you want to appear in the pop-up message box.
- ❏ nSecondsToWait—Optional. A numeric value indicating the maximum length of time (in seconds) you want the pop-up message box displayed.
- ❏ strTitle—Optional. A string value that contains the text you want to appear as the title of the pop-up message box.
- ❏ nType—Optional. A numeric value indicating the type of buttons and icons you want in the pop-up message box. These determine how the message box is used.
- ❏ IntButton—An integer value indicating the number of the button the user clicked to dismiss the message box. This is the value returned by the Popup method.

The Popup method is used to display a message box regardless of which host executable file is running the script (wscript.exe or cscript.exe).

If nSecondsToWait is equal to zero (the default), the pop-up message box remains visible until it is closed by the user. If nSecondsToWaitis is greater than zero, the pop-up message box closes after nSecondsToWait seconds.

If you don't supply the argument strTitle, the title of the pop-up message box is set to the default string "Windows Script Host".

The function of nType is the same as in the Microsoft Win32 application programming interface MessageBox function. The following tables show the values and their meanings. To get different results you can combine various values from these tables.

To display text properly in RTL (Right-to-Left) languages such as Hebrew or Arabic, add hex &h00100000 (decimal 1048576) to the nType parameter.

## Button Types

| Value | Description |
|---|---|
| 0 | Show the OK button |
| 1 | Show the OK and Cancel buttons |
| 2 | Show the Abort, Retry, and Ignore buttons |
| 3 | Show the Yes, No, and Cancel buttons |
| 4 | Show the Yes and No buttons |
| 5 | Show Retry and Cancel buttons |

## Icon Types

| Value | Description |
|---|---|
| 16 | Show the Stop Mark icon |
| 32 | Show the Question Mark icon |
| 48 | Show the Exclamation Mark icon |
| 64 | Show the Information Mark icon |

The return value intButton denotes the number of the button that the user clicked on. If the user does not click a button before nSecondsToWait seconds, intButton is set to –1.

| Value | Description |
|---|---|
| 1 | OK button |
| 2 | Cancel button |
| 3 | Abort button |
| 4 | Retry button |
| 5 | Ignore button |
| 6 | Yes button |
| 7 | No button |

```
Dim WshShell, BtnCode
Set WshShell = WScript.CreateObject("WScript.Shell")

BtnCode = WshShell.Popup("Do you like this code?", 7, "Quick survey:", 4 + 32)

Select Case BtnCode
    case 6     WScript.Echo "Glad to hear it - Thanks!"
    case 7     WScript.Echo "I'm sorry you didn't like it."
    case -1    WScript.Echo "Hellllooooooooo?"
End Select
```

### RegDelete

This method deletes a key or one of its values from the registry.

```
object.RegDelete(strName)
```

❏  object—WshShell object.

❏  strName—A string value that indicates the name of the registry key or key value to delete.

You can specify a key name by ending `strName` with a final backslash or leave it out to specify a value name.

Fully qualified key names and value names are prefixed with a root key. You can also use abbreviated versions of root key names with the `RegDelete` method.

The five possible root keys you can use are listed in the following table.

| Root Key Name | Abbreviation |
| --- | --- |
| HKEY_CURRENT_USER | HKCU |
| HKEY_LOCAL_MACHINE | HKLM |
| HKEY_CLASSES_ROOT | HKCR |
| HKEY_USERS | HKEY_USERS |
| HKEY_CURRENT_CONFIG | HKEY_CURRENT_CONFIG |

The script that follows creates, reads, and then deletes Windows registry keys. The highlighted part of the script does the key deleting.

```
Dim WshShell, bKey
Set WshShell = WScript.CreateObject("WScript.Shell")

WshShell.RegWrite "HKCU\Software\WROX\VBScript\", 1, "REG_BINARY"
WshShell.RegWrite "HKCU\Software\WROX\VBScript\ProgRef", "VBS_is_great", "REG_SZ"

bKey = WshShell.RegRead("HKCU\Software\WROX\VBScript\")
WScript.Echo WshShell.RegRead("HKCU\Software\WROX\VBScript\ProgRef")

WshShell.RegDelete "HKCU\Software\WROX\VBScript\ProgRef"
WshShell.RegDelete "HKCU\Software\WROX\VBScript\"
WshShell.RegDelete "HKCU\Software\WROX\"
```

*It is vitally important to take great care when modifying registry settings. Making incorrect changes to the registry can cause your system to become unstable or render it completely unusable. If you have any doubts about the inner workings of the registry, you are strongly advised to do some reading on the subject before beginning to experiment on your own.*

### RegRead

This method returns the value of a key or value name from the registry.

```
object.RegRead(strName)
```

❑ `object`—`WshShell` object.

❑ `strName`—A string value that indicates the key or value name whose value you want.

The `RegRead` method returns values of the following five types.

| Type | Description | In the Form of |
|------|-------------|----------------|
| REG_SZ | A string | A string |
| REG_DWORD | A number | An integer |
| REG_BINARY | A binary value | A VBArray of integers |
| REG_EXPAND_SZ | An expandable string (for example, `%windir%\\notepad.exe`) | A string |
| REG_MULTI_SZ | An array of strings | A VBArray of strings |

You can specify a key name by ending `strName` with a final backslash or leave it off to specify a value name.

A value entry consists of three parts:

❑     `Name`

❑     `Data type`

❑     `Value`

When you specify a key name (as opposed to a value name) `RegRead` returns the default value. To read a key's default value, specify the name of the key.

Fully qualified key names and value names begin with a root key. You can also use abbreviated versions of root key names with the `RegRead` method. The five possible root keys are listed in the following table.

| Root Key Name | Abbreviation |
|---------------|--------------|
| HKEY_CURRENT_USER | HKCU |
| HKEY_LOCAL_MACHINE | HKLM |
| HKEY_CLASSES_ROOT | HKCR |
| HKEY_USERS | HKEY_USERS |
| HKEY_CURRENT_CONFIG | HKEY_CURRENT_CONFIG |

The script that follows creates, reads, and then deletes Windows registry keys. The highlighted part of the script does the key reading.

```
Dim WshShell, bKey
Set WshShell = WScript.CreateObject("WScript.Shell")
```

```
WshShell.RegWrite "HKCU\Software\WROX\VBScript\", 1, "REG_BINARY"
WshShell.RegWrite "HKCU\Software\WROX\VBScript\ProgRef", "VBS_is_great", "REG_SZ"

bKey = WshShell.RegRead("HKCU\Software\WROX\VBScript\")
WScript.Echo WshShell.RegRead("HKCU\Software\WROX\VBScript\ProgRef")

WshShell.RegDelete "HKCU\Software\WROX\VBScript\ProgRef"
WshShell.RegDelete "HKCU\Software\WROX\VBScript\"
WshShell.RegDelete "HKCU\Software\WROX\"
```

### RegWrite

This method creates a new key, adds another value name to an existing key (and assigns it a value), or changes the value of an existing value name.

```
object.RegWrite(strName, anyValue [,strType])
```

- ❑ object—WshShell object.

- ❑ strName—A string value that indicates the key name, value name, or value you want to create, add, or change.

- ❑ anyValue—The name of the new key you want to create, the name of the value you want to add to an existing key, or the new value you want to assign to an existing value name.

- ❑ strType—Optional. A string value indicating the value's data type.

You can specify a key name by ending strName with a final backslash. Do not include the final backslash to specify a value name.

The RegWrite method automatically converts the parameter anyValue to either a string or an integer while the value of strType determines its data type (either a string or an integer) The following table lists the options available for the strType method.

| Converted to | StrType |
|---|---|
| String | REG_SZ |
| String | REG_EXPAND_SZ |
| Integer | REG_DWORD |
| Integer | REG_BINARY |

The REG_MULTI_SZ type is not supported for the RegWrite method.

RegWrite will write at most one DWORD to a REG_BINARY value. Larger values are not supported with this method. Fully qualified key names and value names are prefixed with a root key. You can use abbreviated versions of root key names with the RegWrite method. The five root keys of the Windows registry are listed in the following table.

| Root Key Name | Abbreviation |
|---|---|
| HKEY_CURRENT_USER | HKCU |
| HKEY_LOCAL_MACHINE | HKLM |
| HKEY_CLASSES_ROOT | HKCR |
| HKEY_USERS | HKEY_USERS |
| HKEY_CURRENT_CONFIG | HKEY_CURRENT_CONFIG |

The four possible data types you can specify with strType are listed in the following table.

| Type | Description | In the Form of |
|---|---|---|
| REG_SZ | A string | A string |
| REG_DWORD | A number | An integer |
| REG_BINARY | A binary value | A VBArray of integers |
| REG_EXPAND_SZ | An expandable string (for example, %windir% \\notepad.exe) | A string |

```
Dim WshShell, bKey
Set WshShell = WScript.CreateObject("WScript.Shell")

WshShell.RegWrite "HKCU\Software\WROX\VBScript\", 1, "REG_BINARY"
WshShell.RegWrite "HKCU\Software\WROX\VBScript\ProgRef", "VBS_is_great", "REG_SZ"

bKey = WshShell.RegRead("HKCU\Software\WROX\VBScript\")
WScript.Echo WshShell.RegRead("HKCU\Software\WROX\VBScript\ProgRef")

WshShell.RegDelete "HKCU\Software\WROX\VBScript\ProgRef"
WshShell.RegDelete "HKCU\Software\WROX\VBScript\"
WshShell.RegDelete "HKCU\Software\WROX\"
```

> It is vitally important to take great care when modifying registry settings. Making incorrect changes to the registry can cause your system to become unstable or render it completely unusable. If you have any doubts about the inner workings of the registry, you are strongly advised to do some reading on the subject before beginning to experiment on your own.

### Run

The Run method runs a program in a new process.

```
object.Run(strCommand, [intWindowStyle], [bWaitOnReturn])
```

- ❏  object—WshShell object.

- ❏  strCommand—A string value indicating the command line you want to run. You must include any parameters you want to pass to the executable file.

- ❏  intWindowStyle—Optional. An integer value indicating the appearance of the program's window. Not all programs make use of this information.

- ❏  bWaitOnReturn—Optional. A Boolean value indicating whether the script should wait for the program to finish executing before continuing to the next statement in your script. If set to True, script execution halts until the program finishes, and Run returns any error code returned by the program. If set to False (the default), the Run method returns immediately after starting the program, automatically returning 0 (this is not an error code).

The Run method returns an integer. The Run method starts a program running in a new Windows process. You can have your script wait for the program to finish executing before it continues, which allows you to run scripts and programs synchronously. If a file type has been properly registered to a particular program, calling Run on a file of that type executes the program. For example, calling Run on a *.txt file starts Notepad and loads the text file into it. The following table lists the available settings for intWindowStyle.

| IntWindowStyle | Description |
| --- | --- |
| 0 | Hides the window and activates another window. |
| 1 | Activates and displays a window. |
| | If the window is minimized or maximized, the system restores it to its original size and position. |
| | An application should specify this flag when displaying the window for the first time. |
| 2 | Activates the window and displays it as a minimized window. |
| 3 | Activates the window and displays it as a maximized window. |
| 4 | Displays a window in its most recent size and position. |
| | The active window remains active. |
| 5 | Activates the window and displays it in its current size and position. |
| 6 | Minimizes the specified window and activates the next top-level window in the Z order. |
| 7 | Displays the window as a minimized window. |
| | The active window remains active. |
| 8 | Displays the window in its current state. |
| | The active window remains active. |

*Continues*

337

| IntWindowStyle | Description |
|---|---|
| 9 | Activates and displays the window. |
| | If the window is minimized or maximized, the system restores it to its original size and position. |
| | An application should specify this flag when restoring a minimized window. |
| 10 | Sets the show-state based on the state of the program that started the application. |

```
Dim oShell
Set oShell = WScript.CreateObject ("WSCript.shell")
oShell.run "cmd /K CD C:\ & Dir"
Set oShell = Nothing
```

### SendKeys

The SendKeys method sends one or more keystrokes to the active window (as if typed on the keyboard).

```
object.SendKeys(string)
```

❑ object—WshShell object.

❑ string—A string value that indicates the keystroke or keystrokes that you want to send.

You use the SendKeys method to send keystrokes to applications that have no in-built automation interface. Most keyboard characters are represented by a single keystroke while some keyboard characters are made up of combinations of keystrokes (Alt + F4, for example).

To send a single keyboard character, you simply send the character itself as the string argument. For example, to send the letter v, send the string argument "v". To send a space, send the string " ".

You can also use the SendKeys method to send multiple keystrokes. You do this by creating a compound string argument that represents the sequence of keystrokes by appending each keystroke in the sequence to the one before it. For example, to send the keystrokes x, y, and z, you would send the string argument "xyz".

The SendKeys method uses some characters as modifiers of other characters. This set of special characters consists of parentheses, brackets, braces, and the following.

| | |
|---|---|
| Plus sign | "+" |
| Caret | "^" |
| Percent sign | "%" |
| Tilde | "~" |

To send these characters you enclose them inside curly braces "{}". So if you want to send the plus sign, send the string argument "{+}".

Square brackets " [] " have no special meaning when used with SendKeys, but you must enclose them within braces to accommodate applications that do give them a special meaning (Dynamic Data Exchange for example).

To send the square bracket characters, send the string argument "{[}" for the left bracket and "{]}" for the right one. To send curly brace characters, send the string argument "{{}" for the left brace and "{}}" for the right one.

Some keystrokes do not generate characters (such as Enter and Tab). Some keystrokes represent actions (such as Backspace and Break). To send these kinds of keystrokes, send the arguments shown in the following table.

| Key | Argument |
| --- | --- |
| Backspace | {BACKSPACE}, {BS}, or{BKSP} |
| Break | {BREAK} |
| Caps Lock | {CAPSLOCK} |
| Del or Delete | {DELETE} or {DEL} |
| Down Arrow | {DOWN} |
| End | {END} |
| Enter | {ENTER} or ~ |
| Esc | {ESC} |
| Help | {HELP} |
| Home | {HOME} |
| Ins or Insert | {INSERT} or {INS} |
| Left Arrow | {LEFT} |
| Num Lock | {NUMLOCK} |
| Page Down | {PGDN} |
| Page Up | {PGUP} |
| Print Screen | {PRTSC} |
| Right Arrow | {RIGHT} |
| Scroll Lock | {SCROLLLOCK} |
| Tab | {TAB} |
| Up Arrow | {UP} |
| F1 | {F1} |
| F2 | {F2} |

*Continues*

| Key | Argument |
|-----|----------|
| F3 | {F3} |
| F4 | {F4} |
| F5 | {F5} |
| F6 | {F6} |
| F7 | {F7} |
| F8 | {F8} |
| F9 | {F9} |
| F10 | {F10} |
| F11 | {F11} |
| F12 | {F12} |
| F13 | {F13} |
| F14 | {F14} |
| F15 | {F15} |
| F16 | {F16} |

To send keyboard characters that are composed of a regular keystroke in combination with a Shift, Ctrl, or Alt, you will need to create a compound string argument to represent the keystroke combination. You do this by preceding the regular keystroke with one or more of the following special characters.

| Key | Special Character |
|-----|-------------------|
| Alt | % |
| Ctrl | ^ |
| Shift | + |

When used for this purpose, these special characters are not enclosed within a set of braces.

To specify that a combination of Shift, Ctrl, and Alt should be held down while several other keys are pressed, you create a compound string argument with the modified keystrokes enclosed in parentheses. For example, to send the keystroke combination that specifies that the Shift key is held down while:

❑    V and B are pressed, send the string argument "+(VB)".

❑    V is pressed, followed by a lone B (with no Shift), send the string argument "+VB".

You can use the SendKeys method to send a pattern of keystrokes that consists of a single keystroke pressed multiple times. This is done by creating a compound string argument that specifies the keystroke you want to repeat, followed by the number of times you want the keystrokes repeated. You do this using a compound string argument of the form {keystroke number}. For example, to send the letter "V" ten times, you would send the string argument "{V 10}".

The only keystroke pattern you can send is the kind that is composed of a single keystroke pressed several times. For example, you can send "V" ten times, but you cannot do the same for "Ctrl+V". Note that you cannot send the Print Screen key {PRTSC} to an application.

```
<package>
    <job id="vbs">
        <script language="VBScript">
        set WshShell = WScript.CreateObject("WScript.Shell")
        WshShell.Run "calc"
        WScript.Sleep 100
        WshShell.AppActivate "Calculator"
        WScript.Sleep 100
        WshShell.SendKeys "1{+}"
        WScript.Sleep 500
        WshShell.SendKeys "2"
        WScript.Sleep 500
        WshShell.SendKeys "~"
        WScript.Sleep 500
        WshShell.SendKeys "*9"
        WScript.Sleep 500
        WshShell.SendKeys "~"
        WScript.Sleep 2500
        </script>
    </job>
</package>
```

### Exec

The Exec method runs an application in a child command shell, which provides access to the StdIn, StdOut, and StdErr streams.

```
object.Exec(strCommand)
```

❑ object—WshShell object.

❑ strCommand—A string value that indicates the command line used to run the script.

The Exec method returns a WshScriptExec object, which provides status and error information about a script run with Exec along with access to the StdIn, StdOut, and StdErr channels. The Exec method allows the execution of command-line applications only and cannot be used to run remote scripts.

# The WshNamed Object

The WshNamed object provides access to the named arguments from the command line.

The Named property of the WshArguments object returns the WshNamed object, which is a collection of arguments that have names. This collection uses the argument name as the index to retrieve individual argument values. There are three ways to access sets of command-line arguments:

❑ Access the entire set of arguments with the WshArguments object.

❑   Access the arguments that have names with the WshNamed object.

❑   Access the arguments that have no names with the WshUnnamed object.

## Accessing the WshNamed Object

This is accessed by creating an instance of WScript.Named.

```
Set argsNamed = WScript.Arguments.Named
```

## WshNamed Properties

The WshNamed object has two properties:

❑   Item property

❑   Length property

### Item

The Item property provides access to the items in the WshNamed object.

```
Object.Item(key)
```

❑   Object—WshNamed object

❑   key—The name of the item you want to retrieve.

The Item property returns a string. For collections, it returns an item based on the specified key. When entering the arguments at the command line, you can use spaces in string arguments as long as you enclose the string in quotes. The following line is typed at the command prompt to run the script.

```
sample.vbs /a:arg1 /b:arg2
```

If the following code is executed inside the script

```
WScript.Echo WScript.Arguments.Named.Item("b")
WScript.Echo WScript.Arguments.Named.Item("a")
```

then the following output is produced.

```
arg2
arg1
```

### Length

The Length property is a read-only integer that you use in scripts when you write in JScript. As such, this is beyond the scope of this book.

## WshNamed Methods

The WshNamed object has two methods:

❑   Count method

❑   Exists method

### Count

The Count method returns the number of switches in the WshNamed or WshUnnamed objects.

```
object.Count
```

❑   object—Arguments object.

The Count method is used to return an integer value. The Count method is intended for VBScript users, and JScript users should use the length property instead.

```
For x = 0 to WScript.Arguments.Count-1
    WScript.Echo WScript.Arguments.Named(x)
Next x
```

### Exists

The Exists method indicates whether a specific key value exists in the WshNamed object.

```
object.Exists(key)
```

❑   object—WshNamed object.

❑   Key—String value indicating an argument of the WshNamed object.

This method returns a Boolean value. It returns True if the requested argument was specified on the command line (otherwise, it returns False). The following line is typed at the command prompt to run the script.

```
sample.vbs /a:arg1 /b:arg2
```

The following code could be used to discover whether the arguments /a, /b, and /c were used.

```
WScript.Echo WScript.Arguments.Named.Exists("a")
WScript.Echo WScript.Arguments.Named.Exists("b")
WScript.Echo WScript.Arguments.Named.Exists("c")
```

# The WshUnnamed Object

The WshUnnamed object provides access to the unnamed arguments from the command line. It is a read-only collection that is returned by the Unnamed property of the WshArguments object. All individual argument values are retrieved from this collection using zero-based indexes.

There are three ways to access sets of command-line arguments:

❑   Access the entire set of arguments with the WshArguments object.

❑   Access the arguments that have names with the WshNamed object.

❑   Access the arguments that have no names with the WshUnnamed object.

## Accessing the WshUnnamed Object

This is accessed by creating an instance of WScript.Arguments.Unnamed.

```
Set argsUnnamed = WScript.Arguments.Unnamed
```

## WshUnnamed Properties

The WshUnnamed object has two properties:

- ❑ Item property
- ❑ Length property

Both these are similar to that of the WshNamed object and as such don't need to be covered again here.

## WshUnnamed Methods

The WshUnnamed object has one method:

- ❑ Count method

This method is similar to that of the WshNamed object and as such doesn't need to be covered again here.

# The WshNetwork Object

The WshNetwork object provides access to the shared resources on the network to which the computer is connected.

You will need to create a WshNetwork object when you want to connect to network shares and network printers, disconnect from network shares and network printers, map or remove network shares, or access information about a user on the network.

## Accessing the WshNetwork Object

This is accessed by creating an instance of WScript.Network.

```
Set WshNetwork = WScript.CreateObject("WScript.Network")
```

## WshNetwork Properties

The WshNetwork object has three properties:

- ❑ ComputerName property
- ❑ UserDomain property
- ❑ UserName property

### ComputerName

The ComputerName property returns the name of the computer system.

```
object.ComputerName
```

- ❑ object—WshNetwork object.

The ComputerName property contains a string value that indicates the name of the computer system.

```
<package>
    <job id="vbs">
        <script language="VBScript">
            Set WshNetwork = WScript.CreateObject("WScript.Network")
```

```
        WScript.Echo "Domain = " & WshNetwork.UserDomain
        WScript.Echo "Computer Name = " & WshNetwork.ComputerName
        WScript.Echo "User Name = " & WshNetwork.UserName
        </script>
    </job>
</package>
```

### UserDomain

The UserDomain property returns a user's domain name.

```
object.UserDomain
```

❑ object—WshNetwork object.

The UserDomain property will not work on Windows 98 and Windows Me unless the USERDOMAIN environment variable is set. This variable is not set by default.

```
<package>
    <job id="vbs">
        <script language="VBScript">
        Set WshNetwork = WScript.CreateObject("WScript.Network")
        WScript.Echo "Domain = " & WshNetwork.UserDomain
        WScript.Echo "Computer Name = " & WshNetwork.ComputerName
        WScript.Echo "User Name = " & WshNetwork.UserName
        </script>
    </job>
</package>
```

### UserName

The UserName property returns the name of a user.

```
object.UserName
```

❑ object—WshNetwork object.

The UserName property returns the name of a user as a string.

```
<package>
    <job id="vbs">
        <script language="VBScript">
        Set WshNetwork = WScript.CreateObject("WScript.Network")
        WScript.Echo "Domain = " & WshNetwork.UserDomain
        WScript.Echo "Computer Name = " & WshNetwork.ComputerName
        WScript.Echo "User Name = " & WshNetwork.UserName
        </script>
    </job>
</package>
```

## WshNetwork Methods

The WshNetwork object makes available the following eight methods:

❑ AddWindowsPrinterConnection method

❑ AddPrinterConnection method

345

- ❏ EnumNetworkDrives method
- ❏ EnumPrinterConnection method
- ❏ MapNetworkDrive method
- ❏ RemoveNetworkDrive method
- ❏ RemovePrinterConnection method
- ❏ SetDefaultPrinter method

### AddWindowsPrinterConnection

The AddWindowsPrinterConnection method adds a Windows printer connection to your computer system.

#### Windows NT/2000/XP

```
object.AddWindowsPrinterConnection(
    strPrinterPath
)
```

#### Windows 9x/Me

```
object.AddWindowsPrinterConnection(
    strPrinterPath,
    strDriverName[,strPort]
)
```

- ❏ object—WshNetwork object.
- ❏ strPrinterPath—A string value indicating the path to the printer connection.
- ❏ strDriverName—A string value indicating the name of the driver (this is ignored on Windows NT/2000/XP).
- ❏ strPort—Optional. A string value that specifies a printer port for the printer connection (this is ignored on Windows NT/2000/XP systems).

Using this method is very similar to using the Printer option on Control Panel to add a printer connection. This method allows you to create a printer connection without the inconvenience of having to direct it to a specific port.

If the connection fails, an error is generated.

```
Set WshNetwork = WScript.CreateObject("WScript.Network")
PrinterPath = "\\printerserver\DefaultPrinter"
WshNetwork.AddWindowsPrinterConnection PrinterPath
```

### AddPrinterConnection

The AddPrinterConnection method adds a remote MS-DOS printer connection to your computer system.

```
object.AddPrinterConnection(strLocalName,
    strRemoteName[,bUpdateProfile][,strUser][,strPassword])
```

- ❏ object—WshNetwork object.
- ❏ strLocalName—A string value that indicates the local name to assign to the connected printer.

❏ strRemoteName—A string value that indicates the name of the remote printer.

❏ bUpdateProfile—Optional. A Boolean value that indicates whether the printer mapping is stored in the current user's profile. If bUpdateProfile is supplied and is True, the mapping is stored in the user profile. The default value is False.

❏ strUser—Optional. A string value that indicates the user name. If you are mapping a remote printer using the profile of someone other than current user, you can specify strUser and strPassword.

❏ strPassword—Optional. A string value that indicates the user password. If you are mapping a remote printer using the profile of someone other than current user, you can also specify strUser and strPassword.

## EnumNetworkDrives

The EnumNetworkDrives method returns the current network drive mapping information.

```
objDrives = object.EnumNetworkDrives
```

❏ object—WshNetwork object.

❏ objDrives—A variable that holds the network drive mapping information.

This method returns a collection which is an array that associates pairs of items—network drive local names and their associated UNC (Universal Naming Convention) names. Even-numbered items in the collection represent local names of logical drives while odd-numbered items represent the associated UNC share names.

The first item in the collection is at index zero (0).

## EnumPrinterConnection

The EnumPrinterConnections method returns the current network printer mapping information.

```
objPrinters = object.EnumPrinterConnections
```

❏ object—WshNetwork object.

❏ objPrinters—A variable that holds the network printer mapping information.

The EnumPrinterConnections method returns a collection that consists of an array that associates pairs of items—network printer local names and their associated UNC names. Even-numbered items in the collection represent printer ports while odd-numbered items represent the networked printer UNC names.

The first item in the collection is at index zero (0).

## MapNetworkDrive

The MapNetworkDrive method adds a shared network drive to your computer system.

```
object.MapNetworkDrive(strLocalName, strRemoteName, [bUpdateProfile],
[strUser], [strPassword])
```

❏ object—WshNetwork object.

❏ strLocalName—A string value that indicates the name by which the mapped drive will be known locally.

❑ strRemoteName—A string value that indicates the share's UNC name (\\xxx\yyy).

❑ bUpdateProfile—Optional. A Boolean value indicating whether the mapping information is stored in the current user's profile. If bUpdateProfile is supplied and has a value of True, the mapping is stored in the user profile (the default is False).

❑ strUser—Optional. A string value that indicates the user name. You must supply this argument if you are mapping a network drive using the credentials of someone other than the current user.

❑ strPassword—Optional. A string value that indicates the user password. You must supply this argument if you are mapping a network drive using the credentials of someone other than the current user.

An attempt to map a nonshared network drive will result in an error being generated.

### RemoveNetworkDrive

The RemoveNetworkDrive method removes a shared network drive from your computer system.

```
object.RemoveNetworkDrive(strName, [bForce], [bUpdateProfile])
```

❑ object—WshNetwork object.

❑ strName—A string value that indicates the name of the mapped drive you want to remove. The strName parameter can be either a local name or a remote name depending on how the drive is mapped.

❑ bForce—Optional. A Boolean value indicating whether to force the removal of the mapped drive. If bForce is supplied and its value is True, this method removes the connections whether the resource is used or not.

❑ bUpdateProfile—Optional. A string value indicating whether to remove the mapping from the user's profile. If bUpdateProfile is supplied and its value is True, this mapping is removed from the user profile. bUpdateProfile is False by default.

If the drive has a mapping between a local name (drive letter) and a remote name (UNC name) then strName must be set to the local name. If the network path does not have a local name mapping, then strName must be set to the remote name. The following script removes the network drive "G:".

```
Dim WshNetwork
Set WshNetwork = WScript.CreateObject("WScript.Network")
WshNetwork.RemoveNetworkDrive "G:"
```

### RemovePrinterConnection

The RemovePrinterConnection method removes a shared network printer connection from a computer.

```
object.RemovePrinterConnection(strName, [bForce], [bUpdateProfile])
```

❑ object—WshNetwork object.

❑ strName—A string value that indicates the name that identifies the printer. It can be a UNC name (in the form \\xxx\yyy) or a local name (such as LPT1).

❑ bForce—Optional. A Boolean value indicating whether to force the removal of the mapped printer. If this is set to True (the default is False), the printer connection is removed whether or not a user is connected.

❑ bUpdateProfile—Optional. A Boolean value. If set to `True` (the default is `False`), the change is saved in the user's profile.

The `RemovePrinterConnection` method will remove both Windows- and MS-DOS-based printer connections.

If the printer was connected using the method `AddPrinterConnection`, `strName` must be the printer's local name.

If the printer was connected using the `AddWindowsPrinterConnection` method or was added manually, then `strName` must be the printer's UNC name.

### SetDefaultPrinter

The `SetDefaultPrinter` method assigns a remote printer as the default printer.

```
object.SetDefaultPrinter(strPrinterName)
```

❑ object—`WshNetwork` object.

❑ strPrinterName—A string value that indicates the UNC name of the remote printer.

The `SetDefaultPrinter` method will fail when using a DOS-based printer connection. Also, you cannot use the `SetDefaultPrinter` method to determine the name of the currently installed default printer.

# The WshEnvironment Object

The `WshEnvironment` object provides access to the collection of Windows environment variables.

This object is a collection of environment variables that are returned by the `WshShell` object's `Environment` property. This collection contains the entire set of environment variables (both those with names and those without).

To retrieve individual environment variables (and their values) from this collection, you would use the environment variable name as the index.

## Accessing the WshEnvironment Object

This is accessed by creating an instance of `WScript.Environment`. The following script returns the number of processors installed on the system running the script.

```
Set WshShell = WScript.CreateObject("WScript.Shell")
Set WshSysEnv = WshShell.Environment("SYSTEM")
WScript.Echo WshSysEnv("NUMBER_OF_PROCESSORS")
```

## WshEnvironment Properties

The `WshEnvironment` object has two properties:

❑ Item property

❑ Length property

### Item

The Item property exposes a specified item from a collection.

```
Object.Item(natIndex)
```

❑　Object—The result of the EnumNetworkDrive or EnumPrinterConnections method, or the object returned by the Environment or SpecialFolders property.

❑　natIndex—Sets the item to retrieve.

Item is the default property for each collection. For EnumNetworkDrive and EnumPrinterConnections collections, index is an integer, while for the Environment and SpecialFolders collections, index is a string.

WshShell.SpecialFolders.Item (strFolderName) returns "Empty" in VBScript if the requested folder (strFolderName) is not available.

```
<package>
    <job id="vbs">
       <script language="VBScript">
       Set WshShell = WScript.CreateObject("WScript.Shell")
       Set WshSpecialFolders = WshShell.SpecialFolders
       For x = 0 To WshSpecialFolders.Count - 1
           WScript.Echo WshSpecialFolders.Item(x)
       Next
       </script>
    </job>
</package>
```

### Length

The Length property is a read-only integer that you use in scripts when you write in JScript. As such, this is beyond the scope of this book.

## WshEnvironment Methods

The WshEnvironment object has two methods:

❑　Count method

❑　Remove method

### Count

The Count method returns a Long value, which is the number of items in the collection.

```
object.Count
```

❑　object—Arguments object.

The Count method returns an integer value. The Count method is intended for VBScript users, and JScript users should use the Length property.

```
For x = 0 to WScript.Arguments.Count-1
    WScript.Echo WScript.Arguments.Named(x)
Next x
```

### Remove

The `Remove` method removes an existing environment variable.

```
object.Remove(strName)
```

❑   `object`—WshEnvironment object.

❑   `strName`—A string value that indicates the name of the environment variable that you want to remove.

The `Remove` method removes environment variables from the following types of environments:

❑   PROCESS

❑   USER

❑   SYSTEM

❑   VOLATILE

Environment variables removed with the `Remove` method are not permanently removed and are restored at the end of the current session.

```
Dim WshShell, WshEnv
Set WshShell = WScript.CreateObject("WScript.Shell")
Set WshEnv = WshShell.Environment("PROCESS")
WshEnv("tVar") = "VBScript is Cool!"
WScript.Echo WshShell.ExpandEnvironmentStrings("The value of the test
variable is: '%tVar%'")
WshEnv.Remove "tVar"
WScript.Echo WshShell.ExpandEnvironmentStrings("The value of the test
variable is: '%tVar%'")
```

# The WshSpecialFolders Object

The `WshSpecialFolders` object provides access to the collection of Windows special folders.

The `WshShell` object's `SpecialFolders` property returns the `WshSpecialFolders` object. This collection contains references to Windows special folders (for example, the Desktop folder and Start Menu folder).

This collection retrieves the paths to special folders using the special folder name as the index. The path of a special folder depends on the user environment. If there are several different users on the same computer, several different sets of special folders will exist on the hard drive.

The following special folders are available:

❑   AllUsersDesktop

❑   AllUsersStartMenu

❑   AllUsersPrograms

❑   AllUsersStartup

- ❑ Desktop

- ❑ Favorites

- ❑ Fonts

- ❑ MyDocuments

- ❑ NetHood

- ❑ PrintHood

- ❑ Programs

- ❑ Recent

- ❑ SendTo

- ❑ StartMenu

- ❑ Startup

- ❑ Templates

```vbscript
<package>
    <job id="vbs">
        <script language="VBScript">
        set WshShell = WScript.CreateObject("WScript.Shell")
        strDesktop = WshShell.SpecialFolders("Desktop")
        set oShellLink = WshShell.CreateShortcut(strDesktop & "\Shortcut
Script.lnk")
        oShellLink.TargetPath = WScript.ScriptFullName
        oShellLink.WindowStyle = 1
        oShellLink.Hotkey = "CTRL+SHIFT+N"
        oShellLink.IconLocation = "notepad.exe, 0"
        oShellLink.Description = "A Script Generated Shortcut to Notepad"
        oShellLink.WorkingDirectory = strDesktop
        oShellLink.Save
        </script>
    </job>
</package>
```

## WshSpecialFolders Properties

The WshSpecialFolders object has one property:

- ❑ Item property

### Item

The Item property exposes a specified item from a collection.

```
Object.Item(natIndex)
```

- ❑ Object—The result of the EnumNetworkDrive or EnumPrinterConnections method, or the object returned by the Environment or SpecialFolders property.

- ❑ natIndex—Sets the item to retrieve.

Item is the default property for each collection. For EnumNetworkDrive and
EnumPrinterConnections collections, index is an integer, while for the Environment and
SpecialFolders collections, index is a string.

```
<package>
    <job id="vbs">
        <script language="VBScript">
        Set WshShell = WScript.CreateObject("WScript.Shell")
        Set WshSpecialFolders = WshShell.SpecialFolders
        For x = 0 To WshSpecialFolders.Count - 1
            WScript.Echo WshSpecialFolders.Item(x)
        Next
        </script>
    </job>
</package>
```

## WshSpecialFolders Methods

The WshSpecialFolders object has one method:

❑   Count property

### Count

The Count method returns the number of switches in the WshNamed or WshUnnamed object.

```
object.Count
```

❑   object—Arguments object.

The Count method returns an integer value. The Count method is intended for VBScript users, and
JScript users should use the Length property.

# The WshShortcut Object

The WshShortcut object allows you to create shortcuts using script.

```
<package>
    <job id="vbs">
        <script language="VBScript">
        set WshShell = WScript.CreateObject("WScript.Shell")
        strDesktop = WshShell.SpecialFolders("Desktop")
        set oShellLink = WshShell.CreateShortcut(strDesktop & "\Shortcut
Script.lnk")
        oShellLink.TargetPath = WScript.ScriptFullName
        oShellLink.WindowStyle = 1
        oShellLink.Hotkey = "CTRL+SHIFT+N"
        oShellLink.IconLocation = "notepad.exe, 0"
        oShellLink.Description = "Shortcut Script"
        oShellLink.WorkingDirectory = strDesktop
        oShellLink.Save
        </script>
    </job>
</package>
```

## WshShortcut Properties

The `WshShortcut` object has eight properties:

- ❏ `Arguments` property
- ❏ `Description` property
- ❏ `FullName` property
- ❏ `Hotkey` property
- ❏ `IconLocation` property
- ❏ `TargetPath` property
- ❏ `WindowStyle` property
- ❏ `WorkingDirectory` property

### Arguments

The `Arguments` property contains the `WshArguments` object (a collection of arguments). Use a zero-based index to retrieve individual arguments from this collection.

```
Set objArgs = WScript.Arguments
For x = 0 to objArgs.Count - 1
    WScript.Echo objArgs(x)
Next
```

### Description

The `Description` property returns a description of a shortcut.

```
object.Description
```

- ❏ `object`—WshShortcut object.

The `Description` property contains a string value describing a shortcut.

```
<package>
    <job id="vbs">
        <script language="VBScript">
        set WshShell = WScript.CreateObject("WScript.Shell")
        strDesktop = WshShell.SpecialFolders("Desktop")
        set oShellLink = WshShell.CreateShortcut(strDesktop & "\Shortcut
Script.lnk")
        oShellLink.TargetPath = WScript.ScriptFullName
        oShellLink.WindowStyle = 1
        oShellLink.Hotkey = "CTRL+SHIFT+N"
        oShellLink.IconLocation = "notepad.exe, 0"
        oShellLink.Description = "Script generated shortcut to Notepad"
        oShellLink.WorkingDirectory = strDesktop
        oShellLink.Save
        </script>
    </job>
</package>
```

## FullName

The `FullName` property returns the fully qualified path of the shortcut object's target.

```
object.FullName
```

❑   `object`—`WshShortcut` object.

The `FullName` property contains a read-only string value that gives the fully qualified path to the shortcut's target.

```
<package>
    <job id="vbs">
        <script language="VBScript">
        set WshShell = WScript.CreateObject("WScript.Shell")
        strDesktop = WshShell.SpecialFolders("Desktop")
        set oShellLink = WshShell.CreateShortcut(strDesktop & "\Shortcut
Script.lnk")
        oShellLink.TargetPath = WScript.ScriptFullName
        oShellLink.WindowStyle = 1
        oShellLink.Hotkey = "CTRL+SHIFT+N"
        oShellLink.IconLocation = "notepad.exe, 0"
        oShellLink.Description = "Shortcut Script"
        oShellLink.WorkingDirectory = strDesktop
        oShellLink.Save
        WScript.Echo oShellLink.FullName
        </script>
    </job>
</package>
```

## Hotkey

The `Hotkey` property is used to assign a key combination to a shortcut, or identifies the key combination assigned to a shortcut. A *hotkey* is a combination of keys that starts a shortcut when all associated keys are held down at the same time.

```
object.Hotkey = strHotkey
```

❑   `object`—`WshShortcut` object.

❑   `strHotkey`—A string that represents the key combination to assign to the shortcut.

The following is the syntax of `strHotkey`.

```
[KeyModifier]KeyName
```

`KeyModifier`—`KeyModifier` can be any one of the following: Alt+, Ctrl+, Shift+, Ext+.

*Ext+ means "Extended key." This has been added in case a new type of Shift key is added to the character set in the future.*

*KeyName—a . . . z, 0 . . . 9, F1 . . . F12, . . .*

*The KeyName is not case-sensitive.*

```
<package>
    <job id="vbs">
        <script language="VBScript">
```

```
        set WshShell = WScript.CreateObject("WScript.Shell")
        strDesktop = WshShell.SpecialFolders("Desktop")
        set oShellLink = WshShell.CreateShortcut(strDesktop & "\Shortcut
Script.lnk")
        oShellLink.TargetPath = WScript.ScriptFullName
        oShellLink.WindowStyle = 1
        oShellLink.Hotkey = "CTRL+SHIFT+N"
        oShellLink.IconLocation = "notepad.exe, 0"
        oShellLink.Description = "Shortcut Script"
        oShellLink.WorkingDirectory = strDesktop
        oShellLink.Save
        WScript.Echo oShellLink.FullName
        </script>
    </job>
</package>
```

### IconLocation

The `IconLocation` property is used to assign an icon to a shortcut, or identify the icon assigned to a shortcut.

```
object.IconLocation = strIconLocation
```

❑   object—WshShortcut object.

❑   strIconLocation—A string that specifies the icon to use. The string should contain a fully qualified path and an index associated with the icon. The index is used to select the appropriate icon when more than one exists. The index begins at zero (0).

```
<package>
    <job id="vbs">
        <script language="VBScript">
        set WshShell = WScript.CreateObject("WScript.Shell")
        strDesktop = WshShell.SpecialFolders("Desktop")
        set oShellLink = WshShell.CreateShortcut(strDesktop & "\Shortcut
Script.lnk")
        oShellLink.TargetPath = WScript.ScriptFullName
        oShellLink.WindowStyle = 1
        oShellLink.Hotkey = "CTRL+SHIFT+N"
        oShellLink.IconLocation = "notepad.exe, 0"
        oShellLink.Description = "Shortcut Script"
        oShellLink.WorkingDirectory = strDesktop
        oShellLink.Save
        WScript.Echo oShellLink.FullName
        </script>
    </job>
</package>
```

### TargetPath

The `TargetPath` property gives the path to the shortcut's executable file.

```
object.TargetPath
```

❑   object—WshShortcut or WshUrlShortcut object.

This property is for the shortcut's target path only. Any arguments provided must be placed in the Argument's property.

```
<package>
    <job id="vbs">
        <script language="VBScript">
        set WshShell = WScript.CreateObject("WScript.Shell")
        strDesktop = WshShell.SpecialFolders("Desktop")
        set oShellLink = WshShell.CreateShortcut(strDesktop & "\Shortcut
Script.lnk")
        oShellLink.TargetPath = WScript.ScriptFullName
        oShellLink.WindowStyle = 1
        oShellLink.Hotkey = "CTRL+SHIFT+N"
        oShellLink.IconLocation = "notepad.exe, 0"
        oShellLink.Description = "Shortcut Script"
        oShellLink.WorkingDirectory = strDesktop
        oShellLink.Save
        WScript.Echo oShellLink.FullName
        </script>
    </job>
</package>
```

### WindowStyle

The `WindowStyle` property is used to either assign a window style to a shortcut or identify the type of window style used by a shortcut.

```
object.WindowStyle = intWindowStyle
```

❑ `object`—WshShortcut object.

❑ `intWindowStyle`—This sets the window style for the program being run.

The `WindowStyle` property returns an integer.

The following table lists the available settings for `intWindowStyle`.

| InWindowStyle | Description |
| --- | --- |
| 1 | Activates and displays a window. |
| | If the window is minimized or maximized, the system restores it to its original size and position. |
| | An application should specify this flag when displaying the window for the first time. |
| 3 | Activates the window and displays it as a maximized window. |
| 7 | Displays the window as a minimized window. |
| | The active window remains active. |

```
<package>
    <job id="vbs">
        <script language="VBScript">
        set WshShell = WScript.CreateObject("WScript.Shell")
        strDesktop = WshShell.SpecialFolders("Desktop")
```

```
        set oShellLink = WshShell.CreateShortcut(strDesktop & "\Shortcut
Script.lnk")
        oShellLink.TargetPath = WScript.ScriptFullName
        oShellLink.WindowStyle = 1
        oShellLink.Hotkey = "CTRL+SHIFT+N"
        oShellLink.IconLocation = "notepad.exe, 0"
        oShellLink.Description = "Shortcut Script"
        oShellLink.WorkingDirectory = strDesktop
        oShellLink.Save
        WScript.Echo oShellLink.FullName
        </script>
    </job>
</package>
```

### WorkingDirectory

The WorkingDirectory property is used to assign a working directory to a shortcut, or to identify the working directory used by a shortcut.

```
object.WorkingDirectory = strWorkingDirectory
```

❑   object—WshShortcut object.

❑   strWorkingDirectory—A string. The directory in which the shortcut starts.

```
<package>
    <job id="vbs">
        <script language="VBScript">
        set WshShell = WScript.CreateObject("WScript.Shell")
        strDesktop = WshShell.SpecialFolders("Desktop")
        set oShellLink = WshShell.CreateShortcut(strDesktop & "\Shortcut
Script.lnk")
        oShellLink.TargetPath = WScript.ScriptFullName
        oShellLink.WindowStyle = 1
        oShellLink.Hotkey = "CTRL+SHIFT+N"
        oShellLink.IconLocation = "notepad.exe, 0"
        oShellLink.Description = "Shortcut Script"
        oShellLink.WorkingDirectory = strDesktop
        oShellLink.Save
        WScript.Echo oShellLink.FullName
        </script>
    </job>
</package>
```

## WshShortcut Methods

The WshShortcut object has one method:

❑   Save method.

### Save

The Save method saves a shortcut object to disk.

```
object.Save
```

❑   object—WshShortcut or WshUrlShortcut object.

After you have used the `CreateShortcut` method to create a shortcut object and set the shortcut object's properties, you use the `Save` method to save the shortcut object to the hard drive. The `Save` method uses the information in the shortcut object's `FullName` property to determine where to place the shortcut object on a hard drive.

Shortcuts can only be created to system objects—files, directories, and drives. Shortcuts cannot be created to printer or scheduled tasks.

# The WshUrlShortcut Object

The `WshUrlShortcut` object allows you to create shortcuts to Internet resource using script. It is a child object of the `WshShell` object. You must use the `WshShell` method's `CreateShortcut` to create a `WshUrlShortcut` object. This file would be saved as a `.wsf` Windows Script file.

```
WshShell.CreateShortcut(strDesktop & "\URLShortcut.lnk")

<package>
    <job id="vbs">
        <script language="VBScript">
        set WshShell = WScript.CreateObject("WScript.Shell")
        set oUrlLink = WshShell.CreateShortcut(strDesktop & "\Wrox Web
Site.url")
        oUrlLink.TargetPath = "http://www.wrox.com"
        oUrlLink.Save
        </script>
    </job>
</package>
```

## WshUrlShortcut Properties

The `WshUrlShortcut` object has two properties:

❑   `FullName` property

❑   `TargetPath` property

### FullName

The `FullName` property returns the fully qualified path of the shortcut object's target.

```
object.FullName
```

❑   object—WshUrlShortcut object.

The `FullName` property contains a read-only string value that gives the fully qualified path to the shortcut's target. This file would be saved as a `.wsf` Windows Script file.

```
<package>
    <job id="vbs">
        <script language="VBScript">
        set WshShell = WScript.CreateObject("WScript.Shell")
        set oUrlLink = WshShell.CreateShortcut(strDesktop & "\Wrox Web
Site.url")
```

```
            oUrlLink.TargetPath = "http://www.wrox.com"
            oUrlLink.Save
            WScript.Echo oUrlLink.FullName
            </script>
        </job>
    </package>
```

### TargetPath

The `TargetPath` property gives the path to the shortcut's executable file.

```
    object.TargetPath
```

❑    object—`WshUrlShortcut` object.

This property is for the shortcut's target path only. Any arguments provided must be placed in the `Argument`'s property. This file would be saved as a `.wsf` Windows Script file.

```
<package>
    <job id="vbs">
        <script language="VBScript">
        set WshShell = WScript.CreateObject("WScript.Shell")
        set oUrlLink = WshShell.CreateShortcut(strDesktop & "\Wrox Web Site.url")
        oUrlLink.TargetPath = "http://www.wrox.com"
        oUrlLink.Save
        WScript.Echo oUrlLink.FullName
        </script>
    </job>
</package>
```

## WshUrlShortcut Methods

The `WshUrlShortcut` object has one method:

❑    `Save` method.

### Save

The `Save` method saves a shortcut object to disk.

```
    object.Save
```

❑    object—`WshUrlShortcut` object.

After you have used the `CreateShortcut` method to create a shortcut object and set the shortcut object's properties, you use the `Save` method to save the shortcut object to the hard drive. The `Save` method uses the information in the shortcut object's `FullName` property to determine where to place the shortcut object on a hard drive. This file would be saved as a `.wsf` Windows Script file.

```
<package>
    <job id="vbs">
        <script language="VBScript">
        set WshShell = WScript.CreateObject("WScript.Shell")
        set oUrlLink = WshShell.CreateShortcut(strDesktop & "\Wrox Web
Site.url")
        oUrlLink.TargetPath = "http://www.wrox.com"
```

```
         oUrlLink.Save
         WScript.Echo oUrlLink.FullName
         </script>
     </job>
</package>
```

# Summary

We have covered a lot in this chapter. Here's a recap of the topics we've looked at:

- ❏  The tools needed to get started writing scripts with Windows Script Host
- ❏  Ways in which WSH can be used, including the creation of custom solutions which integrate scripting with COM components
- ❏  The cscript.exe and wscript.exe execution environments and how they differ
- ❏  How to customize the behavior of individual scripts through the use of .wsh configuration files
- ❏  A detailed examination of the object model available to WSH developers

# Windows Script Components

## Overview

In this chapter, we'll be examining Windows Script Components. We will examine their structure and also how to create and register them. Later in the chapter, we'll look at how we can use classes in our components.

If you are used to using XML then the structure of the script here will be familiar to you and that will be a huge advantage, if not, work carefully through the examples and all will become clear!

## What Are Windows Script Components?

Windows Script Components are interpreted COM components (they have to be interpreted because VBScript and all other scripting languages are interpreted). Structurally, they are XML-based files that contain script code. Within the files themselves you can use VBScript, JScript, Python, PScript, PERLScript, or any other scripting language. As always, we will focus on using VBScript in this chapter (for obvious reasons), but it is possible to use the script language of your choice.

The script components are interpreted by the Script Component Runtime which exposes the internal properties and methods, fires the events, and makes the component look like a compiled COM component to the calling application. We will look at the Script Component Runtime in more detail in the next section.

Script components are full COM components, and have the ability to call other COM components. Script components have some built-in interfaces into the Active Server Pages library and Internet Explorer DHTML behaviors that make it very easy to build these components for the Web.

One important point to note is that script components are not designed for use as early bound access objects. If you reference a script component as an early bound component then your application will generate a runtime error. This is a common issue when using script components, which crops up all the time. Keep them late bound and you will have fewer problems implementing them.

Late bound access means that there is no information available at compile time about the object being accessed, and everything is evaluated dynamically at runtime. Early bound access provides you with information about the object you are accessing while you are building your program. It is normally faster when running your program to use early bound access, but in this case it cannot be used.

You might be wondering, why you would want to use these when you could use Visual Basic to build a standard COM component instead. The main reason is that Windows Script Components don't require a compiler. The minimum that you will need to build script components is the good old Windows Notepad or another simple text editor. Script components are also a quick and easy way to encapsulate functions and routines that you write in VBScript. By doing this you can create a library of your source code. Finally, if you still need convincing, the ASP interfaces allow you to directly access the Active Server Pages library for quick and easy integration with your Internet or intranet sites.

*If you're not familiar with ASP, don't worry—Chapter 18 is an introduction to that subject.*

## What Tools Do You Need?

Before we move on, let's get your toolkit in order. You can create Windows Script Components with nothing more than Notepad and your imagination, but if you plan on doing a lot of scripting, you may find it a little tedious to do it all by hand. Microsoft provides the Script Component Wizard (which you can find at www.microsoft.com/scripting/—the precise URL for this varies but if you access the download section of the scripting area you will find it there. You are looking for a file called wz10en.exe) to help speed up the creation of the script component framework. You need to have the VBScript 5.0 libraries (preferably the latest 5.6 libraries) on your machine to run script components properly. Script components use the Windows Script Host when they run, so you'll also need that. Luckily, all this will be installed with the scripting libraries.

Here's a list of items that you must have to create script components.

- ❏ VBScript 5.0 libraries or later (5.6 libraries if possible)
- ❏ Internet Explorer 5.0 or later (Internet Explorer 6.0 preferred)
- ❏ The Script Component Wizard (optional)
- ❏ A copy of the Script Component documentation (optional)

*All these downloads are available free of charge from the Microsoft Web site.*

## The Script Component Runtime

Since Script Components are interpreted during runtime (as they are run) there is need for an interpreter to be installed on the client system. The Script Component Runtime (scrobj.dll) is the interpreter used to control calls between clients and script components. The runtime implements the basic COM interfaces for the component (IUnknown) and handles some of the basic COM methods (QueryInterface, AddRef) in the same way that the Visual Basic runtime handles the low-level COM routines of Visual Basic components.

Since we are running though an interpreter, our script components will look different from other COM components in the registry. Let's examine this in a little more detail. We will assume that our object is called "Math.WSC" and that we are calling this object through script.

```
Set objMath = CreateObject("Math.WSC")
```

The first thing that happens is that the registry will be searched for the Math.WSC entry under HKEY_CLASSES_ROOT. The registry entry of this is shown in Figure 13-1.

**Figure 13-1**

If we look up the GUID (Globally Unique IDentifier) under HKEY_CLASSES_ROOT\CLSID then it brings us to our information for our COM component.

Notice that in Figure 13-2 the InprocServer32 key is actually scrobj.dll, not the script component file itself. We are actually creating the scrobj.dll component when we call our CreateObject statement.

The scrobj.dll file knows to look at the ScriptletURL key for the location of our component. It now knows that we need to look at that path for the actual object for the method calls. The registry entry that corresponds to this is shown in Figure 13-3.

Notice that the key is named ScriptletURL. This implies that these can be called over the Internet. Don't worry about this just yet, because we won't cover this until later in the chapter. There is a bit more to know about script components first.

# Script Component Files

Now let's look at how to create the actual script component. As we've already said, you can build script files by hand, however, Microsoft makes a free wizard available for building a script component file, automating a lot of the laborious tasks when creating script components. The wizard simply builds the XML framework that defines your component. There's nothing at all to stop you creating this yourself if

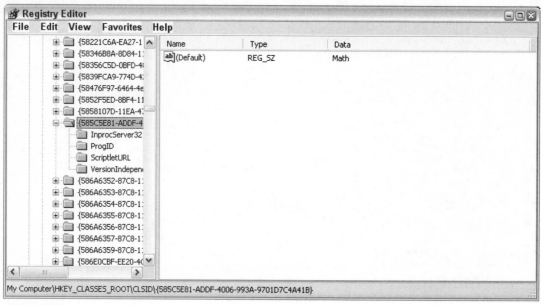

Figure 13-2

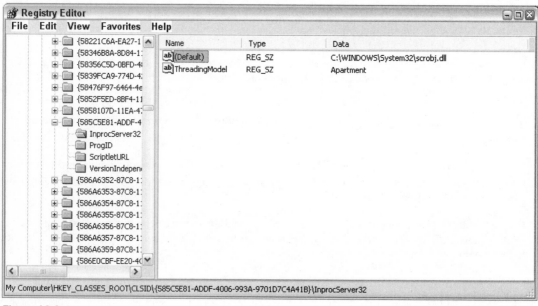

Figure 13-3

you know how it's done, however, XML is very strict and mistakes are easily made. Of course, the best way to find out how it's done is to use the wizard first, so let's do that.

## The Script Component Wizard

We invoke the wizard under XP from the Start ⇨ All Programs ⇨ Microsoft Windows Script ⇨ Windows Script Component Wizard shortcut (for other operating systems go Start ⇨ Programs ⇨ Microsoft Windows Script ⇨ Windows Script Component Wizard shortcut). First, we will tell the wizard the name of the component, along with its ProgID. One point to note is that script components use a special ProgID that defines the component. By default, the ProgID of the component will be componentname.WSC. Don't worry though, this can be changed in this step or after the component file has been created.

Script components can also maintain version information just like any other COM component, as you can see in the Version field. This is very useful for keeping track of updates.

Note that the Location in this dialog is simply the location of the source files that the wizard produces. The location of the source files will not be important to the actual Windows operating system until you register the component.

Step 1 of the Script Component Wizard is shown in Figure 13-4.

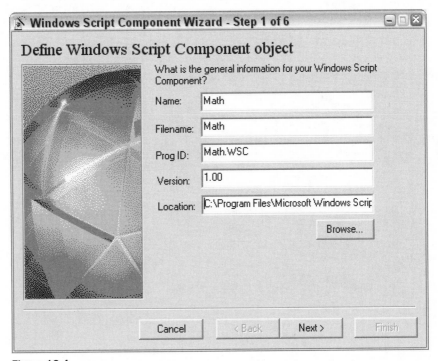

**Figure 13-4**

Once you are satisfied with the settings that you have chosen for the various options (some you have huge scope over, such as version, others less so), select the Next button to go to the second step of the wizard.

Windows Script Components can use VBScript or JScript natively, but other scripting platforms such as Python and PERL can be used as well if the proper interpreter is installed on the computer. There are two options under the implements section that need a little extra background information. These are DHTML behaviors and Active Server Pages.

DHTML behaviors are simple, lightweight components that interface with some of the DHTML objects and events of Internet Explorer. DHTML components are beyond the scope of this chapter, but for more information you can refer to the Microsoft Scripting site and the MSDN Web Workshop (http://msdn.microsoft.com/library).

Active Server Pages support will be covered in more detail in this chapter, and ASP itself will be covered later on in the book. Basically, ASP support allows a script component to gain direct access to the ASP object model. The ASP object model exposes the vast ASP Request, Response, Application, Session, and Server objects.

Finally, error checking and debugging can be selected as options. If you select debugging, you'll be allowed to use the script debugger. The script debugger can be found at http://msdn.microsoft.com/scripting/, and using it is the only way to debug a script component. It gives you the ability to check variables and view data, and works in a way very similar to the Visual Basic debugging tools.

Step 2 of the Script Component Wizard is shown in Figure 13-5.

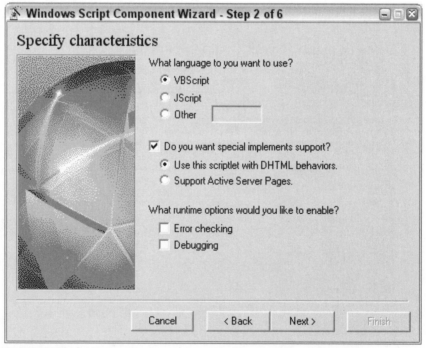

**Figure 13-5**

When you have selected the options that you want, select the Next button to move to step 3 of the wizard.

This screen allows you to define the properties of your object. You are able to define the name, type, and default values for the component. The `Type` setting is not the data type, but the property type, which can be one of the following:

- ❑   Read/Write
- ❑   Read-Only
- ❑   Write-Only

The `Default` entry allows you to specify a default value for the property. The following code listing shows a read/write property with a default value of 5.

```
Dim ReadWriteProperty
ReadWriteProperty = 5
```

Note that this is how the wizard declares a variable that will be accessed by a property. This should be changed to read.

```
Private ReadWriteProperty
ReadWriteProperty = 5
```

This will make sure that the variable is private to the script component. If this isn't done the variable would be public, as would the property accessing it, which could in turn lead to problems and conflicts.

Step 3 of the Script Component Wizard is shown in Figure 13-6.

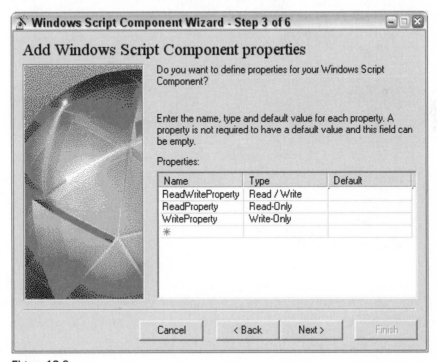

**Figure 13-6**

Press the Next button to proceed to step 4 in the wizard.

The fourth step of the wizard brings us to the methods of our component. You can specify the name of the method as well as the parameter list. When adding parameters, be sure to separate them with a comma, so that the parameter list looks like the following:

```
param1, param2, param3, ...
```

Again, remember that VBScript uses only variants, so you don't need to specify a type. If you go as far as trying to specify a type you will get an error. For similar reasons, you also can't specify a return type. The use of variant data types does reduce overall performance somewhat because variants are the largest data type that can be used, and are designed to represent any other data type, so each time a variant is called the application must decide what format the variable should be in. But since there is nothing we can do about that, there's no point worrying about it.

We will add a few methods here for our Math component. The Script Component Wizard will generate all methods as functions. If you want you can manually change these to subprocedures later if you don't need return values. It is an inconvenience that this can't be set in the wizard but again since there is nothing we can do about that, there's no point worrying about it here.

Step 4 of the Script Component Wizard is shown in Figure 13-7.

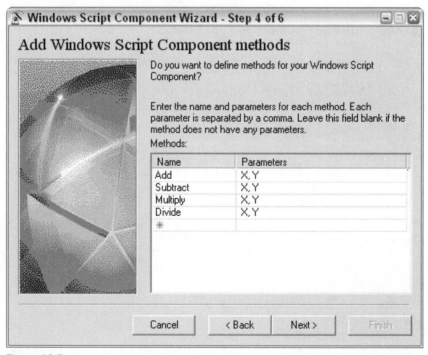

Figure 13-7

The fifth step of the wizard allows us to specify the events for our component. This is one of the most exciting areas of script components. We will see a little more on events in script components later in this section. Our `Math` component won't actually use events as such. If you do want to have events in your objects, enter one event name per line.

> *A previous version of the Script Component Wizard had a bug that ignored any entries in this section. If you discover that you are affected by this, will need to add events manually once the component has been created. We will go into more detail later in this chapter. If you are affected by this we suggest that you upgrade to the latest release of the Script Component Wizard.*

Step 5 of the Script Component Wizard is shown in Figure 13-8.

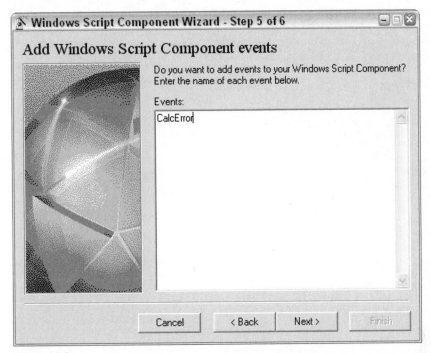

**Figure 13-8**

Once you are satisfied with the layout of the events, press the `Next` button to move to the final step of the wizard.

The final step of the wizard gives us some information about our component and some of the settings that we have selected. If you find any errors or omissions at this point then you can press the `Back` button to return to the previous steps and make the necessary changes.

Step 6 of the Script Component Wizard is shown in Figure 13-9.

Once we click `Finish`, the wizard will create a skeleton component like that in the following code sample:

```
<?xml version="1.0"?>
<component>

<registration
  description="Math"
```

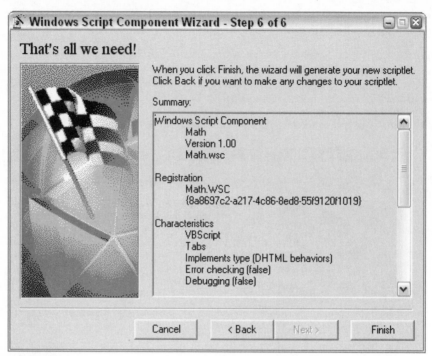

**Figure 13-9**

```
progid="Math.WSC"
version="1.00"
classid="{585c5e81-addf-4006-993a-9701d7c4a41b}"
>
</registration>

<public>
 <property name="ReadOnlyProperty">
        <get/>
</property>
<property name="WriteOnlyProperty">
        <put/>
</property>
<property name="ReadWriteProperty">
        <get/>
        <put/>
</property>
<method name="Add">
        <PARAMETER name="X"/>
        <PARAMETER name="Y"/>
</method>
<method name="Subtract">
        <PARAMETER name="X"/>
        <PARAMETER name="Y"/>
</method>
<method name="Multiply">
```

```
        <PARAMETER name="X"/>
        <PARAMETER name="Y"/>
</method>
<method name="Divide">
        <PARAMETER name="X"/>
        <PARAMETER name="Y"/>
</method>
<event name="CalcError"/>
</public>

<implements type="Behavior" id="Behavior"/>

<script language="VBScript">
<![CDATA[

dim ReadOnlyProperty
dim WriteOnlyProperty
dim ReadWriteProperty

function get_ReadOnlyProperty()
 get_ReadOnlyProperty = ReadOnlyProperty
end function

function put_WriteOnlyProperty(newValue)
 WriteOnlyProperty = newValue
end function

function get_ReadWriteProperty()
 get_ReadWriteProperty = ReadWriteProperty
end function

function put_ReadWriteProperty(newValue)
 ReadWriteProperty = newValue
end function

function Add(X, Y)
 Add = "Temporary Value"
end function

function Subtract(X, Y)
 Subtract = "Temporary Value"
end function

function Multiply(X, Y)
 Multiply = "Temporary Value"
end function

function Divide(X, Y)
 Divide = "Temporary Value"
end function

]]>
</script>

</component>
```

If your code looks like the earlier listing, you have now created a Windows Script COM Component. Now let's take a look at it in a little more detail.

# Exposing Properties, Methods, and Events

The next thing to do is to actually define the properties, methods, and events that your component needs to contain.

## Properties

Properties within script components can be read/write, read-only, or write-only. They are implemented within the script file using <property></property> tags. Within these tags you set the get and put options for the property. Gets are used for reading the values and puts are for writing to the properties. The following code sample lists the structure that's created to first "declare" the three types of properties.

```
<property name="ReadOnlyProperty">
      <get/>
</property>
<property name="WriteOnlyProperty">
      <put/>
</property>
<property name="ReadWriteProperty">
      <get/>
```

The properties are then actually defined within script code later in the script file.

```
<script language="VBScript">
<![CDATA[

dim ReadOnlyProperty
dim WriteOnlyProperty
dim ReadWriteProperty

function get_ReadOnlyProperty()
 get_ReadOnlyProperty = ReadOnlyProperty
end function

function put_WriteOnlyProperty(newValue)
 WriteOnlyProperty = newValue
end function

function get_ReadWriteProperty()
 get_ReadWriteProperty = ReadWriteProperty
end function

function put_ReadWriteProperty(newValue)
 ReadWriteProperty = newValue
end function

function Add(X, Y)
 Add = "Temporary Value"
end function
```

```
function Subtract(X, Y)
 Subtract = "Temporary Value"
end function

function Multiply(X, Y)
 Multiply = "Temporary Value"
end function

function Divide(X, Y)
 Divide = "Temporary Value"
end function

]]>
</script>
```

You can script any additional logic within the get and put functions of the properties. For this example we haven't included any real properties. Later on, when we look at classes, we'll actually see an example that does use properties.

Remember that script components can implement other COM objects, so you can create an ADO component, access LDAP and Exchange, or even call Microsoft Word and Excel. The sky is the limit with script components!

# Methods

Methods in script components are defined in <method></method> tags in the object definition section of the script file. Parameters for a method use a <parameter> definition for the values, as you can see in the following code sample.

```
<public>
    <method name="mNoParameters">
    </method>
    <method name="mWithParameters">
        <PARAMETER name="var1"/>
        <PARAMETER name="var2"/>
    </method>
</public>
```

The <parameter> tag simply defines the name of the input parameters. Remember that everything that comes from the Script Component Wizard is, by default, a function within the script components and no return type is specified since all variables are of the variant data type. We are, however, free to use subprocedures as our methods in place of functions.

The actual method code is within the script tags of the script component.

```
<script language="VBScript">
<![CDATA[

Function mNoParameters()
    mNoParameters = "Temporary Value"
End Function
```

```
Function mWithParameters(var1, var2)
    mWithParameters = "Temporary Value"
End Function

]]>
</script>
```

Note that all methods that are created though the Windows Script Component Wizard return the value "Temporary Value". You will probably need to change this (unless you really need a function that returns "Temporary Value"!). You will also need to declare any temporary variables before the function definitions.

Let's add our real methods to our Math component.

```
<script language="VBScript">
<![CDATA[

Private ReadOnlyProperty
Private WriteOnlyProperty
Private ReadWriteProperty

function get_ReadOnlyProperty()
 get_ReadOnlyProperty = ReadOnlyProperty
end function

function put_WriteOnlyProperty(newValue)
 WriteOnlyProperty = newValue
end function

function get_ReadWriteProperty()
 get_ReadWriteProperty = ReadWriteProperty
end function

function put_ReadWriteProperty(newValue)
 ReadWriteProperty = newValue
end function

function Add(X, Y)
 Add = X + Y
end function

function Subtract(X, Y)
 Subtract = X - Y
end function

function Multiply(X, Y)
 Multiply = X * Y
end function

function Divide(X, Y)
 Divide = X / Y
end function

]]>
</script>
```

Something that is not documented in the WSC documentation (because it's specific to the scripting language you use) is that you can use the byval (by value) and byref (by reference) keywords within the parameter declaration of the method. By default in VBScript all values are passed byref, so any changes to the variables in the method will change the underlying value in the calling function.

*JScript variables are all passed byval since JScript cannot pass a variable byref.*

## Events

Events are defined within <event></event> tags within the object definition of the script file.

There was a bug in an older release (we can't call it a version because the Windows Script Component Wizard is still in version 1.0) of Windows Script Component Wizard, which meant that it did not create the events you specified. All event declarations had to be created manually within a script file. The latest release of the Windows Script Component Wizard behaves correctly.

```
<public>
    <method name="mNoParameters">
        </method>
    <event name="MethodCalled">
        </event>
</public>
```

The event is actually fired through the FireEvent() method. FireEvent() is called within the script of the script component. The event itself should also be described here, using the form ComponentName_EventName.

```
<script language="VBScript">
<![CDATA[

function mNoParameters()
  FireEvent("MethodCalled")
  mNoParameters = "Temporary Value"
end function

sub MyComponent_MethodCalled()
  'some event handling code
end sub

]]>
</script>
```

Script components can also handle events using an <implements> tag within the script definition. The syntax for capturing events in a script component is defined as

```
<implements type="COMHandlerName" [id="internalName"] [default=fAssumed]>
    handler-specific information here
</implements>
```

The `COMHandlerName` is the name of the handler (ASP or behavior) or the COM object that is being handled. `InternalName` is an optional parameter that allows you to define a variable name for the COM handler. The `fAssumed` property is a Boolean flag (the default value is `True`) that indicates `InternalName` is assumed in scripts. If you set this to `False` you would hide some members in the `<implements>` tag.

There are two built-in COM handlers, ASP and Behaviors. We will look at the ASP COM handler later in the next section.

# Registration Information

To be able to register a Windows Script Component you will need to have the Script Component Runtime (`scrobj.dll`) on your machine and have it properly registered. This file is automatically registered when you install the VBScript or JScript script engines. Once you have the scripting runtime and a valid script component (`.wsc`) file then you can register the component. There are three methods available for properly registering a WSC file.

The easiest way to register and unregister a script component is to right-click the component file in Windows Explorer and select `Register` or `Unregister` from the popup menu. This is shown in Figure 13-10 and is both easy and convenient to use.

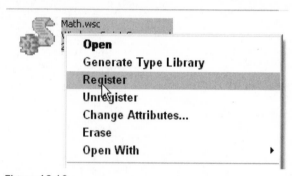

Figure 13-10

In the event that you need to manually register and unregister a component you can still use `regsvr32 .exe`. If you are using an old version of `regsvr32` that comes with Windows or Visual Studio then you can use the following command.

```
regsvr32 scrobj.dll /n /i:Path/component_name.wsc
```

New versions of `regsvr32` that ship with the script component packages can directly register the script component file.

```
regsvr32 path/component_name.wsc
```

You can also add a registration entry into the script component that defines the registration behavior. You can add the `<registration>` tag to the component as defined in the following code.

```
<registration progid="progID" classid="GUID" description="description"
    version="version" [remotable=remoteFlag]>
<script>
    (registration and unregistration script)
</script>
</registration>
```

Within the `<script>` tags you can add a `Register()` and `Unregister()` event that will be fired whenever the component is registered or unregistered on the system. The `progID` attribute is optional, but you must have data for either the `classid` or `progID` in order for the component to register.

If you leave either `classid` or `progID` out then it will be automatically generated when the component is registered.

All of these methods will properly register a script component file on your system. This is nice, but what about remote components? Well, the short and simple (and sweet!) answer is that Windows Script Components can be registered remotely.

In order to make the components DCOM-ready, you need to follow these four simple steps:

1. Determine the `progid` and `clsid` of the component. Local components do not need an entry for a `clsid`. If it is absent this tells the component to create a `clsid` entry at registration time.

2. On every local machine that needs to access the component, add an entry into the registry under `HKEY_CLASSES_ROOT\componentProgID`. Here `ComponentProgID` is the `ProgID` of the script component. This is a job ideally suited to Windows Script Host.

3. Beneath this entry, create a `CLSID` key and set the value to that of the `clsid` of the script component.

4. Set `remotable=true` within the `<registration>` tags of the component.

Another way to simplify this process would be to register the component on the server and export the registry key information using `regedit`. You can then copy the exported `.reg` file from `regedit` to each machine that needs the component. Once the file has been copied to the local machine, double-click the `.reg` file to merge the data into the registry. You now have a DCOM-ready script component that can be used throughout the enterprise.

Let's quickly test the component with a short test script. Save the following code as a file called `testmathcomp.vbs` and then run it after you've registered your `Math` component:

```
dim obj
set obj = wscript.createobject("math.wsc")
msgbox obj.add(15, 9)
msgbox obj.subtract(15, 9)
msgbox obj.multiply(15, 9)
msgbox obj.divide(28, 4)
set obj = nothing
```

# Creating the Script Component Type Libraries

Script components are no different to any other COM component and can have type libraries generated. Type libraries are used in some environments (such as Visual Basic) for enabling events or for enabling the use of IntelliSense by programs such as Visual InterDev. Type libraries contain descriptions of the COM components and also help with early binding of objects or using tools such as OLE2VIEW to view the declarations and constants in a component.

To generate a type library for a script component, simply right-click on the script component file and select the Generate Type Library option from the popup context-sensitive menu, as shown in Figure 13-11.

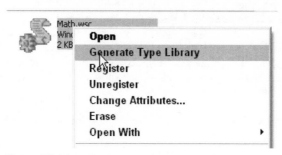

**Figure 13-11**

Though there is another way to generate a type library within a script component. Script components can automatically generate a type library for themselves when the Register method is called. When this method is called, the component uses the information that exists within the <registration> tags. The syntax of the <registration> tag is as follows.

```
<registration progid="progID" classid="GUID" description="description"
    version="version" [remotable=remoteFlag]>
    <script>
    (registration and unregistration script)
    </script>
</registration>
```

Remember that both the progID and classid items are optional, but one of the two must be specified for the tags to be valid. The progID is the component name while the classid entry is for the GUID of the component. If the classid entry is left blank, then a GUID will be assigned to the component at registration time by the system.

Both description and version are optional as well. If we used a registration entry with our previous Math component, then we would add the following <registration> tags.

```
<registration
    description="My Simple Math Component"
    progid="Math.WSC"
    version="1.0"
    classid="{585C5E81-ADDF-4006-993A-9701D7C4A41B}">
```

```
  <script language="VBScript">
  <![CDATA[
  Function Register()
     Set oComponent = CreateObject("Scriptlet.GenerateTypeLib")
     oComponent.AddURL "C:\Program Files\Microsoft Windows Script\Math.wsc"
```

AddURL allows us to add other component files into the type library. If we used or exposed other components then we would want to add them into one type library rather than using multiple files.

```
  oComponent.Path = "C:\Program Files\Microsoft Windows Script\Math.tlb"
```

We add the path indicating where the component will be stored. If this is left blank the type library will be written to the current location of the script component.

```
  oComponent.Doc = "Math component typelib" ' Documentation string.
  oComponent.GUID = "{a1e1e3e0-a252-11d1-9fa1-00a0c90fffc0}"
  oComponent.Name = "MathComponent" ' Internal name for tlb.
  oComponent.MajorVersion = 1
  oComponent.MinorVersion = 0
  oComponent.Write
```

Here is the code that writes the type library to the hard drive.

```
     oComponent.Reset
  End Function
  ]]>
  </script>
  </registration>
```

Remember, if you plan to use this component through DCOM then you would also need to add this line.

```
  remotable=true
```

This line of code tells the component that it needs to set itself up in the registry for DCOM.

# How to Reference Other Components

A script component file can contain multiple components within itself. You can easily create a library of components just as you would in Visual Basic, however, you cannot use the Windows Script Component Wizard to do this and you would need to do this manually. The script components use a series of <package></package> tags to create script libraries. For example, you would define a series of components within a file as follows.

```
  <package>
     <component id="COMObj1">

     </component>

     <component id="COMObj2">
```

```
        </component>

        <component id="COMObj3">

        </component>
    </package>
```

Within each script you would add the appropriate properties, methods, and events for each component. You would also need to add the necessary registration information as well.

You can reference another component within the package by using the `CreateComponent` function. If we want to reference `COMObj2` in the preceding code, we would set a reference to an object using `CreateComponent`.

```
    Set oComponent = CreateComponent("COMObj2")
```

This will give us a runtime reference of `COMObj2`. How does this help? It allows you to add components that implement ASP interfaces and DHTML behaviors, while at the same time exposing properties and methods to other client applications. Your ASP and DHTML components can access all of the properties and methods of the COM component and will reduce the amount of redundant code.

While the Windows Script Component Wizard can't help you with all of it, it can build the individual objects for you. Once all of the objects have been created, you can then build a package and cut and paste the contents of the individual files into the one package.

# Script Components for ASP

ASP script components include the functionality of the Active Server Pages library to allow for Web enabled script components. These script components are called from within ASP pages and can contribute greatly to code reuse of ASP components and business logic and also save time by separating functional code from the Web page that displays it.

In order to ASP-enable a script component, you will need to add an `<implements>` tag with a reference to the ASP COM handler.

```
    <implements type="ASP">
    </implements>
```

Once the `<implements>` tag has been set up, the script component will have a reference to ASP and can make use of the `Response`, `Request`, `Session`, `Application`, and `Server` ASP objects. For example, we can have a component that outputs the current date and time to an ASP page. The script component would look like the following.

```
    <component id="ASPDateTimeObject">
    <registration progid="ASPDateTimeObject"/>

    <public>
      <method name="OutputDateTime"/>
    </public>
```

```
<implements type="ASP"/>
<script language="VBScript">
<![CDATA[

Sub OutputDateTime()
  Response.Write("Is is currently " & Time & " on " & Date)
End Sub

]]>
</script>
</component>
```

The code for out ASP page would create this object and call the `OutputDateTime` method.

```
<html>
<head>
<title>ASP Script Objects</title>
</head>
<body>
<h1>ASP Script Objects</h1>

<%

Set objDateTime = CreateObject("ASPDateTimeObject")%>

objDateTime.OutputDateTime()

set objDateTime = nothing

%>

</body>
</html>
```

An ASP script component can also contain complex database functions, which can be reused for generic database output. Since script objects can call other COM components, we have access to all ADO functions, Office COM libraries, and third party objects. That is a lot of power!

So, how do ASP script components operate? When the script object is called from an ASP page, the script object is run in the same namespace (or process space) as the calling page. This gives the script component direct access to the page, so it can use all of the intrinsic ASP objects, and all output back to ASP is directed back to the page. The script component and the ASP page both see the exact same objects. This is similar to creating a Visual Basic COM component that implements the `OnStartPage` method. When a Visual Basic COM component has this method, ASP will call it automatically and send a reference to the ASP library, thus giving Visual Basic full control over ASP.

If you're familiar with using ASP, you might be wondering why is this better than using `#include` directives? Whenever you include a library into ASP files, the entire contents of the file is merged with the source file. As an example, say that you have a library that contains 50 relatively complicated functions. A library like this can easily run into several hundred, if not thousands, of lines of source code. If you only wanted to use one function out of the 50, you are still forced into a position where you have to add all of the remaining lines of redundant code, code that will need processing. What if you don't happen to use any of the functions due to the way the page is processed? Too bad, because ASP must still merge all of the included files in order to process the page. This isn't an effective use of system resources that might be better needed elsewhere.

An ASP script component, on the other hand, can contain all of the library functions that you use, but it is only loaded when it is needed. If the page logic does not require a function then the object is never loaded and the page contains less code and needs less processing which makes it smaller and faster. ASP script components are by far a better design choice for ASP pages because you can organize individual components with related functions, you're not required to add #include directives for every page that might need a function. You can also remotely execute complex scripts on middle tier servers. Included files, on the other hand, run directly on the Web server and cannot take advantage of n-tier architectures in intranet and Internet applications.

# Compile-Time Error Checking

When you register your script component something else happens at the same time. The script syntax is also validated. You will receive error messages if there are scripting errors or if the XML cannot be validated. The error messages are not very verbose and give you little more than a position in the file and possibly a snippet of the affected code.

As an example, I've added a semicolon to my script (let's pretend we were converting the source from JScript).

```
function Add(X,Y)
   Add = X + Y;
end function
```

What we get when we register the component are the dialog boxes shown in Figures 13-12 and 13-13, which show that there has been an error and that registration wasn't successful.

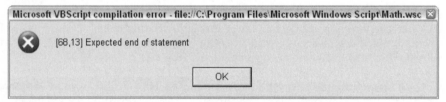

Figure 13-12

Figure 13-13

The text shown in the error message gives the approximate location (expressed as line number followed by column number) of the error in the component. Unfortunately this is not usually completely accurate, but it's close. Also, it's not easy to count lines, let alone columns, in Notepad and this is where a text editor that give line and column numbers comes in handy.

For example, the location quoted earlier is actually pointing to the plus sign in our code, rather than the semicolon at the end of our line.

Compile-time error checking is far from perfect, but it will point you in the general direction of any errors that exist in your code.

# Using VBScript Classes in Script Components

As you have seen previously, VBScript includes the ability to declare classes and class constructs. You can integrate a standard VBScript class into a Windows Script Component within the `<script></script>` tags in the data portion of the XML file. You still use the standard construct for classes.

```
class <classname>

    <internal class declaration>

end class
```

## Limitations of VBScript Classes

There is one key limitation of using VBScript classes in Windows Script Components that you should be aware of: class information is not exposed automatically. In essence, script components know nothing about the structure of an internal class. In order to expose the class to the outside world you must wrap the class information around methods and properties declared in the script component file.

So, why use a class in a script component? Well, classes will not provide a lot of functionality for a small component, but a complex component can benefit from a class by helping a developer to organize the object structure in a more meaningful way. Large script components can get very complex due to the reliance on XML parsing, so your component may become harder to maintain over time. A well-defined class will always provide a more familiar structure to developers.

As we will see later , you can include external source files. If you have defined many classes you can simply include the source file and provide a COM wrapper for the class definition. Remember that VBScript classes cannot be exposed automatically to COM, so you must provide a mechanism for other objects to access your class.

## Using Internal Classes

Internal classes in script components need a class construct and a series of methods and properties that wrap the internal class. We can take the Math component that we built earlier in the chapter and use it as a class wrapper. Initially our script component had the following form.

```
<?xml version="1.0"?>
<component>
```

```
<?component error="true" debug="true"?>

<registration
  description="Math"
  progid="Math.Scriptlet"
  version="1.00"
  classid="{b0a847a0-63c2-11d3-aa0e-00a0cc322d8b}"
>
</registration>
<public>
    <method name="Add">
        <PARAMETER name="X"/>
        <PARAMETER name="Y"/>
    </method>
    <method name="Subtract">
        <PARAMETER name="X"/>
        <PARAMETER name="Y"/>
    </method>
    <method name="Multiply">
        <PARAMETER name="X"/>
        <PARAMETER name="Y"/>
    </method>

    <method name="Divide">
        <PARAMETER name="X"/>
        <PARAMETER name="Y"/>
    </method>
</public>

<script language="VBScript">
<![CDATA[

function Add(X,Y)
    Add = X + Y
end function

function Subtract(X,Y)
    Subtract = X - Y
end function

function Multiply(X,Y)
    Multiply = X * Y
end function

function Divide(X,Y)
    Divide = X / Y
end function

]]>
</script>

</component>
```

Within our <script> tags we can build a class that handles the methods of the script component.

```
<script language="VBScript">
<![CDATA[

Class clsMath

  Public Function Add(X, Y)
      Add = X + Y
  End Function

  Public Function Subtract(X, Y)
      Subtract = X - Y
  End Function

  Public Function Multiply(X, Y)
      Multiply = X * Y
  End Function

  Public Function Divide(X, Y)
      Divide = X / Y
  End Function

End Class

Private oMath
set oMath = new clsMath

Function Add(X,Y)
    Add = oMath.Add(X,Y)
End Function

Function Subtract(X,Y)
    Subtract = oMath.Subtract(X,Y)
End Function

Function Multiply(X,Y)
    Multiply = oMath.Multiply(X,Y)
End Function

Function Divide(X,Y)
    Divide = oMath.Divide(X,Y)
End Function

]]>
</script>
```

You can see that we have built a VBScript class and we have wrapped the functionality into the script component. This can provide a new level of flexibility to a script component, as you will see in the next section.

# Including External Source Files

We are not required to have our class declarations (or our source for that matter) in the file itself. There is a declaration within the <script> tag that allows us to include an external source file.

The `src=` declaration acts as an include for another file. This gives us the ability to move our class declarations to a `.vbs` (or a `.txt` file for that matter) file for later use. We can then leverage our external source files across both the Windows Script Host as well as within Active Server Pages and script components.

We can move the class declaration from our math sample to `math.vbs`. The text of `math.vbs` is simply the entire class declaration.

```
Class clsMath

    Public Function Add(X, Y)
        Add = X + Y
    End Function

    Public Function Subtract(X, Y)
        Subtract = X - Y
    End Function

    Public Function Multiply(X, Y)
        Multiply = X * Y
    End Function

    Public Function Divide(X, Y)
        Divide = X / Y
    End Function

End Class
```

We then change the text of the `Math` component to include the new source file.

```
<script language="VBScript" src="math.vbs">
<![CDATA[

private oMath
set oMath = new clsMath
```

When the component is instantiated we parse the script file, add any included files into the `<script>` tag and continue processing. As far as COM is concerned, both internal class declaration and the external class declaration are identical.

# Summary

Windows Script Components provide added flexibility to Web pages and can tightly integrate into your ASP code. You can use these objects as stand alone COM components or you can have them interact directly with ASP pages. All you need is some scripting, a little bit of XML know-how, basic understanding of the Script Component Wizard, and a quick run through `regsvr32` and you have a perfectly formed and ready-to-run script component!

14

# Script Encoding

## Overview

One thing that becomes immediately obvious to those who come to writing script from a programming background is that anything they create using script is easily and readily visible to anyone and everyone else. There is no compiler that turns the code into code that only a machine can make sense of. This was a real worry, but on the whole it didn't stop people writing and using scripts. It also had massive advantages for scripting in general. Just as the open, plain-text nature of HTML made learning Web design easier than say learning C++, the same "open book" format for scripts encouraged a huge explosion of script use on the Web. Okay, thinking back to those times, some of it was pretty bad and looked pretty ugly, but we didn't care because it was scripting and it made our pages look more exciting than the others out there. Because it was so easy to see how scripts worked (and to copy the code from one page and paste it into another), the future of scripting was guaranteed.

However, now with the future of script use well established, a bit of privacy isn't a bad thing. Programmers who use script want to regain some of the mystique that they once had when using C++ or VB (using script to solve a problem is a bit like a magician in a see-through jacket). Things have moved on a little bit from the days of scripts being a total free-for-all and there are a few things you can do to make it harder for those script snoopers to see your secrets!

## Limitations of Script Encoding

It's only fair that we inject a bit of reality and caution here. None of the methods that we will look at there for making it harder for the script snoopers to peek at your code are 100 percent guaranteed. In fact, the best of them, the Microsoft Script Encoder, isn't very robust at all. Why? Because ultimately the browser must still be able to execute the script. This means any technique you use will be a weak one. Of course, if you want to protect a script from viewing you could take an encryption program, such as PGP, and run that on your script. Taking all the proper precautions you could be pretty guaranteed that your script would be safe—the problem is that it's so safe the browser can't do anything with it anymore!

Fortunately, script snoopers come in a variety of forms:

- ❑ Someone that wants to take a look at how it works
- ❑ Someone wanting to learn how the script works
- ❑ Someone who wants to use or modify the script for a benign purpose
- ❑ Someone who wants to modify the script for malicious purposes

They also come in a variety of skill levels:

- ❑ The lower skilled "casual" snooper
- ❑ The skilled "interested" snooper
- ❑ The skilled "determined" snooper

It doesn't really matter why someone is trying to snoop on your script (although that might factor into why you might want to protect the script), the real factor here is how skilled they are and how determined. Taking simple precautions will deter the casual snooper and send them on their way but if someone is really determined to see your script, and they are skilled, nothing here will stop them. That's the plain truth and while it sounds harsh, it is much harsher to find out the hard way.

# Why Encode Scripts?

Protecting your scripts is much more than just protecting your intellectual property—although there's nothing wrong with doing that!

Most people out there are honest and few even bother to look at plain-text scripts anyway. But even so, taking precautions against accidental changes with some script (such as Windows Script Host scripts) makes sense. If you have a WSH script that searches folders for particular files, copies them and then deletes the originals, you wouldn't want that script tampered with, ending up with it just deleting files (I've seen this happen and it wasn't an example of someone doing it maliciously instead a genuine accident caused by someone who was unfamiliar with the script.). If you use the Microsoft Script Encoder, you have the added advantage that if an encoded script is modified, just one character changed, it will no longer work. Encoding scripts can help protect curious users from themselves as much as from malicious attack.

# How to Encode Script

Let's see how scripts can be encoded. We'll be looking at how VBScript code can be encoded with the Microsoft Script Encoder primarily, but we will also look at some other things that you can do to discourage script snooping. These won't be as effective as the Microsoft Script Encoder but they are nonetheless worth bearing in mind and can be quite effective in appropriate circumstances.

# The Microsoft Script Encoder

The Microsoft Script Encoder is a simple, easy to use command line tool that script programmers can use to encode the scripts that they have created so that the source cannot be viewed or modified. (This works with JScript too, although we'll only be looking at VBScript here.)

*Note: The application is a Script Encoder. It encodes the script, but doesn't encrypt it. Encryption is different to encoding, but the difference is subtle. With both you take a file and change its format but with encryption the file is unusable until it is decrypted. Encoding changes the file from the point of view of a human reader but the script engine can still understand what the file does.*

## Availability

The Microsoft Script Encoder installation file is available free from Microsoft as a small download (approximately 130KB) from www.microsoft.com/scripting. It is available in English, Chinese (traditional), German, and Korean.

## Installation

Installing the Microsoft Script Encoder is easy. Locate the download (the English language version is called sce10en.exe while the Chinese version is called sce10cht.exe, the German version sce10de.exe, and the Korean version sce10ko.exe). Double click it and follow the prompts. The default installation location for the command line application and the help files is C:\Program Files\ Windows Script Encoder.

As well as installing the command line application and the help file, the installation application also modifies the Windows registry so that the system recognizes.vbe and.jse files (VBScript Encoded Script files and JScript Encoded Script files).

*Note: Installation of the Microsoft Script Encoder is not required for running encoded script files. Only the programmer needs to install the decode.*

## Using the Microsoft Script Encoder

The Microsoft Script Encoder is, as we mentioned earlier, a command line utility and doesn't come with a Windows interface. This means that it's not as easy to use as a GUI application. However, it's not particularly difficult to start using it and you will find that having it as a command line tool gives the added advantage that it can be easily integrated into batch files.

The Microsoft Script Encoder doesn't do any encoding itself but rather uses the scripting runtime module (scrrun.dll) to do the encoding for it. All the Script Encoder executable does is provide a command-line mechanism for calling the scripting.encoder object implemented in the scripting runtime. This is very handy indeed because it provides the programmer with an extensible mechanism for using encoding in their applications or in third-party applications. This was done by Microsoft to ensure that the programmer could use script encoding wherever they wanted, rather than only in a few specific areas.

Because scripting.encoder is simply a COM object, it may be used wherever any other COM object would be. This means you could extend on the functions provided by the Script Encoder in your own applications.

Because the installation program doesn't add the path to the encoder to the PATH system variable, it isn't available from every folder in a command prompt window. So that using the Microsoft Script Encoder is smooth and trouble-free, we recommend you do one of the following:

❑    Add the path to the Microsoft Script Encoder (the default path is C:\Program Files\Windows Script Encoder) to the PATH system variable

❑ Copy the Microsoft Script Encoder executable (screnc.exe) to the folder you will be using for script encoding

❑ Copy all of the scripts you want to encode to the folder used by the Microsoft Script Encoder

For clarity and simplicity, we will copy all the scripts that we'll be encoding to the folder used by the Microsoft Script Encoder.

### Syntax

The easiest way to familiarize yourself with the syntax of the Microsoft Script Encoder is to begin using it. Open a command prompt window and navigate to `C:\Program Files\Windows Script Encoder`. (The Microsoft Script Encoder can also be run from the Run dialog box in the Start Menu of Windows.) Once there, type the following:

```
screnc \?
```

This will make the application list the Help for the application. This can be a very useful reference when you are in a hurry! The output is shown in Figure 14-1.

The syntax for the Microsoft Script Encoder is as follows.

```
screnc [/s] [/f] [/xl] [/l defLanguage ] [/e defExtension] source destination
```

Here is a run through of the switches supported by the application:

❑ /?—Optional. The switch that lists the Help for the Script Encoder.

❑ /s—Optional. The switch that specifies that the Script Encoder is to work silently, that is, it produces no screen output. If this switch is omitted, the default is to provide verbose output.

❑ /f—Optional. This switch specifies that the input file is to be overwritten by the output file. Note that this option will destroy your original input source file, and perhaps your only unencoded copy of the script! If omitted, the output file is not overwritten.

❑ /xl—Optional. This switch specifies that the @language directive is not added at the top of .ASP files. If omitted, @language directive is added at the top of all .ASP files.

❑ /l defLanguage—Optional. This switch specifies the default scripting language (JScript or VBScript) to be used during encoding. Script blocks within the file being encoded that do not contain a language attribute are assumed to be of this specified language. If omitted, JScript is the default language for HTML pages and scriptlets, while VBScript is the default for active server pages. For plain-text files, the file extension (either .js or .vbs) is used to determine the default scripting language.

❑ /e defExtension—Optional. This switch associates the input file with a specific file type. You should use this switch when the input file's extension doesn't make the file type clear, that is, when the input file extension is not one of the recognized extensions, but the file content does fall into one of the recognized types. There is no default for this option. If a file with an unrecognized extension is encountered and this option is not specified, the Script Encoder fails for that unrecognized file. Recognized file extensions are asa, asp, cdx, htm, html, js, sct, and vbs.

❑ source—Required. This is the name of the input file to be encoded, and it can include any necessary path information relative to the current directory.

```
C:\WINDOWS\System32\cmd.exe                                          _ |□| ×|

C:\Program Files\Windows Script Encoder>screnc /?

Usage:    screnc [/?] [/s] [/f] [/xl] [/l ScriptLanguage] [/e DefaultExtension]
                 <source> <destination>

Encode embedded script.

/? -      Help
/s -      Silent: display no messages
/f -      Force: allow file(s) overwrite (source == destination)
/xl -     Exclude Language: does not add the language directive in asp files
/l ScriptLanguage -
          Script Default Language: specify the default script language to be
          used when encoding
/e DefaultExtension -
          Default Extension: override actual file extension. Control the
          encoder to be loaded.
<source>
          The file to encode. It can have wildcard characters.
<destination>
          The destination file. When <source> contains wildcard characters,
          <destination> is the directory where to place the encoded
          files; files will keep the same name. When <source> and
          <destination> are the same /f must be used.

Examples:
          screnc test.html encode.html
                  encode test.html into encode.html
          screnc /f test.html
                  encode and override test.html
          screnc /e html test.txt test1.txt
                  treat text.txt as an html file, encode it into text1.txt
          screnc test.asp c:\myDir\test.asp
                  encode test.asp into c:\myDir\test.asp
          screnc *.asp c:\myDir
                  encode all the asp files in the current directory and place
                  them in c:\myDir
          screnc -s -f *.sct
                  encode all the scriptlet files in the current directory and
                  override them. No message is displayed
          screnc -e asp *.* c:\myDir
                  encode *all* the files in the current directory as asp files.
                  Place these files in c:\myDir
          screnc -e asp -xl *.inc c:\myDir
                  encode all the files with .inc extension as asp files.
                  Does not add the @LANGUAGE directive at the top of the file
          screnc -l vbscript test.html encode.html
                  encode test.html into encode.html. When a script tag with
                  no language attribute is found, VBScript is assumed to be
                  the default language. If -l is not specified, JScript is
                  assumed for html and VBScript is the default for asp

C:\Program Files\Windows Script Encoder>
```

**Figure 14-1**

❑   destination—Required. This is the name of the output file to be produced, and it can include any
    necessary path information relative to the current directory.

Let's now look at how to put the above together with some examples. What follows are a few examples of
the use of the Microsoft Script Encoder, each accompanied by a brief explanation of the results.

To encode the input file unencoded.htm and produce an output file called encoded.htm, use:

```
screnc unencoded.html encoded.html
```

To encode the input file test.htm and overwrite the input file with the encoded output file, use:

```
screnc /f test.htm
```

To encode all files with the .ASP file extension in the current directory and place the encoded output files in c:\output, use:

```
screnc *.asp c:\output
```

To encode all files in the current directory as .asp files and place them in c:\output, use:

```
screnc /e asp *.* c:\output
```

To encode input file unencoded.htm and produce output file encoded.htm, while ensuring that all script blocks that don't have a specified language attribute are encoded as VBScript, use:

```
screnc /l vbscript unencoded.htm encoded.htm
```

To encode every scriptlet file (.sct) in the current directory and overwrite each of them with encoded files, while not displaying a message, use:

```
screnc /s /f *.sct
```

## What Files Can I Encode?

There are four kinds of files than can be processed by the Script Encoder: HTML, ASP, Plain text, and Scriptlets.

### HTML Files

Any HTML file can be processed by the Microsoft Script Encoder, but remember that it only acts on the script in the page, so encoding an HTML page that doesn't contain any script won't have any effect on it but also won't generate any message to say that it doesn't contain script.

Let's look at encoding an HTML page containing VBScript. Following is the code of page we will use.

```
<html>
<head>
<title>Simple VBScript Example</title>
<script language="vbscript">
    Sub ButtonClicked
        window.alert("You clicked on the button!")
    End Sub
</script>
</head>
<body>
  <button name="Button1" type=BUTTON onclick="ButtonClicked">
  Click Me If You Can!!!
  </button>
</body>
</html>
```

We have named the preceding file `unencoded.htm` for clarity. Let's now take a look at how to use to the Microsoft Script Encoder to encode this file.

As we mentioned earlier, we will copy this file to the folder that contains the Microsoft Script Encoder. Then we open a command prompt window and navigate to that folder. Once there you type in the following, followed by *Enter*.

```
screnc unencoded.htm encoded.htm
```

If everything has worked and there were no errors of faults, there will be no error messages displayed and the command prompt returns as shown in Figure 14-2. Many people are surprised by this and expect some sort of confirmation that everything has worked out right.

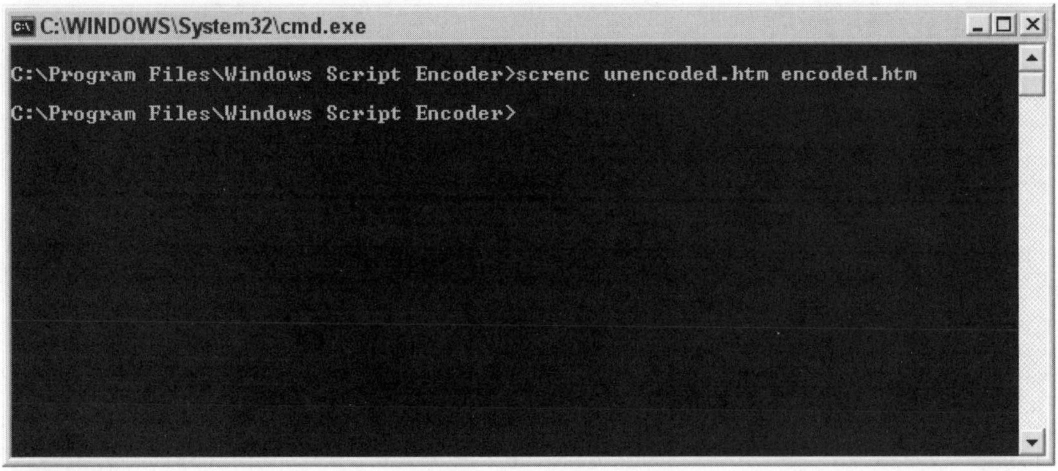

**Figure 14-2**

However, where in the beginning you had just the one HTML file (called `unencoded.htm`) you now have another new one—this one called `encoded.htm`. If you open up a text editor and take a look at the source code for this new HTML page you will see some key differences.

```
<html>
<head>
<title>Simple VBScript Example</title>
<script
language="VBScript.Encode">#@~^YgAAAA==@#@&P~,PUE4,A!OYKx/VbmVn9@#@&,~P,PP,~Ak
  NKh lsnMYcJIGE,msr13+[~Kx~Y4n,4;DYKx"r#@#@&P,P~2
N~j!4@#@&DBoAAA==^#~@</script>
</head>
<body>
  <button name="Button1" type=BUTTON onclick="ButtonClicked">
  Click Me If You Can!!!
  </button>
</body>
</html>
```

In fact, two significant changes have been made: The script that previously was unencoded is now encoded (pretty obvious!) and the script language attribute value has been changed from VBScript to

VBScript.Encoded. Do not be alarmed by this as this is exactly as it now would be and the browser will understand it. To prove this, open the page in the browser and see if it still works. Click on the button and a message box should be displayed as shown in Figure 14-3 to show that indeed the VBScript code does still work!

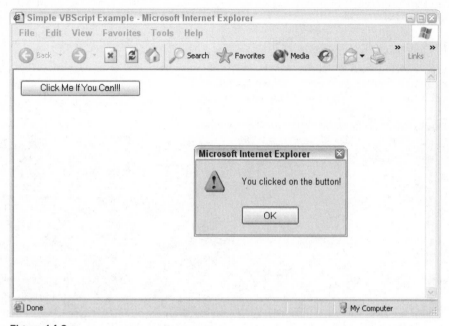

**Figure 14-3**

The great thing about the Microsoft Script Encoder is that you don't have to encode all the script on the page. You can choose where the encoding should start using the following encoding marker in your VBScript code:

'**Start Encode**

*Note: For JScript the encoding marker would be //**Start Encode***

Take a look at this modified example that follows. This example uses the encoding marker to begin encoding at the second subprocedure.

```
<html>
<head>
<title>Simple VBScript Example</title>
<script language="vbscript">
    Sub ButtonClicked
        window.alert("This is not encoded!")
    End Sub
'**Start Encode**
        Sub ButtonClicked2
        window.alert("This is encoded!")
    End Sub
```

```
    </script>
    </head>
    <body>
      <button name="Button1" type=BUTTON onclick="ButtonClicked">
      Click Me If You Can!!!
      </button>

        <button name="Button2" type=BUTTON onclick="ButtonClicked2">
      Click On Me Too!!!
      </button>
    </body>
    </html>
```

Encoding the file alters any code that appears below the encoding marker. This results in the following output.

```
    <html>
    <head>
    <title>Simple VBScript Example</title>
    <script language="VBScript.Encode">
        Sub ButtonClicked
            window.alert("This is not encoded!")
        End Sub
    '**Start Encode**#@~^YQAAAA==~,P~@#@&,PP,P,~PUE8P~EOOKxZ^rm0+Ny@#@&P,P,
    P~P~Abx[WSl^+.OvJK4rkPr/,nmG9+9"J*@#@&~P,P3x9Pj;(@#@&fhcAAA==^#~@</script>
    </head>
    <body>
      <button name="Button1" type=BUTTON onclick="ButtonClicked">
      Click Me If You Can!!!
      </button>

        <button name="Button2" type=BUTTON onclick="ButtonClicked2">
      Click On Me Too!!!
      </button>
    </body>
    </html>
```

Both subprocedures work as exactly normal. There is no difference between the encoded code and the unencoded code when the page is loaded into Internet Explorer and the script run. The only difference is a visual one, that you can understand the unencoded script but not the encoded script.

Here's a great trick to prevent others making changes to your copyright notices in scripts. Make your copyright notice part of the script! Place the copyright notice string into a variable and check to see if that variable is unaltered at runtime.

```
    <html>
    <head>
    <title>Simple VBScript Example</title>
    <script language="vbscript">

    Dim strCopyright
    strCopyright = "This script is copyright to me, 2003!"
```

```
'**Start Encode**
    Sub ButtonClicked
    If strCopyright = "This script is copyright to me, 2003!" Then
        MsgBox "Copyright notice is unaltered. Script cleared to continue ..."
        MsgBox "Script continues ..."
    Else
        MsgBox "Copyright notice is altered!!! Script halted!"
    End If
    End Sub
</script>
</head>
<body>
  <button name="Button1" type="BUTTON" onclick="ButtonClicked">
  Check copyright notice
  </button>
</body>
</html>
```

Encoding this script gives you the following:

```
<html>
<head>
<title>Simple VBScript Example</title>
<script language="VBScript.Encode">
Dim strCopyright
strCopyright = "This script is copyright to me, 2003!"
'**Start Encode**#@~^VAEAAA==~,P~@#@&,PP,?!8P~EOYKx/sbm3□[@#@&PP,~
(0,/DD/W2zMkLtD~',JP4b/Pd^
Mk2Y,rkP^KwHDkTtD~YKPh+BP+TZ&"r~K4+x@#@&~P,P,P~P\dTAG6,EZKwz.botO~    WOk1n,kd,E
 lVD+MnNcP~?1Dr2DPm^n1M+N,OGP1W          Yrx;n,R
Rr~@#@&P~~,PP~~t/LAKa,Jj1DbwY,P1GxDkUE□/~
cRJ,@#@&,PP,3s/□@#@&P~P~~,P~HkLAK6~E;Wwz.bo4Y,UKYr1+,k/,1^O+M+ ["e"~~UmDb2Y,
tl^OnNeJ
,@#@&P~~,2UN,(0i@#@&~,PP3U9PjE(@#@&7V0AAA==^#~@</script>
</head>
<body>
  <button name="Button1" type="BUTTON" onclick="ButtonClicked">
  Check copyright notice
  </button>
</body>
</html>
```

Now, when you run the script with the unaltered copyright notice, the script proceeds normally. However, just making one small change to the copyright notice halts the script.

```
...
Dim strCopyright
strCopyright = "This script is copyright to you instead, 2003!"
...
```

Figure 14-4 shows the result of such tampering! A message is shown indicating that the script has been tampered with. This message would be very hard to get rid of (certainly too hard for someone who wanted to borrow your code in the first place.).

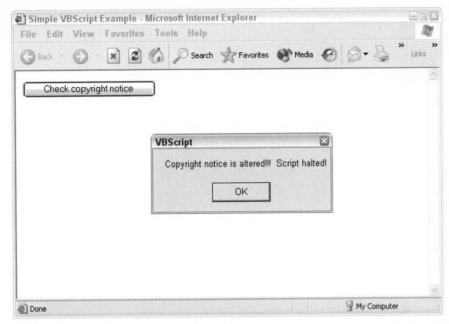

Figure 14-4

### ASP Files

Encoding ASP files is a little more complex than encoding HTML. This is because the ASP file format provides more information about script. However, if you have a relatively simple ASP file that contains a single script element, you should be able to run it through the Script Encoder and have it encoded without much trouble.

ASP lets you embed script code using the <%...%> notation and many ASP pages use this method rather than the alternate <SCRIPT runat="Server">. This presents a potential problem when encoding an ASP page because the <%...%> notation doesn't contain any language information, and the encoding mechanism needs that information to be able to perform proper encoding. As it happens, the vast majority of ASP developers use VBScript as their programming language of choice. VBScript is also the default language for ASP. Based on these factors, the script encoder will assume that the default language is set to VBScript.

Here is a simple example so you can see the output you can expect. First, this is the unencoded page.

```
<html>
<head>
<title>Client/server Information</title>
</head>
<body>
<p>
<b>You are browsing this site with:</b>
<%Response.Write(Request.ServerVariables("http_user_agent"))%>
</p>
```

```
<p>
<b>Your IP address is:</b>
<%Response.Write(Request.ServerVariables("remote_addr"))%>
</p>
<p>
<b>The DNS lookup of the IP address is:</b>
<%Response.Write(Request.ServerVariables("remote_host"))%>
</p>
<p>
<b>The method used to call the page:</b>
<%Response.Write(Request.ServerVariables("request_method"))%>
</p>
<p>
<b>The server's domain name:</b>
<%Response.Write(Request.ServerVariables("server_name"))%>
</p>
<p>
<b>The server's port:</b>
<%Response.Write(Request.ServerVariables("server_port"))%>
</p>
</body>
</html>
```

Once passed through the Script Encoder, a few changes are made.

```
<%@ LANGUAGE = VBScript.Encode %>
<html>
<head>
<title>Client/server Information</title>
</head>
<body>
<p>
<b>You are browsing this site with:</b>
<%#@~^OgAAAA==]□/2Kxk
+RqDbO+vIn;!+dOc?+M-+M.lMrC4^+k`EtOOa{;/□.{monUDJ#b4RUAAA==^#~@%>
</p>
<p>
<b>Your IP address is:</b>
<%#@~^NgAAAA==]□/2Kxk+RqDbO+vIn;!+dOc?+M-+M.lMrC4^+k`EDnhKYn{m
[NMJbbGxQAAA==^#~@%>
</p>
<p>
<b>The DNS lookup of the IP address is:</b>
<%#@~^NgAAAA==]□/2Kxk+RqDbO+vIn;!+dOc?+M-+M.lMrC4^+k`EDnhKYn{4G/
DJbbPhQAAA==^#~@%>
</p>
<p>
<b>The method used to call the page:</b>
<%#@~^OQAAAA==]□/2Kxk+RqDbO+vIn;!+dOc?+M-+M.lMrC4^+k`EDn5!+dY|h+DtG
[r##fhUAAA==^#~@%>
</p>
<p>
<b>The server's domain name:</b>
<%#@~^NgAAAA==]□/2Kxk+RqDbO+vIn;!+dOc?+M-+M.lMrC4^+k`E/n.7+
```

```
.{C:□JbbLBQAAA==^#~@%>
</p>
<p>
<b>The server's port:</b>
<%#@~^NgAAAA==]□/2Kxk+RqDbO+vIn;!+dOc?+M-+M.lMrC4^+k`E/n.7+
.{aGDDJbbUBQAAA==^#~@%>
</p>
</body>
</html>
```

Apart from the script being encoded, the other change is the addition of the language tag to the top of the page, which is used by the script engine to identify the encoding used.

ASP pages can have a number of different file extensions, but this won't bother the Script Encoder because it can, by default, handle all the commonly used ones: asp, asa, cdx.

If you have created your own file extensions and want to use the Script Encoder to encode them, you will have to use the defExtension argument (/e) to specify the file extension you want the encoder to use on your files. For example, if you use a .spa extension for your ASP pages, you would encode the page using the following command line command.

```
screnc unencoded.spa encoded.spa /e ASP
```

## Plain Text

The plain-text format consists of text file that contains nothing but script. This script will have no surrounding tags. Hosts utilizing scripting format include Windows Scripting Host and Microsoft Outlook. The recognized file extension for a plain-text file containing VBScript is .vbs before it is encode and .vbe after encoding.

*Note: These are easy to distinguish from plain-text JScript files, which have the file extension .js prior to encoding and .jse after encoding.*

Basically, expect nothing different here to what you've already seen. Script goes into the encoder looking like the following:

```
' Kathie Kingsley-Hughes
' 27 Oct 2003
' This script prompts the user for their name.
' It incorporates various greetings depending on input by the user.
'
' Added alternative greeting
' Changed variable names to make them more readable

Dim PartingGreeting
Dim VisitorName

VisitorName = PromptUserName

If VisitorName <> "" Then
    PartingGreeting = "Hello, " & VisitorName & ". Nice to have met you."
```

```
Else
    PartingGreeting = "I'm glad to have met you, but I wish I knew your name."
End If

MsgBox PartingGreeting

Function PromptUserName

    ' This Function prompts the user for their name.
    ' It incorporates various greetings depending on input by the user.
    Dim YourName
    Dim Greeting

    YourName = InputBox("Hello! What is your name?")

    If YourName = "" Then
        Greeting = "OK. You don't want to tell me your name."
    Else
        Greeting = "Hello, " & YourName & ", great to meet you."
    End If

    MsgBox Greeting

    PromptUserName = YourName

End Function
```

. . . and encoded script is outputted.

```
#@~^eQQAAA==v,b[MkmxPLPnrxT/s+HOu;Tt+k@#@&EP
F~6mDPy!T&@#@&EPPtbdPkm.raYP2.K:2Yk~Dtn,Ek+D,OK.PDtnkMPUCs+R@#@&B,qY,
rUmKDaW.lOnkP-
lMrW!/~LM++Or    odP9na+U9k
oPKx,rxaEOP(X~O4+P!d+MR@#@&v~@#@&B,b[Nn[,lsY□.xmYr-□Po.n□YrxT@#@&B~;tmxo□N,-
lMkC4^+~Um:+k~YKP:mVnPDt□:~:G.□P.+m[l(Vn~@#@&@#@&9b:~nm.DkUTMM++Dk
 L@#@&fr:,.rdbYWMHls+@#@&@#@&.b/bYGDHCs+~',KDK:2O`/+.Hm:nP@#@&@#@&(6Pjk/
bYK.1m:nP@!@*~ErPK4nx@#@&P,~~nmDDkUo!.□+Ok
   LP{PEu□VVGS,J~[,#b/rDWM1ls+,'PrR~1bmn~DWP4C\□P:□O~XKEcJ@#@&~@#@&@#@&2^d+
@#@&~~,PnC
.DkUoV.□+ObxTP',J&v:,osl9POG,tl7nPs+Y,zGEBP(EOP(~Skdt,(P0xnA,XW;.,xC:□
r@#@&Ax9Pq6@#@&@#@&t/LAK6~KmDYbUoVD+□OrxT@#@&@#@&@#@&@#@&s;x1OkKx~KMW:2O`/
nDgCs+@#@
&@#@&PP,PE~K4kdPwEU^DkW ~wMW:aOdPDt□P;/n.,0GD,Ot□k.~  l:n
@#@&~P,~EP(DPbxmKDaGDmYn/,\C.bWEk~oM++DrUokP9+2+U[bxLPKUPbx2;DP4z~DtnP!d□D
@#@&,PP,fbhPIW;Dglhn,@#@&,~P,fks~!D□+DkUo@#@&@#@&~P,~5KE.Hm:+~x,qUw!O~WavJ_
+V^We~Pq
tCY,kd~HWEM~xm:+QEb@#@&@#@&P~P~(6PeW!.1m:n~{PJE~:tnx@#@&,P~,P,PPVD□nYbxLP

{PE6nRP,eW!PNKUvY,hmxOPOG,YnV^~:□PzG!DPUCs+ J@#@&,P~,2^/+@#@&,~P,P~P,M.n□Yk
  LP{PJ_nsVK~,J~[~eKE.1mh+,[~EBPo.nmY~YK~s+nDPHWEcJ@#@&P,P~2
N~(6@#@&@#@&P,PPtdLAK6,M.+nObxL@#@&@#@&,P~~hDWh2Djd+MHm:n,',5W!DgC:□
@#@&@#@&2U[,sE^YbWxh0UBAA==^#~@
```

Again, you can use the encoding marker to control where the encoding begins.

```
' Kathie Kingsley-Hughes
' 27 Oct 2003
' This script prompts the user for their name.
' It incorporates various greetings depending on input by the user.
'
' Added alternative greeting
' Changed variable names to make them more readable

Dim PartingGreeting
Dim VisitorName

VisitorName = PromptUserName
'**Start
Encode**#@~^IAMAAA==@#@&qW,.b/kDWMHls+~@!@*PEE,Kt□U@#@&PP,~KlMYbxLM.n□YrxT~',
Jun^VW
S~rP'PjrkkOKDgl:□PL~JcPHk1+~OKPtm-+,:+D~zW!Rr@#@&P@#@&@#@&3Vkn@#@&P~~,nl.ObxL
MMn□Yr
 o,'PrqEhPTVCN,YG~41\□~:□YPHG;~,4!Y~q~Ab/4P&~3        +A~HWE.~           lh+cE@#@&3
N,q0@#@&@#@&Hko$WXPKCMYk        LMM++DrUo@#@&@#@&@#@&@#@&wEUmDrW
 PK.K:wOik+.1mh□@#@&@#@&,PP,B,Ptb/~s!x ObWx,2DK:wDd~Y4+,Ed+.~6W.PD4+bD~Um:+
@#@&P~P,v,qO,k  mWMwK.1D+dP71.rKE/,LD□+YbUL/,N□wnx[r  o~W    ~k
 w;O,4X~O4+~EknMR@#@&P,PPGks~5KE.1m:n~@#@&P,~PGk:,!.+□YbxL@#@&@#@&P~P,eW!DHCs
 +Px~&x
2ED$K6crC□VVK",~□41OPb/~zKED,Uls+grb@#@&@#@&,P~P(W,5GEMHls+~x,JJ~P4+U@#@&~,P~,
P,PMM+□Ok    o~',J6FcPPIGE,NW     vOPS1
 Y~YG~D+sV,h+,XG;MPxCh□RE@#@&~,P~AVk+@#@&P,~P,P~PVDnnDkxT~',JC□ssWBPrP'PeG!DH
lsnPLPES,oDnCDPOW,h□+O,XKERr@#@&~P,P3x9P(W@#@&@#@&~P,PHkL$WXPVDn+Or
o@#@&@#@&P,P~KMW:20`/nDgCs+~{PIWEM1mh+@#@&@#@&Ax[~wEx1OkKxyNoAAA==^#~@
```

Make sure that you fully test all scripts after encoding to ensure that they still work properly!

### Scriptlets

*Note: Scriptlet technology was deprecated by Microsoft in late 1998 and replaced by HTC components (behaviors). However, you can still use scriptlet technology.*

A scriptlet consists of a text file that contains valid scriptlet code within <SCRIPT>...</SCRIPT> tags. The recognized file extensions are .sct and .wsh; nothing new in the way that things work here. The main thing to remember is to make sure that VBScript code contained within a scriptlet is properly identifies using the language attribute.

```
<scriptlet>

<Registration

    Description="TempConvert"
    ProgID="TempConvert.Scriptlet"
    Version="1.00"
>
</Registration>

<implements id=Automation type=Automation>
```

```
        <method name=Celsius>
            <PARAMETER name=F/>
        </method>
        <method name=Fahrenheit>
            <PARAMETER name=C/>
        </method>
</implements>

<script language="VBScript">

Function Celsius(F)
    Celsius = 5/9 * (F - 32)
End Function

Function Fahrenheit(C)
    Fahrenheit = (9/5 * C) + 32
End Function

</script>
</scriptlet>
```

Encoding the script generated the expected output.

```
<scriptlet>

<Registration
    Description="TempConvert"
    ProgID="TempConvert.Scriptlet"
    Version="1.00"
>
</Registration>

<implements id=Automation type=Automation>
        <method name=Celsius>
            <PARAMETER name=F/>
        </method>
        <method name=Fahrenheit>
            <PARAMETER name=C/>
        </method>
</implements>

<script language="VBScript.Encode">#@~^pAAAAA==@#@&@#@&wE      mYbW
 ~Z□Vdk!/co*@#@&,~P,Z+^drEkP{PXz1~CPcs,RP2 b@#@&2x[~wEUmDrKx@#@&@#@&sE     mDrW
 Pol4DnU4+kDcZ*@#@&,~~Pwl4Dnx4nbY~',c,J*~M,Z#~Q,&+@#@&3       N~wE    mYbW
 @#@&@#@&WCYAAA==^#~@</script>
</scriptlet>
```

# Encoded Scripts–Do's and Don'ts

Before and after encoding there are a few do's and don'ts you should follow to ensure trouble-free scripts after encoding:

❑   Do keep an unencoded backup of the script.

- ❏ Do take care over correctly specifying the script language used, is there an ambiguity or you have not used the default.

- ❏ Do remove comments prior to encoding—after encoding they are useless and add significant bulk to the script.

- ❏ Do test the script before and after it is encoded to make sure it works.

- ❏ Don't make any changes to the script once encoded.

- ❏ Don't leave testing and debugging until the script is encoded!

- ❏ Don't expect script encoding to offer 100 percent code security. There are ways that the "determined" script snooper can get around it.

# Decoding the Script

One question you may be asking is "If you use the Script Encoder to encode a script, what decodes it before it is executed?" Good question! In fact, version 5 of Windows Script brought with it the ability for any application that uses VBScript and JScript to use the encoding feature. Once the language name is set to VBScript.Encode (or JScript.Encode) the ability to interpret encoded scripts is activated in the script engine while the debugging features are deactivated to prevent people simply loading up the script debugger and taking a look at your code that way. So all the decoding is handled by the script engine. The command line Script Encoder is only used to encode the script and nothing else.

# Other Methods of Script Obfuscation

Here is a quick rundown of a few alternatives to using the Microsoft Script Encoder. None of these alternatives are as effective. They do, however, help make the code more "confusing" to follow and will deter the casual viewer from using or altering the script.

Remember to keep at least one copy of the script in its original format so that you can understand and make changes to it easily!

# Remove Comment Tags

Seems simple but it can be quit effective. Removing all comment tags before making the code live can aid in adding an obstacle in the way of a code snooper. Comments are generally designed for internal consumption so why offer assistance to others in reading and deciphering your scripts!

# Substitute Good Variable Names for Bad Ones

Here's another good idea, but one you should leave until the script is finished. This goes against the concept of using clear, well-defined variable names but by using a simple find and replace you could change clear variable names (such as TaxRate or Your Name) to more obscure ones (such as var1 and var2).

# Add/Remove White Space

White space is critical in making code readable. If you remove indents the code becomes harder to read. Likewise, erratic indentation will make the code more complex.

Some programmers add a lot of white space at the top of code so that when the code is opened in a text editor, it appears to be a blank file.

# Summary

In this chapter you've been introduced to a few ways through which you can make code harder to read by people who you don't want reading your code. Without doubt, the best method of protecting code both from viewing and changing is the Microsoft Script Encoder. You've seen how the Microsoft Script Encoder can be used to encode scripts that reside in plain-text files (usually Windows Script Host files), HTML pages, ASP pages, and scriptlet files. The Microsoft Script Encoder doesn't offer 100 percent protection but it does offer a level of protection that makes using it worthwhile.

We also briefly touched on other methods which aren't anywhere near as effective as using the Windows Script Encoder, but which may help to protect your code from the casual code snoopers.

We hope that this chapter has made you realize that your code need not be released unprotected and that there are steps you can take to protect both your time invested in your code and your intellectual property.

# Remote Scripting

## Overview

The remote scripting technology was created in order to make Web applications substantially more powerful and to make them more closely resemble client/server applications developed using languages like C++, Visual Basic, or Java. By doing this, programmers can overcome the inherent limitations of Web applications. Without remote scripting, a Web browser has only one way to request new information from the server—to load an entirely new page. With remote scripting it becomes possible for the client page to execute a method on an ASP page without navigating away from the current page. More importantly, the requested data is available as the return value of the remote method called by the client page.

Combined with DHTML, this technology greatly simplifies all the applications that were previously forced to use cookies, hidden HTML input fields, or other dirty tricks to rebuild the new page as similar as possible to the previous one.

## The Influence of JScript on Remote Scripting

Unfortunately for VBScript users, the current implementation of remote scripting was created for JScript (the Microsoft equivalent of JavaScript). Microsoft developed remote scripting as part of a larger project called the Microsoft Scripting Library. In fact, the current implementation is a library of functions to enable remote scripting features, plus a little something else—a Java applet. Many users are very surprised when they come across these files and think that they must be having the wrong files or that different files relate to them. Don't worry—you have the right files!

Three files constitute the implementation of the remote scripting technology:

❑   RS.HTM—a collection of JScript functions to be used on the client page

❑   RS.ASP—a collection of JScript functions to be used on the server ASP page

❑   RSPROXY.CLASS—a Java applet that plays the vital role

These files, along with the official documentation, can be downloaded from the Microsoft Scripting Technologies site (www.microsoft.com/scripting/).

# How Remote Scripting Works

Remote scripting is implemented as a library of functions that you call from a client-side script when you want to run a server method. When a server method is called, the request is routed to a proxy process that runs asynchronously in the browser (in the current implementation of remote scripting, the proxy is implemented as a Java applet). The proxy process then sends a request to the server for the ASP page containing the method that has been called.

The server loads the ASP page, and a special routine on the ASP page sends the requests to the correct function. If the method returns a value, this is then sent back to the proxy process, which packages it as an object called a call object. This contains properties for the return value, as well as other useful information. A call is made with client-side script to a server method in one of two ways:

❑ Synchronously—The script calls the remote procedure and waits for it to return. This is useful if you need the results of the remote procedure before you proceed.

❑ Asynchronously—The script makes the call to a remote script, and then continues processing. The page remains available for users to work with. Asynchronous calls are very useful when a call might take a long time.

Security is a key factor nowadays. Remote scripting offers the same level of security as a Java applet or IFrames. To ensure remote scripting does not breach server security, you cannot pass structured data (which includes objects) as parameters to a server script for execution. In addition, the server to which remote scripting calls are made must be the same server that delivered the client page. What do the remote scripting files do?

Staying within the scope of this chapter (and the book) let's take a look at the role of the three files listed above so we can get a more clear idea of what's 'under the hood' of remote scripting

Here is a look at what the three files are and how they fit into remote scripting:

❑ The Java applet RSPROXY.CLASS is inserted automatically in the client page during initialization by the RSEnableRemoteScripting function. The role of this Java applet is to send the HTTP request to the server and receive the response.

❑ The RS.HTM file implements functions that marshal the remote method name and parameters into a buffer to be sent "over the net."

❑ RS.ASP implements functions that unmarshall such data from the receiving buffer. In a complementary way the returned value is marshalled by RS.ASP function and unmarshalled by RS.HTM functions.

These three files are everything that you need for remote scripting to work. In the remainder of this chapter we will look at how you use scripting to control these files and make remote scripting work for you.

# Using VBScript for Remote Scripting

Lucky for us, the major power and benefits of remote scripting are equally available to VBScript users as well as JScript users.

The remainder of this chapter provides a few guidelines to permit VBScript developers to make use of remote scripting, while at the same time avoiding features that have been shown to work with JScript only. The guidelines show you how to:

- ❑ Install the remote scripting files
- ❑ Enable the remote scripting engine on the server side
- ❑ Enable the remote scripting engine on the client side
- ❑ Call a remote method from a client page using VBScript
- ❑ Fetch the data returned from the remote method call
- ❑ Transform an asp page into a VBScript remote object

To be able to use remote scripting, the remote script files need to be installed on the server.

# Installing Remote Script on the Server

The default location for the remote scripting files is in a folder called `_ScriptLibrary`. This folder must be located in the root directory of your Web server.

> *All the samples in this section will assume that the files used for remote scripting are stored in a folder which is itself located in the root directory of your Web server.*

The remote scripting files can be located elsewhere but if you choose to do this then you will have to specify the location while initializing the remote scripting engine both on the client and server side. To avoid any difficulties arising from this, follow the following format while building your first remote scripting project.

| | |
|---|---|
| If the root directory of your Web server is: | `c:\inetpub\wwwroot\` |
| The three remote scripting files (`rs.htm`, `rs.asp`, `rsproxy.class`) should be located in the directory: | `c:\inetpub\wwwroot\_ScriptLibrary` |
| Any file in your project using remote scripting should be located in a directory like: | `c:\inetpub\wwwroot\YourScriptProject` |

# Enabling Remote Scripting on the Server

On the server the code will be included inside an ASP page. We suggest you use the following skeleton to encapsulate your server-side scripting code and at the same time enable remote scripting.

```
<%@ language="VBSCRIPT" %>
<%

' Write your VBScript remote methods in here...
```

```
' Remember to call RSDispatch to initialize the remote scripting engine
RSDispatch

%>
<!-- #INCLUDE FILE="../_scriptlibrary/rs.asp" -->
```

As you can see, two steps are required:

1. To invoke the function RSDispatch once in the lifetime of the ASP page to initialize the remote scripting engine

2. To include the file RS.ASP that contains the implementation of the RSDispatch function.

## Enabling Remote Scripting on the Client Side

The remote scripting engine must be initialized on every client page that needs to call remote methods. In this case there is a standard header to be applied just after the <body> HTML element.

```
...
<body>
<script language="JavaScript" src="../_ScriptLibrary/rs.htm"></script>
<script language="JavaScript">
RSEnableRemoteScripting("../_ScriptLibrary");</script>
...
```

This is the only place where we will use JavaScript in this chapter. It is necessary because the file RS.HTM is a file of JavaScript functions despite its .HTM extension. Furthermore, RSEnableRemoteScripting is an initializing function contained in that file.

## Invoking a Remote Method

Once the remote scripting has been properly initialized we can start invoking VBScript remote methods, entering the sample "Hello (Remote) World!"

The sample requires two files that should be located in the same directory on your Web server. For example they could be located at:

- ❑ d:\inetpub\wwwroot\rs\16\rsclient01.htm
- ❑ d:\inetpub\wwwroot\rs\16\hello.asp

While the remote scripting library (RS.HTM, RS.ASP, and RSPROXY.CLASS) is located in d:\inetpub\wwwroot\rs\_ScriptLibrary

The ASP page that hosts the remote method is called HELLO.ASP. The following is its source code.

```
<%@ language="VBSCRIPT" %>
<%

Function HRW()
    HRW = "Hello Remote World!"
End Function
```

```
RSDispatch

%>
<!-- #INCLUDE FILE="../_scriptlibrary/rs.asp" -->

<script runat="server" language="JavaScript">

    var public_description = new ExposeRemoteMethods();

    function ExposeRemoteMethods()
    {
        this.HRW = Function( 'return HRW()' );
    }

</script>
```

A little bit of JavaScript code is used to build this sample and make it as simple as possible, for now. But we'll get rid of this need for JavaScript after introducing VBScript classes. JavaScript is needed to expose the HRW method as a remote function.

VBScript cannot expose remote functions, but it can expose remote objects (with their methods), that give us more power and flexibility. By the way, the remote method is called HRW (and stands for "Hello Remote World").

```
...
Function HRW()
    HRW = "Hello Remote World!"
End Function
...
```

A client page named RSCLIENT01.HTM calls the remote method. The following is its source code.

```
<html>
<head>
<script language="VBScript">

Function InvokeHRW()
    Dim retObj
    set retObj = RSExecute("http://me/rs/16/hello.asp", "HRW")
    MsgBox retObj.return_value
End Function

</script>
</head>

<body onload="InvokeHRW">

<script language="JavaScript" src="../_ScriptLibrary/rs.htm"></script>
<script language="JavaScript">
RSEnableRemoteScripting("../_ScriptLibrary");
</script>

</body>
</html>
```

The remote method is called by the VBScript function.

```
...
Function InvokeHRW()
    Dim retObj
    Set retObj = RSExecute("http://me/rs/16/hello.asp", "HRW")
    MsgBox retObj.return_value
End Function
...
```

The function RSExecute is implemented in the RS.HTM file and gives the developer the power to invoke remote methods on the server without leaving the current client page. It returns an object with an important property called the return_value. This property contains the data retrieved from the server without loading a new page.

The remote method HRW simply returns a constant string "Hello Remote World", but it could be attached to a database via ADO, or it could have retrieved data on the server by other means, returning more meaningful and critical information.

We are now going to introduce a technique to get rid of the JavaScript public_description object using VBScript classes (after all, who wants JavaScript in a VBScript book!).

## Transforming an ASP Page into a VBScript Object

In the previous code sample a little JavaScript was required. So, let's get rid of the JavaScript, introduce a fully VBScript sample, and then discuss the importance and benefits of this approach. We'll call the sample "Hello (VBScript Remote) World!"

Changes are required in both the client and the server page. Using the model directory structure we introduced earlier, the two new files could be located in the directories.

❑   d:\inetpub\wwwroot\rs\16\rsclient02.htm

❑   d:\inetpub\wwwroot\rs\16\vbhello.asp

While the remote scripting library (RS.HTM, RS.ASP, and RSPROXY.CLASS) is still located in d:\inetpub\wwwroot\rs\_ScriptLibrary

Here's the server page, so you can immediately appreciate that there is no more JavaScript. The following is the VBHELLO.ASP code.

```
<%@ LANGUAGE= "VBSCRIPT" %>
<%

Class clsHello
    Public Function HRW()
        HRW = "Hello Remote World!"
    End Function
End Class
```

```
Set public_description = New clsHello

RSDispatch

%>
<!-- #INCLUDE FILE="../_scriptlibrary/rs.asp" -->
```

In this version, the HRW remote method has become a method of a VBScript class named clsHello. The nice issue is that VBScript classes can be used to define a working public_description object.

Modifications are required in the client page. Now we must invoke a VBScript object and not just a remote function. The RSCLIENT02.HTM code is as follows:

```
<html>
<head>
<script language="VBScript">

Function InvokeHRW()
    Dim aspObj
    Dim retObj
    Set aspObj = RSGetASPObject("vbhello.asp")
    Set retObj = aspObj.HRW()
    MsgBox retObj.return_value
End Function

</script>
</head>

<body onload="InvokeHRW">

<script language="JavaScript" src="../_ScriptLibrary/rs.htm">
</script>
<script language="JavaScript">
RSEnableRemoteScripting("../_ScriptLibrary");
</script>

</body>
</html>
```

In this case we are no longer using RSExecute but a different function available in the remote scripting engine: RSGetASPObject, as you can see from the following line.

```
        Set aspObj = RSGetASPObject("vbhello.asp")
```

The RSGetAspObject function takes only one parameter that is our ASP page. It actually converts an ASP page into a remote object; in fact, we can call the HRW remote method without using RSExecute.

```
        Set retObj = aspObj.HRW()
```

All programmers familiar with implementing the object-oriented model will immediately understand the benefits arising from this technique.

The functionality of an ASP page can be divided into remote methods and encapsulated inside an object. On the client side, all the scripting code will invoke remote methods as if they were local.

```
aspObj.aRemoteMethod
```

The numbers of applications of this technique are then just limited by your imagination. Once again, experimentation is the mother of learning and invention. Enjoy!

# Summary

In this chapter we discussed how to make Web applications using VBScript perform like applications developed using more complicated compiled languages. Specifically, we've looked at using remote scripting technologies and saw how to:

❑   Install the remote scripting files

❑   Enable the remote scripting engine on the server side

❑   Enable the remote scripting engine on the client side

❑   Call a remote method from a client page using VBScript

❑   Fetch the data returned from the remote method call

❑   Transform an asp page into a VBScript remote object

Again, remember that remote scripting is a massive subject. Whole volumes can (and have) been devoted to this topic. This chapter is but a brief taster of what you can do with it. We've covered the basics here, but if you want to learn more you will need to refer to more specialized sources.

# 16

# HTML Applications

The previous chapters focused on Web development, but there are times when you don't want your application to look like a Web page with all of the browser components, such as toolbars, exposed. In the past, C/C++, Java, and Visual Basic programmers had the market cornered for traditional Windows applications. With the introduction of HTML applications in Internet Explorer, that has now changed. Now you can use the skills you already have of technologies such as Dynamic HTML (DHTML), Cascading Style Sheets (CSS), and scripting to write fully fledged Windows applications. HTML applications are often referred to as HTAs. This refers to the file extension (.hta) that HTML applications use. The full name for the technology is HTML Applications.

## What is an HTML Application?

An HTML application is essentially what it sounds like. It is an HTML-based application. The parent process of mshta.exe (the application that actually runs an HTA) is Internet Explorer; so almost anything (we'll talk about exceptions later) that you can do using Internet Explorer 5 or later, you can do in HTA. These functions include scripting, CSS, behaviors, XML, and XSL.

You can control everything that is shown on the screen with an HTA. You don't have to see Internet Explorer menus or toolbars if you don't want them to be present. For example, take a look at the simple application (shown in Figure 16-1) that we'll be using to help us explore HTAs in this chapter. All it does is navigate to a few select sites, but as you can see, this application really doesn't look like it's running under Internet Explorer at all because there are no toolbars or menus present.

You may be thinking that's great, but what about the security warnings that come up when you embed other objects in a browser? The great thing about HTAs is that they are fully trusted applications. All of the restrictions that you worry about with a Web page are not a problem with HTAs. You can, if you want, modify the registry while running an HTA. However, do bear in mind that if you don't have standard security restrictions, you need to be aware of the problems that may arise from your code or another site that is used within the HTA. We'll look into security issues in more depth later in this chapter.

OK, with that covered, the next question you probably have is how do you run an HTA? All you need is Internet Explorer installed (not a problem on most systems as it is built into the Windows

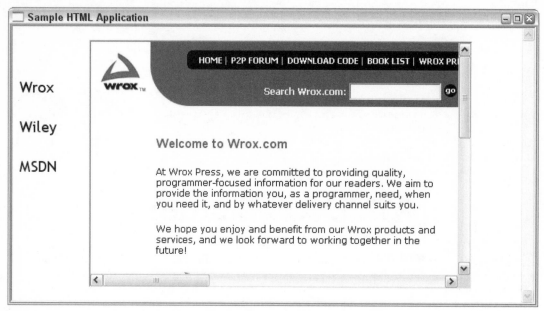

**Figure 16-1**

operating system), and you're ready. Once you have an HTA created, you can simply double-click on the file and the application will run, just like any other program. Another huge advantage of HTAs is that they can be run from both the server and the client machine, as we'll see later on. This gives HTA technology wide appeal with both client-side and server-side developers.

# What Tools Do You Need?

You don't need much to start creating HTAs:

❑ A text editor—any will do, from the simple but robust Windows Notepad to something more fancy and easier to use, such as UltraEdit32 (http://www.ultraedit.com)

❑ The latest version of the script engines (download this free from http://www.microsoft.com/scripting—if you already haven't!)

❑ Internet Explorer 5 or later (HTAs are supported automatically when you install Internet Explorer 5. Previous versions of Internet Explorer do not support HTAs.)

# How to Create a Basic HTA

It's actually very simple to create HTAs. All you need to do is create an HTML file, add the script, and change the file extension of your HTML file to .hta. There are no additional constraints over what you can or can't do.

Let's take a look at an example. We will go through the steps of first creating the HTML file, then a CSS file that controls the formatting of the HTML file, and finally rename the file with the right file extension.

## Sample HTML File

We'll start with an HTML file that navigates a frame to a Web site. Since it's a normal HTML file at the moment, it'll have the file extension .htm. There are three <span> elements that, when clicked, navigate the <iframe> (which will act as our viewer).

The three Web sites we'll be using are:

❑   www.wrox.com

❑   www.wiley.com

❑   msdn.microsoft.com

When the page is loaded into the Internet Explorer browser, the Web page will navigate to the Wrox Web site by default and display it.

```
<html>
<head>

<title>Sample HTML Application</title>

<link rel="stylesheet" type="text/css" href="HTA.css">
</head>
<body>

<br>
<br>
</span
    onclick="Viewer.document.location.href='http://www.wrox.com'">
    Wrox
</span>
<br>
<br>
<span
    onclick="Viewer.document.location.href='http://www.wiley.com'">
    Wiley
</span>
<br>
<br>
<span
    onclick="Viewer.document.location.href='http://msdn.microsoft.com'">
    MSDN
</span>

<iframe id="Viewer" src="http://www.wrox.com">
</iframe>

</body>
</html>
```

Next we have to create the `HTA.css` file. This CSS file controls the formatting of the HTA file. Here's the code contained in this file.

```css
body
{

    FONT-FAMILY: 'Trebuchet MS';
    FONT-SIZE: 20px;
    POSITION: absolute

}

span
{

    CURSOR: hand;
    POSITION: absolute;
    WIDTH: 15%

}

iframe
{

    HEIGHT: 95%;
    LEFT: 15%;
    OVERFLOW: scroll;
    POSITION: absolute;
    TOP: 5%;
    WIDTH: 80%

}
```

Our style sheet sets the default font as Trebuchet MS with a font size of 20px (pixels). We define positioning as absolute. For our `<span>` tags, we turn the mouse pointer into a hand.

We refer to a number of size parameters in percentages. This sets the dimension as a percentage of the size of its parent element. If the length of the parent element changes, the length of the child element will be changed as well. Let's say we give the parent element a width of 900px. If the width of the child element is 10%, then the absolute width of the child element will be 90px.

Our completed Web page looks like Figure 16-2.

*Note that we have all of the standard Internet Explorer toolbars and menus.*

Although the script may look correct, we do have a few problems. When an HTML file has a `<frame>` or `<iframe>`, there are some security restrictions that aren't necessarily obvious right away.

If a frame navigates away from the domain in which the original file is located, the properties and methods of the frame, and the elements within it, are no longer accessible to the parent element. An example of this is once the `<iframe>` has been navigated to another URL, such as the MSDN site, we

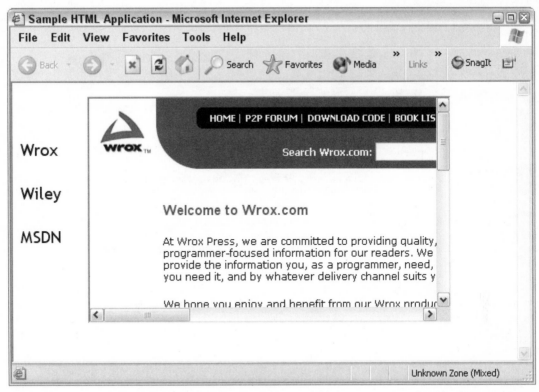

**Figure 16-2**

can't change the `document.location` of the `<iframe>`. In fact the document of the `<iframe>` is not accessible at all. This is not an error, it is by design.

Basically, if you try clicking on MSDN or any other link, you will receive an error message. This restriction is there to limit the ability of one site to track your subsequent navigation.

This might not seem reasonable, but let's think about it a little bit more. Let's say that you have search results in one panel of a page, generated from a search engine. The search panel can know where you are going from the `<iframe>`, but once you get to the site in the opposite frame, the search engine can't track anything else. It's all revolves around privacy issues—do you really want a search engine site to know about everything that you do on the Internet? Probably not!

## Turning an HTML File into an HTML Application

Let's try renaming our file from `HTA.htm` to `HTA.hta`. This small change now gives our application an entirely different look (as shown in Figure 16-3).

By default, we have a title bar and minimize, maximize, and restore buttons, but we don't have any of the Internet Explorer toolbars. The title bar of the application even picked up the title that we put in.

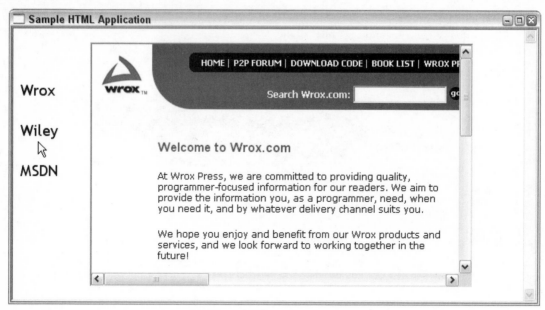

**Figure 16-3**

Also, you can now navigate to other sites through the main application. That was a quick fix to some painful issues.

Now, that looks great. All we needed to do was change the file extension, and our file is recognized as an application. We don't have to deal with all the security issues any more. But we might want to get rid of the title bar, or have the application launch in full screen.

Well, we can solve those problems, too. Let's look at the HTA:APPLICATION element.

# The HTA:APPLICATION Element

We want to modify the look of our application even further. Fortunately, there is an HTML element called HTA:APPLICATION. With this tag we can choose not to display a caption, or to maximize the window, as well as a few other things. In our sample application, let's try some of these options.

You can embed the HTA:APPLICATION tag anywhere within the document, but for performance reasons, it's recommended that you embed it within the head of the document. Since the browser parses information in the order that it is found on the page, if you place the HTA element at the end of the document, the browser won't recognize the HTA attributes you've set until it has completely parsed the document. For example, let's say you've sized elements by percentages—by doing this, the browser will now need to calculate these parameters over again.

The HTA:APPLICATION element requires a closing tag.

```
<HTA:APPLICATION ... > ... </HTA:APPLICATION>
```

Because the HTA:APPLICATION element is an empty tag, it can also be closed using the following shortcut.

```
<HTA:APPLICATION ... />
```

We'll set the Caption attribute to no and the windowState attribute of the HTML tag to maximize. Now our application loads in full screen mode without a title bar. We can close the application using the Windows task bar.

```
<head>

<title>Sample HTML Application</title>

<HTA:APPLICATION
    Caption="no"
    windowState="maximize" />

<link rel="stylesheet" type="text/css" href="HTA.css">
</head>
<body>

<br>
<br>
<span
    onclick="Viewer.document.location.href='http://www.wrox.com'">
    Wrox
</span>
<br>
<br>
<span
    onclick="Viewer.document.location.href='http://www.wiley.com'">
    Wiley
</span>
<br>
<br>
<span
    onclick="Viewer.document.location.href='http://msdn.microsoft.com'">
    MSDN
</span>

<iframe id="Viewer" src="http://www.wrox.com">
</iframe>

</body>
</html>
```

# Do File Extensions Still Matter?

If you use an .htm file extension, but an HTA tag is embedded, will the application act like an HTML application? The answer is no. Without the .hta file extension, the HTA:APPLICATION tag will not be recognized by the browser. The file extension is the only thing that truly defines an HTML application.

## Changing Parameters from the Command Line

We will now try launching an HTA from the command line. First, we need to have an ID for our HTA to be able to access attributes of our HTA through script. We are also going to put our caption back in, but we'll discuss that further in the next section.

We'll also create a script that creates an array from our commandLine property. The commandLine property is only available through scripting. It returns the location of the HTA launched and any other parameters specified on the command line. It cannot be specified within the HTA:APPLICATION tag.

*Please note that this script requires that there are no spaces in the name of the location used to launch the application.*

You can use this in your existing HTA if you simply replace the existing HTA tag with the following one, and add the script under the new HTA tag.

```
<HTA:APPLICATION
    ID="MySampleHTA"
    Caption="yes"
    windowState="maximize">

<script language="VBScript">
    Option Explicit

    Sub LoadPage

    Dim cmdLineArray
    Dim WebSite

    ' fill array with elements of commandLine attribute
    cmdLineArray = Split(MySampleHTA.commandLine)

    ' check if first element of array is equal to commandLine attribute
    ' if so, no Web site was specified, so go to the Wrox site.
        If cmdLineArray(0) = MySampleHTA.commandLine Then
            WebSite = "http://www.wrox.com"

    ' Otherwise, there is a specified Web site. Need to see
    ' if it's properly formatted. If :// isn't present in
    ' the second element of the array, we add http://
        ElseIf InStr(1, cmdLineArray(1), "://" ) = 0 Then
            WebSite = cmdLineArray(1)
            WebSite = "http://" & WebSite
        Else
            WebSite = cmdLineArray(1)
        End If

        Viewer.document.location.href = WebSite

    End Sub

</script>
```

You'll also need to change your HTML <body> tag to read

```
<body onload="LoadPage">
```

Now, when we launch the application from the command line with

```
d:\wrox\hta\hta.hta www.kingsley-hughes.com
```

the site will be displayed in the <iframe>. If a specific Web site is not specified at the command line, the default will be MSDN.

Let's just see how we did that. First, this line:

```
cmdLineArray = Split(MySampleHTA.commandLine)
```

This creates an array that accesses the commandLine attribute of our HTA and splits it into separate pieces wherever it finds a space. Then, we check to see if the first element of the array is the same as the commandLine attribute of the HTA. If it is, that means that the string had no spaces, which in turn means that no Web site was specified. So we go to the Wrox site.

```
If cmdLineArray(0) = MySampleHTA.commandLine Then
    WebSite = "http://www.wrox.com"
```

Otherwise, we know that a Web site has been specified, so we need to see if it is properly formatted. If we don't find "://" in the second element of the array, we'll add "http://".

```
ElseIf InStr(1, cmdLineArray(1), "://" ) = 0 Then
    WebSite = cmdLineArray(1)
    WebSite = "http://" & WebSite
```

Finally, what if the URL is formed correctly? Here, we assume that if the Else statement is reached, then the command line must contain a properly formatted URL that we can use.

```
Else
    WebSite = cmdLineArray(1)
```

After we've done all that, we send the <iframe> to the Web site we specified.

```
Viewer.document.location.href = WebSite
```

And that's it—all done! You have a fully completed and fully functioning HTA file. What you should notice is how the actual representation of your code in the browser changed by simply changing the file extension from .htm to .hta. With a .htm file the browser displays the file as a Web page, but using the .hta extension changes this and the page is displayed as a more stand-alone application.

# All HTA:APPLICATION Attributes

There are a number of other properties that we can access for the HTA:APPLICATION element. The full list of properties for the HTA:APPLICATION element appears in the following table.

| Property | Values | Description |
|---|---|---|
| ApplicationName | User-defined string | Sets the name of the HTA. |
| Border | thick (Default)<br>thin<br>none<br>dialog | The border size for the application. |
| BorderStyle | normal (Default)<br>static<br>raised<br>sunken<br>complex | The style of the border. The static border style is normally used for windows that don't allow user input. |
| Caption | yes (Default)<br>no | Displays a caption in the title bar. |
| CommandLine | | Path used to launch the HTA. This is a read-only property. |
| ContextManu | yes (Default)<br>no | Sets or retrieves whether the context menu is displayed when the right mouse button is clicked. |
| Icon | Path to .bmp or .ico file | Icon to be displayed in the task bar and title bar when the application is running. |
| ID | User-defined string | ID that can be used to access the HTA through script. |
| InnerBorder | yes (Default)<br>no | Sets or retrieves whether the inside 3-D border is displayed. |
| MaximizeButton | yes (Default)<br>no | Displays the maximize button. |
| MinimizeButton | yes (Default)<br>no | Displays the minimize button. |
| Navigable | no (Default)<br>yes | Sets or retrieves whether linked documents will be loaded in the main HTA window or into a new browser window. |
| Scroll | yes (Default)<br>no<br>auto | Sets or retrieves whether the scroll bars are displayed. |
| ScrollFlat | no (Default)<br>yes | Sets or retrieves whether the scroll bar is 3-D or flat. |
| Selection | yes (Default)<br>no | Sets or retrieves whether the content can be selected with the mouse or keyboard. |

| Property | Values | Description |
|---|---|---|
| ShowInTaskBar | yes (Default)<br>no | Sets or retrieves a value that indicates whether the HTA is displayed in the Microsoft Windows taskbar. |
| SingleInstance | no (Default)<br>yes | Sets or retrieves a value that indicates whether only one instance of the specified HTA can run at a time. |
| SysMenu | yes (Default)<br>no | Sets or retrieves a Boolean value that indicates whether a system menu is displayed in the HTA. |
| Version | User-defined string | Sets or retrieves the version number of the HTA. |
| WindowState | normal (Default)<br>minimize<br>maximize | Sets or retrieves the initial size of the HTA window. The normal state will size the window to the same size Internet Explorer starts up at, whatever that may be. |

## Interdependent Attributes

A number of attributes are dependent upon each other. If the border attribute is not set to thick, the HTA cannot be resized. If the ID of the application is not specified, other attributes of the HTA cannot be accessed.

❑ If the caption is set to no, then the minimize and maximize buttons aren't displayed, the system menu is not available, and the program icon is not seen in the title bar.

❑ If the system menu is turned off, then the minimize and maximize buttons are not visible. The icon in the title bar won't be visible either.

❑ If you choose not to display a border, there is no title bar, and so the minimize and maximize buttons (along with the title bar icon in the title bar) are not visible.

This may seem a little confusing, but the goal is to match the current Windows user interface.

### Examples of Interdependency

Let's look at a few examples. We'll start by setting the minimize and maximize buttons, and then add an icon, a caption, a border, and a system menu. We can also see the system menu from the task bar. This is all done by changing the HTA:APPLICATION element as seen next.

```
<html>
<head>

<title>Sample HTML Application</title>
<HTA:APPLICATION
    ID=MySampleHTA
    icon="hta.ico"
    caption="yes"
    minimizeButton="yes"
```

```
       maximizeButton="yes"
       sysMenu = "yes"
       border="thick"
       windowState="maximize" />

   <script language="VBScript">
       Option Explicit
```

Now let's try setting the `sysMenu` property to `no`, as shown.

```
   <HTA:APPLICATION
       ID=MySampleHTA
       icon="hta.ico"
       caption="yes"
       minimizeButton="yes"
       maximizeButton="yes"
       sysMenu="no"
       border="thick"
       windowState="maximize" />
```

With this simple change, our HTA no longer displays the icon in the title bar and in the taskbar. This is shown in Figure 16-4. Now we aren't able to resize our window and the minimize, maximize, and close buttons are no longer visible.

*From www.wrox.com. Copyright © 2004 by Wiley Publishing, Inc. All rights reserved. Reproduced here by permission.*

**Figure 16-4**

Now let's change the `sysMenu` attribute back to `yes`, but set the `caption` to `no`.

```
   <HTA:APPLICATION
       ID=MySampleHTA
       icon="hta.ico"
       caption="no"
       minimizeButton="yes"
       maximizeButton="yes"
       sysMenu="yes"
       border="thick"
       windowState="maximize" />
```

Figure 16-5 shows what this looks like in the browser.

**Figure 16-5**

Now we can no longer see the minimize, maximize, and close buttons. This time, since the `windowState` is also set to `maximize`, the task bar is no longer visible.

Finally, we'll set the `caption` attribute back to `yes`, and see what happens when we set the `border` to `none`.

```
<HTA:APPLICATION
    ID=MySampleHTA
    icon="hta.ico"
    caption="yes"
    minimizeButton="yes"
    maximizeButton="yes"
    sysMenu="yes"
    border="none"
    windowState="maximize" />
```

In fact, as Figure 16-6 shows, we have the same result as if we set the `caption` attribute to `no`.

**Figure 16-6**

There isn't a way to specifically set the close button on the application. Although the minimize and maximize buttons can be set to `no` without losing the close button, if the caption or the system menu are set to `no` or if the border is set to `none`, the close button will not be visible.

This may not seem important at first glance, but if you choose certain options, you will have to close the application using Ctrl+Alt+Del. You probably don't want all of your users to be required to use this method (many might not even know how to do this). Therefore you will need to provide another method to close your application through scripting, with the `window.close` function for example.

# Helpful Hints

Some references may show that the yes/no values could be replaced by true or false. This does not appear to work and as such we recommend using yes or no.

The document's location href is not updated until the application is completely loaded. If you try to access this property before the onload event fires, you will be given the href of the previous frame. It is recommended that you use the document.URL property if you need access to the location of the document before it is loaded. For example, you could use document.URL and retrieve the same result you'd have expected from the document.location.href property.

# HTAs and Security

We've already seen that HTAs aren't limited by browser security because the executable file that runs the HTA (mshta.exe) overrides Internet Explorer's standard security. HTAs are considered fully trusted applications, and all of the restrictions on the client machine and its file system are removed. The registry of the client machine is even accessible.

> *If this seems like a very unsafe thing to you, bear in mind that the same power is available to standard programs written in, say, C++ and Visual Basic.*

ActiveX controls can be embedded without warnings. This is extremely helpful when using even standard scripting controls such as the FileSystemObject or the XMLDOM. Keep in mind when disabling security warnings, though, that you should make sure that security issues won't be a problem.

But what if you want to apply some restrictions when navigating to another Web site? There are certainly no guarantees that the site you are navigating to doesn't have a virus or some other problem.

Typically, both <frame> and <iframe> are used to navigate to another site within a document. These tags are generally used because they can have a source. In fact, frames have their own document object. <div>, <span>, and other frequently used tags do not have this capability.

Let's look at security for frames.

# Frames without Trust

In the past, <frame> and <iframe> have supported an attribute called TRUSTED to indicate if normal browser security would apply to a frame. With Internet Explorer 5 and beyond, the TRUSTED attribute is no longer functional. Although there is still quite a bit of documentation that refers to the TRUSTED attribute, it doesn't work.

How are you supposed to change a frame's security options in Internet Explorer 6 (or 5 for that matter)? First of all, when you are not using a frame within an HTML application, the answer is that you can't.

> *All <frame> and <iframe> not in HTML applications are considered untrusted. Normal browser security applies to the frame.*

But what if you are in an HTML application? You may want a frame to be trusted. How do we do that? Well, that's where the APPLICATION attribute of the frames comes in.

# APPLICATION Attribute

The APPLICATION attribute has been added to the <frame> and <iframe> tags. The APPLICATION attribute indicates whether a frame should be treated like an HTML application, disabling security warnings. The possible values for the attribute are yes, meaning the application is trusted, and no (the default), meaning that standard security warnings apply.

If, by default, frames are untrusted, why were the security issues in the example simply by changing the file extension? It is because untrusted frames in an HTA are unaware of both the parent window and the URL that opened the external frame. The untrusted content can't then use that information in any way. When the document within the untrusted frame tries to access the top element of the document, the frame's window is returned. That way, there are no access violations that would occur in the HTML file with frames in different domains.

If frames within an HTML document are in different URL domains, the script for one domain cannot access the properties and methods in another domain. The HTA itself is considered trusted and has access to the frame's properties and methods.

Let's take a look at a page that contains an ActiveX control. We'll create a simple VBScript object, the FileSystemObject. This is just a simple demonstration page, though, and we aren't going to actually use the FileSystemObject in any way. We'll call this page ActiveXControl.htm.

```
<html>
<head>

<title>ActiveX Control</title>

<link rel="stylesheet" type="text/css" href="HTA.css">

<script language="VBSCRIPT">

    Dim FileSystem
    ' Creates the FileSystemObject
    Set FileSystem = CreateObject("Scripting.FileSystemObject")

</script>
</head>

<body>

<p>This page contains the ActiveX control FileSystemObject.</p>

</body>
</html>
```

Let's look at what happens when we try to load this page into the browser. We get a security warning (shown in Figure 16-7) that asks the user if they want to download the ActiveX control.

**Figure 16-7**

After we answer yes, our page looks like the one shown in Figure 16-8.

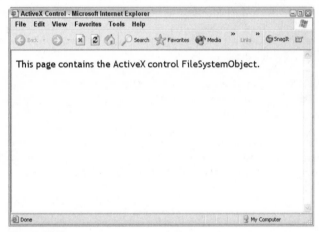

**Figure 16-8**

Let's try adding this page into our HTA and see what happens. We'll add a fourth span that is linked to our new page. For now, everything else will stay the same. Just add these lines under the other three spans.

```
<br>
<br>
<span
    onclick="Viewer.document.location.href='ActiveXControl.htm'">
    Control
</span>
```

When we click on our new span, we see the same security warning. But now let's set our `<iframe>` `APPLICATION` attribute to `yes`.

```
<iframe ID='Viewer' APPLICATION="yes">
</iframe>
```

Now when we navigate to our new page, we don't see any security warnings. The resulting HTA should look like the one shown in Figure 16-9.

Figure 16-9

## Nested Frames

What if you want to have nested frames? Let's add an <iframe> into the body of ActiveXControl
.htm. The source for the <iframe> will be NestedFrame.htm.

```html
<html>
<head>
<title>ActiveX Control</title>

<LINK rel="stylesheet" type="text/css" href="HTA.css">

<script language="VBScript">

    Dim FileSystem
    ' Creates the FileSystemObject
    Set FileSystem = CreateObject("Scripting.FileSystemObject")

</script>
</head>

<body>

<iframe src="NestedFrame.htm">
</iframe>

</body>
</html>
```

Let's create NestedFrame.htm. This file also creates the FileSystemObject. The body of the
document contains text. When we try to load the file ActiveXControl.htm, we receive two security
warnings, one for each frame.

Now let's try loading the frame from the HTA instead. Since we already changed the APPLICATION
attributes of the <iframe> in the HTA to yes, we'll only see one warning; if we hadn't, we'd have seen
two. Interestingly, if we set the APPLICATION attribute of the <iframe> in the HTA to no, and the one in
the ActiveXControl to yes, we still get two sets of security warnings. This is because the
APPLICATION attribute isn't recognized by Internet Explorer unless the parent element is an
APPLICATION. For nested frames, the APPLICATION attribute will not be recognized, and will mean the
frame is untrusted, if its parent window is not trusted.

Now if we set both APPLICATION attributes to yes, we won't have any security warnings at all, which is a far more desirable outcome.

# HTA Deployment Models

HTAs are very exciting, but by now you're probably wondering how you can distribute them.

HTAs can be accessed in a couple of ways, including via the Web and as a package with all of the referenced files in the HTA (in much the same way that you would install a standard Windows application). You can even create a combination of the two. Let's look at all these models in more depth.

## Web Model

In a Web model, an HTA can be referenced just as you might reference any other file with a URL. The user is asked to verify that they want to download the file, and no further security warnings occur. The application, and any other relevant files, are downloaded by the browser and cached.

Since the files live on the server, the user will always receive the most recent version when they download it. If the user elects to run from the current location, they don't even need to install or configure anything because the browser will do all of the work. The application doesn't even need to be uninstalled afterwards.

The server does need to have the MIME type "application:hta" registered for the file to be successfully downloaded through the http: protocol. Bear in mind that the client machine must also be running Internet Explorer 5 or later to run HTAs, as these are the only browsers that supports HTAs.

### Web Model Issues

When you are thinking about running the application from the server, there are a few things to consider:

❑ Since you have to go to the server to retrieve the application, the application isn't available when the user isn't connected to the Internet. If your network isn't that reliable, that is certainly going to be an issue.

❑ If you aren't on a high-speed network, and particularly if your application is large, the speed of your application is going to suffer. While DSL and ADSL are starting to replace standard modems, the new technology hasn't reached everyone yet.

❑ Every time the application is run, the user is prompted with a screen about downloading the file. This can get pretty frustrating if the application is started frequently.

However, on a high-speed corporate intranet where all users have the latest Internet Explorer, the Web model is extremely useful. Changes can be made to code without any of the hassles that are seen with traditional Windows applications.

## Package Model

An HTML application doesn't need to run through the Web. In many cases, that's not necessary at all. All that is required is to have Internet Explorer 5 or later installed. Since an HTML application is a set of files, the files can be installed on a user's local drive or even at a network location. If your application doesn't contain custom ActiveX controls, you can use a simple zip file to place the files on the client's machine.

If you do have custom Active X controls, you will need to register them. You could use applications such as Wise or InstallShield to register controls and create an installation process.

The advantages of this model are that you don't need to be online, the application will run faster, and you don't need to deal with security warnings after the initial installation.

### Package Model Issues

The disadvantage of using a package model is that the updates are not automatically transferred to the user like they are in the Web model. You would need to manually update the files on the local machine.

Also, if you do have ActiveX controls to register, you will need to provide a way to uninstall the controls. If you choose to install controls, you will probably want to use programs that have uninstall utilities, such as Wise or InstallShield.

## Hybrid Model

You can also combine the two models, forming a kind of "hybrid" model. You can install part of the application locally, and part of the application on the server. Anything that you want to reference on the server, such as images, style sheets, sources for frames, XML data, and so on, can be referenced from the HTML application on the client machine.

Our example application could be seen as a kind of hybrid-model HTA, as it accesses URLs on the Internet, while the application and corresponding style sheet are stored locally. Using an approach such as this one may better meet your needs.

For example, if your concern is speed, you might choose to store larger files locally. If you want to limit the number of updates that are manually sent to the user, you might choose to make the HTA file itself a fairly simple file, possibly by using frames that have their sources on the server. That way, any content changes can be made to the frame files in their central location.

## What Isn't Supported with HTAs?

Many of the references on HTML applications state that all of the features available in Internet Explorer 5 or 6 are also available in HTAs. This isn't entirely accurate. For example, the HTA doesn't know anything about the application or site that launched the HTA. As a result, there are a number of properties and methods of the window object that aren't available within the HTA.

## The Window Object

The window object's opener property is not available to the user. The external property (which normally allows the window access to its referring window) is also unavailable, as is the menuArguments property.

Most of the methods that aren't available are those that would give the HTA unreasonable access to other programs, like Internet Explorer. Since an HTA is in fact an application, it makes sense that the user wouldn't have access to another application, even Internet Explorer.

Here's a list of the unavailable methods in HTAs.

| Method | Description |
| --- | --- |
| AddChannel | Presents a dialog box that allows the user to either add the channel specified, or change the channel URL if it is already installed. |
| AddDesktopComponent | Adds a Web site or image to the Microsoft Active Desktop. |
| AddFavorite | Adds a page to the Favorites list. |
| AutoCompleteSaveForm | Saves the form to the auto complete data. |
| AutoScan | Tries to connect to the Web server with queries. |
| ImportExportFavorites | Imports or exports Internet Explorer's favorites list. |
| IsSubscribed | Indicates if a user is subscribed to an Active Channel. |
| NavigateAndFind | Opens a Web page, and highlights a specific string. |
| ShowBrowser | Opens the browser's dialog box. |

## Default Behaviors

There are also a few default behaviors in Internet Explorer that are not available within an HTML application. As in the previous section, they are related to browser modifications and involve data storage by the browser.

These include saveFavorite, saveHistory, saveSnapshot, and userData.

## Summary

I'm sure by now you will feel pretty good about using HTML applications. They provide a simple way to get the most out of HTML and script, and they give you even more control over the user interface of your application.

HTML applications are a powerful technique for quickly developing Windows applications. They provide a great way for HTML and other programming languages to come together. HTAs are also a good way for you to use your skills on both the server and client machines. The problems that surround standard security warnings that are usually encountered with browsers are now a thing of the past.

In addition to creating full-blown Windows applications, HTAs are an excellent tool for prototyping. Application designers can easily build an interface, and demonstrate the interactions that they want built without having to learn a complex programming language like C++ or VB.

# Server-Side Web Scripting

## Overview

Talk to most people about VBScript and usually the first thing that pops into their heads is Active Server Pages (ASP). The two technologies are linked together in the minds of many Web developers. Sure, you can do a lot with VBScript on the client side and even create stand-alone applications, but ASP is where all the power is!

In the preceding chapter, we've been focusing mainly on client-side scripting and applications. Now it's time to take a look at the server side of things. Creating Web sites with only client-side scripting is all well and good, but your functionality and power are severely limited. By adding server-side scripting, you add a whole new dimension to the Web site and gain a huge advantage. You are able to draw upon the wealth of data available to you on the server and across the enterprise in various databases. You are able to customize pages to the needs of each different user that comes to your Web site. In addition, by keeping your code on the server side you can build a library of functionality. This library can be drawn from again and again to further enhance other Web sites. Best of all, using server-side script libraries will allow your Web sites to scale to multitier, or distributed, Web applications.

To do this, you'll need a good understanding of the HTTP protocol, and how an HTTP server interacts with a browser. This model is important to understand when developing Web applications that exist on the client and server side.

Next, we'll introduce you to Active Server Pages. ASP is Microsoft's server-side scripting environment. ASP can be used to create everything from simple, static Web pages to database-aware dynamic sites, using HTML and scripting. Another important use is as "programming glue." Through the use of ASP you can create and manipulate server-side components. These components can perhaps provide data to your application such as graphic image generation, or may link to a mainframe database. The important thing to always remember is that the ASP code does nothing more than to facilitate the use of these components on the Internet.

ASP comes with some built-in objects that are important to understand before their full potential can be unleashed. We will cover these objects in depth.

Finally, we'll look at some real-world examples of using ASP on a Web site. These should give you some idea of the power and beauty of server-side scripting with ASP.

# The Anatomy of the HTTP Protocol

As you know, surfing the Web is as simple as clicking links on your browser. But do you know what really goes on beneath the hood of your Web browser? It can be quite complex, but isn't too difficult to understand. More importantly, it will help you to understand the intricacies of client and server-side scripting.

## Overview

The Hypertext Transfer Protocol, or HTTP, is an application level TCP/IP protocol. An application level protocol is one that travels on top of another protocol. In this instance, HTTP travels on top of TCP, which is also a protocol. When two computers communicate over a TCP/IP connection, the data is formatted and processed in such a manner that it is guaranteed to arrive at its destination. This elaborate mechanism is the TCP/IP protocol.

HTTP takes for granted, and largely ignores, the entire TCP/IP protocol. It relies instead on a set of text commands such as GET and PUT. Application level protocols are implemented, usually, within an application (as opposed to at the driver level), hence the name. Some other examples of application level protocols are the File Transfer Protocol (FTP) and the mail protocols, Standard Mail Transfer Protocol (SMTP) and the Post Office Protocol (POP3). Pure binary data is rarely sent via these protocols, but when it is, it is always encoded into an ASCII format. This is inefficient at best, and future versions of the HTTP protocol may attempt to rectify this problem. The most up-to-date version of HTTP is version 1.1, and almost all Web servers available today support this version.

*For more information on the HTTP/1.1 protocol, visit the W3 Website at www.w3.org/protocols/.*

## The HTTP Server

To carry out an HTTP request, there must be an HTTP or Web server running on the target machine. This server is an application that listens for and responds to HTTP requests on a certain TCP port (by default this is port 80). An HTTP request is for a single item from the Web server. The item may be anything from a Web page to a sound file. The server, upon receipt of the request, attempts to retrieve the data asked for. If the server finds the correct information, it formats and returns the data to the client. If the requested information could not be found, the server will return an error message.

Pulling up a single Web page in your browser may cause dozens of HTTP transactions to occur. Each element on a Web page that is not text needs to be requested from the HTTP server individually. The main point of all this is that each HTTP transaction consists of a request and a response.

And it is in this transaction model that you must place yourself when you are programming Web applications.

# Protocol Basics

There are four basic states that make up a single HTTP transaction. They are:

❑ The Connection

❑ The Request

❑ The Response

❑ The Disconnection

A client connects to a server and issues the request. It waits for a response, then disconnects. A connection typically lasts only for a few seconds. On Web sites where the data is not laden with graphics, and the information is fairly static, requests will last less than one second.

## The Connection

The client software, a Web browser in this case, creates a TCP/IP connection to an HTTP server on a specific TCP/IP port. Port 80 is used if one is not specified. This is considered the default port for an HTTP server. A Web server may, however, reside on any port allowed. It is completely up to the operator of the Web server, and port numbers are often deliberately changed as a first line of defense against unauthorized users.

## The Request

Once connected, the client sends a request to the server. This request is in ASCII, and must be terminated by a carriage-return/line-feed pair. Every request must specify a method, which tells the server what the client wants. In HTTP 1.1, there are eight methods:

❑ OPTIONS

❑ GET

❑ HEAD

❑ POST

❑ PUT

❑ DELETE

❑ TRACE

❑ CONNECT

For more information about the different methods and their use, please check out the HTTP specification on the W3C Web site. For the purpose of this chapter, we are going to focus on the GET method.

The GET method asks the Web server to return the specified page. The format of this request is as follows:

```
GET <URL> <HTTP Version>
```

You can make HTTP requests yourself with the telnet program. Telnet is a program that is available on most computer systems and it was originally designed for use on UNIX systems. Since basic UNIX is character-based, one could log in from a remote site and work with the operating system. Telnet is the program that allows you to connect to a remote machine and all versions of Windows come with a telnet program. Figure 17-1 shows a telnet application in action.

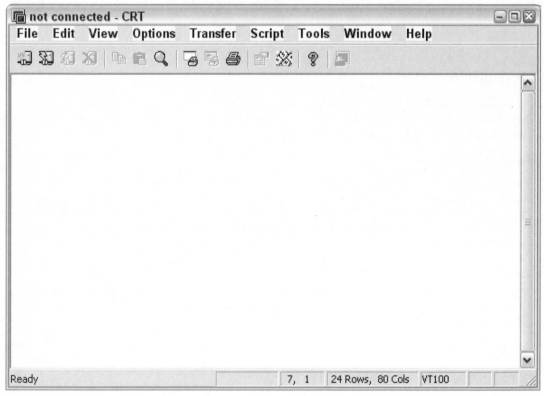

**Figure 17-1**

> *Microsoft's telnet program leaves much to be desired. However, there are many third-party commercial products available that you can use. One is made by a company called Van Dyke Technologies (www.vandyke.com) and it is called CRT (current version is version 4.0).*

Telnet defaults to using TCP/IP port 23. On UNIX systems, in order to telnet into a machine, that machine must be running a telnet server. This server listens for incoming telnet connections on port 23. However, almost all telnet programs allow you to specify the port on which to connect. It is this feature that we can utilize to examine HTTP running under the hood.

If you choose not to download the Van Dyke telnet client, you can test this by running Window's own telnet.

In the Van Dyke telnet client select Quick Connect from the File menu and you'll be presented with the dialog box shown in Figure 17-2, which requires filling in before proceeding.

Next, type in the name of any Web server and then enter the Web server's port. This is almost always 80. An example of these settings is shown in Figure 17-3.

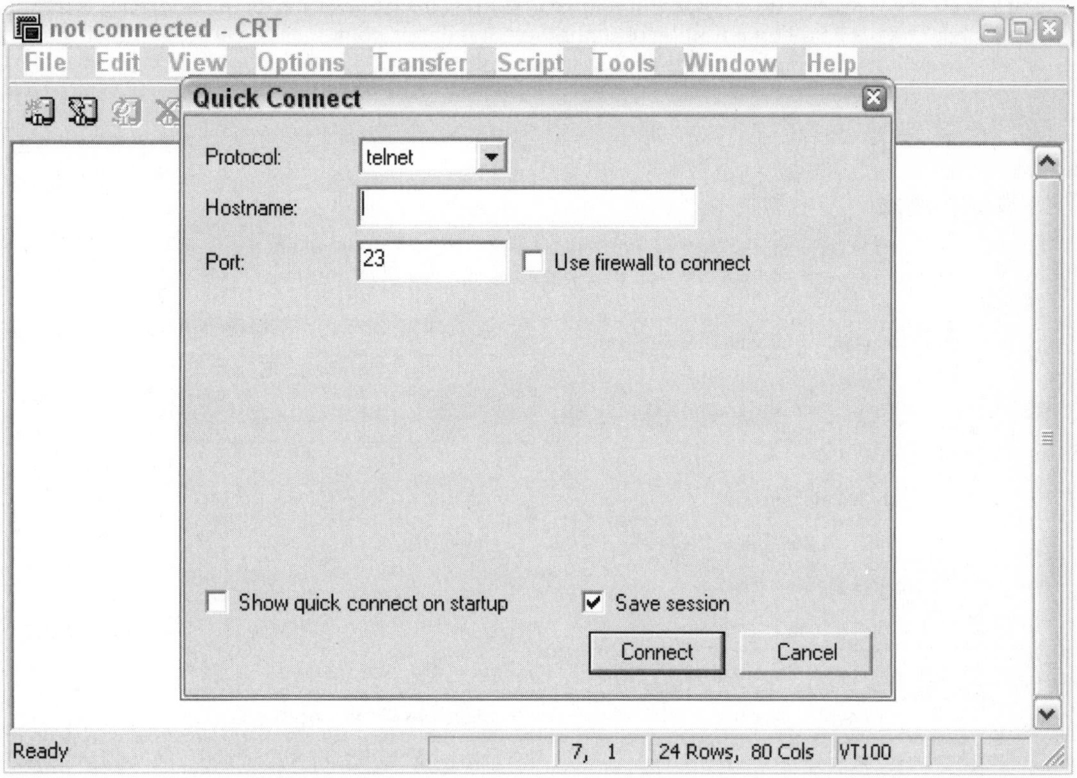


Figure 17-2

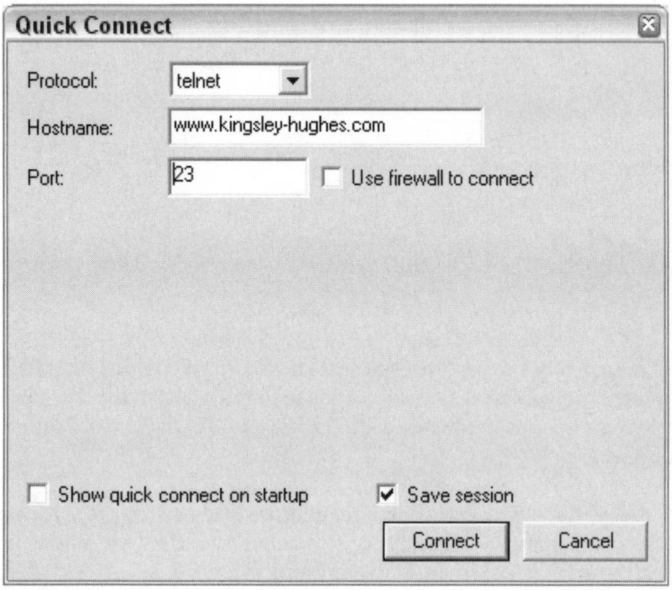


Figure 17-3

Once you are connected, the title bar will change to contain the name of the server to which you are connected. There is no other indication of connection. It is at this point that you need to type in your HTTP command. Type in the following, all in upper case.

```
GET / HTTP/1.0
```

## The Response

Upon receipt of the request, the Web server will answer. This will most likely result in some sort of HTML data as shown previously. However, you may get an error as shown in Figure 17-4.

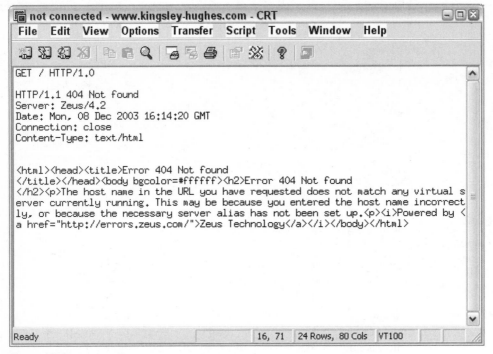

Figure 17-4

Again, the response is in HTML, but the code returned is an error code (404) instead of an OK (200).

### HTTP Headers

What was actually returned is a two-part response. The first part consists of HTTP headers. These headers provide information about the actual response to the request, the most important header being the status header. In the previous listing, it reads HTTP/1.1 404 Object Not Found. This indicates the actual status of the request.

The other headers that were returned with this request are `Server`, `Date`, `Connection`, and `Content-Type`. There are many different types of headers, and they are all designed to aid the browser in easily identifying the type of information that is being returned.

### The Disconnect

After the server has responded to your request, it closes the connection thus disconnecting you. Subsequent requests require you to reestablish your connection with the server.

# Introducing Active Server Pages

With the HTTP architecture laid out in the last section, you can clearly see that the real heart of the HTTP protocol lies in the request and the response. The client makes a request to the server, and the server provides the response to the client. What we're looking at here is really the foundations of client/server computing. A client makes a request from a server and the server fulfills that request. We see this pattern of behavior throughout the programming world today, not only in Web programming.

Microsoft recognized this pattern and developed a new technology that rendered Web programming a much more accessible technique. This technology is Active Server Pages or ASP. ASP is a server-side scripting environment that comes with Microsoft's Internet Information Services.

ASP allows you to embed scripting commands inside your HTML documents. The scripting commands are interpreted by the server and translated into the corresponding HTML and sent back to the server. This enables the Web developer to create content that is dynamic and fresh. The beauty of this is that it does not matter which browser your Web visitor is using when they visit the pages because the server returns only pure HTML. Sure, you can, if you want, extend your returned HTML with browser specific programming, but that is your choice. By no means is this all that ASP can do, but we'll cover more of its capabilities such as form validation and data manipulation later in this chapter.

Although you can use languages such as JavaScript or even Perl, by default the ASP scripting language is . . . yes, you've guessed it, VBScript!

# How the Server Recognizes ASPs

ASP pages do not have an `.html` or `.htm` extension; instead they have an `.asp` extension. The reason for this is twofold. First, in order for the Web server to know to process the scripting in your Web page, it needs to know that there is some script in there. Well, by setting the extension of your Web page to `.asp`, the server can assume that there are scripts in your page.

A nice side-effect of naming your ASP pages with the `.asp` extension is that the ASP processor knows that it does not need to process your HTML files. It used to be the case, as in ASP 2.0, that any page with the `.asp` extension, no matter whether it contained any server-side scripting code or not, was automatically sent to the server, and would thereby take longer to process. With ASP 3.0, introduced in Windows 2000, the server is now able to determine the presence of any server-side code and process or not process the page accordingly. This increases the speed of your HTML file retrieval and makes your Web server run more efficiently.

Secondly, using an `.asp` extension (forcing interpretation by the ASP processor every time your page is requested) hides your ASP scripts. If someone requests your `.asp` file from the Web server, all he is going to get back is the resultant processed HTML. If you put your ASP code in a file called `mycode.scr` and requested it from the Web server, you'll see all of the code inside.

# ASP Basics

ASP files are just HTML files with scripting embedded within them. When a browser makes a request for an ASP file from the server, it is passed on to the ASP processing DLL for execution. After processing, the resulting file is then sent on to the requesting browser. Any scripting commands embedded from the original HTML file are executed and then are removed from the results. This is excellent because all of your scripting code is hidden from the person viewing your Web pages with a browser. That is why it is so important that files containing ASP scripts have an .asp extension.

## The Tags of ASP

To distinguish the ASP code from the HTML inside your files, ASP code is placed between <% and %> tags. This convention should be familiar to you if you have ever worked with any kind of server-side commands before in HTML. The tag combination implies to the ASP processor that the code within should be executed by the server and removed from the results. Depending on the default scripting language of your Web site, this code could be VBScript, JScript, or any other language you've installed. Since this book is for the VBScript programmer, all of our ASP scripts will be in VBScript.

In the following snippet of HTML, you'll see an example of some ASP code between the <% and %> tags:

```
<table>
<tr>
<td>
<%
  x = x + 1
  y = y - 1
  ans = x * y
%>
</td>
</tr>
</table>
```

## <SCRIPT> Blocks

You may also place your ASP code between <script></script> blocks. However, unless you direct the script to run at the server level, code placed between these tags will be executed at the client as normal client-side scripts. To direct your script block to execute on the server, use the runat command within your <script> block as follows:

```
<script language="VBScript" runat="Server">
' Your Script Goes Here
</script>
```

## The Default Scripting Language

As stated previously, the default scripting language used by ASP is VBScript. However, you may change it for your entire site, or just a single Web page. Placing a special scripting tag at the beginning of your Web page does this. This tag specifies the scripting language to use for this page only.

```
<%@ language="ScriptingLanguage" %>
```

"ScriptingLanguage" can be any language for which you have the scripting engine installed. ASP comes with JScript, as well as VBScript.

## Mixing HTML and ASP

You've probably guessed by now that one can easily mix HTML code with ASP scripts. The power of this feature is quite phenomenal! VBScript, as you know, has all of the control flow mechanisms such as If Then, For Next, and Do While loops. But with ASP you can selectively include HTML code based on the results of these operators. Let's look at an example.

Suppose you are creating a Web page that greets the viewer with a "Good Morning," "Good Afternoon," or "Good Evening" depending on the time of day. This can be done quite easily as follows:

```
<html>

<head>
<title>Sample ASP Page</title>
</head>

<body>
<p>The time is now <%=Time()%></p>
<%
 Dim iHour

 iHour = Hour(Time())

 If (iHour >= 0 And iHour < 12 ) Then
%>
Good Morning!
<%
 ElseIf (iHour > 11 And iHour < 16 ) Then
%>
Good Afternoon!
<%
 Else
%>
Good Evening!
<%
End If
%>

</body>
</html>
```

First, we print out the current time. The <%= notation is shorthand to print out the value of an ASP variable or the result of a function call. We then move the hour of the current time into a variable called iHour. Based on the value of this variable we write our normal HTML text.

Notice how the HTML code is outside of the ASP script tags. When the ASP processor executes this page, the HTML that lies between control flow blocks that aren't executed is discarded, leaving you with only the correct code. Here is the source of what is returned from our Web server after processing this page.

```
<html>

<head>
<title>Sample ASP Page</title>
</head>

<body>
<p>The time is now 15:27:12 PM</p>

Good Afternoon!
</body>
</html>
```

As you can see, the scripting is completely removed leaving only the HTML and text.

The other way to output data to your Web page viewer is using one of ASPs built-in objects called `Response`. We'll cover this approach in the next section as you learn about the ASP object model.

## Commenting Your ASP Code

As with any programming language, it is of utmost importance to comment your ASP code as much as possible. Try looking back at code you wrote a few days, weeks, or months ago and you'll then appreciate the comments! Do remember to make comments clear and concise—unclear comments are not worth putting in your code.

Comments in ASP are identical to comments in VBScript. When ASP comes across the single quote character it will graciously ignore the rest of the line.

```
<%
Dim iNumber

'Here is a comment
iNumber = iNumber + 1
%>
```

# The Active Server Pages Object Model

ASP, like most Microsoft technologies, utilizes the Component Object Model, or COM, to expose functionality to consumer applications. ASP is actually an extension to your Web server that allows server-side scripting. At the same time it also provides a compendium of objects and components, which manage interaction between the Web server and the browser. These objects form the Active Server Pages Object Model. These "objects" can be manipulated by scripting languages.

ASP neatly divides up into six objects, which manage their own part of the interaction between client and server. At the heart of the interaction between client and server are the `Request` and `Response` objects, which deal with the HTTP request and response; but we will be taking a quick tour through all of the different objects and components that are part of ASP.

Four of the six core objects of the object model (the `Request`, `Response`, `Application`, and `Session` objects) can use collections to store data. Before we look at each object in turn we need to take a quick overview of collections.

# Collections

Collections in ASP are very similar to their VBScript namesakes. They act as data containers that store their data in a manner close to that of an array. The information is stored in the form of name/value pairs.

The `Application` and the `Session` objects have a collection property called `Contents`. This collection of variants can hold any information you wish to place in it. Using these collections allow you to share information between Web pages.

To place a value into the collection, simply assign it a key and then assign the value

```
Application.Contents("Name") = "Homer Simpson"
```

Or you can follow this for numerical values:

```
Session.Contents("Age") = 39
```

Fortunately for us, Microsoft has made the Contents collection the default property for these two objects. Therefore, the following shorthand usage is perfectly acceptable:

```
Application("Name") = "Homer Simpson"
Session("Age") = 39
```

Having entered this data, you will want to retrieve it. To read values from the Contents collections just reverse the call:

```
sName = Application("Name")
sAge = Session("Age")
```

## Iterating the Contents Collection

Because the `Contents` collections work like regular VBScript collections, they are easily iterated. You can use the collections `Count` property or use the `For Each` iteration method.

```
for x = 1 to Application.Contents.Count
  ...
next

for each item in Application.Contents
  ...
next
```

*Note that the `Contents` collections are 1 based. That is to say that the first element in the collection is at position 1, not 0.*

To illustrate this, the following ASP script will dump the current contents of the `Application` and `Session` objects' `Contents` collections.

```
<html>

<head>
<title>Sample ASP Page 2</title>
</head>

<body>
<p>The Application.Contents</p>
<%
  Dim Item

  For Each Item In Application.Contents
  Response.Write Item & " = [" & Application(Item) & "]<br>"
  Next
%>
<p>The Session.Contents</p>
<%
  For Each Item In Session.Contents
  Response.Write Item & " = [" & Session(Item) & "]<br>"
  Next
%>

</body>
</html>
```

## Removing an Item from the Contents Collection

The Application Object's Contents collection contains two methods, and these are Remove and RemoveAll. These allow you to remove one or all of the items stored in the Application.Contents collection.

Let's add an item to the Application.Contents collection, and then remove it.

```
<%
  Application("MySign") = "Gemini"
  Application.Contents.Remove("MySign")
%>

Or we can just get rid of everything...

<%
  Application.Contents.RemoveAll
%>
```

Not all of the collections of each object work in this way, but the principles remain the same and we will explain how each differs when we discuss each object.

# The Request Object

When your Web page is requested, along with the HTTP request, information such as the URL of the Web page request and the format of the data requested is passed. It can also contain feedback from the user such as the input from a text box or drop-down list box. The Request object allows you to get at information passed along as part of the HTTP request. The corresponding output from the server is returned as part of the `Response`. The `Request` object has several collections to store information that warrant discussion.

## The Request Object's Collections

The `Request` object has five collections. Interestingly, they all act as the default property for the object. That is to say, you may retrieve information from any of the five collections by using the abbreviated syntax:

```
ClientIPAddress = Request("REMOTE_ADDR")
```

The `REMOTE_ADDR` value lies in the `ServerVariables` collection. However, through the use of the collection cascade, it can be retrieved with the previous notation. Please note that for ASP to dig through each collection, especially if they have many values, to retrieve a value from the last collection is extremely inefficient. It is always recommended that you use the fully qualified collection name in your code. Not only is this faster, but it improves your code in that it is more specific and less cryptic.

ASP searches through the collections in the following order:

- ❑ QueryString
- ❑ Form
- ❑ Cookies
- ❑ ClientCertificate
- ❑ ServerVariables

If there are variables with the same name, only the first is returned when you allow ASP to search. This is another good reason for you to fully qualify your collection.

### QueryString

This contains a collection of all the information attached to the end of an URL. When you make an URL request, the additional information is passed along with the URL to the Web page appended with a question mark. This information takes the following form.

```
URL?item=data[&item=data][...]
```

The clue to the server is the question mark. When the server sees this, it knows that the URL has ended and variables are starting. So an example of a URL with a query string might look like this:

```
http://www.kingsley-hughes.com/book.asp?bookname=VBScriptProgrammersReference
```

We stated earlier that the collections store information in name/value pairs. Despite this slightly unusual method of creating the name/value pair, the principle remains the same; `bookname` is the `name` and `VBScriptProgrammersReference` is the `value`. When ASP gets hold of this URL request, it breaks apart all of the name/value pairs and places them into this collection for easy access. This is another excellent feature of ASP. Query strings are built up using ampersands to delimit each name/value pair so if you wished to pass the user information along with the book information, you could pass the following:

```
http://www.kingsley-
hughes.com/book.asp?bookname=VBScriptProgrammersReference&buyer=HSimpson
```

Query strings can be generated in one of three ways. The first is, as discussed, by a user typed URL. The second is as part of a URL specified in an Anchor tag.

```
<a href="book.asp?bookname=VBScriptProgrammersReference">Buy this book!</a>
```

So when you click on the link, the name/value pair is passed along with the URL. The third and final method is via a form sent to the server with the GET method.

```
<form action="book.asp" method="GET">
Type your name: <input type="TEXT" name="buyer"><br>
Type your requested book: <input type="TEXT" name="bookname" SIZE=50><br>
<input type="SUBMIT" value="Submit">
</form>
```

This form that the last code generates is shown in Figure 17-5.

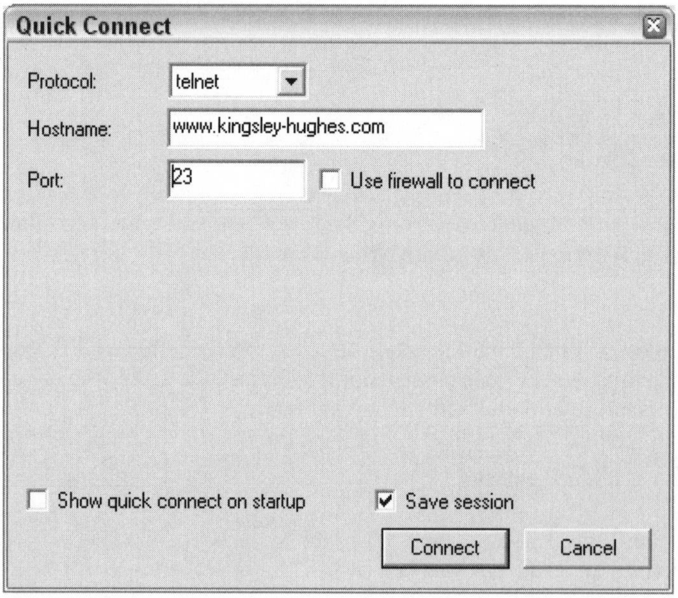

Figure 17-5

Next, you need to be able to retrieve information, and you use this technique to retrieve from each of the three methods used to generate a query string.

```
Request.QueryString("buyer")
Request.QueryString("bookname")
```

Please note that these lines won't display anything by themselves, you need to add either the shorthand notation (equality operator) to display functions in front of a single statement, or when a number of values need displaying then use `Response.Write` to separately display each value in the collection. For example:

```
<%=Request.QueryString("buyer")%> or Response.Write(Request.QueryString
("bookname"))
```

The first of the two `Request` object calls should return the name of `HSimpson` on the page and the second of the two should return `VBScript Programmers Reference`. Of course, you could always store this information in a variable for later access.

```
sBookName = Request.QueryString("bookname")
```

## Form

Contains a collection of all the form variables posted to the HTTP request by an HTML form. Query strings aren't very private as they transmit information via a very visible method, the URL. If you want to transmit information from the form more privately then you can use the form collection to do so which sends its information as part of the HTTP Request body. The easy access to form variables is one of ASPs best feature.

If we go back to our previous example, the only alteration we need to make to our HTML form code is to change the `METHOD` attribute. Forms using this collection must be sent with the `POST` method and not the `GET` method. It is actually this attribute that determines how the information is sent by the form. So we change the method of the form as follows.

```
<form action="book.asp" method="POST">
Type your name: <input type="TEXT" name="buyer"><br>
Type your requested book: <input type="TEXT" name="bookname" size="40"><br>
<input type="SUBMIT" value="Submit">
</form>
```

Once the form has been submitted in this style, then we can retrieve and display the information using the following:

```
=Request.Form("buyer")
```

## Cookies

Contains a read-only collection of cookies sent by the client browser along with the request. Because the cookies were sent from the client, they cannot be changed here. You must change them using the `Response.Cookies` collection. A discussion of cookies can be found in the discussion of the `Response` object.

## ClientCertificate

When a client makes a connection with a server requiring a high degree of security, either party can confirm who the sender/receiver is by inspecting their digital certificate. A digital certificate contains a number of items of information about the sender, such as the holder's name, address, and length of time the certificate is valid for. A third party, known as the Certificate Authority or CA, will have previously verified these details.

The `ClientCertificate` collection is used access details held in a client-side digital certificate sent by the browser. This collection is only populated if you are running a secure server, and the request was via an `https://` call instead of an `http://` call. This is the preferred method to invoke a secure connection.

### ServerVariables

When the client sends a request and information is passed across to the server, it's not just the page that is passed across, but also information such as who created the page, the server name, and the port that the request was sent to. The HTTP header that is sent across together with the HTTP request also contains information of this nature such as the type of browser and type of connection. This information is combined into a list of variables that are predefined by the server as environment variables. Most of them are static and never really change unless you change the configuration of your Web server. The rest are based on the client browser.

These server variables can be accessed in the normal method. For instance, the server variable HTTP_USER_AGENT, which returns information about the type of browser being used to view the page, can be displayed as follows.

```
<%=Request.ServerVariables("HTTP_USER_AGENT")%>
```

Alternatively you can printout the whole list of server variables and their values with the following ASP code.

```
For Each key in Request.ServerVariables
   Response.Write "<b>" & (Key) &"</b> "
   Response.Write (Request.ServerVariables(key)) & "<br>"
Next
```

Server variables are merely informative, but they do give you the ability to customize page content for specific browsers, or to avoid script errors that might be generated.

### Request Object Properties and Methods

The `Request` object contains a single property and a single method. They are used together to transfer files from the client to the server. Uploading is accomplished using HTML forms.

### TotalBytes Property

When the request is processed, this property will hold the total number of bytes in the client browser request. Most likely you'd use it to return the number of bytes in the file you wish to transfer. This information is important to the `BinaryRead` method.

### BinaryRead Method

This method retrieves the information sent to the Web server by the client browser in a POST operation. When the browser issues a POST, the data is encoded and sent to the server. When the browser issues a GET, there is no data other than the URL. The `BinaryRead` method takes one parameter, the number of bytes to read. So if you want it to read a whole file, you pass it the total number of bytes in the file, generated by the `TotalBytes` property.

It's very rarely applied because `Request.QueryString` and `Request.Form` are much easier to use. This is because `BinaryRead` wraps its answer in a safe array of bytes. For a scripting language that essentially only handles variants, this makes life a little complicated. However this format is essential for file uploading.

*You can find full details on how to upload files and then decode a safe array of bytes in an excellent article at 15seconds.com (`www.15seconds.com/Issue/981121.htm`).*

# The Response Object

After you've processed the request information from the client browser, you'll need to be able to send information back. The `Response` object is just the ticket. It provides you with the tools necessary to send anything you need back to the client.

## The Response Object's Collection

The `Response` object contains only one collection: Cookies. This is the version of the `Request` object's `Cookies` collection that can be written to.

If you've not come across them before, cookies are small (limited to 4KB of data) text files stored on the hard drive of the client that contain information about the user, such as whether they have visited the site before and on what date they last visited the site. There are lots of misapprehensions about cookies being intrusive as they allow servers to store information on the user's drive. However, you need to remember that firstly, the user has to voluntarily accept cookies or activate an Accept Cookies mechanism on the browser for them to work; secondly, this information is completely benign and cannot be used to determine the user's e-mail address or such like. They are used to personalize pages that the user might have visited before.

*Examples of things to store in cookies are unique user IDs, or user names; then, when the user returns to your Web site, a quick check of cookies will let you know if this is a return visitor or not.*

You can create a cookie on the user's machine as follows:

```
Response.Cookies("BookBought") = "VBScript Programmers Reference"
```

You can also store multiple values in one cookie using an index value key. The cookie effectively contains a VBScript Dictionary object and using the key can retrieve individual items. Its functioning is very close to that of an array.

```
Response.Cookies("BookBought")("1") = "VBScript Programmers Reference "
Response.Cookies("BookBought")("2") = "XSLT Programmers Reference"
```

A cookie will automatically expire—disappear from the user's machine—the moment a user ends their session. To extend the cookie beyond this natural lifetime, you can specify a date with the `Expires` property. The date takes the following format `WEEKDAY DD-MON-YY HH:MM:SS`.

```
Response.Cookies("BookBought").Expires = #31-Dec-04#
```

The # sign can be used to delimit dates in ASP (as in VBScript).

Other properties that can be used in conjunction with this collection are:

❑   `Domain`: a cookie is only sent to page requested within the domain from which it was created

❑   `Path`: a cookie is only sent to pages requested within this path

❑    HasKeys: specifies whether the cookie uses an index/dictionary object or not

❑    Secure: specifies whether the cookie is secure. A cookie is only deemed secure if sent via the HTTPS protocol

You can retrieve the cookies information using the Request object cookies collection, mentioned earlier. To do this you could do the following:

```
You purchased <%=Request.Cookies("BookBought")%> last time you visited
the site.
```

If there were several cookies in the collection you could iterate through each cookie and display the contents as follows ASP code:

```
For Each cookie in Request.Cookies
   Response.Write (Request.Cookies(cookie))
Next
```

# The Response Object's Methods

To understand what the Response Object's methods and properties do, we need to examine the workings of how ASP sends a response in more detail. When an ASP script is run, an HTML output stream is created. This stream is a receptacle for the Web server to store details and create the dynamic/interactive Web page. As mentioned before, the page has to be created entirely in HTML for the browser to understand it (excluding client-side scripting, which is ignored by the server).

The stream is initially empty when created. New information is added to the end. If any custom HTML headers are required then they have to be added at the beginning. Then the HTML contained in the ASP page is added next to the script, so anything not encompassed by <%%> tags is added. The Response object provides two ways of writing directly to the output stream, either using the Write method or its shorthand technique.

### Write

Probably the most used method of all the built-in objects, Write allows you to send information back to the client browser. You can write text directly to a Web page by encasing the text in quotation marks.

```
Response.Write "Hello World!"
```

Or to display the contents of a variant you just drop the quotation marks.

```
sText = "Hello World!"
Response.Write sText
```

For single portions of dynamic information that only require adding into large portions of HTML, you can use the equality sign as shorthand for this method, as specified earlier, for example:

```
My message is <% =sText %>
```

This technique reduces the amount of code needed, but at the expense of readability. There is nothing to choose between these techniques in terms of performance.

### AddHeader

This method allows you to add custom headers to the HTTP response. For example, if you were to write a custom browser application that examined the headers of your HTTP requests for a certain value, you'd use this method to set that value. Usage is as follows:

```
Response.AddHeader "CustomServerApp", "CustomApp/1.2"
```

This would add the header `CustomServerApp` to the response with the value of `CustomApp/1.2`. There are no restrictions regarding headers and header value.

### AppendToLog

Calling this method allows you to append a string to the Web server log file entry for this particular request. This allows you to add custom log messages to the log file.

### BinaryWrite

This method allows you to bypass the normal character conversion that takes place when data is sent back to the client. Usually, only text is returned, so the Web server cleans it up. By calling `BinaryWrite` to send your data, the actual binary data is sent back, bypassing that cleaning process.

### Clear

This method allows you to delete any data that has been buffered for this page so far. See discussion of the `Buffer` property for more details.

### End

This method stops processing the ASP file and returns any currently buffered data to the client browser.

### Flush

This method returns any currently buffered data to the client browser and then clears the buffer. See discussion of the `Buffer` property for more details.

### Redirect

This method allows you to relinquish control of the current page to a different Web page. For example, you can use this method to redirect users to a login page if they have not yet logged on to your Web site.

```
<%
If (Not Session("LoggedOn") ) Then
    Response.Redirect "login.asp"
End If
%>
```

## The Response Object's Properties

Let's take a look at the properties of the `Response` object.

### Buffer

You may optionally have ASP buffer your output for you. This property tells ASP whether or not to buffer output. Usually, output is sent to the client as it is generated. If you turn buffering on (by setting this property to `True`), output will not be sent until all scripts have been executed for the current page, or the `Flush` or `End` methods are called.

`Response.Buffer` has to be inserted after the language declaration, but before any HTML is used. If you insert it outside this scope you will most likely generate an error. A correct use of this method would look like:

```
<@ language="VBScript">
<% Response.Buffer = True %>
<html>
...
```

The `Flush` method is used in conjunction with the `Buffer` property. To use it correctly you must set the `Buffer` property first and then at places within the script you can flush the buffer to the output stream, while continuing processing. This is useful for long queries, which might otherwise worry the user that nothing was being returned.

The `Clear` method erases everything in the buffer that has been added since the last `Response.Flush` call. It erases only the response body however, and leaves intact the response header.

### CacheControl

Generally when a proxy server retrieves an ASP Web page, it does not place a copy of it into its cache. That is because by their very nature ASP pages are dynamic and, most likely, a page will be stale the next time it is requested. You may override this feature by changing the value of this property to `Public`.

### Charset

This property will append its contents to the HTTP content-type header that is sent back to the browser. Every HTTP response has a content-type header that defines the content of the response. Usually the content-type is "`text/html`". Setting this property will modify the type sent back to the browser.

### ContentType

This property allows you to set the value of the content-type that is sent back to the client browser.

### Expires

Most Web browsers keep Web pages in a local cache. The cache is usually good as long as you keep your browser running. Setting this property allows you to limit the time the page stays in the local cache. The value of the `Expires` property specifies the length of time in minutes before the page will expire from the local cache. If you set this to zero, the page will not be cached.

### ExpiresAbsolute

Just like the `Expires` property, this property allows you to specify the exact time and date on which the page will expire.

### IsClientConnected

This read-only property indicates whether or not the client is still connected to the server. Remember that the client browser makes a request then waits for a response. Well, imagine you're running a lengthy script and during the middle of processing, the client disconnects because he was waiting too long. Reading this property will tell you if the client is still connected or not.

### Status

This property allows you to set the value returned on the status header with the HTTP response.

# The Application and Session Objects

The Application and Session objects like Request and Response work together very closely. Application is used to tie all of the pages together into one consistent application, while the Session object is used to track and present a user's series of requests to the Web site as a continuous action, rather than an arbitrary set of requests.

## Scope

Normally, you will declare a variable for use within your Web page. You'll use it, manipulate it, then perhaps print out its value or whatever. But when your page is reloaded or the viewer moves to another page, the variable and its value are gone forever. By placing your variable within the Contents collection of the Application or Session objects, you can extend the life span of your variable!

Any variable or object that you declare has two potential scopes: procedure and page. When you declare a variable within a procedure, its life span is limited to that procedure. Once the procedure is executed, your variable is gone. You may also declare a variable at the Web page level but like the procedure-defined variable, once the page is reloaded the value is reset.

The Contents collections of these two objects allow you to extend the scope of your variables to session-wide and application-wide. If you place a value in the Session object, it will be available to all Web pages in your site for the life span of the current session (more on sessions later). Good session scope variables are user IDs, user names, login time, and other data items that pertain only to the session. Likewise, if you place your value into the Application object, it will exist until the Web site is restarted. This allows you to place application-wide settings into a conveniently accessible place. Good application scope variables are font names and sizes, table colors, system constants, and other data that pertains to the application as a whole.

## The global.asa File

Every ASP application may utilize a special script file. This file is named global.asa and it must reside in the root directory of your Web application. It can contain script code that pertains to the application as a whole or each session. You may also create ActiveX objects for later use in this scripting file.

## The Application Object

ASP works on the concept that an entire Web site is a single Web application. Therefore, there is only one instance of the Application object available for use in your scripting at all times.

*Please note that it is possible to divide up your Web site into separate applications, but for the purposes of this discussion we'll assume there is only one application per Web site.*

### Collections

The Application object contains two collections: Contents and StaticObjects. The Contents collection is discussed earlier. The StaticObjects collection is similar to Contents, but only contains the objects that were created with the <object> tag in the scope of your application. This collection can be iterated just like the Contents collection.

You cannot store references to ASPs built-in objects in the Application collections.

### Methods

The Application object contains two methods as detailed in the following table.

| Method | Description |
|--------|-------------|
| Lock | The Lock method is used to "lock-down" the Contents collection so that it cannot be modified by other clients. This is useful if you are updating a counter, or perhaps grabbing a transaction number stored in the Application's Contents collection |
| Unlock | The Unlock method "unlocks" the Application object thus allowing others to modify the Contents collection |

### Events

The Application object generates two events: Application_OnStart and Application_OnEnd.

The Application_OnStart event is fired when the first view of your Web page occurs. The Application_OnEnd event is fired when the Web server is shut down. If you choose to write scripts for these events they must be placed in your global.asa file.

The most common use of these events is to initialize application-wide variables. These would include items such as font names, table colors, and database connection strings. This could also include writing information to a system log file. The following is an example of global.asa file with script for these events:

```vbscript
<script language="VBScript" runat="Server">
Sub Application_OnStart
    'Globals...
    Application("ErrorPage") = "handleError.asp"
    Application("SiteBanAttemptLimit") = 10
    Application("AccessErrorPage") = "handleError.asp"
    Application("RestrictAccess") = False

    'Keep track of visitors...
    Application("NumVisits") = Application("NumVisits") + 1
End Sub
</script>
```

## The Session Object

Each time a visitor comes to your Web site, a Session object is created for the visitor if the visitor does not already have one. Therefore, there is an instance of the Session object available to you in your scripting as well. The Session object is similar to the Application object in that it can contain values. However, the Session object's values are lost when your visitor leaves the site. The Session object is most useful for transferring information from Web page to Web page. Using the Session object, there is no need to pass information in the URL.

The most common use of the Session object is to store information in its Contents collection. This information would be session-specific in that it would pertain only to the current user.

Many Web sites today offer a "user personalization" service. That is, to customize a Web page to their preference. This is easily done with ASP and the Session object. The user variables are stored in the client browser for retrieval by the server later. Simply load the user's preferences at the start of the session and then, as the user browses your site, utilize the information regarding the user's preferences to display information.

Suppose your Web site displays stock quotes for users. You could allow users to customize the start page to display their favorite stock quotes when they visit the site. By storing the stock symbols in your Session object, you can easily display the correct quotes when you render your Web page.

This session management system relies on the use of browser cookies. The cookies allow the user information to be persisted even after a client leaves the site. Unfortunately, if a visitor to your Web site does not allow cookies to be stored, you will be unable to pass information between Web pages within the Session object.

## Collections

The Session object contains two collections, Contents and StaticObjects.

We discussed the Contents collection earlier in this chapter. The StaticObjects collection is similar to Contents, but only contains the objects that were created with the <object> tag in your HTML page. This collection can be iterated just like the Contents collection.

## Properties

Following are the properties that the Session object exposes for your use.

| Property | Description |
| --- | --- |
| CodePage | Setting this property will allow you to change the character set used by ASP when it is creating output. This property could be used if you were creating a multinational Web site |
| LCID | This property sets the internal locale value for the entire Web application. By default, your application's locale is your server's locale. If you server is in the United States, then your application will default to the United States. Much of the formatting functionality of ASP utilizes this locale setting to display information correctly for the country in question. For example, the date is displayed differently in Europe versus the United States. So based on the locale setting, the date formatting functions will output the date in the correct format. |
| | You can also change this property temporarily to output data in a different format. A good example is currency. Let's say your Web site had a shopping cart and you wanted to display totals in U.S. dollars for U.S. customers, and Pounds Sterling for U.K. customers. To do this you'd change the LCID property to the British locale setting and then call the currency formatting routine |
| SessionID | Every session created by ASP has a unique identifier. This identifier is called the SessionID and is accessible through this property. It can be used for debugging ASP scripts. |

*Continues*

| Property | Description |
|---|---|
| Timeout | By default, an ASP session will timeout after 20 minutes of inactivity. Every time a Web page is requested or refreshed by a user, this internal ASP time clock starts ticking. When the time clock reaches the value set in this property, the session is automatically destroyed. You can set this property to reduce the timeout period if you wish |

### Methods

The Session object contains a single method, Abandon. This instructs ASP to destroy the current Session object for this user. This method is what you would call when a user logs off your Web site.

### Events

The Session object generates two events, Session_OnStart and Session_OnEnd. The Session_OnStart event is fired when the first view of your Web page occurs. The Session_OnEnd event is fired when the Web server is shut down. If you choose to write scripts for these events they must be placed in your global.asa file. The most common use of these events is to initialize session-wide variables, items such as usage counts, login names, real names, user preferences, and so on.

The following is an example global.asa file with script for these events.

<script language="VBScript" runat="Server">

```
Sub Session_OnStart
    Session("LoginAttempts") = 0
    Session("LoggedOn") = False
End Sub

Sub Session_OnEnd
    Session("LoggedOn") = False
End Sub
</script>
```

# The Server Object

The next object in the ASP object model is the Server object. The Server object enables you to create and work with ActiveX controls in your Web pages. In addition, the Server object exposes methods that help in the encoding of URLs and HTML text.

Let's take a look at the properties and methods associated with it.

## ScriptTimeout

This property sets the time, in seconds, that a script will be allowed to run. The default value for all scripts on the system is 90 seconds. That is to say, that if a script has run for more than 90 seconds, the Web server will intervene and let the client browser know something is wrong. If you expect your scripts to run for a long time, you will want to use this property.

# CreateObject

This method is the equivalent to VBScript's `CreateObject`, or using the `New` keyword—it instantiates a new instance of an object. The result can be placed into the `Application` or `Session` `Contents` collection to lengthen its life span.

Generally you'll create an object at the time the session is created and place it into the `Session` `.Contents` collection. For example, let's say you've created an ActiveX DLL with a class that converts Fahrenheit to Celsius and vice versa. You could create an instance of this class with the `CreateObject` method and store it in the `Session.Contents` collection like the following:

```
Set Session("MyConverter") = Server.CreateObject("MyDLL.CDegreeConverter")
```

This object would be around as long as the session is and will be available for you to call. As you'll see in later chapters, this method is invaluable when working with database connections.

ASP comes with its own built in set of components that you can create instances of using the `CreateObject` method. These are:

❏    Ad Rotator—used to display a random graphic and link every time a user connects to the page.

❏    Browser Capabilities—manipulates a file `browscap.ini` contained on the server computer to determine the capabilities of a particular client's browser.

❏    Content Linker—provides a central repository file from where you manage a series of links and their URLs, and provide appropriate descriptions about them.

❏    Content Rotator—a cut down version of the Ad Rotator that provides the same function but without optional redirection.

❏    Page Counter—counts the number of times a page has been hit.

❏    Permission Checker—checks to see if a user has the permission before allowing them to access a given page.

❏    Counters—counts any value on an ASP page from anywhere within an ASP application.

❏    MyInfo—can be used to store personal information about a user within an XML file.

❏    Status—used to collect server profile information.

❏    Tools—a set of miscellaneous methods that are grouped under the generic heading of Tools.

❏    IIS Log—allows you to create an object that allows your applications to write to and otherwise access the IIS log.

# Execute

This method executes an ASP file and inserts the results into the response. You can use this call to include snippets of ASP code, such as subroutines.

# GetLastError

This method returns an `ASPError` object that contains all of the information about the last error that has occurred.

## HTMLEncode

This method encodes a string for proper HTML usage. This is useful if you want to actually display HTML code on your Web pages.

## MapPath

This method returns a string that contains the actual physical path to the file in question. Subdirectories of your Web site can be virtual. That is to say that they don't physically exist in the hierarchy of your Web site. To find out the true whereabouts of a file, you can call this method.

## Transfer

The Transfer method allows you to immediately transfer control of the executing page to another page. This is similar to the Response.Redirect method except for the fact that the Transfer method makes all variables and the Request collections available to the called page.

## URLEncode

This method, as the title says, encodes a URL for transmission. This encoding includes replacing spaces with a plus sign (+) and replacing unprintable characters with hexadecimal values. You should always run your URLs through this method when redirecting.

# The ObjectContext Object

The final object we shall consider is the ObjectContext object, which comes into play when you use transactions in your Web page. When an ASP script has initiated a transaction, it can either be committed or aborted by this object. It has two methods to do this.

## SetAbort

SetAbort is called when the transaction has not been completed and you don't want resources updated.

## SetComplete

SetComplete is called when there is no reason for the transaction to fail. If all of the components that form part of the transaction call SetComplete, then the transaction will complete.

# Using Active Server Pages Effectively

Is it true that a little bit of knowledge is a bad thing? In the realm of ASP, I think not. A little bit of knowledge is probably just enough to get you interested in learning more!

For the final part of this chapter we're going to build a Web site to demonstrate some of the features of ASP. This sample site will demonstrate many of the ASP features and principles described earlier in this chapter.

## Designing the Site

Before we start creating our new Web site, we should discuss the design. For your first ASP application, we'll keep it quite simple. What we want to create is an HTML form that accepts for input the following information:

- ❑ First name
- ❑ Last name
- ❑ E-mail address

After the user submits the form, our ASP page will reformat the first and last name and check the e-mail address for proper syntax.

## Creating the global.asa file

The first step in creating a new ASP application is to create your `global.asa` file. This is the file that houses your event handlers for the `Application` and `Session` objects. In addition, in this file you may set application and session-wide variables to their default values. To create this file, in the root of your Web server directory create a file called `global.asa`. Following is the content of our sample `global.asa`.

```
<script language="VBScript" runat="Server">
Sub Application_OnStart
    Application("AllowedErrorsBeforeWarning") = 3
End Sub

Sub Session_OnStart
    Session("ErrorCount") = 0
End Sub

Sub Session_OnEnd
    'Nothing to do here...
End Sub

Sub Application_OnEnd
    'Nothing to do here...
End Sub
</script>
```

Our file has handlers defined for `Application_OnStart`, `Application_OnEnd`, `Session_OnStart`, and `Session_OnEnd`. The `Application_OnEnd` and `Session_OnEnd` events are shown earlier for completeness but are not used in this example.

We want to set a limit on the number of submissions the user gets before a warning message is shown. Since this is a feature of the application and affects all users, we will store this constant in the `Application.Contents` collection. This is done in the `Application_OnStart` event. We add to the collection an item named `AllowedErrorsBeforeWarning` and set its value to 3.

Now that we know how many times a user can try to get it right, we need a place to store the number of times the user has tried to get it right. Since this counter is different for each user, we'll place this into the `Session.Contents` collection. We initialize our variable to 0. This is done in the `Session_OnStart` event. We add to the collection an item named, appropriately, `ErrorCount`, with a value of 0.

# Creating Our Main Page

Now that we've laid the groundwork for our ASP application, it's time to build the main page. Since this is a simple example, we will only utilize a single Web page. Let's begin by creating this single page.

Create a new Web page on your site and name it `default.asp`. This is the file name used by IIS as the default Web page. The default Web page is the page that is returned by a Web server when no Web page is specified. For example, when you call up `www.wrox.com/`, you aren't specifying a Web page. The server looks through its list of default file names and finds the first match in the Web site's root directory.

The following shows the contents of your `default.asp` page.

```
<%@ language="VBScript" %>
<%
Dim txtFirstName, txtLastName, txtEmailAddr
Dim sMessage

'*********************************************************************
'* Main
'*
'* The main subroutine for this page...
'*********************************************************************

Sub Main()
  'Was this page submitted?
  if ( Request("cmdSubmit") = "Submit" ) Then
    'Reformat the data into a more readable format...
    txtFirstName = InitCap(Request("txtFirstName"))
    txtLastName = InitCap(Request("txtLastName"))
    txtEmailAddr = LCase(Request("txtEmailAddr"))

    'Check the email address for the correct components...
    if (Instr(1, txtEmailAddr, "@") = 0 _
        or Instr(1, txtEmailAddr, ".") = 0 ) Then
      sMessage = "The email address you entered does not " _
        & "appear to be valid."
    Else
      'Make sure there is something after the period..
      if ( Instr(1, txtEmailAddr, ".") = Len(txtEmailAddr) _
        or Instr(1, txtEmailAddr, "@") = 1 or _
        (Instr(1, txtEmailAddr, ".") = Instr(1, txtEmailAddr, "@") + 1) ) Then
          sMessage = "You must enter a complete email address."
      end if
    End If
    'We passed our validation, show that all is good...
```

```
      if ( sMessage = "" ) Then
        sMessage = "Thank you for your input. All data has " _
          & "passed verification."
      else
        Session("ErrorCount") = Session("ErrorCount") + 1

        if ( Session("ErrorCount") > _
            Application("AllowedErrorsBeforeWarning") ) then
          sMessage = sMessage & "<P><Font Size=1>You have exceeded " _
            & "the normal number of times it takes to get this right!</Font>"
        end if
      End If
    Else
      'First time in here? Set some default values...
      txtFirstName = "Enter Your First Name"
      txtLastName = "Enter Your Last Name"
      txtEmailAddr = "Enter Your Email Address"
    End If
End Sub

'*********************************************************************
'* InitCap
'*
'* Capitalizes the first letter of the string
'*********************************************************************

Function InitCap(sStr)
 InitCap = UCase(Left(sStr, 1)) & LCase(Right(sStr, Len(sStr) - 1))
End Function

'*********************************************************************
'* Call our main subroutine
'*********************************************************************

Call Main()
%>

<html>
<head>
  <title>My First ASP Application</title>
</head>

<body>

<table border="0" cellPadding="0" cellSpacing="0" width="600">
<tbody>
   <tr>
     <td width="100"><a href="http://www.wrox.com" target="_blank" border=0
alt><img border=0 title="Check out the Wrox Press Web Site!"
src="images/wroxlogo.gif" WIDTH="56" HEIGHT="56"></a></td>
     <td width="500"><center><font size="5" face="Trebuchet MS">My First ASP
Application</font></center></td>
   </tr>
```

```
        <tr>
          <td width="100"> </td>
          <td width="500" align="left"><font face="Trebuchet MS"><br>
          Please fill out the following form and press the [Submit] button. The
information you enter will be reformatted and the email address will be
verified.</font><form action="default.asp" id="FORM1" method="post"
name="frmMain">
            <table border="0" cellPadding="1" cellSpacing="5" width="100%">
              <tr>
                <td width="100" nowrap align="right"><font size="2" face="Trebuchet
MS">First Name:</font></td>
                <td width="350"><font size="2" face="Trebuchet MS">
                  <input title="Enter your first name here" name="txtFirstName"
size="30"
value="<%=txtFirstName%>" tabindex="1"></font></td>
                  <td width="50"><div align="right"><font size="2" face="Trebuchet MS">
                  <input type="submit" title="Submit this data for processing..."
value="Submit" name="cmdSubmit" tabindex="4"></font></td>
              </tr>

              <tr>
                <td width="100" nowrap align="right">
                  <font size="2" face="Trebuchet MS">Last Name:</font></td>
                <td width="400" colspan="2">
                  <font size="2" face="Trebuchet MS">
                  <input title="Enter your last name here" name="txtLastName" size="30"
value="<%=txtLastName%>" tabindex="2"></font></td>
              </tr>

              <tr>
                <td width="100" nowrap align="right"><font size="2" face="Trebuchet
MS">Email Address:</font></td>
                <td width="400" colspan="2"><font size="2" face="Trebuchet MS"><input
title="Enter your valid email address here" name="txtEmailAddr"
                  size="40" value="<%=txtEmailAddr%>" tabindex="3"></font></td>
              </tr>
              <tr>
                <td nowrap width=500 colspan="3" align="center"><font face="Trebuchet
MS"><br>
                <strong><%=sMessage%></strong> </font></td>
              </tr>
            </table>
          </form>
          <p> </td>
        </tr>
      </tbody>
    </table>
  </body>
</html>
```

As you can see, the page is quite long. But it breaks logically into two distinct sections: the ASP/VBScript portion and the HTML portion. Let's examine each section individually.

# The ASP/VBScript Section

The top half of our file is where the ASP code lives. This code is executed by the server before the page is returned to the browser that requested it. As you've seen, any code that is to be executed on the server before returning is enclosed in the special <% and %> tags.

For clarity (and sanity!) the ASP code has been divided into subroutines. This not only makes the code more readable, but also will aid in its reuse. Our code has two routines: Main and InitCap. Before we do anything however, we declare some variables.

```
Dim txtFirstName, txtLastName, txtEmailAddr
Dim sMessage
```

When variables are declared outside of a subroutine in an ASP page, the variables retain their data until the page is completely processed. This allows you to pass information from your ASP code to your HTML code as you'll see.

After our variables have been declared, we have our Main routine. This is called by our ASP code every time a browser retrieves the page. The Main subroutine is not called automatically: we must explicitly call it ourselves.

```
'**************************************************************
'* Main
'*
'* The main subroutine for this page...
'**************************************************************

Sub Main()
  '  Was this page submitted?
  if ( Request("cmdSubmit") = "Submit" ) Then
  ' Reformat the data into a more readable format...
    txtFirstName = InitCap(Request("txtFirstName"))
    txtLastName = InitCap(Request("txtLastName"))
    txtEmailAddr = LCase(Request("txtEmailAddr"))

    '  Check the email address for the correct components...
    if ( Instr(1, txtEmailAddr, "@") = 0 or Instr(1, txtEmailAddr, ".") _
        = 0  ) Then
      sMessage = "The email address you entered does not appear to be valid."
    Else
      '  Make sure there is something after the period..
      if ( Instr(1, txtEmailAddr, ".") = Len(txtEmailAddr) _
          or Instr(1, txtEmailAddr, "@") = 1 or & _
          (Instr(1, txtEmailAddr, ".") = Instr(1, txtEmailAddr, "@") + 1) ) _
          Then
        sMessage = "You must enter a complete email address."
      end if
    End If

  ' We passed our validation, show that all is good...
    if ( sMessage = "" ) Then
```

```
              sMessage = "Thank you for your input. All data has " _
                 & "passed verification."
           else
              Session("ErrorCount") = Session("ErrorCount") + 1

              if ( Session("ErrorCount") > _
                  Application("AllowedErrorsBeforeWarning") ) then
                 sMessage = sMessage & "<P><Font Size=1>You have exceeded " _
                    & "the normal number of times it takes to get this right!</Font>"
              end if
           End If
        Else
           '    First time in here? Set some default values...
           txtFirstName = "Enter Your First Name"
           txtLastName = "Enter Your Last Name"
           txtEmailAddr = "Enter Your Email Address"
        End If
     End Sub
```

First, we see if the form was actually submitted by the user, otherwise we initialize our variables. To determine if the page has been submitted, we check the value of the cmdSubmit Request variable. This is the button on our form. When pressed, the form calls this page and sets the value of the cmdSubmit button to Submit. If a user just loads the page without pressing the button, the value of cmdSubmit is blank (" "). There are other ways to determine if a Web page was submitted, but this method is the simplest.

After we have determined that the page was in fact submitted, run the names through the second function on this page: InitCap. InitCap is a quick little function that will format a word to proper case. That is to say that the first letter will be capitalized and the rest of the word will be lowercase. Following is the function.

```
'****************************************************************
'* InitCap
'*
'* Capitalizes the first letter of the string
'****************************************************************

Function InitCap(sStr)
    InitCap = UCase(Left(sStr, 1)) & LCase(Right(sStr, Len(sStr) - 1))
End Function
```

Now that we've cleaned up the names, we need to check the e-mail address for validity. To do this we ensure that it contains an "@" sign and a period ( . ). Once past this check, we make sure that there is data after the period and before the "@" sign. This is "quick and dirty" e-mail validity checking.

If either of these checks fails, we place a failure message into the string sMessage. This will be displayed in our HTML section after the page processing is complete.

Now, if our e-mail address has passed the test, we set the message (sMessage) to display a thank you note. If we failed our test, we increment our error counter that we set up in the global.asa file. Here we also check to see if we have exceeded our limit on errors. If we have, a sterner message is set for display.

Finally, the last thing in our ASP section is our call to `Main`. This is what is called when the page is loaded.

```
'****************************************************************
'* Call our main subroutine
'****************************************************************

Call Main()
```

# The HTML Section

This section is a regular HTML form with a smattering of ASP thrown in for good measure. The ASP that we've embedded in the HTML sets default values for the input fields and displays any messages that our server-side code has generated.

The most important part of the HTML is where the ASP code is embedded. The following snippet illustrates this.

```
<input title="Enter your first name here" name="txtFirstName" size="30"
 value="<%=txtFirstName%>" tabindex="1">
```

Here we see a normal text input box. However, to set the value of the text box we use the `Response` `.Write` shortcut (`<%=`) to insert the value of the variable `txtFirstName`. Remember that we dimensioned this outside of our ASP functions so that it would have page scope. Now we utilize its value by inserting it into our HTML.

We do exactly the same thing with the Last Name and Email Address text boxes:

```
<input title="Enter your last name here" name="txtLastName" size="30"
 value="<%=txtLastName%>" tabindex="2">
<input title="Enter your valid email address here" name="txtEmailAddr"
 size="40" value="<%=txtEmailAddr%>" tabindex="3">
</tr>
```

The last trick in the HTML section is the display of our failure or success message. This message is stored in the variable called `sMessage`. At the bottom of the form, we display the contents of this variable.

```
<td nowrap width=500 colspan="3" align="center">
    <font face="Trebuchet MS">
    <br>
    <strong>
    <%=sMessage%>
    </strong>
    </font>
</td>
```

The beauty of this code is that if `sMessage` is blank then nothing is shown, otherwise the message is displayed.

# Summary

You have learned much in this chapter! We first covered how HTTP is the transaction system that sends Web pages to requesting clients. It is a very important piece of the puzzle. We then discussed Active Server Pages or ASP. You learned how ASP pages are created, and what special HTML tags you need to include in your files to use ASP.

We looked through the ASP object model and saw that the `Request` and `Response` objects are used to manage details of the HTTP request and responses. We saw that the `Application` object is used to group pages together into one application and we saw that the `Session` is used to create the illusion that the interaction between user and site is one continuous action. Finally, we created a small application that demonstrates two uses for ASP: form validation and data manipulation.

# 18

# Adding VBScript to Your VB Applications

## Overview

By now, it should be clear that VBScript is useful in many contexts within Windows. Not surprisingly, along with a variety of different technologies, Microsoft provides yet another component capable of supporting VBScript—the Script Control. This *ActiveX control* provides a simple way for your application written in Visual Basic (or any other language that supports ActiveX controls) to host its own scripting environment, allowing you, or your users, to customize the application.

In the past, programmers had to struggle to provide customizability to their projects, or pay license fees for other products such as Microsoft's portable VB variant, Visual Basic for Applications (VBA). In 1997, Microsoft released Windows Script Interfaces (WSI) as an interface to scripting engines, and eventually followed up with Script Control. Although WSI provides greater control over how your application interfaces with a scripting engine, WSI was intended for C++ programmers. The Script Control, on the other hand, is tailor made for Visual Basic (VB).

## Why Add Scripting to Your Application?

Allowing customization of your application through scripting can open many opportunities—not only to you, the programmer (allowing you to change or customize your application's behavior without having to recompile and redistribute), but also to your end users, who will be able to do more with your application. The possibilities of scripting are almost endless, but, as usual, adding this capability to your application will require additional time and effort for design, coding, testing.

> Note: This chapter assumes that you are familiar with the fundamentals of using the Visual Basic language and its Integrated Development Environment (IDE) to create executables and DLLs, including the use of external libraries.

Adding scripting support to your application is most appropriate when you want to allow customization of the application from within—as opposed to from without. Adding customization from without is often what you really want. For example, consider Microsoft Excel, which offers customization through scripting both from within and from without. Customization of Excel from without comes from the fact that Excel exposes a public, COM-based programming interface that programmers in any other COM-enabled language (like Visual Basic or VBScript) can code against, all without even starting the Excel graphical interface. From within, however, you can add macros and VBA code that add customizations to the behavior of Excel from within Excel itself.

In your Visual Basic application, you can accomplish customization from without simply by creating ActiveX DLLs or EXEs that expose published interfaces. This technique does not necessarily require any additional coding or testing time, though you do need to design your program and segregate your code in a particular way in order to do it right. For many applications, this level of customization is all that is needed.

However, you can also, like Excel, offer customization from within by using the Script Control. There are different approaches to this, and you have to design the internals of your program (at least the parts you want to expose to scripting) a little differently than you are used to. In this chapter we will discuss these techniques and introduce a freely downloadable sample Visual Basic projects that implements the Script Control.

# Macro and Scripting Concepts

Before we dig into the details of the Script Control, it is helpful to conceptualize how the Script Control can be used inside an application. There are two approaches: first, using externally stored "scriptlets" that are executed at certain times for very targeted purposes; and second, exposing whole sections of an application to customization and automation through scripting. In both approaches, you have the option of sharing some or all your application's internal object model with your application's hosted scripts.

Both approaches are similar in that your application gives up control over some portion of its logic or functionality to scripts that are loaded at runtime as opposed to being compiled into your application. They are different primarily in terms of scope. Let's look at two examples.

As an example of the smaller scope approach, imagine an application that has a complex algorithm coded as a series of steps spread across several procedures and/or classes. Let's say this complex algorithm computes the amounts of a series of invoices over time, calculated based on a series of subformulas that have different inputs and outputs depending on the portion of the total invoice amount being computed. Lets say there are 10 subformulas required to compute the amount of one month's invoice. Imagine that nine of these formulas are static, meaning that they are the same in all cases and can therefore be hard coded.

However, one of the formulas is different based on the type of invoice. Sometimes the formula must work one way, sometimes another. Also, the company paying for this application adds new types of invoices all the time, each with unique requirements for this tenth formula. The company wants to be able to add new invoice types without having to add unique, hard-coded versions of this formula for each invoice type. They don't want to have to redeploy the application each time a new invoice type is added.

The application designers decide to use the Script Control to solve this quandary. They add a column called `ForumlaScript` to the `InvoiceTypes` table in the database. In this column they store "scriptlets," written in VBScript, that compute the result for this tenth subformula in a unique way for each invoice type. Each scriptlet is different based on the requirements for each invoice type. When the invoice amount calculation algorithm reaches the step for the tenth subformula it loads the appropriate scriptlet from the `InvoiceType` table and uses the Script Control to dynamically execute the scriptlet.

As you can see, in this first example, the application uses scripting capability for a very targeted purpose, adding just the necessary amount of customizability. In a larger scope example, a whole section of the application might be opened up for scripting and automation. The scripts used by the application might be more complex, like the Windows Script Host (WSH) and ASP scripts we've been looking at in this book. The scripts could have access to the entire object model of the hosting application, much in the way that the WSH and ASP engines expose objects like `WScript` and `Server` to the scripts they host.

This larger scope approach might be used to allow users to write their own macros to control the user interface of the application. Or the application might expose an object model that allows users to write and plug in their own scripts to generate reports.

Large scope or small scope, the possibilities are endless, and an application you are tasked with designing may or may not have a use for the Script Control at all. If you are trying to add customizability for your end users, then the Script Control may indeed be the best thing because you probably want to allow your users to create and edit scripts from within your application, and you have no control over how or which users to choose to add scripting to the application. Or maybe your application is deployed at the customer's site, and your deployment consultants (who may not be expert programmers) need the flexibility to customize the application on the spot, right when they are in the customer's office installing the application.

However, if you are trying to achieve a design that simply allows for "plug in" components to ease deployment of bug fixes and new features into your production environment, upon further consideration of your design options, and perhaps a little research, you may decide that an object-oriented polymorphic design that utilizes interfaces and the class factory design pattern might be a better, more stable, and more predictable alternative.

That's a mouthful. Unfortunately, there is no room here to explain what we exactly mean by "an object-oriented polymorphic design that utilizes interfaces and the class factory design pattern." The point is that the Script Control is not the solution to every design problem. Consider carefully *why* you are thinking of using the Script Control. What requirements exactly are you trying to implement? You may find that another solution that achieves the same thing without some of the downsides of the Script Control, namely the fact that script code will almost always run slower than you application's native compiled code and that you do not have any control over syntax errors and poor programming practices that people might insert into the scripts.

# Adding the Script Control to a VB Application

If you have not alreadydownload the Script Control you can download it from this address on the Microsoft Web site: `http://msdn.microsoft.com/downloads/list/webdev.asp`. The installation program automatically adds the control to your machine and registers it.

When you are ready (you might want to read ahead some first, and perhaps take some time to go through this chapter's downloadable sample project), the Script Control can be easily added to a VB project as an ActiveX control (attached to a form) or as a normal COM object that you declare and instantiate in code. In the former case, you would add the control to a form as normal from the Component Toolbox in the VB IDE. In the latter case, you would instead add a reference to the Script Control using the Project ⇨ References menu.

When you attach the control to a form, it is an invisible control. That means it does not add any visual properties to your form, much like the native Timer control you may have used before. Unlike the Timer control, which can *only* be used as a control attached to a form, the Script Control is not limited in this way. In fact, using the Script Control as an object rather than as a control attached to a form offers more flexibility, as demonstrated by the sample project discussed later in the chapter.

# Script Control Reference

This middle part of the chapter is a complete reference for the Script Control, including the objects, collections, properties, methods, method syntax, and examples. After the reference, the chapter continues with some additional explanation, followed by an example Visual Basic application that makes use of the Script Control.

## Object Model

The Script Control object model is illustrated in Figure 18-1. The details of these objects and their properties and methods are documented in the upcoming sections.

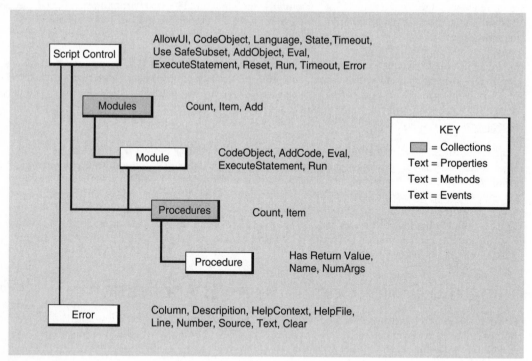

**Figure 18-1**

## Objects and Collections

The Script Control component has several objects and collections (which are a special kind of multivalued object) that work together to provide a wide range of capabilities for adding scripts to a Visual Basic application. For each object and collection, we will describe the object in general; document its properties, methods, and events; and, where appropriate, provide example code.

## ScriptControl Object

ScriptControl is the main element that enables scripting in an application. It provides a simple interface for hosting scripting engines such as VBScript or JScript. All of the other available objects depend on an instance of ScriptControl. ScriptControl can be instantiated in three different ways:

❑ Early bound, on a form (add it through the Components dialog)

❑ Early bound, through code (add it through the References dialog)

❑ Late bound (at any time)

### Declaration Syntax

This is the syntax to declare an early bound variable for the ScriptControl object (this is preferred over the late bound syntax.).

```
Dim|Private|Public [WithEvents] objSC As [MSScriptControl.]ScriptControl
```

This is the syntax to declare a late bound variable for the ScriptControl object. A late bound variable will not be able to handle events. If using a late bound variable, the Script Control does not need to be referenced in the project.

```
Dim|Private|Public objSC [As Object|Variant]
```

### Properties

The properties of the ScriptControl object are described in the following table.

| Name | Accepts/ Returns | Access | Description |
|------|------------------|--------|-------------|
| AllowUI | Boolean | Read/Write | Sets or returns the value indicating whether or not visual elements such as MsgBox or InputBox can be displayed. When this is set to False, the only way to communicate visually with the user is directly through the hosting application |
| Error | Error object | Read-only | Returns a reference to the Error object for a ScriptControl instance. |
| Language | String | Read/Write | Sets or returns the name of the scripting language used by the ScriptControl object. "VBScript" and "JScript" are natively supported. If other compatible scripting languages are installed, the name of other scripting languages can be used as well. Setting this property resets all other members of the ScriptControl and its child objects |

*Continues*

| Name | Accepts/ Returns | Access | Description |
|------|------------------|--------|-------------|
| Modules | Modules object | Read-only | Returns a reference to the Modules collection of the ScriptControl object |
| Name | String | Read-only | If the ScriptControl object is attached to a form, this property returns the name assigned to the control on its properties page |
| Procedures | Procedures object | Read-only | Returns a reference to the Procedures collection of the default "Global" Module object. To access the Procedures collection of other modules, access the module directly through the Modules collection and use the Module.Procedures property |
| SitehWnd | Long | Read/Write | Sets or returns the "handle" to the parent window used by the executing code. When the Script Control is used as an ActiveX Control, placed on a form, the default value of SitehWnd is the hWnd property of the container of the control. Otherwise, when the Script Control is used as an object (not attached to a form), SitehWnd is always 0, which corresponds to the Desktop. This property may impact which window (or control) has UI control over the scripted UI elements. You may change this property to make the Script Control dependent upon a specific window rather than, in some cases, the Desktop (for example, you might want the Script Control to freeze a part of your application and not the Desktop). Circumstances under which you would need to change this property should be rare |
| State | Long (States) | Read/Write | Sets or returns the mode of the ScriptControl object; uses the States enumerated constant. When this value is set to Connected (1), the ScriptControl will be able to sink events generated by objects added using the AddObject method. Thus, changing the state gives you some control over the handling of events |

| Name | Accepts/ Returns | Access | Description |
|------|------------------|--------|-------------|
| TimeOut | Long | Read/Write | Sets or returns a number representing time in milliseconds, indicating how long the ScriptControl object will wait before aborting a script that is taking a long time. This property can be set to a constant NoTimeout (−1) which removes time restrictions placed on the execution of script code; turning off the timeout can be dangerous, however, because someone might, for instance, create a script that contains an endless loop. The default value is 10,000 milliseconds (10 seconds). When the timeout expires, a Timeout event may occur (depending on whether or not the ScriptControl can handle events), and at that time, if the ScriptControl has the AllowUI property enabled, the user is alerted with a dialog box, permitting the user to continue execution of the script. Otherwise, the script is terminated and an error is raised. When this property is set to 0 (not recommended), a Timeout event occurs as soon as the script stops Windows messaging for slightly more than 100 milliseconds |
| UseSafeSubset | Boolean | Read/Write | Sets or returns a Boolean value indicating whether or not the Script Control may run components that are not marked as "Safe for Scripting." For example, a script may try to use the scripting runtime FileSystemObject, which is not "Safe for Scripting" since it allows access to the file system. You may set this property to True when you are concerned about the ability of the script to create damage on the client computer. When the Script Control is used in a host that requires that components are "Safe for Scripting" (such as Internet Explorer), this property defaults to True and is read-only |

## Methods

The methods of the `ScriptControl` object are described in the following table.

| Name | Arguments | Returns | Description |
|------|-----------|---------|-------------|
| AddCode | *code*—String value representing a valid script | N/A | This is the primary method of adding script to the Script Control. When called on the `ScriptControl` object, automatically adds the new code to the default "Global" module. Calls on an individual `Module` object to add code to a particular module. When adding code for entire procedures and blocks of code, the code must be added in a single call to the `AddCode` method. Each statement in the block can be separated by colons (:) or the line break characters `vbNewLine` (preferred), `vbCr`, `vbLf`, and `vbCrLf` |
| AddObject | *name*Unique String name for the object being added<br><br>*object*—Any object within the scope of your application<br><br>*addmembers*—Optional Boolean value indicating whether or not the object's public members should be accessible to the `ScriptControl` object and its scripts | N/A | Allows the script to access the host's runtime object model as exposed by the object(s) added through this method. Objects added to the `ScriptControl` are available globally within the `ScriptControl` object. The optional *addmembers* parameter indicates whether or not the members of the added object are also available to the scripts within |
| Eval | *expression*—A String value representing a valid "expression," meaning any script fragment that can be compiled and executed | The output of the expression, if any | Evaluates an expression. Similar to `Eval` function in VBScript. This is one of the best ways to evaluate dynamic expressions provided by the user. When comparing `Eval` to the `ExecuteStatement` method, be aware that the "=" operator will be treated as a comparison operator when used with `Eval`, but as an assignment operator when used with `ExecuteStatement`. Hence, $x = y$ will evaluate to a `Boolean` subtype when used with `Eval`, but when used with `ExecuteStatement`, the value of $y$ will be assigned to variable $x$, and nothing will be returned. The expression evaluated can take advantage of any members within scope of the `Module` or `ScriptControl` object |

| Name | Arguments | Returns | Description |
|------|-----------|---------|-------------|
| Execute Statement | *statement*—String value representing the statement to executed | N/A | Unlike the Eval method, ExecuteStatement only executes a statement and does not return any value. When comparing Eval to the ExecuteStatement method, be aware that the "=" operator will be treated as a comparison operator when used with Eval, but as an assignment operator when used with ExecuteStatement. Hence, x = y will evaluate to a Boolean subtype when used with Eval, but when used with ExecuteStatement, the value of y will be assigned to variable x, and nothing will be returned. The statement executed can take advantage of any members within scope of the Module or ScriptControl object. In order to obtain a return value from a procedure, you should use either the Eval or Run methods |
| Reset | None | N/A | Discards all the members and child objects of the ScriptControl object and initializes them to their default state. When the Reset method is called, the State property is reset to Initialized (0) |
| Run | *procedurename*—String name of the procedure or function to run<br><br>*paramarray()*—optional array of parameter values, as accepted by the procedure or function | If a function is called, returns the return value of that function | When called on the ScriptControl object, attempts to run the named procedure or function in the default "Global" module. When called on a Module object, attempts to run the named procedure or function within that module. Alternatively, you can use the CodeObject property call procedures and functions directly |

### Events

The events of the ScriptControl object are described in the following table.

| Name | Arguments | Description |
|------|-----------|-------------|
| Error | None | Occurs when the ScriptObject encounters an error while running a script. In order to receive notification of this event, you must declare the ScriptControl object variable "early bound" and using the WithEventskeyword |

*Continues*

477

| Name | Arguments | Description |
|------|-----------|-------------|
| Timeout | None | Occurs when script execution exceeds the time allotted in the Timeout property, and the user decides to stop the execution of the script. When several ScriptControl objects are present, a Timeout event will occur only for the first ScriptControl object to timeout |

## Examples

This line of code shows how to instantiate a new early bound Script Control object.

```
Set objSC = New [MSScriptControl.]ScriptControl
```

This line of code shows how to instantiate a new late bound Script Control object.

```
Set objSC = CreateObject("[MSScriptControl.]ScriptControl")
```

This script fragment shows how variables and procedures that are outside the scope of a procedure or function can be added in separate steps using the AddCode method. Entire procedures and functions should be added in one call.

```
strCode = "Option Explicit" & vbNewLine & vbNewLine
objSC.AddCode strCode

strCode = "Dim x, y" & vbNewLine & vbNewLine
objSC.AddCode strCode

strCode = "x = 15" & vbNewLine & "y = 2"
objSC.AddCode strCode

strCode = "Function MultiplyXY(): MultiplyXY = x * y : End Function"
objSC.AddCode strCode
```

The Eval function allows you to execute code fragments at runtime. Eval is simple but effective, capable of achieving tasks nearly impossible in VB.

```
MsgBox objSC.Eval(InputBox$( _
        "Enter Numeric Expression", _
        "Eval Example", "5 * 3 - 1"))
```

Depending upon the type of a procedure, you may call the Run method in several different ways, depending on return values and parameters.

```
strCode = "Sub TwoArg(a,b): MsgBox CInt(a + b)" & " : End Sub"
objSC.AddCode strCode
objSC.Run "TwoArg", 1, 2
strCode = "Function ManyArg(a,b,c,d): ManyArg = a * b + c - d"
strCode = strCode & ": End Function"
objSC.AddCode strCode
lngResult = objSC.Run("ManyArg", 1, 2, 3, 4)
```

The following script fragment illustrates the use of the `Error` event.

```
Private WithEvents objSC As ScriptControl

Private Sub Main()
    Set objSC = New ScriptControl
    ...
    objSC.Run "MyProc"
End Sub

Private Sub objSC_Error
    MsgBox "Script error occurred:" & vbNewLine & _
        "Number: " & objSC.Error.Number & vbNewLine & _
        "Description: " & objSC.Error.Description & vbNewLine & _
        "Line: " & objSC.Error.Line & vbNewLine & _
        "Column: " & objSC.Error.Column & vbNewLine & _
        "Script Text: " & objSC.Error.Text
End Sub
```

The script following fragment illustrates the use of the `Timeout` event.

```
Private WithEvents objSC As ScriptControl

Private Sub Main()
    Set objSC = New ScriptControl
    ...
    objSC.Timeout = 10000
    objSC.Run "MyProc"
End Sub

Private Sub objSC_TimeOut
    MsgBox "The script has timed out."
End Sub
```

## Module Object

The `Module` object, a member of the `Modules` collection (see below), contains procedure, type, and data declarations used in a script. The Script Control has a default `Global` module, which is automatically used unless specific member calls are made to other modules that have been added. You can add code to a Module object using the `AddCode` method. Individual `Module` objects, on the other hand, are added by using the `Add` method of the `Modules` collection. Since the code in each module is private in scope to its module, you can repeat variable and procedure names across modules. This is useful when you have several similar scripts that are only partially different from each other.

### Declaration Syntax

This is the syntax to declare a variable for a `Module` object.

```
Dim|Private|Public objModule [As [MSScriptControl.]Module|Object]
```

### Properties

The properties of the `Module` object are described in the following table.

| Name | Accepts/ Returns | Access | Description |
|------|------------------|--------|-------------|
| CodeObject | Object | Read-only | Returns an object that can be used to call the public procedures and functions in a Module object. This is a late bound object, but it is useful in that it allows direct calls to procedures in the script without using the Run method. Procedures and functions in the module will appear as public methods of the object returned by this property |
| Name | String | Read/Write | The logical name of a Module object. Also used as its Modules collection key, so must be unique within the Modules collection. If you add another Module object of the same name to the collection, the new object will overwrite the original object |
| Procedures | Procedures object | Read-only | Returns a reference to the Procedures collection of a Module object |

### Methods

The methods of the Module object are described in the following table.

| Name | Arguments | Returns | Description |
|------|-----------|---------|-------------|
| Eval | *expression*—A String value representing a valid "expression," meaning any script fragment that can be compiled and executed | The output of the expression, if any | Evaluates an expression. Similar to Eval function in VBScript. This is one of the best ways to evaluate dynamic expressions provided by the user. When comparing Eval to the ExecuteStatement method, you should be aware that the "=" will be treated as a comparison operator when used with Eval, but as an assignment operator when used with ExecuteStatement. Hence, x = y will evaluate to a Boolean subtype when used with Eval, but when used with ExecuteStatement, the value of y will be assigned to variable x, and nothing will be returned. The Eval method may be used against the ScriptControl or Module object, and take advantage of its members |

| Name | Arguments | Returns | Description |
|------|-----------|---------|-------------|
| AddCode | *code*—String value representing a valid script | N/A | This is the primary method of adding script to the Script Control. When called on the ScriptControl object, automatically adds the new code to the default "Global" module. Call on an individual Module object to add code to a particular module. When adding code for entire procedures and blocks of code, the code must be added in a single call to the AddCode method. Each statement in the block can be separated by colons (:) or the line break characters vbNewLine (preferred), vbCr, vbLf, and vbCrLf |
| Execute Statement | *statement*—String value representing the statement to executed | N/A | Unlike the Eval method, ExecuteStatement only executes a statement and does not return any value. When comparing Eval to the ExecuteStatement method, be aware that the "=" operator will be treated as a comparison operator when used with Eval, but as an assignment operator when used with ExecuteStatement. Hence, x = y will evaluate to a Boolean subtype when used with Eval, but when used with ExecuteStatement, the value of y will be assigned to variable x, and nothing will be returned. The statement executed can take advantage of any members within scope of the Module or ScriptControl object. In order to obtain a return value from a procedure, you should use either the Eval or Run methods |
| Run | *procedurename*—String name of the procedure or function to run<br><br>*paramarray()*—optional array of parameter values, as accepted by the procedure or function | If a function is called, returns the return value of that function | When called on the ScriptControl object, attempts to run the named procedure or function in the default "Global" module. When called on a Module object, attempts to run the named procedure or function within that module. Alternatively, you can use the CodeObject property call procedures and functions directly |

## Examples

The script following fragment illustrates the use of the `Module.Run` method to call a procedure contained in a module.

```
Set objModule = objSC.Modules.Add("NewModule")
objModule.AddCode "Sub Test(): " & _
    vbNewLine & vbTab & "MsgBox ""Hello, world.""" & _
    vbNewLine & "End Sub"
objModule.Run "Test"
```

The following script fragment illustrates the use of the `Module.CodeObject` to call code within the module. You may find that calling procedures this way is more natural, and perhaps more readable than using the `ScriptControl.Run` method since procedures are exposed as methods of the `CodeObject` object.

```
Set objModule = objSC.Modules.Add("TestMod")

objModule.AddCode "Sub TestProc(): " & _
    vbNewLine & vbTab & "MsgBox ""Hello, world.""" & _
    vbNewLine & "End Sub"
objModule.AddCode "Function TestFunction(a) : & _
    vbNewLine & vbTab & "TestFunction = a * a " & _
    vbNewLine & "End Function"

Set objCodeObject = objModule.CodeObject
objCodeObject.TestProc
lngVal = objCodeObject.TestFunction(2)
```

This script fragment shows how variables and procedures that are outside the scope of a procedure or function can be added in separate steps. Entire procedures and functions should be added in one call.

```
strCode = "Option Explicit" & vbNewLine & vbNewLine
objModule.AddCode strCode

strCode = "Dim x, y" & vbNewLine & vbNewLine
objModule.AddCode strCode

strCode = "x = 15" & vbNewLine & "y = 2"
objModule.AddCode strCode

strCode = "Function MultiplyXY(): MultiplyXY = x * y : End Function"
objModule.AddCode strCode
```

The `Eval` function allows you to execute code fragments at runtime. `Eval` is simple but effective, capable of achieving tasks nearly impossible in VB.

```
MsgBox objSC.Eval(InputBox$( _
        "Enter Numeric Expression", _
        "Eval Example", "5 * 3 - 1"))
```

Depending upon the type of a procedure, you may call the `Run` method in several different ways, depending on return values and parameters.

```
strCode = "Sub TwoArg(a,b): MsgBox CInt(a + b)" & " : End Sub"
objSC.AddCode strCode
objSC.Run "TwoArg", 1, 2

strCode = "Function ManyArg(a,b,c,d): ManyArg = a * b + c - d"
strCode = strCode & ": End Function"
objSC.AddCode strCode
lngResult = objSC.Run("ManyArg", 1, 2, 3, 4)
```

## Modules Collection

The `Modules` collection contains all the `Module` objects for a `ScriptControl` object, including the default `Global` module. Calls to the members of the `Global` module can be made directly through the `ScriptControl` object without iterating through the `Modules` collection. It also has an index matching the value of the constant `GlobalModule`.

`Module` objects can be added to the `Modules` collection using the `Add` method. Specific `Module` objects can be accessed through the default `Modules.Item` method. The `Count` property provides the number of `Module` objects in the collection. The entire collection can be iterated in various ways, most commonly using the `For Each...Next` loop. Since there is no way of deleting individual modules, you will have to use the `Reset` method of the `ScriptControl` object to delete unwanted modules, which clears the entire collection.

### Properties

The single property of the `Modules` collection object is described in the following table.

| Name | Accepts/ Returns | Access | Description |
|------|------------------|--------|-------------|
| Count | Long | Read-only | Returns the number of `Module` objects in the `Modules` collection |

### Methods

The methods of the `Modules` collection object are described in the following table.

| Name | Arguments | Returns | Description |
|------|-----------|---------|-------------|
| Add | *name*—String value representing the name of the `Module` object being added; will be used as the `Modules` collection key<br><br>*module*—optional `Module` object to be added to the collection | If *module* argument omitted, returns new `Module` object | Use this method to add a new `Module` object to the collection of `Modules`; if your project has a relatively small set of scripts, you may wish to just use the default "Global" module, but if you have a larger set of scripts, you may find it beneficial to break them up into separate modules—especially if you need to repeat procedures and functions with the same name in different modules |

*Continues*

| Name | Arguments | Returns | Description |
|------|-----------|---------|-------------|
| Item | *index*—A `Long` or `String` value, representing an index or key, respectively | Returns a `Module` object from the collection if one matching the *index* exists | This is the default property of the collection, so many programmers omit the actual name of the item method: `Set objModule = objSC.Modules("MyModule")` |

### Examples

The following line of code shows how to access the `Global` module directly. The same syntax, using different module names, can be used with other named modules.

```
Set objModule = sc.Modules("Global")
```

The following script fragment illustrates how to iterate through the `Modules` collection.

```
For Each objModule In objSC.Modules
    strModuleList = strModuleList & vbNewLine & objModule.Name
Next
```

Modules allow the use of separate scripts and provide separate namespaces. The following script fragment shows how two different modules can contain scripts with the same name.

```
' Add code to separate modules, using same sub names.

Set objModule = objSC.Modules.Add("Maine")
objModule.AddCode "Sub ShowState" & _
    vbNewLine & vbTab & "MsgBox ""In Maine""" & _
    vbNewLine & "End Sub"
Set objModule = Nothing

Set objModule = objSC.Modules.Add("Ohio")
objModule.AddCode "Sub ShowState" & _
    vbNewLine & vbTab & "MsgBox ""In Ohio""" & _
    vbNewLine & "End Sub"
```

## Procedure Object

The `Procedure` object defines a logical unit of code, which in case of VBScript can be either a `Sub` or a `Function`. The `Procedure` object contains a number of useful properties that allow us to inspect a procedure's name, the number of arguments, and whether or not the procedure returns any values. Entry to the script code is also provided via the `Procedure` object.

### Declaration Syntax

This is the syntax to declare a variable for a `Procedure` object.

```
Dim|Private|Public objProc [As [MSScriptControl.]Procedure|Object]
```

## Properties

The properties of the `Procedure` object are described in the following table.

| Name | Accepts/ Returns | Access | Description |
|---|---|---|---|
| HasReturnValue | Boolean | Read-only | Returns whether or not a procedure returns a value (in other words, whether it is a procedure or a function) |
| Name | String | Read-only | The name of a `Procedure` object, which will match the actual name of the procedure or function contained in the object. Also used as the `Procedures` collection key, so must be unique within the `Procedures` collection. If you use the `AddCode` method to add another procedure of the same name to a module, the new procedure will overwrite the original procedure in that module |
| NumArgs | Long | Read-only | Returns the number of arguments accepted by a procedure or function in a `Procedure` object |

## Methods

The methods of the `Procedure` object are described in the following table.

| Name | Arguments | Returns | Description |
|---|---|---|---|
| It m | *index*—A Long or String value, representing an index or key, respectively. | Returns a Procedure object from the collection if one matching the *index* exists | This is the default property of the collection, so many programmers omit the actual name of the item method: `Set objProc = objMod.Procedures("MyProc")` |

Note that the `Procedures` collection does not have an `Add` method. New procedures are added to a module using the `AddCode` method; `Procedure` objects are created and added to the collection behind the scenes.

## Procedures Collection

The `Procedures` collection holds all of the procedures in a given `Module` object. It provides a convenient way to iterate through all of the procedures in a module and access the code therein. Individual procedures are added through the `Module` object's `AddCode` method, not through the `Procedures` collection directly. Also, you can't remove an individual procedure once it has been added, as there is no `Remove` method on the `Procedures` collection.

## Properties

The single property of the `Procedures` collection object is described in the following table.

| Name | Accepts/ Returns | Access | Description |
|------|------------------|--------|-------------|
| Count | Long | Read-only | Returns the number of `Procedure` objects in the `Procedures` collection |

## Methods

The `Procedures` collection object does not have any methods.

## Examples

The following script fragment iterates through the `Procedures` collection using the `For Each` loop syntax.

```
For Each objProcedure In objModule.Procedures
    strList = strList & "Name: " & objProcedure.Name
    strList = strList & vbNewLine & vbTab

    strList = strList & "Argument Count: " & objProcedure.NumArgs
    strList = strList & vbNewLine & vbTab

    strList = strList & "Has Return: " & objProcedure.HasReturnValue
    strList = strList & vbNewLine & vbNewLine
Next
```

# Error Object

The `Error` object provides information about syntax and runtime errors associated with the Script Control. Although information provided by the `Error` object is similar to that of the `Err` object in VB and VBScript, there are additional properties (`Column`, `Text`, `Line`) that are invaluable when diagnosing problems associated with the script. Although it is possible to declare and initialize the `Error` object in VB, it is common to access members of the `Error` object directly through the `ScriptControl` object.

Unlike the `Err` object, the `Error` object is not global in scope and only handles errors associated with a single instance of a `ScriptControl` object. The `Error` object is reset each time you change the `ScriptControl.Language` property, or when you call the `Reset`, `AddCode`, `Eval`, `ExecuteStatement`, or `Clear` methods of the `ScriptControl` object. Use the `Clear` method to explicitly reset the `Error` object properties. Runtime errors handled internally by the script will not be raised to the application level.

The section called *Error Handling with the Script Control* provides additional information about error handling strategies. Chapter 6, "Error Handling and Debugging," is also a good reference if you need a primer on VBScript error handling.

## Properties

The properties of the `Error` object are described in the following table.

| Name | Accepts/ Returns | Access | Description |
|---|---|---|---|
| Column | Long | Read-only | Returns the column number indicating the place where a syntax error occurred while adding script code |
| Description | String | Read-only | Returns a description of a script error |
| HelpContext | Long | Read Only | If the error raised from a script has a help file available (which is highly unlikely), this property returns the identifier for the section within the help file that has information about the error |
| HelpFile | String | Read-only | If the error raised from a script has a help file available (which is highly unlikely), this property returns the pathname to the help file |
| Line | Long | Read-only | Returns the line number indicating the place where a syntax error occurred while adding script code |
| Number | Long | Read-only | Returns the error number of a script error |
| Source | String | Read-only | Returns the name of the source where a script error occurred |
| Text | String | Readonly | Returns a string containing a snippet of code where a script syntax error has occurred. If you allow your users to add or edit scripts from within your application, you can use this property along with Description, Line, and Column to help the user understand how to fix the syntax error. Also useful for debugging scripts |

## Methods

The single method of the Error object is described in the following table.

| Name | Arguments | Returns | Description |
|---|---|---|---|
| Clear | None | N/A | Resets all of the properties of the Error object. This method is called implicitly when the ScriptControl.Language property is changed, or when the Reset, AddCode, Eval, or ExecuteStatement methods are called |

# Constants

The following named constants and enumerated constants are available to projects with a reference to the Script Control. These constants are globally available within any Visual Basic application that has a reference to the Script Control. For each of the constants, we explain the type, value(s), and where the constant is used.

## GlobalModule Named Constant

**Type:** `String`

**Value:** "Global"

When using the Script Control with scripting engines (like VBScript or Jscript) that support more than one module, use the `GlobalModule` constant to access the default "global" module in the `ScriptControl.Modules` collection.

## NoTimeout Named Constant

**Type:** `Long`

**Value:** `-1`

This constant can be used to set the `Timeout` property of the `ScriptControl` object, and prevent the execution from timing out. Please refer to the `ScriptControl.Timeout` property reference (previous) for more specifics.

## ScriptControlState Enumerated Constant

This enumerated constant is intended for use with the `ScriptControl.State` property. The purpose of the `State` property is to control how events raised by objects is added to the `ScriptControl` through the `AddObject` method. The default value, `Initialized` (0), means that the `ScriptControl` will *not* respond to events raised by these objects. The other possible value, `Connected` (1) means that the `ScriptControl` *will* respond to raised events.

# Error Handling with the Script Control

Error handling can never be underestimated, especially when dealing with several sources of code. This is especially true for dynamically generated scripts, and user-entered expressions. In order to handle the errors, you may have to work with both VBs `Err` object and the Script Control's `Error` object. If you are working with several instances of the Script Control, each will have a separate `Error` object. When an error occurs, if you have a proper strategy to handle the error, you may always clear the error and continue execution of the program. You should use all possible script error-handling techniques in your scripts (especially the scripts you load from files), and handle them internally as much as possible.

*Note: Depending on VBs settings, your error handlers may not work properly in debug mode (check Break on Unhandled Errors in IDEs General Options tab). In addition, error handlers in script will depend on the Disable Script Debugging option set in Internet Explorer, and on the availability of the debugger. Script errors may automatically invoke the debugger, bypassing your error handling code. Consult Chapter 6 for more information on script debugging.*

# Common Errors

The Script Control may raise several types of errors when setting global properties.

| Error | Description |
|-------|-------------|
| Can't execute; script is running | An attempt has been made to modify one of `ScriptControl` object's members while the script is running |
| Can't set `UseSafeSubset` property | The application hosting the Script Control may force it into safe mode |
| Executing script has timed out | Script execution has ended because it went over the time allotted in the `Timeout` property |
| Language property not set | Certain properties can only be set after the `Language` property is set |
| Member is not supported by selected scripting engine | When working with languages other than VBScript or JScript, not all of the properties and methods may be supported |
| Object is no longer valid | When the Script Control is reset (caused by call to the `Reset` method or change to `Language` property), objects that have been set previously are released |

These errors can most probably be avoided by careful programming, and should not be a big factor of your error handling strategy. The two cases when errors will be a major nuisance are when adding the scripting code to the Script Control (syntax errors in the script), and when executing it (runtime errors in the script). When an error occurs, you may inspect both the `Err` and `Error` objects; however, the Script Control's `Error` object provides additional information about the nature of the error. The following example shows hypothetical error handling through VB.

```
Dim strCode As String
Dim strValue As String
sc.Reset

On Error GoTo SyntaxErrorHandler
strCode = InputBox("Enter Function (name it Test(a))", _
    "Syntax Error Testing", _
    "Sub Test(a): MsgBox ""Result: "" & CStr(a*a): End Sub")

sc.AddCode strCode

On Error GoTo RuntimeErrorHandler
strValue = InputBox("Enter a Value for Test function", _
    "Runtime Error Testing", _
    "test")
sc.Run "Test", strValue

Exit Sub

SyntaxErrorHandler:
    MsgBox "Error # " & Err.Number & ": " & _
```

```
            Err.Description, vbCritical, "Syntax Error in Script"

    Exit Sub

RuntimeErrorHandler:
    MsgBox "Error # " & Err.Number & ": " & _
        Err.Description, vbCritical, "Runtime Error in Script"
```

There are several different ways in which VB can handle errors: through use of On Error GoTo [Label], and, as in VBScript, through On Error Resume Next and immediate testing of Err.Number. The following example illustrates the use of On Error Resume Next, combined with an inspection of the Err object as well as Script Control's Error object, which provides us with more information.

```
On Error Resume Next
    sc.AddCode strCode
    If Err Then
        With sc.Error
            MsgBox "Error # " & .Number & ": " _
                & .Description & vbCrLf _
                & "At Line: " & .Line & " Column: " & .Column _
                & " : " & .Text, vbCritical, "Syntax Error"
        End With
    Else
        MsgBox "No Error, result: " & CStr(sc.Run("Test", _
            strValue))
        If Err Then
            With sc.Error
                MsgBox "Error # " & .Number & ": " _
                & .Description & vbCrLf _
                & "At Line: " & .Line _
                    , vbCritical, "Runtime Error"
            End With
        End If
    End If
```

Finally, you may also use two of the events exposed by the ScriptControl object/control, Event and Timeout, to handle some of the errors; however, in some circumstances it may be a nuisance, and the use of the On Error... statement may be preferred because:

❑   The Timeout event will only occur for the initial ScriptControl object if more than one is in use

❑   The Script Control either has to be attached to a form, or has to be initialized using the WithEvents keyword, which may not always be desirable

❑   You may lose the granularity required when executing certain scripts that are likely to cause errors

You should use the Error event when you do not plan on adding any other error-handling script code to your application, as the following example code shows.

```
Private Sub sc_ Error()
    Dim strMsg As String

    With sc.Error
        strMsg = "Script error has occurred:" & vbCrLf & vbCrLf
```

```
            strMsg = strMsg & .Description & vbCrLf
            strMsg = strMsg & "Line # " & .Line
            ' Syntax errors have additional properties
            If InStr(.Source, "compilation") > 0 Then
                strMsg = strMsg & ", Column# " & .Column
                strMsg = strMsg & ", Text: " & .Text
            End If
            strMsg = strMsg & vbCrLf
        End With

        MsgBox strMsg, vbCritical, "Script Error"
        sc.Error.Clear
    End Sub
```

Note that when using the `ScriptControl Error` event, the event handler is invoked *before* any `On Error...` code. Hence, use of both error-handling techniques may produce double error messages and disable any effective error handling.

# Debugging

A quick note on debugging scripts hosted by your application using the Script Control: you can debug your native Visual Basic code in the VB IDE. However, in order to debug the code inside of a script, you have to use the freely downloadable Microsoft Script Debugger. When the debugger is installed, any unhandled errors or `Stop` statements inside of a script will invoke the debugger, just as with any other script. Please read Chapter 6, "Error Handling and Debugging," for more information on the Script Debugger and script debugging techniques.

Also, keep in mind that if the debugger is invoked during script execution, the script execution time as it relates to the `Timeout` property continues to accumulate. In other words, if your `Timeout` is set to 10,000 milliseconds (10 seconds) and the debugger comes up and the script pauses for more than 10 seconds, the Script Control will bring up the timeout dialog box.

For this reason, while you are debugging, you might want to set the `Timeout` property to `NoTimeout` (−1) and then set it to another value when you release to production. A good way to do this is to use a named constant for setting the Timeout value, but control the value of this constant using a conditional compilation flag and the `#IFDEF` statement, such as the following.

```
#IFDEF blnDebugging
        Const TIMEOUT_ VAL = -1
#ELSE
        Const TIMEOUT_ VAL = 15000
#ENDIF
...
objSC.Timeout = TIMEOUT_ VAL
...
```

# Using Encoded Scripts

The Script Control does support encoded scripts (see Chapter 14). There are two things to keep in mind.

First, when setting the Language property for an encoded script, set the property to "VBScript.Encode" instead of the normal "VBScript."

Second, if you are loading an encoded script from a file or database, you may have to use alternative techniques to account for the fact that an encoded script will have a lot of special characters. For loading from a file, you might want to use the scripting runtime TextStream object with the FileSystemObject.OpenTextFile method (see Chapter 7) rather than using native Visual Basic functions to open the file. For storing in and loading from a database, your best bet is to store the script as binary data rather than in a normal Char or VarChar column.

# Sample Project

The sample project, ComplexSC, demonstrates the basics of the Script Control, including how an application can share its objects with the script and pass static events—because of this requirement, the project is an ActiveX EXE type.

*You can download this sample project, and all of the other code in this book, from* wrox.com.

When building database applications that depend on an outside database, we always encounter the problem of feeding the application with the connection string associated with the appropriate database and the appropriate server. Often, this information is retrieved from the system registry, identifying the software author and the application, and then by a custom key:

*Sample Registry Path*: SOFTWARE\Company Name\App Name\

*Sample Key Name*: MyAppConnection

The sample project provides a way to create, store, and edit registry settings for application settings such as connection strings. The Visual Basic form and code in the ComplexSC project are designed to be generic and customized through a script. This means that you can distribute a new script without having to recompile or redistribute the VB application.

Figure 18-2 shows the main form of the ComplexSC project.

The possibilities here are almost endless: by exposing the objects in the application, and passing some of the events to the script, the script can act as a macro and adapt to your needs. There are some idiosyncrasies, especially when it comes to passing events between the form and the script. To make this possible, all of the controls are placed on the form at design time, some of them in control arrays. The script can easily control all of the properties and methods of all controls, but when the control arrays (optional connection string tags and their values) are used, dynamic modification of the form members is simplified. Here, depending on the choice of connection (OLE DB, ODBC, and DSN) we can display different labels and editable values associated with the connection type.

Sharing of the form members is easily achieved through the CShared class, which allows us to share the main form and all of its members with a script (shown below). Although we could expose individual elements as opposed to the entire form, and prevent the script from manipulating any of the elements we want protected, in the case of this application it is simply not necessary.

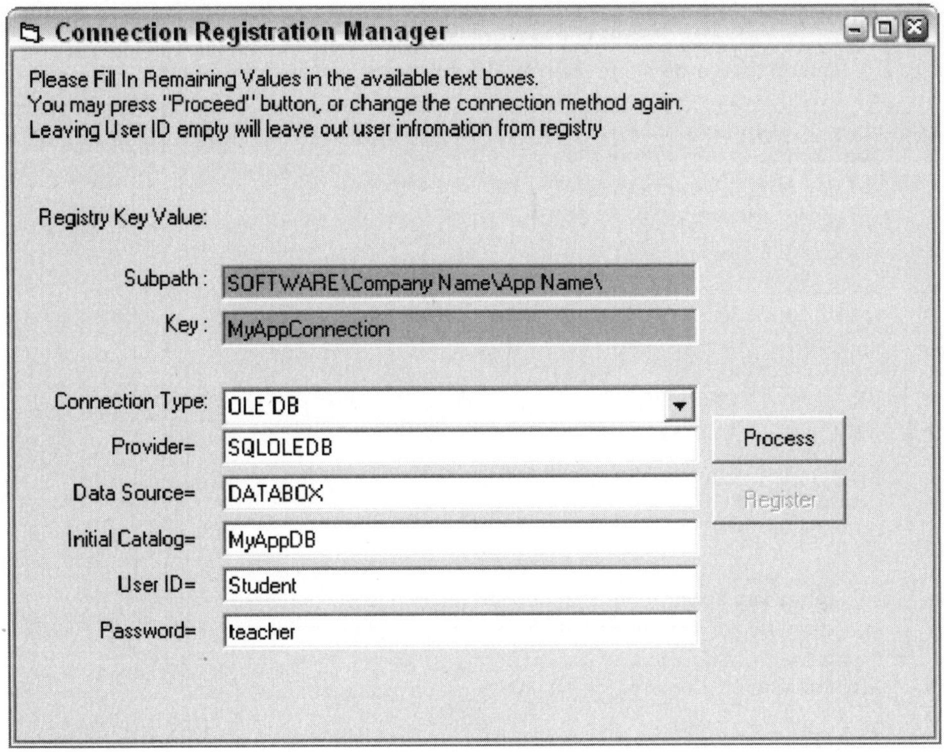

**Figure 18-2**

```
Option Explicit

Private m_Form As Form

Public Property Get Form() As Object
    Set Form = m_Form
End Property

Friend Property Set Form(ByVal newValue As Object)
    Set m_Form = newValue
End Property
```

What we are doing here is wrapping the form in the CShared class. With the CShared class in place, we need to use the AddObject method of the Script Control to share the form with the script. This is done via the InitScriptControl procedure, which is executed when the form is loaded (called from the Form_Load event handler). We are passing the reference to the VB form, exposed through the CShared .Form property.

```
Private Sub Form_Load()
    Set objScript = InitScriptControl(Me)
End Sub
```

The `InitScriptControl` instantiates the `ScriptControl` object, loads the script, instantiates the `CShared` object, and exposes it to the Script Control. Because we set the third parameter of the `AddObject` method to true, all of the members of the form are shared too.

```
Function InitScriptControl(frmForm As Form) As ScriptControl
    Dim objSC As ScriptControl
    Dim fileName As String, intFnum As Integer
    Dim objShare As New CShared

    ' create a new instance of the control
    Set objSC = New ScriptControl
    objSC.Language = "VBScript"
    objSC.AllowUI = True
    Set objShare.Form = frmForm
    objSC.AddObject "share", objShare, True

    ' load the code into the script control
    fileName = App.Path & "\ regeditor.scp"
    intFnum = FreeFile
    Open fileName For Input As #intFnum

    objSC.AddCode Input$(LOF(intFnum), intFnum)
    Close #intFnum

    ' return to the caller
    Set InitScriptControl = objSC

End Function
```

After the Script Control is initialized, the `Form_Load` code calls the `Init` procedure in the script, which sets up all of the necessary controls on the form. In actuality, some of the controls are pre-set with certain properties (such as background color, enabled, and so on.), while others are initialized by the script by accessing the members of the form exposed by `CShared.Form`.

```
Sub Init()
    Dim i, strTmp

    Form.Caption = "Connection Registration Manager"
    strTmp = "This application saves the database connection"
    strTmp = strTMP & string in the registry. " & vbCrLf
    Form.lblExplanation = strTmp
    Form.lblRegistry.Caption = ""

    ' this information should be reflected in your application
    ' the standard is to store the registry keys in subhives
    ' for different companies and projects
    Form.txtSubpath.Text = "SOFTWARE\ Company Name\ App Name\ "

    ' finally the name of the key
    ' you could similarly extend this application so it would
    ' work like a wizard, and register several keys
    Form.txtKey.Text = "MyAppConnection"
    Form.lblRegistry.Caption = ""
    Form.cmdRegister.Enabled = False
```

```
            Form.cmdProcess.Enabled = True
            For i = 0 To 5
                Form.lblLabel(i).Visible = False
                Form.txtText(i).Visible = False
            Next

            Form.cboCombo.Clear
            Form.cboCombo.AddItem "OLE DB"
            Form.cboCombo.AddItem "ODBC"
            Form.cboCombo.AddItem "DSN"
    End Sub
```

Next, we need to respond to events generated by the application. In this simple case, we simply pass the events as intercepted by the application directly to the script. Hence, our application may have the following events passed to the script.

```
    Private Sub cboCombo_Click()
        objScript.Run "cboCombo_Click"
    End Sub

    Private Sub txtText_KeyPress(Index As Integer, KeyAscii As Integer)
        KeyAscii = objScript.Run("txtText_KeyPress",Index, KeyAscii)
    End Sub
```

As the example shows, we pass the events directly to the script, optionally passing along the parameters generated by the event. Because in certain cases we might want to modify one of the parameters, we should treat the event-handling procedure as a function, which would return the modified value. This is probably the simplest mechanism for modifying such parameters. Although this functionality is not required by our application, the following function inside the script would capitalize each character entered into one of the text boxes.

```
    Function txtText_KeyPress(Index , KeyAscii)
      txtText_KeyPress = Asc(Ucase(Chr(KeyAscii)))
    End Function
```

This approach is a little different from what you'd expect in VB code, because even if we pass the value of KeyAscii by reference (normal VB code would be KeyAscii = Asc(Ucase(Chr(KeyAscii)))), the script will not update this value back in VB. Hence, we employ a simple work around by turning the event handler from procedure into a function.

It is also possible to override the default event handling, or to provide optional event handling in the script. When the script does not have the member procedure, an error is generated, which provides us with a possibility of either ignoring events or providing default events, in case the script does not have an appropriately named procedure. The following example shows the simplest error trapping, which allows us to create a default event handler. Moreover, when the error handler is disabled (with On Error Resume Next), the script must contain an appropriately named procedure with the correct number of parameters.

```
    Private Sub cboCombo_Click()
        On Error Resume Next
            objScript.Run "cboCombo_Click"
        If Err = 0 Then Exit Sub
        ' default event handler goes here...
    End Sub
```

Details of the application lie in the script itself, so rather than copying the entire code listing, the following example only shows partial implementation of the cboCombo_Click procedure within the script. After the key controls are reset, we set up values of the labels and the associated text that would correspond to an OLE DB type connection string.

```
Sub cboCombo_Click()
    Dim strComboSelection, strTmp

    ' Clean Up in case this was pressed already
    Form.cmdRegister.Enabled = False
    Form.cmdProcess.Enabled = True
    Form.lblRegistry.Caption = ""
    For i = 0 To 5
        Form.lblLabel(i).Visible = False
        Form.txtText(i).Visible = False
    Next

    strComboSelection = _
            Trim(Form.cboCombo.List(Form.cboCombo.ListIndex))
    Select Case strComboSelection
        Case "OLE DB"
            For i = 0 To 4
                Form.lblLabel(i).Visible = True
                Form.txtText(i).Visible = True
            Next
            Form.lblLabel(0).Caption = "Provider="
            Form.lblLabel(1).Caption = "Data Source="
            Form.lblLabel(2).Caption = "Initial Catalog="
            Form.lblLabel(3).Caption = "User ID="
            Form.lblLabel(4).Caption = "Password="
            Form.txtText(0).Text = "SQLOLEDB"
            Form.txtText(1).Text = "DATABOX"
            Form.txtText(2).Text = "MyAppDB"
            Form.txtText(3).Text = "Student"
            Form.txtText(4).Text = "teacher"

    [...]

    End Select
    strTmp = "Please Fill In Remaining Values in the available"
    strTmp = strTmp & " text boxes. " & vbCrLf
    strTmp = strTmp & "You may press ""Proceed"" button, or"
    strTmp = strTmp & " change the connection method again. "
    strTmp = strTmp & "Leaving User ID empty will leave out"
    strTmp = strTmp & " user infromation from registry"
    Form.lblExplanation = strTmp
End Sub
```

The remainder of the application responds to the end-user events, and builds the connection string as required by the core application, enabling and disabling controls, and modifying values on the form, depending on the "stage." The last action is actually carried out directly by the application itself; a value is written to the registry based on the string that is stored in one of the labels on the form.

This little application can be further extended to take advantage of several scripts, and provide wizard-like functionality that can easily be scripted.

# Summary

The Script Control is a free control provided by Microsoft that enables your application to host a scripting engine. Uses of the Script Control can range from simple dynamic evaluation of expressions, to a full-fledged macro language add-on capable of automating your applications.

This chapter covered the following topics:

- ❑ What the Script Control is
- ❑ How the Script Control can be a useful addition to your Visual Basic application
- ❑ Why you would want to consider using the Script Control (or why not)
- ❑ The Script Control object model, including its properties, methods, and events
- ❑ Error handling and debugging
- ❑ A sample project demonstrating the use of the Script Control

# VBScript Functions and Keywords

This appendix contains a complete reference of functions and keywords in VBScript 5.6. You will also find a list of the VB/VBA functions and keywords that are not supported in VBScript. Where appropriate an alternative to an unsupported function or keyword is shown.

## Operators

An operator acts on one or more operands when comparing, assigning, concatenating, calculating, and performing logical operations.

## Assignment Operator

The assignment operator is simply used for assigning a value to a variable or property. See the `Set` keyword for an explanation of how to reference and assign objects.

| = | Name | Assignment |
|---|---|---|
| | Description | Assigns the result of an expression, the value of a constant, or the value of another variable to a variable or property. |
| | Syntax | `Variable = value` |

## Arithmetic Operators

The arithmetic operators are all used to calculate a numeric value, and are normally used in conjunction with the assignment operator and/or one of the comparison operators; they are listed in order of operator precedence.

| ^ | Name | Exponentiation |
|---|---|---|
| | Description | Raises a number to the power of an exponent. |
| | Syntax | `Result = number ^ exponent`<br><br>`number` and `exponent` is any valid numeric expression. |
| | Example | `MsgBox 5 ^ 5`<br><br>MsgBox displays 3125, which is the result of raising the number 5 to the exponent 5. |

| * | Name | Multiplication |
|---|---|---|
| | Description | Multiplies two numbers. |
| | Syntax | `Result = number1 * number2`<br><br>`number1` and `number2` is any valid numeric expression. |
| | Example | `MsgBox 5 * 5`<br><br>MsgBox displays 25, which is the result of multiplying the number 5 by 5. |

| / | Name | Floating-point division |
|---|---|---|
| | Description | Returns a floating-point result when dividing two numbers. |
| | Syntax | `Result = number1/number2`<br><br>`number1` and `number2` is any valid numeric expression. |
| | Example | `MsgBox 5 / 4`<br><br>MsgBox displays 1.25, which is the result of dividing the number 5 by 4. |

| \ | Name | Integer division |
|---|---|---|
| | Description | Returns the integer part of the result when dividing two numbers. |
| | Syntax | `Result = number1\number2`<br><br>`number1` and `number2` is any valid numeric expression. |

| | Example | `MsgBox 5\4` |
|---|---|---|
| | | MsgBox displays 1, which is the integer part of the result, when dividing the number 5 with 4. |
| | Notes | The numeric expressions are rounded to `Byte`, `Integer`, or `Long` subtype expressions, before the integer division is performed. They are rounded to the smallest possible subtype; that is, a value of 255 will be rounded to a `Byte`, 256 will be rounded to an `Integer`, and so on. |
| Mod | Name | Modulus division |
| | Description | Returns the remainder when dividing two numbers. |
| | Syntax | `Result = number1 Mod number2`<br>number1 and number2 is any valid numeric expression. |
| | Example | `MsgBox 5 Mod 4`<br>MsgBox displays 1, which is the remainder part of the result, when dividing the number 5 with 4. |
| | Notes | The numeric expressions are rounded to `Byte`, `Integer`, or `Long` subtype expressions, before the modulus division is performed. They are rounded to the smallest possible subtype; that is, a value of 255 will be rounded to a `Byte`, 256 will be rounded to an `Integer`, and so on. |
| + | Name | Addition |
| | Description | Sums two expressions. |
| | Syntax | `Result = expression1 + expression2`<br>expression1 and expression2 is any valid numeric expression. |
| | Example | `MsgBox 5 + 5`<br>MsgBox displays 10, which is the result of adding the expression 5 to 5. |

*Continues*

| | Notes | If one or both expressions are numeric, the expressions will be summed, but if both expressions are strings, they will be concatenated. This is important to understand, especially if you have a Java background, in order to avoid runtime errors. In general, use the & operator (see under *Concatenation Operators*) when concatenating, and the + operator when dealing with numbers. |
|---|---|---|
| − | Name | Subtraction |
| | Description | Subtracts one number from another or indicates the negative value of an expression. |
| | Syntax (1) | `Result = number1 - number2`<br>`number1` and `number2` is any valid numeric expression. |
| | Example (1) | `MsgBox 5 - 4`<br><br>`MsgBox` displays 1, which is the result of subtracting the number 4 from 5. |
| | Syntax (2) | `-number`<br>`number` is any valid numeric expression. |
| | Example (2) | `MsgBox -(5 - 4)`<br><br>`MsgBox` displays −1, which is the result of subtracting the number 4 from 5 and using the unary negation operator (−) to indicate a negative value. |

## Concatenation Operators

Concatenation operators are used for concatenating expressions; they are listed in order of operator precedence.

| & | Name | Ampersand |
|---|---|---|
| | Description | Concatenates two expressions. |
| | Syntax | Returns the concatenated expressions.<br>`Result = expression1 &`<br>`expression2` |

| | Example | If expression1 is "WROX" and expression2 is "Press" then the result is "WROX Press". |
|---|---|---|
| | Notes | The expressions are converted to a String subtype, if they are not already of this subtype. |

| + | Name | + Operator |
|---|---|---|
| | Description | Does the same as the & operator if both expressions are strings. |
| | Syntax | Returns the concatenated or summed expressions.<br><br>`Result = expression1 + expression2` |
| | Example | `1 + "1" = 2`<br>`"1" + "1" = "11"` |
| | Notes | If one or both expressions are numeric, the + operator will work as an arithmetic + operator and sum the expressions. A runtime error occurs if one expression is numeric and the other a string containing no numbers. It is recommended that + should be used only for numeric addition and never for concatenation purposes (use & instead). |

## Comparison Operators

The comparison operators are used for comparing variables and expressions against other variables, constants, or expressions; they are listed in order of operator precedence.

| = | Name | Equal to |
|---|---|---|
| | Description | Returns True if expression1 is equal to expression2; False otherwise. |
| | Syntax | `Result = expression1 = expression2` |

| <> | Name | Not equal to |
|---|---|---|
|  | Description | Returns `True` if expression1 is not equal to expression2; `False` otherwise. |
|  | Syntax | `Result = expression1 <> expression2` |

| < | Name | Less than |
|---|---|---|
|  | Description | Returns `True` if expression1 is less than expression2; `False` otherwise. |
|  | Syntax | `Result = expression1 < expression2` |

| > | Name | Greater than |
|---|---|---|
|  | Description | Returns `True` if expression1 is greater than expression2; `False` otherwise. |
|  | Syntax | `Result = expression1 > expression2` |

| <= | Name | Less than or equal to |
|---|---|---|
|  | Description | Returns `True` if expression1 is less than or equal to expression2; `False` otherwise. |
|  | Syntax | `Result = expression1 <= expression2` |

| >= | Name | Greater than or equal to |
|---|---|---|
|  | Description | Returns `True` if expression1 is greater than or equal to expression2; `False` otherwise. |
|  | Syntax | `Result = expression1 >= expression2` |

| Is | Name | Compare objects |
|---|---|---|
| | Description | Returns `True` if `object1` and `object2` refer to the same memory location (if they are in fact the same object). |
| | Syntax | `Result = object1 Is object2` |
| | Note | Use the `Not` operator (see under *Logical Operators*) with the `Is` operator to get the opposite effect. |
| | | `Result = object1 Not Is object2` |
| | | Use the `Nothing` keyword with the `Is` operator to check if an object reference is valid. Returns `True` if object has been destroyed (`Set object = Nothing`). |
| | | `Result = object Is Nothing` |
| | | Be careful, `Nothing` is *not* the same as `Empty`. `Nothing` references an invalid object reference, whereas `Empty` is used for any variable, which has been assigned the value of `Empty`, or has not yet been assigned a value. |

## Logical Operators

The logical operators are used for performing logical operations on expressions; they are listed in order of operator precedence. All logical operators can also be used as bitwise operators (see under *Bitwise Operators*).

| Not | Used to | Negate the expression |
|---|---|---|
| | Returns | Returns the logical negation of an expression. |
| | Syntax | `Result = Not expression` |
| | Note | Result will be `True` if expression is `False`; and `False` if expression is `True`. `Null` will be returned if expression is `Null`. |

| And | Used to | Check if both expressions are true. |
|---|---|---|
| | Returns | Returns `True` if both expressions evaluate to `True`; otherwise, `False` is returned. |
| | Syntax | `Result = expression1 And expression2` |

| Or | Used to | Check if one or both expressions are true. |
|---|---|---|
| | Returns | Returns `True` if one or both expressions evaluate to `True`; otherwise `False` is returned. |
| | Syntax | `Result = expression1 Or expression2` |

| Xor | Used to | Check if one and only one expression is true. |
|---|---|---|
| | Returns | `Null` will be returned if either expression is `Null`. |
| | Syntax | `Result = expression1 Xor expression2` |
| | Note | Returns `True` if only one of the expressions evaluates to `True`; otherwise `False` is returned. |

| Eqv | Used to | Check if both expressions evaluate to the same value. |
|---|---|---|
| | Returns | Returns `True` if both expressions evaluate to the same value (`True` or `False`). |
| | Syntax | `Result = expression1 Eqv expression2` |
| | Note | `Null` will be returned if either expression is `Null`. |

| Imp | Used to | Perform a logical implication. |
|---|---|---|
| | Returns | Returns these values: |
| | | `true Imp true = true` |
| | | `false Imp true = true` |
| | | `false Imp false = true` |
| | | `false Imp Null = true` |
| | | `Null Imp true = true` |
| | | `true Imp false = false` |
| | | `true Imp Null = Null` |
| | | `Null Imp false = Null` |
| | | `Null Imp Null = Null` |
| | Syntax | `Result = expression1 Imp expression2` |

# Bitwise Operators

Bitwise operators are used for comparing binary values bit-by-bit; they are listed in order of operator precedence. All bitwise operators can also be used as logical operators (see under *Logical Operators*).

| Not | Used to | Invert the bit values. |
|---|---|---|
| | Returns | Returns 1 if bit is 0 and vice versa. |
| | Syntax | `Result = Not expression`<br>If expression is 101 then result is 010. |

| And | Used to | Check if both bits are set to 1. |
|---|---|---|
| | Returns | Returns 1 if both bits are 1; otherwise 0 is returned. |
| | Syntax | `Result = expression1 And expression2`<br>If expression1 is 101 and expression2 is 100 then result is 100. |

| Or | Used to | Check if one of the bits is set to 1. |
|---|---|---|
| | Returns | Returns 1 if one or both bits are 1; otherwise 0 is returned. |
| | Syntax | `Result = expression1 or expression2`<br>If expression1 is 101 and expression2 is 100 then result is 101. |

| Xor | Used to | Check if one and only one of the bits is set to 1. |
|---|---|---|
| | Returns | Returns 1 if only one of the bits is 1; otherwise 0 is returned. |
| | Syntax | `Result = expression1 Xor expression2`<br>If expression1 is 101 and expression2 is 100 then result is 001. |

| Eqv | Used to | Checks if both bits evaluate to the same value. |
|---|---|---|
| | Returns | Returns 1 if both the bits have the same value; otherwise 0 is returned. |
| | Syntax | `Result = expression1 Eqv expression2`<br>If expression1 is 101 and expression2 is 100 then result is 110. |

| Imp | Used to | Performs a logical implication on 2 bits. |
|---|---|---|
| | Returns | Returns these values: <br> `0 Imp 0 = 1` `0 Imp 1 = 1` <br> `1 Imp 1 = 1` <br> `1 Imp 0 = 0` |
| | Syntax | `Result = expression1 Imp expression2` <br> If `expression1` is `101` and `expression2` is `100` then result is `110`. |

## Operator Precedence

When more than one operation occurs in an expression they are normally performed from left to right. However, there are several rules.

Operators from the arithmetic group are evaluated first, and then concatenation, comparison, and logical operators.

This is the complete order in which operations occur (operators in brackets have the same precedence):

❑ `^, −, (*, /), \, Mod, (+, −)`

❑ `&`

❑ `=, <>, <, >, <=, >=, Is`

❑ Not, And, Or, Xor, Eqv, Imp

This order can be overridden by using parentheses. Operations in parentheses are evaluated before operations outside the parentheses, but inside the parentheses, the normal precedence rules apply.

## Unsupported Operators

The following VB/VBA operator is not supported in VBScript:

❑ `Like`

## Math Functions

The following listing is in alphabetical order.

| Abs | Returns the absolute value of a number, that is, its unsigned magnitude. |
|---|---|
| Syntax | `Abs (number)` <br> `number` is any valid numeric expression. |
| Note | `Null` will be returned if number contains `Null`. |
| Example | `Abs(-50)  ' 50` <br> `Abs(50)  ' 50` |
| See also | `Sgn` |

| | |
|---|---|
| Atn | Returns the arctangent of a number as `Variant` subtype `Double(5)`. |
| Syntax | `Atn(number)`<br>number is any valid numeric expression. |
| Note | This function takes the ratio of two sides of a right-angled triangle (number) and returns the corresponding angle in radians. The ratio is the length of the side opposite the angle divided by the length of the side adjacent to the angle. The range of the result is $-\pi/2$ to $\pi/2$ radians. |
| Example | ```<br>Dim dblPi<br><br>' Calculate the<br>' value of Pi<br>dblPi = 4 * Atn(1)<br>``` |
| See also | Cos, Sin, and Tan |

| | |
|---|---|
| Cos | Returns the cosine of an angle as `Variant` subtype `Double(5)`. |
| Syntax | `Cos(number)`<br>number is any valid numeric expression that expresses an angle in radians. |
| Note | This function takes an angle and returns the ratio of two sides of a right-angled triangle. The ratio is the length of the side adjacent to the angle divided by the length of the hypotenuse (dblSecant). The result is within the range $-1$ to $1$, both inclusive. |
| Example | ```<br>Dim dblAngle, dblSecant<br>Dim dblLength<br><br>dblLength = 10<br>        ' Convert 30° to radians<br>dblAngle = (30 * 3.14 / 180)<br>dblSecant = dblLength /<br>Cos(dblAngle)<br>``` |
| See also | Atn, Sin, and Tan |

| | |
|---|---|
| Exp | Returns a `Variant` subtype `Double(5)` specifying e (the base of natural logarithms) raised to a power. |
| Syntax | `Exp(number)`<br>Number is any valid numeric expression. |
| Note | A runtime error occurs if number is larger than 709.782712893. e is approximately 2.718282.<br><br>Sometimes this function is referred to as the antilogarithm, and complements the action of the Log function. |

*Continues*

| | |
|---|---|
| Example | ```
Dim dblAngle, dblHSin

dblAngle = 1.3
dblHSin = (Exp( dblAngle) - Exp( -1 * dblAngle)) / 2
```
Here the Exp function is used to return e raised to a power. |
| See also | Log |

| | |
|---|---|
| Fix | Returns the integer part of a number. |
| Syntax | Fix(number) |
| Note | Fix is internationally aware, which means that the return value is based on the locale settings on the machine.

Null is returned if number contains Null. The data type returned will be decided from the size of the integer part. Possible return data types in ascending order:

Integer

Long

Double

If number is negative, the first negative integer equal to or greater than number is returned. |
| Example | ```
Dim vntPosValue
Dim vntNegValue

vntPosValue = Fix(5579.56)
vntNegValue = Fix(-5579.56)
```

vntPosValue now holds the value 5579, and vntNegValue the value –5579.

Fix is the equivalent of Int when dealing with nonnegative numbers. When you handle negative numbers, Fix returns the first negative integer, greater than, or equal to the number supplied. |
| Note | Int, Round, and the conversion functions CInt and CLng |

| | |
|---|---|
| Int | Returns the integer part of a number. |
| Syntax | Int(number)

Number is any valid numeric expression. |
| Note | Int is internationally aware, which means that the return value is based on the locale settings on the machine.

Null is returned if number contains Null. The data type returned will be decided from the size of the integer part. Possible return data types in ascending order:

Integer

Long

Double |

If `number` is negative, the first negative integer equal to or less than number is returned.

| | |
|---|---|
| Example | ```
Dim vntPosValue
Dim vntNegValue

    vntPosValue = Int(5579.56)
    vntNegValue = Int(-5579.56)
``` |

`vntPosValue` now holds the value 5579, and `vntNegValue` the value –5580.

`Int` is the equivalent of `Fix` when dealing with nonnegative numbers. When you handle negative numbers, `Int` returns the first negative integer, less than, or equal to the number supplied.

| | |
|---|---|
| See also | `Fix`, `Round`, and the conversion functions `CInt` and `CLng` |

| | |
|---|---|
| `Log` | Returns the natural logarithm of a number. |
| Syntax | `Log(number)`<br><br>`number` is any valid numeric expression greater than zero. |
| Example | ```
Dim vntValueBase10

    vntValueBase10 = Log(5) / Log(10)
```<br><br>This sample code calculates the base-10 logarithm of the number 5, which is 0.698970004336019. |
| See also | `Exp` |

| | |
|---|---|
| `Randomize` | Initializes the random number generator, by giving it a new seed-value. A *seed-value* is an initial value used for generating random numbers. |
| Syntax | `Randomize[number]`<br><br>`Number` is any valid numeric expression. |
| Note | You can repeat a sequence of random numbers, by calling the `Rnd` function with a negative number, before using the `Randomize` statement with a numeric argument. |
| Example | ```
Const LNG_UPPER_BOUND = 20
Const LNG_LOWER_BOUND = 1

Dim intValue
Dim lngCounterIn
Dim lngCounterOut

    For lngCounterOut = 1 To 3
        Rnd -1
``` |

*Continues*
```

```
                    Randomize 3

                For lngCounterIn = 1 To 3
                    intValue =
            Int((LNG_UPPER_BOUND -
            LNG_LOWER_BOUND + 1) * _
                    Rnd + LNG_LOWER_BOUND)
                    MsgBox intValue
                Next
            Next
```

This sample has an inner loop that generates three random numbers and an outer loop that calls the Rnd function with a negative number, immediately before calling Randomize with an argument. This makes sure that the random numbers generated in the inner loop will be the same for every loop the outer loop performs.

| See also | Rnd |
|---|---|

| Rnd | Returns a random number, less than 1 but greater than or equal to 0. |
|---|---|
| Syntax | Rnd[(number)] |

number (Optional) is any valid numeric expression that determines how the random number is generated; if number is:

< 0—uses same number every time

> 0 or missing—uses next random number in sequence

= 0—uses most recently generated number.

| Note | Use the Randomize statement, with no argument, to initialize the random-number generator with a seed based on the system timer, before calling Rnd. |
|---|---|

The same number sequence is generated for any given initial seed, because each successive call to Rnd uses the previous number as the seed for the next number in the sequence.

Call Rnd with a negative argument immediately before using Randomize with a numeric argument, in order to repeat sequences of random numbers.

| Example | ``` |
|---|---|

```
            Const LNG_UPPER_BOUND = 20
            Const LNG_LOWER_BOUND = 1

            Dim intValue
            Dim lngCounter

                For lngCounter = 1 To 10
                    intValue = Int( _
                                (LNG_UPPER_BOUND
            - _
```

```
                              LNG_LOWER_BOUND + 1) * _
                              Rnd + LNG_LOWER_BOUND)

                        MsgBox intValue
                    Next
```

This produces 10 random integers in the range 1–20.

| | |
|---|---|
| See also | `Randomize` |

| | |
|---|---|
| Round | Returns a number rounded to a specified number of decimal places as a `Variant` subtype `Double(5)`. |
| Syntax | `Round(number, [numdecimalplaces])`<br><br>`number` is any valid numeric expression.<br><br>`numdecimalplaces` (Optional) indicates how many places to the right of the decimal separator should be included in the rounding. |
| Note | An integer is returned if `numdecimalplaces` is missing. |
| Example | `Round(10.4)        ' Returns 10`<br>`Round(10.456)      ' Returns 10`<br>`Round(-10.456)     ' Returns -10`<br>`Round(10.4, 1)     ' Returns 10.4`<br>`Round(10.456, 2)   ' Returns 10.46`<br>`Round(-10.456, 2)  ' Returns -10.46` |
| See also | `Int` and `Fix` |

| | |
|---|---|
| Sgn | Returns an integer indicating the sign of a number. |
| Syntax | `Sgn(number)`<br><br>`Number` is any valid numeric expression. |
| Note | `Sgn` returns the following when number is:<br>`< 0  —  -1`<br>`= 0  —  0`<br>`> 0  —  1` |
| Example | `Sgn(10.4) ' Returns 1`<br>`Sgn(0)     ' Returns 0`<br>`Sgn(-2)    ' Returns -1` |
| See also | `Abs` |

| | |
|---|---|
| Sin | Returns a `Variant` subtype `Double(5)` specifying the sine of an angle. |
| Syntax | `Sin(number)`<br><br>`number` is any valid numeric expression that expresses an angle in radians. |

*Continues*

| | |
|---|---|
| Note | This function takes an angle and returns the ratio of two sides of a right-angled triangle. The ratio is the length of the side opposite the angle (`dblCosecant`) divided by the length of the hypotenuse (`dblSecant`). The result is within the range −1 to 1, both inclusive. |
| Example | ```
Dim dblAngle, dblCosecant
Dim dblSecant
    dblSecant = 11.545
            ' Convert 30° to radians
    dblAngle = (30 * 3.14 / 180)
    dblCosecant = dblSecant *
Sin(dblAngle)
```<br><br>Here the `Sin` function is used to return the sine of an angle. |
| See also | `Atn`, `Cos`, and `Tan` |

| | |
|---|---|
| `Sqr` | Returns the square root of a number. |
| Syntax | `Sqr(number)`<br><br>`number` is any valid numeric expression greater than or equal to zero. |
| Example | `Sqr(16)  ' Returns 4` |

| | |
|---|---|
| `Tan` | Returns a `Variant` subtype `Double(5)` specifying the tangent of an angle. |
| Syntax | `Tan(number)`<br><br>`number` is any valid numeric expression that expresses an angle in radians. |
| Note | This function takes an angle and returns the ratio of two sides of a right-angled triangle. The ratio is the length of the side opposite the angle (`dblCosecant`) divided by the length of the side adjacent to the angle (`dblLength`).<br><br>The result is within the range −1 to 1, both inclusive. |
| Example | ```
Tan(10.4) ' Returns 1.47566791425166
Tan(0)    ' Returns 0
Tan(-2)   ' Returns 2.18503986326152
``` |
| See also | `Atn`, `Cos`, and `Sin` |

# Date and Time Functions and Statements

There are a number of ways to display and represent dates and times. This includes date literals, which are valid date expression, enclosed in number signs (#). You need to be careful when using date literals because VBScript lets you use only the US date format, mm/dd/yyyy. This is true even if a different locale is being used on the machine. This might lead to problems when trying to use date literals in other formats, because in most cases the date will be accepted although converted to a different date. #10/12/2003# will be interpreted as October 12, 2003, but you might in fact want December 10, 2003, because your locale settings interpret dates as dd/mm/yyyy. Date literals accept only the forward slash (/) as the date separator.

The data range for a date is January 1, 100, to December 31, 9999, both inclusive. Internally, dates are stored as part of real numbers or to be more specific as a `Variant` subtype `Double(5)`. The digits to the left of the decimal separator represent the date and the digits to the right of the decimal separator represent the time. Negative numbers are used internally for representing dates prior to December 30, 1899.

The following is a list of functions used for converting and formatting dates and times.

| | |
|---|---|
| `Cdate` | Returns an expression converted to `Variant` subtype `Date(7)`. |
| Syntax | `CDate(date)`<br>`date` is any valid date expression. |
| Note | `CDate` is internationally aware, which means that the return value is based on the locale settings on the machine. Dates and times will be formatted with the appropriate time and date separators, and for dates the correct order of year, month, and day are applied. Date and time literals are recognized. |
| Example | `Dim dtmValue`<br><br>`dtmValue = CDate( #12/10/2003#)`<br><br>`dtmValue` now holds the value `10-12-03`, if your locale settings use the dash (–) as the date separator and the short date format is dd/mm/yy. |
| See also | `IsDate` |

| | |
|---|---|
| `Date` | Returns a `Variant` subtype `Date(7)` indicating the current system date. |
| Syntax | `Date` |
| Example | `MsgBox Date`<br><br>Assuming that today is February 28, 2004, the `MsgBox` now displays 28-02-04, if your locale settings use the dash (–) as the date separator and the short date format is dd/mm/yy. |
| See also | `Now` and `Time` |

| | |
|---|---|
| DateAdd | Adds or subtracts a time interval to a specified date and returns the new date. |
| Syntax | DateAdd(interval, number, date)<br>Interval can have these values: |

d    Day
h    Hour
m    Month
n    Minute
q    Quarter
s    Second
w    Weekday
ww   Week of year
y    Day of year
yyyy Year

number is a numeric expression that must be positive if you want to add or negative if you want to subtract.

number is rounded to the nearest whole number if it's not a Long value.

date must be a Variant or Date literal to which interval is added.

| | |
|---|---|
| Note | DateAdd is internationally aware, which means that the return value is based on the locale settings on the machine. Dates and times will be formatted with the appropriate time and date separators and for dates the correct order of year, month, and day are applied. An error occurs if the date returned is less than the year 100. |
| Example | MsgBox DateAdd("m", 3, "1-Jan-04")<br><br>This will add 3 months to January 1, 2004, and the MsgBox now displays 01-04-04, if your locale settings use the dash (–) as the date separator and the short date format is dd/mm/yy. |
| See also | DateDiff and DatePart |

| | |
|---|---|
| DateDiff | Returns the interval between two dates. |
| | DateDiff(interval, date1, date2, [firstdayofweek], [firstweekofyear])<br>Interval can have these values: |

d    Day
h    Hour
m    Month
n    Minute
q    Quarter
s    Second
w    Weekday
ww   Week of year
y    Day of year
yyyy Year

date1 and date2 are date expressions.

firstdayofweek (Optional) specifies the first day of the week. Use one of the following constants:

vbUseSystemDayOfWeek 0 (National Language Support (NLS) API setting. NLS functions help Win32-based applications support the differing language- and location-specific needs of users around the world)

| | |
|---|---|
| vbSunday | 1 (Default) |
| vbMonday | 2 |
| vbTuesday | 3 |
| vbWednesday | 4 |
| vbThursday | 5 |
| vbFriday | 6 |
| vbSaturday | 7 |

firstweekofyear (Optional) specifies the first week of the year. Use one of the following constants:

vbUseSystem 0 (Use NLS API setting)

vbFirstJan1 1 (Default)

(Week in which January 1 occurs)

vbFirstFourDays 2 (First week in the new year with at least four4 days)

vbFirstFullWeek 3 (First full week of the new year)

| | |
|---|---|
| Note | A negative number is returned if date1 is later in time than date2. |
| Example | MsgBox DateDiff("yyyy", #06-12-1972#, Now) |
| | This will calculate the number of years between 06/12/1972 and now. In 2004, the MsgBox will display 32. |
| See also | DateAdd and DatePart |

| | |
|---|---|
| DatePart | Returns a specified part of a date. |
| Syntax | DatePart(interval, date, [firstdayofweek], [firstweekofyear]) |
| | Interval can have these values: |

| | |
|---|---|
| d | Day |
| h | Hour |
| m | Month |
| n | Minute |
| q | Quarter |
| s | Second |
| w | Weekday |
| ww | Week of year |
| y | Day of year |
| yyyy | Year |

date is a date expression.

firstdayofweek (Optional) specifies the first day of the week. Use one of the following constants:

*Continues*

| | |
|---|---|
| | `vbUseSystemDayOfWeek` 0 (NLS API setting) |
| | `vbSunday`                    1 (Default) |

`vbUseSystemDayOfWeek` 0 (NLS API setting)
`vbSunday`                1 (Default)
`vbMonday`                2
`vbTuesday`               3
`vbWednesday`             4
`vbThursday`              5
`vbFriday`                6
`vbSaturday`              7

`firstweekofyear` (Optional) specifies the first week of the year. Use one of the following constants:

`vbUseSystem` 0 (Use NLS API setting)
`vbFirstJan1` 1 (default) (Week in which January 1 occurs)`vbFirstFourDays` 2
(First week in the new year with at least 4 days)

`vbFirstFullWeek` 3 (First full week of the new year)

| | |
|---|---|
| Example | `MsgBox DatePart("ww", Now, vbMonday, vbFirstFourDays)` |
| | This will extract the week number from the current system date. On July 29, 2004, the `MsgBox` will display 31. |
| See also | `DateAdd` and `DateDiff` |

| | |
|---|---|
| `DateSerial` | Returns a `Variant` subtype `Date(7)` for the specified year, month, and day. |
| Syntax | `DateSerial(year, month, day)` |
| | `year` is an expression that evaluates to a number between 0 and 9999. Values between 0 and 99, both inclusive, are interpreted as the years 1900–1999. |
| | `month` is an expression that must evaluate to a number between 1 and 12. |
| | `day` is an expression that must evaluate to a number between 1 and 31. |
| Note | If an argument is outside the acceptable range for that argument, it increments the next larger unit. Specifying 13 as the month will automatically increment year by 1 and subtract 12 from month leaving a value of 1. The same is true for negative values and a value of 0. However, instead of incrementing, the next larger unit is decremented. |
| | An error occurs if any of the arguments is outside the `Variant` subtype `Integer` range, which is −32768 to +32767. The same is true if the result is later than December 31, 9999. If you specify the year as 0, and the month and day as 0 or a negative value, the function wrongly assumes that the year is 100 and decrements this value. |
| | So `DateSerial(0, 0, 0)` returns 11/30/99. |
| Example | `MsgBox DateSerial( 2004, 07, 29)` |
| | The `MsgBox` will display 29-07-04, if your locale settings use the dash (–) as the date separator and the short date format is dd/mm/yy. |
| See also | `Date, DateValue, Day, Month, Now, TimeSerial, TimeValue, Weekday,` and `Year` |

| DateValue | Returns a Variant subtype Date(7) |
|---|---|
| Syntax | DateValue(date)<br><br>date is an expression representing a date, a time, or both, in the range January 1, 100, to December 31, 9999. |
| Note | Time information in date is not returned, but invalid time information will result in a runtime error. DateValue is internationally aware and uses the locale settings on the machine when recognizing the order of a date with only numbers and separators. If the year is omitted from date, it is obtained from the current system date. |
| Example | ```
DateValue("06/12/2004")
DateValue("June 12, 2004")
DateValue("Jun 12, 2004")
DateValue("Jun 12")
```<br><br>All of these will return the same valid date of 06/12/04. |
| See also | Date, DateSerial, Day, Month, Now, TimeSerial, TimeValue, Weekday, and Year |

| Day | Returns a number between 1 and 31 representing the day of the month. |
|---|---|
| Syntax | Day(date)<br><br>date is any valid date expression. |
| Note | A runtime error occurs if date is not a valid date expression. Null will be returned if date contains Null. |
| Example | ```
MsgBox Day("June 12, 2004")
```<br><br>The MsgBox will display 12. |
| See also | Date, Hour, Minute, Month, Now, Second, Weekday, and Year |

| FormatDateTime | See under *String Functions* |
|---|---|

| Hour | Returns an integer between 0 and 23, representing the hour of the day. |
|---|---|
| Syntax | Hour(time)<br><br>time is any valid time expression. |
| Note | A runtime error occurs if time is not a valid time expression. Null will be returned if time contains Null. |
| Example | ```
MsgBox Hour("12:05:12")
```<br><br>The MsgBox will display 12. |
| See also | Date, Day, Minute, Month, Now, Second, Weekday, and Year |
```

| IsDate | Returns a `Variant` subtype `Boolean(11)` indicating whether an expression can be converted to a valid date. |
|---|---|
| Syntax | `IsDate(expression)`<br><br>`expression` is any expression you want to evaluate as a date or time. |
| Example | ```MsgBox IsDate(Now)        ' true```<br>```MsgBox IsDate("")         ' false```<br>```MsgBox IsDate(#6/12/2004#) ' true``` |
| See also | `CDate`, `IsArray`, `IsEmpty`, `IsNull`, `IsNumeric`, `IsObject`, and `VarType` |

| Minute | Returns a number between 0 and 59, both inclusive, indicating the minute of the hour. |
|---|---|
| Syntax | `Minute(time)`<br><br>`time` is any valid time expression. |
| Note | A runtime error occurs if time is not a valid time expression. `Null` will be returned if time contains `Null`. |
| Example | ```MsgBox Minute("12:45")```<br><br>The `MsgBox` will display 45. |
| See also | `Date`, `Day`, `Hour`, `Month`, `Now`, `Second`, `Weekday`, and `Year` |

| Month | Returns a number between 1 and 12, both inclusive, indicating the month of the year. |
|---|---|
| Syntax | `Month(date)`<br><br>`date` is any valid date expression. |
| Note | A runtime error occurs if date is not a valid date expression. `Null` will be returned if date contains `Null`. |
| Example | ```MsgBox Month(#7/29/1999#)```<br><br>The `MsgBox` will display 7. |
| See also | `Date`, `Day`, `Hour`, `Minute`, `Now`, `Second`, `Weekday`, and `Year` |

| MonthName | Returns a `Variant` subtype `String(8)` for the specified month. |
|---|---|
| Syntax | `MonthName(month, [abbreviate])`<br><br>`month` is a number between 1 and 12 for each month of the year beginning with January.<br><br>`abbreviate` (Optional) is a `Boolean` value indicating if the month name should be abbreviated or spelled out (default). |

| Note | A runtime error occurs if month is outside the valid range (1–12). `MonthName` is internationally aware, which means that the returned strings are localized into the language specified as part of your locale settings. |
|---|---|
| Example | ```
MsgBox MonthName(2)  ' February
MsgBox MonthName(2, true) ' Feb
``` |
| See also | `WeekDayName` |

| Now | Returns the system's current date and time. |
|---|---|
| Syntax | `Now` |
| Example | ```
Dim dtmValue
        dtmValue = Now
```<br><br>`dtmValue` now holds the current system date and time. |
| See also | `Date`, `Day`, `Hour`, `Month`, `Minute`, `Second`, `Weekday`, and `Year` |

| Second | Returns a `Variant` subtype `Date(7)` indicating the number of seconds (0–59) in the specified time. |
|---|---|
| Syntax | `Second(time)`<br>`time` is any valid time expression. |
| Note | A runtime error occurs if time is not a valid time expression. `Null` will be returned if time contains `Null`. |
| Example | ```
MsgBox Second("12:45:56")
```<br><br>The `MsgBox` will display 56. |
| See also | `Date`, `Day`, `Hour`, `Minute`, `Month`, `Now`, `Weekday`, and `Year` |

| Time | Returns a `Variant` subtype `Date(7)` indicating the current system time. |
|---|---|
| Syntax | `Time` |
| Example | ```
Dim dtmValue
        dtmValue = Time
```<br><br>`dtmValue` now holds the current system time. |
| See also | `Date` and `Now` |

| | |
|---|---|
| Timer | Returns a `Variant` subtype `Single(5)` indicating the number of seconds that have elapsed since midnight. This means that it is "reset" every 24 hours. |
| Syntax | `Timer` |
| Example | ```
Dim dtmStart, dtmStop

dtmStart = Timer
' Do processing here
dtmStop = Timer
' Display how many
' seconds the operation
' took
MsgBox dtmStop - dtmStart
``` |

| | |
|---|---|
| TimeSerial | Returns a `Variant` subtype `Date(7)` for the specified hour, minute, and second. |
| Syntax | `TimeSerial(hour, minute, second)` |
| | `hour` is an expression that evaluates to a number between 0 and 23. |
| | `minute` is an expression that must evaluate to a number between 0 and 59. |
| | `second` is an expression that must evaluate to a number between 0 and 59. |
| Note | If an argument is outside the acceptable range for that argument, it increments the next larger unit. Specifying 61 as minute will automatically increment hour by 1 and subtract 60 from minute leaving a value of 1. The same is true for negative values and a value of 0. However, instead of incrementing, the next larger unit is decremented. |
| | An error occurs if any of the arguments is outside the `Variant` subtype `Integer` range, which is $-32768$ to $+32767$. |
| Example | `MsgBox TimeSerial(23, 07, 29)` |
| | The `MsgBox` will display 23:07:29. |
| See also | `Date`, `DateSerial`, `DateValue`, `Day`, `Month`, `Now`, `TimeValue`, `Weekday`, and `Year` |

| | |
|---|---|
| TimeValue | Returns a `Variant` subtype `Date(7)` containing the time. |
| Syntax | `TimeValue(time)` |
| | `time` is an expression in the range 0:00:00 to 23:59:59. |
| Note | Date information in time is not returned, but invalid date information will result in a runtime error. `Null` is returned if time contains `Null`. You can use both 24- and 12-hour representations for the time argument. |
```

| | |
|---|---|
| Example | `TimeValue("23:59")`<br>`TimeValue("11:59 PM")`<br><br>Both will return the same valid time. |
| See also | `Date`, `DateSerial`, `DateValue`, `Day`, `Month`, `Now`, `TimeSerial`, `Weekday`, and `Year` |

| | |
|---|---|
| Weekday | Returns a number indicating the day of the week. |
| Syntax | `Weekday(date, [firstdayofweek])`<br><br>`date` is any valid date expression.<br><br>`firstdayofweek` (Optional) specifies the first day of the week. Use one of the following constants:<br><br>`vbUseSystemDayOfWeek`  0 (Use NLS API setting)<br>`vbSunday`       1 (Default)<br>`vbMonday`       2<br>`vbTuesday`      3<br>`vbWednesday`  4<br>`vbThursday`    5<br>`vbFriday`       6<br>`vbSaturday`    7 |
| Note | `Null` is returned if date contains `Null`. A runtime occurs if date is invalid. Possible return values are:<br><br>`vbSunday`       1<br>`vbMonday`       2<br>`vbTuesday`      3<br>`vbWednesday`  4<br>`vbThursday`    5<br>`vbFriday`       6<br>`vbSaturday`    7 |
| Example | `Weekday(#July 29, 1999#)`<br><br>Returns 5 for Thursday. |
| See also | `Date`, `Day`, `Month`, `Now`, and `Year` |

| | |
|---|---|
| WeekdayName | Returns a `Variant` subtype `String(8)` for the specified weekday. |
| Syntax | `WeekdayName(weekday, [abbreviate], [firstdayofweek])`<br><br>`weekday` is a number between 1 and 7 for each day of the week. This value depends on the `firstdayofweek` setting.<br><br>`abbreviate` (Optional) is a `Boolean` value indicating if the weekday name should be abbreviated or spelled out (default)<br><br>`firstdayofweek` (Optional) is a numeric value indicating the first day of the week. Use one of the following constants: |

*Continues*

523

| | |
|---|---|
| | vbUseSystemDayOfWeek 0 (Use NLS API setting) |
| | vbSunday              1 (Default) |
| | vbMonday             2 |
| | vbTuesday            3 |
| | vbWednesday        4 |
| | vbThursday          5 |
| | vbFriday             6 |
| | vbSaturday          7 |
| Note | A runtime error occurs if weekday is outside the valid range (1–7). WeekdayName is internationally aware, which means that the returned strings are localized into the language specified as part of your locale settings. |
| Example | WeekdayName(2, , vbSunday) ' Monday<br>WeekdayName(1, , vbMonday) ' Monday |
| See also | MonthName |

| | |
|---|---|
| Year | Returns a number indicating the year. |
| Syntax | Year(date)<br><br>date is any valid date expression. |
| Note | A runtime error occurs if date is not a valid date expression. Null will be returned if date contains Null. |
| Example | MsgBox Year(#6/12/2004#)<br><br>The MsgBox will display 2004. |
| See also | Date, Day, Month, Now, and Weekday |

# Unsupported Date Functions and Statements

The following VB/VBA statements are not supported in VBScript.

| Function/Statement Name | Alternatives |
|---|---|
| Date statement | Sets the system date, which is not possible in VBScript. |
| Time statement | Sets the system time, which is not possible in VBScript. |

# Array Functions and Statements

One major difference between VB/VBA and VBScript is the way you can declare your arrays. VBScript does not support the Option Base statement and you cannot declare arrays that are not zero-based.

The following is a list of functions and statements that you can use for array manipulation in VBScript.

| | |
|---|---|
| Array | Returns a comma-delimited list of values as a `Variant` subtype `Array` (8192). |
| Syntax | `Array(arglist)`<br><br>`arglist` is a comma-delimited list of values that is inserted into the one-dimensional array in the order they appear in the list. |
| Note | An array of zero length is created if `arglist` contains no arguments.<br><br>All arrays in VBScript are zero-based, which means that the first element in the list will be element 0 in the returned array. |
| Example | ```Dim arrstrTest```<br><br>```    ' Create an array with three```<br>```elements```<br>```            arrstrTest = Array( _```<br>```                    "Bart", "Lisa",```<br>```"Maggie")```<br>```     ' Show the first list element```<br>```     ' now in the array```<br>```     MsgBox arrstrTest(0)```<br><br>`MsgBox` displays Bart. |
| See also | `Dim` |

| | |
|---|---|
| Erase | Reinitializes the elements if it is a fixed-size array and deallocates the memory used if it is a dynamic array. |
| Syntax | `Erase array`<br><br>`array` is the array to be reinitialized or erased. |
| Note | You must know if you are using a fixed-size or a dynamic array, because this statement behaves differently depending on the array type.<br><br>Because the memory is deallocated when using `Erase` with dynamic arrays, you must redeclare the array structure with the `ReDim` statement, before you use it again.<br><br>Fixed-size arrays are reinitialized differently depending on the contents of the elements:<br><br>`Numeric`    Set to 0<br>`Strings`     Set to `""`<br>`Objects`    Set to `Nothing` |
| Example | ```Dim arrstrDynamic()```<br>```Dim arrstrFixed(3)```<br><br>```         ' Allocate space for the```<br>```         ' dynamic array```<br>```         ReDim arrstrDynamic(3)```<br>```         ' Free the memory used by``` |

*Continues*

```
                                          ' the dynamic array
                                      Erase arrstrDynamic
                                      ' Reinitialize the elements
                                      ' in the fixed-size array
                                      Erase arrstrFixed
```

| | |
|---|---|
| See also | Dim and ReDim |

| | |
|---|---|
| For Each | Performs a group of statements repeatedly for each element in a collection or an array. |
| Syntax | For Each element In group<br><br>[statements]<br><br>[Exit For]<br><br>Next [element]<br><br>element is a variable used for iterating through the elements in a collection or an array.<br><br>group is the name of the object or array.<br><br>statements is one or more statements you want to execute on each item in the group. |
| Note | The For Each loop is only entered if there is at least one element in the collection or array. All the statements in the loop are executed for all the elements in the group. You can control this by executing the Exit For statement if a certain condition is met. This will exit the loop and start executing on the first line after the Next statement.<br><br>The For Each loops can be nested, but you must make sure that each loop element is unique. |
| Example | ```
Dim arrstrLoop
Dim strElement

    ' Create the array
    arrstrLoop = Array _
( "Bart", "Lisa", "Maggie")
        ' Loop through the array
      For Each strElement In _
arrstrLoop
          ' Display element content
        MsgBox strElement
      Next
``` |

| | |
|---|---|
| IsArray | Returns a Variant subtype Boolean(11) indicating if a variable is an array. |
| Syntax | IsArray(varname)<br><br>varname is a variable you want to check is an array. |
```

| | |
|---|---|
| Note | Only returns `True` if varname is an array. |
| Example | ```
Dim strName
Dim arrstrFixed(3)

strName = "Wrox is Great!"
MsgBox IsArray( strName)
        ' false
MsgBox IsArray( arrstrFixed)
        ' true
``` |
| See also | `IsDate`, `IsEmpty`, `IsNull`, `IsNumeric`, `IsObject`, and `VarType` |

| | |
|---|---|
| Lbound | Returns the smallest possible subscript for the dimension indicated. |
| Syntax | `LBound(arrayname[,dimension])`<br><br>`arrayname` is the name of the array variable.<br><br>`dimension` is an integer indicating the dimension you want to know the smallest possible subscript for. The dimension starts with 1, which is also the default that will be used if this argument is omitted. |
| Note | The smallest possible subscript for any array is always 0 in VBScript. `LBound` will raise a runtime error if the array has not been initialized. |
| Example | ```
Dim arrstrFixed(3)

MsgBox LBound(arrstrFixed)
```<br><br>`MsgBox` displays 0. |
| See also | `Dim`, `ReDim`, and `UBound` |

| | |
|---|---|
| ReDim | This statement is used to size or resize a dynamic array. |
| Syntax | `ReDim [Preserve] varname(subscripts[,`<br>`varname(subscripts)]...)`<br><br>`Preserve` (Optional) is used to preserve the data in an existing array, when you resize it. The overhead of using this functionality is quite high and should only be used when necessary.<br><br>`varname` is the name of the array variable.<br><br>`subscripts` is the dimension of the array variable `varname`. You can declare up to 60 multiple dimensions. The syntax is:<br><br>`upper[, upper]...`<br><br>where you indicate the upper bounds of the `subscript`. The lower bound is always 0. |

*Continues*

| | |
|---|---|
| Note | A dynamic array must already have been declared without dimension subscripts, when you size or resize it. If you use the `Preserve` keyword, only the last array dimension can be resized and the number of dimensions will remain unchanged. |
| | Since an array can be made smaller when resizing, you should take care that you don't lose any data already in the array. |
| Example | |

```
Dim arrstrDynamic()

  ' Size the dimension to
  ' contain one dimension
  ' with 3 elements
  ReDim arrstrDynamic(2)
  ' Put data in the array
  arrstrDynamic(0) = "1"
  arrstrDynamic(1) = "2"
  arrstrDynamic(2) = "3"
  ' Resize the array, but
  ' keep the existing data
  ReDim Preserve arrstrDynamic(5)
  ' Display the 3rd element
  MsgBox arrstrDynamic(2)
```

MsgBox displays 3.

| | |
|---|---|
| See also | Dim and Set |

| | |
|---|---|
| Ubound | Returns the largest possible subscript for the dimension indicated. |
| Syntax | UBound(arrayname[, dimension]) |
| | arrayname is the name of the array variable. |
| | dimension is an integer indicating the dimension you want to know the largest possible subscript for. The dimension starts with 1, which is also the default that will be used if this argument is omitted. |
| Note | UBound will raise a runtime error if the array has not been initialized. |
| | If the array is empty, −1 is returned. |
| Example | |

```
Dim arrstrFixed(3)

        MsgBox UBound(arrstrFixed)
```

MsgBox displays 3.

| | |
|---|---|
| See also | Dim, Ubound, and ReDim |

# Unsupported Array Functions and Statements

The following VB/VBA constructs are not supported in VBScript:

❑   Option Base

# String Functions and Statements

| | |
|---|---|
| FormatCurrency | Formats an expression as a currency value with the current currency symbol. The currency symbol is defined in Regional Settings in Windows Control Panel |
| Syntax | FormatCurrency(expression [,numdigitsafterdecimal [,includeleadingdigit [,useparensfornegativenumbers [,groupdigits]]]]) |
| | expression is the expression that you want formatted. |
| | numdigitsafterdecimal (Optional) is a numeric value that indicates how many places to the right of the decimal separator should be displayed. If you omit this argument, the default value (−1) will be assumed and the settings from Control Panel will be used. |
| | includeleadingdigit (Optional) indicates if a leading zero is displayed for fractional values. Use one of the following constants: |
| | vbUseDefault 2 (Uses the settings from the Number tab in Control Panel) |
| | vbtrue -1<br>vbfalse 0 |
| | useparensfornegativenumbers (Optional) indicates if negative numbers are enclosed in parentheses. Use one of the following constants: |
| | vbUseDefault 2 (Uses the settings from the Regional Settings tab in Control Panel) |
| | vbTrue -1<br>vbFalse 0 |
| | groupdigits (Optional) indicates if numbers are grouped using the thousand separator specified in Control Panel. Use one of the following constants: |
| | vbUseDefault 2 (Uses the settings from the Regional Settings tab in Control Panel) |
| | vbtrue -1<br>vbfalse 0 |
| Note | The way the currency symbol is placed in relation to the currency value is determined by the settings in the Regional Settings tab in Control Panel—Is the currency symbol placed before the number or after the number, is there a space between the symbol and the number, and so on. |
| Example | MsgBox FormatCurrency(7500000)<br>MsgBox FormatCurrency(7500000, , vbtrue)<br>MsgBox FormatCurrency(7500000, 2, vbtrue)<br><br>If the currency symbol is a dollar sign ($), the thousand separator a comma (,), and the currency symbol placed in front of the number with no spaces between, then MsgBox will display $7,500,000.00 in all these statements. |
| See also | FormatDateTime, FormatNumber, and FormatPercent |

| | |
|---|---|
| `FormatDateTime` | Returns a string formatted as a date and/or time. |
| Syntax | `FormatDateTime(date, [namedformat])` |
| | `date` is any valid date expression. |
| | `namedformat` (Optional) is a numeric value that indicates the date/time format used. Use one of the following constants: |
| | `vbGeneralDate 0` (Format date (if present) and time (if present) using the short date and long time format from the machine's locale settings) |
| | `vbLongDate 1` (Format date using the long date format from the machine's locale settings) |
| | `vbShortDate 2` (Format date using the short date format from the machine's locale settings) |
| | `vbLongTime 3` (Format time using the long time format from the machine's locale settings) |
| | `vbShortTime 4` (Format time using the short time format from the machine's locale settings) |
| Note | A runtime error occurs if date is not a valid date expression. `Null` will be returned if date contains `Null`. |
| Example | `MsgBox FormatDateTime(Now, vbShortDate)` |
| | On June 12, 2004, the `MsgBox` will display 06/12/04, if the locale settings use mm/dd/yy as the short date order and the forward slash (/) as the date separator. |
| See also | `FormatCurrency`, `FormatNumber`, and `FormatPercent` |

| | |
|---|---|
| `FormatNumber` | Returns a string formatted as a number. |
| Syntax | `FormatNumber (expression,` |
| | `[, numdigitsafterdecimal` |
| | `[, includeleadingdigit` |
| | `[, useparensfornegativenumbers [, groupDigits]]]])` |
| | `expression` is the expression that you want formatted. |
| | `numdigitsafterdecimal` (Optional) is a numeric value that indicates how many places to the right of the decimal separator should be displayed. If you omit this argument, the default value (−1) will be assumed and the settings from `Control Panel` will be used. |
| | `includeleadingdigit` (Optional) indicates if a leading zero is displayed for fractional values. Use one of the following constants: |
| | `TristateUseDefault -2` (Uses the settings from the `Number` tab in `Control Panel`) |
| | `TristateTrue -1` |
| | `TristateFalse 0` |

useparensfornegativenumbers (Optional) indicates if negative numbers are enclosed in parentheses. Use one of the following constants:

TristateUseDefault -2 (Uses the settings from the Number tab in Control Panel)

TristateTrue -1

TristateFalse 0

groupdigits (Optional) indicates if numbers are grouped using the thousand separator specified in Control Panel. Use one of the following constants:

TristateUseDefault -2 (Uses the settings from the Number tab in Control Panel)

TristateTrue -1

TristateFalse 0

| | |
|---|---|
| Note | The Number tab in Regional Settings in Control Panel supplies all the information used for formatting. |
| Example | `MsgBox FormatNumber("50000", 2,`<br>`vbtrue, vbfalse, vbtrue)`<br>`MsgBox FormatNumber("50000")`<br><br>The MsgBox will display 50,000.00, if the locale settings use a comma (,) as the thousand separator and a period (.) as the decimal separator. |
| See also | FormatCurrency, FormatDateTime, and FormatPercent |

| | |
|---|---|
| FormatPercent | Returns a string formatted as a percentage, such as 45%. |
| Syntax | FormatPercent(expression,<br><br>[, numdigitsafterdecimal<br><br>[, includeleadingdigit<br><br>[, useparensfornegativenumbers [, groupDigits]]]])<br><br>expression is any valid expression that you want formatted.<br><br>numdigitsafterdecimal (Optional) is a numeric value that indicates how many places to the right of the decimal separator should be displayed. If you omit this argument, the default value ($-1$) will be assumed and the settings from Control Panel will be used.<br><br>includeleadingdigit (Optional) indicates if a leading zero is displayed for fractional values. Use one of the following constants:<br><br>TristateUseDefault -2 (Uses the settings from the Number tab in Control Panel)<br><br>TristateTrue -1<br><br>TristateFalse 0 |

*Continues*

| | |
|---|---|
| | useparensfornegativenumbers (Optional) indicates if negative numbers are enclosed in parentheses. Use one of the following constants:<br><br>TristateUseDefault -2 (Uses the settings from the Number tab in Control Panel)<br><br>TristateTrue -1<br><br>TristateFalse 0<br><br>groupdigits (Optional) indicates if numbers are grouped using the thousand separator specified in Control Panel. Use one of the following constants:<br><br>TristateUseDefault -2 (Uses the settings from the Number tab in Control Panel)<br><br>TristateTrue -1<br><br>TristateFalse 0 |
| Note | The Number tab in Regional Settings in Control Panel supplies all the information used for formatting. |
| Example | ```MsgBox FormatPercent(4 / 45)``` <br> ```MsgBox FormatPercent(4 / 45, 2,``` <br> ```vbtrue, vbtrue, vbtrue)``` <br><br> The MsgBox will display 8.89%, if the locale settings use a period (.) as the decimal separator. |
| See also | FormatCurrency, FormatDateTime, and FormatNumber |

| | |
|---|---|
| InStr | Returns an integer indicating the position for the first occurrence of a substring within a string. |
| Syntax | InStr([start,] string1, string2[, compare])<br><br>start (Optional) is any valid nonnegative expression indicating the starting position for the search within string1. Noninteger values are rounded. This argument is required if the compare argument is specified.<br><br>string1 is the string you want to search within.<br><br>string2 is the substring you want to search for.<br><br>compare (Optional) indicates the comparison method used when evaluating. Use one of the following constants:<br><br>vbBinaryCompare 0 (Default) (Performs a binary comparison, that is, a case-sensitive comparison)<br><br>vbTextCompare 1 (Performs a textual comparison, that is, a non-case-sensitive comparison) |
| Note | A runtime error will occur, if start contains Null. If start is larger than the length of string2 (> Len(string2)) 0 will be returned. |

Possible return values for different `stringx` settings:

| string1 | Zero-length | 0 |
|---------|-------------|---|
| string1 | Null | Null |
| string2 | Zero-length | start |
| string2 | Null | Null |
| string2 | Not found | 0 |
| string2 | Found | Position |

**Example**

```
Dim lngStartPos
Dim lngFoundPos
Dim strSearchWithin
Dim strSearchFor

    ' Set the start pos
    lngStartPos = 1
    ' Initialize the strings
    strSearchWithin = _
      "This is a test string"
    strSearchFor = "t"
    ' Find the first occurrence
    lngFoundPos = InStr( _
      lngStartPos, _
      strSearchWithin, _
      strSearchFor)
    ' Loop through the string
    Do While lngFoundPos > 0
       ' Display the found position
       MsgBox lngFoundPos
       ' Set the new start pos to
       ' the char after the found
       ' position
       lngStartPos = lngFoundPos + 1
       ' Find the next occurrence
       lngFoundPos = InStr( _
         lngStartPos, _
         strSearchWithin, _
         strSearchFor)
    Loop
```

This code finds all occurrences of the letter t in `string1`, at position 11, 14, and 17. Please note that we use binary comparison here, which means that the uppercase T will not be "found." If you want to perform a case-insensitive search, you will need to specify the compare argument as `vbTextCompare`.

**See also**

`InStrB` and `InStrRev`

| InStrB | Returns an integer indicating the byte position for the first occurrence of a substring within a string containing byte data. |
|---|---|
| Syntax | InStrB([start,] string1, string2[, compare]) |
| | start (Optional) is any valid nonnegative expression indicating the starting position for the search within string1. Noninteger values are rounded. This argument is required, if the compare argument is specified. |
| | string1 is the string containing byte data you want to search within. |
| | string2 is the substring you want to search for. |
| | compare (Optional) indicates the comparison method used when evaluating. Use one of the following constants: |
| | vbBinaryCompare -0 (Default) (Performs a binary comparison, that is, a case-sensitive comparison) |
| | vbTextCompare -1 (Performs a textual comparison, that is, a non-case-sensitive comparison) |
| Note | A runtime error will occur, if start contains Null. If start is larger than the length of string2 (> Len(string2)), 0 will be returned. |
| | Possible return values for different stringx settings: |

| | | |
|---|---|---|
| string1 | Zero-length | 0 |
| string1 | Null | Null |
| string2 | Zero-length | start |
| string2 | Null | Null |
| string2 | Not found | 0 |
| string2 | Found | Position |

Example

```
Dim lngStartPos
Dim lngFoundPos
Dim strSearchWithin
Dim strSearchFor

    ' Set the start pos
    lngStartPos = 1
    ' Initialize the strings
    strSearchWithin = _
     "This is a test string"
    strSearchFor = ChrB(0)

    ' Find the first occurrence
    lngFoundPos = InStrB( _
      lngStartPos, _
```

```
                    strSearchWithin, _
                    strSearchFor)
' Loop through the string
Do While lngFoundPos > 0
    ' Display the found position
    MsgBox lngFoundPos
    ' Set the new start pos to
    ' the char after the
    ' found position
    lngStartPos = lngFoundPos + 1
    ' Find the next occurrence
    lngFoundPos = InStrB( _
        lngStartPos, _
        strSearchWithin, _
        strSearchFor)
Loop
```

This code finds all occurrences of the byte value 0 in string1, at position 2, 4, 6, ..., 40, and 42. This is because only the first byte of the Unicode character is used for the character. If you use a double-byte character set like the Japanese, the second byte will also contain a nonzero value.

| See also | InStr and InStrRev |
|---|---|

| InStrRev | Returns an integer indicating the position of the first occurrence of a substring within a string starting from the end of the string. This is the reverse functionality of InStr. |
|---|---|
| Syntax | InStrRev(string1, string2[, start[, compare]]) |
| | string1 is the string you want to search within. |
| | string2 is the substring you want to search for. |
| | start (Optional) is any valid nonnegative expression indicating the starting position for the search within string1; −1 is the default and it will be used if this argument is omitted. |
| | compare (Optional) indicates the comparison method used when evaluating. Use one of the following constants: |
| | vbBinaryCompare −0 (Default) (Performs a binary comparison, that is, a case-sensitive comparison) |
| | vbTextCompare −1 (Performs a textual comparison, that is, a non-case-sensitive comparison) |
| Note | A runtime error will occur, if start contains Null. If start is larger than the length of string2 (> Len(string2)), will be returned. |

*Continues*

Possible return values for different `stringx` settings:

| | | |
|---|---|---|
| string1 | Zero-length | 0 |
| string1 | Null | Null |
| string2 | Zero-length | start |
| string2 | Null | Null |
| string2 | Not found | 0 |
| string2 | Found | Position |

`InStrRev` and `InStr` do not share the same syntax.

**Example**

```
Dim lngStartPos
Dim lngFoundPos
Dim strSearchWithin
Dim strSearchFor

    ' Set the start pos
    lngStartPos = -1
    ' Initialize the strings
    strSearchWithin = _
     "This is a test string"
    strSearchFor = "t"

    ' Find the first occurrence
    lngFoundPos = InStrB( _
        strSearchWithin, _
        strSearchFor, lngStartPos)
    ' Loop through the string
    Do While lngFoundPos > 0
        ' Display the found
        ' position
        MsgBox lngFoundPos
        ' Set the new start pos to
        ' the char before the
        ' found position
        lngStartPos = lngFoundPos -1
        ' Find the next occurrence
        lngFoundPos = InStrB( _
          strSearchWithin, _
          strSearchFor, _
          lngStartPos)

    Loop
```

This code finds all occurrences of the letter t in `string1`, at position 17, 14, and 11. Please note that we use binary comparison here, which means that the uppercase T will not be "found." If you want to perform a case-insensitive search, you will need to specify the compare argument as `vbTextCompare`.

**See also**

`InStr` and `InStrB`

| Join | Joins a number of substrings in an array to form the returned string. |
|------|------------------------------------------------------------------------|
| Syntax | `Join(list[, delimiter])`<br><br>`list` is a one-dimensional array that contains all the substrings that you want to join.<br><br>`delimiter` (Optional) is the character(s) used to separate the substrings. A space character " " is used as the delimiter if this argument is omitted. |
| Note | All the substrings are concatenated with no delimiter if a zero-length string is used as delimiter. If any element in the array is empty, a zero-length string will be used as the value. |
| Example | ```
Dim strLights
Dim arrstrColors(3)

    ' Fill the array
    arrstrColors(0) = "Red"
    arrstrColors(1) = "Yellow"
    arrstrColors(2) = "Green"

    ' Join the array into a string
    strLights = Join( arrstrColors, ",")
```<br>`strLights` contains `"Red,Yellow,Green"`. |
| See also | `Split` |

| Lcase | Converts all alpha characters in a string to lowercase. |
|-------|---------------------------------------------------------|
| Syntax | `LCase(string)`<br>`string` is the string you want converted to lowercase. |
| Note | `Null` is returned if string contains `Null`. Only uppercase letters are converted. |
| Example | `MsgBox LCase("ThisIsLowerCase")`<br>`MsgBox` displays thisislowercase. |
| See also | `Ucase` |

| Left | Returns length number of leftmost characters from string. |
|------|-----------------------------------------------------------|
| Syntax | `Left(string, length)`<br><br>`string` is the string you want to extract a number of characters from.<br><br>`length` is the number of characters you want to extract starting from the left. The entire string will be returned if length is equal to or greater than the total number of characters in string. |
| Note | `Null` is returned if string contains `Null`. |

*Continues*
```

| | |
|---|---|
| Example | ```
Dim strExtract

strExtract = "LeftRight"
MsgBox Left(strExtract, 4)
```<br><br>`MsgBox` displays Left. |
| See also | `Len`, `LenB`, `Mid`, `MidB`, and `Right` |

| | |
|---|---|
| `Len` | Returns the number of characters in a string. |
| Syntax | `Len(string)`<br><br>`string` is any valid string expression you want the length of. |
| Note | `Null` is returned if string contains `Null`. |
| Example | ```
Dim strLength

strLength = "1 2 3 4 5 6 7 8 9"
MsgBox Len(strLength)
```<br><br>`MsgBox` displays 17. |
| See also | `Left`, `LenB`, `Mid`, `MidB`, and `Right` |

| | |
|---|---|
| `LenB` | Returns the number of bytes used to represent a string. |
| Syntax | `LenB(string)`<br><br>`string` is any valid string expression you want the number of bytes for. |
| Note | `Null` is returned if string contains `Null`. |
| Example | ```
Dim strLength

strLength = "123456789"
MsgBox LenB(strLength)
```<br><br>`MsgBox` displays 18. |
| See also | `Left`, `Len`, `Mid`, `MidB`, and `Right` |

| | |
|---|---|
| `Ltrim` | Trims a string of leading spaces; " " or `Chr(32)`. |
| Syntax | `LTrim(string)`<br><br>`string` is any valid string expression you want to trim leading (leftmost) spaces from. |
| Note | `Null` is returned if string contains `Null`. |
| Example | ```
Dim strSpaces

strSpaces = " Hello again *"
MsgBox LTrim(strSpaces)
```<br><br>`MsgBox` displays Hello again *. |
| See also | `Left`, `Mid`, `Right`, `Rtrim`, and `Trim` |

| Mid | Returns a specified number of characters from any position in a string. |
|---|---|
| Syntax | `Mid(string, start[, length])` |
| | `string` is any valid string expression you want to extract characters from. |
| | `start` is the starting position for extracting the characters. A zero-length string is returned if it is greater than the number of characters in string. |
| | `length` (Optional) is the number of characters you want to extract. All characters from start to the end of the string are returned if this argument is omitted or if length is greater than the number of characters counting from start. |
| Note | `Null` is returned if string contains `Null`. |
| Example | `Dim strExtract`<br><br>`strExtract = "Find ME in here"`<br>`MsgBox Mid(strExtract, 6, 2)`<br><br>`MsgBox` displays ME. |
| See also | `Left`, `Len`, `LenB`, `LTrim`, `MidB`, `Right`, `Rtrim`, and `Trim` |

| MidB | Returns a specified number of bytes from any position in a string containing byte data. |
|---|---|
| Syntax | `MidB(string, start[, length])` |
| | `string` is a string expression containing byte data you want to extract characters from. |
| | `start` is the starting position for extracting the bytes. A zero-length string is returned if it is greater than the number of bytes in string. |
| | `length` (Optional) is the number of bytes you want to extract. All bytes from start to the end of the string are returned if this argument is omitted or if length is greater than the number of bytes counting from start. |
| Note | `Null` is returned if string contains `Null`. |
| Example | `Dim strExtract`<br><br>`strExtract = "Find ME in here"`<br>`MsgBox MidB(strExtract, 11, 4)`<br><br>`MsgBox` displays ME because VBScript uses 2 bytes to represent a character. The first byte contains the ANSI character code when dealing with "normal" ANSI characters like M, and the next byte is 0. So byte 11 in the string is the first byte for the letter M and then we extract 4 bytes/2 characters. |
| See also | `Left`, `Len`, `LTrim`, `Mid`, `Right`, `Rtrim`, and `Trim` |

| | |
|---|---|
| Replace | Replaces a substring within a string with another substring a specified number of times. |
| Syntax | `Replace(expression, find, replacewith[, start[, count[, compare]]])` |

`expression` is a string expression that contains the substring you want to replace.

`find` is the substring you want to replace.

`replacewith` is the substring you want to replace with.

`start` (Optional) is the starting position within expression for replacing the substring. 1 (default), the first position, will be used if this argument is omitted. You must also specify the `count` argument if you want to use start.

`count` (Optional) is the number of times you want to replace `find`. −1 (default) will be used if this argument is omitted, which means all find in the expression. You must also specify the `start` argument if you want to use `count`.

`compare` (Optional) indicates the comparison method used when evaluating. Use one of the following constants:

`vbBinaryCompare` – 0 (Default) (Performs a binary comparison, that is, a case-sensitive comparison)

`vbTextCompare` – 1 (Performs a textual comparison, that is, a non-case-sensitive comparison)

| | |
|---|---|
| Note | If `start` and `count` are specified, the return value will be the original expression, with `find` replaced `count` times with `replacewith`, from start to the end of the expression, and not the complete string. A zero-length string is returned if `start` is greater than the length of expression (`start > Len(expression)`). All occurrences of `find` will be removed if `replacewith` is a zero-length string (""). |

Possible return values for different argument settings:

| | | |
|---|---|---|
| expression | Zero-length | zero-length |
| expression | Null | Error |
| find | Zero-length | expression |
| count | 0 | expression |

| | |
|---|---|
| Example | ```
Dim strReplace

strReplace = Replace( _
 "****I use binary", _
 "I", "You", 5, 1, _
 vbBinaryCompare)
   ' You use binary
strReplace = Replace( _
 "****I use text", "i", _
 "You", , , _
 vbTextCompare)
   ' ****You use text
``` |
| See also | `Left`, `Len`, `LTrim`, `Mid`, `Right`, `Rtrim`, and `Trim` |
```

| Right | Returns length number of rightmost characters from string. |
|---|---|
| Syntax | Right(string, length) |
| | string is the string you want to extract a number of characters from. |
| | length is the number of characters you want to extract starting from the right. The entire string will be returned if length is equal to or greater than the total number of characters in string. |
| Note | Null is returned if string contains Null. |
| Example | ``` Dim strExtract strExtract = "LeftRight" MsgBox Right(strExtract, 5) ``` |
| | MsgBox displays Right. |
| See also | Left, Len, LenB, Mid, and MidB |

| RTrim | Trims a string of trailing spaces; " " or Chr(32). |
|---|---|
| Syntax | RTrim(string) |
| | string is any valid string expression you want to trim trailing (rightmost) spaces from. |
| Note | — |
| Example | ``` Dim strSpaces strSpaces = "* Hello again " MsgBox RTrim(strSpaces) ``` |
| | MsgBox displays * Hello again. |
| See also | Left, LTrim, Mid, Right, and Trim |

| Space | Returns a string made up of a specified number of spaces (" "). |
|---|---|
| Syntax | Space(number) |
| | number is the number of spaces you want returned. |
| Example | ``` Dim strSpaces strSpaces = "Hello again" MsgBox "*" & Space(5) & strSpaces ``` |
| | MsgBox displays * Hello again. |
| See also | String |

| | |
|---|---|
| Split | Returns a zero-based one-dimensional array "extracted" from the supplied string expression. |
| Syntax | `Split(expression[,delimiter[,count[,compare]]])` |
| | `expression` is the string containing substrings and delimiters that you want to split up and put into a zero-based one-dimensional array. |
| | `delimiter` (Optional) is the character that separates the substrings. A space character will be used if this argument is omitted. |
| | `count` (Optional) indicates the number of substrings to return. −1 (default) means all substrings will be returned. |
| | `compare` (Optional) indicates the comparison method used when evaluating. Use one of the following constants: |
| | `vbBinaryCompare −0` (Default) (Performs a binary comparison, that is, a case-sensitive comparison) |
| | `vbTextCompare −1` (Performs a textual comparison, that is, a non-case-sensitive comparison) |
| Note | An empty array will be returned if expression is a zero-length string. The result of the `Split` function cannot be assigned to a variable of `Variant` subtype `Array (8192)`. A runtime error occurs if you try to do so. |
| Example | <pre>Dim arrstrSplit
Dim strSplit

    ' Initialize the string
    strSplit = _
    "1,2,3,4,5,6,7,8,9,0"
    ' Split the string using _
    ' comma as the delimiter
    arrstrSplit = Split( _
      strSplit, ",")</pre> |
| | The array `arrstrSplit` now holds 10 elements, 1,2, ... , 0. |
| See also | `Join` |

| | |
|---|---|
| StrComp | Performs a string comparison and returns the result. |
| Syntax | `StrComp(string1,string2[,compare])` |
| | `string1` is a valid string expression. |
| | `string2` is a valid string expression. |
| | `compare` (Optional) indicates the comparison method used when evaluating. Use one of the following constants: |

vbBinaryCompare –0 (Default) (Performs a binary comparison, that is, a case-sensitive comparison)

vbTextCompare –1 (Performs a textual comparison, that is, a non-case-sensitive comparison)

| | |
|---|---|
| Note | Possible return values for different `stringx` settings: |

`string1 < string2`     –1

`string1 = string2`      0

`string1 > string2`      1

`Null` is returned if `string1` or `string2` is `Null`.

| | |
|---|---|
| Example | |

```
Dim intResult

intResult = StrComp( _
    "abc", "ABC", _
    vbTextCompare)
        ' 0
intResult = StrComp( _
    "ABC", "abc", _
    vbBinaryCompare)
        ' -1
intResult = StrComp( _
    "abc", "ABC")
        ' 1
```

| | |
|---|---|
| See also | `String` |

| | |
|---|---|
| `String` | Returns a string with a substring repeated a specified number of times. |
| Syntax | `String(number, character)` |

`number` indicates the length of the returned string.

`character` is the character code or string expression for the character used to build the returned string. Only the first character of a string expression is used.

| | |
|---|---|
| Note | `Null` is returned if number or character contains `Null`. The character code will automatically be converted to a valid character code if it is greater than 255. The formula is `character Mod 256`. |

| | |
|---|---|
| Example | |

```
Dim strChars

strChars = "Hello again"
MsgBox String(5, "*") & _
strChars
```

`MsgBox` displays *****Hello again.

| | |
|---|---|
| See also | `Space` |

| | |
|---|---|
| StrReverse | Returns a string with the character order reversed. |
| Syntax | StrReverse(string) |
| | string is the string expression you want reversed. |
| Note | A runtime error occurs if string is Null. If string is a zero-length string, a zero-length string will be returned. |
| | The case of the characters is not changed. |
| Example | MsgBox StrReverse("Hello again") |
| | MsgBox displays niaga olleH. |

| | |
|---|---|
| Trim | This trims a string of leading and trailing spaces; " " or Chr(32). |
| Syntax | Trim(string) |
| | string is any valid string expression you want to trim leading (leftmost) and trailing (rightmost) spaces from. |
| Note | Null is returned if string contains Null. |
| Example | Dim strSpaces |
| | strSpaces = " *Hello again* " <br> MsgBox Trim(strSpaces) |
| | MsgBox displays *Hello again*. |
| See also | Left, Ltrim, Mid, Right, and RTrim |

| | |
|---|---|
| UCase | Converts all alpha characters in a string to uppercase and returns the result. |
| Syntax | UCase(string) |
| | string is the string you want converted to uppercase. |
| Note | Null is returned if string contains Null. Only lowercase letters are converted. |
| Example | MsgBox UCase("ThisIsUpperCase") |
| | MsgBox displays THISISUPPERCASE. |
| See also | Lcase |

# Unsupported String Functions, Statements, and Constructs

The following VB/VBA string functions/statements and constructs are not supported in VBScript.

| Function/Statement Name | Alternative |
|---|---|
| Format | FormatCurrency, FormatDateTime, FormatNumber, and FormatPercent |
| Mid (statement) | Left, Mid, and InStr functions, or the Replace function. |

Here is how to replace a substring identified by characters using the Replace function.

```
Dim strText
Dim strFind
Dim strSubstitute
   strText = "This is the text I want
to replace a substring in"
   strFind = "want to replace"
   strSubstitute = "have replaced"
   strText = Replace(strText, _
strFind, strSubstitute)
```

strText now holds "This is the text I have replaced a substring in".

Here is how to replace a substring identified by position and length using the InStr, Left, and Mid functions.

```
Dim strText
Dim strSubstitute
   strText = "This is the text + _
   I want to replace a + _
   substring in"
   strSubstitute = "have replaced"
   strText = Left$(strText, 19) &
strSubstitute & Mid$(strText, _
   35, Len(strText) - 34)
```

strText now holds "This is the text I have replaced a substring in".

| Function/Statement Name | Alternative |
|---|---|
| StrConv | It is very unlikely that this will be needed as all variables are Variant and this will be done implicitly. |

Fixed length strings (Dim strMessage As String * 50) are not supported.

# String Constants

| Constant | Value | Description |
|---|---|---|
| vbCr | Chr(13) | Carriage Return. |
| vbCrLf | Chr(13) & Chr(10) | A combination of Carriage Return and line feed. |

*Continues*

| Constant | Value | Description |
|---|---|---|
| vbFormFeed | Chr(12) | Form Feed* |
| vbLf | Chr(10) | Line Feed |
| vbNewLine | Chr(13) & Chr(10) or Chr(10) | New line character. This is platform-specific, meaning whatever is appropriate for the current platform |
| vbNullChar | Chr(0) | Character with the value of 0 |
| vbNullString | String with the value of 0 | This is not the same as a zero-length string (""). Mainly used for calling external procedures |
| vbTab | Chr(9) | Tab (horizontal) |
| VbVerticalTab | Chr(11) | Tab (vertical)* |

*Not useful in Microsoft Windows.

# Conversion Functions

| Asc | Returns the ANSI character code for the first character in a string. |
|---|---|
| Syntax | Asc(string)<br><br>string is any valid string expression. |
| Note | A runtime error occurs if string doesn't contain any characters. string is converted to a String subtype if it's a numeric subtype. |
| Example | intCharCode = Asc("WROX")<br><br>intCharCode now holds the value 87, which is the ANSI character code for "W." |
| See also | AscB, AscW, Chr, ChrB, and ChrW |

| AscB | Returns the ANSI character code for the first byte in a string containing byte data. |
|---|---|
| Syntax | AscB(string)<br><br>string is any valid string expression. |
| Note | A runtime error occurs if string doesn't contain any characters. For normal ANSI strings this function will return the same as the Asc function. Only if the string is in Unicode format will it be different from Asc. Unicode characters are represented by 2 bytes as opposed to ANSI characters that only need 1. |
| Example | intCharCode = AscB("WROX")<br><br>intCharCode now holds the value 87, which is the ANSI character code for "W." |
| See also | Asc, AscW, Chr, ChrB, and ChrW |

| AscW | Returns the Unicode character code for the first character in a string. |
|---|---|
| Syntax | `AscW(string)`<br>`string` is any valid string expression. |
| Note | A runtime error occurs if string doesn't contain any characters. `string` is converted to a `String` subtype if it's a numeric subtype. For use on 32-bit Unicode enabled platforms only, to avoid conversion from Unicode to ANSI. |
| Example | `intCharCode = AscW("WROX")`<br><br>`intCharCode` now holds the value 87, which is the Unicode character code for "W." |
| See also | `Asc`, `AscB`, `Chr`, `ChrB`, and `ChrW` |

| Cbool | Returns a `Boolean` value (`Variant` Subtype 11) corresponding to the value of an expression. |
|---|---|
| Syntax | `CBool(expression)`<br>`expression` is any valid expression. |
| Note | A runtime error occurs if expression can't be evaluated to a numeric value.<br><br>If expression evaluates to zero then `False` is returned; otherwise, `True` is returned. |
| Example | `Dim intCounter, blnValue`<br>`    intCounter = 5`<br>`    blnValue = CBool(intCounter)`<br><br>`blnValue` now holds the value `True`, because `intCounter` holds a nonzero value. |
| See also | `CByte`, `CCur`, `CDbl`, `CInt`, `CLng`, `CSng`, and `CStr` |

| Cbyte | Returns an expression converted to `Variant` subtype `Byte(17)`. |
|---|---|
| Syntax | `CByte(expression)`<br>`expression` is any valid numeric expression. |
| Note | A runtime error occurs if expression can't be evaluated to a numeric value or if expression evaluates to a value outside the acceptable range for a byte (0–255). Fractional values are rounded. |
| Example | `Dim dblValue, bytValue`<br>`    dblValue = 5.456`<br>`    bytValue = CByte(dblValue)`<br><br>`bytValue` now holds the value 5, because `dblValue` is rounded. |
| See also | `CBool`, `CCur`, `CDbl`, `CInt`, `CLng`, `CSng`, and `CStr` |

| | |
|---|---|
| Ccur | Returns an expression converted to Variant subtype Currency (6). |
| Syntax | CCur(expression) |
| | expression is any valid expression. |
| Note | CCur is internationally aware, which means that the return value is based on the locale settings on the machine. Numbers will be formatted with the appropriate decimal separator and the fourth digit to the right of the separator is rounded up if the fifth digit is 5 or higher. |
| Example | ``` Dim dblValue, curValue dblValue = 724.555789 curValue = CCur(dblValue) ``` |
| | curValue now holds the value 724.5558 or 724,5558, depending on the separator. |
| See also | CBool, CByte, CDbl, CInt, CLng, CSng, and CStr |

| | |
|---|---|
| Cdate | See under *Date and Time Functions and Statements* |

| | |
|---|---|
| CDbl | Returns an expression converted to Variant subtype Double (5). |
| Syntax | CDbl(expression) |
| | expression is any valid expression. |
| Note | CDbl is internationally aware, which means that the return value is based on the locale settings on the machine. Numbers will be formatted with the appropriate decimal separator. A runtime error occurs if expression lies outside the range ($-1.79769313486232E308$ to $-4.94065645841247E-324$ for negative values, and $4.94065645841247E-324$ to $1.79769313486232E308$ for positive values) applicable to a Double. |
| Example | ``` Dim dblValue dblValue = CDbl("5,579.56") ``` |
| | dblValue now holds the value 5579.56 or 5,57956, depending on the thousand and decimal separators in use. |
| See also | CBool, CByte, CCur, CInt, CLng, CSng, and CStr |

| | |
|---|---|
| Chr | Returns the ANSI character corresponding to character code. |
| Syntax | Chr(charactercode) |
| | charactercode is a numeric value that indicates the character you want. |

| Note | Supplying a `charactercode` from 0 to 31 will return a standard nonprintable ASCII character. |
|---|---|
| Example | ```
Dim strChar
    strChar = Chr(89)
```
`strChar` now holds the character Y, which is number 89 in the ANSI character table. |
| See also | `Asc`, `AscB`, `AscW`, `ChrB`, and `ChrW` |

| ChrB | Returns the ANSI character corresponding to `charactercode`. |
|---|---|
| Syntax | `ChrB(charactercode)`<br><br>`charactercode` is a numeric value that indicates the character you want. |
| Note | Supplying a `charactercode` from 0 to 31 will return a standard nonprintable ASCII character. This function is used instead of the `Chr` (returns a 2-byte character) function when you want only the first byte of the character returned. |
| Example | ```
Dim strChar
    strChar = ChrB(89)
```
`strChar` now holds the character Y, which is number 89 in the ANSI character table. |
| See also | `Asc`, `AscB`, `AscW`, `Chr`, and `ChrW` |

| ChrW | Returns the Unicode character corresponding to `charactercode`. |
|---|---|
| Syntax | `ChrW(charactercode)`<br><br>`charactercode` is a numeric value that indicates the character you want. |
| Note | Supplying a `charactercode` from 0 to 31 will return a standard nonprintable ASCII character. This function is used instead of the `Chr` function when you want to return a 2-byte character. It is for use on 32-bit Unicode enabled platforms only, to avoid conversion from Unicode to ANSI. |
| Example | ```
Dim strChar
    strChar = ChrW(89)
```
`strChar` now holds the character Y, which is number 89 in the Unicode character table. |
| See also | `Asc`, `AscB`, `AscW`, `Chr`, and `ChrB` |
```

| | |
|---|---|
| Cint | Returns an expression converted to `Variant` subtype `Integer (2)`. |
| Syntax | `CInt(expression)`<br><br>`expression` is any valid expression. |
| Note | `CInt` is internationally aware, which means that the return value is based on the locale settings on the machine. Please note that decimal values are rounded, before the fractional part is discarded. A runtime error occurs if expression lies outside the range ($-32,768$ to $32,767$) applicable to an `Integer`. |
| Example | ```Dim intValue      intValue = CInt("5,579.56")```<br><br>`intValue` now holds the value 5580, 6, 56, 558, or more, depending on the thousand and decimal separators in use. |
| See also | `CBool`, `CByte`, `CCur`, `CDbl`, `CLng`, `CSng`, `CStr`, and the math functions `Fix` and `Int` |

| | |
|---|---|
| CLng | Returns an expression converted to `Variant` subtype `Long (3)`. |
| Syntax | `CLng(expression)`<br><br>`expression` is any valid expression. |
| Note | `CLng` is internationally aware, which means that the return value is based on the locale settings on the machine. Please note that decimal values are rounded, before the fractional part is discarded. A runtime error occurs if expression lies outside the range ($-2,147,483,648$ to $2,147,483,647$) applicable to a `Long`. |
| Example | ```Dim lngValue      lngValue = CLng("5,579.56")```<br><br>`lngValue` now holds the value 5580, 6, 56, 558, or more, depending on the thousand and decimal separators in use. |
| See also | `CBool`, `CByte`, `CCur`, `CDbl`, `CInt`, `CSng`, `CStr`, and the math functions `Fix` and `Int` |

| | |
|---|---|
| CSng | Returns an expression converted to `Variant` subtype `Single (4)`. |
| Syntax | `CSng(expression)`<br><br>`expression` is any valid expression. |
| Note | `CSng` is internationally aware, which means that the return value is based on the locale settings on the machine. A runtime error occurs if expression lies outside the range ($-3.402823E38$ to $-1.401298E-45$ for negative values, and $1.401298E-45$ to $3.402823E38$ for positive values) applicable to a `Single`. |

| | |
|---|---|
| Example | ```
Dim sngValue
    sngValue = CSng("5,579.56")
``` |
| | sngValue now holds the value 5579.56 or 5,57956, depending on the thousand and decimal separators in use. |
| See also | CBool, CByte, CCur, CDbl, CInt, CLng, CStr, and the math functions Fix and Int |

| | |
|---|---|
| CStr | Returns an expression converted to Variant subtype String(8). |
| Syntax | CStr(expression) |
| | expression is any valid expression. |
| Note | CStr is internationally aware, which means that the return value is based on the locale settings on the machine. A runtime error occurs if expression is Null. Numeric and Err values are returned as numbers, Boolean values as True or False, and Date values as a short date. |
| Example | ```
Dim strValue
    strValue = CStr("5,579.56")
``` |
| | strValue now holds the value 5,579.56. |
| See also | CBool, CByte, CCur, CDbl, CInt, CLng, CSng, and the math functions Fix and Int |

| | |
|---|---|
| Fix | See under *Math Functions* |

| | |
|---|---|
| Hex | Returns the hexadecimal representation (up to 8 characters) of a number as a Variant subtype String(8). |
| Syntax | Hex(number) |
| | number is any valid expression. |
| Note | number is rounded to nearest even number before it is evaluated. Null will be returned if number is Null. |
| Example | ```
Dim strValue
    strValue = Hex(5579.56)
``` |
| | strValue now holds the value 15CC. |
| See also | Oct |

| | |
|---|---|
| Int | See under *Math Functions* |
```

| | |
|---|---|
| Oct | Returns the octal representation (up to 11 characters) of a number as a `Variant` subtype `String(8)`. |
| Syntax | `Oct(number)` |
| | `expression` is any valid expression. |
| Note | `number` is rounded to nearest whole number before it is evaluated. `Null` will be returned if number is `Null`. |
| Example | `Dim strValue` |
| | `        strValue = Oct(5579.56)` |
| | `strValue` now holds the value 12714. |
| See also | `Hex` |

## Unsupported Conversion Functions

The following VB/VBA conversion functions are not supported in VBScript.

| Function Name | Alternative |
|---|---|
| `Cvar` | Not needed since conversion to a `Variant` is implicit |
| `CVDate` | `CDate`, `Date` |
| `Str` | `CStr` |
| `Val` | `CDbl`, `CInt`, `CLng`, and `CSng` |

## Miscellaneous Functions, Statements, and Keywords

Some functionalities do not fit under any of the other categories, and so they have been gathered here.

In the following table you will find descriptions of various functions for handling objects, user input, variable checks, output on screen, and so on.

| | |
|---|---|
| CreateObject | Returns a reference to an Automation/COM/ActiveX object. The object is created using COM object creation services. |
| Syntax | `CreateObject(servername.typename[, location])` |
| | `servername` is the name of the application that provides the object. |
| | `typename` is the object's type or class that you want to create. |
| | `location` (Optional) is the name of the network server you want the object created on. If this is missing the object is created on the local machine. |

| Note | An Automation/COM/ActiveX object always contains at least one type or class, but usually several types or classes are contained within. servername and typename are often referred to as progid. Note that a progid is not always a two part one, like servername.typename. It can have several parts, like servername.typename.version. |
|------|------|

| Example | |
|---------|---|

```
Dim objRemote
Dim objLocal

    ' Create an object from class
    ' MyClass contained in the
    ' COM object MyApp on a
    ' remote server named FileSrv
    Set objRemote = CreateObject( _
        "MyApp.MyClass", "FileSrv")

    ' Create an object from class
    ' LocalClass contained in the
    ' COM object LocalApp on the
    ' local macine
    Set objLocal = CreateObject( _
        "LocalApp.LocalClass")
```

| See also | GetObject |
|----------|-----------|

| Dim | Declares a variable of type Variant and allocates storage space. |
|-----|------|

| Syntax | Dim varname[([subscripts])][, |
|--------|------|

varname[([subscripts])]]...

varname is the name of the variable

subscripts (Optional) indicates the dimensions when you declare an array variable. You can declare up to 60 multiple dimensions using the following syntax:

upperbound[, upperbound]...

upperbound specifies the upper bounds of the array. Since the lower bound of an array in VBScript is always zero, upperbound is one less than the number of elements in the array.

If you declare an array with empty subscripts, you can later resize it with ReDim; this is called a dynamic array.

| Note | This statement is scope specific; that is, you need to consider when and where you want to declare your variables. Variables that are used only in a specific procedure should be declared in this procedure. This will make the variable invisible and inaccessible outside the procedure. |
|------|------|

You can also declare your variables with script scope. This means that the variables will be accessible to all procedures within the script. This is one way of sharing data between different procedures.

Dim statements should be put at the top of a procedure to make the procedure easier to read.

*Continues*

| | |
|---|---|
| Example | ``` ' Declare a dynamic array Dim arrstrDynamic() ' Declare a fixed size array ' with 5 elements Dim arrstrFixed(4) ' Declare a non-array variable Dim vntTest ``` |

| | |
|---|---|
| See also | ReDim and Set |

| | |
|---|---|
| Eval | Evaluates and returns the result of an expression. |
| Syntax | result = Eval(expression) |
| | result (Optional) is the variable you want to assign the result of the evaluation to. Although result is optional, you should consider using the Execute statement, if you don't want to specify it. |
| | expression is a string containing a valid VBScript expression. |
| Note | Because the assignment operator and the comparison operator are the same in VBScript, you need to be careful when using them with Eval. Eval always uses the equal sign (=) as a comparison operator; so if you need to use it as an assignment operator, you should use the Execute statement instead. |
| Example | ``` Dim blnResult Dim lngX, lngY     ' Initialize the variables     lngX = 15: lngY = 10     ' Evaluate the expression     blnResult = Eval( _       "lngX = lngY") ``` |
| | blnResult holds the value False, because 15 is not equal to 10. |

| | |
|---|---|
| See also | Execute |

| | |
|---|---|
| Execute | Executes one or more statements in the local namespace. |
| Syntax | Execute statement |
| | statement is a string containing the statement(s) you want executed. If you include more than one statement, you must separate them using colons or embedded line breaks. |
| Note | Because the assignment operator and the comparison operator are the same in VBScript, you need to be careful when using them with Execute. Execute always uses the equal sign (=) as an assignment operator; so if you need to use it as a comparison operator, you should use the Eval function instead. |

All in-scope variables and objects are available to the statement(s) being executed, but you need to be aware of the special case when your statements create a procedure.

```
Execute "Sub ExecProc: MsgBox ""In
here"": End Sub"
```

The scope of `ExecProc` is global and thus everything from the global scope is inherited. The context of the procedure itself is only available within the scope it is created. This means that if you execute the aforementioned Execute statement in a procedure, the `ExecProc` procedure will only be accessible within the procedure where the Execute statement is called. You can bypass this by simply moving the Execute statement to the script level or using the `ExecuteGlobal` statement.

| | |
|---|---|
| Example | ```
Dim blnResult
Dim lngX, lngY

    ' Initialize the variables
    lngX = 15: lngY = 10
    ' Execute the statement
    Execute("lngResult = + _
      lngX + lngY")
``` |

`lngResult` holds the value 25.

| | |
|---|---|
| See also | `Eval` and `ExecuteGlobal` |

| | |
|---|---|
| `ExecuteGlobal` | Executes one or more statements in the global namespace. |
| Syntax | `ExecuteGlobal statement`<br><br>`statement` is a string containing the statement(s) you want executed. If you include more than one statement, they need to be separated using colons or embedded line breaks. |
| Note | Because the assignment operator and the comparison operator are the same in VBScript, you need to be careful when using them with `ExecuteGlobal`. `ExecuteGlobal` always uses the equal sign (=) as an assignment operator; so if you need to use it as a comparison operator, you should use the `Eval` function instead.<br><br>All variables and objects are available to the statement(s) being executed. |
| Example | ```
Dim lngResult
Dim lngX, lngY

    ' Initialize the variables
    lngX = 15: lngY = 10
    ' Execute the statement
    ExecuteGlobal("lngResult = + _
      lngX + lngY")
``` |

`lngResult` holds the value 25.

| | |
|---|---|
| See also | `Eval` and `Execute` |

| | |
|---|---|
| Filter | Returns an array that contains a subset of an array of strings. The array is zero-based as are all arrays in VBScript and it holds as many elements as are found in the filtering process. The subset is determined by specifying a criterion. |
| Syntax | Filter(inputstrings, value[, include[, compare]]) |
| | inputstrings is a one-dimensional string array that you want to search. |
| | value is the string you want to search for. |
| | include (Optional) is a Boolean value indicating if you want to include (True) or exclude (False) elements in inputstrings that contains value. |
| | compare (Optional) indicates the comparison method used when evaluating. Use one of the following constants: |
| | vbBinaryCompare -0 (Default) (Performs a binary comparison, that is, a case-sensitive comparison) |
| | vbTextCompare -1 (Performs a textual comparison, that is, a non-case-sensitive comparison) |
| Note | An empty array is returned if no matches are found. A runtime error occurs if inputstrings is not a one-dimensional array or if it is Null. |
| Example | ```
Dim arrstrColors(3)
Dim arrstrFilteredColors

    ' Fill the array
    arrstrColors(0) = "Red"
    arrstrColors(1) = "Green"
    arrstrColors(2) = "Blue"

    ' Filter the array
    arrstrFilteredColors = _
Filter(arrstrColors, "Red")
``` |
| | arrstrFilteredColors now holds one element (0) which has the value Red. |
| See also | See the string function Replace |

| | |
|---|---|
| GetObject | Returns a reference to an Automation object. |
| Syntax | GetObject([pathname][, class]) |
| | pathname (Optional) is a string specifying the full path and name of the file that contains the object you want to retrieve. You need to specify class if you omit this argument. |
| | class (Optional) is a string that indicates the class of the object. You need to specify pathname if you omit this argument. The following syntax is used for class: |
| | appname.objecttype |
| | appname is a string indicating the application that provides the object. |
| | objecttype is a string specifying the object's type or class that you want created. |
```

| Note | You can use this function to start the application associated with pathname and activate/return the object specified in the pathname. A new object is returned if pathname is a zero-length string ("") and the currently active object of the specified type is returned if pathname is omitted. Note that if the object you want returned has been compiled with Visual Basic, you cannot obtain a reference to an existing object by omitting the pathname argument. A new object will be returned instead. The opposite is true for objects that are registered as single-instance objects; the same instance will always be returned. However, you should note the aforementioned problems with ActiveX DLLs compiled using Visual Basic. |
|---|---|
| | Some applications allow you to activate part of a file and you can do this by suffixing pathname with an exclamation mark (!) and a string that identifies the part of the object you want. |
| | You should only use this function when there is a current instance of the object you want to create, or when you want the object to open up a specific document. Use `CreateObject` to create a new instance of an object. |

| Example | |
|---|---|

```
Dim myobj
Set myobj = 
CreateObject("Excel.Application")
Dim objAutomation

    ' Create a reference to an
    ' existing instance of an
    ' Excel application (this
    ' call will raise an error
    ' if no Excel.Application
    ' objects already exists)
    Set objAutomation = _
GetObject(, "Excel.Application")

    ' Create a reference to a
    ' specific workbook in a new
    ' instance of an Excel
    ' application
    Set objAutomation = _
    GetObject( "C:\Test.xls ")
```

| See also | `CreateObject` |
|---|---|

| GetRef | Returns a reference to a procedure. This reference can be bound to an object event. This will let you bind a VBScript procedure to a DHTML event. |
|---|---|
| Syntax | `Set object.eventname = GetRef(procname)`<br><br>`object` is the name of the object in which `eventname` is placed.<br><br>`eventname` is the name of the event to which the procedure is to be bound.<br><br>`procname` is the name of the procedure you want to bind to `eventname`. |

*Continues*

| Example | |
|---|---|
| | ```
Sub NewOnFocus()
    ' Do your stuff here
End Sub

' Bind the NewOnFocus
' procedure to the
' Window. OnFocus event
Set Window.OnFocus = _
    GetRef("NewOnFocus ")
``` |

| InputBox | Displays a dialog box with a custom prompt and a text box. The content of the text box is returned when the user clicks OK. |
|---|---|
| Syntax | InputBox(prompt[, title][, default][, xpos][, ypos], [helpfile, context]) |

prompt is the message you want displayed in the dialog box. The string can contain up to 1024 characters, depending on the width of the characters you use. You can separate the lines using one of these VBScript constants.

vbCr, vbCrLf, vbLf, or vbNewLine

title (Optional) is the text you want displayed in the dialog box title bar. The application name will be displayed, if this argument is omitted.

default is the default text that will be returned, if the user doesn't type in any data. The text box will be empty if you omit this argument.

xpos (Optional) is a numeric expression that indicates the horizontal distance of the left edge of the dialog box measured in twips (1/20 of a printer's point, which is 1/72 of an inch) from the left edge of the screen. The dialog box will be horizontally centered if you omit this argument.

ypos (Optional) is a numeric expression that indicates the vertical distance of the upper edge of the dialog box measured in twips from the upper edge of the screen. The dialog box will be vertically positioned approximately one third of the way down the screen, if you omit this argument.

helpfile (Optional) is a string expression that indicates the help file to use when providing context-sensitive help for the dialog box. This argument must be used in conjunction with context. This is not available on 16-bit platforms.

context (Optional) is a numeric expression that indicates the help context number that makes sure that the right help topic is displayed. This argument must be used in conjunction with helpfile. This is not available on 16-bit platforms.

| Note | A zero-length string will be returned if the user clicks Cancel or presses Esc. |
|---|---|
```

| | |
|---|---|
| Example | ```
Dim strInput
    strInput = InputBox( _
        "Enter User Name:", "Test")
    MsgBox strInput
``` |

The `MsgBox` will display either an empty string or whatever the user entered into the text box.

| | |
|---|---|
| See also | `MsgBox` |

---

| | |
|---|---|
| IsEmpty | Returns a `Boolean` value indicating if a variable has been initialized. |
| Syntax | `IsEmpty(expression)`<br><br>`expression` is the variable you want to check has been initialized. |
| Note | You can use more than one variable as expression. If, for example, you concatenate two `Variants` and one of them is empty, the `IsEmpty` function will return `False`, because the expression is not empty. |
| Example | ```
Dim strTest
Dim strInput
    strInput = "Test"
    MsgBox IsEmpty(strTest) ' true
    MsgBox IsEmpty(strInput & _
    strTest)            ' false
``` |
| See also | `IsArray`, `IsDate`, `IsNull`, `IsNumeric`, `IsObject`, and `VarType` |

---

| | |
|---|---|
| IsNull | Returns a `Boolean` value indicating if a variable contains `Null` or valid data. |
| Syntax | `IsNull(expression)`<br><br>`expression` is any expression. |
| Note | This function returns `True` if the whole of expression evaluates to `Null`. If you have more than one variable in expression, all of them must be `Null` for the function to return `True`.<br><br>Please be aware that `Null` is not the same as `Empty` (a variable that hasn't been initialized) or a zero-length string (""). `Null` means no valid value.<br><br>You should always use the `IsNull` function when checking for `Null` values, because using the normal operators will return `False` even if one variable is `Null`. |
| Example | ```
Dim strInput
    strInput = "Test"
    MsgBox IsNull( strInput _
        & Null) ' false
    MsgBox IsNull(Null)       ' true
``` |
| See also | `IsArray`, `IsDate`, `IsEmpty`, `IsNumeric`, `IsObject`, and `VarType` |
```

| IsNumeric | Returns a `Boolean` value indicating if an expression can be evaluated as a number. |
|---|---|
| Syntax | `IsNumeric(expression)`<br><br>`expression` is any expression. |
| Note | This function returns `True` if the whole expression evaluates to a number. A `Date` expression is not considered a numeric expression. |
| Example | ```MsgBox IsNumeric(55.55)```<br>``` ' true```<br>```MsgBox IsNumeric("55.55")```<br>``` ' true```<br>```MsgBox IsNumeric("55.55aaa")```<br>``` ' false```<br>```MsgBox IsNumeric( "March 1, 1999")```<br>``` ' false```<br>```MsgBox IsNumeric(vbNullChar)```<br>``` ' false``` |
| See also | `IsArray`, `IsDate`, `IsEmpty`, `IsNull`, `IsObject`, and `VarType` |

| IsObject | Returns a `Boolean` value indicating if an expression is a reference to a valid `Automation` object. |
|---|---|
| Syntax | `IsObject(expression)`<br><br>`expression` is any expression. |
| Note | This function returns `True` only if expression is in fact a variable of `Variant` subtype `Object (9)` or a user-defined object. |
| Example | ```Dim objTest```<br><br>```MsgBox IsObject(objTest)```<br>```          ' false```<br>```Set objTest = CreateObject( _```<br>```   "Excel.Application")```<br>```MsgBox IsObject(objTest)```<br>``` ' true``` |
| See also | `IsArray`, `IsDate`, `IsEmpty`, `IsNull`, `IsNumeric`, `Set`, and `VarType` |

| LoadPicture | Returns a picture object. |
|---|---|
| Syntax | `LoadPicture(picturename)`<br><br>`picturename` is a string expression that indicates the filename of the picture you want loaded. |

| Note | This function is available only on 32-bit platforms. |
|------|------|

The following graphic formats are supported:

```
Bitmap - .bmp
Icon - .ico
Run-length encoded - .rle
Windows metafile - .wmf
Enhanced metafile - .emf
GIF - .gif
JPEG - .jpg
```

A runtime error occurs if `picturename` doesn't exist or if it is not a valid picture file. Use `LoadPicture("")` to return an "empty" picture object in order to clear a particular picture.

| Example | |
|---------|---|

```
Dim objPicture

' Load a picture into
' objPicture
objPicture = LoadPicture( _
    "C:\Test.bmp")
' Clear objPicture
objPicture = LoadPicture("")
```

| MsgBox | Displays a dialog box with a custom message and a custom set of command buttons. The value of the button the user clicks is returned as the result of this function. |
|--------|------|
| Syntax | `MsgBox(prompt[, buttons][, title [, helpfile, context])` |

`prompt` is the message you want displayed in the dialog box. The string can contain up to 1024 characters, depending on the width of the characters you use.

You can separate the lines using one of these VBScript constants.

`vbCr`, `vbCrLf`, `vbLf`, or `vbNewLine`

`buttons` (Optional) is the sum of values indicating the number and type of button(s) to display, which icon style to use, which button is the default, and if the `MsgBox` is modal.

The settings for this argument are:

`vbOKOnly` –0 (Displays OK button)

`vbOKCancel` –1 (Displays OK and Cancel buttons)

`vbAbortRetryIgnore` –2 (Displays Abort, Retry, and Ignore buttons)

`vbYesNoCancel` –3 (Displays Yes, No, and Cancel buttons)

`vbYesNo` –4 (Displays Yes and No buttons)

*Continues*

vbRetryCancel -5 (Displays Retry and Cancel buttons)

vbCritical -16 (Displays critical icon)

vbQuestion -32 (Displays query icon)

vbExclamation -48 (Displays warning icon)

vbInformation -64 (Displays information icon)

vbDefaultButton1 -0 (Makes the first button the default one)

vbDefaultButton2 -256 (Makes the second button the default one)

vbDefaultButton3 -512 (Makes the third button the default one)

vbDefaultButton4 -768 -(Makes the fourth button the default one)

vbApplicationModal -0 (When the MsgBox is application modal, the user must respond to the message box, before he or she can continue)

vbSystemModal -4096 (The same effect as vbApplicationModal)

Buttons (values 0–5)

Icon (values 16, 32, 48, and 64)

Default button (values 0, 256, 512, and 768)

Modal (values 0 and 4096)

You should only pick one value from each group when creating your MsgBox.

title (Optional) is the text you want displayed in the dialog box title bar. The application name will be displayed if this argument is omitted.

helpfile (Optional) is a string expression that indicates the help file to use when providing context-sensitive help for the dialog box. This argument must be used in conjunction with context. This is not available on 16-bit platforms.

context (Optional) is a numeric expression that indicates the help context number that makes sure that the right help topic is displayed. This argument must be used in conjunction with helpfile.

Note

The following values can be returned:

vbOK (1)

vbCancel (2)

vbAbort (3)

vbRetry (4)

vbIgnore (5)

vbYes (6)

vbNo (7)

The Esc key has the same effect as the Cancel button. Clicking the Help or pressing F1 will not close the MsgBox.

| | |
|---|---|
| Example | ```
Dim intReturn

intReturn = MsgBox( "Exit the _
application?", vbYesNoCancel + _
                 vbQuestion)
``` |

The `MsgBox` will display the message `"Exit the application?"`, the buttons `Yes`, `No`, and `Cancel`, and the question mark icon. This `MsgBox` will be application modal.

| | |
|---|---|
| See also | `InputBox` |

---

| | |
|---|---|
| RGB | Returns an integer that represents an RGB color value. |
| | The RGB color value specifies the relative intensity of red, green, and blue to cause a specific color to be displayed. |
| Syntax | `RGB(red, green, blue)` |
| | `red` is the red part of the color. Must be in the range 0–255. |
| | `green` is the green part of the color. Must be in the range 0–255. |
| | `blue` is the blue part of the color. Must be in the range 0–255. |
| Note | 255 will be used, if the value for any of the arguments is larger than 255. |
| | A runtime error occurs if any of the arguments cannot be evaluated to a numeric value. |
| Example | ```
' Returns the RGB number for white
RGB(255, 255, 255)
``` |

---

| | |
|---|---|
| `ScriptEngine` | Returns a string indicating the scripting language being used. |
| Syntax | `ScriptEngine` |
| Note | The following scripting engine values can be returned: |
| | `VBScript` MS VBScript |
| | `JScript`  MS JScript |
| | `VBA`      MS Visual Basic for Applications |
| | Other third-party ActiveX Scripting engines can also be returned, if you have installed one. |
| See also | `ScriptEngineBuildVersion,`<br>`ScriptEngineMajorVersion,` and<br>`ScriptEngineMinorVersion` |

| | |
|---|---|
| `ScriptEngineBuildVersion` | Returns the build version of the script engine being used. |
| Syntax | `ScriptEngineBuildVersion` |
| Note | This function gets the information from the DLL for the current scripting language. |
| See also | `ScriptEngine`, `ScriptEngineMajorVersion`, and `ScriptEngineMinorVersion` |

| | |
|---|---|
| `ScriptEngineMajorVersion` | Returns the major version number of the script engine being used. The major version number is the part before the decimal separator, for example 5 if the version is 5.6. |
| Syntax | `ScriptEngineMajorVersion` |
| Note | This function gets the information from the DLL for the current scripting language. |
| See also | `ScriptEngine`, `ScriptEngineBuildVersion`, and `ScriptEngineMinorVersion` |

| | |
|---|---|
| `ScriptEngineMinorVersion` | Returns the minor version number of the script engine being used. The minor version number is the part after the decimal separator, for example 6 if the version is 5.6. |
| Syntax | `ScriptEngineMinorVersion` |
| Note | This function gets the information from the DLL for the current scripting language. |
| See also | `ScriptEngine`, `ScriptEngineBuildVersion`, and `ScriptEngineMajorVersion` |

| | |
|---|---|
| `Set` | Returns an object reference, which must be assigned to a variable or property, or returns a procedure reference that must be associated with an event. |
| Syntax | `Set objectvar = {objectexpression | New classname | Nothing}` |
| | `objectvar` is the name of a variable or property. |
| | `objectexpression` (Optional) is the name of an existing object or another variable of the same object type. It can also be a method or function that returns either. |
| | `classname` (Optional) is the name of the class you want to create. |
| | `Set object.eventname = GetRef(procname)` |
| | `object` is the name of the object that `eventname` is associated with. |
| | `eventname` is the name of the event you want to bind `procname` to. |
| | `procname` is the name of the procedure you want to associate with `eventname`. |

| Note | objectvar must be an empty variable or an object type consistent with objectexpression being assigned. |
|---|---|
| | Set is used to create a reference to an object and not a copy of it. This means that if you use the Set statement more than once on the same object, you will have more than one reference to the same object. Any changes made to the object will be "visible" to all references. |
| | New is used only in conjunction with classname, when you want to create a new instance of a class. |
| | If you use the Nothing keyword, you release the reference to an object, but if you have more than one reference to an object, the system resources are released only when all references have been destroyed (by setting them to Nothing) or they go out of scope. |
| Example | ```
Dim objTest1
Dim objTest2
Dim objNewClass

    ' Create a new dictionary object
    Set objTest1 = CreateObject( _
    "Scripting.Dictionary")
    ' Create a reference to the
    ' newly created dictionary
    ' object
    Set objTest2 = objTest1

    ' Destroy the object reference
    Set objTest1 = Nothing
    ' Although objTest2 was set
    ' to refer to objTest1, you can
    ' still refer to objTest2,
    ' because the system resources
    ' will not be released before
    ' all references have been
    ' destroyed. So let's add a key
    ' and an item
    objTest2.Add "TestKey", "Test"
    ' Destroy the object reference
    Set objTest2 = Nothing

    ' Create an instance of the
    ' class clsTest (created with
    ' the Class keyword)
    Set objNewClass = New clsTest
    ' ...
    ' Destroy the class instance
    Set objNewClass = Nothing
``` |
| See also | Class and GetRef |
```

| TypeName | Returns the `Variant` subtype information for an expression as a `Variant` subtype `String(8)`. |
|---|---|
| Syntax | `TypeName(expression)` |
| | `expression` is the variable or constant you want subtype information for. |
| Note | This function has the following return values (strings): |
| | `Byte` – Byte |
| | `Integer` – Integer |
| | `Long` – Long integer |
| | `Single` – Single-precision floating-point number |
| | `Double` – Double-precision floating-point number |
| | `Currency` – Currency |
| | `Decimal` – Decimal |
| | `Date` – Date and/or time |
| | `String` – Character string |
| | `Boolean` – `True` or `False` |
| | `Empty` – Unitialized |
| | `Null` – No valid data |
| | `<object type>` – Actual type name of an object |
| | `Object` – Generic object |
| | `Unknown` – Unknown object type |
| | `Nothing` – Object variable that doesn't refer to an object instance |
| | `Error` – Error |
| Example | ```
Dim arrstrTest(10)

MsgBox TypeName(10)
        ' Integer
MsgBox TypeName("Test")
        ' String
MsgBox TypeName(arrstrTest)
        ' Variant()
MsgBox TypeName(Null)
        ' Null
``` |
| See also | `IsArray`, `IsDate`, `IsEmpty`, `IsNull`, `IsNumeric`, `IsObject`, and `VarType` |

| VarType | Returns an integer indicating the subtype of a variable or constant. |
|---|---|
| Syntax | `VarType(expression)` |
| | `expression` is the variable or constant you want subtype information for. |
```

| Note | This function has the following return values: |
|------|------|
| | vbEmpty -0 (Uninitialized) |
| | vbNull -1 (No valid data) |
| | vbInteger - 2 (Integer) |
| | vbLong -3 (Long integer) |
| | vbSingle -4 (Single-precision floating-point number) |
| | vbDouble -5 (Double-precision floating-point number) |
| | vbCurrency -6 (Currency) |
| | vbDate -7 (Date) |
| | vbString -8 (String) |
| | vbObject -9 (Automation object) |
| | vbError -10 (Error) |
| | vbBoolean -11 (Boolean) |
| | vbVariant -12 (Variant (only used only with arrays of Variants)) |
| | vbDataObject -13 (A data-access object) |
| | vbByte -17 (Byte) |
| | vbArray -8192 (Array) |

| Example | |
|---------|---|

```
Dim arrstrTest(10)

MsgBox VarType(10)
      ' 2
MsgBox VarType("Test")
      ' 8
MsgBox VarType(arrstrTest)
      ' 8204
MsgBox VarType(Null)
      ' 1
```

| See also | IsArray, IsDate, IsEmpty, IsNull, IsNumeric, IsObject, and TypeName |
|----------|------|

# Variable Naming Convention

Variables are used to hold values. With that goal in mind, it makes sense to choose names for them that describe their purpose or what they contain. The bigger the project you are working on is, the more important it is to be able to keep track of its variables. Here, we offer some things to keep in mind, including standards.

First, you'll want to keep your naming consistent. So, for example if you use `Cnt` as a variable in one part of the script and `Count` in another when you are in fact dealing with the same data, you're very likely to introduce runtime errors by confusing the variables.

Second, it is useful to include the scope of a variable by prefixing with `g` for global, or `l` for local (to a subprocedure), for example, `gstrCompanyName` and `lstrDepartmentName`.

Finally, one of the best ways to organize variable names is to prefix all variable names you use with a shorthand representation of the data type that the variable will hold. The standard prefixes used to accomplish this are called Hungarian notation.

Here is a listing of data types and their associated Hungarian prefixes, complete with examples of use.

| Data Type | Hungarian Prefix | Example | VarType() |
|---|---|---|---|
| Boolean | bln (or bool) | BlnValid | 11 |
| Byte | Byt | bytColor | 17 |
| Currency | Cur | CurTotal | 6 |
| Date or Time | Dtm | dtmMember | 7 |
| Double | Dbl | DblTotal | 5 |
| Error | Err | errInvalidEmailAddress | 10 |
| Integer | Int | intCount | 2 |

*Continues*

| Data Type | Hungarian Prefix | Example | VarType() |
|-----------|-----------------|---------|-----------|
| Long | Lng | lngHeight | 3 |
| Object | Obj | ObjWS | 9 or 13 |
| Single | Sng | sngWidth | 4 |
| String | Str | strName | 8 |
| Variant | Var | varNumber | 12 |

Here is a listing of control types and their associated Hungarian prefixes, complete with examples of use.

| Control Type | Hungarian Prefix | Example |
|--------------|-----------------|---------|
| Animated button | Ani | AniButton |
| Check box | Chk | ChkNo |
| Combo list box | Cbo | CboOS |
| Command button | Cmd | CmdSend |
| Common dialog | Dlg | DlgOpen |
| Frame | Fra | FraOptions |
| Horizontal scroll bar | Hsb | HsbContrast |
| Image control | Img | ImgHeading |
| Label | Lbl | LblText |
| Line | Lin | LinDivide |
| List box | Lst | LstDueBy |
| 3D panel | Pnl | PnlMain |
| Pop-up menu | Mnu | MnuContextSelect |
| Radio/Option button | Opt | OptIncludeFreeGift |
| Slider | Sld | SldSetVolume |
| Spin button | Spn | SpnCounter |
| Tab strip | Tab | TabOptions |
| Text box | Txt | TxtComment |
| Vertical scroll bar | Vsb | VsbSetVolume |

# Coding Convention

This appendix covers coding conventions and, like the previous appendix covering variable naming, will help us to produce code that is easily readable and understandable, minimizing errors, and speeding up the inevitable debugging process.

## Constants

Constants should be clearly identifiable in any code that you write by using either capitals or a `con` prefix. This is done to avoid confusion with variables in the code. For example:

- ❑   `TAX_RATE`
- ❑   `conTaxRate`

## Arrays

Arrays should be prefixed with the letter `a` or letters `arr`, depending on your preference or company policy, as well as adhering to the conventions already detailed earlier. By doing this all arrays in your code will be easier to find later. For example:

- ❑   `astrName`
- ❑   `arrstrName`

## Procedure Naming

Another key to writing easy-to-read, easy-to-debug, and easy-to-reuse code is to give your procedures descriptive names. This makes them easier to find in the code and also allows you to keep sections of code for later use—because the descriptive name makes their purpose easier to understand. One trick to this is to start your procedure names with a verb:

- ❑   `InitValues`
- ❑   `ReadData`
- ❑   `CloseWindow`

Mixed case (that is, the capitalization of the first letter of each word) and consistency (using similar verbs) of use between different routines should also be used.

# Indentation

The single most valuable thing that you can do to make your code more readable and easy to follow is proper indentation. This is the greatest way of enhancing clarity and adding a visual cue to the hierarchy to the script.

After a procedure declaration, opening loop statement, or conditional test, we indent by 2 (or 4) spaces, or use tabs. Similarly, closing statements follow the reverse indentation.

By doing this, you can easily follow the flow of your program, as this example demonstrates. The structure of the code contained within the `For...Next` loop and the `If...End If` statements are clear and easy to follow.

```
Sub ShowIndentation()
    Dim intCount
    Dim strMessage
    For intCount = 1 to 5
        strMessage = strMessage & " " & intCount
        If strMessage = " 1 2" then
            strMessage = strMessage & " -"
        End If
    Next
    MsgBox(strMessage)
End Sub
```

# Commenting

Comments are a must, especially when more than one person is working on a project, with functions that will be used by other team members. Even if you're in a position to write code that only you will ever see, we can guarantee you that after a few months of not dealing with it (or even just certain parts of it), you will forget what it does or how exactly it does it. This is where commenting comes in handy.

You can comment all sorts of aspects of the code. You can add many different comments to your procedures. Here are a few suggestions:

❑   Describing what they do

❑   Pre- and postconditions

❑   Return values

You can also comment things such as important variables (ones that are changed in the procedure or passed by reference) and other parts of your code. Not only will you then be able to remember what it does six months down the line, but another programmer will be able to easily follow your logic when they take over the maintenance of your code after your promotion.

Remember to also make use of the two different types of comments within your code:

- ❑ *Tombstone:* Comments that appear at the beginning of the code and are used to describe the code as a whole.

- ❑ *Inline:* Comments that are specific to particular lines that appear within the code.

What follows is an example of well-commented code.

```
' These comments here describe what the
' function does and what it is for.
' It can also contain information such as
' copyright notices and author name

Sub ShowIndentation()
    Dim intCount
    Dim strMessage ' comment specific to this line
    For intCount = 1 to 5
        strMessage = strMessage & " " & intCount
        If strMessage = " 1 2" then ' another specific comment
            strMessage = strMessage & " -"
        End If
    Next
    MsgBox(strMessage)
End Sub
```

# Visual Basic Constants Supported in VBScript

This appendix is primarily aimed at the Visual Basic programmer who wants to make the jump into VBScript. This appendix covers all of the Visual Basic constants that are supported in VBScript. Constants are useful in script because they allow us to use a specific value without explicitly writing it.

## Color Constants

These constants are used within script code to specify particular colors.

| Constant | Value | Description |
|----------|-------|-------------|
| VbBlack | &h00 | Black |
| VbRed | &Hff | Red |
| VbGreen | &hFF00 | Green |
| VbYellow | &hFFFF | Yellow |
| VbBlue | &hFF0000 | Blue |
| VbMagenta | &hFF00FF | Magenta |
| VbCyan | &hFFFF00 | Cyan |
| VbWhite | &hFFFFFF | White |

## Comparison Constants

These constants are used to switch between binary or textual comparisons.

| Constant | Value | Description |
| --- | --- | --- |
| VbBinaryCompare | 0 | Perform a binary comparison |
| VbTextCompare | 1 | Perform a textual comparison |
| VbSunday | 1 | Sunday |
| VbMonday | 2 | Monday |
| VbTuesday | 3 | Tuesday |
| VbWednesday | 4 | Wednesday |
| VbThursday | 5 | Thursday |
| VbFriday | 6 | Friday |
| VbSaturday | 7 | Saturday |
| vbUseSystemDayOfWeek | 0 | Use the day of the week specified for your computer as the first day of the week. |
| vbFirstJan1 | 1 | Use the week in which January 1 occurs as the first week of the year (this is the default) |
| VbFirstFourDays | 2 | Use the week that has at least 4 days in the new year |
| VbFirstFullWeek | 3 | Use the first full week of the year |

# Date Format Constants

These constants determine how a date is displayed.

| Constant | Value | Description |
| --- | --- | --- |
| VbGeneralDate | 0 | Displays a date and/or time. The format is determined by your system settings. |
| VbLongDate | 1 | Display a date using your system's long date format. |
| VbShortDate | 2 | Display a date using your systems short date format. |
| VbLongTime | 3 | Display a time using your system's long time format. |
| VbShortTime | 4 | Display a time using your system's short time format. |

# Miscellaneous Constants

| Constant | Value | Description |
| --- | --- | --- |
| VbObjectError | –2147221504 | Used as the base for user-defined error numbers. |

# MsgBox Constants

These constants specify which buttons and icons appear on the message box, and which button is the default. Some of the constants are also used to determine the modality of the MsgBox.

| Constant | Value | Description |
| --- | --- | --- |
| VbOKOnly | 0 | Display the OK button only. |
| VbOKCancel | 1 | Display the OK and Cancel buttons. |
| VbAbortRetryIgnore | 2 | Display the Abort, Retry, and Ignore buttons. |
| VbYesNoCancel | 3 | Display the Yes, No, and Cancel buttons. |
| VbYesNo | 4 | Display the Yes and No buttons. |
| VbRetryCancel | 5 | Display the Retry and Cancel buttons. |
| VbCritical | 16 | Display the Critical Message icon. |
| VbQuestion | 32 | Display the Warning Query icon. |
| VbExclamation | 48 | Display the Warning Message icon. |
| VbInformation | 64 | Display the Information Message icon. |
| VbDefaultButton1 | 0 | The first displayed button is the default. |
| VbDefaultButton2 | 256 | The second displayed button is the default. |
| VbDefaultButton3 | 512 | The third displayed button is the default. |
| VbDefaultButton4 | 768 | The fourth displayed button is the default. |
| VbApplicationModal | 0 | The user must respond to the message box. |
| VbSystemModal | 4096 | The user must respond to the message box. The message box is always on top in all other windows. |

The following determine which MsgBox button the user has selected. These constants must be explicitly declared within your code before they can be used.

| Constant | Value | Description |
|---|---|---|
| VbOK | 1 | The OK button was clicked. |
| VbCancel | 2 | The Cancel button was clicked. |
| VbAbort | 3 | The Abort button was clicked. |
| VbRetry | 4 | The Retry button was clicked. |
| VbIgnore | 5 | The Ignore button was clicked. |
| VbYes | 6 | The Yes button was clicked. |
| VbNo | 7 | The No button was clicked. |

# String Constants

These constants allow for the convenient insertion of nonvisible characters into strings.

| Constant | Value | Description |
|---|---|---|
| VbCr | Chr(13) | Carriage return. |
| VbCrLf | Chr(13) & Chr(10) | Carriage return and linefeed combination. |
| VbFormFeed | Chr(12) | Form feed. This is not useful from within Windows applications. |
| VbLf | Chr(10) | Line feed. |
| VbNewLine | Chr(13) & Chr(10) or Chr(10) | Platform-specific newline character. |
| VbNullChar | Chr(0) | Character having the value 0. |
| VbNullString | String having value 0 | Not the same as a zero-length string (" "). This is used for calling external procedures. |
| VbTab | Chr(9) | Horizontal tab. |
| VbVerticalTab | Chr(11) | Vertical tab. This is not useful from within Windows applications. |

# Tristate Constants

These constants are used to switch arguments on or off, or to use the default setting.

| Constant | Value | Description |
| --- | --- | --- |
| TristateUseDefault | -2 | Use default from computer's regional settings |
| TristateTrue | -1 | True |
| TristateFalse | 0 | False |

## VarType Constants

The VarType constants are used to determine the subtype of a Variant. These constants must be explicitly declared within your code before they can be used.

| Constant | Value | Description |
| --- | --- | --- |
| VbEmpty | 0 | Uninitialized (this is the default) |
| VbNull | 1 | Contains no valid data |
| VbInteger | 2 | Integer subtype |
| VbLong | 3 | Long subtype |
| VbSingle | 4 | Single subtype |
| VbDouble | 5 | Double subtype |
| VbCurrency | 6 | Currency subtype |
| VbDate | 7 | Date subtype |
| VbString | 8 | String subtype |
| VbObject | 9 | Object |
| VbError | 10 | Error subtype |
| VbBoolean | 11 | Boolean subtype |
| VbVariant | 12 | Variant (used only for arrays of Variants) |
| VbDataObject | 13 | Data access object |
| vbDecimal | 14 | Decimal subtype |
| vbByte | 17 | Byte subtype |
| vbArray | 8192 | Array |

# VBScript Error Codes and the Err Object

Here you'll find all the error codes associated with VBScript along with the Err object.

## Runtime Errors

Runtime errors occur wherever your script attempts to perform an invalid action. The vast majority of these errors should be caught during the debugging and testing stage. VBScript contains 43 runtime errors, which are listed in the following table with their decimal and hexadecimal representations.

| Decimal | Hexadecimal | Description |
| --- | --- | --- |
| 5 | 800A0005 | Invalid procedure call or argument |
| 6 | 800A0006 | Overflow |
| 7 | 800A0007 | Out of memory |
| 9 | 800A0009 | Subscript out of range |
| 10 | 800A000A | This array is fixed or temporarily locked |
| 11 | 800A000B | Division by zero |
| 13 | 800A000D | Type mismatch |
| 14 | 800A000E | Out of string space |
| 17 | 800A0011 | Can't perform requested operation |
| 28 | 800A001C | Out of stack space |
| 35 | 800A0023 | Sub or Function not defined |
| 48 | 800A0030 | Err in loading DLL |

*Continues*

| Decimal | Hexadecimal | Description |
|---------|-------------|-------------|
| 51 | 800A0033 | Internal error |
| 91 | 800A005B | Object variable not set |
| 92 | 800A005C | For loop not initialized |
| 94 | 800A005E | Invalid use of Null |
| 424 | 800A01A8 | Object required |
| 429 | 800A01AD | ActiveX component can't create object |
| 430 | 800A01AE | Class doesn't support Automation |
| 432 | 800A01B0 | File name or class name not found during Automation operation |
| 438 | 800A01B6 | Object doesn't support this property or method |
| 445 | 800A01BD | Object doesn't support this action |
| 447 | 800A01BF | Object doesn't support current locale setting |
| 448 | 800A01C0 | Named argument not found |
| 449 | 800A01C1 | Argument not optional |
| 450 | 800A01C2 | Wrong number of arguments or invalid property assignment |
| 451 | 800A01C3 | Object not a collection |
| 458 | 800A01CA | Variable uses an Automation type not supported in VBScript |
| 462 | 800A01CE | The remote server machine does not exist or is unavailable |
| 481 | 800A01E1 | Invalid picture |
| 500 | 800A01F4 | Variable is undefined |
| 502 | 800A01F6 | Object not safe for scripting |
| 503 | 800A01F7 | Object not safe for initializing |
| 504 | 800A01F8 | Object not safe for creating |
| 505 | 800A01F9 | Invalid or unqualified reference |
| 506 | 800A01FA | Class not defined |
| 507 | 800A01FB | An exception occurred |
| 5008 | 800A1390 | Illegal assignment |
| 5017 | 800A1399 | Syntax error in regular expression |

| Decimal | Hexadecimal | Description |
|---|---|---|
| 5018 | 800A139A | Unexpected quantifier |
| 5019 | 800A139B | Expected ']' in regular expression |
| 5020 | 800A139C | Expected ')' in regular expression |
| 5021 | 800A139D | Invalid range in character set |

## Syntax Errors

Syntax errors occur wherever your script contains statements that do not follow the pre-defined rules for that language. This type of error should be caught during development. VBScript contains 49 syntax errors, listed in the following table with their decimal and hexadecimal representations.

| Decimal | Hexadecimal | Description |
|---|---|---|
| 1001 | 800A03E9 | Out of memory |
| 1002 | 800A03EA | Syntax error |
| 1005 | 800A03ED | Expected '(' |
| 1006 | 800A03EE | Expected ')' |
| 1010 | 800A03F2 | Expected identifier |
| 1011 | 800A03F3 | Expected '=' |
| 1012 | 800A03F4 | Expected 'If' |
| 1013 | 800A03F5 | Expected 'To' |
| 1014 | 800A03F6 | Expected 'End' |
| 1015 | 800A03F7 | Expected 'Function' |
| 1016 | 800A03F8 | Expected 'Sub' |
| 1017 | 800A03F9 | Expected 'Then' |
| 1018 | 800A03FA | Expected 'Wend' |
| 1019 | 800A03FB | Expected 'Loop' |
| 1020 | 800A03FC | Expected 'Next' |
| 1021 | 800A03FD | Expected 'Case' |
| 1022 | 800A03FE | Expected 'Select' |
| 1023 | 800A03FF | Expected expression |
| 1024 | 800A0400 | Expected statement |

*Continues*

| Decimal | Hexadecimal | Description |
|---------|-------------|-------------|
| 1025 | 800A0401 | Expected end of statement |
| 1026 | 800A0402 | Expected integer constant |
| 1027 | 800A0403 | Expected 'While' or 'Until' |
| 1028 | 800A0404 | Expected 'While', 'Until', or end of statement |
| 1029 | 800A0405 | Expected 'With' |
| 1030 | 800A0406 | Identifier too long |
| 1013 | 800A0407 | Invalid number |
| 1014 | 800A0408 | Invalid character |
| 1015 | 800A0409 | Unterminated string constant |
| 1034 | 800A040A | Unterminated comment |
| 1037 | 800A040D | Invalid use of 'Me' keyword |
| 1038 | 800A040E | 'loop' without 'do' |
| 1039 | 800A040F | Invalid 'exit' statement |
| 1040 | 800A0410 | Invalid 'for' loop control variable |
| 1041 | 800A0411 | Name redefined |
| 1042 | 800A0412 | Must be first statement on the line |
| 1044 | 800A0414 | Cannot use parentheses when calling a Sub |
| 1045 | 800A0415 | Expected literal constant |
| 1046 | 800A0416 | Expected 'In' |
| 1047 | 800A0417 | Expected 'Class' |
| 1048 | 800A0418 | Must be defined inside a Class |
| 1049 | 800A0419 | Expected Let or Set or Get in property declaration |
| 1050 | 800A041A | Expected 'Property' |
| 1051 | 800A041B | Number of arguments must be consistent across properties specification |
| 1052 | 800A041C | Cannot have multiple default property/method in a Class |
| 1053 | 800A041D | Class initialize or terminate do not have arguments |
| 1054 | 800A041E | Property Set or Let must have at least one argument |
| 1055 | 800A041F | Unexpected 'Next' |

| Decimal | Hexadecimal | Description |
|---------|-------------|-------------|
| 1057 | 800A0421 | 'Default' specification must also specify 'Public') |
| 1058 | 800A0422 | 'Default' specification can only be on Property Get |

# The Err Object

Errors usually make their way into code and as such it's important to be able to spot them and remove them. At the core of this is error handling using the Err object.

Let's take a quick tour of the Err object and the On Err statement and look at ways to make use of them in VBScript code.

# Err Object

The Err object is the heart and soul of error handling in VBScript, and exposes information about runtime errors through its properties. Unlike other objects in VBScript, it is an intrinsic object with global scope; hence, there is no need to declare and initialize the Err object.

Initially the Err properties are either zero-length strings or 0, and when a runtime error occurs the properties of the Err object get populated by the generator of the error (e.g. VBScript, an Automation object, or by the programmer). Err.Number contains an integer, and Number is the default property of the Err object. It is easy to test whether the error actually occurred with an If Err Then statement because of automatic conversion between integer and Boolean subtypes: the integer 0 (no error) converts to Boolean False, and all other numbers evaluate to True.

The following example illustrates a partial IE VBScript (although it could just as easily be from a .wsc, or .hta file) in which the programmer raises one of the predefined VBScript errors. Note that the Err object is not declared and it cannot be created as a separate object.

```
<script language="VBScript">
On Error Resume Next
Err.Raise 11 ' Division by Zero
MsgBox ("Error # " & CStr(Err.Number) & " " & Err.Description)
</script>
```

## Err Object Properties

Let's take a look at the Err object properties.

### Description

The Description property returns or sets a descriptive string associated with an error. By default this is a zero-length string until the property is set by the programmer or by the generator of an error. The description is useful when displaying or logging errors and when raising custom errors. If the programmer raises one of the default runtime errors, the Description property contains the string associated with the error.

**Syntax**

```
Err.Description [= stringexpression]
```

| Name | Subtype | Description |
|---|---|---|
| Err | Err Object | This is always the Err Object |
| Stringexpression | String | A string expression containing a description of the error |

**Example Usage**

```
<script language="VBScript">
Option Explicit
On Error Resume Next

IntTest = 5
MsgBox ("Error Description: " & Err.Description)
</script>
```

This sample script will produce Variable in undefined inside a message box.

## HelpContext

The HelpContext property is used to automatically display the Help topic specified in the HelpFile property. This property either sets or retrieves the value of the help context. If both HelpFile and HelpContext are empty, the value of Number is checked. If Number corresponds to a VBScript runtime error value, then the VBScript help context ID for the error is used.

This property is rarely used, and requires coordination between the person authoring the Help system and the scripter.

Finally, use of the HelpFile and HelpContext only make sense in a non-IE setting with the older .hlp system. Newer HTML help simply uses HTML documents, which may be displayed under most circumstances using techniques discussed in HTML Help manuals.

The following sample illustrates the use of the traditional .hlp files with the Windows Script Host.

**Syntax**

```
Err.HelpContext [= contextID]
```

| Name | Subtype | Description |
|---|---|---|
| Err | Err Object | This always is the Err Object |
| ContextID | Integer | Optional. A valid identifier for a Help topic within the Help file |

## Example Usage

```
On Error Resume Next
Dim Msg
Err.Clear
Err.Raise 6 ' Generate "Overflow" error.
Err.Helpfile = "c:\windows\help\yourHelp.hlp"
Err.HelpContext = 21
If Err.Number <> 0 Then
    Msg = "Press Help to see " & Err.Helpfile & " topic for" & _
    " the following HelpContext: " & Err.HelpContext
    MsgBox Msg, , "error: " & Err.Description, Err.Helpfile, Err.HelpContext
End If
```

### *HelpFile*

The HelpFile property is used to set and retrieve a fully qualified path to a programmer-authored Help File. Often it is used in conjunction with the HelpContext property—see the notes and the earlier example. The most common way of setting the value is through the Err.Raise method.

#### Syntax

```
Err.HelpFile [= filepath]
```

| Name | Subtype | Description |
|------|---------|-------------|
| Err | Err Object | This always is the Err Object |
| Filepath | String | Optional. Fully qualified path to the Help File |

### *Number*

This is the default property of the Err object, and returns or sets a numeric value specifying an error. Custom error handling functions utilize the Number property to diagnose the runtime error.

When setting or retrieving a custom error, the vbObjectErr constant is used to ensure that custom errors do not conflict with VBScript and common Automation Errs.

#### Syntax

```
Err.Number [= errornumber]
```

| Name | Subtype | Description |
|------|---------|-------------|
| Err | Err Object | This is always the Err Object |
| Errornumber | Integer | An integer representing a VBScript error number or an SCODE error value. SCODE is a long integer value that is used to pass detailed information to the caller of an interface member or API function |

## Example Usage

```
On Error Resume Next
Err.Raise vbObjectError + 16, ,"CustomObject Error" ' Raise Custom Error #16.
If Err.Number <> 0 Then         ' (If Err Then) can be used too
    MsgBox ("Error # " & CStr(Err.Number) & " " & Err.Description)
End If
```

The preceding sample code sets a custom error number in `Err.Number` through the `Err.Raise` method, and then displays the return value through a Message Box (`MsgBox`).

## Source

The `Source` property sets or returns the name of the object or application that reported the error. Most commonly the source is the class name or `ProgID` of the object generating the error.

Most of the time the `Source` property will show "Microsoft VBScript", but in cases where the error occurs while accessing a property or method of an Automation object, the source property will show the component's class name. This is not only useful because it allows for a greater degree of granularity (or visibility) in error handling, but it also allows for better error display and logging possibilities. This property can be set through the `Err.Raise` method in both VBScript and in custom COM components.

### Syntax

```
Err.Source [= stringexpression]
```

| Name | Subtype | Description |
|------|---------|-------------|
| Err | Err Object | This always is the Err Object |
| Stringexpression | Integer | A string expression representing the application that generated the error |

### Example Usage

```
On Error Resume Next
Err.Raise vbObjectError + 1, "cTestClass", "CustomObject Error"
If Err.Number <> 0 Then           ' (If Err Then) can be used too
    MsgBox ("Error # " & CStr(Err.Number) & " " & Err.Description &
" Source: " & Err.Source)
End If
```

# Err Object Methods

Let's take a look at the `Err` object methods.

## Clear

The `Clear` method resets all of the properties of the `Err` object to either 0 or a zero-length string. The `Err` object should ideally be reset after an error has been handled because of the deferred nature of error handling in VBScript, to avoid the potential mistake of handling the same error twice.

The Err object is additionally cleared by any of the following statements:

- ❏   On Error Resume Next
- ❏   On Error Goto 0
- ❏   Exit Sub
- ❏   Exit Function

Therefore, error-handling functions must be called before any of the preceding statements are executed.

### Syntax

```
Err.Clear
```

| Name | Subtype | Description |
|------|---------|-------------|
| Err | Err Object | This always is the Err Object |

### Example Usage

```
On Error Resume Next        ' The Err Object is Reset
Err.Raise 5
Err.Clear
If Err.Number = 0 Then      ' (If Err Then) can be used too
    MsgBox ("Error has been reset: Err.Number - " & CStr(Err.Number))
End If
```

## Raise

The Raise method generates a runtime error. All of the parameters of the Raise method, except for its number, are optional. When optional parameters are not specified, and the Err object has not been cleared, old values may appear.

The best practice is to use Err.Clear after error handling, and to inspect the Err object before using Err.Raise (in case an error has occurred in the meantime). When raising custom error numbers, the vbObjectErr constant should be added.

The HelpFile and HelpContext parameters are used with the traditional .hlp help, and not with the HTML help systems.

Raising errors is a popular technique to stop the execution of a procedure, and handle it via some error handling function. You may raise errors when data is invalid, and when you want to pass an error up the call stack. This is a popular technique when you want to change one error into another, so that it can be handled properly.

### Syntax

```
Err.Raise (number, source, description, helpfile, helpcontext)
```

| Name | Subtype | Description |
|------|---------|-------------|
| Err | Err Object | This is always the Err Object |
| Number | Long | This identifies the nature of the error. All VBScript (predefined and user-defined) error numbers are in the range 0–65535 |
| Source | String | This identifies the name of the object or application that generates the error. When setting this property for Windows Script Components, use the ProgID form. If nothing is specified, the current ID of the project is used; often, it just defaults to 'Microsoft VBScript' |
| Description | String | This is the description of the error. If unspecified, the value in number is examined. If it can be mapped to a VBScript runtime error code, a string provided by VBScript is used as the description. If there is no VBScript error corresponding to number, a generic error message is used |
| Helpfile | String | This is the fully qualified path to a customized help file in which help on this error can be found. If unspecified, VBScript uses the fully qualified drive, path, and file name of the VBScript help file |
| Helpcontext | Integer | This is the context ID identifying a topic within helpfile that provides help for the error. If omitted, the VBScript help file context ID for the error corresponding to the number property is used, if it exists |

### Example Usage

```
Dim strMsg
On Error Resume Next
Err.Raise vbObjectError + 1, "prjProject.clsClass", "Custom Error",
"c:\windows\YourHelpfile.hlp", 1
If Err.Number <> 0 Then
    strMsg = "Error Number: " & CStr(Err.Number) & vbCrLf
    strMsg = strMsg & "Description: " & Err.Description & vbCrLf
    strMsg = strMsg & "Source: " & Err.Source
    If Err.HelpFile <> "" Then
        strMsg = strMsg & vbCrLf & "Press Help to see the help file"
        MsgBox strMsg, , "Error: " & Err.Description, Err.Helpfile, Err
.HelpContext
    End If
    MsgBox strMsg    ' No Help file available here
    Err.Clear
End If
```

This example shows a common way of raising an error in Windows Script Host, where the help file is readily available.

### vbObjectError Constant

This is a built-in constant that can be used in conjunction with programmer-defined errors and
Err.Raise. It does not have to be declared or initialized; its decimal value is −2147221504 (or
−0 × 8004000 in hexadecimal). Whereas previous examples have shown how to use the vbObjectError
constant with the Err.Raise method, the following example shows a skeleton of a centralized error
handler that combines Select Case with custom errors.

### Example Usage

```
If Err.Number <> 0 Then              ' this should call separate subs
    Select Case Err.Number
        Case vbObjectError + 1
        ' call sub handling error 1
        Case vbObjectError + 3
        ' call sub handling error 3
        Case Else
        ' call reporting sub to display errors
    End Select
End If
```

### On Error Resume Next

This statement enables error handling within the scope of a script or a procedure. Without the On Error
Resume Next statement, the default runtime error handler displays the error and stops the execution of
the script.

On Error Resume Next continues the execution of the script on the next line following the error. The
error handling routine has to exist within the same scope as this statement. The statement becomes
inactive with a call to another procedure or when an On Error Goto 0 statement is used.

### Syntax

```
On Error Resume Next
```

*When Internet Explorer's advanced option Disable Script Debugging is not selected and the Script
Debugger is installed on the same system, On Error Resume Next does not go into effect; instead, the
browser automatically goes into the "debug" mode. So, when testing the effectiveness of your error handler
through Internet Explorer, make sure that this option is selected.*

### On Error Goto 0

The On Error Goto 0 statement disables the error handling that was enabled by On Error Resume
Next. This statement is especially useful in the testing stage, when there is a need to identify certain
errors and yet handle others. On Error Goto 0 can be placed immediately after the error handling
procedure is called.

Like On Error Resume Next, this statement is also scope dependent.

### Syntax

```
On Error Goto 0
```

## Scope of On Error Statement and Differences Between VBScript's and VBs (or VBAs) Error Handling

It is important to understand the scope of the On Error statement; otherwise your error handling procedures may never execute. VBScript—unlike its parent language—does not support labels, and it does not support the VB On Error Goto label. Thus, VBScript provides support only for in-line error handlers that can cause understandable grief. Basically, in order to mimic a block of code in VB that would respond to an On Error Goto label statement you might be inclined to use several If Err Then statements in order to check for an error with each single line of execution. However, with a little bit of programming, this can easily be achieved by enabling an error handler around a given procedure. Should one of the lines in the procedure fail, the error can be thrown up the calling stack. Of course, there is no Resume statement, which complicates some of the scripting. This can only be circumvented by trying to correct the problem that generated the error and attempting to call the procedure again.

Before we look at some error handling techniques, let's examine the scope of error handling. The following script illustrates an important concept behind the scope of the error-enabling and error-disabling statements, as well as showing the differences in scope and the importance in clearing of errors.

```
Sub TestError()
    On Error Resume Next
    Err.Raise 6              ' Execution will continue
    MsgBox ("TestError: Error # " & CStr(Err.Number) & " " & Err.Description)
Err.Clear
End Sub


Sub TestError2()
    Err.Clear                ' Execution stops, moves up in scope
    MsgBox ("TestError2: This will never Show Up")
End Sub

' Main body of the script
' TestError() has local Error Handler no need for global Handler
On Error Resume Next
Call TestError()
If Err.Number <> 0 Then
    MsgBox ("Global: Error # " & CStr(Err.Number) & " " & Err.Description)
    Err Clear
Else
    MsgBox ("Global: No Error, It was handled locally and cleared")
End If


' TestError2 has no local error handler
Call TestError2()
If Err.Number <> 0 Then
    MsgBox ("Global: Error # " & CStr(Err.Number) & " " & Err.Description)
    Err.Clear
End If
' Global script Error handling is turned off, cause crash
On  Error  goto  0
Call TestError2()
```

Upon execution, the error is first handled locally, and after it is cleared, it is ignored. Next, the calls to the TestError2() subroutine are first handled by the global error handler and, after it is disabled on the second-last line, a runtime error appears.

Now, to consider the importance of clearing errors and the scope of On Error Resume Next, we make two adjustments, commenting out certain code.

```
Sub TestError()
    On Error Resume Next
    Err.Raise 6               ' Execution will continue
    MsgBox ("TestError: Error # " & CStr(Err.Number) & " " & Err.Description)
    REM Err.Clear
End Sub

Sub TestError2()
    Err.Clear               ' Execution stops, moves up in scope
    MsgBox ("TestError2: This will never Show Up")
End Sub

' Main body of the script
' TestError() has local Error Handler no need for global Handler
REM On Error Resume Next
```

With these changes, an error message is still displayed after the call to TestError(), but the first call to the TestError2() subprocedure results in an invocation of the default error handler, and stoppage of the script immediately after the call, that is, the On Error Resume Next statement was local in scope to the TestError() subprocedure.

The following code illustrates the possibility of mimicking the On Error Goto label statement by encompassing a block of code in a procedure, rather than trapping errors inline, as in VB. Here the scripter can invoke an error handler at a higher level rather than at the level where the error occurred (in this case, a procedure without a local error handler).

```
Option Explicit
Dim intZero, intNonZero, intResult
intZero = 0
intNonZero = 1

Sub TestError()
    ' Statements that will execute
    MsgBox ("This will always execute")
    ' now cause an error
    intResult = intNonZero / intZero          ' causes error 11
    ' Statements that will not execute if error occurs
    MsgBox ("Finally executed, Result = " & CStr(intResult) )
End Sub

' simulate On Error Goto Label by having a block of code in a sub
On Error Resume Next
Call TestError()
If Err.Number = 11 Then
    MsgBox "Division By Zero - may still continue" & vbCrLf & Err.Description
    Err.Clear
    intZero = 1
    TestError()
End If
On Error Goto 0                               'kill other error handling
```

## Error Handling in Internet Explorer

Besides VBScript itself, some Web authors might also turn to DHTML events. Internet Explorer's DHTML object model supports a variety of events, including events occurring as a result of an error. Essentially, this allows for a different degree of control when authoring scripts for IE. Thanks to the `GetRef()` function, which returns a pointer to a function, it is now possible to bind VBScript procedures to an event.

For instance, the following line will execute the `RunMySub` procedure in response to the `Window`.`Onload` event in IE.

```
Set Window.Onload = GetRef("RunMySub")
```

Similarly, you can write procedures that will execute when the `OnError` event is fired, either for an element or for the window object.

There are two additional techniques for error handling in IE:

❑ Centralized, through the use of the `window.onerror` event

❑ Decentralized, through the use of the `element.onerror` event

The following code example illustrates the old and the new syntax for handling DHTML errors.

### Old Syntax

```
Function element_onerror ( message, url, line)
```

`element` is the name of the element or window.

```
<script language="VBScript">
Function window_onerror ( message, url, line )
    ' handle error here
    window_onerror = true
End Function
</script>
```

### New Syntax

```
Set element.onerror = GetRef("functionName")
```

The new syntax allows us to bind functions to events, just like in JScript. Again, `element` is the name of the element or window, and `functionName` is an actual function or a sub.

```
<script language="VBScript">
Function onErrorHandler ( message, url, line )
    ' handle error here
    onErrorHandler = True
End Function
set window.onerror = GetRef("onErrorHandler")
</script>
```

There are a few important differences between the VBScript's error handling and the use of the onerror event in IE. Following is the list of a summary of the onerror IE handlers:

- ❏ Execution does not resume on the next line. The script may resume with the next user action or handled event—for example, the user "clicks" on another element. If you want greater error-handling control in individual procedures executed in the browser, the On Error Resume Next statement should be used.

- ❏ All errors pertaining to the element (or window) are handled by the event unless handled via VBScript's On Error Resume Next technique.

- ❏ Errors can be passed to a higher-level element via event bubbling.

- ❏ Custom errors cannot be created; there is no Err.Raise counterpart in the DHTML object model.

# The Scripting Runtime Library Object Reference

The default scripting languages installed with Microsoft Windows XP, Office XP, ASP 3.0, and many other applications provide a scripting runtime library in the file scrrun.dll, which implements a series of objects that can be used in ASP on the server and in client-side code running on the client.

❑ The *Dictionary* object provides a useful storage object that we can use to store values, accessed and referenced by their name rather than by index as would be the case in a normal array—it's ideal for storing the name/value pairs that we retrieve from the ASP Request object, for example.

❑ The *FileSystemObject* object provides us with access to the underlying file system on the server (or on the client in Internet Explorer 5/6 when used in conjunction with a special type of page named HTML Application or HTA)—we can use the FileSystemObject object to iterate through the machine's local and networked drives, folders and files.

❑ The *TextStream* object provides access to files stored on disk, and is used in conjunction with the FileSystemObject object—it can read from or write to text (sequential) files.

## The Scripting.Dictionary Object

The Dictionary object provides a useful storage object that we can use to store values, accessed and referenced by their name rather than by index, as would be the case in a normal array. The properties and methods exposed by the Dictionary object are:

## Properties

| Property | Description |
|---|---|
| Count | Returns the number of key/item pairs in the Dictionary (read-only) |
| Item (key) | Sets or returns the value of the item for the specified key |
| Key (key) | Sets or returns the value of a key |

## Methods

| Method | Description |
|---|---|
| `Add (key, item)` | Adds the key/item pair to the Dictionary. You can also add items with a simple assignment, and in fact, you must use this syntax in order to store object references in a dictionary:<br><br>`Set objDict("keyname") = objMyObject` |
| `Exists (key)` | Returns true if the specified key exists or false if not |
| `Items ()` | Returns an array containing all the items in a `Dictionary` object |
| `Keys ()` | Returns an array containing all the keys in a `Dictionary` object |
| `Remove (key)` | Removes a single key/item pair specified by `key` |
| `RemoveAll ()` | Removes all the key/item pairs |

> An error will occur if we try to add a key/item pair when that key already exists, remove a key/item pair that doesn't exist, or change the **CompareMode** of a **Dictionary** object that already contains data.

# The Scripting.FileSystemObject Object

The `FileSystemObject` object provides us with access to the underlying file system on the server (or on the client in Internet Explorer 5/6 when used in conjunction with a special type of page named an HTML Application or HTA). The `FileSystemObject` object exposes a series of properties and methods of its own, some of which return other objects that are specific to objects within the file system. These subsidiary objects are:

❑ The `Drive` object, provides access to all the drives available on the machine

❑ The `Folder` object, provides access to the folders on a drive

❑ The `File` object, provides access to the files within each folder

While these three objects form a neat hierarchy, the `FileSystemObject` object also provides methods that can bridge the hierarchy by creating instances of the subsidiary objects directly.

## The FileSystemObject Object

The `FileSystemObject` object provides overall access to the underlying file system and is used as a starting point when navigating the file system.

## Properties

| Property | Description |
| --- | --- |
| Drives | Returns a collection of `Drive` objects that are available from the local machine. This includes network drives that are mapped from this machine |

## Methods

| Method | Description |
| --- | --- |
| BuildPath (path, name) | Adds the file or folder specified in name to the existing path, adding a path separator character ('\') if required. This does not check for valid or existing path |
| CopyFile (source, destination, overwrite) | Copies the file or files specified in source (wildcards can be included) to the folder specified in destination. If source contains wildcards or destination ends with a path separator character ('\') then destination is assumed to be a folder; otherwise, it is assumed to be a full path and name for the new file. |
| | Note that leaving off the last '\' when the source doesn't contain wildcards throws a "Permission denied" error since the name (assumed to be a filename without an extension) exists as a folder name. An error will occur if the destination file already exists and the optional overwrite parameter is set to False. |
| | The default for overwrite is True |
| CopyFolder (source, destination, overwrite) | Copies the folder or folders specified in source (wildcards can be included) to the folder specified in destination, including all the files contained in the source folder(s). If source contains wildcards or destination ends with a path separator character ('\') then destination is assumed to be a folder into which the copied folder(s) will be placed; otherwise, it is assumed to be a full path and name for a new folder to be created. An error will occur if the destination folder already exists and the optional overwrite parameter is set to False. The default for overwrite is True |

*Continues*

| Method | Description |
|---|---|
| CreateFolder (foldername) | Creates and returns a reference to a new folder, which has the path and name specified in foldername. Only the last folder in the path is created—all parent folders must exist. An error occurs if the specified folder already exists. |
| CreateTextFile (filename, overwrite, unicode) | Creates a new text file on disk with the specified file-name and returns a TextStream object that refers to it. If the optional overwrite parameter is set to True any existing file with the same path and name will be overwritten. The default for overwrite is False. If the optional unicode parameter is set to True, the content of the file will be stored as Unicode text. The default for unicode is False for an ASCII file |
| DeleteFile (filespec, force) | Deletes the file or files specified in filespec (wildcards can be included). If the optional force parameter is set to True the file(s) will be deleted even if the read-only attribute is set. The default for force is False |
| DeleteFolder (folderspec, force) | Deletes the folder or folders specified in folderspec (wildcards can be included in the final component of the path) together with all their contents. If the optional force parameter is set to True the file(s) will be deleted even if the read-only attribute is set. The default for force is False |
| DriveExists (drivespec) | Returns true if the drive specified in drivespec exists, or False if not. The drivespec parameter can be a drive letter as a string or a full absolute path for a folder or file |
| FileExists (filespec) | Returns True if the file specified in filespec exists, or False if not. The filespec parameter can contain an absolute or relative path for the file, or just the file name to look in the current folder |
| FolderExists (folderspec) | Returns True if the folder specified in folderspec exists, or False if not. The folderspec parameter can contain an absolute or relative path for the folder, or just the folder name to look in the current folder |
| GetAbsolutePathName (pathspec) | Takes a path that unambiguously identifies a folder and, taking into account the current folder's path, returns a full unambiguous path specification for the pathspec folder. For example, if the current folder is "c:\docs\sales\" and pathspec is "jan" the returned value is "c:\docs\sales\jan". Wildcards and the ".", ".." and "\\" path operators are accepted |

| Method | Description |
| --- | --- |
| GetBaseName (filespec) | Returns just the name of a file or folder specified in filespec, that is, with the path and file extension removed |
| GetDrive (drivespec) | Returns a Drive object corresponding to the drive specified in drivespec. The format for drivespec can include the colon, path separator or be a network share, that is, "c", "c:","c:\" or "\\machine\sharename" |
| GetDriveName (drivespec) | Returns the name of the drive specified in drivespec as a string. The drivespec parameter must be an absolute path to a file or folder, or just the drive letter such as "c:" or just "c" |
| GetExtensionName (filespec) | Returns just the extension of a file or folder specified in filespec, that is, with the path and file name removed |
| GetFile (filespec) | Returns a File object corresponding to the file specified in filespec or the last folder name if there is no file. This can be a relative or absolute path to the required file |
| GetFileName (pathspec) | Returns the name part (that is, without the path or file extension) of the path and filename specified in pathspec, or the last folder name of which there is no file name. This does not check for existence of the file or folder |
| GetFileVersion (filespec) | Returns the version information from a file in Windows 2000, XP and Windows Script Host 2.0 and 5.6 |
| GetFolder (folderspec) | Returns a Folder object corresponding to the folder specified in folderspec. This can be a relative or absolute path to the required folder |
| GetParentFolderName (pathspec) | Returns the name of the parent folder of the file or folder specified in pathspec. This does not check for existence of the folder |
| GetSpecialFolder (folderspec) | Returns a Folder object corresponding to one of the special Windows folders. The permissible values for folderspec are: WindowsFolder (0) SystemFolder (1) TemporaryFolder (2) |
| GetTempName () | Returns a randomly generated file name that can be used for performing operations that require a temporary file or folder |

*Continues*

| Method | Description |
|---|---|
| MoveFile (source, destination) | Moves the file or files specified in source to the folder specified in destination. Wildcards can be included in source but not in destination. If source contains wildcards or destination ends with a path separator character ('\') then destination is assumed to be a folder; otherwise, it is assumed to be a full path and name for the new file. |
| | Note that leaving off the last '\' when the source doesn't contain wildcards throws a "Permission denied" error since the name (assumed to be a filename without an extension) exists as a folder name. An error will occur if the destination file already exists |
| MoveFolder (source, destination) | Moves the folder or folders specified in source to the folder specified in destination. Wildcards can be included in source but not in destination. If source contains wildcards or destination ends with a path separator character ('\') then destination is assumed to be the folder in which to place the moved folders; otherwise, it is assumed to be a full path and name for a new folder. An error will occur if the destination folder already exists |
| OpenTextFile (filename, iomode, create, format) | Creates a file named filename, or opens an existing file named filename, and returns a TextStream object that refers to it. The filename parameter can contain an absolute or relative path. The iomode parameter specifies the type of access required. The permissible values are ForReading (1), (the default), ForWriting (2), and ForAppending (8). If the create parameter is set to True when writing or appending to a file that does not exist, a new file will be created. The default for create is False. The format parameter specifies the format of the data to be read from or written to the file. Permissible values are TristateFalse (0), (the default) to open it as ASCII, TristateTrue (-) to open it as Unicode, and TristateUseDefault (-2) to open it using the system default format |

# The Drive Object

The Drive object provides access to all the drives available on the machine. The properties (note that it has no methods) exposed by the Drive object are:

| Property | Description |
|---|---|
| AvailableSpace | Returns the amount of space in bytes available to this user on the drive, taking into account quotas and/or other restrictions |
| DriveLetter | Returns the drive letter of the drive |
| DriveType | Returns the type of the drive<br><br>The values are:<br><br>Unknown (0)<br><br>Removable (1)<br><br>Fixed (2)<br><br>Network (3)<br><br>CDRom (4)<br><br>RamDisk (5) |
| FileSystem | Returns the type of file system for the drive. The values include "FAT", "NTFS", and "CDFS" |
| FreeSpace | Returns the actual amount of free space in bytes available on the drive |
| IsReady | Returns a Boolean value indicating if drive is ready (True) or not (False) |
| Path | Returns the path for the drive as a drive letter and colon, that is, "C:" |
| RootFolder | Returns a Folder object representing the root folder of the drive |
| SerialNumber | Returns a decimal serial number used to uniquely identify a disk volume |
| ShareName | Returns the network share name for the drive if it is a networked drive |
| TotalSize | Returns the total size in bytes of the drive |
| VolumeName | Sets or returns the volume name of the drive if it is a local drive |

# The Folder Object

The Folder object provides access to the folders on a drive.

## Properties

| Property | Description |
|---|---|
| Attributes | Returns the attributes of the folder |
| | Can be a combination of any of the values |
| | Normal (0) |
| | ReadOnly (1) |
| | Hidden (2) |
| | System (4) |
| | Volume (name) (8) |
| | Directory (folder) (16) |
| | Archive (32) |
| | Alias (1024) |
| | Compressed (2048) |
| | Can also be used to set the ReadOnly, Hidden, System, and Archive attributes |
| DateCreated | Returns the date and time that the folder was created where available |
| DateLastAccessed | Returns the date and time that the folder was last accessed |
| DateLastModified | Returns the date and time that the folder was last modified |
| Drive | Returns the drive letter of the drive on which the folder resides |
| Files | Returns a Files collection containing File objects representing all the files within this folder |
| IsRootFolder | Returns a Boolean value indicating if the folder is the root folder of the current drive |
| Name | Sets or returns the name of the folder |
| ParentFolder | Returns the Folder object for the parent folder of this folder |
| Path | Returns the absolute path of the folder using long file names where appropriate |
| ShortName | Returns the DOS-style 8.3 version of the folder name |
| ShortPath | Returns the DOS-style 8.3 version of the absolute path of this folder |
| Size | Returns the total combined size of all files and subfolders contained in the folder |

*Continues*

| Property | Description |
|----------|-------------|
| SubFolders | Returns a `Folders` collection consisting of all folders contained in the folder, including hidden and system folders |
| Type | Returns a string that is a description of the folder type (such as "Recycle Bin"), if available |
| DateCreated | Returns the date and time that the folder was created where available |

## Methods

| Method | Description |
|--------|-------------|
| Copy (destination, overwrite) | Copies this folder and all its contents to the folder specified in `destination`, including all the files contained in this folder. If `destination` ends with a path separator character ( '\' ) then destination is assumed to be a folder into which the copied folder will be placed; otherwise, it is assumed to be a full path and name for a new folder to be created. An error will occur if the `destination` folder already exists and the optional `overwrite` parameter is set to `False`. The default for `overwrite` is `True` |
| Delete (force) | Deletes this folder and all its contents. If the optional `force` parameter is set to `True` the folder will be deleted even if the read-only attribute is set on it or on any contained files. The default for `force` is `False` |
| Move (destination) | Moves this folder and all its contents to the folder specified in `destination`. If `destination` ends with a path separator character ( '\' ) then `destination` is assumed to be the folder in which to place the moved folder; otherwise, it is assumed to be a full path and name for a new folder. An error will occur if the destination folder already exists |
| CreateTextFile (filename, overwrite, unicode) | Creates a new text file within this folder with the specified `filename` and returns a `TextStream` object that refers to it. If the optional `overwrite` parameter is set to `True` any existing file with the same name will be overwritten. The default for `overwrite` is `False`. If the optional `unicode` parameter is set to `True`, the content of the file will be stored as Unicoded text. The default for `unicode` is `False` |

# The File Object

The File object provides access to the files within each folder.

## Properties

| Property | Description |
| --- | --- |
| Attributes | Sets or returns the attributes of the file |
| | Can be a combination of any of the values: |
| | Normal (0) |
| | ReadOnly (1) |
| | Hidden (2) |
| | System (4) |
| | Volume (name) (8) |
| | Directory (folder) (16) |
| | Archive (32) |
| | Alias (1024) |
| | Compressed (2048) |
| | Can also be used to set the ReadOnly, Hidden, System, and Archive attributes |
| DateCreated | Returns the date and time that the file was created where available |
| DateLastAccessed | Returns the date and time that the file was last accessed |
| DateLastModified | Returns the date and time that the file was last modified |
| Drive | Returns the drive letter of the drive on which the file resides |
| Name | Sets or returns the name of the file |
| ParentFolder | Returns the Folder object for the parent folder of this file |
| Path | Returns the absolute path of the file using long file names where appropriate |
| ShortName | Returns the DOS-style 8.3 version of the file name |
| ShortPath | Returns the DOS-style 8.3 version of the absolute path of this file |
| Size | Returns the size of the file in bytes |
| Type | Returns a string that is a description of the file type (such as "Text Document" for a .txt file) if available |

## Methods

| Method | Description |
|---|---|
| Copy (destination, overwrite) | Copies this file to the folder specified in destination. If destination ends with a path separator character ('\') then destination is assumed to be a folder into which the copied file will be placed; otherwise, it is assumed to be a full path and name for a new file to be created. |
| | Note that leaving off the last '\' when the source doesn't contain wildcards throws a "Permission denied" error since the name (assumed to be a filename without an extension) exists as a folder name. An error will occur if the destination file already exists and the optional overwrite parameter is set to False. The default for overwrite is True |
| Delete (force) | Deletes this file. If the optional force parameter is set to True the file will be deleted even if the read-only attribute is set. The default for force is False |
| Move (destination) | Moves this file to the folder specified in destination. If destination ends with a path separator character ('\') then destination is assumed to be the folder in which to place the moved file; otherwise, it is assumed to be a full path and name for a new file. An error will occur if the destination file already exists |
| OpenAsTextStream (iomode, format) | Opens a specified file and returns a TextStream object that can be used to read from, write to, or append to the file. The iomode parameter specifies the type of access required. |
| | The permissible values are: |
| | ForReading (1) (the default) |
| | ForWriting (2) |
| | ForAppending (8) |
| | If the create parameter is set to True when writing or appending to a file that does not exist, a new file will be created. The default for create is False. The format parameter specifies the format of the data to be read from or written to the file. Permissible values are TristateFalse (0) (the default) to open it as ASCII, TristateTrue (-1) to open it as Unicode, and TristateUseDefault (-2) to open it using the system default format |

# The TextStream Object

The TextStream object provides access to files stored on disk, and is used in conjunction with the FileSystemObject object.

# Properties

| Property | Description |
|---|---|
| AtEndOfLine | Returns true if the file pointer is at the end of a line in the file |
| AtEndOfStream | Returns true if the file pointer is at the end of the file |
| Column | Returns the column number of the current character in the file starting from 1 |
| Line | Returns the current line number in the file starting from 1 |

Note: The *AtEndOfLine* and *AtEndOfStream* properties are only available for a file that is opened with the *iomode* parameter set with the value *ForReading*. Referring to them otherwise causes an error to occur.

# Methods

| Method | Description |
|---|---|
| Close () | Closes an open file |
| Read (numchars) | Reads numchars characters from the file |
| ReadAll () | Reads the entire file as a single string |
| ReadLine () | Reads a line from the file as a string |
| Skip (numchars) | Skips and discards numchars characters when reading from the file |
| SkipLine () | Skips and discards the next line when reading from the file |
| Write (string) | Writes string to the file |
| WriteLine (string) | Writes string (optional) and a newline character to the file |
| WriteBlankLines (n) | Writes n newline characters to the file |

# The Windows Script Host Object Model

This Appendix gives details about the Windows Script Host objects. Further details and examples can also be found in Chapter 12.

Windows Script Host has 14 objects outlined.

- ❑ `WScript` Object:
  This object provides access to most of the objects, methods, and properties contained in the WSH object model.

- ❑ `WshArguments` Object:
  This object gives the programmer access to the entire collection of command-line parameters in the order in which they were originally entered.

- ❑ `WshController` Object:
  This object exposes the method `CreateScript()` that creates a remote script process.

- ❑ `WshEnvironment` Object:
  This object gives the programmer access to the collection of Microsoft Windows system environment variables.

- ❑ `WshNamed` Object:
  This object provides access to the named command-line script arguments contained within the `WshArguments` object.

- ❑ `WshNetwork` Object:
  This object gives the programmer access to the shared resources on the network to which the host computer is connected.

- ❑ `WshRemote` Object:
  This object provides access to the remote script process.

- ❑ `WshRemoteError` Object:
  This object is used to expose the error information available when a remote script terminates as a result of a script error.

❏ WshScriptExec Object:
This object provides status and error information about a script.

❏ WshShell Object:
This object is used to give the programmer access to the native Windows shell functionality.

❏ WshShortcut Object:
This object allows the programmer to create shortcuts.

❏ WshSpecialFolders Object:
This object is used to access Windows Special Folders.

❏ WshUnnamed Object:
This object provides access to unnamed command-line script arguments within the WshArguments object.

❏ WshUrlShortcut Object:
This allows the programmer to create a shortcut to an Internet resource.

# The WScript Object

The root of the WSH object model is the WScript object. This object provides properties and methods that give the developer access to a variety of information, such as:

❏ Name and path information for the script file being executed

❏ Version of the Microsoft Scripting engines

❏ Links to external objects

❏ User interaction

❏ The ability to delay or terminate script execution

# WScript Properties

The WScript object has 11 properties:

❏ Arguments Property

❏ FullName Property

❏ Interactive Property

❏ Name Property

❏ Path Property

❏ ScriptFullName Property

❏ ScriptName Property

❏ StdErr Property

❏ StdIn Property

❏ StdOut Property

❏ Version Property

## WScript Methods

The WScript object has seven methods:

- ❑ CreateObject Method
- ❑ ConnectObject Method
- ❑ DisconnectObject Method
- ❑ Echo Method
- ❑ GetObject Method
- ❑ Quit Method
- ❑ Sleep Method

# The WshArguments Object

This object gives the programmer access to the entire collection of command-line parameters.

## WshArguments Properties

The WshArguments object has four properties:

- ❑ Item Property
- ❑ Length Property
- ❑ Named Property
- ❑ Unnamed Property

## WshArguments Methods

The WshArguments object has two methods:

- ❑ Count Method
- ❑ ShowUsage Method

# WshController Object

This object is used to expose the method CreateScript() that creates a remote script process.

## WshController Properties

The WshController object has no properties.

## WshController Methods

The `WshController` object has one method:

- ❑ `CreateScript` Method

# WshEnvironment Object

This object provides access to the collection of Windows environment variables.

## WshEnvironment Properties

The `WshEnvironment` object has two properties.

- ❑ `Item` Property
- ❑ `Length` Property

## WshEnvironment Methods

The `WshEnvironment` object has two methods:

- ❑ `Count` Method
- ❑ `Remove` Method

# WshNamed Object

This object is used to provide access to named arguments from the command line.

## WshNamed Properties

The `WshNamed` object has two properties:

- ❑ `Item` Property
- ❑ `Length` Property

## WshNamed Methods

The `WshNamed` object has two methods:

- ❑ `Count` Method
- ❑ `Exists` Method

# The WshNetwork Object

The WshNetwork object provides access to the shared resources on the network to which the computer is connected.

## WshNetwork Properties

The WshNetwork object has three properties:

- ❏ ComputerName Property
- ❏ UserDomain Property
- ❏ UserName Property

## WshNetwork Methods

The WshNetwork object has eight methods:

- ❏ AddWindowsPrinterConnection Method
- ❏ AddPrinterConnection Method
- ❏ EnumNetworkDrives Method
- ❏ EnumPrinterConnection Method
- ❏ MapNetworkDrive Method
- ❏ RemoveNetworkDrive Method
- ❏ RemovePrinterConnection Method
- ❏ SetDefaultPrinter Method

# WshRemote Object

This object is used to provide access to the remote script process.

## WshRemote Properties

The WshRemote object has two properties:

- ❏ Status Property
- ❏ Error Property

## WshRemote Methods

The WshRemote object has two methods:

- ❏ Execute Method
- ❏ Terminate Method

# WshRemoteError Object

This object provides access to the error information available when a remote script terminates because of a script error.

## WshRemoteError Properties

The WshRemoteError object has six properties:

- ❑ Description Property
- ❑ Line Property
- ❑ Character Property
- ❑ SourceText Property
- ❑ Source Property
- ❑ Number Property

## WshRemoteError Methods

The WshRemoteError object has one method:

- ❑ WshRemote Object

# WshScriptExec Object

The WshScriptExec object provides status information about a script run with Exec when used in conjunction with the StdIn, StdOut, and StdErr streams.

## WshScriptExec Properties

The WshScriptExec object has four properties:

- ❑ Status Property
- ❑ StdOut Property
- ❑ StdIn Property
- ❑ StdErr Property

## WshScriptExec Methods

The WshScriptExec object has one method:

- ❑ Terminate Method

# The WshShell Object

Windows Script Host provides a convenient way to gain access to system environment variables, create shortcuts, access Windows special folders such as the Windows Desktop, and add or remove entries from the registry. It is also possible to create more customized dialogs for user interaction by using features of the Shell object.

## WshShell Properties

The WshShell object has three properties:

- ❑ CurrentDirectory Property
- ❑ Environment Property
- ❑ SpecialFolders Property

## WshShell Methods

The WshShell object has 11 methods:

- ❑ AppActivate Method
- ❑ CreateShortcut Method
- ❑ ExpandEnvironmentStrings Method
- ❑ LogEvent Method
- ❑ Popup Method
- ❑ RegDelete Method
- ❑ RegRead Method
- ❑ RegWrite Method
- ❑ Run Method
- ❑ SendKeys Method
- ❑ Exec Method

# The WshShortcut Object

The WshShortcut object allows you to create shortcuts using script.

## WshShortcut Properties

The WshShortcut object has eight properties:

- ❑ Arguments Property
- ❑ Description Property

- ❏ FullName Property
- ❏ Hotkey Property
- ❏ IconLocation Property
- ❏ TargetPath Property
- ❏ WindowStyle Property
- ❏ WorkingDirectory Property

## WshShortcut Methods

The WshShortcut object has one method:

- ❏ Save Method

# The WshSpecialFolders Object

The WshSpecialFolders object provides access to the collection of Windows special folders. The following special folders are available:

- ❏ AllUsersDesktop
- ❏ AllUsersStartMenu
- ❏ AllUsersPrograms
- ❏ AllUsersStartup
- ❏ Desktop
- ❏ Favorites
- ❏ Fonts
- ❏ MyDocuments
- ❏ NetHood
- ❏ PrintHood
- ❏ Programs
- ❏ Recent
- ❏ SendTo
- ❏ StartMenu
- ❏ Startup
- ❏ Templates

## WshSpecialFolders Properties

The WshSpecialFolders object has one property:

❑ Item Property

## WshSpecialFolders Methods

The WshSpecialFolders object has one method:

❑ Count Method

# The WshUnnamed Object

The WshUnnamed object provides access to the unnamed arguments from the command line. The WshUnnamed object is a read-only collection that is returned by the Unnamed property of the WshArguments object. All individual argument values are retrieved from this collection using zero-based indexes.

There are three ways to access sets of command-line arguments:

❑ Access the entire set of arguments with the WshArguments object.

❑ Access the arguments that have names with the WshNamed object.

❑ Access the arguments that have no names with the WshUnnamed object.

## WshUnnamed Properties

The WshUnnamed object has two properties:

❑ Item Property
❑ Length Property

## WshUnnamed Methods

The WshUnnamed object has one method:

❑ Count Method

# The WshUrlShortcut Object

The WshUrlShortcut object allows you to create shortcuts to Internet resource using script. The WshUrlShortcut object is a child object of the WshShell object. You must use the WshShell method CreateShortcut to create a WshUrlShortcut object.

# WshUrlShortcut Properties

The WshUrlShortcut object has two properties:

❑ FullName Property
❑ TargetPath Property

# WshUrlShortcut Methods

The WshUrlShortcut object has one method:

❑ Save Method

# Regular Expressions

A regular expression is a pattern of text that consists of ordinary characters (such as letters a through z) and special characters that are known as *metacharacters*. The pattern is used to describe one or more strings to match when searching a body of text. The regular expression acts as a template for matching a character pattern to the string that is being searched for.

The following table contains the complete list of metacharacters and their behavior in the context of a regular expression.

| Character | Description |
|---|---|
| \ | Marks the next character as either a special character or a literal |
| ^ | Matches the beginning of input |
| $ | Matches the end of input |
| * | Matches the preceding character zero or more times |
| + | Matches the preceding character one or more times |
| ? | Matches the preceding character zero or one time |
| . | Matches any single character except a newline character |
| (pattern) | Matches pattern and remembers the match. The matched substring can be retrieved from the resulting Matches collection, using Item [0] . . . [n]. To match the parentheses characters themselves, precede with slash—use "\(" or "\)" |
| (?:pattern) | Matches pattern but does not capture the match, that is, it is a noncapturing match that is not stored for possible later use. This is useful for combining parts of a pattern with the "or" character (\|). For example, 'anomol(?:y\|ies)' is a more economical expression than 'anomoly\|anomolies' |

*Continues*

| Character | Description |
|---|---|
| `(?=pattern)` | Positive lookahead matches the search string at any point where a string matching pattern begins. This is a noncapturing match, that is, the match is not captured for possible later use. For example 'Windows (?=95\|98\|NT\|2000\|XP)' matches "Windows" in "Windows XP" but not "Windows" in "Windows 3.1" |
| `(?!pattern)` | Negative lookahead matches the search string at any point where a string not matching pattern begins. This is a noncapturing match, that is, the match is not captured for possible later use. For example, "Windows (?!95\|98\|NT\|2000\|XP)" matches "Windows" in "Windows 3.1" but does not match "Windows" in "Windows XP" |
| `x\|y` | Matches either x or y |
| `{n}` | Matches exactly n times (n must always be a nonnegative integer) |
| `{n,}` | Matches at least n times (n must always be a nonnegative integer—note the terminating comma) |
| `{n,m}` | Matches at least n and at most m times (m and n must always be nonnegative integers) |
| `[xyz]` | Matches any one of the enclosed characters (xyz represents a character set) |
| `[^xyz]` | Matches any character not enclosed (^xyz represents a negative character set) |
| `[a-z]` | Matches any character in the specified range (a-z represents a range of characters) |
| `[^m-z]` | Matches any character not in the specified range (^m-z represents a negative range of characters) |
| `\b` | Matches a word boundary, that is, the position between a word and a space |
| `\B` | Matches a nonword boundary |
| `\d` | Matches a digit character. Equivalent to `[0-9]` |
| `\D` | Matches a nondigit character. Equivalent to `[^0-9]` |
| `\f` | Matches a form-feed character |
| `\n` | Matches a newline character |
| `\r` | Matches a carriage return character |
| `\s` | Matches any white space including space, tab, form-feed, and so on. Equivalent to "`[\f\n\r\t\v]`" |

| Character | Description |
|---|---|
| \S | Matches any nonwhite space character. Equivalent to "[^\f\n\r\t\v]" |
| \t | Matches a tab character |
| \v | Matches a vertical tab character |
| \w | Matches any word character including underscore. Equivalent to "[A-Za-z0-9_]" |
| \W | Matches any nonword character. Equivalent to "[^A-Za-z0-9_]" |
| \. | Matches . |
| \| | Matches \| |
| \{ | Matches { |
| \} | Matches } |
| \\ | Matches \ |
| \[ | Matches [ |
| \] | Matches ] |
| \( | Matches ( |
| \) | Matches ) |
| $num | Matches num, where num is a positive integer. A reference back to remembered matches (note the $ symbol—differs from some Microsoft documentation) |
| \n | Matches n, where n is an octal escape value. Octal escape values must be 1, 2, or 3 digits long |
| \uxxxx | Matches the ASCII character expressed by the UNICODE xxxx |
| \xn | Matches n, where n is a hexadecimal escape value. Hexadecimal escape values must be exactly two digits long |

# VBScript Features not in VBA

The following appendix lists VBScript features that are not available in VBA.

| Category | Feature/Keyword |
| --- | --- |
| Declarations | Class |
| Miscellaneous | Eval |
| | Execute |
| Objects | RegExp |
| Script Engine Identification | ScriptEngine |
| | ScriptEngineBuildVersion |
| | ScriptEngineMajorVersion |
| | ScriptEngineMinorVersion |

# VBA Features not in VBScript

The following appendix lists VBA features that are not available in VBScript.

| Category | Omitted Feature/Keyword |
|---|---|
| Array handling | `Option Base`<br>Declaring arrays with lower bound <> 0 |
| Collection | `Add`, `Count`, `Item`, `Remove`<br>Access to collections using the ! character |
| Conditional compilation | `#Const`<br>`#If...Then...#Else` |
| Control flow | `DoEvents`<br>`GoSub...Return`, `GoTo`<br>`On Error GoTo`<br>`On...GoSub`, `On...GoTo`<br>Line numbers, line labels |
| Conversion | `CVar`, `CVDate`<br>`Str`, `Val` |
| Data types | All intrinsic data types except `Variant`<br>`Type...End Type` |
| Date/time | `Date` statement<br>`Time` statement |
| DDE | `LinkExecute`, `LinkPoke`, `LinkRequest`, `LinkSend` |
| Debugging | `Debug.Print`<br>`End`, `Stop` |

*Continues*

| Category | Omitted Feature/Keyword |
|---|---|
| Declaration | `Declare` (used to declare DLLs)<br>`Optional`<br>`ParamArray`<br>`Static` |
| Error handling | `Erl`<br>`Error`<br>`Resume`, `Resume Next` |
| File input/output | All standard Basic file I/O |
| Financial | All financial functions |
| Object manipulation | `TypeOf` |
| Objects | `Clipboard`<br>`Collection` |
| Operators | `Like` |
| Options | `Deftype`<br>`Option Base`<br>`Option Compare`<br>`Option Private Module` |
| Select case | Expressions containing `Is` keyword or any comparison operators<br>Expressions containing a range of values using the `To` keyword |
| Strings | Fixed-length strings<br>`LSet`, `Rset`<br>`Mid` statement<br>`StrConv` |
| Using objects | Collection access using `!` |

# The Variant Subtypes

The reference material in this appendix is a companion to the detailed explanation of data types and the VBScript Variant in Chapter 3. However, a brief description of these concepts is as follows.

VBScript is what is known as a *weakly typed* programming language, which is the opposite of a "strongly typed" language. A weakly typed language does not allow you to declare variables with specific data types such as String, Date, or Boolean. Instead, in VBScript all variables are automatically and implicitly assigned a special data type called Variant. The Variant data type is actually many data types in one. VBScript still has the concept of data types such as String, Date, and Boolean, but these data types are somewhat hidden inside the Variant type.

The mechanism by which the Variant type encompasses many data types in one is called the *subtype*. A Variant variable can have one of many different subtypes—but only one subtype at a time. The subtype of a Variant variable can change in one of two ways: implicitly and explicitly.

An implicit change in subtype occurs when a new value is assigned to a Variant variable and VBScript uses some intelligence to examine the new value and automatically decides what the subtype should be. If the new value fits within the bounds of the already assigned subtype, VBScript will not change it. This automatic subtype change process is called *implicit type coercion*. As a VBScript programmer, it is very important to understand how implicit type coercion works and when and how it occurs.

A programmer can also explicitly force a change in subtype. The primary way of doing this is with one of VBScript's *conversion functions*. For example, the CLng() function will change the subtype to Long. Similarly, the CStr() function will change it to String. Sometimes it is necessary to use a conversion function to force a subtype change so that a particular operation or function call will work properly.

The Variant data type, the subtypes, and the ins and outs of implicit and explicit type coercion are covered in great detail in Chapter 3. Even an experienced programmer coming from another language would do well to read this chapter. Management of the `Variant` subtypes in your scripts is a key to your success as a VBScript programmer.

The following table lays out the particulars of all of the `Variant` subtypes. This is intended as a reference for those times when you're not sure which subtype you might need or when you're not sure if a particular value is too big for a certain subtype.

Following the Variant Subtypes table is a table of the Visual Basic data types. Visual Basic is a strongly typed language. Visual Basic also supports the `Variant` data type, but many others besides. The list of Visual Basic data types lines up pretty closely with the list of `Variant` subtypes. The reason we include this information on the Visual Basic data types is that often your VBScript code will be calling components that use specific data types as parameters or return values. When communicating with external components that expose these standard data types, it is important to make sure that your `Variant` subtype corresponds to the Visual Basic data type required by the external component.

# The Variant Subtypes

| Subtype | Visual Basic Data Type Equivalent | Conversion Function to Force the Subtype | Test Function (Other than VarType and TypeName) | VarType() Function Return Value (with Named Constant Equivalent) | TypeName() Function Return Value |
|---|---|---|---|---|---|
| Empty | N/A | N/A | IsEmpty() | 0 (vbEmpty) | Empty |
| Null | N/A | N/A | IsNull() | 1 (vbNull) | Null |
| Integer | Integer | CInt() | IsNumeric() | 2 (vbInteger) | Integer |
| Long | Long | CLng() | IsNumeric() | 3 (vbLong) | Long |
| Single | Single | CSng() | IsNumeric() | 4 (vbSingle) | Single |
| Double | Double | CDbl() | IsNumeric() | 5 (vbDouble) | Double |
| Currency | Currency | CCur() | IsNumeric() | 6 (vbCurrency) | Currency |
| Date | Date | CDate() | IsDate() | 7 (vbDate) | Date |
| String | String | CStr() | None | 8 (vbString) | String |
| Object | Object | N/A | IsObject() | 9 (vbObject) | Object |
| Error | N/A | * | None | 10 (vbError) | Error |
| Boolean | Boolean | CBool() | None | 11 (vbBoolean) | Boolean |
| Variant | Variant | CVar() | None | 12 (vbVariant) | Variant |
| Decimal | N/A | * | IsNumeric() | 14 (vbDecimal) | Decimal$ |

*Continues*

| Subtype | Visual Basic Data Type Equivalent | Conversion Function to Force the Subtype | Test Function (Other than VarType and TypeName) | VarType() Function Return Value (with Named Constant Equivalent) | TypeName() Function Return Value |
|---|---|---|---|---|---|
| Byte | Byte | CByte() | IsNumeric() | 17 (vbByte) | Byte |
| Array | N/A | N/A | IsArray() | 8192 (vbArray)# | Array |

*Visual Basic supports conversion functions for the *Error* and *Decimal* subtypes called *CVErr()* and *CDec()*, respectively. VBScript, however, does not support these conversion functions. See the sidebar later in this section for more information.

$Because of a bug in VBScript, the *TypeName()* function does not support the *Decimal* subtype (although *VarType()* does). See the sidebar later in this section for more information.

#This value is actually returned from the *VarType()* function in combination with the value for *Variant (12)*. See the section on arrays at the end of this chapter.

# The Visual Basic Data Types

| Data Type | Storage Required | Range of Allowable Values | Comments |
|---|---|---|---|
| Byte | 1 byte | 0 to 255 | Often used to store binary data in the form of a "Byte array" |
| Integer | 2 bytes | $-32,768$ to 32,767 | None |
| Long | 4 bytes | $-2,147,483,648$ to $2,147,483,647$ | The most commonly used numeric data type |
| Single | 4 bytes | Negative values:<br>$-3.402823E38$ to $-1.401298E-45$<br>Positive values:<br>$1.401298E-45$ to $3.402823E38$ | For storing IEEE 32-bit single precision floating point numbers (in other words, numbers with decimals) |
| Double | 8 bytes | Negative values:<br>$-1.79769313486232E308$ to $4.94065645841247E-324$<br>Positive values:<br>$4.94065645841247E-324$ to $1.79769313486232E308$ | For storing IEEE 64-bit double precision floating point numbers; offers greater precision than the Single |
| Currency | 8 bytes | $-922,337,203,685,477.5808$ to $922,337,203,685,477.5807$ | Automatically rounds to four decimal places |

*Continues*

| Data Type | Storage Required | Range of Allowable Values | Comments |
|---|---|---|---|
| Decimal | 14 bytes | With no decimal point: +/−79,228,162,514,264,337,593,543,950,335 With 28 decimal places: +/−7.9228162514264337593543950335 Smallest nonzero number: +/−0.0000000000000000000000000001 | Can only be stored in a variant; use when maximum floating point accuracy is needed |
| Boolean | 2 bytes | True or False | Only has two possible values; False can also be represented as zero (0), and True can also be represented as −1 (or, really, any nonzero value); often used as a success/failure return value for functions; also very common for procedure arguments |
| String | 10 bytes + string length | 0 to approximately 2 billion characters | Can be used to store any kind of text characters, numbers, or symbols |
| Date | 8 bytes | January 1, 100 to December 31, 9999 | When displayed, by default uses the Windows "Short Date" format setting |
| Object | 4 bytes | Any object reference | A generic data type that can hold a "late bound" reference to any COM object |
| Variant | 16 or 22 bytes | Any data within the range of any of the above data types | Takes up 16 bytes when storing numeric data, 22 bytes when storing string data; can have a different "subtype" depending on the type of value stored within it; also takes up a little more space when storing an array; equivalent to the VBScript Variant type |

# ActiveX Data Objects

The purpose of this appendix is to provide a brief overview of ActiveX Data Objects (ADO), which is the standard component provided by Microsoft for accessing databases and other structured data sources. Since ADO is a provided as a library of COM objects, you can use ADO in your VBScript programs to write to and read from databases. Our purpose here is not to discuss all of the details and powerful features of ADO. Rather, since ADO is so often used in combination with VBScript, our goal is to provide a brief overview and reference.

ADO is too large a subject to cover thoroughly in one appendix. If you are making significant use of ADO in your scripts, you may want to purchase a book dedicated to ADO. Given the brevity of this overview, we also assume that you are familiar with basic relational database concepts such as tables, columns, queries, stored procedures, and so on.

This guide to ADO covers ADO 2.8, which is the latest version of ADO available at press time. Please note that, since VBScript is a pre-.NET technology, we will not be discussing ADO.NET, which is the latest version of ADO. ADO.NET is intended for use by .NET languages such as C# and VB.NET. It is not natively compatible with VBScript. If you want to ensure that you have the latest version of ADO, you can download the latest release of Microsoft Data Access Components (MDAC) from msdn.microsoft.com/data.

Our discussion will include the following ADO objects:

- ❑ `Connection`—Used to connect to a data source and manage transactions.

- ❑ `Command`—Used to execute commands such as queries and stored procedures against a data source.

- ❑ `Parameters` and `Parameter`—`Parameter` objects are stored in the `Command` object's `Parameters` collection. Together, `Parameter` and `Parameters` are used to specify parameters for a stored procedure being called through a `Command` object.

- ❑ `Recordset`—Used to store a series of structured data—usually data returned from a query or stored procedure—represented as a series of rows and columns. You can also use the `Recordset` object to manually construct a data set that you wish to submit to a database.

❑ Error—If one or more errors occur while using any of the ADO objects, the Connection object's Errors collection will contain one or more Error objects. An Error object has information about an error such as the number, description, and source.

Please note that we are not covering the Record or Stream objects as these are more advanced than our basic ADO overview. Also, we do not have separate sections for the Fields and Field objects, but the basic usage of these are covered in the section on the Recordset object.

The example code in this appendix is based on the Northwind sample database that ships with Microsoft Access. The downloadable script files are designed for running under the Windows Script Host (see Chapter 12), but the code is easily transferable to other hosts. Our discussion will focus on using ADO for relational database access, since that it by far the most common use for ADO, but keep in mind that since ADO is part of Microsoft's "Universal Database" strategy, it can be used to access other structured data formats such as spreadsheets, e-mail systems, text files, and so on.

Finally, please note that certain advanced or seldom used properties and methods may be excluded for some objects.

# The Connection Object

The Connection object is almost always required in order to do anything interesting with the other ADO objects. The Connection object represents the primary access point to a data source. If you want to read from or write to a data source, you need to use the Connection object to establish a connection with that data source. The following example script (ADO_CONNECTION.VBS) illustrates the basic technique for opening a connection.

```
Option Explicit

Const adStateOpen = 1

Dim cnNorthwind
Dim strStatus

Set cnNorthwind = CreateObject("ADODB.Connection")

cnNorthwind.ConnectionString = _
    "Provider=Microsoft.Jet.OLEDB.4.0;" & _
    "User ID=Admin;Password=;Data Source=" & _
    "C:\Program Files\Microsoft Office\Office\Samples\" & _
    "Northwind.mdb"

cnNorthwind.Open

If cnNorthwind.State = adStateOpen Then
    MsgBox "Connection is open."
Else
    MsgBox "Connection is not open."
End If

cnNorthwind.Close
Set cnNorthwind = Nothing
```

After instantiating the `Connection` object, this code sets the `ConnectionString` property. The connection string is how you tell the `Connection` object what kind of data source to connect to (`Provider=`), how to locate that data source (`Data Source=`), and security information for logging into the data source (`User ID=` and `Password=`). To get this connection string to work on your machine, you may have to change the path to the `Northwind.mdb` file.

Unfortunately, there are many different "provider" types for different data source types and many different versions of these providers. There are also different styles of connection strings that different providers may or may not support. Unfortunately, there is not enough space here to include information on the dozens of different providers and connection string formats. Please consult the documentation for the type of database you are using. There is also an excellent comprehensive connection string reference available online at `http://www.able-consulting.com/ADO_Conn.htm`.

Going back to the script, after setting the connection string, we call the `Open` method, which tells the `Connection` object to attempt to connect to the data source. Finally, just to prove that our connection was successful, we check the `State` property to find out the status of the connection. Notice also that we call the `Close` method when we are done with the connection. It is always a good idea to close any database connections as soon as you are done with them.

The following two sections describe in detail the important `Connection` object properties and methods.

## Connection Object Properties

| Name | Accepts/Returns | Access | Description |
| --- | --- | --- | --- |
| CommandTimeout | Long | Read/Write | Used to set or obtain the number of seconds a `Connection` object will wait when executing a command (see `Execute` method) before giving up; has no effect on the `CommandTimeout` property of the `Command` object. |
| ConnectionString | String | Read/Write | Used to set or obtain the connection details for a data source, including provider type, data source location, user name, and password. |
| ConnectionTimeout | Long | Read/Write | Used to set or obtain the number of seconds a `Connection` object will wait when connecting to a data source (see `Open` method) before giving up. |
| CursorLocation | Long (CursorLocationEnum) | Read/Write | Used to set or obtain the location of the "cursor" of |

*Continues*

| Name | Accepts/Returns | Access | Description |
|---|---|---|---|
| | | | any Recordset objects opened with a Connection object; a cursor can be "client-side" or "server-side." |
| Errors | Collection | Read Only | If an error occurs during usage of a Connection object, this collection will contain one or more Error objects, which have properties exposing error number, description, source, and so on. |
| State | Long (ObjectStateEnum) | Read Only | Returns information about the status of a connection to a data source. Most often, the status is either "open" or "closed"; other statuses apply when using asynchronous methods on ADO objects using the connection. |

## Connection Object Methods

| Name | Arguments | Returns | Description |
|---|---|---|---|
| BeginTrans | None | Long | Used to begin a transaction at the data source; must be followed, eventually, by a call to either CommitTrans or RollbackTrans; the Long return value (seldom used) indicates the "nesting level" of the new transaction |
| CommitTrans | None | N/A | Used to "commit" a transaction that was started with a call to BeginTrans |
| RollbackTrans | None | N/A | Used to abort a transaction that was started with a call to BeginTrans |
| Cancel | None | N/A | Used to abort a method call (such as Connection.Execute or Recordset.Open) that was executed asynchronously |

| Name | Arguments | Returns | Description |
|------|-----------|---------|-------------|
| Close | None | N/A | Used to close an open connection; important to call this when done using a `Connection` object, before setting it to `Nothing` |
| Execute | `CommandText`—`String` value containing an SQL query, stored procedure call, or URL to execute at the data source<br><br>`RecordsAffected`—Optional `Long` in/out argument that will contain the number of records returned by the data source<br><br>`Options`—Optional `Long` value indicating the type of command in the `CommandText` argument; can be any combination of values from `CommandTypeEnum` and `ExecuteOptionEnum` | `Recordset` object | To execute a command on a data source, you can use either the `Execute` method of the `Connection` object or the `Command` object; use a `Command` object when you need to pass parameters to a stored procedure; otherwise `Connection.Execute` is a convenient shortcut; for an SQL query, use adCmdText (1) in the `Options` argument; for a stored procedure, use adCmdStoredProc (4) |
| Open | `ConnectionString`—Optional `String` value that can be used in place of, or to override, the `ConnectionString` property<br><br>`UserID`—Optional `String` value that can be used in place of specifying a user ID in the connection string<br><br>`Password`—Optional `String` value that can be used in place of specifying a password in the connection string<br><br>`Options`—Optional `Long` (`ConnectOptionEnum`) value; default value of adConnectUnspecified causes normal, synchronous connection; adAsyncConnect will cause asynchronous connection | N/A | Opens a connection object; traditionally, most programmers set the `ConnectionString` property before calling `Open` instead of using the arguments of the `Open` method |

# The Command Object

The Command object is an optional alternative to using the Execute and Open methods of the Connection object. Some programmers prefer the explicitness of using a Command object instead of Connection.Execute and Connection.Open. Other programmers prefer the brevity of using the Connection object. The choice is up to you. Note, however, that if you are calling a stored procedure that uses parameters, you pretty much have to use the Command object instead of Connection. Execute or Connection.Open.

The following script (ADO_COMMAND.VBS) demonstrates the basic technique of using an SQL query to open a Recordset object from the Northwind database's Suppliers table. This script example borrows from the Connection object example in the previous section and will be continued in the Recordset object section, later.

```
Option Explicit

Const adCmdText = 1
Const adStateOpen = 1

Dim cnNorthwind
Dim cmdQuery
Dim rsSuppliers

Set cnNorthwind = CreateObject("ADODB.Connection")

cnNorthwind.ConnectionString = _
    "Provider=Microsoft.Jet.OLEDB.4.0;" & _
    "User ID=Admin;Password=;Data Source=" & _
    "C:\Program Files\Microsoft Office\Office\Samples\" & _
    "Northwind.mdb"

cnNorthwind.Open

Set cmdQuery = CreateObject("ADODB.Command")
With cmdQuery
    Set .ActiveConnection = cnNorthwind
    .CommandText = "SELECT [SupplierID], [CompanyName] " & _
                   "FROM Suppliers " & _
                   "WHERE [Country] = 'Australia'"
    .CommandType = adCmdText
    Set rsSuppliers = .Execute
End With

If rsSuppliers.State = adStateOpen Then
    MsgBox "Recordset opened successfully."
    rsSuppliers.Close
End If

Set rsSuppliers = Nothing
Set cmdQuery = Nothing
cnNorthwind.Close
Set cnNorthwind = Nothing
```

Notice that once we have an open Connection object, we instantiate a Command object and set the ActiveConnection property of the Command to the Connection object. This gives the Command object its link to the data source. Next we set the CommandText property to an SQL query and set the CommandType to 1, which is the value for the adCmdText enumerated constant (see *ADO Enumerated Constants* at the end of this appendix). Then we use the Execute method to run the query and return a Recordset object.

The Execute method may or may not return a Recordset depending on the type of command sent through CommandText. For example, an SQL UPDATE statement would not return a Recordset. In that case, you would just call the Execute method as a procedure instead of as a function.

Another common use of the Command object is calling a stored procedure (which may or may not return a Recordset). In this case, most programmers use the Parameters collection to specify any parameters accepted by the stored procedure. The Parameter object section later includes an example of this syntax. (You can also pass parameters to a stored procedure in two other ways: one, as part of the CommandText or CommandStream property; and two, using the Parameters argument of the Execute method (which is not the same as the Parameters collection). Keep in mind that these alternative methods only support input-only parameters.

The following two sections describe in detail the important Command object properties and methods.

## Command Object Properties

| Name | Accepts/Returns | Access | Description |
|---|---|---|---|
| ActiveConnection | Connection object (in a Variant) | Read/Write | Used to set or obtain a reference to a Connection object used by the Command; all ADO objects must go through a Connection object to get to the data source; this is usually the first property you would set after instantiating a Command object |
| CommandStream | Stream object | Read/Write | A mutually exclusive alternative to the CommandText property; whereas CommandText accepts/returns a String value and CommandStream accepts/returns a Stream object |
| CommandText | String | Read/Write | Used to set or obtain the string representing the "command" that you wish the |

*Continues*

| Name | Accepts/Returns | Access | Description |
|------|-----------------|--------|-------------|
| | | | Command object to execute; can be an SQL query, stored procedure call, or URL; you should also set the CommandType property to the type value corresponding to the type of command |
| CommandTimeout | Long | Read/Write | Used to set or obtain the number of seconds a Command object will wait before giving up on a call to the Execute method |
| CommandType | Long (CommandTypeEnum) | Read/Write | Must be set to match the type of command value placed into the CommandText or CommandStream property; use 1 (adCmdText) for SQL queries and 4 (adCmdStoredProc) for stored procedure calls |
| NamedParameters | Boolean | Read/Write | If the Command object is using the Parameters collection to pass parameters to a stored procedure, this property controls how those parameters are interpreted; True means that the parameters will be matched up by Parameter.Name with the parameter names defined in the stored procedure; False (the default) means that Parameter.Name is ignored and the parameters will be sent to the stored procedure in the order in which they are added to the Parameters collection |
| Parameters | Collection of Parameter objects | Read/Write | Holds a collection of Parameter objects; used when calling stored procedures that accept parameters; initially the |

| Name | Accepts/Returns | Access | Description |
|------|-----------------|--------|-------------|
| | | | collection is empty; `Parameter` objects must be added manually or can be auto-populated using the `Parameters.Refresh` method |
| Prepared | Boolean | Read/Write | Used to set or obtain whether the `Execute` method should tell the data source to cache a compiled version of the command, which can increase performance when repeatedly executing the same command |

## Command Object Methods

| Name | Arguments | Returns | Description |
|------|-----------|---------|-------------|
| Cancel | None | N/A | If the `Execute` method was called asynchronously, a call to this method will abort the pending or in-progress command |
| CreateParameter | Name—Optional `String` value representing the parameter name<br><br>Type—Optional `Long` value (`DataTypeEnum`) representing the data type of the parameter<br><br>Direction—Optional `Long` value (`Parameter DirectionEnum`) indicating whether the parameter is input, output, or both<br><br>Size—Optional `Long` value indicating the maximum parameter value length in bytes or characters<br><br>Value—Optional `Variant` representing the value for the parameter (must correspond to the `Type` argument) | Parameter object | When calling a stored procedure and manually creating `Parameter` objects to add to the `Parameters` collection, use this method to create a new `Parameter` object; note that this method returns only a `Parameter` object—it does not add it to the `Parameters` collection; you can either use the arguments to initialize the `Parameter` object or omit the arguments and manually set the properties on the returned `Parameter` object; if you use the arguments, the returned `Parameter` object will already have its properties set |

*Continues*

| Name | Arguments | Returns | Description |
|------|-----------|---------|-------------|
| Execute | RecordsAffected— Optional Long in/out argument that ADO will use to return the number of records affected by the command<br><br>Parameters—Optional Variant array of parameters to pass to a stored procedure; does not support in/out parameters<br><br>Options—Optional Long value indicating the type of command in the CommandText argument; can be any combination of values from CommandTypeEnum and ExecuteOptionEnum | Either returns a Recordset object, a Stream object, or Nothing, depending on the command sent to the data source | When you have prepared a Command object with properties such as CommandText, CommandType, and the Parameters collection, the Execute method will actually issue the command to the data source; depending on the content of the command, the data source may or may not return data, which influences the return type of the Execute method |

# The Parameters and Parameter Objects

The Parameter object is used in conjunction with the Command object and its Parameters collection. "Parameter" in this context refers to parameters/arguments expected by a stored procedure that is being called with a Command object. There are actually a few ways to pass parameters to a stored procedure.

❑ Embedding the parameters in the text of CommandText or CommandStream

❑ Passing them in a Variant array to the Execute method's Parameters argument

❑ Explicitly creating Parameter objects and adding them to the Command object's Parameters collection

Only the third technique actually involves the use of the Parameter object. Using the third technique has two advantages: one, the code is more explicit and a little more readable; and two, it supports in/out parameters, which the other two methods do not. On the downside, using the third method is a little slower since you have to instantiate (potentially) several Parameter objects for a single call to a stored procedure.

Using Parameter objects for passing parameters to a stored procedure involves these steps:

1.  Create a new Parameter object using Command.CreateParameter (using the arguments of the CreateParameter method to set the properties of the Parameter object)

2.  Adding the Parameter object to the Parameters collection using the Parameters.Append method

3.  Repeating the first two steps for as many times as the stored procedure's parameter list requires

All this must be done before calling the `Execute` method and, ideally, after setting the `CommandText` or `CommandStream` property of the `Command` object. Also, many programmers prefer to expedite the process by performing the first and second steps simultaneously. The following code snippet illustrates this technique (please note that this code is not included in the downloadable code for this chapter since we are using Access for our examples and Access does not support stored procedures).

```
Const adCmdStoredProc = 4
Const adVarChar = 200
Const adParamInput = 1

Set cmdStoredProc = CreateObject("ADODB.Command")

With cmdStoredProc
    Set .ActiveConnection = cnConnection
    .CommandText = "GetSuppliersByCountry"
    .CommandType = adCmdStoredProc

    .Parameters.Append .CreateParameter("strCountry", _
        adVarChar, adParamInput, 15, "Australia")

    Set rsSuppliers = .Execute
End With
```

The benefit of the shortcut used here is that you do not have to explicitly declare or instantiate any `Parameter` objects. The `CreateParameter` method returns a `Parameter` object that is immediately passed to the `Parameters.Append` method.

Another technique is to call the `Command.Parameters.Refresh` method after setting the stored procedure name in `CommandText` or `CommandStream`. The `Refresh` method will retrieve the parameter list from the data source and automatically populate the `Parameters` collection. Then you can loop back through the `Parameters` collection to set all of the `Value` properties. However, while this is a cool technique, it is usually avoided because of the extra round trip to the database.

The following two sections describe in detail the important `Parameter` object properties and methods.

## Parameter Object Properties

| Name | Accepts/Returns | Access | Description |
|------|----------------|--------|-------------|
| Direction | Long (ParameterDirectionEnum) | Read/Write | Used to set or obtain the "direction" for a stored procedure parameter; parameters can be input only (adParamInput), output only (adParamOutput), both input and output (adParamInputOutput), or return values (adParamReturn) |

*Continues*

| Name | Accepts/Returns | Access | Description |
|---|---|---|---|
| Name | String | Read/Write before appended to Parameters, Read Only after appended | Depending on the value of Command .NamedParameters, the Name of a Parameter object may or may not be used in the execution of the stored procedure; if NamedParameters is True, Parameter.Name must match exactly the name of one of the stored procedure's parameters |
| NumericScale | Byte | Read/Write | Used to set or obtain the number of decimal places to which numeric parameter values are resolved |
| Precision | Byte | Read/Write | Used to set or obtain the precision for numeric parameters |
| Size | Long | Read/Write | Used to set or obtain the maximum size, in characters or bytes (depending on the Type), for a parameter |
| Type | Long (DataTypeEnum) | Read/Write | Used to set or obtain the data type of a parameter |
| Value | Variant | Read/Write | Used to set or obtain the value of a parameter; for output or input/output parameters, the value will be set by the stored procedure |

## Parameter Object Methods

| Name | Arguments | Returns | Description |
|---|---|---|---|
| AppendChunk | Data—Variant value to be appended to the Value property of the Parameter | N/A | In situations in which you are sending large amounts of text or binary data in a Parameter object, use the AppendChunk method to gradually build up the Value property rather than setting the Value property directly; |

| Name | Arguments | Returns | Description |
|---|---|---|---|
| | | | for example, if you have 10,000 bytes of data you might call `AppendChunk` 10 times in a loop, appending 1000 bytes each time; can only be used when `Type` is `adFldLong` |

## Parameters Object Properties

| Name | Accepts/Returns | Access | Description |
|---|---|---|---|
| Count | Long | Read Only | Used to obtain the number of `Parameter` objects in the `Parameters` collection |
| Item | Parameter | Read Only | Used to obtain a reference to a certain `Parameter` object based on its index in the `Parameters` collection |

## Parameters Object Methods

| Name | Arguments | Returns | Description |
|---|---|---|---|
| Append | Parameter—A `Parameter` object that has already been initialized with `Name`, `Type`, `Value`, and so on | N/A | Used to add a new `Parameter` object to the `Parameters` collection; the `Parameter` object should have been created with `Command.Create Parameter`; its `Type` and `Name` properties must be set, but the `Value` can optionally be set or changed after appending |
| Delete | Index—The numeric collection index of the `Parameter` object you wish to remove from the `Parameters` collection | N/A | Used to remove a `Parameter` object from the `Parameters` collection |
| Refresh | None | N/A | If the (`Command .CommandText`) or `CommandStream` property has already been set with the |

*Continues*

| Name | Arguments | Returns | Description |
|------|-----------|---------|-------------|
| | | | name of a stored procedure, the `Parameters.Refresh` method will make a trip to the database to obtain the parameter list for the stored procedure and automatically populate the `Parameters` collection, after which you can loop through the collection to set the `Value` properties, if necessary |

# The Recordset Object

In general, setting aside the `Stream` object for a moment (see later), the `Recordset` is where a programmer can work with actual data. The typical scenario for the use of the `Recordset` object is that a programmer creates `Connection` and `Command` objects in order to execute a query or stored procedure in a database. The query or stored procedure returns a set of data, formatted as rows and columns, which is stored in a `Recordset` object. Then the programmer can use the `Recordset` object to read, update, add, or delete the data.

The `Recordset` object is also quite versatile beyond this typical scenario. It has a long list of properties and methods, and we could go on explaining all the cool things you can do with a `Recordset`. For example, you can programmatically create a `Recordset` object from scratch, create fields for it, and fill it up with data—all without using a data source at all. You can also save a `Recordset` to disk and re-create it later without having to connected to the original source of the `Recordset`. `Recordset` objects can even be nested inside of other `Recordset` objects. However, our focus here will be on the primary properties and methods used to work with `Recordset` objects that are returned by queries and stored procedures.

We will look at two example scripts: one that opens a `Recordset` from a query and loops through the data one time; and another that opens a `Recordset`, changes some of the data it contains, and updates the database with the changes. The following example script (ADO_RECORDSET_READ.VBS) illustrates the open and read technique.

```
Option Explicit

Const adCmdText = 1
Const adStateOpen = 1
Const adOpenForwardOnly = 0
Const adUseClient = 3
Const adLockReadOnly = 1

Dim cnNorthwind
Dim cmdQuery
Dim rsSuppliers
Dim strMsg
```

```
Set cnNorthwind = CreateObject("ADODB.Connection")

cnNorthwind.ConnectionString = "Provider=Microsoft.Jet.OLEDB.4.0;" & _
    "User ID=Admin;Password=;Data Source=" & _
    "C:\Program Files\Microsoft Office\Office\Samples\" & _
    "Northwind.mdb"

cnNorthwind.Open

Set cmdQuery = CreateObject("ADODB.Command")
With cmdQuery
    Set .ActiveConnection = cnNorthwind
    .CommandText = "SELECT [SupplierID], [CompanyName] " & _
                   "FROM Suppliers " & _
                   "WHERE [Country] = 'Australia'"
    .CommandType = adCmdText
End With

Set rsSuppliers = CreateObject("ADODB.Recordset")
Set rsSuppliers.Source = cmdQuery
rsSuppliers.CursorType = adOpenForwardOnly
rsSuppliers.CursorLocation = adUseClient
rsSuppliers.LockType = adLockReadOnly
rsSuppliers.Open

If rsSuppliers.State = adStateOpen Then
    Do While Not rsSuppliers.EOF
        strMsg = strMsg & rsSuppliers.Fields("SupplierID").Name
        strMsg = strMsg & ":" & vbTab
        strMsg = strMsg & rsSuppliers.Fields("SupplierID").Value
        strMsg = strMsg & vbNewLine

        strMsg = strMsg & rsSuppliers.Fields("CompanyName").Name
        strMsg = strMsg & ":" & vbTab
        strMsg = strMsg & rsSuppliers.Fields("CompanyName").Value
        strMsg = strMsg & vbNewLine & vbNewLine

        rsSuppliers.MoveNext
    Loop
    rsSuppliers.Close

    MsgBox strMsg
Else
    MsgBox "Recordset not opened."
End If

Set rsSuppliers = Nothing
Set cmdQuery = Nothing
cnNorthwind.Close
Set cnNorthwind = Nothing
```

If you've been following along, you'll see that this is an extension of the example script from the previous Command object section. However, notice that we have changed the way we open the Recordset. Instead of using Command.Execute, we use CreateObject to instantiate an empty Recordset and then set the Command object to the Recordset.Source. A few lines later, when we call Recordset.Open, the Command object we put in the Source property (and its Connection object) is used to communicate with the database. This alternative method is necessary if you want to have control over some important properties of the Recordset *before* opening it.

In this example, we have set the CursorType property to adOpenForwardOnly, the CursorLocation to adUseClient., and the LockType to adLockReadOnly. What this means is that we only intend to loop through this Recordset one time and that we want to do this as fast as possible while using the least amount of resources. Other cursor types, such as adOpenDynamic and adOpenKeyset, are more flexible in that they allow you to move back and forth between records and to loop through the Recordset more than one, but these cursor types incur more overhead and are therefore slower.

As far as CursorLocation, server-side cursors can enable certain Recordset features, such as the ability to receive dynamic updates to the data in the Recordset as it changes in the data source, but use more resources on the server. In this case we're not using those features, so we use a client-side cursor since it puts less of a tax on the database.

Finally, we set the LockType to adLockReadOnly since we do not intend to make any updates to the data. This is not strictly necessary since adLockReadOnly happens automatically when using adOpenForwardOnly, but it illustrates the point that CursorType, CursorLocation, and LockType have primary influence over what you can and can't do with a Recordset, how fast you'll be able to do it, and how much resource overhead you're incur.

When working with the Recordset object, it is important to have in mind how you plan to use the Recordset and then to set properties such as CursorType, CursorLocation, and LockType so that the Recordset will have the features you need while at the same time using the least amount of resources and offering the best performance. If you want to experiment to find out which capabilities are supported by which cursor types and locations (and this different depending on the "Provider" specified in the connection string), you can use the Recordset.Supports method with CursorOptionEnum to find out if a feature you want (such as "move previous" support or the ability to update the Recordset) is supported by a certain cursor type and location.

After we open the Recordset, we use a Do loop to move through each of the records. One key to making this work is that we use the EOF property to make sure that we stop looping when we have reached the end (and that we don't *start* looping if the Recordset is empty). Another key to the loop is the call to Recordset.MoveNext right before the Loop statement. MoveNext moves the cursor to the next record. This call is essential or you will create an endless loop that reads the first record in the Recordset over and over again.

Inside the loop, we use the Fields collection, which returns a Field object based on the Name of the field, to read the data out of each record. The two important Field properties for us here are Name and Value. The Name is the same as the column name we used in the SQL query. The Value is the value that came back from the data source for that column on that row.

We turn now to our second example (ADO_RECORDSET_WRITE.VBS), which uses a Recordset object to update data.

```
Option Explicit

Const adCmdText = 1
```

```
Const adStateOpen = 1
Const adOpenKeyset = 1
Const adUseServer = 2
Const adLockOptimistic = 3

Dim cnNorthwind
Dim cmdQuery
Dim rsOrders
Dim datOrder

Set cnNorthwind = CreateObject("ADODB.Connection")

cnNorthwind.ConnectionString = "Provider=Microsoft.Jet.OLEDB.4.0;" & _
    "User ID=Admin;Password=;Data Source=" & _
    "C:\Program Files\Microsoft Office\Office\Samples\" & _
    "Northwind.mdb"

cnNorthwind.Open

Set cmdQuery = CreateObject("ADODB.Command")
With cmdQuery
    Set .ActiveConnection = cnNorthwind
    .CommandText = "SELECT [OrderDate] " & _
                   "FROM Orders " & _
                   "WHERE [ShipCountry] = 'Italy'"
    .CommandType = adCmdText
End With

Set rsOrders = CreateObject("ADODB.Recordset")
Set rsOrders.Source = cmdQuery
rsOrders.CursorType = adOpenKeyset
rsOrders.CursorLocation = adUseServer
rsOrders.LockType = adLockOptimistic
rsOrders.Open

If rsOrders.State = adStateOpen Then
    Do While Not rsOrders.EOF
        datOrder = rsOrders("OrderDate")
        If Not IsNull(datOrder) Then
            'Add one second to the OrderDate
            datOrder = DateAdd("s", 1, datOrder)
            rsOrders("OrderDate") = datOrder
            rsOrders.Update
        End If

        rsOrders.MoveNext
    Loop
    rsOrders.Close

    MsgBox "Finished updating recordset."
Else
    MsgBox "Recordset not opened."
End If
Set rsOrders = Nothing
```

```
Set cmdQuery = Nothing
cnNorthwind.Close
Set cnNorthwind = Nothing
```

First, notice that we have changed our query to return a list of order dates that are to be shipped to Italy. We did this because we want to be able to demonstrate an update operation without messing up your Northwind database if you decide to run this script on your machine. As we'll explain in a minute, and as you can see from reading the code, to keep the update as harmless as possible, we are adding one second to the OrderDate value.

Second, we have change the values we are using for the CursorType, CursorLocation, and LockType properties to a combination that will open an updateable Recordset. The adOpenKeyset cursor type will give us an updateable cursor that will detect any new records that are added while we have the Recordset open, but that does not use as many resources as adOpenDynamic. We changed the cursor location to adUseServer to support the adOpenKeyset cursor, which needs to run on the server in order to detect new records. Finally, we changed the lock type to adLockOptimistic to indicate that we want to update records but that we don't care if other users update the same records while we have the Recordset open. (If we did care, we would use adLockPessimistic.)

Inside of the loop, we retrieve the value of the OrderDate field, add one second to the date, and then write the new date value back to the field. We call the Update method to save to the database the change to the current record. Notice that we have altered the syntax we use to access the Recordset.Fields collection. This new syntax is a shorthand that takes advantage of the fact that the Fields property is the default property of the Recordset object and that the Value property is the default property of the Field object. Typing rsOrders.Fields("OrderDate") is equivalent to just typing rsOrders("OrderDate").

The following two sections describe in detail the important Recordset object properties and methods.

## Recordset Object Properties

| Name | Accepts/Returns | Access | Description |
|------|------------------|--------|-------------|
| BOF and EOF | Boolean | Read Only | Indicates whether the cursor is at the beginning of the Recordset or at the end; if the cursor is one position *before* the first record, BOF will be True; if one after the last record, EOF will be True; if directly on one of the records, both BOF and EOF will be False |
| CursorLocation | Long (CursorLocationEnum) | Read/Write before open; Read Only after open | As explained in the "Overview" section above, CursorLocation is one of the essential properties for controlling cursor behavior and |

| Name | Accepts/Returns | Access | Description |
|------|-----------------|--------|-------------|
| | | | feature support; value can be either `adUseClient` or `adUseServer` |
| CursorType | Long (`CursorTypeEnum`) | Read/Write before open; Read Only after open | As explained in the previous section *Overview*, `CursorType` is one of the essential properties for controlling cursor behavior and feature support; different cursor types support different features; set the `CursorType` based on the features you need |
| Fields | `Fields` collection holding `Field` objects | Read Only | A `Recordset` is a matrix of columns and rows; the `Fields` property exposes the collection of columns, represented as `Field` objects; when reading a `Recordset` returned by a data source, you do not add or remove `Field` objects from the collection, but this can be done when working with a `Recordset` that is not associated with a data source |
| LockType | Long (`LockTypeEnum`) | Read/Write before open; Read Only after open | As explained in the previous section *Overview*, `CursorType` is one of the essential properties for controlling cursor behavior and feature support; if you do not need to update the data in the `Recordset`, use `adLockReadOnly`; for updates use either `adLockOptimistic` or `adLockPessimistic`, depending whether you need to protect against other processes changing data at the same time |
| RecordCount | Long | Read Only | Returns the number of records in the `Recordset`; will return −1 if the `CursorType` and `CursorLocation` do not support this feature; count may not be reliable if the cursor does not support "approximate positioning" or "bookmarks" |

*Continues*

| Name | Accepts/Returns | Access | Description |
|------|-----------------|--------|-------------|
| | | | (see `Supports` method); you must use the exactly correct combination of `CursorType` and `CursorLocation` in order to depend on this property based on the underlying provider |
| Source | `String` or `Command` object | Read/Write before open; Read Only after open | If you wish to set properties such as `CursorType` and `CursorLocation` before opening the `Recordset`, create a `Command` object and set it into this property; you can also put an SQL query or stored procedure call string in this property if you also set the `ActiveConnection` property to a `Connection` object, but using a `Command` object that already has a `Connection` is more explicit |
| State | `Long` (`ObjectStateEnum`) | Read Only | Indicates the status of the `Recordset`; for example, `adStateOpen` or `adStateClosed` |

## Recordset Object Methods

| Name | Arguments | Returns | Description |
|------|-----------|---------|-------------|
| AddNew | `FieldList`—Optional `String` or array of names or ordinal positions that must correspond to the fields in the `Recordset`. `Fields` collection<br><br>`Values`—Optional `String` or array of values for the fields; elements must line up with the `FieldList` | N/A | If you are working with an updateable `Recordset`, use this to add a new record; you can either pass the fields and values as arguments to this method or omit the arguments and then set the value of each field as separate calls |
| Close | None | N/A | Closes an open `Recordset`; it's a good idea to always close a `Recordset` when you're done |

| Name | Arguments | Returns | Description |
|------|-----------|---------|-------------|
| | | | with it; will return an error if the Recordset is not open, so check the State property before calling Close |
| Delete | AffectRecords— Optional Long (AffectEnum) value indicating which records to include in the delete operation | N/A | Use this method to delete records from an updateable Recordset; most often, you would call this method while the cursor is positioned on the record you wish to delete—in which case you can omit the AffectRecords argument since the default is adAffectCurrent |
| MoveFirst MoveLast MoveNext MovePrevious | None | N/A | These four methods are used to move the cursor from its current position to another position; MoveNext is most often used since normally you start at the beginning of the Recordset and move through it one row at a time; if the CursorType and CursorLocation settings support it, you can use MoveFirst and MovePrevious to move the cursor backwards |
| Open | Source—Optional Variant that can contain a Command object, SQL string, or stored procedure call string; can be omitted if Source property is set<br><br>ActiveConnection— Optional Variant that can contain an open Connection object or a connection string; can be omitted if ActiveConnection property is set or if the Command object has an open connection | N/A | As demonstrated in the *Overview* section earlier, used to open a Recordset using a certain source with certain options; you can either set the properties you want first and call Open with the arguments omitted, or you can pass the arguments to Open, which will set the corresponding properties automatically |

*Continues*

| Name | Arguments | Returns | Description |
|------|-----------|---------|-------------|
| | CursorType—Optional Long (CursorTypeEnum) indicating desired cursor type; can be omitted if CursorType property is set | | |
| | LockType—Optional Long (LockTypeEnum) indicating desired locking behavior; can be omitted if LockType property is set | | |
| | Options—Optional Long value indicating how to treat Source argument if other than a Command object; can be any combination of values from CommandTypeEnum and ExecuteOptionEnum | | |
| Supports | CursorOptions—Long (CursorOptionEnum) value indicating which feature/behavior you wish to test | Boolean | Since the various features and behaviors of a Recordset object may or may not be available depending on CursorType and CursorLocation, this method is helpful in determining whether a given operation is supported |
| Update | Fields—Optional Variant containing a single field name or an array of field names or ordinal positions that must correspond to the fields in the Recordset.Fields collection | N/A | Call this method after performing any edits of Field.Value or after a call to AddNew and before moving the cursor; data will not be saved until Update is called |
| | Values—Optional Variant containing a single value or an array of values; elements must line up with Fields | | |

# ADO Enumerated Constants

A note regarding enumerated constants: enumerated constants are not directly supported by VBScript. This is unfortunate since they are an easy way to keep your code readable. For example, instead of setting Command.CommandType with the value of 1, you can set it to the value of adCmdText, making it a lot easier to understand what's going on in your code. However, there are two workarounds that can help you achieve that same code readability.

First, if you are writing an ASP (Active Server Pages) application, you can add this line to each of your pages that are going to include ADO code.

```
<!--#include File="adovbs.inc"-->
```

This include file is provided by Microsoft and should already be installed on your machine. This include file contains constant declarations equivalent to the ADO enumerated constants so that you can use them in your code just as if VBScript supported enumerated constants.

Second, if you are using another host, such as the Windows Script Host, you can declare named constants of your own as you need. We have used this technique with the example Windows Script Host scripts included with this appendix. Manually declaring your constants is a little tedious, but worth the trouble. Besides, you have to only declare the few that you're going to need in any given script. Take a look at these two equivalent lines of code and decide which one is more readable.

```
.Parameters.Append .CreateParameter("strCountry", _
    200, 4, 15, "Germany")
```

```
.Parameters.Append .CreateParameter("strCountry", _
    adVarChar, adParamInput, 15, "Germany")
```

If you're not using ASP, all that's required to achieve the improved readability of the second line is to add these two lines to your script.

```
Const adVarChar = 200
Const adParamInput = 1
```

Here are the ADO enumerated constants referred to in this ADO object reference.

| Name | Values |
| --- | --- |
| AffectEnum | adAffectAll—3<br>adAffectAllChapters—4<br>adAffectCurrent—1<br>adAffectGroup—2 |
| CommandTypeEnum | adCmdUnspecified—1<br>adCmdText—1<br>adCmdTable—2<br>adCmdStoredProc—4<br>adCmdUnknown—8 (Default)<br>adCmdFile—256<br>adCmdTableDirect—512 |
| ConnectOptionEnum | adAsyncConnect—16<br>adConnectUnspecified—1 |
| CursorLocationEnum | adUseClient—3<br>adUseNone—1 (obsolete—do not use)<br>adUseServer—2 |
| CursorOptionEnum | adAddNew—16778240<br>adApproxPosition—16384<br>adBookmark—8192 |

*Continues*

| Name | Values |
|---|---|
| | adDelete—16779264<br>adFind—524288<br>adHoldRecords—256<br>adIndex—1048576<br>adMovePrevious—512<br>adNotify—262144<br>adResync—131072<br>adSeek—2097152<br>adUpdate—16809984<br>adUpdateBatch—65536 |
| CursorTypeEnum | adOpenDynamic—2<br>adOpenForwardOnly—0<br>adOpenKeyset—1<br>adOpenStatic—3<br>adOpenUnspecified—1 |
| DataTypeEnum | adArray—8192<br>adBigInt—20<br>adBinary—128<br>adBoolean—11<br>adBSTR—8<br>adChapter—136<br>adChar—129<br>adCurrency—6<br>adDate—7<br>adDBDate—133<br>adDBTime—134<br>adDBTimeStamp—135<br>adDecimal—14<br>adDouble—5<br>adEmpty—0<br>adError—10<br>adFileTime—64<br>adGUID—72<br>adInteger—3<br>adLongVarBinary—205<br>adLongVarChar—201<br>adLongVarWChar—203<br>adNumeric—131<br>adPropVariant—138<br>adSingle—4<br>adSmallInt—2<br>adTinyInt—16<br>adUnsignedBigInt—21<br>adUnsignedInt—19<br>adUnsignedSmallInt—18 |

| Name | Values |
|------|--------|
| | adUnsignedTinyInt—17<br>adUserDefined—132<br>adVarBinary—204<br>adVarChar—200<br>adVarNumeric—139<br>adVarWChar—202<br>adWChar—130 |
| ExecuteOptionEnum | adAsyncExecute—16<br>adAsyncFetch—32<br>adAsyncFetchNonBlocking—64<br>adExecuteNoRecords—128<br>adExecuteStream—1024<br>adOptionUnspecified—1 |
| LockTypeEnum | adLockBatchOptimistic—4<br>adLockOptimistic—3<br>adLockPessimistic—2<br>adLockReadOnly—1<br>adLockUnspecified—1 |
| ObjectStateEnum | adStateClosed—0<br>adStateOpen—1<br>adStateConnecting—2<br>adStateExecuting—4<br>adStateFetching—8 |
| ParameterDirectionEnum | adParamInput—1<br>adParamInputOutput—3<br>adParamOutput—2<br>adParamReturnValue—4<br>adParamUnknown—0 |

# Index

# Index

## Symbols & Numbers

# A